Learning to Teach in the Secondary School

Learning to teach might sound easy but the reality involves hard work and careful preparation. To become an effective teacher requires subject knowledge, an understanding of your pupils and how they learn and the confidence to respond to dynamic classroom situations.

This book offers a sound and practical introduction to the skills needed to qualify as a teacher, and is designed to help you to develop those qualities that lead to good practice and a successful future in education. This 4th edition has been updated to include changes to the National Curriculum for schools in England, an introduction to the Scottish system as well as developments in the curriculum for early professional development.

With a focus on evidence-based practice, the book contains many examples of how to analyse practice to ensure pupil learning is maximized. Activities or tasks in each chapter also provide opportunities for student teachers to analyse their own learning and performance and provide an analytical toolkit for the beginner teacher. Web-based links to sources of new knowledge that supports evidence-based practice are also included.

As well as containing useful strategies and ideas for enhancing teaching and learning, *Learning to Teach in the Secondary School* covers many of the situations and potential challenges faced by the student teacher and the newly qualified teacher.

The book contains 29 units, organised into 9 chapters, each covering a key concept or skill, including:

- managing behaviour to support learning;
- ways pupils learn;
- planning lessons and schemes of work;
- differentiation, progression and pupil grouping;
- assessment;
- inclusion and special educational needs;
- using ICT in teaching and learning;
- getting your first teaching post.

This book is the core text for the subject-specific *Learning to Teach* series by the same editors, also published by Routledge, and is an essential buy for every student teacher.

Susan Capel is a professor in the School of Sport and Education at Brunel University. **Marilyn Leask** is head of effective practices and research dissemination at the Teacher Training Agency. **Tony Turner** was senior lecturer in education at the Institute of Education, University of London.

Related titles

Learning to Teach Subjects in the Secondary School Series

Series Editors

Susan Capel, Marilyn Leask and Tony Turner

Designed for all students learning to teach in secondary schools, and particularly those on school-based initial teacher training courses, the books in this series complement *Learning to Teach in the Secondary School* and its companion, *Starting to Teach in the Secondary School*. Each book in the series supports students in school and college learning how to teach their subject, applying underpinning theory to address practical issues.

Learning to Teach English in the Secondary School, 2nd edition
Jon Davison and Jane Dowson

Learning to Teach Modern Foreign Languages in the Secondary School, 2nd edition
Norbert Pachler and Kit Field

Learning to Teach History in the Secondary School, 2nd edition
Terry Haydn, James Arthur and Martin Hunt

Learning to Teach Physical Education in the Secondary School, 2nd edition
Edited by Susan Capel

Learning to Teach Science in the Secondary School, 2nd edition
Jenny Frost and Tony Turner

Learning to Teach Mathematics in the Secondary School, 2nd edition
Edited by Sue Johnston-Wilder, Peter Johnston-Wilder, David Pimm and John Westwell

Learning to Teach Religious Education in the Secondary School
Edited by Andrew Wright and Ann-Marie Brandom

Learning to Teach Art and Design in the Secondary School
Edited by Nicholas Addison and Lesley Burgess

Learning to Teach Geography in the Secondary School
David Lambert and David Balderstone

Learning to Teach Design and Technology in the Secondary School
Edited by Gwyneth Owen-Jackson

Learning to Teach Music in the Secondary School
Edited by Chris Philpott

Learning to Teach in the Secondary School, 3rd edition
Edited by Susan Capel, Marilyn Leask and Tony Turner

Learning to Teach ICT in the Secondary School
Edited by Steve Kennewell, John Parkinson and Howard Tanner

Learning to Teach Citizenship in the Secondary School
Edited by Liam Gearon

Starting to Teach in the Secondary School, 2nd edition
Edited by Susan Capel, Ruth Heilbronn, Marilyn Leask and Tony Turner

Learning to Teach in the Secondary School, 4th edition
Edited by Susan Capel, Marilyn Leask and Tony Turner

Learning to Teach Using ICT in the Secondary School, 2nd edition
Edited by Marilyn Leask and Norbert Pachler

Learning to Teach in the Secondary School

A companion to school experience

4th edition

Edited by
Susan Capel, Marilyn Leask
and Tony Turner

Routledge
Taylor & Francis Group

LONDON AND NEW YORK

Fourth edition published 2005
by Routledge
2 Park Square, Milton Park, Abingdon, Oxon OX14 4RN

Simultaneously published in the USA and Canada
by Routledge
270 Madison Ave, New York, NY 10016

Reprinted 2006 (twice)

First published 1995 by RoutledgeFalmer
Second edition published 1999 by RoutledgeFalmer
Third edition published 2001 by RoutledgeFalmer

Routledge is an imprint of the Taylor & Francis Group, an informa business

Typeset in Bembo by
H WA Text and Data Management, Tunbridge Wells
Printed and bound in Great Britain by
Bell & Bain Ltd., Glasgow

British Library Cataloguing in Publication Data
A catalogue record for this book is available from the British Library

Library of Congress Cataloging in Publication Data
A catalog record for this book has been requested

ISBN-10: 0-415-36392-6
ISBN-13: 978-0-415-36392-1

Contents

Illustrations

FIGURES

TABLES

TASKS

Contributors

Françoise Allen is a lecturer in education at Brunel University, where she is PGCE Secondary Course leader.

Steve Bartlett is currently reader in education at University of Wolverhampton.

Rob Batho is a senior regional director for the Key Stage 3 National Strategy where his current responsibilities are for ITT and English.

Richard Bennett is currently senior lecturer in education at University College Chester where he is the ICT co-ordinator for the School of Education.

Diana Burton is professor and dean of the Faculty of Education, Community and Leisure at Liverpool John Moores University.

Graham Butt is senior lecturer in geography education and head of curriculum and pedagogy at the School of Education, University of Birmingham.

Susan Capel is professor in the School of Sport and Education at Brunel University.

Jon Davison is currently dean of initial teacher education and continuing professional development at the Institute of Education, University of London.

Philip Garner is currently professor of education at Nottingham Trent University.

Misia Gervis is a senior lecturer in sport psychology and coaching at Brunel University.

Terry Haydn is a senior lecturer in education at the School of Education and Professional Development at the University of East Anglia.

Graham Haydon is a lecturer in the philosophy of education at the Institute of Education, University of London.

Susan Heightman is an experienced teacher and teacher educator and she manages a Graduate Teacher Programme.

Ruth Heilbronn is subject leader for the PGCE in modern foreign languages at the Institute of Education, University of London.

Judith Ireson is reader in psychology and education, School of Psychology and Human Development, Institute of Education, University of London.

Margaret Jepson is a principal lecturer at Liverpool John Moores University.

Julia Lawrence is a lecturer in physical education in the School of Sport and Education at Brunel University.

Marilyn Leask is head of effective practices and research dissemination at the Teacher Training Agency in London. She was previously at De Montfort University.

Hilary Lowe is principal lecturer in education and an academic development director at the Westminster Institute of Education, Oxford Brookes University.

John McCormick is manager of the secondary PGCE programme at Liverpool John Moores University.

Catherine Moorhouse is a national casework official for the Association of Teachers and Lecturers.

John Moss is head of department of Postgraduate Initial Teacher Education, Canterbury Christ Church University College.

Andrew Noyes is a lecturer in education at the University of Nottingham.

Nick Peacey is co-ordinator of the Special Educational Needs Joint Initiative for Training (SENJIT), Institute of Education, University of London.

Alexis Taylor is a lecturer in education at Brunel University, where she is deputy head of Postgraduate Studies.

Allen Thurston is a senior lecturer in education in the Faculty of Education and Social Work, University of Dundee.

Keith Topping is professor of educational and social research and associate dean of research in the Faculty of Education and Social Work, University of Dundee.

Tony Turner: Until full retirement in September 2000 Tony Turner was senior lecturer in education at the Institute of Education, University of London.

Bernadette Youens is a lecturer in science education at the School of Education, University of Nottingham.

Paula Zwozdiak-Myers is head of professional studies at De Montfort University Bedford.

Introduction

Susan Capel, Marilyn Leask and Tony Turner

Teaching is both an art and a science. In this book we show that there are certain essential elements of teaching that you can master through practice that help you become an effective teacher. However, there is no one correct way of teaching, no one specific set of skills, techniques and procedures that you must master and apply mechanically. This is, in part, because your pupils are all different and each day brings a new context in which they operate. Every teacher is an individual and brings something of their own unique personality to the job and their interactions with pupils. We hope that this book helps you to develop skills, techniques and procedures appropriate for your individual personality and style and provides you with an entry to ways of understanding what you do and see. An effective, reflective teacher is one who can integrate theory with practice. We also hope that the text provides the stimulus for you to want to continue to learn and develop throughout your career as a teacher. There is a website associated with this text where you will find documents and information to extend what is available in the text – <http://www.routledge.com/textbooks/0415363926>.

DEVELOPING YOUR PHILOSOPHY OF TEACHING

On your initial teacher training course much of your time is spent in school. You can expect your initial teacher training to provide not merely *training* but also to introduce you to wider educational issues. What we mean by this is that teacher training is not an apprenticeship but a journey of personal development in which your skills of classroom management develop alongside an emerging understanding of the teaching and learning process. This is a journey of discovery that begins on the first day of your course and may stop only when you retire. Thus, we use the term initial teacher *education* rather than initial teacher training throughout this book.

The school-based element of your course provides the opportunity to appreciate at first hand the complex, exciting and contradictory events of classroom interactions without the constant immediacy of having to teach all the time. It should allow you time to make sense of experiences, both in the classroom and the wider school, that demand explanations. Providing such explanations requires you to have a theory of teaching and learning.

By means of an organized course that provides for practical experience, structured observation and reflective activity suitably interwoven with theoretical inputs, student teachers can begin to develop their own theory of teaching and learning. Theoretical inputs can come from tutors and teachers, from lectures and from print and web-based resources. Theory also arises from practice, the better to inform and develop practice.

Everyone who teaches has a theory of how to teach effectively and of how pupils learn. The theory may be implicit in what the teacher does and the teacher may not be able to tell you what their theory is. For example, a teacher who is a disciplinarian is likely to have a different theory about the conditions for learning than a teacher who is liberal in their teaching style. Likewise, some teachers may feel that they do not have a philosophy of education. What these teachers are really saying is that they have not examined their views, or cannot articulate them. What is your philosophy? For example, do you consider that your job is to transfer the knowledge of your subject to pupils? Or are you there to lead them through its main features? Are you 'filling empty vessels' or are you the guide on a 'voyage of discovery'? On the other hand, perhaps you are the potter, shaping and moulding pupils.

It is recognized that an initial teacher education course only enables you to start developing your own personal understanding of the teaching and learning process. There are a number of different theories about teaching and learning. You need to be aware of what these are, reflect on them and consider how they help you to explain more fully what you are trying to do and why. Through the process of theorizing about what you are doing, reflecting on a range of other theories as well as your own, you understand your practice better and develop into a reflective practitioner, that is, a teacher who makes conscious decisions about the teaching strategies to employ and who modifies their practice in the light of experiences.

An articulated, conscious philosophy of teaching emerges only if a particular set of habits is developed. In particular, the habit of reviewing your own teaching from time to time. It is these habits that need to be developed from the start of your initial teacher education course. This is what many authors mean when they refer to 'the reflective practitioner'. This is why we (as well as your course tutors) ask you to evaluate your own teaching, to keep a diary, and to develop a professional development portfolio to record your development and carry that forward from your initial teacher education course to your first post. Part of this reflection is included in your career entry and development profile if you are learning to teach in England.

HOW TO USE THIS BOOK

Structure of the book

The book is laid out so that elements of appropriate background information and theory along with evidence from research introduce each issue. These are interwoven with tasks designed to help you identify key features of the behaviour or issue. A number of different inquiry methods are used to generate data, e.g. reflecting on reading and observation or on an activity you are asked to carry out, asking questions, gathering data, discussing with a tutor or another student teacher. Some of the tasks involve you in activities that impinge on other people, for example, observing a teacher in the classroom, or asking for information. If a task requires you to do this, *you must first of all seek permission of the person concerned*. Remember that you are a guest in school(s); you cannot walk into any teacher's classroom to observe. In addition, some information may be personal or sensitive and you need to consider issues of confidentiality and professional behaviour in your inquiries and reporting.

The main text is supported by a glossary of terms to help you interpret the jargon of education. An appendix on writing and reflection is also included to help you with the written assignments on your initial teacher education course.

We call school children 'pupils' to avoid confusion with students, by which we mean people in further and higher education. The important staff in your life are those in school and higher education institution; we have called all these people 'tutors'. Your institution will have its own way of referring to staff. Where appropriate, we have used the words 'he' or 'she', and other gender words, trying to effect a balance without recourse to the use of he/she or justifying the use of the male pronoun as a substitute for all humans.

Developing your competence

The range and type of competences/standards you are expected to become aware of and develop during your initial teacher education course will have been derived from those for student teachers in the country in which you are learning to teach. The units in this book are designed to help you work towards developing these competences/standards. Your tutors in school and in your higher education institution help you identify levels of competence appropriate to your status as a student teacher and as a newly qualified teacher. At appropriate points in the text you should relate the work directly to the specific competences/standards to which you are working.

Your diary of reflective practice

As you read through the book and complete the tasks, we ask you to keep a reflective diary. This diary can be used to record the outcomes of tasks and your thoughts on the reading, analyses undertaken as part of that reading, or other activities that arise as part of your course. The diary can also be used to record your reactions to events, both good and bad, as a way of letting off steam! It enables you to analyse strengths and areas for development, hopes for the future, and elements of your emerging personal philosophy of teaching and learning. It provides a record of your development that can be very useful in developing your professional development portfolio and writing the relevant sections of your career entry and development profile. Thus, we strongly recommend that you start to keep a diary of reflective practice now.

Your professional development portfolio

Your professional development portfolio provides a selective record of your development as a teacher, your strengths as well as areas for further development, and is something that you continue to develop throughout your teaching career. It is likely that your institution has a set format for a professional development portfolio, in which case you will be told about it. If not, you should develop your own. You can use any format and include any evidence you think appropriate. However, to be truly beneficial, it should contain evidence beyond the minimum required for your course. This further evidence could be work of value to you, a response to significant events, extracts from your diary of reflective practice, good lesson plans, evaluations of lessons, teaching reports, observations on you made by teachers, outcomes of tasks undertaken, assessed and non-assessed course work.

At the end of your course you can use your portfolio to reflect on your learning and achievements. It is also used as the basis for completing applications for your first post; and to take to interview. It can form the basis of a personal statement describing aspects of your development as a teacher during your course. This would include reference to teaching reports written by teachers, tutors and yourself. It can also help provide the basis of your continuing professional development as it enables you to identify competences/standards in need of development and thus targets for induction and continuing professional development in your first post, first through your career entry and development profile then as part of the appraisal process you will be involved with as a teacher.

Ways you might like to use this book

With much (or all) of your course being delivered in school, you may have limited access to a library, to other student teachers with whom to discuss problems and issues at the end of the school day, and, in some instances, limited access to a tutor to whom you can refer. There are likely to be times when you are faced with a problem in school which has not been addressed up to that point within your course and you need some help immediately, for example before facing a class the next day or next week. This book is designed to help you address some of the issues or difficulties you are faced with during your initial teacher education, by providing supporting knowledge interspersed with a range of tasks to enable you to link theory with practice.

The book can be used in a number of ways. It is designed more for you to dip in and out of, to look up a specific problem or issue that you want to consider, rather than for you to read from cover to cover (although you may want to use it in both ways of course). You can use it on your own as it provides background information and supporting theory along with evidence from research about a range of issues you are likely to face during your initial teacher education course. Reflecting on an issue faced in school with greater understanding of what others have written and said about it, alongside undertaking some of the associated tasks, may help you to identify some potential solutions. The book can also be used in association with your tutors. The tasks are an integral part of the book and you can complete most individually. Most tasks do, however, benefit from wider discussion, which we encourage you to do whenever possible. However, some tasks can be carried out only with other student teachers and/or with the support of a tutor. You should select those tasks that are appropriate to your circumstances.

This book will not suffice alone; we have attempted to provide you with guidance to further reading by two methods. The first, by references to print and web-based material in the text, the details of which appear at end of the book. The second, by readings related to the units. These further readings, to direct and develop understanding, appear at the end of the units. There is a considerable amount of educational material available on the internet. We make reference to this throughout the book and we urge you to keep a record of useful websites. The government sites are a useful start (e.g. in England <http://www.teachernet.gov.uk> and the Qualifications and Curriculum Authority <http://www.qca.org.uk>) as are those of subject associations. In addition, you should use this book alongside your course handbook, which outlines specific course requirements, agreed ways of working, roles and responsibilities.

If you see each unit as potentially an open door leading to whole new worlds of thought about how societies can best educate their children, then you will have achieved one of our goals - to provide you with a guide book on your journey of discovery about teaching and learning. Remember, teaching is about the contribution you make to your pupils, to their development and their learning.

Finally, we hope that you find the book useful, and of support in school. If you like it, tell others; if not, tell us.

1 Becoming a Teacher

Through the units in this chapter, the complexity and breadth of the teacher's role and the nature of teaching are explored. You are posed questions about your values and attitudes because these influence the type of teacher you become. Society is constantly changing and so the demands society places on teachers change. Consequently as your career progresses you will find you need new skills and knowledge about teaching and learning (pedagogy). Professional development is therefore a lifelong process for the teacher which is aided by regular reflection on practice and continuing education, e.g. through continuing professional development.

Each unit in this chapter examines different facets of the work of student teachers and experienced teachers. Unit 1.1 covers wider aspects of the teacher's role, including academic and pastoral roles and we consider the necessity for regular curriculum review as society changes.

In Unit 1.2 we discuss the expectations which the tutors responsible for your training have of you. The meaning of professionalism is discussed and the idea that you will have your own philosophy of teaching is introduced. Phases which mark your development as a teacher are identified. We suggest that as your own confidence and competence in managing the classroom grow, you can expect the focus of your work to move from your self-image and the mechanics of managing a lesson, to the learning taking place generally and, as you become more experienced, to the learning for the individual pupil.

Unit 1.3 provides advice for managing time, both inside and outside the classroom, and for preventing stress. There are a variety of competing demands made on your time and if you learn to use your time effectively, you will have more time to enjoy your work as a teacher and more leisure time.

Unit 1.4 provides an introduction to ways in which information and communications technology can be used to support teaching and learning.

To become a teacher you need to supplement your *subject content knowledge* with *professional pedagogic knowledge* (about teaching and learning) and to develop your *professional judgement*, e.g. about managing situations which arise with pupils. Ways of developing your professional knowledge and judgement provide themes running throughout the book.

In the UK, you can find a wealth of material on government supported websites to support you as a teacher. Starting places are for England <http://www.teachernet.gov.uk>; for Scotland <http://www.scotland.gov.uk>; for Wales <http://www.cymru.gov.uk>; and for Northern Ireland <http://www.deni.gov.uk>. International curricula are available on <http://www.inca.org.uk>; European and Commonwealth education networks can be found on <http://www.eun.org>; and <http://www.col.org/cense>.

You may come to recognise your situation in the following poem called 'Late'.

> You're late, said miss
> The bell has gone,
> dinner numbers done
> and work begun.
>
> What have you got to say for yourself?
>
> Well, it's like this, miss
> Me mum was sick,
> me dad fell down the stairs,
> the wheel fell off my bike
> and then we lost our Billy's snake
> behind the kitchen chairs. Earache
> struck down me grampy, me gran
> took quite a funny turn.
> Then on the way I met this man
> whose dog attacked me shin –
> look, miss you can see the blood
> it doesn't look too good,
> does it?
>
> Yes, yes sit down –
> and next time say you're sorry
> for disturbing all the class.
> Now get on with your story
> fast!
>
> Please miss, I've got nothing to write about.

(Judith Nicholls in Batchford (1992) *Assemblies for the 1990s*)

Unit 1.1

What Do Teachers Do?

Marilyn Leask with Catherine Moorhouse

INTRODUCTION

The answer to this question depends on where and when the question is being asked. You will be teaching in the twenty-first century. We'd like to take you back in time, just for a moment, to English schools in the Middle Ages.

Curtis (1967: 23–4) writes that in England in the twelfth century,

> theology was considered the queen of studies, to which philosophy served as an introduction. The studies which led to the supreme study of theology were known generally as the Seven Liberal Arts. The Arts (or sciences) were termed liberal from liber, free and constituted the course of study suitable for the freeman as contrasted with the Practical and Mechanical Arts which were learned and practised by slaves in the classical period. The arts were divided into the Trivium and Quadrivium. … The subjects of the Trivium consisted of Grammar, Rhetoric and Dialectic (logic); and of the Quadrivium, Arithmetic, Geometry, Astronomy and Music – the subjects of the Trivium were taught to younger pupils and the Quadrivium to older pupils. There were grammar schools (providing preparation for university work), song schools (for teaching singing in Latin at church services) and reading and writing schools (effectively providing a primary education). The three schools were often housed under the one roof and the language of instruction changed with political changes – from Latin to Norman-French to the vernacular.

Clearly what teachers teach reflects the times in which they live so change is essential in education. Without change, we would have a fossilised, out-of-date curriculum – what Peddiwell (1939, cited in Goddard and Leask, 1992) called the 'sabre-toothed curriculum'. Peddiwell describes a prehistoric community which successfully taught its youngsters how to deal with sabre-toothed tigers. Unfortunately, the curriculum wasn't updated when the sabre-toothed tigers died out, with the result that the pupils' education didn't prepare them for the new challenges facing the community. This illustrates the necessity for regular review of the curriculum and, for similar reasons, teachers' knowledge and skills should be regularly updated. So what teachers do depends on what is happening in the wider community. Curriculum change is to be expected through your working life, with new subjects being introduced and old subjects phased out or altered to make way for the new. Naturally what is taught in schools is of concern to society in general. Curriculum change is discussed in more detail in Chapter 7.

OBJECTIVES

By the end of this unit you should:

- be aware of the range of skills and forms of knowledge which a teacher uses in planning and giving lessons;
- have considered the relationship between subject knowledge and effective teaching;
- have an understanding of various aspects of a teacher's role and responsibilities including academic and pastoral roles, administration and health and safety;
- be developing your own philosophy of teaching.

CLASSROOM PRACTICE: AN INTRODUCTION TO HOW TEACHERS TEACH

The teacher's job is first and foremost to ensure that pupils learn. To a large extent, *what* (i.e. the lesson content) pupils should learn in maintained (state) schools in England and Wales and Scotland is determined through legislation and the requirements are set out in various national curriculum documents. Other countries may give schools and teachers much more autonomy. On the other hand, *how* you teach so that the pupils learn effectively (i.e. the methods and materials used) is more often left to the professional judgement of the individual teacher, department and school.

Task 1.1.1
Focusing on competences/standards

To understand what is expected of newly qualified teachers you need to be familiar with the competences/standards you are required to reach by the end of your course. These can be found in your course handbook and other documentation provided by your institution and we suggest you look at them now.

Teaching is a very personal activity and while certain teaching styles and strategies might suit one teacher, they might not be appropriate for another. However, although there exists a core of good practice to which most teachers would subscribe, there are differences between teachers which relate to personality, style and philosophy. Moreover, observers of the same teacher might well disagree about the strengths and weaknesses of that teacher. In your first days in school, it is likely that you will spend time observing a number of experienced teachers. It is highly unlikely that you will see two teachers who teach identically. Perhaps you will see teaching styles which you feel more at home with, while others do not seem as appropriate to your own developing practice. Of course, there is no one way to teach. Provided effective teaching and learning takes place, a whole range of approaches from didactic (formal, heavy on content) to experiential (learning by doing) is appropriate – often in the same lesson. Unit 5.3 provides more details about teaching styles. Increasingly, training institutions are able to offer trainees the opportunity to use video to analyse teaching styles and to have videos of their own lessons which can be analysed and used to improve practice (see <http://www.ttrb.ac.uk> and <http://www.teachers.tv> for video materials related to teaching).

Learning to manage the classroom is similar in many ways to learning to drive. At the outset there seems so much to remember. How do you manage to: depress the clutch; brake; change gear; be aware of oncoming traffic and cars following you; look in the mirror; indicate; obey the speed limit; observe traffic signs and signals; be aware of and sensitive to changing road and weather conditions; anticipate problems and steer simultaneously? After a short time, however, such skills become part of subconscious patterns of behaviour.

Much of what many experienced teachers do to manage their classes has become part of their unconscious classroom behaviour. Their organization of the lesson so that pupils learn is implicit in what they do rather than explicit. So much so that often teachers find it hard to articulate exactly what it is they are doing or why it is successful. This situation, of course, does not help the student teacher. It also gives weight to the spurious notion that teachers are born rather than made and that nobody can tell you how to teach.

Undoubtedly some teachers may well begin teaching with certain advantages such as a 'good' voice or organizational skills. Nevertheless there are common skills and techniques to be learned that, when combined with an awareness of and sensitivity to the teaching and learning contexts, enable student teachers to manage their classes effectively.

Teaching is a continuously creative and problem-solving activity. Each learner or each group of learners has their own characteristics which the experienced teacher takes into account in planning the relevant learning programme. For example, if there has been recent controversy over environmental issues in the local area or the school has taken refugees fleeing from civil war, an effective teacher will adapt their approach to the discussion of such matters to make lessons more relevant and to allow the pupils to draw on their experience. Although lessons with different groups may have similar content, a lesson is rarely delivered in the same way twice. Variations in interactions between the pupils and the teacher affect the teaching strategy chosen.

THE WORK IN THE CLASSROOM: THE TIP OF THE ICEBERG

On the surface, teaching may appear to be a relatively simple process – the view that the teacher stands in front of the class and talks and the pupils learn appears to be all too prevalent. (Ask friends and family what they think a teacher does.) The reality is somewhat different.

Classroom teaching is only the most visible part of the job of the teacher. The contents of this book are designed to introduce you to what we see as the invisible foundation of the teacher's work: *professional knowledge* about teaching and learning and *professional judgement* about the routines, skills and strategies which support effective classroom management. Your *subject knowledge* comes from your degree and from your continuing professional development. An effective teacher draws on these three factors in planning each and every lesson; and the learning for a particular class is planned ahead – over weeks, months and years – so that there is *continuity and progression* in the pupils' learning. Each lesson is planned as part of a sequence of learning experiences.

The following analogy may help you understand what underpins the work in the classroom. Think of a lesson as being like an iceberg – 70 to 80 per cent, the base, is hidden (Figure 1.1.1). The work in

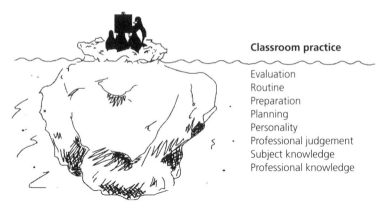

Figure 1.1.1   The tip of the iceberg (Acknowledgement: Simon Beer)

the classroom represents the tip of the iceberg. Supporting this tip, but hidden, are many elements of the teacher's professional expertise. These include:

- evaluation of previous lessons;
- established routines and procedures which ensure that the work of the class proceeds as planned;
- preparation for the lesson;
- planning of a sequence of lessons to ensure learning progresses;
- personality – including the teacher's ability to capture and hold the interest of the class, to establish their authority;
- professional judgement built up over time through reflection on experience;
- subject knowledge;
- professional knowledge about effective teaching and learning.

During your course, you will often see experienced teachers and student teachers teaching. But what are you really seeing? You need to learn to 'read the classroom' – to train yourself to look beyond what is readily visible so that you come to understand the variety of skills and strategies which the teacher brings to bear in order to maximize the learning taking place. Some of these skills and strategies are easily identifiable, others require you to observe more carefully. Any classroom observation you undertake must have a purpose, be focused, generate information and should provoke thought. We hope to sensitize you to what happens behind the scenes of the classroom so that you can build on that knowledge in your own classroom work.

Throughout your course, you should expect to develop confidence and new levels of competence in all the areas in Figure 1.1.1.

SUBJECT KNOWLEDGE AND EFFECTIVE TEACHING

A common misunderstanding about teaching is that if you know your subject then you automatically can teach it well. In the same way that delivering milk to the doorstep provides no guarantee that it will be taken into the house, so too is it with the subject content of a lesson. You cannot assume that pupils will automatically take in what you had hoped to teach them. The fact that you are an expert in a subject is no guarantee that you can help others learn that subject.

It is usually assumed that student teachers on a one-year post-graduate course have an appropriate level of subject knowledge and their initial teacher education course usually concentrates on subject application to the classroom. These student teachers often find they have to relearn aspects of their subject which they may not have thought about for years as well as material which is new to them. You can expect to have to widen your knowledge base so that you have a deeper understanding of the subject than is required by the syllabus. Wider knowledge enables you to develop differentiated tasks for pupils with differing abilities much more easily and gives you confidence that you will be able to answer questions.

Teaching requires you to transform the knowledge you possess into suitable tasks which lead to learning. Acquiring appropriate up-to-date knowledge requires some effort on your part and this is just part of the work of the teacher. The English National Curriculum <http://nc.uk.net/> provides a useful starting point for student teachers in England and most subject associations produce relevant materials and run annual conferences which help you keep up with developments. See Unit 7.5 for Scottish curriculum references. The subject association for your subject will be able to provide help with resources and advice, much of which may be accessed online. Ask colleagues for details. Alternatively, look at the website for this book <http://www.routledge.com/textbooks/0415363926>. Addresses of subject associations can also be found in *The Education Year Book* (published annually).

However, to teach effectively, you need more than good subject knowledge.

Task 1.1.2
Subject knowledge competences/standards

Identify the competences/standards in subject knowledge required by your course. Now look at the curriculum for your subject. Analyse it to identify the areas of knowledge that you can cope with now, those you could learn with some effort and those areas which require totally new learning. Where there are areas which are unfamiliar to you, set yourself goals for improving this aspect of your knowledge. You may find it helpful to discuss these goals with more experienced colleagues. Make sure to check your progress regularly, e.g. before school experience and after your final school experience. For those teaching in England, a profile of your developing knowledge of subject matter could be included in your career entry and development profile, which you take to your first post. Your knowledge needs may be able to be further addressed in your first post as a newly qualified teacher through continuing professional development.

As already indicated, *personality and personal style* influence your effectiveness as a teacher but many skills and strategies can be learned and practised until they become part of your professional repertoire. We introduce you to theories underpinning educational practice and ideas which can provide a foundation for your development as an effective teacher whatever your subject. But what do we mean by effective teaching?

Effective teaching occurs where the learning experience structured by the teacher matches the needs of the learner, i.e. tasks develop the individual pupil's knowledge, skills, attitudes and/or understanding in such a way that the pupil is applying past knowledge as appropriate and laying the foundation for the next stage of learning. A key feature of effective teaching is balancing the pupils' chance of success against the level of difficulty required to challenge them. Effective teaching depends on complex interrelationships of a whole range of factors, a major one of which is the teacher's understanding of the different ways in which pupils learn. Chapter 5 provides further information about pupil learning. Understanding about the ways in which learning takes place is essential to your work as a teacher of a subject and this understanding provides the foundations on which to build your professional knowledge about teaching and learning. The more closely the teaching method matches the preferred learning style of the pupils the more effective the teaching will be.

As a student teacher you have the opportunity to develop a repertoire of teaching styles and strategies and to test these out in the classroom. The information in various chapters should help you in this process. It may take you some considerable time before you can apply the principles of effective teaching to your classroom practice but you can monitor your development through regular evaluation of lessons (see Unit 5.4). We aim to provide a basic introduction to what are complex areas and it is up to you to develop systematically your professional knowledge and judgement through analysing your experience (i.e. through reflection) and wider reading. Figure 1.1.2 illustrates what we see as the interconnections between effective teaching, subject knowledge, professional knowledge and professional judgement.

Figure 1.1.2   Subject knowledge is just part of the effective teacher's professional tool kit

THE WIDER ROLE

The success of a school depends on the qualities and commitment of the staff as well as the pupils. A teacher's work is very varied and probably no one teacher's job is exactly the same as another's.

Most staff have responsibilities beyond their subject specialism: they may become involved in cross-curricular issues; personal, social and health education; school development planning; work experience; liaison with primary schools; careers advice; links with industry; planning educational trips and social events; curriculum planning and development; pupil performance monitoring; assessment; planning and implementing school policies; extra-curricular activities. In addition, teachers have a role to play in supporting the school ethos by reinforcing school rules and routines, e.g. on behaviour, dress and in encouraging pupils to develop self-discipline so that the school can function effectively and pupils can make the most of opportunities available to them.

Under the 1988 Education Reform Act, teachers in England and Wales have responsibility for implementing the National Curriculum and for the spiritual and moral welfare of their pupils so most

Table 1.1.1   Some of the activities which teachers undertake in their academic and pastoral roles

The academic role	*The pastoral role and spiritual and moral welfare*
The academic role of the teacher encompasses a variety of activities including:	Pastoral duties vary from school to school They often include:
<ul><li>subject teaching;</li><li>lesson preparation;</li><li>setting and marking of homework;</li><li>assessing pupil progress in a variety of ways, including marking tests and exams;</li><li>writing reports;</li><li>recording achievement;</li><li>working as part of a subject team;</li><li>curriculum development and planning;</li><li>undertaking visits, field courses;</li><li>reporting to parents;</li><li>keeping up to date (often through work with the subject association);</li><li>implementing school policies;</li><li>extra-curricular activities;</li><li>examining for public examination boards, e.g. GSCE and A level boards.</li></ul>	<ul><li>working as part of a pastoral team;</li><li>teaching pastoral, social and health education;</li><li>taking part in the daily act of worship required by legislation;</li><li>getting to know the pupils as individuals;</li><li>helping pupils with problems;</li><li>being responsible for a form; registering the class, following up absences;</li><li>monitoring sanctions and rewards given to form members;</li><li>reinforcing school rules and routines, e.g. on behaviour;</li><li>writing reports, ensuring records of achievement and/or profiles are up to date;</li><li>house/year group activities (plays/sports);</li><li>liaising with parents;</li><li>ensuring school information is conveyed to parents via pupils;</li><li>giving careers and subject guidance;</li><li>extra-curricular activities.</li></ul>

teachers have both a specialist academic role and a pastoral role. Both roles encompass administrative as well as teaching responsibilities.

The role of the teacher is changing in England due to an agreement reached between teaching unions and the government about the introduction of higher level teaching assistants who undertake many administrative tasks previously undertaken by teachers. So your administrative responsibilities may be shared. Record keeping (marks for homework, tests, classwork, attendance), marking, producing pupils' profiles and helping with records of achievement, writing references, attending meetings and planning all need to be undertaken for the classes for which you are responsible. From the beginning of your school experiences, it is worth developing efficient ways of dealing with administration to save time. Developing your word processing and spreadsheet skills will be useful in helping you prepare teaching materials and record and monitor progress. Some teachers keep their mark books electronically using spreadsheets and many schools have management information systems, which are used to monitor pupil performance and asessment (Chapter 1 of Leask and Pachler, 2005, gives guidance about how to set up an electronic mark book). Unit 1.3 on time management provides further advice. Later units provide more detailed information on a variety of aspects of the academic and pastoral roles.

HEALTH AND SAFETY

All teachers are responsible for the health and safety of the pupils in their charge. Legally, as a student teacher you cannot take on that responsibility. Whenever you are teaching, the ultimate responsibility lies with the class teacher.

Nevertheless in planning your lessons you must take into account the health and safety of your pupils by appropriate planning, e.g. identifying activities that endanger pupils, such as climbing on chairs; or for science and related subjects following the COSHH (Control Of Substances Hazardous to Health) regulations. Sharing your lesson plans in advance with your class teacher is an essential feature of your responsibility to both the pupils and your teachers. If you have any doubts about the safety of the lesson, ask for advice. If advice is not available, then don't use that strategy.

While you are teaching, an experienced teacher must always be available in the classroom or nearby. If the lesson has special safety considerations, e.g. in physical education or science, then if the class teacher or a suitably qualified teacher is not available, you must not proceed as if they were. Have an alternative lesson up your sleeve which does not require specific subject specialist support but could be carried out with the support of another teacher. Sometimes you may have to cancel your planned lesson.

It follows from this situation that, legally, you cannot act as supply teacher to fill in if the regular teacher is absent.

Task 1.1.3
Health and safety procedures

Find out who is responsible for health and safety in your school experience school. Find the school and departmental policies on health and safety. Check the procedures you will be expected to apply – for example, in science, find out how you should check the safety of the chemicals or other equipment you may use, locate the eyewash bottle and gas, water and electricity isolating taps/switches; in physical education check that you know how to test the safety of any apparatus pupils might use. Find out the names of the first aiders in the school, where the first aid box is, what you are permitted to do if an incident occurs and what forms have to be filled in to record any accident.

We suggest that you take a first aid course and find out how to deal with, for example, faints, nose bleeds, fits, asthma attacks, epilepsy, diabetic problems, burns, bleeding and common accidents. But you should not administer first aid yourself unless qualified and, even then, only the minimum necessary. You should report any incident and make a written record. There will usually be a record book in school for this purpose. Your subject association should be able to provide you with subject-specific safety information and St John Ambulance produce a first aid text for schools and provide first aid courses for school staff (see <http://www.sja.org.uk/training/courses/schools/ea.asp>).

You also need to consider the following health and safety issues that may affect you.

Your voice

A common problem for teachers new to the profession is voice strain, particularly amongst those teaching foreign languages or English as an Additional Language (EAL). If you start developing hoarseness, a sore throat or problems in projecting your voice, ask your GP to refer you for specialist help. Drinking water between lessons will help.

See the end of this unit for details of the Voice Care Network from which you can obtain further free advice on protecting your voice.

VDUs

You may find yourself needing to spend a substantial amount of time working with a visual display unit (VDU), particularly when report writing time comes round. It is important that you adjust your chair so that your spine is straight and that you take frequent breaks to stretch your limbs.

See the end of this unit for information about free guidance on working with VDUs.

Health and safety policy

The school has a legal 'duty of care' towards you as well as pupils with regard to your personal health and safety. Your school should have a health and safety policy and member of staff and a governor with a particular remit for ensuring that your working environment is safe and suitable for the activities you undertake. You also have a legal responsibility to make sure that you do not put yourself or your pupils at risk of injury by practising or allowing unsafe behaviour, or failing to report damage which could cause an accident, e.g. a hole in stair covering. Equally, you need to make sure that you look after your own safety. For example, it is not a good idea to agree to lift heavy boxes or furniture on your own and without making sure you are using the correct technique for doing so. The school site-manager and staff should be willing and able to deal with heavy lifting and it is reasonable for you to expect help.

It is also advisable take steps to protect your personal safety should you have reason to leave school or a work-related meeting late at night. As a student teacher you are not likely to visit a pupil's home. Teachers should always make sure someone, be it a family member, a friend or a colleague, knows the location of the meeting and their expected arrival home. See the end of this unit for details of the Suzy Lamplugh Trust which provides advice on personal safety practice.

> **Task 1.1.4**
> **Health and safety – what should you know?**
>
> What should you know and be able to do if you are to discharge your duties as a student teacher and as a teacher in your subject area? Discuss this with your tutor and other student teachers in your specialist area. To what extent do school and department rules help staff and pupils understand their duties in the area of safety?

Teachers also have a wide range of statutory duties set out, for England, in the document School Teachers Pay and Conditions <http://www.teachernet.gov.uk/paysite/>.

SUMMARY AND KEY POINTS

In the UK, while the curriculum is to a large extent determined centrally, the choice of teaching strategies and materials is largely in the hands of the individual teacher. Your own philosophy of teaching affects the way you approach your work – this philosophy will develop over time as you acquire further professional knowledge and your professional judgement develops.

Clearly there are certain skills which an effective teacher possesses and you can identify many of these by skimming through the contents of each chapter. As a student teacher, you have to move from knowing about these skills to being able to exercise them flexibly so that the planned learning can take place. Lists of competences/standards for newly qualified teachers which those training you will show you, are best regarded as highlighting areas for development in which you will improve your capability. There are no ready-made patterns for success in teaching. Key elements in becoming a successful teacher, i.e. ensuring your pupils learn, include:

- adequate, secure subject and pedagogic knowledge;
- attention to planning;
- awareness of pupil needs;
- concern for the welfare of pupils;
- careful monitoring of pupil achievement.

A range of different solutions can be employed in most situations and different strategies succeed with different pupils.

FURTHER READING

Hay McBer (2000) *Research into Teacher Effectiveness*, London: DfEE, <http://www.teachernet.gov.uk/haymcber>. This comprehensive report into effective teaching proposes a model of teacher effectiveness comprising teaching skills and professional characteristics. The early sections are particularly useful in relation to the preparation and planning of lessons.

Moore, A. (2004) *The Good Teacher: Dominant Discourses in Teaching and Teacher Education*, London: RoutledgeFalmer. Hayes, D. (ed.) (2004) *The RoutledgeFalmer Guide to Key Debates in Education*, London: RoutledgeFalmer. Wragg, E.C. (ed.) (2004) *The Routledgefalmer Reader in Teaching and Learning*, London: RoutledgeFalmer. These three texts provide a useful background to educational issues and overviews of key debates.

White, J. (ed.) (2004) *Rethinking the School Curriculum: Values, Aims and Purposes*, London: Routledge Falmer. This text contains series of essays discussing the place of each subject in the curriculum in England and giving an overview of curriculum developments within each subject.

Gordon, P. and Lawton, D. (2003) *Dictionary of British Education*, London: Woburn. This text gives an overview of education systems in the UK and definitions of hundreds of educational terms.

Shayer, M. and Adey, P. (2002) *Learning Intelligence: Cognitive Acceleration across the Curriculum from 5 to 15 Years*, Buckingham: Open University Press. The work underpinning the ideas in this text is well grounded in research and practice. This text is essential reading for teachers who will want to return to it over and over as they test out the ideas in their own practice. It is very focused on ways of helping pupils learn more effectively and so enable them to achieve more highly.

Shaffer, R.H. (1997) *Making Decisions About Children*, 2nd edn, Oxford: Blackwell Publishers. Teachers by the fact they are teachers, have been successful in various learning environments. From a privileged position it is easy to lack understanding of the difficult lives that many pupils lead. This book provides a useful framework for teachers to understand the different emotional issues which pupils may be facing. It discusses the impact of divorce and marital conflict, the relationship with step-parents, the relationship between poverty and psychological development and issues of vulnerability in general. Teachers can have a critical impact on pupils' self-esteem at vulnerable points in their lives.

Suzy Lamplugh Trust, 14 East Sheen Avenue, London SW14 8AS provides advice on all aspects of personal safety, e.g. when making professional visits to private homes, travelling home late at night. Tel: 020 8392 1839. Online. Available HTTP: <http://www.suzylamplugh.org>; e-mail: trust@ suzylamplugh.org.

TEACHERLINE and the Teacher Support Network is a 24 hours confidential counseling, support and advice service. This is supported by the Teachers Benevolent Fund, London, tel. 08000 562561. Online. Available HTTP: <http://www.teacherline.org.uk/>.

VDUs: Free guidance on working with VDUs is available from HSE Books, PO Box 1999, Sudbury, Suffolk CO10 2WA. Tel. 01787 881165 . Online. Available HTTP: <http://www.hsebooks.co.uk>.

Voice Care Network. Their booklet 'More Care for your Voice' and a copy of a guidance document with the same title are available from the charity Voice Care Network (VCN), 29 Southbank Road, Kenilworth CV8 1LA. Tel/fax: 01926 864000. Online. Available HTTP: <http://www.voicecare. org.uk>; e-mail: vcnuk@btconnect.com.

Unit 1.2

The Student Teacher's Role and Responsibilities

Marilyn Leask and Catherine Moorhouse

INTRODUCTION

The school-based experiences of the student teacher depend on a three-way partnership between the school, the student teacher and a higher education institution, except in those cases where the school is undertaking teacher education on its own. These experiences include the periods of whole class teaching as well as those occasions when direct class teaching is not the main purpose of the exercise.

In most partnerships between the school and the student teacher, roles and responsibilities have previously been agreed and worked out. It is important that the student teacher is aware of what those are. The same principle applies when two institutions are in partnership with the student teacher. Agreed roles and responsibilities can usually be found in the handbook for the course.

OBJECTIVES

By the end of this unit you should:

- have clarified your own role and that of your tutors in the partnership;
- have an understanding of your working role within the school;
- be aware of your responsibilities and your tutors' expectations of you;
- have developed an understanding of the professional responsibilities and behaviour required of a newly qualified teacher;
- recognize the phases of development you are likely to be going through in the transition from student teacher to effective teacher, including taking on a pastoral role.

In this unit we discuss your tutors' expectations of you and your professional responsibilities. We then go on to discuss the phases of development through which a student teacher is likely to pass.

THE SCHOOL TUTOR OR MENTOR

Schools identify members of staff to support and advise student teachers, often from the student teacher's subject department. Increasingly schools are appointing a general school tutor or mentor to oversee the work of student teachers in the school. You can expect to meet regularly with school staff to discuss your progress, any lessons observed and wider school issues.

ARRANGEMENTS FOR SCHOOL EXPERIENCE

What is expected of you in school?

Your school-based work is usually built up through a series of structured activities:

- detailed observation of experienced teachers: where you look at specific aspects of teaching in a lesson, e.g. how teachers use questions to promote learning;
- team teaching: where you share the lesson with others – planning, giving the lesson and evaluating together;
- micro-teaching: this is a short teaching episode where you teach peers or small groups of pupils – it can be useful to video-tape your micro-teaching so that an analysis of different aspects of your teaching can be carried out;
- whole class teaching with the class teacher present; and finally
- whole class teaching on your own. (As a student teacher, you should always have an experienced teacher nearby.)

An important issue for student teachers on school experience is the way feedback is given on lessons. The amount of feedback student teachers get from teachers watching their lessons varies. If you wish to have feedback on every lesson ask if this can be done. Some student teachers prefer a small amount of very focused feedback, others can cope with a page or more of comments. Written feedback is essential because it provides a record of your progress and ideas for your development. In practice, your course will have agreed conventions governing this aspect of your work. These take into account how you are to achieve the competences/standards required to complete your programme successfully.

You will probably find comments on your teaching divide into those relating to tangible technical issues which can be worked on relatively easily and those relating to less tangible issues relating to pupils' learning. Technical problems such as your use of ICT, audio-visual aids, the quality and clarity of your voice, how you position yourself in the classroom, managing transitions from one activity to another in a lesson are easy to spot, so you may receive considerable advice on these issues. Problems with these aspects of your work are usually resolved early in your course, whereas less tangible issues which are directly related to the quality of pupil learning require ongoing reflection, attention and discussion, e.g. your approach to the explanation of lesson content, your style of questioning, your evaluation of pupil learning. If you have access to videos of yourself teaching, you are advised to spend some time in the detailed analysis of your performance in these different aspects of teaching. More detailed advice related to the teaching of your specific subject is given in the subject-specific texts in the Routledge 'Learning to Teach in the Secondary School' series. The appendix to this chapter gives more detailed advice about preparing for teaching practice, including developing good working relationships with pupils and other teachers.

THE STUDENT TEACHER ROLE

You are expected to play a full part in the life of the school – gradually taking on as many aspects of a teacher's work as possible – and you should take advantage of any opportunities to extend your experience. As well as the *structured teaching activities* identified above, you can expect to undertake a wide range of activities. Table 1.2.1 provides a list illustrating the range of activities teachers undertake.

Teachers have other roles and responsibilities such as planning the curriculum and liaising with outside agencies but these are not usually undertaken by student teachers. However, you may have the opportunity to help to write course materials if your department is developing new areas of work.

In addition to these general responsibilities, staff have expectations relating to: your organization and teaching approach, your professionalism and your social skills. Table 1.2.1 summarises expectations staff may have of you in these areas.

PROFESSIONAL ATTITUDES AND RESPONSIBILITIES

Part (ii) of Table 1.2.1 provides some guidance about professional behaviour but professionalism extends beyond personal behaviour.

What does it really mean to be a professional?

The hallmarks of a profession are that there is a substantial body of knowledge which the professional needs to acquire, that substantial training is required before an individual can be accepted into the profession and that the profession is self-governing as well as publicly accountable. On the basis of this definition, for you, becoming a member of the teaching profession means that you make the following commitments. That you will:

- *Reach an acceptable level of competence and skill* in your teaching by the end of your course. This includes acquiring knowledge and skills which enable you to become an effective teacher and which enable you to understand the body of knowledge about how young people learn and how teachers can teach most effectively.
- *Continuously develop your professional knowledge and professional judgement* through experience, further learning and reflection on your work.
- *Be publicly accountable for your work.* Various members of the community have the right to inspect and/or question your work: the head, governors, parents, inspectors. You have a professional duty to plan and keep records of your work and that of the pupils. This accountability includes implementation of school policies, e.g. on behaviour, on equal opportunities.
- *Set personal standards and conform to external standards* for monitoring and improving your work.

There is a professional code of ethics which is currently unwritten in the UK but which you are expected to uphold. For example, you are expected to treat information about individuals with confidentiality; provide equal opportunities for the pupils in your care; deal with pupils in an objective, professional manner regardless of your personal feelings; keep up to date in your subject; reflect on and develop your teaching; adopt appropriate language and a professional demeanour.

In some countries teachers must have their qualifications accepted and registered with a national or state teachers' council before they are allowed to teach. Their names may be removed from this register if, for example, they are found guilty of professional misconduct. In England and Wales recognition of

Table 1.2.1 The school's expectations of the student teacher

(i) Organization and teaching approach

You will be expected to:

- Be well organized.
- Arrive in plenty of time. And that does not mean arriving just as the bell goes. It means arriving considerably earlier in order to arrange the classroom; check the availability of books and equipment; test out equipment new to you; talk to staff about the work and the children's progress; and clarify any safety issues.
- Plan and prepare thoroughly. Be conscientious in finding our what lesson content and subject knowledge are appropriate to the class you are teaching. In many cases, you will be teaching material which is new to you or which you last thought about many years ago. Staff will expect you to ask if you are not sure but to work conscientiously to improve your subject knowledge. They will not be impressed if you frequently show you have not bothered to read around the subject matter of the lesson.
- Keep good records: have your file of schemes of work and lesson plans, pupil attendance and homework record up to date. Your evaluations of your lessons are best completed on the same day as the lesson.
- Know your subject.
- Try out different methods of teaching. Teaching practice is your opportunity to try out different approaches without having to live with the results of failures, but you have a duty to the class teacher not to leave chaos behind you.

(ii) Professionalism

You will be expected to:

- Act in a professional manner, e.g. with courtesy and tact; and to respect confidentiality of information.
- Be open to new learning: seek and act on advice.
- Be flexible.
- Dress appropriately (different schools have different dress codes).
- Become familiar with and work within school procedures and policies. These include record keeping, rewards and sanctions, uniform, relationships between teachers and pupils.
- Accept a leadership role. You may find imposing your will on pupils uncomfortable but unless you establish your right to direct the work of the class, you will not be able to teach effectively.
- Recognize and understand the roles and relationships of staff responsible for your development.
- Keep up to date with your subject.
- Take active steps to ensure that your pupils learn.
- Discuss pupil progress with parents.

(iii) Social skills

You will be expected to:

- Develop a good relationship with pupils and staff.
- Keep a sense of humour.
- Work well in teams.
- Be able to communicate with children as well as adults.
- Learn to defuse difficult situations.

qualifications by the Department for Education and Skills (DfES) is required before you can teach in government-funded schools and this process is managed by the General Teaching Council for England (GTCE) with which teachers are required to register. In Scotland, there is the GTC Scotland.

As a student teacher you gradually take on the responsibilities of a teacher and develop as a professional. To do this you go through three main phases of development. In the following section, we discuss these so that you can get a sense of progression in your development.

Task 1.2.1
Professional accountability

As a teacher, you are held professionally accountable for your own work. What does this mean in practice? Discuss this question with other student teachers and make a note of the standards which you would wish to govern your own professional conduct.

PHASES OF DEVELOPMENT

Initially most student teachers are concerned with class management issues, how they come across as teachers (self-image), how they are going to control the pupils, if there is sufficient material for the lesson and whether the pupils will ask difficult questions. It is only when you have achieved some confidence in your classroom management skills that you are able to focus on whether the learning outcomes you have planned for have been generally achieved. Your initial focus is on yourself as a teacher, after which you focus on whole class learning, then the individual pupil and their learning.

During your initial teacher education course and in your early teaching career, you can expect to pass through three broad overlapping stages which we identify as:

- phase 1: focus on self-image and class management;
- phase 2: focus on whole class learning;
- phase 3: focus on individual pupil's learning.

Many student teachers are six or eight weeks into their school experience before they feel a level of confidence about their image and the management of the class (phase 1). They can then start to focus on whether the learning taking place is what was intended (phase 2). Once a student teacher feels reasonably competent in classroom management and in achieving global objectives, they should be able to shift their focus to the needs of individuals (phase 3).

Figure 1.2.1 shows how the focus of your work may change over time as you become more effective as a teacher.

As you move to phase 3 we would expect you to become aware of your pupils' personal development as well as their academic development. On school experience you can initially expect to assist the form tutor, who introduces you to this area of work.

PHASE 1: SELF-IMAGE AND CLASS MANAGEMENT

How do I come across?

Do you see yourself as a teacher? Student teachers can find it quite hard to change their self-image from that of learner, in which they may have had a passive role, to the active, managing, authoritative image of a teacher. Up until now, you may have been a learner in most classrooms you've been in and now you have to make the transition from learner to teacher. This requires a change in self-image. Teaching is sometimes likened to acting and thinking of this comparison may enable you to assume a new role more easily. Accompanying this role is a need to change your perspective. As a learner, the teachers were 'in charge', as a student teacher, teachers and tutors are also 'in charge' of you, but as a class teacher, you now become 'the person in charge'. Your role and your perception of it change during your school experience.

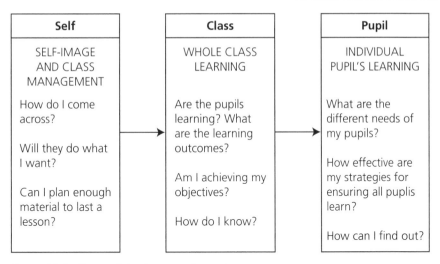

Self	Class	Pupil
SELF-IMAGE AND CLASS MANAGEMENT	WHOLE CLASS LEARNING	INDIVIDUAL PUPIL'S LEARNING
How do I come across?	Are the pupils learning? What are the learning outcomes?	What are the different needs of my pupils?
Will they do what I want?	Am I achieving my objectives?	How effective are my strategies for ensuring all pupils learn?
Can I plan enough material to last a lesson?	How do I know?	How can I find out?

Figure 1.2.1   Phases of development of a teacher

As your experience increases, your professional judgement should develop alongside your store of professional knowledge but confidence and self-belief are also needed to help you carry off the part. Figure 1.2.2 illustrates the interdependency of these different aspects.

There has been much research on what makes teachers effective and the various texts on teaching skills and classroom management listed throughout this book provide a wide range of perspectives on effectiveness (e.g. the subject-specific texts in this 'Learning to Teach in the Secondary School' series, Bleach, 2000). A summary of the attributes of effective teachers drawn from these texts and others is given in Table 1.2.2.

Increasing professional knowledge and judgement

Increasing effectiveness and competence

Increasing confidence and self-belief

Figure 1.2.2   Becoming an effective teacher

Table 1.2.2   Attributes of effective teachers (Munn *et al.*)

Humorous	Enthusiastic	Enjoys the subject
Relaxed	Organized	Makes the work relevant
Imaginative	Supportive	Is active in helping pupils to learn
Warm	Cheerful	Uses a variety of methods
Firm	Flexible	Has high expectations
Listens	Encourages	Explains clearly
Fair	Sympathetic	Gives praise
Friendly	Responsive	Applies sanctions fairly and does not make threats

When pupils' perceptions of teachers were researched as part of a wider study on discipline in Scotland (Munn *et al.*, 1990), pupils identified over 75 per cent of their teachers as being effective in terms of getting the class to work well, although as the authors point out, getting the class to work well is not the same as ensuring that the pupils learn what was intended. Humour as well as use of sanctions and threats were perceived by pupils as important characteristics of effective teachers. The amount of talk between pupils in lessons is usually of concern to staff. Yet pupil comments about the effect of the level of talk were mixed: some felt a high level of talk was a sign that the teacher wasn't in control, while others did not suggest this link. Making it clear to pupils what types of talk you allow in the classroom can be helpful to pupils. 'Partner talk' is an example of what you might allow when pupils are working together, i.e. a soft voice which only one other person can hear.

It is unlikely that any one teacher will have all the attributes listed in Table 1.2.2. In any case, you could probably have many of the attributes listed but still lack authority in the classroom. Neither the attributes themselves nor relationships between teachers and pupils can be developed by ticking off attributes on a checklist. However, you can monitor and evaluate their development. We have included this list in order to give you ideas to consider when you are undertaking your own self-evaluation.

**Task 1.2.2
What kind of teacher do you want to be?**

What image do you want to create? What role do you see yourself assuming? How would you like others to see you as a teacher? If you are at the beginning of your course, write a profile for the 'sort of teacher I want to be' in about 500 words. Base this on your own education and educational experiences.
Repeat the activity at the end of the course when you've had experience.

Will they do what I say? Classroom management and control

Controlling adolescents is one of the biggest worries student teachers have initially. Units 2.3 and 3.3 provide a considerable amount of information to prepare you for this aspect of your work and Unit 2.1 contains guidelines about observing teachers and classrooms. You may find materials on the Behaviour4Learning website <http://www.behaviour4learning.ac.uk> useful. Developing an aura of authority takes time, effort and reflection on what has happened in order to modify your behaviour. The tasks in Unit 2.1 are designed to help you analyse the routines and expectations which appear to be operated, often effortlessly, by the teachers whose classes you take.

To see how these routines and expectations are established you would have to shadow a teacher new to a school from the beginning of the school year. The early weeks that teachers new to a school spend with their classes are crucial to setting up the working relationship as is the way new teachers conduct themselves in the corridors and playground. The pupil grapevine is a powerful means of spreading a teacher's reputation. Teachers who have been at the school for some time are automatically treated in a certain way by pupils because their reputation has gone before them. So you need to work at establishing your reputation. You may find it helpful to review video materials showing how teachers establish routines with new classes. These are available on <http://www. ttrb.ac.uk>.

PHASE 2: WHOLE CLASS LEARNING

Teaching is not the same as learning, nor is telling pupils the same as them learning. Teaching means organizing experiences and activities which cause pupils to engage actively with the material and thus learn. Copying notes, for example, does not in our experience lead to active engagement, whereas constructing notes with help and guidance is good practice. The teacher's role is then to monitor the outcomes from these experiences and activities. Chapter 5 provides further details about learning.

As you become more competent in classroom management, your concerns shift from asking 'Will I survive?' to 'Are the pupils learning anything from me?' The way you present your lesson and explain the material (the exposition) and the methods you use for asking questions about it become the focus of your attention as you try to improve the learning taking place for the whole class. In Unit 2.2 on lesson planning, the importance of setting clear objectives for each lesson is stressed. Unit 7.4 summarizes the advice given in the English Key Stage 3 Strategy initiative about the planning of lessons (Key Stage 3 covers the age range 11–13 years). Objectives are used to identify the learning outcomes which you expect from that lesson such as skill development, mastery of content, development of attitudes, understanding of processes. However, what is important is that the objectives are clear enough for you to identify when the pupil has achieved those objectives, by action or other behaviour. Individual lesson objectives give a cumulative picture of the outcomes that you expect your class to achieve. Assessment is then based on the achievement (or otherwise) of outcomes.

Your lesson evaluations help you monitor the learning of the class. They provide an analysis of what went well and what could have been improved. You can expect your class teachers and tutor to discuss your evaluations. In this second phase of your development, such post-lesson discussions focus more on the learning taking place rather than on the image and management issues which will have preoccupied you initially.

PHASE 3: INDIVIDUAL LEARNING

Later, as your analytical and planning skills develop and you build your confidence and professional knowledge about learning, you become able to design your lessons so that the *academic needs of individual pupils* are better catered for, i.e. you can more easily build differentiation into your teaching.

Effective teachers help individual pupils to grow. If a teacher can manage, in spite of the pressures of time, to give individuals a sense of achievement and self-worth then their pupils' motivation is usually increased. The converse is also true.

Whilst student teachers are expected to analyse their effectiveness in achieving their lesson objectives, the skills and experience required to be able to provide differentiated work usually take longer to develop and opportunities should arise to develop this understanding further after your initial teacher

---

Task 1.2.3
'The average child'

Reflect on the poem below 'The Average Child'. Think about the implications for your own teaching. In your classroom observations and evaluations, focus on an 'average child' for a number of sessions. Plan your interactions with a small group of these pupils so that you leave them feeling 'special'. Discuss your perceptions with other student teachers.

I don't cause teachers trouble, my grades have been okay.
I listen in my classes and I'm in school everyday.
My parents think I'm average, my teachers think so too.
I wish I didn't know that cause there's lots I'd like to do.
I'd like to build a space rocket, I've a book that shows you how.
Or start a stamp collection, well no use trying now.
Cause since I've found I'm average, I'm just not smart enough you see
I know there's nothing special that I should expect of me.
I'm part of that majority that hump part of the bell*,
Who'll just spend all his life in an average kind of hell.

* This refers to the bell shape of a 'normal distribution' curve.

Buscemi (date unknown) in P. Reeve, 'The average child', unpublished dissertation, De Montfort University, Bedford, 1992.

---

education course. Differentiated work is work which is designed to allow pupils with different abilities to achieve preset goals, i.e. it provides the opportunity for pupils to undertake different tasks or to achieve different outcomes depending on ability. Unit 4.1 provides further information about how you may differentiate work.

Task 1.2.4
What have the pupils learned?

Towards the end of your school experience, arrange to interview a small group of pupils before you teach them about what they know and understand about a topic. Have specific questions in terms of knowledge and understanding that you expect them to achieve through their work on the topic. Then interview them after the lesson to find out what they know and understand about it after being taught. Consider the implications of the findings for your teaching.

SUMMARY AND KEY POINTS

In this unit we have introduced you to some of the complexities of your role as a student teacher. The role of a teacher is diverse but with practice, support, increasing experience and ongoing learning, you can expect your level of competence to rise and with it satisfaction.

Because of the dynamic nature of educational practice you should expect to go on learning throughout your career. Your initial teacher education course only provides a foundation on which to build your professional knowledge and your professional judgement.

In becoming a teacher, you can expect to move through the three phases (self-image and class management, class learning, individual learning) as your experience, confidence and competence increase. We hope, by identifying each phase, that we have helped you understand the task ahead of you. Evaluation through critical reflection is one of the tools in your professional tool kit which you can use to analyse your effectiveness in helping pupils learn (see Unit 5.4). The professional knowledge and judgement of experienced teachers with whom you work also provide a rich resource on which to draw in developing your own knowledge and judgement about how to support pupil learning effectively.

APPENDIX TO UNIT 1.2: WORKING RELATIONSHIPS

As a student teacher on school experience, you are in schools with established ways of working and established working relationships between staff. You have opportunities to become part of the social organization of the school and it helps you settle in if you spend some time understanding the social and physical environment that you are moving into. You also need to develop a professional relationship with your pupils. This appendix considers issues you need to be aware of when you start a new school experience (and later as a newly qualified teacher).

Unit 1.2 introduces you to general issues related to starting your school experience. In this appendix, specific advice is given based on the experiences of student teachers in the past. Issues covered are:

- how to find out about the social and physical environment of the school;
- how to develop a professional working relationship with pupils;
- the need to manage working relationships with colleagues.

Preparing for school experience: learning about your school

It is worth finding out as much as you can about your school experience school and its organization, as well as the specific department before you start. Ideally, you will have visited your school at least once before you start your school experience. It is helpful on such a visit to have a list of things you want to find out about the school. It is likely that your tutor will have given you a list of information to gather and questions to ask to help you with this.

This visit also enables you to familiarize yourself with the geography of the building – particularly if you are going to teach in a large school, maybe one with several different blocks or even one that operates on more than one site. Secondary schools vary immensely not just in size but also in physical features, ranging from the small rural or special school with under 100 pupils to the very large school with 1,000–2,000 pupils. Some schools are modern, or comparatively modern, while others are old, dating back to the 1880s. Each type of building has advantages and disadvantages. Whichever type of school you are in on school experience, it is important that you locate important facilities such as the office, lavatories and the staff room, before you start. The last thing you need to do on your first day is to get lost! If you are planning to drive to school, check out the parking facilities and conventions – there may be reserved spots for some staff.

Take similar care in the staff room. Some staff rooms are like lounges where teachers can relax and chat safely away from work and pupils during break and lunch times. Others have an additional function as a workroom (with or without allocated work spaces) where teachers can do marking and lesson preparation during their free periods. There are still some schools where the same staff have sat in the same chairs for ten, twenty or even thirty years! Colleagues may have brought in their own mugs for tea/coffee. There may or may not be a 'tea/coffee club'. Check it out, that way you will avoid upsetting anyone.

There is a lot of paperwork associated with teaching! During your visit you may or may not be introduced to the head teacher. However, you can expect to talk to the professional tutor and staff with specific areas of responsibility in the school. There are a large number of policy and procedure documents in every school, covering a wide range of subjects, e.g. school uniform; equal opportunities; behaviour management; marking policy; risk management. Often these can be found in a staff handbook. You may be issued with a copy of this, or there may be a copy in the staff room or school office. Your tutor may discuss the most relevant sections in the handbook which you can then read in your own time after the visit. This discussion and further reading provides you with useful practical information about how the school operates and what you need to do to comply with its policies and procedures. The staff handbook should also include a diagram showing the school's management structure and lines of accountability. Your training institution and its partner schools will have an agreed procedure if you are sick or have another important reason (e.g. an interview) to be off school.

You will also talk to the head of faculty or department and others in the department about the curriculum, schemes of work and your teaching timetable. These discussions are likely to include specific aspects of teaching in the department, e.g. safety issues, organization of equipment and pupils, schemes of work, lesson plans, homework routines, access to texts and resources including ICT.

You can gather further information about schools in England in Office for Standards in Education (OFSTED) inspection reports. These are public documents that you can find on the OFSTED website, or the school may be able to lend you a copy. The school's last inspection report will provide you with a wealth of information about all aspects of the school as it was assessed at the time of the inspection. This will provide you with questions to discuss with staff and areas to follow up as you learn more about the school.

Developing professional relationships with pupils

Teaching can be exhilarating and satisfying, particularly when everything goes well, you like your class(es) and they like you. As a student teacher, you may receive a sympathetic response from pupils. Pupils often respond well to young teachers because they may appear less remote from them. On the other hand they may sense your inexperience and try to take advantage of it by 'playing up'. You need to adopt a firm but fair hand from the start (see the discussion in Unit 3.3).

Use your common sense in developing your professional relationships with pupils. Always treat pupils with respect. You should model appropriate language with your pupils – be careful about the language you use. Always be polite to pupils (and expect them to be polite back to you). You may need to practise this in some situations, e.g. where pupils' behaviour, attitude or effort is not what you accept. Pupils need to learn the relationship between cause and effect in their conduct. If a pupil's behaviour is poor, explain why it is unacceptable and the outcomes it could lead to. It is the *behaviour* that is unacceptable, not the pupil. Your school should have a behaviour management policy that states the actions you can take and the support you can expect to receive in addressing disruptive behaviour (see Unit 3.3). Never 'name call' pupils using terms such as 'stupid', 'lazy', etc. Where work or effort is less than satisfactory, a response to the effect that 'I know you can do better than that' followed by encouragement and advice on how to improve it is more likely to be received without resentment than remarks such as 'This is a load of rubbish'. Pupils do not always hear or remember communications in the way you express them, particularly if they are less than complimentary. This can lead to your having said 'That's a stupid answer' being reported at home as 'the teacher called me stupid' and angry parents arriving in the head's office the next morning.

Remember you are a professional. It is important that you retain a professional distance between you and the pupils and not to become over friendly with them, particularly those who might be comparatively close to you in age. Remarks and gestures you may intend as friendly banter can be badly misconstrued, possibly seen as indicating 'special regard' for one or more pupils. These may ultimately lead to trouble. Male teachers can be particularly vulnerable in this respect. As a student teacher (and later as a teacher), you should not visit pupils' homes on your own (unless you have sought the agreement of the headteacher and there is a good professional reason why you need to do so). If you happen to be involved in the running of youth organizations outside school, you may come across members who are pupils at your school experience school. Again, be cautious in how you behave towards these pupils and do not single them out for special treatment of any kind. Sometimes adolescent pupils develop serious 'crushes' on teachers and write affectionate notes, cards or even e-mails and text messages. Do not respond to these and, if you are concerned about the content, inform the pupil's pastoral tutor or year head. They will advise you about how to handle the problem and may offer to deal with the pupil concerned in a sensitive way. See the extension to this unit on the website for further advice. One of the hazards of teaching as a profession is that teachers can be subject to allegations from pupils and/or parents. Prevention is better than cure. There are steps you can take to minimize the likelihood of serious allegations being made against you. Teachers usually avoid being in a classroom alone with a single pupil or, if they need to do so, they keep the door open. We suggest you avoid making physical contact with pupils (even in jest) unless you need to for teaching or safety purposes (e.g. in a physical education or other practical lesson in which there is a safety issue, or if the pupil becomes violent). Your school should have a policy and procedures on the use of physical restraint on pupils for their, other pupils' or your own safety. However, as a student teacher your tutor or other experienced teacher in your lesson should know what to do on such occasions and you should have the chance to receive training in the accepted techniques.

Relationships with colleagues

Teaching is also a physically and emotionally demanding job even though you do not teach a full timetable on school experience. It is the one profession where you can find yourself alone in charge of 30 pupils for long periods and every hour and minute of that time is supposed to be a positive and productive experience for them. As discussed in Unit 1.3, it is very important that you try to achieve a sensible work/life balance, ensuring that you make enough time to relax at the end of the evening as well as to have sufficient sleep.

Your tutor's role is to advise and support you so that you have an enjoyable and successful school experience. Your tutor should be someone who is an experienced teacher who is committed to the mentoring role and ready and available to you to listen to any problems you might have and to offer you practical advice.

Other colleagues in school, e.g. year or departmental/faculty heads and their deputies; curriculum, subject and Key Stage leaders; and members of the senior management team are also able to help you with any queries you may have. You are also likely to find friends amongst the other colleagues you work with who are willing to answer your questions and offer you advice. As a student teacher (and later as a teacher) you are part of a subject or department team and working together with other people is an essential part of team activity. Frequent dialogue with colleagues can be invigorating as well as helpful.

Whilst the profile of teaching staff is becoming increasingly young, there may well be teachers in your school who have 30+ years of service and may even have been in the same school throughout their careers. They have enormous experience and in many cases enjoy much respect from colleagues and pupils. Whilst some individuals may have had a very different training from yours and some may appear to you sceptical, they have an enormous amount of wisdom to offer, especially on issues of pupil management and the expectations of the school.

You need to be aware that teaching is such a strenuous job that problems do sometimes arise in working relationships. Sometimes they are trivial and based on no more than a genuine misunderstanding or a mistake made as a result of lack of experience, and good will is easily restored after an explanation and an apology. As a student teacher you may become aware of professional disagreements between teachers in a department. These can range from how something should be taught; how lessons are organized; behaviours on the part of a colleague that are undermining or otherwise unacceptable, such as addressing another teacher in a disrespectful way in front of pupils or colleagues. Occasionally there is bullying or harassment, but this usually occurs without witnesses. Such events are rare but are very distressing.

SUMMARY AND KEY POINTS

The advice in this appendix is intended to help you as a student teacher (and later as a new teacher), quickly settle into your school experience school. It is also designed to help you develop a professional relationship with your pupils and to start to feel a member of your team of colleagues and enjoy your teaching as well as the camaraderie of the staffroom. Social contact with your colleagues can enhance working relationships and ensure that you have one or more people from whom you can seek advice during your school experience.

USEFUL ADDRESSES, PUBLICATIONS AND HELPLINES

In the UK there are four main teachers' professional associations (unions).

Association of Teachers and Lecturers (ATL), 7 Northumberland Street, London WC2N 5RD; tel: 020 7930 6441; website: <http://www.atl.org.uk>; e-mail: info@atl.org.uk.

National Association of Schoolmasters Union of Women Teachers (NASUWT), Hillscourt Education Centre, Rednal, Birmingham, B45 8RS; tel: 0121 453 6150; website: <http://www.teachersunion.org.uk>; e-mail: nasuwt.org.uk .

National Union of Teachers (NUT), Hamilton House, Mabledon Place, London WC1H 9BJ; tel: 0207 388 6191; website: <http://www.teachers.org.uk>; e-mail: j.friedlander@ nut.org.uk.

Professional Association of Teachers (PAT), 2 St James' Court, Friars Gate, Derby DE1 1BT; tel: 01322 373337; website: <http://www.pat.org.uk>; e-mail: hq@pat.org.uk.

In addition to offering direct advice and support to members on employment related matters, the associations produce useful newsletters and publications on a range of topics, offer special concessions, e.g. on car and travel insurance, and training courses.

Teacher Support Line is an independent charity which provides a 24-hour information, support and counselling service. Tel. 08000 562 561.

Copies of OfSTED reports and other DfES information and publications can be accessed on the OFSTED and DfES websites: <http://www.ofsted.gov.uk>; <http://www.dfes.gov.uk>.

The Andrea Adams Trust is a charity which has a helpline for victims of workplace bullying on 01273 704900 (Mondays to Fridays 10.00–16.00) and its website can be found at <http://www. andreaadamstrust.org>.

Association of Teachers and Lecturers (ATL) (1999) 'Bullying at Work, A Guide for Teachers' – order online at <http://www.atl.org.uk>.

The General Teaching Council of England governs professional standards in teaching (you will be required to register). Its address is Whittington House, 19–30 Alfred House, London WC1E 7EA; tel: 0870 001 0308; fax: 020 7023 3909; website: <http://www.gtce.org.uk>; e-mail: info@gtc.org.uk.

Your local telephone directory will provide contact details of the nearest Citizens Advice Bureau, Law Centre, Race Equality Council and other help agencies in your area.

FURTHER READING

Frobisher, L., Monaghan, J., Orton, A., Orton, J., Roper, T. and Threfall, J. (1999) *Learning to Teach Numbers: A Handbook for Students and Teachers in the Primary School*, Cheltenham: Stanley Thornes. Many teachers, whatever their subject, will use number work in their teaching. This text provides a useful understanding of how to teach number and can provide valuable underpinning to the work of a secondary teacher.

Howe, M.J.A. (1998) *A Teacher's Guide to the Psychology of Learning*, 2nd edn, Oxford: Blackwell Publishers. This is a valuable text to add to a teachers' professional toolbox. This book addresses the issues of the importance of rehearsing and practising activities as well as the importance of a teacher providing material of personal relevance. It addresses the structuring of information in ways that aid learning and deals with issues such as motivation, intelligence and extending writing skills.

Joyce, B., Calhoun, E. and Hopkins, D. (2002) *Models of Learning – Tools for Teaching*, 2nd edn, Buckingham: Open University Press. This is a comprehensive text focusing on different models of teaching and learning.

Voice Care Network. Their booklet 'More Care for your Voice' is available from the following address: 29 Southbank Road, Kenilworth, Warwickshire CU8 1LA; tel: 01926 864000. Online. Available HTTP: <http://www.voicecare.org.uk>; e-mail: vcnuk@btconnect.com. This organization is a registered charity with subscribing members. They focus on teachers' problems and encourage teachers to contact them for advice. They also provide training sessions.

Unit 1.3

Managing your Time and Stress

Susan Capel

INTRODUCTION

Although teaching can be rewarding and exciting, it can also be demanding and stressful. You may be surprised by the amount of time and energy you use while on school experience (and later as a teacher), inside and outside the classroom and outside the school day. There is little time within a school day in which you can relax.

Although you may feel as though you have to keep running faster to keep up with all that is required of you as a student teacher (and later as a teacher), this is not going to help you – indeed, it is likely to increase your stress. You need to plan to use your time and energy effectively over the week. You must not spend so much time preparing one lesson that you do not have time to prepare others well (there are, of course, times when you want to take extra time planning one particular lesson, e.g. for a difficult class with whom the last lesson did not go well or if you are less familiar with the material). Likewise, you must use your energy wisely, so that you have enough energy to teach each lesson well.

Undoubtedly you will be tired. Many student teachers have told us that they are so tired when they get home from school that they have to force themselves to stay awake. If your teaching commitment is not to take over your whole life, you need to manage your time and energy and the stress associated with your school experience and teaching.

There is increasing investment nationally to resolve issues which result in low retention of teachers (some of which cause high levels of stress) – including workload. This includes transferring some tasks from teachers to teaching assistants to lighten teachers' workload. Thus, there is likely to be a change in initial teacher education (ITE) to enable student teachers to see themselves as part of a team of professionals and paraprofessionals. These changes should help student teachers (and also teachers), although you still need to manage your time and stress effectively, otherwise you are not going to benefit from these changes.

> **OBJECTIVES**
>
> By the end of this unit you should be able to:
>
> * identify ways you can use your time effectively in the classroom;
> * develop ways to manage your time effectively;
> * identify factors that may cause you stress;
> * develop methods of coping with stress.

MANAGING YOUR TIME

As Amos (1998) emphasized, everyone has the same amount of time. It cannot be lost, increased, saved, delegated, reallocated nor reclaimed by turning the clock back. Time can easily be misused or wasted, therefore it is especially important to consider what you do in your teaching and how you do it.

First, pupils spend little time in school each year. Assuming six hours contact time per day and 200 days per year, pupils spend less than 14 per cent of their time in lessons (Arnold (1993) calculated that primary school pupils spend less than 12 per cent of their time in lessons (assuming five hours contact each day)). Over 12 years of compulsory schooling pupils spend about 92 weeks in total in lessons. Calculate how much (or little) time pupils spend in lessons in your subject over a year. It is therefore very important that you use this time effectively.

Second, the three main reasons given by teachers as factors which are demotivating and lower morale (e.g. GTC, 2003; PriceWaterhouseCoopers, 2001; School Teachers' Review Body, 2002) and by teachers who leave the profession within the first few years (e.g. Spear *et al.*, 2000; Wilhelm *et al.*, 2000) are related to time and stress. These three factors are: too heavy a workload; work is too pressurized and stressful; and too much administration. These reasons are also causes of concern for student teachers.

Managing your time in the classroom

To use classroom time effectively and economically you need to plan to maximize the amount of time available in the lesson, reduce the time it takes for pupils to get to lessons, to settle down and to pack up at the end and to manage pupils' behaviour in the lesson. Ways of doing this include:

* allocating a high proportion of available time for academic work (sometimes called academic learning time);
* maintaining a good balance in the use of time on teaching, supervisory and organizational activities;
* spending a high proportion of time in 'substantive interaction' with pupils (i.e. explaining, questioning, describing, illustrating);
* regularly reviewing the conduct of lessons in terms of effective use of your own and pupils' time;
* devising simple, fast procedures for routine events and dealing with recurring problems;
* eliminating unnecessary routines and activities from your own performance;
* delegating (to teaching assistants or pupils) responsibilities and tasks that are within their capability (adapted from Waterhouse, 1983: 46).

This should enable pupils to:

- spend a high proportion of their time engaged on learning tasks; and
- experience a high degree of success during this engaged time.

These time management principles can be applied in many ways in the classroom. For example:

- Spending time at the start of the first lesson with the pupils (and as a teacher at the start of the academic year) establishing rules and routines – to save time on organization and management – including behaviour management, as you proceed through the unit (or year). Pay special attention here to safety issues. See Unit 3.3 for further information about managing pupils behaviour and Units 1.2 and 2.2 for further information about organization, rules and routines in the classroom.
- Teaching pupils to seek answers themselves rather than putting their hand up as soon as they get stuck.
- Organizing your files and other work so that you can locate it easily (throw away paper you do not need again).
- Using teaching assistants or pupils to help give out and collect textbooks, pupils' books or equipment, to mark straightforward homework tests in class, make sure the classroom is left ready for the next class with the chairs tidy, floor clear, board clean and books tidied away.
- Carrying a marking pen with you as you move around the class checking the work that is going on. As you skim pupils' work and comment to them, you can make brief notes on the work. It is easier to pick up mistakes and check work when it is fresh in your mind. This not only provides formative feedback to pupils to promote learning, it saves you having to go back to the work at a later stage which, in itself, wastes time.
- Collecting in books which are open at the page where you should start marking.
- Ensuring that work is dated and that homework is clearly identified so that it is easy for you to check what work has been done and what is missing. Ruling off each lesson's work helps you to check this.
- Keeping one page of your mark book for comments about progress (folding the page over ensures that comments are not seen inadvertently by pupils). As you see pupils' work in class or when you are marking, you can make brief notes which are then immediately at hand for discussions with parents, head of year, report writing, etc.

There are many other ways of managing time effectively in classrooms which you develop as you gain experience.

Task 1.3.1
How you spend your time in lessons

Observe how several experienced teachers use their time effectively in lessons. For example, look at how they divide time between teaching, supervisory and organizational activities, time spent managing pupils' behaviour, time spent on explaining and questioning, time spent on procedures for routine events such as collecting in homework or giving back books, what is delegated to teaching assistants or pupils. Ask another student teacher or your tutor to observe how you use time in the classroom in one lesson or over a series of lessons. Discuss with the observer the findings and possible ways of using your or the pupils' lesson time more effectively and economically. Try these ideas out systematically in your teaching.

Planning outside the classroom

Carefully plan the use of time in each lesson. This planning takes time – indeed, it takes more time when you start out than it does later in your teaching career. Use a time line in your lesson plan, allocating time for each activity, as described in Unit 2.2. Allow time for pupils moving from one part of the school to another for the lesson (and in physical education time for changing), getting the class settled, particularly at the beginning of the day, after a break or lunch. You may find initially that you under- or over-estimate the time needed for each activity, including organization and management activities. In your reflection and evaluation at the end of each lesson compare the time taken for each activity with that allocated. Although this helps you gradually to become realistic about how long different activities in a lesson take, early in learning to teach you take longer to organize and manage your classes. It is therefore important that you do not base your planning on the time it takes to organize and manage classes initially; rather you should work hard to develop routine procedures to reduce this time as much as possible so that you maximize the learning time in the lesson.

Similarly, in planning a series of lessons, allocate time carefully. You have a certain amount of work to cover over a given period of time. If you do not plan carefully, you may find yourself taking too long over some of the content and not leaving yourself with enough time to cover all the content. Pupils' knowledge and understanding develop over a period of time; therefore if they do not complete the content required, their learning may be incomplete. Unit 2.2 provides more information about lesson planning and schemes of work.

In order to use your time outside the classroom effectively you need to plan your use of time and prioritize your work. Keeping records of activities can help with this, for example, keep a file of activities for the week – which you clear at the end of each week (e.g. lessons to plan, marking to do, assignments for your course, completing specific records of your work, including how you have met certain standards). You may also want to make a list of activities you are going to complete each day. If there are activities left on the list at the end of the week or the day, why is this, e.g. you are spending too much time on each activity, you are unrealistic in how much you can achieve in a day?

Also leave time for reflection on your teaching overall and your development as a teacher (what have you learned and how are you going to develop further?).

Task 1.3.2
Planning how to use lesson time

> When planning your lessons, deliberately think about how best you can use the time available. Determine what proportion of time to allocate to each activity and indicate, next to each activity, the amount of time to be allocated to it. When you evaluate the lesson and each activity in it, look specifically at how the time was used. Ask yourself how you can organize pupils and establish routines to make more time available for teaching and learning. Include these in future lesson plans.

Managing your own time effectively

However well you use time in the classroom, you may not be using the time you put into your work and your own time to best advantage. Some people always seem to work long hours but achieve little, whereas others achieve a great deal but still appear to have plenty of time to do things other than work.

One explanation for this could be that the first person wastes time, through, for example, being unsystematic in managing time or handling paperwork, putting off work rather than getting on and doing it, trying to do it all rather than delegating appropriately or not being able to say no to tasks, whereas the second person uses time well by, for example, having clear objectives for work to be done, prioritizing work, completing urgent and important tasks first and writing lists of tasks to achieve during the day. Which of these descriptions fits you? To check – you need to analyse the way you work and, if necessary, try to make changes. Task 1.3.3 is designed to help with this.

Task 1.3.3
Planning your use of time outside the classroom

Record for one week the amount of time you spend on school work outside the classroom, e.g. planning, preparation, marking, record keeping, extra-curricular activities, meetings – both at school and at home. You might want to use a grid such as the one here.

Day	Work undertaken (along with time for each activity)	Total time
Monday		
Tuesday		
Wednesday		
Thursday		
Friday		
Saturday		
Sunday		
Total time for one week		

Consider whether the time spent outside the classroom and total hours worked during the week is reasonable; whether you are using this time effectively, i.e. whether the balance of time spent on the activities is right, e.g. whether you are spending more time on record keeping than on planning and preparation, whether you need to spend more time on some activities and whether you could reduce time on some activities, e.g. can some of the work be delegated to pupils (e.g. mounting and displaying work)?

If time spent is excessive (48 hours is the maximum working week in the European Union working time directive), plan what action you are going to take to reduce the time spent on school-related work each week. Recheck the use of time outside the classroom by repeating the log for one week to see whether this has worked and in light of the results what further action you need to, and can, take.

Fontana (1993) stressed that if we could use our time effectively at work we would be more efficient and more productive, be better able to plan long term, be more satisfied with our work and our job, be less stressed, have more time for ourselves and more opportunity to switch off out of work. There are many different techniques you can use to manage your time effectively. Figure 1.3.1 highlights some of these. Draw your own clock and insert your own techniques to avoid working around the clock.

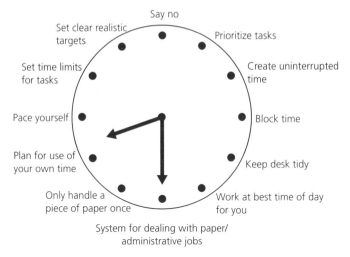

Figure 1.3.1   Working round the clock

Task 1.3.4
Balancing your work and leisure time

In Task 1.3.3 you recorded the time spent outside the classroom over the course of a week on school experience. Now do the same for the time spent, on, and use of, leisure time. You may want to use a table similar to the one in Task 1.3.3. Looking at both tables, why is the balance between school-related work and leisure time as it is? Is this balance acceptable? If not, is it because of, for example, inefficiency, lack of experience or overload? How can you improve it? Discuss the balance of work and leisure with other student teachers and discuss with teachers how they achieve a balance between work and leisure time.

PREVENTING, MANAGING AND COPING WITH STRESS

'Teacher stress may be defined as the experience by a teacher of unpleasant, negative emotions, such as anger, anxiety, tension, frustration or depression, resulting from some aspect of their work as a teacher' (Kyriacou, 2001: 28). Compared to other social welfare professions, teachers experience the highest levels of stress (e.g. Dunham and Varma, 1998; Kyriacou, 2000b; Travers and Cooper, 1996). Other studies have suggested that between a quarter and a third of teachers report their job to be (extremely) stressful (e.g. Gold and Roth, 1993; Mills, 1995). It would therefore be surprising if student teachers did not find teaching stressful.

Although it is preferable if you can prevent stress, this is not always possible therefore it is important that you identify causes of stress for you and develop strategies to be able to cope with it.

Causes of stress

Many causes of teacher stress (including time factors and demanding work conditions) have been identified (see e.g. Benmansour, 1998; Brown and Ralph, 2002). Stokking *et al.* (2003) identified shock and stress when starting to teach as a result of lack of preparation, which they suggested might be due to student teachers having false expectations of the profession (which may be for a range of reasons). Likewise, Terry (1997) found that unrealistic expectations as a result of lack of preparation caused by inadequate training were one source of stress. This can be exacerbated by 'being thrown in at the deep end' or alleviated by gradually growing into more independent roles. On the other hand, research indicates that good preparation for teaching has been found to reduce stress (e.g. Dussault et. al., 1997; Terry, 1997). You need to check the causes of stress for you as a student teacher and work to eliminate them.

Student teachers are likely to have different concerns at different stages in learning to teach. Fuller and Bown (1975) classified changes in concerns over time in learning to teach as a three-way process, i.e. concerns about self; concerns about tasks/situations; concerns about impact on pupils) (see also Unit 1.1). Thus, being concerned about specific aspects of your teaching or your development as a teacher at specific times is a natural part of learning to teach. As you go through your ITE year, reflect on your own development as a teacher, particularly whether your concerns are the same or different at different times of the year.

Studies of stress in student teachers (e.g. Capel, 1996, 1997, 1998; Kyriacou and Stephens, 1999; Morton *et al.*, 1997) have shown that major causes of stress for student teachers include:

- not being regarded as a real teacher;
- control and discipline and dealing with disruptive behaviour;
- motivating pupils and maintaining pupils' interest;
- conflict with pupils;
- coping with the ability range of pupils within a class;
- practical skills of teaching, techniques of lesson preparation and getting the teaching and/or planning right;
- disagreement with the tutor;
- coping with a heavy workload;
- observation, evaluation and assessment of teaching by the tutor, particularly receiving the tutor's or class teacher's opinion of classroom competence;
- role ambiguity, role conflict and role overload.

There are, of course, many other aspects of your teaching that may cause you stress or anxiety, e.g. delivering material with which you are not very familiar or reprimanding a pupil. Later units in this book identify practical ways to help you overcome many of these anxieties. The last two in the list above are considered briefly below because they are particularly relevant to student teachers.

When you are being observed, evaluated and assessed, you are 'on show'. You are vulnerable because your developing skills are analysed and criticised constructively. This may be exacerbated where teachers' take on the role of tutors in ITE. According to Pateman (1994) the role of teachers in assessing the teaching competence of student teachers means that many student teachers feel unable to talk freely and openly to teachers about other concerns. Thus, the role of the teacher-tutor in assessment does not take account of student teachers' needs for friendship, counselling and tutoring. This may cause stress for student teachers. This finding is supported in other research on stress in student teachers, e.g. Capel (1994).

Often your role is ambiguous, so you are not quite sure how to perform in the role of a student teacher.

Role conflict can result from doing a number of different activities within your job, each requiring different responsibilities, demands and skills, e.g. teaching, form tutoring, talking to parents, administration (clerical work and committee duties), other tasks within the department, continuing professional development (inter-role conflict) or from trying to meet the different expectations of a number of people with whom you are working, e.g. pupils, your tutor, other teachers, head of department, senior managers, parents (intra-role conflict).

Role overload can occur because there are so many things for you to do as a teacher and too little time in which to do them. Indeed, in a study by Kyriacou *et al.* (2003) less than 10 per cent of student teachers were absolutely certain that they would have enough time to do a good job. Overload can result in not doing a good job, working very long hours to get the task done and not having enough time mentally and physically to relax for work the following day or week. You can help with this by e.g. spending five minutes identifying what you need for the next day (this also helps to save time – see above).

Role ambiguity, conflict and overload may affect student teachers more than qualified teachers for a number of reasons. For example, student teachers may, at any one time, be answering to and trying to please a number of people, who expect different things. They may also take longer to prepare each lesson than more experienced teachers. Further, they may be unsure of their role in a lesson, a department or the school as a whole.

It may be that stressors outside work, e.g. tensions of home and family or finances, are brought to and add to stress at work and make a person more vulnerable to stressors at work. Job stress may vary during the year according to the demands of a job, personal circumstances and/or other factors at any one time. A significant stressor at a particular time could account for differences in stress experienced by people at different times of a school year.

Task 1.3.5
Causes of stress for student teachers

In your diary write a list of factors that cause stress for you – both stressors as a student teacher and stressors outside your ITE course. Compare these with causes of stress identified by another student teacher. Discuss similarities and differences. Use this list for Task 1.3.7.

How can you cope with your stress?

If you cannot prevent stress, you need to be able to cope with it. As there are different causes of stress for different people and for the same person at different times, there is no one way to cope with stress; you have to find out what works for you or for you in particular situations. Different ways of coping with stress, therefore, are appropriate for different people and for the same person at different times. Arikewuyo (2004) classified strategies for coping with stress as: active behavioural strategies (confronting the source of stress and attempting to change these sources by e.g. envisaging that you will get through in any situation whatever the circumstances, becoming more organized and devoting more time and energy to the job); inactive behavioural strategies (behaviours of escape, such as engaging in physical and recreational activities, and avoidance of the source of stress, e.g. those individuals who might create stressful situations); active cognitive strategies (identifying the sources of stress and trying to tackle them by e.g. restructuring priorities, seeking more clarification, to identify strategies to manage and reduce stress); and inactive cognitive strategies (conforming to, and trying to meet, expectations of e.g. mentors and tutors by e.g. meeting all duties and deadlines).

Those active behavioural and cognitive coping strategies identified below have been drawn from a number of sources (e.g. Cains and Brown, 1998; Cockburn, 1996; Head *et al.*, 1996). These lists are by no means exhaustive and you may find other strategies useful.

- *Take account of the amount and variety of work you are doing to reduce both role overload and conflict.* This may mean, for example, that you need to try to take work home less often or take on fewer extra-curricular activities. You may need to work on this over a period of time.
- *Prepare for stressful situations when you are not under pressure*, e.g. prepare lessons before the day on which you are teaching them.
- *Role-play a situation that is causing you anxiety and/or visualize what you can do to overcome the problem.* This helps you to focus on the problem and can be used to rehearse how you are going to cope.
- *Actively prepare for a situation*, e.g. if you are anxious about a particular lesson prepare it more thoroughly than normal. Plan thoroughly how you can reduce the likelihood of a problem occurring or deal with a particular problem. This strategy can help you to identify the reasons for a problem and to focus on possible ways of preventing or dealing with it.
- *Develop effective self-management techniques*, e.g. establish routines so that you can do things automatically, particularly when you are tired.
- *Recognize and try to develop your strengths as well as your weaknesses* so that you can rely on your strengths as you work on improving any weaknesses.
- *Identify where you can get help*. You should get regular feedback on your teaching, but identify other people who may be able to help.
- *Develop support systems which provide a network of people with whom you could talk through problems*, e.g. other student teachers, your tutor, other teachers, a partner or friend. You may want to talk to different people for help with different problems. You may form a group with other student teachers to provide mutual support, talk about your anxieties/concerns, develop a shared understanding of a problem and provide possible alternative solutions and practical help to address a problem, e.g. a lesson being observed then discussed with another student teacher.
- *Do not worry about incidents that have happened in school and keep problems in proportion*. Try not to take problems home.

See also the strategies for managing your time above.

Task 1.3.6
Systematic observation of aspects of your teaching

You should be getting regular feedback on your teaching from your tutor. However, you may want to ask your tutor to focus an observation of one of your lessons and specifically on one aspect of your teaching that is causing you anxiety, e.g. giving feedback to pupils, giving praise, working with individuals in the class and then give you feedback on this, along with ideas about how you might be able to improve in this area. It may help to develop an observation schedule. Plan your next lesson taking into account feedback from your tutor. Ask your tutor to observe another lesson a couple of weeks later to see if there is any difference in your performance. Try this again with another aspect of your teaching.

However, it is important not only to focus on your concerns and fears, but also to pay attention to your aspirations and hopes as a teacher. Conway and Clark (2003: 470) suggested that focusing on resolving immediate concerns can result in 'an unduly pessimistic understanding of teachers and teaching'. Although you might find it difficult as a student teacher to focus on your development as a teacher, on the positive aspects of learning to teach and on your long-term goals and aspirations as a teacher, if you can do this you are likely to have a more balanced view and be able to put things into perspective and therefore reduce your stress.

Task 1.3.7
Coping with your stress

In Task 1.3.5 you listed factors that cause stress for you. Now identify ways that you can cope with this stress. Are the same or different methods appropriate for coping with stress, irrespective of the cause? Try out these coping methods as soon as you can and reflect on and evaluate whether these are effective. If they are not totally successful in all or some situations – what other methods are you going to try? Evaluate the effectiveness of these methods and adapt them or try new methods until you find those that work for you to cope with different stressful situations.

SUMMARY AND KEY POINTS

We would be very surprised if, as a student teacher on school experience, you are not tired. Likewise, we would be very surprised if you do not feel as though you do not have enough time to do everything, are not anxious when someone comes in to watch your lessons, particularly if that person has a say in whether you become a qualified teacher, or if you are not worried about other aspects of your teaching and/or school experience. It may help to know that you are not going to be alone in being tired or feeling anxious or worried about your school experience and many of the causes of tiredness, lack of time and stress are the same for other student teachers. Where you are alone is in developing effective techniques for managing your time and for coping with stress. There are no ready answers for managing time or coping with stress. They are complex processes. Other people can help you with this, but nobody else can do it for you because what works for someone else may not work for you. Finally, you must work at managing your time and stress over time; there are no short-term, one-off solutions to these problems. However, it helps also to focus on the positive aspects of teaching and why you want to become a teacher.

Although you need to manage time and stress throughout your teaching (Capel *et al.*, 2004, for example look at time and stress management in your first year of teaching), the remodelling of the workforce in teaching, aimed at reducing teachers' workload (partly by transferring some tasks from teachers to teaching assistants) should be beneficial. For further information about the national workforce agreement see <http://www.teachernet.gov.uk>.

FURTHER READING

Amos, J.-A. (1998) *Managing Your Time: What to Do and How to Do it in Order to Do More*, Oxford: How to Books. This book looks at techniques to manage your time at work (what to do and how to do it) to use it effectively and efficiently. It includes, for example, understanding time, planning the use of time, delegating and prioritizing work, dealing with paperwork and administration.

Arnold, R. (1993) *Time Management*, Leamington Spa: Scholastic Publications. The practical management ideas in this book focus on how teachers can organize and manage the time available (inside and outside the classroom) so that they can achieve more.

Bubb, S. and Earley, P. (2004) *Managing Teacher Workload: Work–life Balance and Wellbeing*, London: Sage. This book provides guidance, along with a self-audit tool, on managing your workload including, e.g. how long you are working, what you are spending your time on and whether you are working efficiently.

Capel, S., Heilbronn, R., Leask, M. and Turner, T. (2004) *Starting to Teach in the Secondary School: A Companion for the Newly-Qualified Teacher*, London: RoutledgeFalmer. Although this book is written for newly qualified teachers, Chapter 2 'Managing yourself and your workload', provides guidance on managing stress and time which is also appropriate for student teachers.

Child, D. (2004) *Psychology and the Teacher*, 7th edn, London: Continuum. Chapter 8, 'Human motivation', includes a section on stress in teachers and pupils.

Cook, M.J. (1998) *Time Management: Proven Techniques for Making the Most of your Time*, Holbrook, MA: Adams Media Corporation; and Croft, C. (1996) *Time Management*, London: International Thomson Business Press. Although the titles and focus of these books are time management and efficient use of time at work, as well as your personal time management, they also include a chapter on stress – some of which may be due to poor time management and/or having too much to do.

Dunham, J. (1995) *Developing Effective School Management*, London: Routledge. This book is designed to help teachers to identify and develop knowledge and skills to become effective middle managers. It includes chapters on time management and stress management, which should be helpful to you as student teachers.

Eisenberg, R. and Kelley, K. (1997) *Organise Yourself*, London: Macmillan. This book looks at ways in which you can organize yourself to streamline your personal life, an important aspect of being able to manage your time and to have enough time for rest and relaxation.

Fontana, D. (1993) *Managing Time*, Leicester: British Psychological Society Books. This book is based on the premise that good time management can be learned. It combines text and a series of exercises to help you better understand different aspects of time management, including the qualities of a good time manager, determining how you currently use your time and planning how you can use your time better.

Handy, C. (1993) *Understanding Organisations*, 4th edn, London: Penguin. This book includes a section on stress, which provides a broader perspective of stress than that found when looking only at stress in teachers.

Kyriacou, C. (2000) *Stress-Busting for Teachers*, Cheltenham: Stanley Thornes. This book aims to help teachers to develop a range of strategies for coping with stress at work. It looks at what stress is; sources of stress; how to pre-empt stress; how to cope with stress; and what schools can do to minimize stress.

Maitland, I. (1995) *Managing your Time*, London: Institute of Personnel and Development. This book helps you to analyse your use of the following components of time management: your workload; getting organized; delegating successfully; tackling paperwork; handling meetings; controlling time-wasting activities; and making the most of free time.

Unit 1.4

Teaching and Learning with ICT

An Introduction

Richard Bennett and Marilyn Leask

INTRODUCTION

This unit introduces ways in which you can use information and communication technology (ICT) to support and enhance your teaching and pupils' learning, for administration purposes and to contribute to your professional development. Teacher Training Agency (TTA) documentation defines ICT as including 'computers, the internet, CD-ROM and other software, television, radio, video, cameras and other equipment' (TTA, 1998: 1). This unit focuses on ways of making use of ICT resources to support the teaching of your subject and also contribute to the development of pupils' ICT capabilities.

The ideas in the unit are based on practice in innovative schools and the requirements for Qualified Teacher Status (QTS). Student teachers in England are required to pass an online test in ICT to demonstrate basic skills in word processing, databases, spreadsheets, presentation software, e-mail and internet (see Table 1.4.1). This unit is not intended to help student teachers in England pass the ICT test, but is focused on the requirements for you to make effective use of ICT in your teaching and wider professional role. If you are just beginning to use computers, there are many materials providing this information, e.g. Ferrigan (2001); Leask *et al.* (2000); Leask and Pachler (2005); Trend *et al.* (1999); and the BECTA website <http://www.becta.org>. You may wish to take your 'European Computer Driving Licence (ECDL)' (website details given at the end of this unit in [1]). This provides a structured way of developing your skills supported by material freely available from the British Computing Society.

In this unit we focus on pedagogical applications of ICT, particularly, using ICT to support:

- your teaching, through the presentation of information and ideas to pupils (including the use of interactive whiteboards), the preparation of learning materials (such as handouts, worksheets);

- pupils' learning of your specialist subject(s), in the development of ICT capability through meaningful contexts;
- your wider professional role, including administration (such as planning templates, and record keeping and analysis), your professional development and communication (e.g. through access to online resources and information sources).

In recent years there has been considerable investment of time and finances into the development and provision of ICT resources and training. As a consequence most schools are now well equipped with ICT equipment (hardware) and educational programs (software) to support and enhance subject learning and teaching (OFSTED 2001, 2004b). All UK teachers have had the opportunity to participate in ICT training to enable them to develop their personal ICT competences. However, there is still wide variation in the levels of confidence and capability with ICT in practising teachers (see OFSTED, 2004a).

Inspection reports (e.g. OFSTED, 2004b, 2004a) and research projects (e.g. Harrison *et al.*, 2003) have shown that effective use of ICT resources in schools to support subject learning and teaching is patchy. At best, teachers are making highly successful use of ICT-based resources and activities to stimulate and extend the quality of their pupils' learning experiences. At worst, teachers avoid the use of ICT-based resources which could contribute positively to the development of their pupils' learning. In the world outside school, pupils are surrounded by ICT-based information sources and many are well versed in the use of ICT-based technologies in their daily lives. It has been estimated by Smith (n.d.) that 90 per cent of jobs currently require familiarity with basic ICT. Most teachers recognize the importance of making use of ICT to enhance pupils' learning, but have difficulties in gaining access to ICT resources (OFSTED 2004a) or are hampered by the constraints of time (Harrison *et al.*, 2003). However, many successful teachers and schools recognize the added value which ICT can bring to pupils' learning and, increasingly, opportunities are being made for teachers in all areas of the curriculum to make effective use of ICT resources to support and enhance their teaching and, more importantly, enliven and extend pupils' learning.

In this unit you will find references to ICT-based activities and to websites which are recommended by teachers as well as references to texts which may provide you with further ideas. However, these ideas only provide starting points. Websites change regularly, with new ones developing and old ones disappearing. The resources we reference are those which we consider provide a professional service and are likely to have a permanent presence on the internet.

OBJECTIVES

By the end of this unit you should:

- understand a range of ways in which ICT can be deployed for educational purposes;
- have identified specific applications relevant to your subject area and used those available to you;
- have audited your skills and knowledge in this area against those demanded by your course and developed an action plan for improving these.

BACKGROUND

Computers became widely available in schools in the mid-1980s. Initially these offered basic word processing, spreadsheet and database capabilities. Whilst electronic networking was available between some schools at this time, such a resource did not become widely accessible to all schools until the middle to late 1990s when access to the internet became available at prices individual schools could afford. In the meantime CD-ROM technology also developed together with software which made it easy for pupils and teachers to create multimedia presentations and interactive websites. However, it was access to the internet in particular which changed computers from being machines which were used for quite specific purposes in specialist rooms to machines which provided a medium which combined the attributes of video, telephones, television and radio and which could be employed for a range of purposes in all classrooms.

Teachers are expected to use ICT for teaching and learning as well as for professional development. Traditional approaches to teaching, where teachers taught their pupils in the ways they had been taught themselves, must be reviewed in the light of what technology can now offer. However, as with any changes in classroom practice, the one question must always be asked 'What is the most effective approach to take to achieve the desired learning outcomes?' ICT should only be used where its use is justified as a method of achieving the stated learning outcomes for any lesson.

THE SKILLS AND KNOWLEDGE REQUIRED OF STUDENT TEACHERS

In England, as well as the online ICT tests, student teachers must demonstrate that they know how to use ICT to teach their subject and can use ICT resources to support their wider professional role. Those teaching in secondary schools must also show they can incorporate the cross-curricular elements such as ICT into their teaching and demonstrate they can plan opportunities to develop pupils' key skills in the use of information technology. Student teachers in other parts of the UK must also demonstrate similar competences.

As a useful starting point, we suggest that you check the requirements of your course for ICT skills and that you audit your strengths and weaknesses. You may find it helpful to write notes setting out how you are going to become familiar with the ways that ICT can support the work in your own subject.

Task 1.4.1
Auditing your skills and knowledge

Consider the information contained in Table 1.4.1. In addition, your training provider will outline the criteria you will have to satisfy in terms of ICT competences. We suggest you use these different resources to identify the areas in which you are competent and those in which you need to develop further competence.

When you have undertaken Task 1.4.1 we suggest you draw up an action plan which identifies the areas on which you are going to work, the ways in which you are going to develop competence and the timescales you set yourself.

Table 1.4.2 illustrates ways the various facets of ICT, as defined by the English National Curriculum for ICT (finding things out; developing ideas and making things happen; exchanging and sharing information; reviewing, modifying and evaluating work as it progresses) can be applied in different subjects.

As indicated earlier in this unit, there are many materials, courses and programmes which individuals can use or undertake if they wish to learn how to enhance their ICT skills and knowledge.

Table 1.4.1 ICT QTS Skills Test (England). Each test covers the six types of office software and a balance of the following kinds of skills. Put a tick beside each skill indicating your level of competence/confidence (0 = no confidence, 3 = very confident).

General skills	0	1	2	3
Choosing appropriate software to help solve a problem				
Dragging and dropping				
Having more than one application open at a time				
Highlighting				
Making selections by clicking				
Moving information between software (e.g. using the clipboard)				
Navigating around the desktop environment				
Opening items by double clicking with the mouse				
Printing				
Using menus				
How to change the name of files				
Word processing skills	0	1	2	3
Altering fonts: font, size, style (**bold**, *italic*, <u>underline</u>)				
Text justification: left, right and centre				
Using a spellchecker				
Moving text within a document with 'cut', 'copy' and paste				
Adding or inserting pictures to a document				
Counting the number of words in a document				
Adding a page break to a document				
Altering page orientation – (landscape, portrait)				
Using characters/symbols				
Using find and replace to edit a document				
Using styles to organize a document				
Using styles to alter the presentation of a document efficiently				
Adding page numbers to the footer of a document				
Adding the date to the header of a document				
Changing the margins of a document				
E-mail skills	0	1	2	3
Recognising an e-mail address				
Sending an e-mail to an individual				
Sending an e-mail to more than one person				
Replying to an e-mail				
Copying an e-mail to another person				
Forwarding an incoming e-mail to another person				
Adding an address to an electronic address book				
Filing incoming and outgoing e-mails				
Adding an attachment to an e-mail				
Receiving and saving an attachment in an e-mail				

Database skills	0	1	2	3
Searching a database for specific information				
Using Boolean operators (and/or/not) to narrow down searches				
Sorting database records in ascending or descending order				
Adding a record to a database				
Adding fields to a database				
Querying information in a database (e.g. locating all values greater than 10)				
Filtering information in a database (e.g. sorting on all values greater than 10)				
Categorising data into different types (numbers, text, and yes/no (Boolean) types)				
Web browser skills	0	1	2	3
Recognising a web address (e.g. www or co.uk, etc.)				
Using hyperlinks on websites to connect to other websites				
Using the back button				
Using the forward button				
Using the history				
Understanding how to search websites				
Using Boolean operators (and/or/not) to narrow down searches				
Creating bookmarks				
Organising bookmarks into folders				
Downloading files from a website				
Spreadsheet skills	0	1	2	3
Identifying grid squares in a spreadsheet (e.g. B5)				
Inserting columns into a spreadsheet				
Inserting rows into a spreadsheet				
Sorting spreadsheet or database columns in ascending or descending order				
Converting a spreadsheet into a chart				
Labelling a chart				
Adding simple formulae/functions to cells				
Applying formatting to different types of data including numbers and dates				
Presentation skills	0	1	2	3
Inserting text and images on a slide				
Inserting a slide in a presentation				
Adding a transition between slides				
Adding buttons to a presentation				
Using timers in a presentation				

The requirements of teachers listed in Table 1.4.2 are demanding and need you to take an active role in your own professional development. There is research evidence (e.g. BECTA, 2003a; OECD, 2001) which indicates that, when ICT is effectively deployed, pupil motivation and achievement are raised in a number of respects.

Table 1.4.2 Elements of ICT in various subject areas

Art and design		Maths	
Finding things out	Surveys (e.g. consumer preferences), web galleries, online artist/ movement profiles	Finding things out	Databases, surveys, statistics, graphing, calculators, graphical calculators, dynamic geometry, data logging/ measurement (e.g. timing), web-based information (e.g. statistics/ history of maths)
Developing ideas	Spreadsheets to model design specs	Developing ideas	Number patterns, modelling algebraic problems/probability
Making things happen	Embroidery CAD/CAM	Making things happen	Programming – e.g. LOGO turtle graphics
Exchanging and sharing information	Digital imagery/CAD/ multimedia for students' design portfolios	Exchanging and sharing information	Formulae/symbols, presenting investigation findings, multimedia
Reviewing, modifying and evaluating	Real world applications – e.g. commercial art	Reviewing, modifying and evaluating	Comparing solutions to those online, online modelling and information sources
Business and commercial studies		**Technology**	
Finding things out	Pay packages, databases, online profiling,	Finding things out	Product surveys, consumer preferences, environmental data
Developing ideas	Business/financial modelling	Developing ideas	CAD, spreadsheet modelling
Making things happen	Business simulation	Making things happen	CAM, simulations (e.g. environmental modelling), textiles, embroidery, control
Exchanging and sharing information	Business letters, web authoring, multimedia CVs, e-mail	Exchanging and sharing information	Advertising, product design and realisation, multimedia/web presentation
Reviewing, modifying and evaluating	Commercial packages, dot.com, admin. systems	Reviewing, modifying and evaluating	Industrial production, engineering/electronics
Performing arts		**Physical Education**	
Finding things out	Online information sources, surveys	Finding things out	Recording/analysing performance, internet sources (e.g. records)
Developing ideas	Planning performance/ choreographing sequences	Developing ideas	Planning sequences/tactics
Making things happen	Lighting sequences, computer animation, MIDI, multimedia presentations	Making things happen	Modelling sequences/ tactics, sporting simulations

Exchanging and sharing information	Video, audio, digital video, web authoring, multimedia, animation, DTP posters/flyers/ programmes e-mail	Exchanging and sharing information	Reporting events, posters, flyers, web/multimedia authoring, video, digital video
Reviewing, modifying and evaluating	Ticket booking, lighting control, recording/TV studios, theatre/ film industry	Reviewing, modifying and evaluating	Website evaluation, presentation of performance statistics, event diaries, performance portfolios
English		*Modern foreign languages*	
Finding things out	Surveys, efficient searching/keywords, information texts, online author profiles, readability analysis	Finding things out	Class surveys, topic databases, web searching/ browsing
Developing ideas	Authorship, desktop publishing (balancing text and images)	Developing ideas	Concordancing software, interactive video packages, DTP and word processing
Making things happen	Interactive texts/ multimedia/ web authoring	Making things happen	Online translation tools, interactive multimedia
Exchanging and sharing information	Exploring genres (e.g. writing frames), authoring tools, text/images, scripting, presenting, interviewing (audio / video)	Exchanging and sharing information	Word processing, DTP, web/multimedia authoring, e-mail projects, video/audio recording, digital video editing
Reviewing, modifying and evaluating	Website evaluation, online publishing, e-mail projects	Reviewing, modifying and evaluating	Internet communication, website/CD ROM language teaching evaluation, translation software
Humanities		*Science*	
Finding things out	Surveys, databases, internet searching, monitoring environment (e.g. weather), census data etc.	Finding things out	Data recording and analysis, spreadsheets and graphing packages, internet searching (e.g. genetics info.)
Developing ideas	Multimedia, DTP, modelling (spreadsheets/ simulations)	Developing ideas	Modelling experiments/ simulations
Making things happen	Simulations, interactive multimedia/web authoring	Making things happen	Datalogging, modelling experiments, simulations (what if...?)
Exchanging and sharing information	Web authoring, e-mail projects	Exchanging and sharing information	Communicating investigation findings (DTP, web/multimedia authoring, DV
Reviewing, modifying and evaluating	Weather stations, satellite information, website/CD ROM evaluation, archive information	Reviewing, modifying and evaluating	Accessing information (evaluating for bias on issues, e.g. nuclear power)

Task 1.4.2
Identifying ICT resources for your subject area

Find out what ICT resources are available to you to support your subject area. Discuss the application of these to the lessons you are taking with your mentor, tutor and fellow student teachers. Use these resources in lessons and evaluate your success in achieving the learning objectives you set. Identify your strengths and weaknesses in using ICT and draw up and implement an action plan which sets out a strategy for ensuring your weaknesses are addressed.

WHY USE ICT?

Information provided by the British Education and Communication Technology Agency (BECTA) (2001) indicates the following educational benefits in using ICT:

From a learning perspective, the effective use of ICT can lead to benefits in terms of:
- greater motivation
- increased self-esteem and confidence
- enhanced questioning skills
- promoting initiative and independent learning
- improving presentation
- developing problem solving capabilities
- promoting better information handling skills
- increasing time 'on task'
- improving social and communication skills.

More specifically, ICT can enable children to:

- combine words and images to produce a 'professional' looking piece of work
- draft and redraft their work with less effort
- test out ideas and present them in different ways for different audiences
- explore musical sequences and compose their own music
- investigate and make changes in computer models
- store and handle large amounts of information in different ways
- do things quickly and easily which might otherwise be tedious or time-consuming
- use simulations to experience things that might be too difficult or dangerous for them to attempt in real life
- control devices by turning motors, buzzers and lights on or off or by programming them to react to changes in things like light or temperature sensors
- communicate with others over a distance.

They go on to define ICT capability:

Information technology capability is characterised by an ability to use effectively ICT tools and information sources to analyse, process and present information, and to model, measure and control external events. More specifically, a child who has developed ICT capability should:

- use ICT confidently
- select and use ICT appropriate to the task in hand
- use information sources and ICT tools to solve problems
- identify situations where the ICT use would be relevant
- use ICT to support learning in a number of contexts
- be able to reflect and comment on the use of ICT they have undertaken
- understand the implications of ICT for working life and society.

Pupils should be given opportunities to develop and apply their ICT capability in the context of all curriculum subjects.

Task 1.4.3
How does ICT help teaching and learning?

Consider the list above in the light of your experiences in schools. What evidence have you come across of the potential of computer-supported activity, as outlined in this list, being realized? Is there any scope within your school situation for testing some of these features and examining how various forms of ICT could support teaching and learning in your subject area?

In addition to the features outlined above, ICT has been shown to provide specific support for pupils with special educational needs (SEN). Peacey (2005) provides detailed advice about particular forms of ICT which support pupils with SEN. Teachers interested in SEN issues can join the online forum run within the Virtual Teacher Centre by the British Educational Communications Technology Agency (BECTA) [2]. BECTA also produces a number of publications providing detailed advice, including subject-specific advice, to teachers about ICT issues. Much of this information is available on their website including reviews of CD-ROMs. This is listed in the further reading at the end of this unit.

USING ICT TO SUPPORT YOUR TEACHING

The most obvious and hence the most common use of ICT to support teaching is in the production of paper-based resources such as worksheets, template documents, handouts, information leaflets and pupil booklets. Increasingly, teaching resources are being provided online through websites such as the Teacher Resource Exchange [3], which is government sponsored and is aimed at enabling teachers and other education professionals to share their handiwork and ideas with others. Several other organizations, such as TeacherNet [4] and Schoolzone [5] provide similar resources and some commercial companies market their services or provide adaptable paper-based resources on CD-ROM. Also, the websites for subject organizations (e.g. the Maths Association [6], Geography Association [7]) usually provide educational materials and links to other resources. However, as a teacher you must balance the time taken to search for and modify others' resources to meet your pupils' learning needs against the time it might take to produce your own from scratch.

INTERACTIVE WHITEBOARDS

The recent proliferation of data projectors and interactive whiteboards in classrooms has influenced the role ICT can play in supporting interactive whole class teaching. Interactive whole class teaching was developed particularly by educators in the Pacific Rim countries whose pupils demonstrated the impressive learning gains in basic subjects identified in international comparisons of pupils' performance (see OECD, 2001). The basic principles of interactive whole class teaching require teachers to build shared understanding in pupils through careful questioning and the presentation of information and ideas which expose and challenge learners' misconceptions. The teacher channels and develops pupils' thinking interactively, rather than presenting information, solutions and ideas didactically (see Dickenson, 1999).

The use of data projectors and interactive whiteboard technology further enhances this approach by giving teachers and pupils flexible access to resources, including the internet, and provides teachers with opportunities to present challenging information and ideas through the use of text, images, animations, sound and video – i.e. through multi-sensory (multimedia) approaches, thereby enabling pupils to access information in accord with their preferred learning styles.

To facilitate the use of such approaches, as a teacher you will need to develop your skills in finding, accessing, cataloguing and presenting information in a range of formats. Furthermore, interactive whiteboards offer a series of tools, such as the ability readily to highlight and manipulate text and images, to translate handwriting into text and to save and replay screens and sequences of on-screen actions. The BECTA information sheet (2003b) outlines some of the strategies for effective use of interactive whiteboard teaching technology.

USING ICT TO SUPPORT PUPILS' LEARNING

In addition to using ICT resources to support or enhance your role as a teacher, there is an expectation you will contribute to the development of pupils' ICT capabilities by giving pupils hands-on experience of ICT. In most cases, your prime motivation in making use of ICT will be to address learning objectives related to your subject. However, with a slight shift of emphasis you could modify an activity to develop concomitantly aspects of pupils' ICT knowledge and skills. For example, you might produce a word-processed paper-based writing frame for your pupils to structure the presentation of some information associated with your subject. In this case, you have used your ICT skills to research and produce the worksheet, but the children are making no use of ICT to complete it. The activity could be modified as follows:

- The same writing frame is presented on-screen for completion by a pair of pupils working collaboratively, using the features of a word processor to enhance the communication of information (e.g. by reworking sections of text and by selecting and incorporating appropriate images).
- Relevant information is located and copied from two or three websites you have identified and pupils edit the pasted text, shifting the focus of the information or targeting a specific audience. (Pupils need to be aware that they should acknowledge the sources they use.)
- Groups of pupils search websites (or a CD-ROM encyclopedia) to create information leaflets for each other on different aspects of a topic – or to present controversial information from different viewpoints.

Consider the different levels of cognitive demand (i.e. the decision-making) in each of the above examples. Whilst the subject learning in each case might be broadly similar, shifting the ICT focus for the task not only supports the application and development of the pupils' ICT capabilities, it also deepens their learning by helping them engage more with the subject matter.

Task 1.4.4
Making lessons more active

Reflect on an activity which you have observed or taught recently in school which made no use of ICT. How might the activity have been modified to enable the pupils to gain hands-on experience of ICT resources? In what ways might the activity have helped the children engage more fully with the content of the lesson? Use the BECTA list to identify aspects of ICT capability the revised activity could have developed.

The growth in educational resources provided through the internet has unlocked tremendous opportunities for teachers and pupils wishing to:

- access information;
- use interactive tools and resources;
- participate in and/or create online projects;
- communicate with 'experts' and other learners;
- publish and share information and ideas with a potential world audience.

Information sources predominate the world wide web and most pupils will already know how to access them before commencing their secondary education. However, they may not have learned how to search for information efficiently or to discriminate between sources in terms of accuracy, reliability, plausibility and the currency of the information. When using internet-based information sources it is important to help children learn how to search for and locate the most appropriate information for the task in hand. Similarly, it is essential that they adopt safe surfing habits to avoid unsuitable materials and protect them from unwanted attention. The most useful information on 'superhighway safety' is provided online jointly by the DfES and BECTA [8].

Those wanting their pupils to use the internet more systematically for educational purposes should consider making use of, or setting up, a 'webquest' (see Figure 1.4.1).

Alternatively, you might decide to participate in an online project with pupils from other schools, maybe in other parts of the world. The European Schoolnet site [10] provides a partner finding service.

A 'webquest' is a framework made by teachers for pupils for stimulating educational adventures on the web and to help pupils in the acquisition of problem-solving and searching skills. Taking account of curricular goals, the teacher sets up a few guidelines, with a simple structure:

- introduction – context information related with the task/problem/adventure/questions … to be completed by the pupils;
- the task/problem/adventure/questions – what has to be done by the pupils;
- internet resources – location of internet resources like websites, databases, live video cameras for educational purposes (e.g. vulcanology …);
- reporting results and final discussions.

For further information and examples visit the Webquest website [9]

Figure 1.4.1   An example of a 'webquest'

If you are interested in undertaking such projects then starting with something small and achievable will enable you to develop strategies which work for you in your particular subject. For example, a survey on a specific topic carried out by pupils in two countries can be done over a very short time span, perhaps a couple of weeks. This could enable you to avoid problems of timetabling or clashes of holidays. Funding for collaborative work may be available from UK or European Union sources. Table 1.4.3 provides some guidelines for running e-mail projects. For example, Lord Grey School in Bletchley has undertaken sustained ICT curriculum projects across subjects and involving many countries. Holy Cross Convent School in Surrey has undertaken innovative cross-curricular video-conferencing projects with a school in Japan. This work is described further by Lawrence Williams, the director of studies (Leask and Williams, 2005). Further examples of projects with other schools, e.g. virtual field trips [11], virtual art galleries, are given in Leask and Pachler (2005).

Considerable research has gone into ways in which online activities can be used to enhance learning. Communal constructivism is an approach in which pupils construct knowledge through the development of a collaborative online learning community. By drawing upon the knowledge and experience of others, maybe in other parts of the locality or in different communities around the world, learners will become actively engaged in constructing and communicating their own understanding (Holmes *et al.*, 2001).

FINDING PARTNERS FOR E-MAIL/VIDEO-CONFERENCING/INTERNET-BASED PROJECTS

There are a number of ways of finding partners. These include the following:

- by using existing contacts, through, for example, exchanges or through the local community and teachers in the school;
- by e-mailing schools direct; various sites provide lists of schools' e-mails, e.g. European Schoolnet [10] and ePals [15];
- by advertising your project, e.g. by registration on a site such as those mentioned below;
- by searching sites listing school projects and finding projects which seem to fit with your curriculum goals.

Sites such as the Global School House [12] in the USA, OzteacherNet [13] in Australia, Internet Scuola [14] in Italy, provide all three of the last options.

Table 1.4.3 Check-list for planning ICT projects with other schools

1	What learning outcomes do you want the pupils to achieve in terms of knowledge/concepts, skills, attitudes?
2	What is the time scale of the project and how does that fit with school holidays and other events in the partner school?
3	What languages can you work in? (Don't forget that parents, other schools and the local community may be able to help here.)
4	What resources – staff, equipment, time – are involved?
5	Does anyone need to give their permission?
6	How are you going to record and report the outcomes?
7	Do staff need training?
8	Can you sustain the project within the staff, time and material resources available to you?
9	What sorts of partners are you looking for?
10	How are you going to find the partners?
11	How are you going to evaluate the outcomes?

It is too early to predict the extent to which teaching processes are likely to change in response to the opportunities discussed above. In the UK at secondary level, change would accelerate if the examination boards incorporated ICT-based work into assessment requirements. Clearly, pupils have to be taught skills needed for the critical appraisal of material but good teachers will be doing this already. Issues related to plagiarism as pupils download sections of text and incorporate these into assignments are likely to be more problematic for teachers. Whilst teacherless classrooms are unlikely to occur, certainly the positive motivation which some learners feel when using technology is not to be underestimated, but this does depend on the context for learning which the teacher establishes.

MOTIVATION AND CLASSROOM MANAGEMENT

The involvement of technology into lessons requires confidence and competence in the management of the resources and pupils on the part of the teacher. Cox (1999) gives the following advice on the teaching of word processing which applies to many uses of ICT which, if not carefully planned, could result in poor motivation, lack of involvement (or off-task activity) and very little learning benefit:

- tasks must be relevant;
- pupils should be prepared for their tasks before being assigned computers;
- don't let pupils sit at computers while you are talking to them at the introduction of the lesson;
- don't leave pupils for the whole lesson just working on their task with no intervention to remind them of the educational purpose;
- don't expect pupils to print out their work at the end of every lesson;
- end each lesson by drawing pupils together to discuss what they have achieved;
- don't rely on the technology to run the lesson.

As mentioned earlier in this unit, the rapid development of technology means that it may be hard for any individual to claim expert status across a whole range of software and hardware. Selinger (1999: 39–40) observes:

> Classroom dynamics with ICT alters considerably especially when teaching takes place in a computer room. There will be an increase in noise level and pupils may need to move freely around the classroom. It is also not always easy to be sure pupils are on task or not, and you have to find ways of ascertaining this through questions and summing up sessions at the end of the lesson. You may well find yourself in the unusual position of knowing less than your pupils about hardware or software. There is no need to feel threatened by this situation; use it as an opportunity to increase your own knowledge, and to give pupils an opportunity to excel. Some software requires independent learning, but do not feel as though you are no longer teaching, your role as a mediator between the pupils and the machine is often crucial in developing their understanding. Questioning pupils about what they are doing, and why they are doing it in that way, demands that they have to articulate their understanding and in so doing can consolidate their learning.

Selinger also provides advice about how to manage ICT in the classroom with varying numbers of machines (Leask and Pachler, 1999, 2005). Increasingly the use of wireless technology will give teachers flexibility in their use of ICT, as teaching with ICT will not be reliant on access to a computer suite.

USING ICT TO SUPPORT YOUR WIDER PROFESSIONAL ROLE

When teachers have ready access to laptop computers they are not only more likely to use them for the preparation and presentation of teaching materials, they also use them more extensively for recording and analysing pupils' progress and to access educational information and to communicate with colleagues. However, one of the greatest positive effects is that it seems to encourage them to make more effective use of ICT in their teaching while communicating a positive image of constructive and professional use of ICT to their pupils (Cunningham *et al.*, 2003).

Using ICT for administration and monitoring

ICT is useful for recording and analysing pupils' results, or for using computer-based packages to create reports for parents on pupils' progress.

Many schools are now using quite complex computer-based systems for recording and analysing scores, for logging attendance and for various other administrative tasks. The extent to which you will have contact with or a need to use these systems will be largely dependent on the school, the level of responsibility you have and the degree of interest you exhibit.

Task 1.4.5
Using ICT for administration and monitoring

Schools and teachers use a variety of systems for recording, monitoring and analysing pupil progress and teacher effectiveness against targets, and predictions. The example of the electronic mark book in Unit 1.1 illustrates one teacher's record keeping technique. For details see Younie and Moore, 2005. Find out what systems are in use in the school in which you are placed and, if possible, compare these with those used in other schools. This information may be found by talking to teachers or student teachers from other schools.

Using ICT for professional development and communication

The internet is the most prominent source of information for professional development and lends itself particularly to communication at a formal and informal level. However, it should be remembered that broadcast television and radio, and video, CD-ROM or DVD-based materials provide information and offer opportunities for professional development. See e.g. Teachers TV <http://www.teachers.tv>.

The internet provides educators with the following:

1   Access to a huge range of *free and high quality information sources* including the rapid and inexpensive publication of the latest research findings from researchers around the world in all disciplines [23], as well as access to museums, galleries, newspapers, radio stations [19] and libraries. These resources are often available in a variety of languages. In the UK, the National Grid for Learning (NGfL) and the Virtual Teacher Centre (VTC) [16] within it are intended to provide resources to support teachers. Various government supported sites all have information of potential use to teachers.

2   *Teaching and learning resources*, in the form of lesson plans, worksheets and computer-based learning materials. By browsing through the work of others who are tackling the same sorts of problems and issues (e.g. differentiating tasks for pupils), you will not only be gaining material support, you will have the opportunity to appraise others' teaching approaches. For examples, refer to the Teacher Resource Exchange (TRE) [3] and the Schoolzone [5] websites.

3   For teachers and schools *the opportunity to publish and share information* about their work. School websites and intranets provide opportunities for publishing material for a range of purposes. For example, pupils are sometimes set projects to publish material which they have researched themselves. In doing this, both pupils and teachers are developing their knowledge about the use of this technology. Parents can be kept informed more fully about the work their children are doing through website publications and, of course, parents who are seeking schools for their children may find such sites of value in guiding their choice. In addition, the school website can provide a useful resource as colleagues pool ideas and use the website as a form of departmental filing cabinet for resources.

4   *Synchronous (e.g. video-conferencing and online chat/discussion groups) and asynchronous communication (e.g. e-mail)* with single or multiple audiences, e.g. with other teachers, pupils, parents and experts in particular fields regardless of their location. Some schools tap the expertise of parents and local companies to provide experts online for short periods. These are specialists who are able to answer pupils' questions in areas relevant to their expertise. Teachers are using these facilities for a range of purposes, both curriculum-based and for professional development. For example, joint curriculum projects with classes in other countries can be easily maintained through the use of e-mail. Results of such collaboration can also be posted on the school website for participants in both countries to see.

Task 1.4.6
Exploring the potential of the internet to support your professional development

If you have not already done so, we suggest you take this opportunity to find out how teachers of your subject are using the internet to support teaching and learning. You may, for example, ask other teachers for ideas in a chat area. You may wish to undertake a general search for curriculum projects in your area using the TeacherNet [4] site or the Virtual Teacher Centre [16]. It may be of use to know that the term K-12 (kindergarten to Year 12) is used on websites in the USA to refer to the years of compulsory schooling. Ideas are sometimes published on school websites. If you are going to be looking for jobs soon it may be useful to explore the local education authority website for those areas in which you wish to work as well as the inspection and league table information on maintained schools which is available on the DfES [17] and OFSTED sites [18] and, if possible, compare these with those used in other schools. This information may be found by talking to teachers or student teachers from other schools.

SUMMARY AND KEY POINTS

In this unit, it has only been possible to touch on some of the classroom practice and professional development opportunities available through ICT. We recommend that you extend your understanding beyond the guidance here by reading more widely in this area, by experimenting with different types of software of particular use in your subject, by spending some time searching the internet to identify high-quality resources and educational websites which are specifically relevant to your interests and by talking to teachers and student teachers who are themselves exploring the possibilities offered by new technologies. Make sure you know what your subject association website offers.

However, it is important to remember that ICT use in the classroom should be directly related to the achievement of specified learning outcomes. As Cox (1999) points out, using ICT in your classroom provides no guarantee that learning takes place.

FURTHER READING

The subject-specific texts in the 'Learning to Teach' series all contain chapters about the use of ICT in the specific subject area. You may find further ideas for the application of ICT in your subject areas in these texts. The Routledge texts *Learning to Teach Using ICT in the Secondary School* (Leask and Pachler, 1999, 2005) provide detailed guidance. The OFSTED and BECTA websites. Online. Available HTTP: <http://www.ofsted.gov.uk> and <http://www.becta.org.uk> provide reports of practice in schools and classroom. See, for example, on the BECTA site:

A Preliminary Report for the DfEE on the Relationship between ICT and Primary School Standards (2000); Information Sheet: Parents, ICT and Education (2001); Secondary Schools – ICT and Standards: An Analysis of National Data from OFSTED and QCA by BECTA (2003a); What Research Says about Interactive Whiteboards (2003b).

See also background on ICT in schools in the OFSTED reports. Online. Available HTTP: <http://www.ofsted.gov.uk>:

ICT in Schools: The Impact of Government Initiatives: An Interim Report (2001).

Ofsted Subject Reports 2002/03: Information and Communication Technology in Secondary Schools (2004a).

ICT in schools: The Impact of Government Initiatives Five Years on (2004b).

Considerable research is being undertaken about new forms of pedagogy with ICT and the impact of ICT on learning:

Cunningham, M., Kerr, K., McEune, R., Smith, P. and Harris, S. (2003) *Laptops for Teachers: An Evaluation of the First Year of the Initiative*, London: Department for Education and Skills/British Educational Communications and Technology Agency.

Dickenson, P. (1999) *Whole Class Interactive Teaching*. Online. Available HTTP: <http://s13a.math.aca. mmu.ac.uk/Student_Writings/Masters/PaulDickinson.html> (accessed 12 June 2004). Although focusing on maths teaching, the general principles of whole class interactive teaching described here are applicable to all subjects.

Leask, M. and Pachler, N. (1999, 2nd edn 2005) *Learning to Teach using ICT in the Secondary School*, London: Routledge.

Loveless, A. and Ellis, V. (2001) *ICT, Pedagogy and Curriculum: Subject to Change*, London: Routledge.

Somekh, B. and Davis, N. (eds) (1997) *Using Information Technology effectively in Teaching and Learning*, London: Routledge.

Trend, R., Davis, N. and Loveless, A. (1999) *QTS Information Communication Technology*, London: LETTS Educational.

These texts provide advice and challenge your thinking on how and why you use ICT in your lessons.

Smith, I. (n.d.) *Tackling the Digital Divide*, London: Business in the Community. Online. Available HTTP: <http://www.bitc.org.uk/resources/viewpoint/mt_dd_comment.html> (accessed 28 June 2004). Examines the implications for pupils' employment prospects of access to ICT resources.

OECD (2001) *Knowledge and Skills for Life: First Results from the OECD Programme for International Student Assessment (PISA) 2000*, Paris: Organization for Economic Co-operation and Development. Online. Available HTTP: <http://www.pisa.oecd.org/knowledge/download.htm> (accessed 12 June 2004). A detailed comparative analysis, country by country, of pupils' performance across various subjects. This text provides useful guidance about ensuring learning takes place when ICT is used.

TTA (2002) *Qualifying to Teach: Professional Standards for Qualified Teacher Status and Requirements for Initial Teacher Training*, London: Teacher Training Agency. Describes what student teachers must be able to do to reach qualified teacher status (QTS).

TTA (2003) *Qualifying to Teach: Handbook of Guidance*, London: Teacher Training Agency. Additional guidance for training providers and for student teachers on the sorts of evidence which can be used to demonstrate the Standards for QTS.

WEB ADDRESSES

1   The European Computer Driving Licence is supported by the British Computing Society and details can be found at <http://www.ecdl.co.uk/>.
2   Specific information relating to special educational needs is scattered across the web so a starting point that gathers many of them together is useful. Such a site can be accessed through the teachers' area of the BECTA website: <http://www.becta.org.uk/teachers/index.cfm>. Click on the link to Inclusion and Special Needs. Further help and advice for teachers working with gifted pupils can be obtained from the National Association for Gifted Children at <http://www.nagcbritain.org.uk/>.
3   The Teacher Resource Exchange provides opportunities for teachers and other educators to share lesson plans, teaching materials and ideas. Online. Available HTTP: <http://tre.ngfl.gov.uk/>.
4   TeacherNet (DfES) is on <http://www.teachernet.gov.uk>.
5   Schoolzone is an independent organization supported by the National Grid for Learning providing information, resources and ideas for teachers: <http://www. schoolzone.co.uk/>.
6   The Mathematical Association is one example of a professional body providing information, ideas and resources for teachers: <http://www.m-a.org.uk/>.
7   The Geography Association similarly provides resources for teachers: <http://www.geography.org.uk/>.
8   The joint DfES/BECTA Superhighway Safety website provides detailed guidance and resources for schools in helping pupils make safe use of the internet: <http://www.safety.ngfl.gov.uk/>.
9   The home of the webquest, providing background information, research articles and hundreds of examples across a broad range of subjects: <http://www.webquest.org/>.
10   Access to European government supported educational websites is easily found through the European School Net on <http://www.eun.org>.
11   Virtual field trips: <http://www.field-guides.com/>.

12   Global School House: <http://www.gsh.org/>.

13   OzTeacherNet: <http://rite.ed.qut.edu.au/oz-teachernet/>. Click on the link to Global Youth Forums to access a range of e-mail discussion forums.

14   Internet Scuola: <http://www.internetscuola.net/>.

15   See, for example, 'ePALS Classroom Exchange' available at <http://epals.com/> and 'Windows on the Worlds' by the Central Bureau for Educational Visits and Exchanges available at <http://www.wotw.org.uk/>.

16   National Grid for Learning can be found at <http://www.ngfl.gov.uk/>. The Virtual Teachers' Centre is an integral part of the NGfL and can be located on<http://vtc.ngfl. gov.uk/>.

17   The DfES (Department for Education and Skills) website provides up to date information about legislation and initiatives for schools: <http://www.dfes.gov.uk/>.

18   The Office for Standards in Education (OFSTED) website not only provides reports on school inspections, it provides subject summary reports and reports on educational issues: <http://www.ofsted.gov.uk>.

19   Searching through the news and media categories in the Yahoo search engines on the web provides access to thousands of news sites around the world: <http://www.reuters. com>; <http://www.bigissue.com>; <http://www.telegraph.co.uk>; <http://www.guardian. co.uk>. The BBC news site is excellent: <http://www/bbc.co.uk>.

20   TTA: <http://www.teach-tta.gov.uk>; <http://www.tta.gov.uk>.

21   General Teaching Council: <http://www.gtce.org.uk>.

22   The British Educational Research Association provides access through websites to research papers from conferences around the world: <http://www.bera.ac.uk>. In addition, you will find information about research into the use of ICT for educational purposes on BECTA's website:<http://www.becta.org.uk/>.

2 Beginning to Teach

The previous chapter was concerned with the role and responsibilities of the teacher and how you might manage those. In this chapter, we look first at how you might learn from observing experienced teachers and then move on to consider aspects of planning and preparing lessons.

For most students there is a period during which you observe other teachers working, take part in team teaching and take part of a lesson before taking on a whole lesson. During this period, you use observation and critical reflection to build up your professional knowledge about teaching and learning and your professional judgement about managing learning. Unit 2.1 is therefore designed to focus your attention on how to observe the detail of what is happening in classrooms.

It is difficult for a student teacher to become fully aware of the planning that underpins each lesson as planning schemes of work (long-term programmes of work) is usually done by a team of staff over a period of time. The scheme of work then usually stays in place for some time. The extent of the actual planning for each lesson may also be hidden – experienced teachers often internalize their planning so their notes for a lesson are brief in comparison with those that a student teacher needs. Unit 2.2 explains planning processes. Unit 2.3 combines much of the advice of the first two units in an analysis of the issues you probably need to be aware of before taking responsibility for whole lessons.

The quality of lesson planning is crucial to the success of a student teacher in enabling the pupils to learn. Defining clear and specific objectives for the learning in a particular lesson is one aspect of planning that many student teachers initially find difficult. The following story (from Mager, 1990: p. v) reinforces this need to have clear objectives for lessons:

> Once upon a time a Sea Horse gathered up his seven pieces of eight and cantered out to find his fortune. Before he had travelled very far he met an Eel, who said,
> 'Psst. Hey, bud. Where 'ya goin'?'
> 'I'm going out to find my fortune,' replied the Sea Horse, proudly.
> 'You're in luck,' said the Eel. 'For four pieces of eight you can have this speedy flipper and then you'll be able to get there a lot faster.'
> 'Gee, that's swell,' said the Sea Horse and paid the money and put on the flipper and slithered off at twice the speed. Soon he came upon a Sponge, who said,

'Psst. Hey, bud. Where 'ya goin'?'

'I'm going out to find my fortune,' replied the Sea Horse.

'You're in luck,' said the Sponge. 'For a small fee, I will let you have this jet-propelled scooter so that you will be able to travel a lot faster.'

So the Sea Horse bought the scooter with his remaining money and went zooming thru the sea five times as fast. Soon he came upon a Shark, who said,

'Psst. Hey, bud. Where 'ya goin'?'

'I'm going to find my fortune,' replied the Sea Horse.

'You're in luck. If you take this short cut,' said the Shark, pointing to his open mouth, 'you'll save yourself a lot of time.'

'Gee, thanks,' said the Sea Horse and zoomed off into the interior of the Shark and was never heard from again.

The moral of this fable is that if you're not sure where you're going, you're liable to end up someplace else.

We hope that by the end of this chapter, you will be able to plan lessons in which both you and the pupils know exactly what they are meant to be learning.

Explicitly sharing your lesson objectives with pupils provides them with clear goals and potentially a sense of satisfaction from your lesson as they achieve the goals set. You can expect to find processes in place in most schools for the setting of personal targets for pupils.

Unit 2.1

Reading Classrooms

How To Maximize Learning from Classroom Observation

Susan Heightman

INTRODUCTION

How do you actively read a classroom rather than simply watch a teacher at work? This is a question you need to have some answers to if you are going to make the most of observation opportunities. These opportunities may be to watch highly experienced teachers or to watch fellow trainee teachers and newly qualified teachers. Whatever the case, you should not make prior distinctions about what observations are likely to be of greatest value to you professionally because there is so much to learn from every invitation you receive to observe. Equally you should not consider observation to be an activity reserved for the beginner teacher. Lesson observation and the improved professional practice that can be gained from it, is an important continual professional development activity for teachers at all levels of the profession.

Qualified teachers are increasingly used to being observed, especially in the context of appraisal, inspections and preparations for inspections. What they are sometimes less used to is being observed by people with an open, positive approach who are concerned to analyse what is happening during the lesson rather than measure against preconceived ideas about what should be happening. Try to be the open, positive observer: it is important that the teacher experiences your presence and any follow-up discussion within a positive context. To achieve this you need to express appreciation for being able to observe and ask the teacher's guidance on the nature of the observer role that they wish you to adopt. The teacher may wish to give you a participant role or want you to be the non-participant observer. After the lesson not only should you thank the teacher but you should avoid negative comments. Teachers themselves are most likely to begin any discussion of the lesson with reference to the things that went wrong or were not in the plan. Always lead the discussion towards the aspects of the lesson that they were pleased with because it is from this positive discussion that you will learn most about their professional craft, as exemplified in the research of Brown and McIntyre (1993). It is good to remember that observation is a fundamental research activity – seeking to know what is happening, why it is happening and what the impact is likely to be. It is not passive nor is it concerned to confirm judgements. It is perceptive rather than judgemental.

The form in which you record your observations can be varied according to the focus you select. Many schools possess their own observation proformas that may be useful to you. Equally you may be given a general proforma by your college tutors or you can draw up a range of schedules for yourself. There are advantages to having blank proformas to work with because they facilitate the quick recording of information and prompt you to consider specific aspects which, in the flow of the lesson, you might otherwise forget. There are also great advantages to sharing an observation activity with another student teacher because then you can share perceptions and engage in a discussion about the significance of what you have observed.

OBJECTIVES

At the end of this unit you should have:

- practised defining the focus of your observations to achieve specific learning purposes;
- developed different strategies for recording your observations in forms that lend themselves to subsequent analysis;
- practised the analysis of teaching strategies and pupil learning behaviours to enhance your ability to plan and teach your own lessons;
- developed an enlarged understanding of the teaching and learning process and an insight into how you wish to teach.

WHO SHOULD YOU BE OBSERVING AND WHY?

The majority of your observations will be of classes being taught by their established teacher prior to you working more directly with the class yourself.

Here you will naturally be very concerned to study how the pupils interact with each other and with the teacher and will see these observations as of particular value in preparing you for teaching this specific class. However, you should not be observing the teacher with a view to mimicking his/her teaching style. The teacher is unique and has a unique relationship with the class that cannot be replicated. If you attempt to mimic, the pupils are likely to reject this because you have no shared background or relationship with the class. Instead, as a professional in training, you should be seeking to understand and record for analysis, what and how pupils are learning and the routines and teaching strategies of the teacher. This analysis should enable you to make a selection of those aspects that you wish to adapt in developing your own teaching style and purposes. You will also of course be familiarizing yourself with the subject content in action and the resources that the pupils are using in order to learn.

Alternative forms of observation may be of small groups of pupils working with a special needs teacher or teaching assistant. Here you will be learning a particular range of teaching skills and have the opportunity to understand the learning needs of individual pupils in greater depth. In addition, it is valuable to follow a class or pupil across the curriculum and watch teachers working in subject disciplines other than your own. Try to see any opportunities to observe teachers at work with children as learning opportunities for you. Teachers in assembly, on duty at break or working with pupils in an extra curricular club, are all professionally engaged in their work and how they work in these contexts directly relates to their work in the classroom. It is therefore a good idea to carry a small notepad with you at all times to briefly record significant observations and any questions that have occurred to you at the time. These can be followed up later with tutors and colleagues. Effective observation is a matter of intellectual curiosity and being alert. Table 2.1.1 lists some of the research questions you can address through observation. Add any questions of your own. This is followed by a series of activities to help you achieve effective professional learning from a range of observation contexts.

WHAT DO CLASSROOMS LOOK LIKE?

The classroom is more than a room with chairs, desks and a teaching board of some kind. It is a learning environment. It should both promote and support pupil learning.

It should also express the values and ethos of the school. As part of lesson observation, it is useful to 'read' the impact of the appearance and layout of the room on pupil and teacher learning and performance. You may find the planned approach useful in Task 2.1.1.

Task 2.1.1
The learning environment

Is this room a specialist room or a general classroom? Is the room used mainly by one teacher?

Sketch the layout of the room and the seating arrangements. Identify the light source and other features of note such as the board and the teacher's desk/display boards.

What limitations or advantages do you perceive in the desk layout to pupil and teacher, learning and teaching?

Describe any displays in the room. Note the different proportions of pupil work and teacher/published material display. Were the displays colourful and well cared for? Would the displays prompt pupils to value their own work and the work of other pupils more highly?

Comment on whether you would like to be taught in this room and whether the environment promotes the subject and pupil learning. Give reasons for your response.

What suggestions for improvement could you make that were modest in terms of cost? Consider with whom you might share this information and the form your information could take. Appropriate suggestions made by observers can be very constructive in contributing to school improvements of the learning environment.

HOW LESSONS BEGIN

As with all relationships and activities, how lessons begin is very significant to the success or otherwise of the lesson. Experienced teachers are very aware of this and it is important that you spend some time focusing upon the very different ways in which teachers manage lesson beginnings in order that you can begin to establish your own set of routines. Invariably schools have their own school-wide policies on this, e.g. lining up outside the classroom in single file (so as not to block the corridor) until the teacher arrives. As a student teacher you should always know the school and department policies in these respects and follow them.

Table 2.1.1 Research questions that can assist in focusing lesson observations

Briefing and preparing for observation

Have you clearly established the date, time and place of the lesson?

Are you briefed on the topic being taught in the lesson and the composition of the class?

Have you established the role you are to take during observation – participant or non-participant?

Have you established the form in which you are going to note down your observations and your major areas of focus?

Have you established how you are going to feed back to the teacher and any future use you may make of the notes you have made?

Teaching and learning questions

What was the plan/shape of the lesson?

How was the lesson introduced? How did the pupils know the learning aims of the lesson?

What were the different learning activities that the children undertook?

Was there group or pair work during the course of the lesson?

Did any pupils receive different work, degrees of help or resources during the lesson?

What were the different ways that pupils recorded or presented their learning?

How did the teacher direct the pace of the lesson?

What form of question and answer sessions did the teacher initiate?

How were pupils encouraged to ask and answer questions?

What resources were used to assist in learning?

How did the teacher provide visual, auditory and activity learning resources and opportunities in the lesson?

Was ICT a dimension in the lesson?

Pupil and class management dimensions

What were the teacher's expectations about pupil behaviours?

Were there established routines or codes of conduct? What were they?

Were the issues of health and safety referred to during the lesson?

Did the teacher use any assertive behaviour management techniques? Were any sanctions used during the lesson?

How did the teacher use seating plans in the lesson and for what purpose?

How did the teacher use voice and gesture in the lesson to manage pupil response?

How did the teacher assess pupils work during the lesson and how did he/she feedback to the pupils?

Other professional issues

Was a teaching assistant or special education needs teacher also in the room? What was their role and how did they work with the pupils and the teacher?

Have you identified any gaps in your subject knowledge through watching this lesson? How will you fill them?

How has this observation made you reconsider your future professional practice as a teacher?

**Task 2.1.2
Analysing the beginning of a
lesson**

In carrying out this activity it is advisable that you should arrive at least five minutes before the beginning of the lesson. Discuss the nature of your observation with the teacher prior to the lesson and afterwards you should talk to the teacher about what you have noted to check for any misapprehensions and to further discuss the strategies you have seen being used.

There are three stages to the beginning of a lesson:

1 outside the classroom;
2 entrance of pupils and settling;
3 introduction to the lesson and possibly a starter activity.

Useful prompt questions are:

Outside the classroom

- What procedures were used for pupils gathering outside the classroom?
- Were pupils free to enter as they arrived or did they have to line up?
- Did the teacher wait for the class at the classroom door – were they welcomed on arrival outside the classroom or did the teacher stay inside the classroom until the class were directed to enter?

Settling into place

- Did the pupils sit where they pleased or did they have their own places? Did they wait to greet the teacher standing before they were told to sit down?
- Was a register taken and in what manner?
- What signals did the teacher use to indicate that the lesson had begun?

The beginning of the lesson

- How did the teacher explain the learning purpose of the lesson?
- How long was it before the lesson proper began?
- What problems or issues did the teacher have to deal with before the lesson began? How did they do this?
- What praise or reprimands did the teacher use and how did pupils respond?

If possible discuss this list of questions with a colleague and add to them. Then using a similar checklist to that drafted here, record your observations.

Observer name .... Teacher name ....
Class name and subject .... Date ....

Real time	Place	Pupil actions	Teacher actions	Pupil talk	Teacher talk	Other notes

THE SHAPE OF A LESSON AND TRANSITIONS

The shape of a lesson is very important to its effectiveness. When an experienced teacher is delivering a lesson they work to a plan but equally they deviate from the plan when a new learning need becomes apparent. Good teaching is flexible and responsive. When observing an experienced teacher you will often notice how they use transitions in a lesson to summarize the learning at key stages before moving on to the next learning activity. Figure 2.1.1 is a flow diagram of a lesson about communications where the transitions are highlighted in bold.

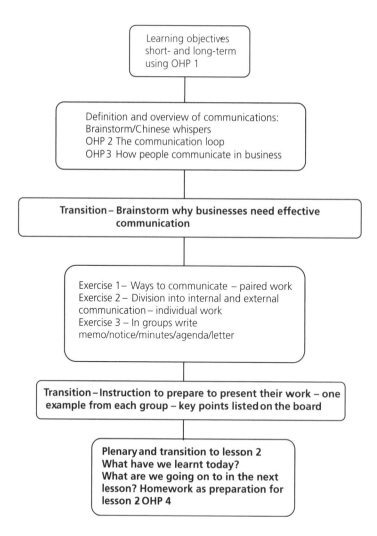

Figure 2.1.1 Flow diagram of a Year 10 business studies lesson which is the first lesson of a double unit of work on communication for business

TEACHER TALK AND ORAL FEEDBACK

It is very useful to focus upon teacher talk and feedback to pupils during a lesson and to begin to estimate its impact on learning and behaviour. There are various ways of doing this, including tape recordings and video recordings of a lesson. The use of a digital camera for detailed observation work is covered towards the end of this section. However, for most occasions you will need to use simple non-technical procedures to capture this kind of data. After the lesson, it is always a good idea to discuss your data with the teacher since a deeper understanding will emerge from the discussion.

Task 2.1.3
Teacher talk analysis

Complete the following checklist for a section of the lesson or the entire lesson.

Oral feedback	Examples observed in the lesson	Learning impact on pupils
Giving information		
Correcting errors or misapprehensions		
Praising		
Questioning to check understanding		
Questioning to deepen understanding		
Asking pupils to focus on specific aspects		
Summarising learning		
Encouraging pupil reflection		
Coaching in skills		
Answering pupil questions		
Correcting poor behaviour		
Guiding pupils back on task		
Outlining next learning tasks		

PUPIL TALK AND INTERACTION

It is equally interesting and highly relevant to analyse pupil talk and interaction which, if you follow a class or group to different lessons, will often change in very significant ways.

You will find it very enlightening simply to use a class list and place a tick in red next to each pupil's name as they ask for information and a tick in black against each pupil's name as they answer a question or offer information. This will give you a clear indication of the degree to which pupils are engaging in pupil talk during a lesson.

A more detailed check that you can make with a small group of pupils, one pupil or the entire class is to complete the checklist in Task 2.1.4 over a 20-minute period where you keep a time record minute by minute. A three-minute exemplar record is shown below.

Task 2.1.4
Analysis of pupil talk

Complete the following checklist to analyse individual, group or whole class pupil talk over a 20-minute period.

Real time – minute intervals	Pupil(s) initiated questions of teacher	Pupil(s) answering teacher questions	Off task(s) discussion with peers	On task discussion with peers	Other notes about the class activity or other events
9.10	John B Mary Y				JB not paying attention Mary Y confused
9.11					
9.12		Mark S	John B		Good recall by Mark
9.13				Mark S Mary Y	

FOCUS UPON PUPIL LEARNING

Often the instinct of student teachers in the classroom is to focus upon the teacher teaching rather than upon how the pupils are learning. This is not surprising. When we first 'go back to school' our memories are those of a pupil who watched and listened to the teacher. However, now you need to shift your focus and observe what and how the pupils are learning. There are so many ways this can be done.

Task 2.1.5
Pupil learning analysis

Before beginning your analysis write down the learning aims of the lesson and identify the task/ activities that you are going to focus upon. If you are a participant observer, you are in the best position to make notes of key information as the lesson unfolds and to look over the work of pupils and be actively engaged with coaching and guiding their learning activities. As you do this you will begin to appreciate what strategies and resources are working effectively for their learning and why. As a non-participant observer, the task becomes more subtle. If you are free to move around once pupils are involved in an activity, then you must move too and oversee their task completion. If it is appropriate, you can ask them brief questions but you must not disengage them from their task. Equally do not be tempted to do the work for them. Always lead them to think through the task with your help. In highly active lessons there may be considerable chat and activity but there may equally be considerable learning taking place. Quiet lessons where the pupils seem attentive to the teacher are not necessarily lessons where learning is happening although they are lessons where some work is being completed! It is not appropriate to have a proforma for recording pupil learning because it is so complex. The most flexible way to record their learning is to make bullet points as you perceive the evidence. Once the lesson is over, you can ask the teacher if you may review the work that the pupils have completed and ideally you could then have a follow-up discussion with the teacher.

FOCUS UPON PUPIL MANAGEMENT AND DEALING WITH DISRUPTIVE BEHAVIOUR

Before beginning lesson observations you should make yourself familiar with the school and the department's behaviour policies. These are important documents that staff rely upon to achieve a common and appropriate way of dealing with disruptive behaviour. It is essential that you work within these policies yourself even if you sometimes notice that some teachers do not follow the policies.

Task 2.1.6
Pupil management and disruptive behaviour

When you identify an example of disruptive behaviour during a lesson observation, make an immediate note of the following things:

• What you thought were the causes that led to the disruption?
• Who was involved?
• How did the teacher react and what impact did this have?
• How did the rest of the class react?
• How was the lesson disrupted?
• What subsequent action or follow up occurred?

At a future time, check on the background of pupils involved to establish what their known problems may be.

FOCUS UPON TEACHER AND PUPIL ASSESSMENT FOR LEARNING

A common weakness identified in school inspections is a lack of focus upon assessment for learning (see also Unit 6.1). Ensure that you know your school's assessment policies and those of the subject department. Discuss assessment with school-based tutors and, after an observation where you have focused on assessment, have a follow-up discussion with the teacher you observed.

Task 2.1.7
Assessment for learning

During the lesson write detailed notes about any activities that the teacher initiates to assess how pupils are understanding the work. The teacher may use many strategies but these are the most common:

• direct questions;
• discussion;
• asking pupils to present their work to their partner, the whole class or a group;
• reviewing work on computer, whiteboard or in exercise books;
• through role-play or display activities;
• setting another task to test understanding;
• posing a problem to solve to evaluate and deepen understanding.

Having identified assessment activities, note down what the teacher does to correct misapprehensions or to advance the learning. How does the teacher reassure and motivate? How does the teacher consolidate the learning?

HOW DOES THE TEACHER USE LEARNING RESOURCES AND AIDS DURING THE LESSON?

It is interesting to map the varied resources and aids that teachers use during lessons to help pupils with different learning styles to learn. Some children learn most easily by activities such as experiments or making things, others learn most easily through visual media while others are very capable of learning through listening. In order to maximize learning and to achieve differentiation to match the lesson activities to the differing abilities of children, teachers use many aids and resources.

Task 2.1.8
Resources and aids used

Map the teaching/learning resources and aids used in a lesson and analyse the pupil learning benefits.

The resource	Learning activity	Learning benefit
Text book		
Prepared study guide or worksheet		
Pictures, mind maps, graphics		
Video, CDs, DVDs		
Computer programs including internet		
Tape recording		
Television programme or film		
Experiment		
Games, puzzles, models and activity cards		
Whiteboard		
Electronic whiteboard and digital camera		

SUBJECT CONTENT FOCUSED OBSERVATION

All teachers during the early stages of their career have to work hard to fill in the gaps in subject knowledge and, as schemes of work and the curriculum change, experienced teachers also need to learn in order to teach. Therefore, focusing upon the subject content of a lesson is an important activity as part of your work to map where you have subject knowledge gaps that need to be filled.

Task 2.1.9
Focusing upon subject content in lessons

Select a lesson for this task where you believe you may have subject knowledge gaps. Prior to observing the lesson, read through schemes of work and any printed materials and other resources that teachers use in teaching the topic to be covered. When watching the lesson, map the subject knowledge and skills that would be necessary to deliver the lesson confidently to ensure that you would be sufficiently informed to stretch more able pupils and deal swiftly with misapprehensions. This is a subject knowledge and skills audit. Once you have created your list then highlight those areas where you need to expand your knowledge and expertise and discuss ways in which you might do this with college and school tutors. The important element that the lesson observation provides is a real experience of how much teachers need to know before they can teach. It is undoubtedly true that you never know anything in depth until you have had to teach it to questioning and interested learners or to people who have difficulty in the subject who need the learning broken down into manageable units.

USING DIGITAL CAMERAS OR VIDEO CAMERAS IN LESSON OBSERVATION

Lesson observation and the subsequent analysis is a very challenging activity. In five minutes of a lesson so much can happen that is of significance and worthy of discussion by the student teacher or any teacher wishing to develop good practice. If you can record part of a lesson for detailed analysis with the teacher concerned, this is an ideal way of learning.

Digital cameras have made a significant difference to the ease with which lessons can be recorded. They are small, easy to use with good sound quality and work well in normal classroom lighting. Lesson observation, if it is not to disturb the natural flow of a lesson needs to be subtle so that the pupils forget that observation is taking place. Many schools use regular video recording of lessons as part of their programme of continual professional development for all teachers and in these circumstances pupils learn to ignore the cameras. Software is available to annotate videos in real time so that key aspects of the lesson, e.g. questions asked, explanations given, can be easily grouped for playback and analysis.

Task 2.1.10
Recording a lesson

Once you begin teaching, you should make every effort to have some of your class or small group lessons recorded for at least part of a lesson. This can be done for you by a teaching assistant, a fellow student teacher, your tutor, the class teacher or even a pupil! Once you have such a record it is unwise simply to view it alone because you need to discuss what is there. It is easy to be overly self-critical and focus on minor shortcomings, taking little note of the things you do really well. A discussion with a colleague whilst you review the film will guard against this and, more importantly, will lead to new insights about teaching. Capture the learning from the discussion with bullet point notes.

COLLABORATIVE TEACHING AS A FORM OF OBSERVATION

In Unit 5.4 you will be introduced to action research where reference is made to paired observation. Collaborative teaching opportunities, where the planning and presentation of a lesson are shared with a colleague, also provide opportunities to observe your colleague. You should seek every opportunity during your school experience to be involved in collaborative teaching because it is a very active and powerful training experience where two-way observation and feedback can be very constructive.

FURTHER INQUIRIES AND OBSERVATIONS: SOME SUGGESTIONS

Many other aspects of teaching can be observed; some examples are given in Tasks 2.1.11 and 2.1.12. You should be able to adapt these for your own use.

Task 2.1.11
Teachers' questions

What types of question do teachers ask? Are they simple questions with one word answers or are they more complex involving explanation? Investigate the frequency of different types of questions. You could classify questions into recall of fact and using prior knowledge to speculate about events or anticipate new ideas. Many writers refer to these sort of questions as 'closed' and 'open'; see Unit 3.1 for further information about 'questioning'.
Do teachers:

- Ask mainly closed questions?
- Ask both open and closed questions according to purpose and circumstance?
- Accept only right answers?
- Dismiss wrong answers?
- Give enough time for pupils to give an answer?
- Encourage pupils to frame a reply?

Explore the way teachers respond to right and wrong answers given by pupils.

Task 2.1.12
Where is the teacher during a lesson?

The movement of teachers in the classroom may say a lot about their relationship with pupils, about how they keep an eye on activity and behaviour and about their interest in the pupils.
Draw an A4 map of the classroom in which you are observing. Mark on the key points: teacher's desk, pupil desk, whiteboard, projector, etc. Have several copies of the blank available. Throughout the lesson at designated times mark on your map where the teacher stands and where she has moved from. Do this at regular intervals, e.g. one minute, and so build up a picture of position and movement. At the same time record the time and what is going on in the lesson. This will enable you to relate teacher movement to lesson activity. Analyse your map and discuss:

- Where is the teacher most likely to be found during the lesson? What reasons can you offer for this: writing on the board; explaining with an overhead projector; helping pupils with written work?

- Does the teacher keep an eye on all the events in the room and, if so, how? Is it done by eye contact from the front or does the teacher move about the room?
- How did the teacher know that pupils were on task for most of the lesson?
- Were some pupils given more attention than others? What evidence do you have for this?
- What explanations are there for this pattern of observations?
- Was the teacher movement related to pupil behaviour in any way? Examine this idea and look for the evidence.
- Did the nature of the subject matter dictate teacher movement? How might movements change in different subject lessons? Give an example.

Share your information with other student teachers. What information does your 'map' give you about 'pupil territory' and 'teacher territory'?

Some teachers use their desk and board and equipment as a barrier between them and the pupils; others get in among the pupils and the desks. Are there 'no-go areas' which the teacher does not invade? Are there similar spaces for teachers which the pupil does not invade? See Unit 3.3 on managing pupil behaviour.

SUMMARY AND KEY POINTS

You have discovered that teachers and pupils have set up a working relationship in which both parties know the rules, the codes of behaviour and their boundaries. You have seen many teachers working smoothly with the class and the boundaries being kept, apparently without great effort; beneath that order you may have realized that there is a history of carefully nurtured practice involving much hard work by the teacher in establishing an appropriate atmosphere.

On occasions you may have seen these boundaries being broken and seen ways in which the teacher restores a working atmosphere. Each and every teacher has their own way of dealing with this problem. Watching the ways other teachers deal with such problems helps you widen your own repertoire of skills. You should find it helpful if you focus on how teachers handle behavioural problems for at least one of your classroom observation tasks.

The class you work with during school experience is someone else's; you are unlikely to break the relationships set up between them. In this respect your job of learning to teach is made more difficult; do you break the established pattern of behaviour or not? It is useful to remember that the school experience is a learning exercise and not one in which you are expected to take on the whole class as if it is yours for the year.

The activities have been designed to help you organize a number of enquiries and get the most out of observation; more importantly, they should enable you to organize other enquiries of interest to you as you seek solutions to problems arising in your own teaching.

Observing can include looking, listening, recording, analysing and selecting; after evaluation some of what you have seen and heard may be incorporated into your own teaching. Unless observing moves on from you merely being in the classroom, letting the events wash over you, observation becomes boring and, more importantly, of little value. So you need to focus on events, strategies, circumstances and observe those; and then do something with the results. Watching other people's lessons is also about feelings: your own because of the task ahead of you; the teachers' because they are under scrutiny and the pupils' because they are wondering what you are there for and what you might be like next week! So the observer is observed, too.

What we see and hear we have to interpret. You need to remember that, as a student teacher, you are likely to be familiar with classrooms. You have spent many years of your life, literally hundreds of hours, in classrooms as a pupil and student and you have a good idea of what you think makes a good classroom. The first point to recognize is that you are biased because of that experience. You are not a neutral observer or one that brings a fresh eye to teaching.

You need to unlearn most of what you know about the classrooms of your adolescence and of your undergraduate days before you can start to understand today's classrooms. Your experience then was that of a learner but that is only half the story; the experience was probably that of a successful learner otherwise you would not be in the position you are in now. In addition you were probably a keen learner, not a reluctant one. All these features of your background may have to be carefully examined and their usefulness evaluated for the task in hand – teaching today's children in today's classrooms.

Observation activities are part of the transition from student teacher to experienced teacher. It is important that observation helps you see classrooms and teachers as you have not seen them before. You bring bias to observations and you may exercise bias in your judgements. Your observations of the lessons of the classroom teacher should be different from those made by the classroom teacher. You each bring a different purpose to the task. The class teacher is looking for quality of learning and is concerned for his performance. At this stage you are not so much concerned with quality but what was done to achieve it and make the lesson run smoothly.

Observation is in one sense a research exercise. It enables you to gather data on teacher performances and pupil learning. By analysing that data, you can begin to identify factors that contribute to effective teaching and learning and so place them in the framework of your own emerging skills. One way of establishing your own framework is to refer to your checklist of competences or standards required of newly qualified teachers.

Observing other teachers working should be a continuing exercise; as your own teaching develops you need to refine and widen your skills and watching others with purpose can aid that development. We have suggested the following:

- All teachers have their own style. An initial teacher education course aims to help you find your own style.
- Your observation and interpretation of teachers and pupils in classrooms is affected by your own past experience. You need to be aware of this bias when you analyse the work of others and in your own teaching.
- When teachers interact with the class then each pupil in the class responds differently to the teacher. Learning and teaching, although carried out in groups, is an intensely personal activity.
- You can learn a lot about aspects of teaching and learning by focusing on particular tasks, events or happenings in the classroom. Understanding those events in terms of the interactions between teacher and pupils and the effect those interactions have on learning allows you to make decisions about your own approaches to teaching and learning.
- You need to evaluate your emerging teaching skills regularly over the course, setting your views against those of staff supporting you and your course requirements.
- Your teaching skills develop throughout your career. You can rarely say 'I can do that' but you should be able to describe the development against the background of new challenges and widening experiences.

So observation is one of the main ways in which we all learn. More importantly it will help you to gain access to the professional expertise of teachers and increase your understanding of their work with pupils. The most productive way in which you can maximize the opportunities school experience provides for classroom observation is to prepare for it just as you would prepare for a lesson. Always decide upon a focus or learning aim for the observation and then plan the approach you are going to take according to the purpose behind your observation. The tasks in this unit have been designed to help you achieve this. Not only should you ensure that the observed colleague is aware of your observation purpose and approves it but, through a positive expression of your appreciation to the observed teacher, you should seek a follow-up discussion where you can reflect upon and contextualize what you have learnt. In observing colleagues, you are also learning to accept and understand the need for your work in the classroom to be observed by others to help you become a reflective teacher. Focused classroom observation is one means by which you will experience education as a process of learning engagement where teachers and pupils transform information and knowledge through its application and the growth of understanding.

FURTHER READING

Brown, S. and McIntyre, D. (1993) *Making Sense of Teaching*, Buckingham: Open University Press.

Barth, R. (1992) *Improving Schools from Within*, San Francisco: Jossey-Bass.

Education Broadcasting Services (2004) *Looking at Learning: Tactics of Questioning*, Condon: Teacher Training Agency (Portland House, London SW1E 5TT) CD-ROM. Two copies have been distributed to all teacher training institutions in England. One copy for loading on the institutional intranet and one copy for their library.

Furlong, J. and Maynard, T. (1995) *Mentoring Student Teachers*, London: Routledge.

Hopkins, D.A. (1985) *A Teachers' Guide to Classroom Research*, Milton Keynes: Open University Press.

Leach, J. and Moon, B. (eds) (1999) *Learners and Pedagogy*, London: Paul Chapman Publishers.

Schon, D. A. (1987*) Educating the Reflective Practitioner*, San Francisco: Jossey-Bass Publishers.

Tilstone, C. (ed.) (1998) *Observing Teaching and Learning: Principles and Practice*, London: David Fulton.

Wragg, E.C. (1999) *An Introduction to Classroom Observation*, London: Routledge.

Unit 2.2

Schemes of Work and Lesson Planning

Jon Davison and Marilyn Leask

INTRODUCTION

> Our lesson observations revealed that in classes run by effective teachers, pupils are clear about what they are doing and why they are doing it. They can see links with their earlier learning and have some ideas about how it could be developed further. The pupils want to know more.
>
> (Hay McBer, 2000: para.1.2.4)

If your time with the pupils is to be used effectively, you need to plan carefully for each lesson – taking account of how pupils learn, the requirements of the curriculum, the most appropriate methods of teaching the topic and the resources available, as well as the evaluations of previous lessons.

There are two levels of planning particularly appropriate to your work in the classroom: the scheme of work and the lesson plan. Examples of lesson plans are available on the web, e.g. on the sites listed in the introduction to Chapter 1. You will quickly gain experience of planning as you plan lessons and schemes of work on your school experience. However, planned activities do not have to be followed through rigidly and at all costs. Because planning is integrally linked to evaluation and development, evaluation of plans for a specific situation may point to the need to change or develop your plans.

OBJECTIVES

By the end of this unit, you should be able to:

- explain what is meant by the terms: 'aims', 'objectives', 'progression', 'differentiation';
- construct schemes of work (also known as programmes or units of work);
- construct effective lesson plans.

Check the competences/standards for your course which relate to lesson planning and schemes of work to make sure you understand what is required of you.

PLANNING WHAT TO TEACH

What should you teach and how should you teach it?

The factors influencing *what* should be taught (lesson content) are discussed in Unit 1.1, but how much you teach in each lesson and *how* you teach it (teaching methods) are the teacher's own decisions.

Lesson content

Recall the 'sabre-toothed curriculum' of the stone age and the 'queen of studies' from medieval times (Unit 1.1). Similarly, the knowledge, skills, understanding and attitudes appropriate for a young person entering the world of work in the twenty-first century are vastly different to those which were considered appropriate even fifteen years ago. Ideas about what teachers should teach change regularly and the curriculum is under constant scrutiny by those responsible for education.

As a student teacher, you are usually given clear guidelines about what to teach and the goals for pupils' learning within your subject. These goals are in part usually set out in government produced documents, e.g. the National Curriculum documents, school documents and syllabuses prepared by examination boards. If you teach in England and Wales, you need to become familiar with the National Curriculum requirements and the terminology (see Chapter 7). However, before you plan individual lessons you need an overall picture of what learning is planned for the pupils over a period of time. This overall plan is called a scheme of work and most departmental schemes of work cover between half a term's work and a couple of years' work.

Teaching methods

However constraining the guidelines on content are, the decision about which teaching methods to use is usually yours. As you become more experienced as a teacher, you acquire your own personal approach to teaching. But as people learn in different ways and different teaching methods are suitable for different types of material, you should become familiar with a range of ways of structuring learning experiences in the classroom. For example, you might choose to use discussion, rote learning, discovery learning, role-play and so on to achieve particular objectives. Chapter 5 gives you detailed advice on teaching styles and strategies appropriate to different approaches to learning.

Task 2.2.1
How do you learn?

Spend a few minutes making notes of the methods which you use to help you learn and the methods of teaching used by teachers from whom you felt you learned a lot. Then make notes about those situations from which you did not learn. Compare these notes with those of other student teachers. People learn in different ways and different areas of learning require different approaches. You need to take account of such differences in planning your lessons and to demonstrate that you can use a range of teaching methods in order to take account of such differences.

SCHEMES OF WORK AND LESSON PLANS

There are two main stages to planning for pupil learning:

1   Preparing an outline of the work to be covered over a period – the scheme of work.
2   Planning each individual lesson – the lesson plan.

A number of formats for both schemes of work and lesson plans are in use. We suggest you read the advice given for the teaching of your subject in the subject-specific texts in this 'Learning to Teach' series. However, whilst the level of detail may vary between different approaches, the purpose is the same: to provide an outline of the work to be done either over an extended period (scheme of work) or in the lesson (lesson plan) so that the planned learning can take place. Try different approaches to planning in order to find those most appropriate to your situation. The best plans are ones which support you in your teaching so that your pupils learn what you intend them to learn. The illustrations in this unit are intended to provide examples with which you can work and later modify.

The scheme of work

This might also be called the 'programme of work' or the 'unit of work'. Different terms may be used in your school or in your subject but the purpose is the same: to devise a long-term plan for the pupils' learning. So a scheme of work sets out the long-term plans for learning and thus covers an extended period of time – this could be a period of years, a term or half a term or weeks, e.g. for a module of work. A scheme of work should be designed to build on the learning which has gone before, i.e. it should ensure continuity of pupil learning.

Schemes of work should be designed to ensure that the knowledge, skills, capabilities, understanding and attitudes of the pupils are developed over a particular period in order to ensure progression in learning. The term 'progression' means the planned development of knowledge, skills, understanding or attitudes over time. In some departments, the schemes of work are very detailed and include teaching materials and methods as well as safety issues.

Using a scheme of work

Usually, you are given a scheme of work. In putting this together, the following questions have been considered:

- What are you trying to achieve? (Aims for the scheme of work and objectives for particular lessons – see the definitions in the numbered paragraphs below.)
- What has been taught before?
- How much time is available to do this work?
- What resources are available?
- How is the work to be assessed?
- How does this work fit in with work pupils are doing in other subjects?
- What is to be taught later?

The scheme itself may be quite brief (Figure 2.2.1 shows a proforma used by student teachers on one course) but it will be based on the above information.

Each of these areas is now discussed in turn. To start with, think about what learning should be taking place.

What are you trying to achieve?

The *aims* of a scheme of work are general statements about the learning that should take place over a period.

Objectives are specific statements which set out what pupils are expected to learn from a particular lesson in a way that allows you to identify if learning has occurred. Objectives are prepared for each lesson and further detail is included under lesson planning later in this unit.

In devising each scheme of work a small aspect of the whole curriculum will have been taken and a route planned through this which provides the best opportunities for pupils to learn. *Progression* in pupil learning should be considered and built into schemes of work.

What has been taught before?

This information should be available from school documentation and from staff. In the case of pupils in their first year of secondary education, there is usually a member of staff responsible for liaising with primary schools who may have this information.

How much time is available to do this work?

The length of lessons and the number of lessons devoted to a topic are decided by the department or school in which you are working. Don't forget that homework has a valuable role to play in enhancing learning and that not all the lessons you expect to have are available for teaching. Some time is taken up by tests, revision, fire drill, special events, lateness.

What resources are available?

Resources include material resources as well as human resources and what is available depends on the school where you are working. You need to find out the procedures for using resources in the school and what is available. You may find there are resources outside the school to draw upon – parents, governors and charities. Many firms provide schools with speakers on current topics. There may be field studies centres or sports facilities nearby. You need to check if there are any safety issues to consider when choosing appropriate resources.

Scheme of work for x topic

Area of work	Ref:

Class	No in class	Age	Key stage

No of lessons	Duration	Dates	

Aims (from the National Curriculum programmes of study)

(Objectives are listed in each lesson plan)

Framework of lessons	NC reference

Assessment strategies

Other notes (safety points)

Figure 2.2.1 Scheme of work proforma

How is the work to be assessed?

Teaching, learning and assessment are interlinked. Most of the work you are doing with pupils is teacher assessed, although some is assessed by outside agencies. A main purpose of teacher assessment is formative – to check pupils' progress, e.g. in relation to lesson objectives. In any case, you should keep good records of the pupils' progress (homework, classwork, test results) in your own record book as well as providing these in the form required by the school or department. Chapter 6 focuses on assessment issues.

Task 2.2.2
Record keeping and assessment
Ask staff in your department how they expect pupil assessment records to be kept and what forms of assessment you should use for the work you are doing.

How does this work fit in with work the pupils are doing in other subjects?

There are many areas of overlap where it is useful to discuss the pupils' work with other departments. For instance, if pupils are having difficulty with measurement in technology, it is worth checking if and when the mathematics department teaches these skills and how they teach them. Cross-curricular dimensions to the curriculum (see Units 7.2 and 7.3) will have been considered by the school and responsibilities for different aspects shared out among departments. Ask staff in your department what responsibilities the department has in this area.

What is to be taught later?

Progression in pupil learning has to be planned for and a scheme of work has to be drawn up for this purpose. From this scheme of work you know what work is to come and the contribution to pupil learning that each lesson is to make.

Task 2.2.3
Drawing up a scheme of work
In consultation with your tutor, draw up a scheme of work to last about six to eight lessons. Focus on one particular class which you are teaching. Use the format provided for your course (or the one we provide in Figure 2.2.1) or one which fits in with the planning methods used in the department.

The lesson plan

The lesson plan provides an outline of one lesson within a scheme of work. In planning a lesson, you are working out the detail required to teach one aspect of the scheme of work. To plan the lesson you use a framework and an example of a lesson planning framework is given in Figure 2.2.2. The following information is required for you to plan effectively.

Overall aim(s) of the scheme of work and the specific objectives for this lesson

Defining objectives which clarify exactly what learning you hope will take place is a crucial skill for the effective teacher. It helps you to be clear about exactly what the pupils should be achieving and it helps the pupils understand what they should be doing. However, drawing up effective objectives requires thought.

At this stage in your career, if you ensure that your lesson objectives focus on what should be achieved from the lesson in terms of pupils' learning, then you have made a good start.

Listing objectives after the following phrase *By the end of this lesson, pupils will be able to …* may help you to devise clear goals and to understand the difference between aims (general statements) and objectives (specific goals).

Words that help you be precise are those such as *state, describe, list, identify, prioritise, solve, demonstrate an understanding of*. These words force you to write statements which can be tested. If you think your

Date .... Class ....

Area of work   ....

Aim ....

Objectives   ....

....

TIme	Teacher activity	Pupil activity	Notes / equipment needed
0–5 min	Class enter and settle	Coats and bags put away	
5–10 min	Homework discussed / recap of work so far / task set / new work explained		
10–25 min	Teacher supports groups / individuals	Pupils work in individual groups to carry out the task	
… and so on			
Ending	Teacher summarises points / sets homework		

Evaluation: Were objectives achieved? What went well? What needs to be addressed next time? How are individuals responding?

Figure 2.2.2   Planning a lesson: one possible approach

objectives are vague, ask yourself whether the objective makes it clear what the pupils must do to achieve them. When you tell the pupils what your objectives are do they understand what is expected of them? Objectives may be related to knowledge, concepts, skills, behaviours and attitudes (see Unit 7.4 for more advice about objective setting).

Task 2.2.4
Writing objectives

There is different terminology in use – some people refer to *behavioural* objectives, some to *learning* objectives. They refer to the observable outcomes of the lesson, i.e. to what pupils are expected to be able to do. Specifying the expected outcomes for the lesson will help you clarify your objectives. Discuss the writing of objectives with other student teachers and your tutor. Choose a particular lesson and, as a group, devise appropriate objectives which relate to changes in pupils' learning or behaviour. Pay particular attention to the quality and type of objectives you are setting – are they focused on the pupils' learning?

Range of abilities of the pupils

As you develop as a teacher, you are expected to incorporate differentiation into your planning. This refers to the need to consider pupils' individual abilities when work is planned so that both the brightest pupils and those with lesser ability are challenged and extended by the work. *Differentiation* can be achieved in different ways depending on the material to be taught. Differentiation may, for example, be achieved by *outcome*, i.e. different types or qualities of work may be produced, or by *task*, i.e. different tasks may be set for pupils of differing abilities. (Unit 4.1 provides further information.) You provide continuity of learning for the pupils by taking account of and building on their existing knowledge, skills, capabilities and attitudes.

Time available

On the examples of a lesson plan provided, a time line is drawn on the left-hand side. If you refer to this in the lesson, you are quickly able to see if it is necessary to adapt the original plan to fit the time available.

Resources available

Staff usually go out of their way to help students have the appropriate resources. But don't forget that others may be needing them so ask in good time for the resources you require. Check how resources are reserved in your department.

Approaches to classroom management

These should be suitable to the topic and subject (see Units 2.3 and 2.4).

Teaching strategies and the learning situations

These should be set up as appropriate to the work being covered (see Chapter 5). Explaining and questioning are two key skills which you should work to improve. It is a good idea to write out questions in advance which you may want to use to test the pupil's grasp of the topic and which develop thinking. Phrasing appropriate questions is a key skill for a teacher (Unit 3.1 has further details).

Assessment methods

Decide which ones to use in order to know whether your objectives have been achieved (see Chapter 6).

Any risks associated with the work

Safety is an important issue in schools. In some subjects, the assessment of risk to the pupils and incorporation of strategies to minimize this risk are a necessary part of the teacher's planning. Departmental and national guidelines are provided to ensure the safety of the pupils and should be followed. Student teachers should consult their head of department or tutor for guidance on safety issues. If you are in doubt about an activity and you cannot discuss your worries with the class teacher or your tutor, do not carry out the activity.

What do the pupils know now?

As your experience of the curriculum and of pupils' learning develops, you will find it easier to answer this question. You need to consider what has been taught before as well as the experience outside school which pupils might have had. It may be appropriate to do some form of testing or analysis of knowledge, skills and understanding or to have a discussion with pupils to discover their prior experience and attitudes to the work in question. As a student teacher you should seek advice from the staff who normally teach your classes.

Lessons have a structure and a rhythm to them. As you read this next section, think about the overall pattern to a lesson and the skills you use at each stage.

Constructing a lesson

Initially, you might find it difficult to see exactly how teachers manage their classes. In order to help you see the underlying structure of a lesson, we have divided the lesson and its planning into five Key Stages: preparation; beginning; moving on; ending, evaluation. Figure 2.2.3 (The structure of a lesson) illustrates this rhythm. Each stage is discussed below.

Task 2.2.5
Planning and giving lessons

As you read about the five stages of a lesson, make notes in your diary to remind you of key points to pay attention to when you are planning and giving lessons. Unit 2.3 provides more details.

1 Preparation

5 Evaluation

2 Beginning

4 Ending

3 Moving on

Figure 2.2.3 The structure of a lesson

Preparation

The most successful lessons are thoroughly planned and structured beforehand and you manage a class more effectively if you carefully consider in advance how to organize yourself and the pupils.

Make sure you have enough of the necessary materials, equipment and resources. Know the exact number of the items you are using so that you know if something has been lost and can take steps to find it immediately. Most departments have developed their own systems of stock control, for example, a useful technique for textbooks is to number them and when you give them to pupils, record the textbook number in your mark book.

Ensure that you know how to operate any equipment you plan to use (e.g. television monitors, videos, computers or subject-specific equipment) and that it is in working order. If you are carrying out a science experiment, you should do it yourself before the lesson. This enables you to anticipate problems pupils might encounter.

Plan a variety of appropriate teaching and learning activities (see Chapter 5). Remember, the concentration span of adults is about 20 minutes and that of most pupils is shorter. Plan extra, related activities in case your chosen approach does not work or pupils complete tasks more quickly than you anticipate.

Give advance warning to pupils of any books, materials, etc., that they need for the lesson. If you have asked them to collect particular items or materials, don't rely on them remembering – bring enough yourself in order for the lesson to proceed just in case or have alternative plans.

Beginning

A good beginning is a crucial part of a successful lesson as it sets the tone, motivates pupils and establishes your authority. There are a number of key points to be kept in mind when you think about beginning your lessons.

Be in the classroom before the pupils arrive and ensure equipment is ready. Undoubtedly, the school you are in has established rules about pupil movement around the school and entry to classrooms. However, in the lower years in particular, it is common to line up pupils outside your teaching room and to usher them inside in an orderly manner.

Settle the class as quickly as possible and ensure that all pupils are facing you – even when they are seated in groups around tables – and are listening in silence before you begin the lesson. Do not begin the lesson when any pupil is talking, but wait calmly, confidently and expectantly for quiet. You will get it! Do not press on until you have established quiet. It is worth taking the time to do so.

Class management is much easier when you know the pupils by name. Make a determined effort to learn their names as quickly as possible. It does not happen by osmosis, so you have to work at it. Seating plans are useful, as is the practice in the early stages of asking pupils to raise their hands when you register them. Although it might appear time consuming, giving out exercise books to pupils individually quickly allows you to put a face to a name.

If you are unable to address pupils by name address them by their class/form designation. For example, 'Right 7G, I want everyone looking this way.' This is far better than 'Right girls/boys/ladies/ lads etc.' Never resort to 'Oi you, blondie!' or some equally unprofessional outburst. Similarly, impersonations of deflating a balloon through continued 'Sshh-sshh-ing' do nothing to enhance your authority.

Pupils like to know what is expected of them. They relax and have a far more positive approach if you explain what you plan to do in the lesson, with a brief rationale of how it fits in with previous and future work and if you let them know what you want them to achieve in the lesson. Establish a crisp, but not rushed, pace from the beginning. Never stand in one place in the room for more than a matter of a few minutes and some teachers suggest that, as a student teacher, you don't sit at the teacher's desk during the lesson except in extremis. Use eye contact, vary the pace and tone of your voice (see Unit 3.1) and monitor pupil reaction continually.

Moving on

Smooth, seamless transitions between one part of the lesson and the next are vital if there is to be overall continuity and coherence. Having introduced the lesson, you need to explain the purpose of the first (and thereafter any subsequent) pupil task. Be very clear about what you want the pupils to do and tell them exactly how long they are to spend on the activity. They then have an idea of the pace they need to work at and how much you expect them to 'produce', and what quality of work you require.

Before they begin the activity, check that all pupils understand exactly what they are expected to do. Deal with any queries before the class begins work. This saves endless repetition of the task to individuals.

Have a definite routine for distributing books and materials. Will you give out equipment? Will pupils come out to collect it row by row, table by table? Will one pupil per table/row collect it? In any event, it is essential that this activity is carried out in a controlled and orderly manner in any classroom. Moreover, if you are teaching a physical education or science subject, the safety aspect of this area of class management is of unequalled importance.

When the pupils are engaged in the activity, move around the room monitoring pupil progress and dealing with questions; but do not interfere unnecessarily. Let them get on with the task. Effective class management depends upon your active involvement. Key skills are: circulation; monitoring progress; the use of proximity to pupils; sensitivity to and awareness of pupil needs. Even when the whole class is engaged in a task, it is rarely appropriate to sit at the teacher's desk and 'switch off'.

Give one or two minutes' warning of the end of the activity. Be vigilant about keeping to the time limit you imposed at the beginning of the activity. Do not let things 'slide'. Be aware that not every pupil will finish the task set. Use your judgement in assessing that, while a few may not have finished within your deadline, most are ready for the next stage. If, however, it becomes clear that the whole class needs longer than you anticipated for an activity, be flexible enough to adjust your planning.

At the end of the activity, settle the class and expect all pupils to be sitting quietly, facing you before you proceed to the next stage of the lesson. Be sure to maintain your business-like manner and the crisp pace you established earlier.

Ending (sometimes called the 'plenary')

It is important that any learning experience is rounded off, that pupils experience a sense of completion. Similarly, pupils need some mental space between lessons. They need to 'come down' from one lesson in order to prepare themselves for the next. Remember, depending upon the timetable, pupils may need to negotiate the conceptual intricacies of between four and eight subjects in a day. Your lesson, therefore, needs to be completed in an organized manner.

Plan enough time at the end of the lesson to: sum up what has been achieved; set homework where appropriate; give a brief idea of what the next lesson will comprise and (if necessary) explain what pupils need to bring to it.

As with the distribution of materials (see the section on 'beginning'), have a definite, orderly routine for collection.

Before pupils leave, make sure the classroom is neat and tidy and remember that the pips or bell are signals for you, not the pupils. Dismiss the pupils by table or row and ensure that they leave the room in a quiet, controlled fashion. Enforcing a quiet orderly departure also adds to the pupils' experience of the standards you expect, i.e. that your classroom provides an orderly and calm learning environment. Take a well-earned 10-second breather before beginning the whole process again with the next class!

Evaluation and planning future lessons

As soon as you can after the lesson, evaluate its success. What went well? What didn't go well? What evidence do you have which allows you to answer with some degree of certainty? (See Unit 5.4.) What should you change next time on the basis of this evaluation and how does this fit in with the scheme of work? If you develop the practice of reflecting on your work as a matter of course, then modifying future practice on the basis of this reflection becomes second nature. In this way, you use your experience systematically to build up your professional knowledge and to develop your professional judgement.

SUMMARY AND KEY POINTS

You should now be able to explain the following terms, aims, objectives, progression, differentiation and have considered how to construct schemes of work and lesson plans which are comprehensive and useful.

At this point, you may like to reflect on criteria used by the Office for Standards in Education (OFSTED) inspectors for judging teaching quality. Although teaching methods vary, the criteria to judge a teacher's effectiveness which are used by OFSTED are standard.

FURTHER READING

Canter, L. and Associates, *Assertive Discipline Programme*. Online. Available HTTP: <http://www.behaviour-learning.com>. Teachers speak highly of this programme which focuses on positive behaviour management strategies. Behaviour Management Ltd, HMA House, 78 Durham Road, London SW20 0TL; tel. 020 8944 6161.

Warburton, N. (2003 edn) *Thinking from A–Z*, London: RoutledgeFalmer. This slim text will help you refine your critical thinking abilities. It provides an easily accessible dictionary of terms describing different types of thinking. The ideas may help you in your teaching of pupils to reason.

Gardner, R., Cairns, J. and Lawton, D. (2000) *Education for Values*, London: RoutledgeFalmer. Bailey, R. (2004) *Teaching Values and Citizenship across the Curriculum*, London: RoutledgeFalmer. Both these texts address the role of the teacher in values education. The first text provides theoretical background and the second provides examples of how you can incorporate values related to citizenship in your lessons.

Hay McBer (2000) *Research Into Teacher Effectiveness*, London: DfEE. This comprehensive report into effective teaching proposes a model of teacher effectiveness comprising teaching skills and professional characteristics. The early sections are particularly useful in relation to the preparation and planning of lessons.

Scottish Consultative Council on the Curriculum (1996) *Teaching for Effective Learning*, Dundee. Online. Available HTTP: <http://claudius.sccc.ac.uk>. The SCCC have produced a very readable booklet on the principles of effective teaching and learning. Discussion forums are available via the website.

Unit 2.3

Taking Responsibility for Whole Lessons

Marilyn Leask

INTRODUCTION

This unit draws attention to issues which have particular relevance to you when you are just starting to take responsibility for whole lessons.

Recall the iceberg image of a teacher's work from Unit 1.1. The delivery of the lesson in the classroom represents the tip of the iceberg, while the bulk of the teacher's work for a lesson – routines, preparation, subject knowledge, professional knowledge and judgement, previous lesson evaluations – is hidden. This unit focuses on particular aspects of planning and teaching which initially cause many student teachers problems.

OBJECTIVES

By the end of this unit, you should have considered the following:

- routines for good class management;
- how your personal attributes contribute to your effectiveness;
- lesson preparation;
- how to avoid common problems.

Concerns common to student teachers who are beginning to teach are also discussed.

ROUTINES FOR CLASS MANAGEMENT

Routines for class and lesson management provide a structure so that learning can take place within a classroom where the rules are understood by all. In time, these routines become instinctive for you. Establishing rules decreases the likelihood of having to waste lesson time disciplining pupils at a later stage.

But your routines are not established in a vacuum. The pupils you teach have been in schools for at least seven years – they expect the teacher to establish 'norms' for classroom work, talk and movement and most pupils are conditioned to accept such classroom routines. This doesn't mean that they won't resist you when you insist on certain types of behaviour but it does mean that they have certain expectations that you will set the rules. Three types of routines in operation are:

- for managing work and movement;
- for managing relationships and reinforcing expectations of attitudes and behaviour;
- for gaining attention – for both the pupils and the teacher.

Routines for managing work and movement

For your early lessons, one of your main goals is to get the pupils down to work fairly promptly by providing them with clear tasks and clear instructions. Your concern is to establish yourself as an organized teacher who sets clear objectives for a lesson and provides work which allows students to achieve those objectives. These lessons will probably go more easily if you can fit in with established routines.

Task 2.3.1
Classroom norms

Make a list of your expectations for the presentation of work, talk and movement for pupils in your classroom. Find out through observation and discussion what the expectations of the experienced teachers are, especially the teachers of the classes you are taking. Update and amend your list as you gain experience with what works for you.

Routines for managing relationships and reinforcing expectations

Adopting a *firm, fair, friendly* approach may help you develop good relationships with pupils. Pupils have certain expectations of you. They expect the teacher to be consistent and fair in applying rules. They expect those who do well to be rewarded and/or acknowledged, e.g. through praise, even just a quiet word or by letting them go first at the end of the lesson. Those who do not abide by your rules expect to be reprimanded. A quiet individual reprimand at the end of a lesson may be sufficient to establish your authority with many pupils. Confrontations in front of the whole class are to be avoided. Remember, the role of routines is to make your lessons run smoothly – everyone should know what your expectations are for classroom behaviour.

It takes time for the student teacher and for any teacher new to a school to find out about influences on classroom relationships which come from the community. Information about the range of group 'norms' of behaviour for teenagers in the local area and background information about other social relationships (e.g. which pupils are cousins, stepsisters or brothers) may help you understand more easily your pupils and their expectations.

Experienced teachers can often sense that trouble is brewing between pupils and defuse the situation. They use their voice sparingly – drawing on a range of other controls, e.g. placing themselves near pupils who need more encouragement to stay on task and using non-verbal gestures to remind pupils to keep working. If needed, there are a number of sanctions which all teachers can use. Beware of giving pupils detentions as a first step. Time is precious to you so don't waste it and, in any case, establishing your authority can be just as easily achieved by using one of a range of other sanctions: e.g.

- the pupil is required to apologise (or face sanctions);
- a verbal warning is given – a brief reprimand or keeping the pupil for a moment at the end of the lesson to indicate your displeasure;
- a couple of pupils tidy up after the others have gone (teachers are wise to protect their professional reputations by not remaining alone in closed classrooms with individual pupils);
- additional work is given.

Task 2.3.2
Sanctions and rewards

Find out about the policies on sanctions and rewards at the school where you are teaching. Make notes of the key issues which affect your work. Check your understanding of the application of these policies with experienced staff.

Routines for gaining attention

Getting the attention of the whole class at points during the lesson is a skill which experienced teachers practise effortlessly. First, act as though you believe the pupils will obey you. One pattern teachers often practise is to call for attention ('Stop what you're doing and just look here for a minute'). They then follow this with a focus on an individual ('Paul, that means you too'), which acts as a reminder to all pupils that if they don't want to be the focus of the teacher's attention they need to stop what they're doing. The time to call the class to attention is not when they're all working well but when the work is flagging and they need to be spurred on or they've come to a difficult point – unless, for example, you wish to draw their attention to a point on safety.

One of the fundamental rules of the classroom is that pupils should not speak when the teacher is speaking. Spending a few minutes in a lesson waiting for silence until you speak saves a lot of time later as pupils know what you expect. Pupils may need reminding of your expectations and you probably need to reinforce the idea that this is one of your basic rules. You must be able to get the class's attention when you require it. When observing classes, the following questions may help you see some of the strategies used by teachers to establish this aspect of their authority.

- What verbal cues does the teacher use to establish quiet? Key phrases such as 'Right then', 'Put your pens down now' establish that the teacher requires the class to listen. Some students make the mistake of thinking the words 'quiet' or 'shush' repeated over and over will gain the required effect. Experienced teachers tend to use more subtle or strident methods, e.g. QUIET! – said once with great emphasis. Units 3.2 and 3.3 provide further advice.
- What non-verbal cues does the teacher use to gain attention? Look at the way teachers use gestures – eyes, face, arms, hands – to establish that they require the class to listen. They may stand still and just wait. Their pupils know that if they keep their teacher waiting they will be penalised. Unit 3.1 contains more ideas.

There are also routines related to the way pupils gain the teacher's attention. The usual routine is that pupils put up their hands and don't call out. Again, we suggest you find out what the current practice is for the classes you are teaching. If you decide to change established practices then you have to put in considerable effort to establish the new rules.

YOUR PERSONAL ATTRIBUTES

Body language plays an important role in your communication with others and is an aspect of the way you present yourself which you should consider. Some personal attributes which may interfere with your teaching may only reveal themselves once you are teaching. For this reason, it is worth keeping this aspect of your interaction with pupils and staff under review.

Try to establish early in your teaching experience:

- whether your voice can be heard at the back of a classroom;
- whether you have any particular habits which may interfere with the developing of a relationship with a class, e.g. do you rattle coins in your pocket as you speak; do you play with your hair; are you able to use facial expressions effectively to indicate enthusiasm; do you speak in a monotone; do you look at people when you speak to them; what do you communicate through your smiling (some people inadvertently smile when they are angry)?
- what messages your posture and your movement in classrooms and corridors convey;
- what gestures you normally use when speaking.

We suggest you ask for feedback occasionally on these aspects in order to check whether you are inadvertently presenting yourself in an unfavourable manner. Increasingly, training providers provide trainees with the opportunity to have some lessons recorded on video. This provides you with evidence of your performance on which you can build. Unit 3.1 on communication provides more detail.

LESSON PREPARATION

> I spent days preparing my first lesson on my first teaching experience – geography with a group of 15-year-olds who weren't exactly enamoured with the subject. Educationally it was a disaster! I was so nervous that I rushed through my carefully prepared 40-minute lesson and at the end of 10 minutes I had nothing more to say. I panicked and told them to draw a map – any map – for the rest of the lesson.

This true story, from a (now) very successful teacher, highlights the nervousness which many student teachers experience when faced with their first lessons. Such nervousness is natural. You are assuming an unfamiliar role – as a teacher – but there are no set lines which you can learn to carry you through the scene. Over time, you build your professional knowledge about teaching and learning (pedagogy) and your professional judgement about how to manage the work in the classroom so that the situation described above does not arise. In the meantime, you are having to learn from each situation you face.

When you are spending hours planning for your first lessons, you may wonder whether you've made a sound choice of career but recall the learner driver mentioned in Unit 1.1. In time, many aspects of driving become automatic; so it is with some features of teaching. In your first lessons, it is a good idea not to try to do anything too ambitious. Limited success is better than unlimited disaster!

It is, of course, possible for a teacher to be in a classroom with a class and for no effective teaching or learning to take place! Effective teaching requires some planned learning to occur in those being taught. Therefore, for your pupils to learn effectively, you must plan carefully.

We suggest you skim through Units 2.2, 5.2 and 5.3 as they provide ideas about the basic teaching skills and planning approaches which you need to employ in your first lessons. You should, of course, be building on your experience of group work, micro-teaching and on the observations you have made.

Following the steps outlined below should ensure that you start your first lessons from a position of being well prepared.

1. Plan the lesson and ask for advice about your plan.

Task 2.3.3
Checking your lesson plan

Look at your plan for one of your lessons. Are you making your expectations of the pupils clear at each stage? Are the pupils actively engaged at each point or are they wasting time waiting for you to organize books or equipment? Are you expecting them to concentrate on you talking for too long; to take in too much new information without the chance to discuss it and assimilate it? Is there scope for pupils to feed back to you what they've learned this lesson, e.g. through question and answer? As a trial run, try to explain the main points of the lesson to another student teacher. The quality of explanation you are able to give affects the learning which takes place, as does the nature of questions you ask. Ask a colleague observing your lesson to give you feedback afterwards on these points.

---

2. Check that you have adequate extension and alternative work. Anticipate that additional work may be needed. You may find that equipment you had planned to use stops working or the specialist in your subject is not available to supervise you.

3. Know the class if possible through your observations and have a strategy for using and learning names. Try to learn names quickly – making notes beside the names in the register may help you remember. Drawing up a seating plan can help; pupils may always, or at least usually, sit in the same places. In any case, you can ask them to sit in the same seats until you know their names.

Tony Buzan (1995) writes extensively on developing memory and he suggests a number of strategies for remembering faces:

- try to link the faces or characteristics of people new to you with existing friends with the same names;
- try to use images to make a mental link between the name and the face of the new person;
- try to repeat the person's name several times during your conversation with them. ('That's an interesting piece of work, David. David, what do you enjoy most about …?')

Unit 2.2 provides additional advice on learning names.

Try to observe the class beforehand and note how the teacher manages potentially noisy or very quiet pupils.

AVOIDING COMMON PROBLEMS

By this point, you know the routines you will use, your lesson is planned. You have also given some thought to where you will stand, when and how you will move around the room. You know to keep scanning the class and, when you talk to children, not to have your back to most of the class.

Judging the timing during a lesson is one of the most difficult problems initially and following a time line on your lesson plan can help you see at a glance how the lesson is progressing in relation to the time allowed.

Unavoidable incidents will occur to interrupt the flow of your carefully prepared lesson but other incidents can be anticipated or at least dealt with effectively if you are prepared. It is as well to anticipate problems so that you are not too distracted from the lesson you planned to deliver. We discuss below some of the more common incidents and possible solutions so that you are not taken by surprise.

One or more pupils won't settle to the work

When some pupils are being disruptive, it is essential to get the bulk of the class working, preferably on work which requires less input from you than normal. This allows you time to deal quietly and firmly with those resisting your authority and thus to establish your authority over them. Ignoring deliberately provocative remarks such as 'This is boring' can help you avoid confrontation. Try to motivate uninterested pupils by linking the work with their interests if possible. Letting them feel you are interested in them as people can promote positive relationships but you still should expect them to work. Ask your experienced colleagues for advice if particular pupils constantly cause you trouble. It is likely that they are also causing some other staff difficulties.

You are asked a question and you don't know the answer

This is bound to happen. You can admit you don't know – 'What an interesting point, I've not thought of it that way'; 'I just can't remember at the moment' – but make arrangements for the answer to be found. The pupil can follow it up for homework, use the library to look for the answer or write to those who might know. You may also be able to find out from other teachers, student teachers or your subject association.

You are asked personal questions

At some point you'll be asked 'Have you got a boyfriend/girlfriend?' 'Are you a student?' (Ask the school if you are to be introduced as a member of staff or a student.) 'Have you ever done this before?' 'How old are you?' – or comments may be made about your car (or lack of one) or what you are wearing.

Don't allow yourself to be distracted from the work in the lesson. You can choose whether or not to answer personal questions but do set boundaries beyond which you won't go. Often a joke deflects the questioner – 'Mine is the Rolls parked around the corner'. Offering to answer the question in the pupils' time, after the lesson, can lead to loss of interest on the part of the questioner.

A pupil swears

As a student teacher, you cannot solve all the problems of the pupils and the school. Usually if a pupil is asked to repeat what they said, they omit the offensive word and feel sufficiently rebuked. You have indicated that swearing is unacceptable.

What you do need to do is to establish a line about what is acceptable and stick to it. Make it clear to your classes what your rule is and link it to school policy which should be 'no swearing'.

However, swearing at teachers or abusing other pupils are serious offences and you must take action. There are different ways in which you might react – depending on the pupils, the context, the school. You may require an apology or you may wish to take the matter further. Take advice from experienced teachers. Act in haste and repent at leisure is good advice for a student teacher. Take a little time to decide on the response. Letting a pupil know an act was unacceptable and that you are thinking about how to respond can be more effective than an ill-considered response from you at the time. Consistency in your approach to discipline is an important facet of establishing your reputation. You want the pupils to know that if they do X, which is unacceptable, some form of action, Y, always follows. (This approach is an application of behaviourist learning theories (Unit 3.2) – you are teaching the pupils to understand that a certain negative action on their part always gets a certain negative response from you. Thus it is perfectly clear to them how to avoid a negative response.)

Task 2.3.4
Swearing

Discuss the following two scenarios with the teachers with whom you're working. What is an appropriate response for you in each case?

1   You overhear a pupil use swear words in conversation with another pupil. The word is not used in an abusive way.
2   A child swears at another child or at you!

What are the routine responses for dealing with these incidents in your school?

Pupils are not properly equipped to do the work – they lack PE kit, pens, books, maths equipment

You should aim to get most of the class working so that you can then direct your attention to those who require individual attention. Many departments have systems in place for dealing with pupils' lack of kit and equipment. In the early days of your teaching, it can be less disruptive to your lesson for you simply to supply the missing item (pencil/paper) so you can keep the flow of the lesson going. But make sure you retrieve what you have loaned and indicate firmly that you expect pupils to provide their own.

Task 2.3.5
Procedures for dealing with poorly equipped pupils

Find out whether there is a system in the department in which you are working for dealing with pupils who are not properly equipped. Plan how you can avoid this problem interfering with the smooth running of your lesson.

Equipment doesn't work

You must check equipment beforehand and, in any case, have an alternative lesson planned if your lesson is dependent on equipment working.

You have too much material

Pupils have to get to their next lesson on time and to have their break on time. So you must let them go on time! Five minutes or so before the end of a lesson (more if they have to change or put equipment away), pull the lesson together, reminding them of what's been achieved and what's expected in the way of homework, perhaps what's coming next. They then pack away and are ready to go at the correct time.

The pupils finish the work earlier than you had anticipated

Inevitably there will be occasions when you have time with a class which you didn't expect. The work may have been finished early or changes in arrangements meant you couldn't do what you had planned. This can be a worrying experience for a student teacher; however, such time can be used to educational advantage in a number of ways:

- Have questions prepared relating to recent work in the area under study.
- Do a quick test of the issues covered in the lesson or a spelling test of new words.
- Use your lesson objectives to devise questions about the work.
- Ask pupils to work in pairs or teams to devise questions to be put to the rest of the class or to other teams. Answers can be written in rough books with the pupils swapping books to mark them.
- Work coming up in subsequent lessons can be introduced so that pupils can see the purpose in what they are doing now – remember repetition is an aid to learning. Introducing concepts briefly in one lesson means they will be more familiar when you go over them in depth later. (This is an example of constructivist learning theory in action – new knowledge is 'scaffolded' on existing knowledge.)
- Pupils' existing knowledge on the next topics could be ascertained by question and answer. (Learning is more certain where you, as the teacher, build on pupils' existing knowledge and experience.)
- You may take the opportunity to check the pupils' ability to apply a range of study skills. There are excellent books on this topic. Plan together with the pupils ways of learning the work you've been covering, e.g. developing a spider diagram for summarizing the key points in a topic in history or geography, producing a mnemonic to aid the recall of key issues.
- Homework (either past or just set) can be discussed in more detail. You may allow the pupils to discuss this together.

Or, in practical subjects:

- You may ask pupils to repeat a sequence they've been working on in PE, perhaps extending it to incorporate another skill; to observe each other performing the sequence and to comment on the performance; or to demonstrate what is coming up in the next lesson.
- Alternatively, if the class is new to you, you may take the opportunity to learn their names.

With experience, you acquire the skill of fitting work to the time available so the problem ceases to cause you anxiety.

MORE GENERAL CONCERNS

There are a number of more general concerns which most students feel at some point or another. We discuss these here so that by anticipating problems and posing solutions, you may be better prepared for dealing with them.

Maintaining good behaviour

This is cited as an area of concern by student teachers more often than any other area and Units 3.2 and 3.3 provide more detailed guidance. See also the website for teacher training <http://www.behaviour4learning.ac.uk>. There are many publications in this area. Pupils are influenced by your confidence, the material, the demands of the work and your ability to enforce rules. The first lesson may be a honeymoon period, where the pupils are sizing you up or, on the other hand, they may test you out. If you insist (in a quiet firm way) that you are in charge of what happens in the classroom, then the vast majority of pupils give way – as long as you are seen as fair and reasonable. Whilst it is important not to see the class as 'them' against 'you', adopting a 'divide and rule' strategy can pay dividends: praise those who work well and reward them – e.g. with privileges or house points or merit slips, using the systems established within the school. Do not expect to win over all pupils immediately; some may take months; a few may never be won over. Discuss any difficulties you have with other teachers – it may be that they have effective strategies for dealing with the pupils who are giving you concern.

Defusing situations

Inexperienced teachers tend to reprimand pupils much more frequently than experienced teachers, probably because they have less well developed subtle control mechanisms, e.g. body language. Techniques used by teachers to defuse situations include:

- Anticipating changes of mood and concentration and moving the lesson on and perhaps increasing the pace of the lesson, e.g. 'Right, let's see what you've understood already …'.
- Scanning the class regularly, even when helping individuals or groups so that potential problems are prevented: 'That's enough, Julia' or 'Have you got a problem over there?' is usually sufficient to remind pupils to keep on task. Pupils are impressed if you can see what they are doing without them realizing you are looking at them. Standing at a pupil's desk perhaps towards the back of the room allows you to monitor the work of pupils close to you as well as to scan the rest of the class without them seeing you.
- Using humour to keep pupils on task – a knowledge of adolescent culture and local activities is useful: 'You're too busying thinking about what you'll be doing on Friday night to concentrate.'
- Using a whole range of non-verbal cues: posture, facial expressions, gestures, positioning in the classroom to reinforce your authority. The children recognize these and you need to recognize them too (see Unit 3.1).

Notice that none of these techniques require the teacher to shout or to be angry in order to keep the pupils on task.

Task 2.3.6
Defusing difficult situations

We suggest that when you are observing experienced teachers you look specifically at how they defuse situations so that reprimands are not required. Note these for future reference.

Retrieving situations

You may have a poor lesson with a class. This doesn't mean that all lessons with that class will be like that. What it does mean, however, is that you must analyse the situation and put into place strategies for ensuring that the next lesson is better. Experienced colleagues should be able to give you advice. Observing an experienced teacher, even if in another discipline, teaching a group that you have difficulty with can be eye opening and can provide you with ideas for the way forward. Discuss what you've seen with the teacher. Ask someone to watch you teach the class with whom you are having difficulty and ask for suggestions about how you can improve.

Personal vulnerability, lack of self-belief and confidence

In becoming a teacher, you are more vulnerable than when being educated for many other professions as you are exposed to a discerning audience (the class) early on. So much of your performance in the classroom depends on your own personal qualities and your ability to form good relationships with pupils from a wide range of backgrounds. Your performance is analysed and commented on by those who observe your teaching. You are forced to face your own strengths and weaknesses as a result of this scrutiny. This can be stressful particularly when you may be given apparently conflicting advice from different observers. As you become more experienced and you develop more analytical skills for use in appraising your performance, you should build your self-belief and confidence.

Dealing with your feelings

Incidents will occur which leave you feeling deflated, unsure or angry. Try to adopt a problem-solving reflective approach to your work so that you maintain some objectivity and can learn from any difficult experiences you have. One group of PGCE students was asked, at the end of their year of initial teacher education, what advice they would give new student teachers. Above all else, they said, keep in touch with other students so that you can discuss your concerns with others in the same situation. It is likely that your concerns are also the concerns of other student teachers.

The challenge to your own values

Most people mix with people who hold similar values and attitudes. As a teacher, you are dealing with children from different backgrounds and with different expectations about education and different values to your own. You need to consider how you can best provide equal opportunities in your classroom and what strategies you might use to motivate disaffected pupils. Chapter 4 provides further advice in these areas. See also the initial teacher training website <http://www.multiverse.ac.uk>.

Loss of books or equipment and breakages

Schools have different approaches to dealing with loss and breakage of equipment by pupils. Seek advice from those with whom you are working. Anticipating and thus avoiding problems makes your life easier. The simple strategy of managing your lesson so that there is sufficient time at the end to check that equipment and books are returned saves you time in the long run.

Having a ready answer

There are a number of routine situations which can throw you off balance in the lesson, e.g. 'Someone's taken my pen/book', 'Sir, she did it too', 'Miss, he started it', 'But Miss, you let her go to the toilet', 'Do you like . . .' (and here they name a pop group about which they all know but of which you've never heard). Discuss these situations with other students and make notes for yourself about how you might deal with them. See how other teachers deal with these.

Time and stress management

These are important enough issues that Unit 1.3 is devoted to them. Here we want to raise three points:

- giving the lesson is only one part of a teacher's job;
- preparing your first lessons takes you a long time;
- if you skimp on lesson preparation, then the stress level you experience in the lesson will be high as you will not feel in control.

SUMMARY AND KEY POINTS

Your first encounters with the pupils are important in setting the tone for your relationships with them. It is worth carefully considering the image you wish to project in these early lessons and planning your work to help reinforce this image. If you want to create the image that you are a disorganized teacher who doesn't know what the lesson is about any more than the pupils do, then this is relatively easy to achieve. Your image is something you should create deliberately and not just allow to happen.

Most student teachers have to work on controlling their nerves and developing their self-confidence. Covering the following points in your preparation should prevent some of the difficulties you would otherwise encounter:

- Set clear, simple objectives for the lesson that are likely to be achieved.
- Plan the lesson carefully and have extension work ready.
- Know the class and obtain pupil lists.
- Check the room layout: are things where you want them? What about safety issues?
- Know the school, class and lesson routines.
- Be on time.

- Prepare board work beforehand if possible (check that it won't be rubbed off if there is a lesson before yours) or use a pre-prepared overhead projector transparency, or computer presentation.
- Act as though you are in charge although you probably won't feel that you are.
- Know the subject and/or make crib notes and put key points on the board, transparency or computer presentation if you're unsure.
- Plan the rhythm of the lesson to give a balance between teacher talk and pupil activity.
- Include a timeline in your lesson plan so that you can check during the lesson how the plan is working. Try not to talk too quickly.
- Be prepared to clamp down on misbehaviour. It is easier to reprimand one pupil who is misbehaving than to wait until they have goaded other pupils into following suit or retaliating.
- Visualize yourself being successful.
- Have a fallback plan for the lesson.

From the observations you've done, you should have established how other teachers deal with minor infringements of school rules – remember there are a number of types of reprimand you can use before you give out detentions.

One of your major problems may be believing that you are indeed a teacher. This is a mental and emotional transition which you need to make. The pupils, parents and staff usually see you as a teacher, albeit a new one and expect you to behave as such.

FURTHER READING

The subject-specific texts in the 'Learning to Teach' series provide you with further advice. Some teachers join chat rooms or discussion groups on the internet to discuss issues related to their teaching. You should be aware that these discussions may be public and may be archived.

Buzan, T. (1995) *Use Your Memory*, London: BBC Books. This is just one of Tony Buzan's books which are packed with ideas for improving memory. Why not draw them to the attention of your pupils?

Olsen, J. and Cooper, P. (2001) *Dealing with Disruptive Students in the Classroom*, London: RoutledgeFalmer. Matheson, K. and Price, M. (2002) *Better Behaviour in Classrooms – A Framework for Inclusive Behaviour Management*, London: RoutledgeFalmer. Both these texts provide background information to help you analyse the reasons behind particular types of behaviours and provide strategies to help you improve your practice.

Reason, R. and Boote, R. (1994) *Helping Children with Reading and Spelling: A Special Needs Manual*, London: RoutledgeFalmer. Pollock, J., Waller, E. and Politt, R. (2004) *Day-to-Day Dyslexia in the Classroom*, 2nd edn, London: RoutledgeFalmer. All teachers have a responsibility to help pupils with their spelling and writing. This text although published some time ago, provides background on how to help pupils on an individual basis. In your teaching career, you can expect to come across pupils with dyslexia. These texts provide activities for class teachers to use with pupils and materials which will deepen your understanding of the structure of the English language and how children learn.

3 Classroom Interactions and Managing Pupils

Effective classroom management is essential to effective learning. Classroom management refers to arrangements made by the teacher to establish and maintain an environment in which learning can occur, e.g. effective organization and presentation of lessons so that pupils are actively engaged in learning.' Classroom management skills and techniques are addressed throughout this book in a number of different chapters and units. This chapter includes three units about different aspects of classroom management related to interacting with pupils. Together they give an insight into the complex relationships which are developed between teachers and pupils, and emphasize the need for well-developed skills and techniques that you can adapt appropriately to the demands of the situation. They reinforce the fact that, although you must plan your lessons thoroughly, not everything you do in the classroom can be planned in advance, as you cannot predict how pupils will react in any situation on any given day.

One commonality of teachers from whom we have learned a lot is their ability to communicate effectively with pupils to enhance their knowledge, skills and understanding. Most of us tend to think we communicate well. However, communication is a complex process. Unit 3.1 is designed to help you communicate effectively in the classroom. The unit looks first at verbal communication including using your voice, the language you use and the importance of active listening. It then considers aspects of non-verbal communication, e.g. appearance, gesture, posture, facial expression and mannerisms, particularly in relation to how you present yourself as a teacher.

Some pupils are motivated to learn and maintain that motivation, others are inherently motivated to learn but various factors result in them losing motivation, others may not be inherently motivated to learn, but their motivation can be increased. A study of motivation therefore is crucial to give you some knowledge and insight into how you can create a motivational climate that helps to stimulate pupils to learn. Unit 3.2 looks at what motivation is, presents a number of theories of motivation and considers how these can inform your teaching and pupils' learning, looks at the motivational learning environment in your classes and how this influences pupil motivation and identifies some specific methods to motivate pupils extrinsically (e.g. the use of praise and punishment, feedback) in order to encourage the development of intrinsic motivation.

We recognize student teachers' concerns about managing behaviour and misbehaviour. Our objective in Unit 3.3 is to help you address these concerns by helping you to reflect on your knowledge and skills in managing pupils' behaviour. It focuses on 'behaviour for learning' – a positive approach to behaviour management by creating positive relationships with pupils and a positive classroom climate in which all pupils can learn effectively. This approach is more consistent with an inclusive schooling approach. Thus, the focus of the unit is on preventing misbehaviour as far as possible rather than on a reactive approach which focuses on 'discipline' for misbehaviour.

Unit 3.1

Communicating with Pupils

Paula Zwozdiak-Myers and Susan Capel

INTRODUCTION

We can all think of teachers who really understand their subject but cannot communicate it with others, as well as teachers from whom we have learned a lot. These teachers may have very different personalities and styles, but they all had in common the ability to communicate effectively with pupils.

Communication is a complex two-way process involving the mutual exchange of information and ideas that can be written, verbal and non-verbal. Clear and effective communication includes not only delivering but also receiving information, which involves listening, observation and sensitivity. Communication can be between pupil and pupil. This is very important, as it can enhance or hinder learning. Pupils can learn from communicating with each other, e.g. through discussion or by talking about a task. Equally, such communication can be irrelevant to, and interfere with the progress of, the lesson, therefore detracting from pupils' learning. Communication can also be between a teacher and pupils. This is the focus of this unit.

Most of us tend to think we communicate well. However, when we study our communication skills systematically, most of us can find room for improvement. You cannot predict how pupils will react to an activity, a conversation or a question asked. Your response, both verbal and non-verbal, in any classroom situation influences the immediate and, possibly, long-term relationship with the class. In order to respond appropriately you need well-developed communication skills, combined with sensitivity to pupils and 'where they are at' in relation to their understanding (Dillon and Maguire, 2001) and judgement.

We first consider aspects of verbal communication, including using your voice (volume, projection, pitch, speed, tone, clarity and expressiveness), the language you use and the importance of active listening. We then consider aspects of non-verbal communication, e.g. appearance, gesture, posture, facial expression and mannerisms, particularly in relation to how you present yourself as a teacher. Further aspects of communication are addressed in Unit 5.2 'Active Learning'.

VERBAL COMMUNICATION

Gaining attention

You need to establish procedures for gaining pupils' attention at the beginning of a lesson and also when you want the class to listen again after they have started an activity. This latter skill is especially important if there is a safety risk in the activity. Before you start talking to a class, make sure that all pupils can see and hear you, that you have silence and that they are paying attention. Establish a means of getting silence, e.g. say 'quiet please', clap your hands, blow a whistle in physical education or bang on a drum in music and use this with the class each time. Wait for quiet and do not speak until there is silence. Once you are talking, do not move around. This distracts pupils, who may pay more attention to the movement than to what you are saying.

Using your voice

A teacher's voice is a crucial element in classroom communication. It is like a musical instrument and if you play it well, then your pupils will be an appreciative and responsive audience. Some people have voices that naturally are easier to listen to than others. Certain qualities are fixed and give your voice its unique character. However, you can alter the volume, projection, pitch, speed, tone, clarity and expressiveness of your voice to use it more effectively and to lend impact to what you say.

The most obvious way you can vary your voice is by altering the *volume*. It is useful to have the whole volume range available, from quiet to very loud, but it is rarely a good thing to be loud when it is not needed. Loud teachers have loud classes. If you shout too much, you may get into the habit of shouting all the time – sometimes people know somebody is a teacher because of their loud voice. Also, if you shout too much, you may lose your voice every September! Of course, you have to be heard, but this is done by projection more than by volume.

You *project* your voice by making sure it leaves your mouth confidently and precisely. This needs careful enunciation and breath control. If your voice is projected well, you are able to make a whisper audible at some distance. Equally, good projection brings considerable volume to your ordinary voice without resort to shouting or roaring.

Each group of words spoken has its own 'tune' that contributes to the meaning. A person may have a naturally high or low voice but everybody varies the 'natural' *pitch* with no pain. Generally speaking, deep voices sound more serious and significant; high voices are more exciting and lively. To add weight to what is being said the pitch should be dropped; to lighten the tone the pitch should be raised. A voice with a lower pitch can create a sense of importance as it comes across as more authoritative and confident than a high-pitched voice. It can also be raised more easily to command attention, whereas raising a naturally high-pitched voice may result in something similar to a squeak, which does not carry the same weight.

Speed variations give contrast to delivery. You can use pause to good effect. It shows confidence if you can hold a silence before making a point or answering a question. Having achieved silence, do not shout into it. Equally, have the patience to wait for a pupil to respond. Research (e.g. Muijs and Reynolds, 2001) suggests that a reasonable time for any such pause is three seconds or slightly longer although up to fifteen seconds might be required for open-ended, higher level questions. Speaking quickly can be a valuable skill on occasion, however, this needs concentration and careful enunciation.

To use your voice effectively these factors need to work together. For example, you do not communicate effectively if the pitch of your voice is right, but you are not enunciating clearly or the volume is wrong, e.g. you are shouting at a group or pupils at the back cannot hear what you are saying. It is also important to put feeling into what you say. Often, pupils respond to HOW you say something rather than WHAT you say. If you are praising, sound pleased; if you are disciplining, sound firm. If you deliver all talk in the same way, do not be surprised if pupil response is undifferentiated.

Task 3.1.1
The quality of your voice

Record your voice either reading from a book or a newspaper or in natural monologue or conversation. Listen to the recording with a friend or another student teacher. If you have not heard yourself before, the experience may be a little shocking! Your voice may sound different from the way you hear it and a common response is to blame the recording equipment. This is probably not at fault. Remember that normally you hear your voice coming back from your mouth. Most of your audience hear it coming forward. As you become used to listening to yourself, try to pick out the good points of your voice. Is it clear? Is it expressive? Is the basic pitch pleasant? When you have built up your confidence, consider areas for improvement. Do you normally speak too fast? Is the tone monotonous?

Repeat the task, but this time trying to vary your voice. For example, try reading at your normal speed, then faster, then as quickly as you can. Remember to start each word precisely and to concentrate on what you are saying. Then try varying the pitch of your voice. You will be surprised at how easy it is. Ask another student teacher to listen to the tape with you, comment on any differences and provide helpful advice for improving. Try these out in your teaching.

Language of the teacher

Teaching involves communicating with pupils from a variety of backgrounds and with different needs. According to the Department for Education and Employment (DfEE, 1999b) approximately 12 per cent of pupils in primary and secondary schools in England belong to minority ethnic groups, with roughly 8 per cent of them using English as an Additional Language (EAL).

All teachers are teachers of language and 'the teaching of English is the responsibility of all teachers' (School Curriculum and Assessment Authority (SCAA), 1996: 2). 'Good oral work enhances pupils' understanding of language … and of the way in which language can be used to communicate' (DfEE, 1998c: 3). In order to develop pupils' language skills, a teacher's language must be accessible. There is no point in talking to pupils in language they do not understand. That does not mean subject-specific vocabulary cannot be introduced, but you gradually introduce your class to the language of the subject. To do this you must not assume that everybody knows the words or constructions that you do, including simple connecting phrases, e.g. 'in order to', 'so that', 'tends to', 'keep in proportion', etc. Start with a simple direct language that makes no assumptions.

It is easier for pupils to understand a new concept if you make comparisons or use examples, metaphors or references to which they can relate. Where appropriate, use a variety of words or explanations that ensures the meaning of what you intend to convey is understood by all pupils. As a teacher your language must be concise. When you are speaking, you stress or repeat important words or phrases. Placing an accent on certain syllables of the words you use gives rise to rhythmic patterns that affect the meaning of your message. These are important techniques in teaching. If they help learning, repetition, accentuation and elaboration are valuable, but filling silence with teacher talk is generally unproductive. You take longer to deliver the same information and pupils' time may not be used most effectively. However, it is generally accepted that pupils understand something and learn it better if they hear it a number of times and if it is explained in different ways. Therefore, as the Chinese proverb says, you should:

- tell them what you are going to tell them;
- tell them;
- then tell them again what you have told them.

Task 3.1.2
The language of your subject

Compile a list of specialist words and phrases used in your subject or in a particular topic that you may be teaching. How many of these might be in the normal vocabulary of an average pupil at your school? In your lesson planning how might you introduce and explain these words and phrases? How might you allow pupils opportunities to practise their use of the words in the lesson? Tape a lesson that you are teaching then replay the tape and consider your use of language, including words and phrases identified above. It can be particularly helpful to listen to this with a student teacher learning to teach another subject who does not have the same subject knowledge and language and who therefore may be nearer to pupils' experience of the subject. How might you improve your use of language in future lessons?

As well as conveying content, a teacher's language is also used to create individual relationships with pupils that make them more interested in learning. Using pupils' names, showing interest in their lives outside the classroom, valuing their experience, are all important in building a positive atmosphere for classroom learning (see also Unit 3.2 for further information).

Teachers also use language to impose discipline. Often, negative terms are used for this. This is not inevitable and a positive approach may have more success. For example, can you suggest a constructive activity rather than condemning a destructive one? Could earlier praise or suggestion have made later criticism unnecessary? (See Unit 3.3 on managing pupils' behaviour.)

Types of communication

There are many different ways in which verbal communication is used in teaching. Explaining, questioning and discussion, are considered briefly below.

Explaining

Teachers spend a lot of time explaining to pupils. In some teaching situations it can be the main form of activity in the lesson, thus being able to explain something effectively is an important skill to acquire. Pupils learn better if they are actively engaged in the learning process and a good explanation actively engages pupils and therefore is able to gain and maintain their attention. You must plan to involve pupils, e.g. mix an explanation with tasks, activities or questions, rather than relying on long lectures, dictating notes or working out something on the board.

Explaining provides information about what, why and how. It describes new terms or concepts or clarifies their meaning. Pupils expect teachers to explain things clearly and become frustrated when they cannot understand an explanation. A good explanation is clear and well structured. It takes account of pupils' previous knowledge and understanding, uses language that pupils can understand, relates new work to concepts, interests or work already familiar to the pupils. Use of analogy or metaphor can also help an explanation.

McCaleb and White (1980) identified five 'aspects of clarity' of an explanation. These are shown in Table 3.1.1, along with questions which may help to achieve clarity.

Teachers often reinforce verbal explanations by providing pupils with a visual demonstration, or model. Modelling is an effective learning strategy as it allows pupils to ask questions about and hear explanations related to each stage of the process as it happens as the teacher can, for example:

Table 3.1.1 Aspects of clarity in explaining

Aspect of clarity	Does the teacher –
Understanding	• Determine pupils' existing familiarity with the information presented? • Use terms that are unambiguous and within the pupils' experience?
Structuring	• Establish the purpose of the lesson? • Preview the organisation of the lesson? • Include internal summaries of the lesson?
Sequencing	• Order the lesson in a logical way, appropriate to the content and the learners?
Explaining	• Define major concepts? • Give examples to illustrate these concepts? • Use examples that are accurate and concrete as well as abstract?
Presenting	• Articulate words clearly and project speech loudly enough? • Pace the sections of the presentation at rates conducive to understanding? • Support the verbal content with appropriate non-verbal communication and visual aids?

- think aloud, making skills, decisions and processes that would otherwise be hidden or unclear, apparent and explicit;
- expose pupils to and show them how to avoid, possible pitfalls of the task in hand;
- demonstrate to pupils that they can make alterations and corrections as part of the process.

(Department for Education and Skills (DfES), 2003a: 3)

Showing learners what to do while talking them through the activity and linking new learning to old through questions, resources/activities and language is sometimes referred to as scaffolding. The idea is that 'learners are supported in carrying out a task by the use of language to guide their action. The next stage in scaffolding is for the learner to talk themselves through the task. Then that talk can, in turn, become an internalised guide to the action and thought of the learner' (Dillon and Maguire, 2001: 145–6). Combining verbal and visual explanations can be more effective than using verbal explanations exclusively, particularly with pupils who prefer a visual learning style or are learning EAL.

Questioning

One technique in the scaffolding process for actively involving pupils in their learning is questioning. Teachers use a lot of questions; indeed 'every day teachers ask dozens, even hundreds of questions, thousands in a single year, over a million during a professional lifetime' (Wragg and Brown 2001: 1).

Asking questions effectively

Effective use of questioning is a valuable part of interactive teaching. However, if not handled effectively, pupils misunderstand and/or become confused. To be able to use questioning effectively in your lessons requires planning (see Unit 2.2 on lesson planning). To use questioning effectively you need to consider:

- why you are asking the question(s);
- what type of question(s) you are going to ask;
- when you are going to ask question(s);
- how you are going to ask question(s);
- of whom you are going to ask a question, how you expect the question answered, how you are going to respond if the pupil does not understand the question or gives an inappropriate answer, and how long you are going to wait for an answer.

However, you cannot plan your questioning rigidly; you must be flexible, adapting your plan during the lesson to take account of the development of the lesson.

Asking questions is not a simple process. Questions are asked for many reasons, e.g. to gain pupils' attention or check that they are paying attention, to check understanding of an instruction or explanation, to reinforce or revise a topic, to deepen understanding, to encourage thinking and problem solving, or to develop a discussion. Wragg and Brown (2001: 16–17) classified the content of questions related to learning a particular subject, rather than procedural issues, as one of three types: *empirical questions* requiring answers based on facts or on experimental findings; *conceptual questions* concerned with eliciting ideas, definitions and reasoning in the subject being studied; and *value questions* investigating relative worth and merit, moral and environmental issues. These broad categories often overlap and some questions may involve elements of all three types of questions.

Another classification that can be used to help you plan questions with specific purposes in mind is Bloom's (1956) 'taxonomy of educational objectives' through which questions can be arranged into six levels of complexity and abstraction. Lower-level questions usually demand factual, descriptive answers whereas higher-level questions are more complex and require more sophisticated thinking from pupils. Bloom's (1956) taxonomy is shown in Table 3.1.2.

Table 3.1.2 Taxonomy of educational objectives (Bloom, 1956)

1. Knowledge	The learner is asked to identify, list, describe or define newly acquired knowledge, for example through identification, recall, labelling or matching tasks
2. Comprehension	The learner is asked to show what knowledge has been acquired, by explaining what has been learnt or summarizing what has been read. This requires them to translate, review, report, restate
3. Application	The learner is asked to make use of his/her existing knowledge by applying it to practical and problem-solving situations. This requires them to interpret, predict, show how, solve, try in a new context
4. Analysis	The learner is asked to break down what they know and make connections between concepts by, for instance, categorising information or identifying patterns. This requires them to explain, infer, analyse, question, test, criticise
5. Synthesis	The learner is asked to respond creatively to a new situation by selecting and combining elements of existing knowledge to arrange, organise, reorganise, construct
6. Evaluation	The learner is asked to use his/her knowledge to form judgements and/ or take up positions which s/he is able to justify and defend. This requires them to assess, compare and contrast, appraise, argue, select

Black and Wiliam (2002) and others have studied the use of the taxonomy in questioning and you might like to refer to this literature.

There are a number of other ways in which questions can be categorized.

Closed and open questions

The most common reason for asking questions is to check that pupils have learned what they are supposed to have learned or that they have memorized certain facts or pieces of information. These are questions like: What is the capital of Peru? What is the atomic weight of nitrogen? How many people are in a netball team? What do we call the main artery leading from the heart? How do you spell 'geranium'? These are called *closed* questions. There is only one correct answer; pupils recall information. The pupil either knows the answer or not, no real thought is required. Closed questions might be given to the whole class, with answers coming instantaneously. A short closed question–answer session might reinforce learning, refresh pupils' memories or provide a link to new work.

On the other hand, *open* questions have several possible answers and it may be impossible to know if an answer is 'correct'. These questions are often used to develop understanding. Examples of open questions are: How could we reduce vandalism in cities? What sort of man was Hamlet? Why did the Roman Empire decline and fall? How might you defeat the offside trap in football? What words could you use to describe a wood in spring?

These questions are much more complex than closed questions. They are designed to extend pupils' understanding of a topic. To answer them the respondent has to think and manipulate information by reasoning or applying information and using knowledge, logic and imagination. Open questions cannot usually be answered quickly. Pupils probably need time to gather information, sift evidence, advance hypotheses, discuss ideas, plan answers.

An example from a religious education lesson shows the difference in purpose between closed and open-ended. 'Where do Muslims go on pilgrimage?' is a closed question requiring factual knowledge but 'Why do Muslims make pilgrimage to Mecca?' requires understanding. Alternatively, a question such as 'Do you think going on pilgrimage is a necessary aspect of being religious?' requires a deeper level of reflection by pupils.

You can ask closed or open questions or a combination of the two as *a series of questions*. The questions in the series can start with a few relatively easy closed questions and then move on to more complex open questions. A series of questions takes time to build up if they are to be an integral part of the learning process. They must therefore be planned as an integral part of the lesson not as a time filler at the end of a lesson where their effect is lost. Questions at the end of the lesson are much more likely to be closed-recall questions to help pupils remember what they have been taught in the lesson. There are implications for assessment of closed and open questions (see Unit 6.1).

There are other aspects of questioning that are important to consider. Questions can be asked to the whole class; to groups; or to specific named individuals. The questions can be spoken, written on a board, or given out on printed sheets. The answers can be given at once or produced after deliberation, either spoken or written. For example, you may set a series of questions for homework and either collect the answers in to mark or go through them verbally with the class at the start of the next lesson.

Effective questioning is a skill you must develop as a teacher. It requires you to be able to ask clear, appropriate questions, use pauses to allow pupils to think about an answer before responding and use prompting to help pupils who are having problems in answering a question. Some key tactics identified by Wragg and Brown (2001: 28) for asking questions include: structuring; pitching and putting clearly; directing and distributing; pausing and pacing; prompting and pacing; listening and responding to replies; sequencing. Muijs and Reynolds (2001: 22) identify three types of prompts to help pupils answer questions: *verbal prompts* (cues, reminders, tips, references to previous lessons or giving part of a sentence for pupils to complete); *gestural prompts* (pointing to an object or modelling a behaviour); and *physical prompts* (guiding pupils through motor skills).

Follow-up questions can be used to probe further, encourage pupils to develop their answers, extend their thinking, change the direction of the questioning and distributing questions to involve the whole class. Non-verbal aspects of communication such as eye contact, gesture, body language, tone of voice, humour, smiles and frowns are important in effective questioning because they go with the words that are used.

Wragg and Brown (2001: 28) identified some common 'errors' in questioning by student teachers:

- asking too many questions at once;
- asking a question and answering it yourself;
- asking questions only of the brightest or most likeable pupils;
- asking a difficult question too early in the sequence of events;
- asking irrelevant questions;
- always asking the same types of questions (e.g. closed ones);
- asking questions in a threatening way;
- not indicating a change in the type of question;
- not using probing questions;
- not giving pupils the time to think;
- not correcting wrong answers;
- ignoring pupils' answers;

- failing to see the implications of pupils' answers;
- failing to build on answers.

Errors of presentation, e.g. not looking at pupils when asking a question, talking too fast, at the wrong volume or not being clear, were identified as the most common errors. One reason for this may be the ease of detection of these errors (Wragg, 1984). The second most common type of error was the way student teachers handled responses to questions, e.g. they only accepted answer(s) to open ended questions that they wanted or expected. Open questions are likely to prompt a range of responses, which may be valid but not correspond to the answer expected. You need to respond appropriately to these. You must avoid the guessing game type of question and answer session where the teacher has a fixed answer in mind and is not open to possible alternative answers. Pupils then spend their time guessing what the teacher wants.

Other errors identified in this study were pupils not knowing why particular questions were being asked, pupils not being given enough background information to enable them to answer questions, teachers asking questions in a disjointed fashion rather than a logical sequence, jumping from one question to another without linking them together and focusing on a small group of pupils and ignoring the rest of the class. Student teachers tended to focus on those pupils sitting in a V-shaped wedge in the middle of the room.

Some aspects of questioning were not identified as common errors, e.g. whether the vocabulary is appropriate for the pupils' level of understanding or whether the questions are too long, complex or ambiguous. Wragg (1984) suggested that one reason for this might be that they are difficult to detect and correct. It is as important to think about and develop these aspects of questioning as it is those that are most obvious.

The use of questioning in a lesson should be considered in relation to the use of other teaching techniques rather than in isolation. For example, you can encourage pupils to participate actively in questioning by listening and responding appropriately to answers, praising good answers, being supportive and respecting answers and not making pupils feel they will be ridiculed if they answer a question incorrectly (see also Unit 3.2 on motivating pupils).

Discussion

Questioning may lead naturally into discussion in order to explore a topic further. Although pupils generally have more control over the material included in, and direction of, a discussion than in many teaching situations the teacher is still in charge. As with all other aspects of your teaching, discussion should be planned. Seating arrangements are important to develop a less structured atmosphere for a discussion, which can encourage as many pupils as possible to contribute to the discussion. You also need to plan how you are going to stimulate the discussion and how you are going to respond if a discussion drifts off its main theme. By interjecting suggestions or key questions you can keep a discussion on the topic.

> For a fruitful discussion which allows pupils some significant say over what is discussed, whilst at the same time covering ground that teacher's judge to be important, it is best to think of questions that may be perplexing, intriguing or even puzzling to pupils. Skilfully chosen encouraging, broad questions are often effective in sparking off animated conversations. The process may begin with recall questions to extend and activate knowledge and then thought questions to lift the discussion.
>
> (Wragg and Brown, 2001: 44)

To maximize pupils' learning through discussion you need to be able to chair a discussion effectively. Before you use discussion in your classes, it is wise to observe another teacher use this technique in their teaching. See also Unit 4.5 and the Appendix to Unit 4.5, 'Handling Discussion with Classes'.

Listening

For effective communication, *being able to listen effectively and take account of the response* is as important as being able to send the message effectively. Learn to recognize and be sensitive to whether or not a message has been received properly by a pupil, e.g. you get a bewildered look or an inappropriate answer to a question. Be able to react appropriately, e.g. repeat the same question or rephrase it. However, also reflect on why the communication was not effective, e.g. was the pupil not listening to you? If so, why? For example, had the pupil 'switched off' in a boring lesson or was the question worded poorly? Do not assume that pupils have your grasp of meaning and vocabulary (see 'Language of the teacher' above). It is all too easy to blame a pupil for not listening properly, but it may be that you had a large part to play in the breakdown of the communication. It is also important that you listen effectively to what pupils are communicating to you.

Wragg and Brown (2001: 34) identify four types of listening:

> *Skim listening* – little more than awareness that a pupil is talking (often when the answer seems irrelevant); *Survey listening* – trying to build a wider mental map of what the pupil is talking about; *Search listening* – actively searching for specific information in an answer; *Study listening* – a blend of survey and search listening to identify the underlying meaning and uncertainties of the words the pupil is using.

It is too easy to ask a question and then 'switch off' while an answer is being given, to think about the next question or next part of the lesson. This lack of interest conveys itself to the pupil. It is distracting to the pupil to know that the teacher is not listening and not responding to what is being said. Also, you may convey boredom or indifference, which has a negative impact on the tone of the lesson. Effective listening is an active process, with a range of non-verbal and verbal responses that convey the message to the pupil speaking that you are listening to what is being said. Effective listening is associated with conveying enthusiasm and generating interest, by providing reinforcement and constructive feedback to pupils. These include looking alert, looking at the pupil who is talking to you, smiling, nodding and making verbal signals to show you have received and understood the message or to encourage the pupil to continue, e.g. 'yes', 'I see what you mean', 'go on', 'Oh dear', 'mmmm', 'uh-huh'.

NON-VERBAL COMMUNICATION

Much teacher–pupil communication is non-verbal (e.g. your appearance, gestures, posture, facial expression and mannerisms). Non-verbal communication supports or detracts from verbal communication, depending on whether or not verbal and non-verbal signals match each other; for example, if you are praising someone and smiling and looking pleased or if you are telling them off and looking stern and sounding firm, you are sending a consistent message and are perceived as sincere. On the other hand, if you are smiling when telling someone off or are looking bored when praising someone, you are sending conflicting messages that cause confusion and misunderstanding. Robertson (1996: 94) expresses this well: 'When non-verbal behaviour is not reinforcing meaning, … it communicates instead the speaker's lack of involvement. Rather than being the message about the message, it becomes the message about the messenger.'

However, non-verbal communication can also have a considerable impact without any verbal communication, e.g. by looking at a pupil slightly longer than you would normally, communicates your awareness that they are talking or misbehaving. This may be enough to make the pupil stop. You can indicate your enthusiasm for a topic by the way you use gestures. You can probably think of a teacher who stands at the front of the class leaning against the board with arms crossed waiting for silence, the teacher marching down between the desks to tell someone off or the teacher who sits and listens attentively to the problems of a particular pupil. The meaning of the communication is clear and there is no need to say anything. Thus, non-verbal communication is important for good communication, classroom management and control.

Effective communication therefore relies not only on appropriate content, but also on the way it is presented.

PRESENTING YOURSELF EFFECTIVELY

There might seem to be some contradiction in discussing ways of presenting yourself as it could indicate that there is a correct way to present yourself as a teacher. However, the heading clearly refers to you as an individual, with your own unique set of characteristics. Herein lies one of the keys to effective teacher self-presentation: while there are some common constituents and expectations, it is also the case that every teacher is an individual and brings something of their own unique personality to the job.

Initial impressions are important and the way you present yourself to a class on first meeting can influence their learning over a period of time. Having prepared the lesson properly, the pupils' impressions of the lesson, and also of you, are important. An important part of the impression created is your appearance. Pupils expect all teachers to wear clothes that are clean, neat and tidy and certain teachers to wear certain types of clothes, e.g. it is acceptable for a physical education teacher to wear a tracksuit but not a history teacher. Thus, first impressions have as much to do with non-verbal as with verbal communication, although both are important considerations.

How teachers follow up the first impression is equally important, e.g. whether you treat pupils as individuals, how you communicate with pupils, whether you have any mannerisms such as constantly flicking a piece of hair out of your eyes or saying 'er' or 'OK' – which reduce or prevent effective communication (pupils tend to focus on any mannerism rather than on what is being said and they may even count the number of times you do it!). It is generally agreed that effective teaching depends on and is enhanced by self-presentation that is *enthusiastic*, *confident* and *caring*. Why are these attributes important? How can you work towards making these part of your self-presentation as a teacher?

Enthusiasm

One of the tasks of a teacher is to enable pupils to learn to do or to understand something. Before many young people will make an effort to get to grips with something new, the teacher needs to 'sell' it to them as something interesting and worthwhile. However, your enthusiasm should be sustained throughout a lesson, and in relation to each activity – not only when you are presenting material but also when you are commenting on a pupil's work, particularly perhaps when a pupil has persevered or achieved a goal.

Your enthusiasm for your subject is infectious. However, there could be a danger of 'going over the top' when showing enthusiasm. If you are over-excited it can give a sense of triviality, so the enthusiasm has to be measured.

There are perhaps three principal ways in which you can communicate enthusiasm both verbally and non-verbally. The first is via *facial expression*:

> An enthusiastic speaker will be producing a stream of facial expressions which convey his excitement, disbelief, surprise or amusement about his message. Some expressions are extremely brief, lasting about one fifth of a second and may highlight a particular word, whereas others last much longer, perhaps accompanying the verbal expression of an idea. The overall effect is to provide a running commentary for the listener on how the speaker feels about the ideas expressed. In contrast, a speaker who is not involved in his subject shows little variation in facial expression. The impression conveyed is that the ideas are brought out automatically and are failing even to capture the attention of the speaker.
>
> (Robertson 1996: 86)

The second way is via the *use of your voice*. The manner in which you speak as a teacher gives a clear indication of how you feel about the topic under debate and is readily picked up by pupils. Your voice needs to be varied and to indicate your feelings about what you are teaching. As you are engaged in something akin to a 'selling job' your voice has to show this in its production and delivery – it has to be persuasive and occasionally show a measure of excitement. A monotone voice is hardly likely to convey enthusiasm. 'Enthusiastic teachers are alive in the room; they show surprise, suspense, joy, and other feelings in their voices and they make material interesting by relating it to their experiences and showing that they themselves are interested in it' (Good and Brophy, 2000: 385).

A third way to convey enthusiasm is via your *poise and movement*. An enthusiastic speaker has an alert posture and accompanies speech with appropriately expressive hand and arm gestures – sometimes to emphasize a point, at other times to reinforce something that is being described through indicating relevant shape or direction, for example an arrangement of apparatus or a tactical move in hockey. If you are enthusiastic you are committed and involved, and all aspects of your posture and movement should display this.

Think back to teachers you have worked with and identify some whose enthusiasm for their subject really influenced your learning. How did these teachers convey their enthusiasm? How do you convey your enthusiasm?

Confidence

It is very important that as a teacher you present yourself with confidence. This is easier said than done because confidence relates both to a sense of knowledgeable mastery of the subject matter and to a sense of assurance of being in control.

There is an irony in pupils' response to teacher confidence. Expression of authority is part of the role pupils expect of a teacher, and where exercised with confidence, pupils feel at ease and reassured. In fact, pupils prefer the security of a confident teacher. However, if they sense at any time that a teacher is unsure or apprehensive, it is in young people's nature to attempt to undermine authority (for further information see Robertson, 1996).

Of course, in many cases it is experience that brings confidence but sadly pupils seldom allow that to influence their behaviour. Although the key to confident self-presentation is to be well planned, both in respect of material and in organization, without the benefit of experience, all your excellent plans may not work and you may have no alternative 'up your sleeve'. Whatever happens you need to cultivate a confident exterior, even if it is something of an act and you are feeling far from assured inside.

Confidence can be conveyed verbally in clear, purposeful instructions and explanations that are not disrupted by hesitation. Instructions given in a direct and business-like manner, such as 'John, please collect the scissors and put them in the red box', convey a sense of confidence. On the other hand, the same instruction put in the form of a question, such as 'John will you collect the scissors and put them in the red box?' can convey a sense of your being less assured, not being confident that, in fact, John *will* co-operate. There is also the possibility of the pupil saying 'No'! Your voice needs to be used in a firm, measured manner. A slower, lower, well-articulated delivery is more authoritative and displays more confidence than a fast, high-pitched method of speaking. Use of voice is particularly important in giving key instructions, especially where safety factors are involved and in taking action to curtail inappropriate pupil behaviour. This is perhaps the time to be less enthusiastic and animated and more serious and resolute in your manner.

Non-verbally, confidence is expressed via, for example, posture, movement and eye contact, both in their own right and as an appropriate accompaniment to verbal language. There is nothing agitated about the movement of confident people. They tend to stand still and to use their arm gestures to a limited extent to reinforce the message being conveyed.

Eye contact is a crucial aspect of conveying confidence to pupils. A nervous person avoids eye contact, somehow being afraid to know what others are thinking, not wanting to develop a relationship that might ultimately reveal their inability or weakness. Clearly it is your role as a teacher to be alert at all times to pupil reaction and to be striving to develop a relationship with pupils that encourages them to seek your help and advice. Steady, committed eye contact is usually helpful for both of these objectives. You must also recognize that the use of eye contact is regarded differently by people of different cultures, e.g. some members of some cultures avoid use of eye contact. You should therefore take into account cultural sensitivities. This also applies to other aspects of non-verbal communication, such as spatial proximity to another person. For further information about cultural differences take advice from your tutor, a staff member of that culture, staff at the local multicultural centre or the Commission for Racial Equality.

Caring

It is not surprising perhaps that young people feel that a caring approach is important in developing an effective relationship with pupils. Wentzel (1997) described caring teachers as those who demonstrate a commitment to their teaching, recognize each pupil's academic strengths and needs and have a democratic style of interaction. Wragg (1984: 82) reported that many more children preferred teachers who were 'understanding, friendly and firm' than teachers who were 'efficient, orderly and firm' or 'friendly, sympathetic and understanding'. It is interesting to note that firmness is also a preferred characteristic.

Notwithstanding young people's preferences, interest in pupils as individuals and in their progress is surely the reason most teachers are in teaching. Your commitment to pupils' well-being and learning should be evident in all aspects of your manner and self-presentation. While this attitude goes without saying, it is not as straightforward as it sounds as it demands sensitivity and flexibility. In a sense it is you as the teacher who has to modify your behaviour in response to the pupils, rather than it always being the pupil who has to fall into line with everything asked for by the teacher. There is a potential conflict, and balance to be struck, between firm confidence and flexible empathy. It is one of the challenges of teaching to find this balance and to be able to respond suitably at the appropriate time.

A caring approach is evident in a range of features of teaching, from efficient preparation through to sensitive interpersonal skills such as listening. Those teachers who put pupils' interests above everything have taken the time and trouble to prepare work thoroughly in a form appropriate to the class. Similarly, the classroom environment shows thoughtful design and organization. In the teaching situation, caring teachers are fully engaged in the task at hand, observing, supporting, praising, alert to the class climate and able to respond with an appropriate modification in the programme if necessary. Above all, however, caring teachers know pupils by name, remember their work, problems and progress from previous lessons and are prepared to take time to listen to them and talk about personal things as well as work. In other words, caring teachers show a real sensitivity to pupils' individual needs. They communicate clearly that each pupil's learning and success are valued.

> **Task 3.1.3**
> **Communicating effectively**
>
> Select in turn each aspect of verbal or non-verbal communication identified above: your use of voice, language, explaining/questioning/discussion, listening, presenting yourself effectively, enthusiasm, confidence, caring. Prepare an observation sheet for your tutor or another student teacher to use when observing a class. Use this as the basis for evaluation and discussion about how you can further develop this aspect of your teaching.

SUMMARY AND KEY POINTS

Good communication is essential for developing good relationships with pupils, a positive classroom climate and effective teaching and learning. This unit has aimed to help you identify both the strengths and weaknesses in your verbal and non-verbal communication and in your self-presentation, to provide the basis for improving your ability to communicate. Your developing professional knowledge and judgement should enable you to communicate sensitively and to best advantage.

ACKNOWLEDGEMENT

The authors would like to acknowledge the significant input of Roger Strangwick and Margaret Whitehead to the first three editions of this chapter.

FURTHER READING

Good, T. and Brophy, J. (2000) *Looking in Classrooms*, 8th edn, New York: Addison-Wesley. Chapter 9 discusses research relating teacher behaviour to pupil achievement and considers its implications for the role of the teacher in actively presenting information to pupils, such as the effectiveness of demonstrations and questioning techniques.

Muijs, D. and Reynolds, D. (2001) *Effective Teaching: Evidence and Practice*, London: Paul Chapman (Sage). Chapter 2 considers the important relationship between interactive teaching and pupils' learning. Elements of effective questioning techniques are identified and then reviewed in relation to class discussion.

Ogborn, J., Kress, G., Martins, I. and McGillcuddy, K. (1996) *Explaining Science in the Classroom*, Buckingham: Open University. This is a very good resource on 'explaining'.

Robertson, J. (1996) *Effective Classroom Control: Understanding Teacher–Student Relationships*, 3rd edn, London: Hodder and Stoughton. This book looks at relationships between teachers and pupils. It considers this in different ways, but includes sections on expressing your authority, establishing authority in first meetings and conveying enthusiasm. The sections consider many aspects of teacher behaviour and effective non-verbal communications in these relationships.

Wragg, E.C. and Brown, G. (2001) *Questioning in the Secondary School*, London: RoutledgeFalmer. This book combines relevant research with practical resources that enable teachers to reflect upon their use of questions; develop approaches to preparing, using and evaluating their own questions; and explore ways in which pupils may be encouraged to question and to provide answers.

Unit 3.2

Motivating Pupils

Susan Capel and Misia Gervis

INTRODUCTION

Pupils' attitudes to school and motivation to learn are a result of a number of factors, including school ethos, class climate, past experiences, future expectations, peer group, teachers, gender, family background, culture, economic status and class. However, the link between motivation and educational performance and achievement is complex.

Some pupils have a more positive attitude to school and to learning, e.g. it is valued at home or they see a link between education and a job. For example, Ford (1992a, 1992b), Mickelson (1990) and Murdock (1999) have found that, if pupils see a relationship between success at school and economic success, they are more likely to work hard, behave in the classroom and be more successful. Many pupils want to learn but depend on teachers to get them interested in a subject. Even though some pupils may not be inherently motivated to learn, the school ethos, teachers' attitudes, behaviour, personal enthusiasm, teaching style and strategies in the classroom can increase their motivation to learn (see Unit 3.1 on 'Communicating with Pupils'). On the other hand, pupils who do not feel valued at school are, in turn, unlikely to value school (e.g. Fine, 1986, 1989; Finn, 1989, 1993). Therefore, although some pupils may be inherently motivated to learn, they may become demotivated or have low motivation because of a learning environment that does not meet the needs of their learning style or does not stimulate them, or a task being too difficult or a negative impact of factors such as those identified above. Pupils for whom the motivational climate is not right are more likely to become disinterested and misbehave. If the teacher does not manage the class and their behaviour effectively, the learning of all pupils in the class can be negatively affected.

Thus, a central aim for you as a teacher is to create a motivational climate that helps to stimulate pupils to learn. There are a range of techniques you can use to increase pupils' motivation to learn, e.g.:

- showing your enthusiasm for a topic, subject or teaching;
- treating each pupil as an individual;
- providing quick feedback by marking work promptly;
- rewarding appropriate behaviour.

In order to use such techniques effectively you need to understand why each technique is used. A study of motivation therefore is crucial to give you some knowledge and insight into ways of motivating pupils to learn. There is a wealth of material available on motivation. This unit tries to draw out some of the material we feel is of most benefit to you as a student teacher. However, the further reading list at the end of this unit, plus other reading in your library, will help you to develop your ability to motivate pupils further.

OBJECTIVES

By the end of the unit you should be able to:

- understand the role and importance of motivation for effective teaching and classroom management;
- appreciate some of the key elements of motivation for effective teaching;
- understand how to motivate pupils effectively.

WHAT IS MOTIVATION?

Motivation 'consists of internal processes and external incentives which spur us on to satisfy some need' (Child, 2004: 176). There are three key elements to motivational behaviour, which it is helpful for you to understand as they can help you to interpret the behaviour of your pupils. These three elements are:

- direction (what activities people start);
- persistence (what activities people continue);
- intensity (the effort they put in).

These three key elements determine the activities that people start (direction) and continue (persistence) and the amount of effort they put into those activities at any particular time (intensity).

Motivation can be intrinsic (motivation from within the person, i.e. engaging in an activity for its own sake for pleasure and/or satisfaction inherent in the activity, e.g. a sense of achievement at having completed a difficult piece of work) or extrinsic (motivation from outside, i.e. engaging in an activity for external reasons, e.g. to receive a reward, such as praise from a teacher for good work, or to avoid punishment). Research (e.g. Lloyd and Fox, 1992) has found that a person intrinsically motivated in an activity or task is more likely to persist and continue with an activity than when extrinsically motivated. This can be illustrated by some (intrinsically motivated) pupils succeeding at school/in a subject despite the quality of the teaching, whereas other (extrinsically motivated) pupils succeed because of good teaching. Therefore, intrinsic motivation is to be encouraged in learning. A teacher's job would certainly be easier if all pupils were motivated intrinsically. However, pupils are asked to do many activities at school which are new to them, which are difficult, at which they may not be immediately successful or which they may perceive to be of little or no relevance to them. In order to become intrinsically motivated, pupils need encouragement along the way, e.g. written or verbal praise for effort, making progress or success, feedback on how they are doing or an explanation of the relevance of the work. For example, the quality of the feedback that pupils receive can directly impact on their self-confidence. Teachers can deliberately plan extrinsic motivators (see below) into their lessons with a view to enhancing both self-confidence and intrinsic motivation (there is a cyclical relationship between self-confidence and intrinsic motivation, such that high self-confidence increases intrinsic motivation whereas low self-confidence decreases intrinsic motivation).

THEORIES OF MOTIVATION

There are a number of theories of motivation. In addition, we adopt our own, often unconscious, theories. Examples of theories of motivation, along with some of their implications for you as a teacher in determining learning activities, are given in Table 3.2.1. Below are several tasks to help you think about the application of these theories. Record the outcomes in your diary so that you can compare these theories of motivation.

What motivates people?

It is often difficult for a teacher to identify the exact reason for a particular pupil's behaviour at a particular time, and therefore what is motivating them. Likewise, it is often difficult for a pupil to identify exactly what is motivating them. As a teacher you can often only infer whether or not pupils are motivated by observing their behaviour. Although there may be other reasons for a pupil not listening to what you are saying, talking, looking bored or staring out of the window, one reason may be that the motivational climate is not right and therefore the pupil is not motivated to learn.

Some of the factors which have been found to be motivating include: positive teacher–pupil relationships (e.g. Midgley *et al.*, 1989; Wentzel, 1997); supportive peer relationships (e.g. Berndt and Keefe, 1995); a sense of belonging (e.g. Anderman and Anderman, 1999; Goodenow, 1993); pupils' beliefs about their abilities (e.g. Bandura, 1977, 1997; Nicholls, 1984, 1990); pupils' beliefs about the control they have over their own learning (e.g. Findley and Cooper, 1983; Skinner, 1995); pupils' interest in the subject (e.g. Krapp *et al.*, 1992; Schiefele, 1996); and the degree to which the subject or specific tasks are valued (e.g. Eccles, 1984). Such factors have been categorized as:

- achievement (e.g. completing a piece of work which has taken a lot of effort);
- pleasure (e.g. getting a good mark or praise from a teacher for a piece of work);
- preventing or stopping less pleasant activities/punishment (e.g. avoiding getting a detention);
- satisfaction (e.g. feeling that you are making progress);
- success (e.g. doing well in a test).

The need for individuals to achieve can be encouraged by creating a learning environment in which 'the need for achievement in academic studies is raised' (Child, 2004: 197). Each individual sets themselves a standard of achievement, according to their level of aspiration. It is therefore important to raise pupils' levels of aspiration. Pupils who are challenged are more likely to improve their performance than those who are not challenged. Thus, setting tasks which are challenging but achievable for each individual pupil, i.e. individualized tasks, can be used to raise aspirations. Tasks on which pupils expect to achieve approximately 50 per cent of the time are the most motivating. However, this means that pupils are likely to fail on the task approximately 50 per cent of the time, so it is important

Table 3.2.1   Important theoretical perspectives and their implications for you as a teacher

Theory	Source	Main points	Implications for teachers
Theory *x* and theory *y*	McGregor, 1960	**Theory *x*** managers assume that the average worker is lazy, lacks ambition, is resistant to change, self-centred and not very bright. **Theory *y*** managers assume that the average worker is motivated, wants to take responsibility, has potential for development and works for the organisation. Any lack of ambition or resistance to change comes from experience.	Your treatment of pupils may be related to whether inherently you believe in theory *x* or theory *y*. A **theory *x*** teacher motivates pupils externally through a controlling environment, e.g. by directing and controlling pupils actions, persuading, rewarding and punishing them to modify their behaviour. A **theory *y*** teacher encourages intrinsic motivation by allowing pupils to develop for themselves. This may be through an autonomy-support environment (see below).
Achievement motivation	Atkinson, 1964; McClelland, 1961	Motivation to perform an achievement-orientated task is related to the: (i) need to achieve on a particular task; (ii) expectation of success on the task; and (iii) strength of the incentive after the task has been completed successfully. This results in individuals setting themselves standards of achievement.	Create a learning environment which raises the need for achievement in academic studies by raising levels of aspiration. Plan tasks that are challenging but attainable with effort. Work should be differentiated according to individual needs.
Achievement goal theory	Ames, 1992a, 1992b; Dweck, 1986; Dweck and Leggett, 1988; Nicholls, 1984, 1989	A social-cognitive perspective which identifies determinants of achievement behaviour; variations of which result from different achievement goals pursued by individuals in achievement situations (Duda, 1993). In achievement settings, an individual's orientation towards one of two incompatible goals by which to judge success underpins how they strive to maximize their demonstration of ability. In a task (or mastery) orientated setting the focus is on skill learning and exerting effort to succeed and success is judged by self-improvement, mastery of a task. In an outcome (ego or performance) orientated setting individuals compare their performance and ability with others and judge success by beating others with little effort to enhance social status.	Pupils' goal orientation may be influenced by the motivational climate created by what teachers do and say (Ames, 1992a, 1992b). Therefore, plan a task orientated learning environment that encourages pupils to improve their performance by trying hard, selecting demanding tasks and persisting when faced with difficulty; rather than an outcome orientated learning environment that encourages pupils to select easy tasks which they can achieve with minimum effort and on which they are likely to give up when facing difficulties.

Table 3.2.1 (continued)

Attribution theory	Weiner, 1972	Success or failure is attributed to ability, effort, difficulty of task or luck, depending on: (i) previous experience of success or failure on the task; (ii) the amount of work put in; or (iii) a perceived relationship between what is done and success or failure on the task.	Reward effort as well as success, as pupils are more likely to try if they perceive success is due to effort, e.g. can give two marks for work, one for the standard of the work, the other for effort. Use teaching and assessment which is individualised rather than competitive.
Expectancy theory	Rosenthal and Jacobson, 1968	A range of cues are used by one person to form expectations (high or low) of another. That person then behaves in a way that is consistent with their expectations. This influences motivation, performance and how the other person attributes success or failure. The other person performs according to the expectations, thus creating a self-fulfilling prophecy.	In order to avoid the self-fulfilling prophesy of pupils performing according to the way teachers expect them to perform (by forming expectations (high or low) based on a range of cues and conveying these expectations), do not prejudge pupils on their past performance. Rather, encourage pupils to work to the best of their ability all the time.
Hierarchy of needs theory	Maslow, 1970	Hierarchy (highest to lowest): 1. Self-actualization (need to fulfil own potential). 2. Self-esteem (need to feel competent and gain recognition from others). 3. Affiliation and affection (need for love and belonging). 4. Need for physical and psychological safety. 5. Physiological needs (e.g. food, warmth). Energy is spent meeting the lowest level of unmet need.	If basic needs, e.g. sleep, food, warmth, are not met, a pupil concentrates on meeting that need first and is unlikely to benefit from attempts by teachers to meet higher level needs. Try to create a classroom environment to fulfil basic needs first, e.g. rules for using dangerous equipment provide a sense of physical safety, routines give a sense of psychological security, group work can give a sense of belonging (affiliation) (Postlethwaite, 1993).
Behavioural learning theories	Skinner, 1953	Activity or behaviour is learned and maintained because of interaction with the environment. An activity or behaviour reinforced by a pleasurable outcome is more likely to be repeated.	Positive reinforcement (reward), e.g. praise, generally increases motivation to learn and behave. This has a greater impact if the reward is relevant to the pupils, they know how to get the reward and it is given fairly and consistently (there are, however, exceptions: see 'Praise', below).

Task 3.2.1
Theory *x* and theory *y*

In two columns, write down your general assumptions about (i) people you work with and (ii) pupils in classes you teach. In another two columns write down your approach to people you are working with or to pupils you are teaching. Do you have the same assumptions of or take the same approach with both sets of people? Which theory do you tend towards – x or y? Reflect on your assumptions as you read through this unit and on whether the approach to your teaching is the most appropriate and effective methods of motivation.

Task 3.2.2
Achievement motivation

Discuss with your tutor how you can differentiate work so that all pupils in a mixed ability class can perceive that they can succeed approximately 50 per cent of the time. How is the work modified to enable each pupil to be able to succeed? What can you do to prevent loss of motivation if pupils are not successful in this work?

to plan to reduce loss of motivation when pupils fail (e.g. by praising effort, giving feedback on performance, etc.).

Intrinsic motivation in pupils is related to interest in the activity and to effort (hard work) (see e.g. Biggs, 1987; Marton and Saljo, 1976; Watkins *et al.*, 2003), which leads to deep learning (Entwistle, 1990; see also deep and surface learning in Units 5.2 and 5.3). Deep learning means that learners try to understand what they are doing, resulting in greater understanding of the subject matter. This is a prerequisite for high-quality learning outcomes, i.e. achievement. According to Achievement Goal Theory, Covington (2000) reported deep learning as being associated with task (or mastery) goals, whereas surface (superficial or rote) learning is associated with outcome (or performance) goals. In line with other studies, Lam *et al.* (2004) found that pupils with an outcome orientation were more likely to sacrifice learning opportunities for better performance.

Pupils' perceptions of the motivational context, i.e. the goal orientation of the classroom and school, has been found (e.g. by Anderman and Maehr, 1994; Maehr and Anderman, 1993; Murdock *et al.*, 2000) to be important for their motivation and adjustment to school. Controlling environments (teachers attempt to guide pupils' thinking by providing specific guidelines for their academic and personal behaviours in class (Manouchehri, 2004)) have been found to have a negative effect on perceived competence and participation, which results in decreased intrinsic and self-motivation (Deci and Ryan, 1985; Deci *et al.*, 1999; Ryan and Deci, 2000). On the other hand, pupils are motivated by teachers who know, support, challenge and encourage them to act independently from each other and from the teacher (Midgley *et al.*, 1989; Wentzel, 1997). An autonomy–support environment is one in which the teacher gives increasing responsibility to pupils, e.g. for choices/options about what they want to do; encourages pupils' decision-making by spending less time talking, more time listening, making less directive comments, asking more questions, and not giving pupils solutions; allows pupils to work in their own way; and offers more praise and verbal approval in class (e.g. Flink *et al.*, 1990; Manouchehri, 2004). Such an environment supports pupils' academic and social growth by increasing intrinsic and self-motivation to succeed at school, self-confidence, perceived competence and self-esteem (e.g. Chirkov and Ryan, 2001; Grolnick *et al.*, 1997; Guay *et al.*, 2001; Reeve and Deci, 1996; Vallerand, 1997; Vallerand *et al.*, 1997). Research by Manouchehri (2004) has found a relationship between the motivational style adopted by teachers of mathematics and their commitment to implementing new teaching methods. Those adopting an autonomy–support style of motivation increase pupil's participation and engagement by, for example, creating more opportunities for pupils to examine and develop their understanding of mathematical ideas, to listen to the arguments, and to ask questions of other pupils.

Figure 3.2.1 illustrates the link between teachers' actions in creating the motivational climate and pupils' responses which influences their intrinsic motivation.

Further, pupils' goal orientations may be influenced by the motivational climate created by what teachers do and say (Ames, 1992a, 1992b; Solmon, 1996; Todorovich and Curtner-Smith, 2002). Research in physical education (e.g. Carpenter and Morgan, 1999; Papaioannou, 1995; Solmon, 1996; Treasure, 1997) has found a relationship between pupils' perceptions of a lesson as being task orientated and adaptive motivational responses, including increased intrinsic motivation. In contrast, a relationship has been found between pupils' perceptions of a lesson as being outcome orientated and maladaptive motivational responses. Such a lesson focuses on individual achievement and competition between individuals. This may foster extrinsic motivation, discourage hard work and effort to achieve success for pupils who fail to achieve the outcome.

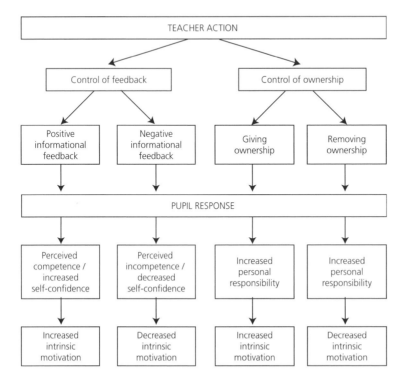

Figure 3.2.1   Creating a motivational climate

Task 3.2.3
Achievement goal theory

Plan a task-orientated learning environment in your classroom. Teach the lesson, asking your tutor to observe and give you feedback on whether and how you could improve the emphasis on task orientation.

Although it changes with age, it is generally accepted that pupils are more likely to try harder if they can see a link between the amount of effort they make and success in the activity. Indeed, there is a link between achievement goal theory and attribution theory (McClelland, 1972; Weiner, 1992) in that pupils with a high need to achieve attribute their success to internal causes (e.g. aptitude and effort), whilst they attribute failure to lack of effort. On the other hand, pupils with a low need to achieve attribute their failure to external factors, e.g. bad luck, or to lack of ability. Therefore, as a teacher, you should design activities which encourage pupils to attribute success or failure to effort. However, this is not always easy. Postlethwaite (1993) identified the difficulty of determining how much effort a pupil has made on a piece of work (especially that done at home) and hence the problems of marking the work. You can no doubt think of occasions where one person has made a lot of effort on a piece of homework, but missed the point and received a low mark, whereas another person has rushed through the homework and managed to achieve a good mark. In 'norm-referenced' marking a certain percentage of the class are given a designated category of mark, no matter how good each individual piece of work. Thus, each pupil's mark for a piece of work is given solely for their performance compared to that of the rest of the group. This encourages success or failure to be attributed to ability or luck. In 'criterion-referenced' marking, all pupils who meet stated criteria for a particular category of mark are marked in that category. Thus, pupils are given a mark which reflects how closely the criteria for the assessment have been met, irrespective of the performance of other pupils. Although this overcomes some of the disadvantages of norm-referenced marking, it does not reflect how much effort the pupil has put into the work. Postlethwaite went on to say that effort can best be judged by comparing different pieces of the same pupil's work, as the standard of work is likely to reflect the amount of effort put in (i.e. ipsative assessment). Giving two marks for the work, one for content and standard of the work and one for effort and presentation can encourage effort. Thus, even if the content and standard are poor, it may be possible to praise the effort. This praise can motivate the pupil to try harder, especially if pupils value the mark for effort. He suggested that another way of encouraging pupils to attribute success to effort is to ask them to write about the way they tackled the task (see also Units 6.1 and 6.2 on assessment).

Task 3.2.4
Attribution theory of motivation

Reflect on one aspect of your educational achievement in which you had success and one in which you were not as successful. For each of these: reflect on whether you attribute (i) success and (ii) less success to ability, effort, difficulty of the task or luck. Also reflect on whether you expect certain grades from assignments and to what you attribute unexpected grades.

According to expectancy theory, a teacher forms an impression of a pupil on which they base their expectations of that pupil; the teacher's verbal and non-verbal behaviour is based, consciously or unconsciously, on those expectations; the pupil recognizes, consciously or unconsciously, the teacher's expectations of them from their behaviour and responds in a way that matches these expectations (Rogers, 1982). Thus, there is a self-fulfilling prophecy. It is generally accepted that if a teacher expects high achievement and good behaviour, pupils perform to the best of their ability and behave well. Murdock (1999) found that where teachers held high expectations of pupils, they were engaged more academically. If, on the other hand, teachers have low expectations of pupils' achievement and behaviour, pupils achieve little and behave badly. In the same way, teachers can develop stereotypes of how different groups of pupils perform or behave; stereotypes can direct expectations. (See also Unit 4.4 'Responding to Diversity'; Gillborn and Gipps, 1996, ch 4; Gillborn and Mirza, 2000, for further information.)

One aspect of the organization of a school that may particularly influence teachers' expectations of pupils is the way pupils are grouped. Pupils streamed by ability remain in the same group throughout the year, whatever their ability in different subjects. Whatever the labels attached to each stream, pupils are perceptive and judge their abilities by the stream they are in. This may be partly because teachers' verbal and non-verbal behaviour communicates clearly their expectations. Teachers expect pupils in the 'top' stream to do well; therefore they behave accordingly, e.g. actively encouraging pupils, setting challenging work. Teachers do not expect pupils in the 'bottom' stream to do as well; therefore they behave accordingly, e.g. constantly nagging pupils, setting easy work (or none at all). Both groups of pupils tend to fulfil the expectations of teachers. No doubt many of you have heard of the notorious 'bottom' stream in a school. Setting (or banding) pupils for different subjects can overcome problems of streaming, i.e. recognizing pupils' ability in different subjects and changing the grouping of pupils according to their ability in a specific subject. The problem can also be overcome by grouping pupils in mixed ability classes and providing differentiated work to enable pupils of different abilities to work alongside each other on tasks that are challenging but achievable for each pupil (see achievement motivation above). For further information about differentiation see Unit 4.1.

Task 3.2.5
Expectancy theory and your teaching

Reflect on whether your expectations of, and behaviour towards, pupils have been influenced by previous knowledge (given to you by the teacher) about the ability or behaviour of particular pupils in a class you are teaching. Ask someone to observe a class you are teaching, looking specifically to see if your behaviour indicates that you might have different expectations of pupils. Discuss their observations.

Task 3.2.6
Hierarchy of needs theory

Consider some of the home conditions likely to leave pupils with unmet needs which prevent effective learning at school. Discuss with your tutor or another student teacher what can be done in the school and what you can do in your lessons that may help pupils to meet these basic needs to provide a foundation for effective learning. Discuss when and to whom you should report if you suspect pupils' most basic needs are not being met, as this may require the skills of other professionals.

Some specific factors which influence pupils motivation to learn

These factors use extrinsic motivation to encourage intrinsic motivation. However, it is important to recognize that motivating pupils extrinsically can have a detrimental effect when a pupil is already motivated intrinsically (see e.g. Deci and Ryan, 1985; Kassin and Lepper, 1984).

Personal achievement (success)

Personal achievement (generally called success in an outcome orientated learning environment) is generally motivating in itself. Some pupils struggle to succeed, whereas others succeed much more quickly. There are many ways to help pupils succeed, e.g. using a technique often called whole–part–whole teaching. In this, pupils are shown the whole activity first so that they know what they are trying to achieve. The activity is then broken down into small, self-contained, achievable parts, which allow pupils to receive reinforcement for each small, successful step. The separate parts of the activity are gradually put together until the whole activity has been built up. Pupils are given appropriate feedback at each stage (see below for more information about giving feedback), therefore when they attempt the whole, they are most likely to succeed. You may relate to this by thinking about when you learned (or tried to learn) front crawl in swimming. You probably practised your arms, legs and breathing separately before you tried to put it all together. What other techniques can you use to help pupils succeed?

Task 3.2.7
Whole–part–whole teaching

As part of your normal lesson planning with a class, select one activity which you can break down into small, self-contained, achievable parts, which can be put together to build up gradually to the whole. Ask your tutor or another student teacher to observe you teaching this activity using whole–part–whole teaching. At the end of the lesson discuss with some of the pupils how this went. Discuss with the observer how the pupils responded and how well they learned the task.

Rewards

Although personal achievement or success is motivating in itself, pupils may not be immediately successful on activities they undertake at school, therefore they may need external rewards (positive reinforcements) to motivate them. Four types of positive reinforcement have been identified (Bull and Solity, 1987). These are listed below in the order in which they are used most often:

- social rewards (social contact and pleasant interactions with other people, including praise, a smile to recognize an action or achievement or to say thank you, encouraging remarks or a gesture of approval);
- token rewards (house points, grades, certificates);
- activity rewards (opportunities for enjoyable activities);
- material rewards (tangible, usable or edible items).

Task 3.2.8
Using rewards

Develop an observation schedule with sections for the four types of reward listed above. Observe a class and mark in the appropriate category any reward used by the teacher in the class. Discuss with the teacher the variety and frequency of use of the different possible methods of reward as well as why a particular type of reward was used to achieve a particular purpose. Ask your tutor or another student teacher to undertake the same observation on one of your lessons. Discuss the differences in variety and frequency of reward used. As you plan your lessons consider how you might use reward. Ask the same person to observe a lesson a couple of months after the first one and see if you have changed your use of reward in your lessons. Relate this to what you know about behavioural learning theories.

Praise

Research findings (e.g. Olweus, 1993) show that pupils generally respond more positively to praise and positive comments about their work or behaviour than to criticism and negative comments. This, in turn, may produce a motivational learning environment in which pupils work harder and behave better. If pupils misbehave in a classroom in which there is a positive motivational learning environment, Olweus (1993: 85) suggested that the use of praise makes pupils feel appreciated, which may make it easier for them to accept criticism of inappropriate behaviour and to attempt to change.

However, the Office for Standards in Education (OFSTED, 1993) reported that teachers give relatively little praise and that their vocabulary is generally more negative than positive. Praise is given more often for academic than social behaviour and social behaviour is more likely to be criticized than praised. One reason for this may be that teachers expect pupils to behave appropriately in the classroom.

Some teachers use very few different words to praise pupils, e.g. 'good', 'well done', 'OK'. What other words can you use to praise someone or give feedback? Try to develop a list of such words because if you use the same word to praise pupils all the time, the word loses its effect. The range of words must be accompanied by appropriate non-verbal communication signals (see Unit 3.1 on communicating with pupils for more information about non-verbal communication), see Task 3.2.9.

Although it is generally accepted that praise aids learning, there are dangers in using praise. There are times when it may not be appropriate. For example, pupils who become lazy about their work as a result of complacency may respond by working harder if their work is gently criticized on occasion. If praise is given automatically, regardless of the work, effort or behaviour, pupils quickly see through it and it loses its effect. Praise should only be used to reward appropriate achievement, effort or behaviour.

Some pupils do not respond positively to praise, e.g. they are embarrassed, especially if they are praised in front of their peers. Others perceive praise to be a form of punishment, e.g. if they are teased or rejected by their peers for being 'teacher's pet' or for behaving themselves in class. Thus, conforming to the behaviours and values promoted in school results in negative social consequences (see e.g. Phelan *et al.*, 1991; Steinberg *et al.*, 1992). Therefore, although pupils know that they will be rewarded for achievement, effort or behaviour, they may also be aware of the norms of the peer-group which discourage them from achieving academically, making an effort or behaving well (Juvonen and Murdock, 1993, 1995).

Other pupils do not know how to respond to praise because they have not received much praise in the past; e.g. because they have continually received low marks for their work or because they have been in the bottom stream. They have therefore learned to fail. Some of these pupils may want to

Task 3.2.9
The language of praise

Use this observation schedule (or develop a similar one of your own with categories for praise and negative comments given to an individual, a group or the whole class, for both academic work and behaviour).

Tick each time praise or negative comment is given in each category					
Praise to individual for academic work					
Praise to group for academic work					
Praise to whole class for academic work					
Praise to individual for behaviour					
Praise to group for behaviour					
Praise to whole class for behaviour					
Negative comment to individual for academic work					
Negative comment to group					
Negative comment to whole class for academic work					
Negative comment to individual for behaviour					
Negative comment to group for behaviour					
Negative comment to whole class for behaviour					

Observe a class taught by an experienced teacher. Sit in a place where you can hear everything that is said. Record the number of times the teacher gives praise and makes negative comments to individuals, groups and the whole class in relation to academic work and behaviour. Observe the same experienced teacher in another lesson. This time write down the different words, phrases and actions the teacher uses to give praise and negative comments in each of these categories and the number of times each is used.

Ask someone to conduct the same observations on your lessons. You might be surprised to find that you use a phrase such as 'good' or 'OK' very frequently in your teaching. Discuss the differences with your tutor and, if appropriate, develop strategies to help you improve the amount of praise you give and the range of words, phrases and actions you use to give praise. Record these strategies in your professional development portfolio and gradually try to incorporate them into your teaching.

attribute failure to not caring or not trying to succeed. One way they may do this is by not making an effort with work, another is misbehaving in the classroom.

Thus, pupils respond differently to praise. In the same class you may have some pupils working hard to receive praise from the teacher or a good mark on their homework, while others do not respond well to praise or are working hard at avoiding praise. You have to use your judgement when giving praise; e.g. if you praise a pupil who is misbehaving to try to encourage better behaviour, you may be seen to be rewarding bad behaviour, thereby motivating the pupil to continue to misbehave in order to get attention. If you are not immediately successful in your use of praise, do not give up using it, but consider whether you are giving it in the right way, e.g. would it be better to have a quiet word, rather than praise pupils out loud in front of their peers? As your professional knowledge and judgement develop you become able to determine how best to use praise appropriately to motivate pupils in your classes.

Punishment

As well as using praise, teachers also use punishment to try to change behaviour. However, reward, most frequently in the form of praise, is generally considered to be more effective because it increases appropriate behaviour, whereas punishment decreases inappropriate behaviour. If pupils are punished, they know what behaviour results in punishment and therefore what not to do, but may not know what behaviour avoids punishment.

However, there are times when punishment is needed. At such times, make sure that you use punishment to best effect; e.g. avoid punishing a whole class for the behaviour of one or a few pupil(s), always make it clear which pupil(s) are being punished for what behaviour, always give punishment fairly and consistently and in proportion to the offence. Also, make sure that the punishment does not include the behaviour that you want exhibited (e.g. do not punish a pupil by requiring them to run round the football pitch if that is what you want them to do). This sends mixed messages and is likely to put the pupil off that activity. Do not make idle threats to pupils, by threatening them with punishment that you cannot carry out. In order to increase appropriate behaviour, identify to the offender any positive aspects of the behaviour being punished and explain the appropriate behaviour. Unit 3.3 provides further information on managing behaviour and Unit 4.5 addresses some ethical and moral dimensions of behaviour.

Feedback

It may be that pupils who do not respond positively to praise are under-performing and have been doing so for a long time. You may be able to check whether they are under performing by comparing assessment data over a period of time to measure current achievement with past achievement. The achievement of all pupils, including under-performing pupils, can be enhanced by receiving feedback on their work. Feedback is a formative process which gives pupils information about how they are doing and whether they are on the right track when learning something. This motivates them to make an effort and to continue. A pupil is more likely to learn effectively or behave appropriately if feedback is used in conjunction with praise. A sequence in which feedback is sandwiched between praise, i.e. praise–constructive feedback–praise, is designed to provide encouragement and motivation, along with information to help the pupil improve the activity or behaviour. Giving praise first is designed to make pupils more receptive to the information and, afterwards, to have a positive approach to try again. Try combining feedback with praise in your teaching.

Feedback can be used effectively with the whole–part–whole teaching method described above. If you give feedback about how a pupil has done on each part, this part can be improved before going on to the next part. If you give feedback immediately (i.e. as an attempt is being finished or immediately after it has finished, but before another attempt is started), pupils can relate the feedback directly to the outcome of the activity. Thus, pupils are more likely to succeed if they take small steps and receive immediate feedback on each step. This success can, in turn, lead to increased motivation to continue the activity.

One problem with giving immediate feedback is how you can provide feedback to individual pupils in a class who are all doing the same activity at the same time. There are several methods which you can use to provide feedback to many pupils at the same time, e.g. getting pupils to work through examples in a book which has the answers in the back, setting criteria and letting pupils evaluate themselves against the criteria or having pupils assess one another against set criteria (see the reciprocal teaching style of Mosston and Ashworth (2002) in Unit 5.3 for more information about this and other teaching styles). If they have been properly prepared for it, pupils are generally sensible and constructive when given responsibility for giving feedback. However, it is not always appropriate to give immediate feedback.

Not all feedback comes from another person, e.g. the teacher or another pupil; feedback also comes from the activity itself. The feedback from an activity may be easier to identify for some activities than others; e.g. a pupil gets feedback about their success if an answer to a mathematics problem matches that given in the book or the wicket is knocked down when bowling in cricket. In other activities, right or wrong, success or failure, is not as clear-cut, e.g. there is often no right or wrong answer to an English essay. In the early stages of learning an activity pupils find it hard to use the feedback from the activity, e.g. they may notice that they were successful at the activity, but not be able to identify why. Normally, therefore, they need feedback from another person. This immediate, external feedback can be used to help pupils become more aware of what they are doing, how they are improving, why they were successful or not at the activity and therefore to make use of feedback from the activity. Later in the learning, e.g. when refining an activity, pupils should be able to benefit from feedback from the activity itself and therefore it is better to encourage this internal feedback by, for example, asking appropriate questions, e.g., how did that feel? In this situation the teacher should not give immediate feedback.

Finally, to be effective, feedback should be given about pupils' work or behaviour, not about the pupils themselves. It must convey to pupils that their work or behaviour is satisfactory or not, not that they are good (or bad) *per se*.

You need to observe pupils very carefully in order to spot small changes or improvements. This allows you to provide appropriate feedback. There is more information about observation techniques in Unit 2.1 and about formative assessment in Unit 6.1. Your developing professional knowledge and judgement will help you to know when and how to use feedback to best effect.

Task 3.2.10
Teaching styles

As an integral part of your lesson planning, select one activity in which pupils can observe each other and provide feedback. Devise a handout with the main points/criteria to be observed. Plan how you are going to introduce this activity into the lesson. Discuss the lesson plan with your tutor. Ask your tutor to observe the lesson. Discuss the effectiveness of the strategy afterwards, determining how you can improve its use. Also try to observe teachers who use this strategy regularly. Try the strategy at a later date in your school experience. Think of other ways in which you can get more feedback to more pupils when they are doing an activity. Include these in your lesson plans, as appropriate (see also teaching styles in Unit 5.3).

Motivating individuals

As the discussion above has highlighted, there is no one correct way to motivate pupils to learn. Different motivation techniques are appropriate and effective in different situations, e.g. pupils of different ages respond differently to different types of motivation, reward, punishment or feedback. Likewise, individual pupils respond differently. Further, any one pupil may respond to the same motivator differently at different times and in different situations.

Pupils need to feel that they are individuals, with their needs and interests taken into account, rather than just being a member of a group. Therefore pupils need to be given opportunities to take ownership of the tasks in which they are engaged. If pupils are not motivated, do not let them avoid doing the task, but try to find ways of motivating them; e.g. try to stimulate the motivation of a pupil bored by work that is being done, by relating it to something in which he or she is interested. You can motivate pupils most effectively by using motivation techniques appropriate for a particular pupil in a particular situation.

Thus, you need to try to find out what motivates each pupil in your class. Learning pupils' names quickly gives you a start in being able to motivate pupils effectively (see Unit 2.3 on taking responsibility for whole lessons, for strategies you can use to learn pupils' names). As you get to know pupils, you can identify what motivates them by finding out what activities they enjoy, what they choose to do and what they try to avoid, what types of reward they work for and to what they do not respond (e.g. by observation, talking to pupils, discussing a pupil with the form tutor or other teachers). The sooner you can relate to pupils individually, the sooner you can manage a class of individuals effectively. However, this does not occur at an early phase in your teaching (see phases of development in Unit 1.2). As a student teacher you are at a disadvantage here because you can only know what motivates each pupil and what rewards they are likely to respond to if you know your pupils well and know something about their needs and interests. As a student teacher, you do not usually spend enough time in one school to get to know the pupils well and therefore you can only try to motivate individual pupils by using your knowledge and understanding of pupils of that age.

SUMMARY AND KEY POINTS

This unit has identified some theoretical underpinnings, general principles and techniques for achieving an appropriate motivational climate in your lessons and therefore to increase pupils' motivation to learn. However, you need to be able to use these appropriately. For example, if you praise a group for working quietly while they are working you may negatively affect their work. It is better in this situation to let the group finish their work and then praise them. In addition, pupils are individuals and therefore respond differently to different forms of motivation, reward, punishment and feedback. Further, the same pupil responds differently at different times and in different situations. To motivate each pupil effectively therefore requires that you know your pupils so you can anticipate how they will respond. Motivation is supported by good formative assessment techniques (see Unit 6.1). Your developing professional knowledge and judgement enables you to combine theory with practice to motivate pupils effectively in your classes, which raises the standard of their work.

FURTHER READING

Chalmers, G. (ed.) (2001) *Reflections on Motivation*, London: Centre for Information on Language Teaching and Research (CILT). By blending theoretical and practical classroom applications, this book provides activities, and a rationale for their use, for motivating learners in modern foreign languages – although these could be used in other subjects.

Child, D. (2004) *Psychology and the Teacher*, 7th edn, London: Continuum. Chapter 8 provides in-depth consideration of motivation in education. It starts by considering three broad types of theories of motivation, then looks specifically at how some of the theories of motivation impact on you as a teacher and on your pupils.

Entwistle, N.J. (1993) *Styles of Learning and Teaching*, 3rd edn, London: David Fulton. Chapters 5 and 9 contain extended discussion about the relationship between personality and motivation and styles of learning.

Gilbert, I. (2002) *Essential Motivation in the Classroom*, London: RoutledgeFalmer. This book covers strategies, ideas and advice to help teachers understand how to motivate pupils and how pupils can motivate themselves.

Kyriacou, C. (1998) *Essential Teaching Skills*, 2nd edn, Cheltenham: Stanley Thornes. This book contains chapters on lesson management and classroom climate, both of which consider aspects of motivation, e.g. whether lesson management helps to maintain pupils' motivation and whether the opportunities for learning are challenging and offer realistic opportunities for success.

Unit 3.3

Behaviour for Learning

A Positive Approach to Managing Classroom Behaviour

Philip Garner

INTRODUCTION

This unit is designed to enable you to reflect on your knowledge and skills in classroom management and to support the enhancement of positive approaches to behaviour. The unit takes account of recent shifts in orientation – in both thinking and policy – regarding the management of pupil behaviour. In doing so, it signals a shift away from reactive approaches, characterized by a preoccupation with 'discipline' as something which the classroom teacher imposes on pupils. This is replaced by the notion of 'behaviour for learning', which is more consistent with an inclusive schooling approach. It emphasizes that subject teachers are integral to creating an appropriate climate in which all pupils can learn effectively. This approach encourages the establishment of positive relationships between pupils and their teacher: this is now seen as the basis of a preventative approach, in which pupils themselves have a key role to play.

This unit does not provide detailed accounts of 'what to do when' or commentaries on individual behavioural needs. There is now a copious literature, both theoretical and practical, relating to 'behaviour management' (see e.g. Ayers and Prytys, 2002; Clough *et al.*, 2004; McSherry, 2001). Rather, the unit is built around an examination of the behaviour for learning approach, and the way that it should be woven into your teaching. It encompasses some key, underpinning principles:

- it is a positive description, emphasizing teacher expectations – it does not focus on behaviours that the teacher does not want;
- it emphasizes the centrality of effective relationships;

- it puts a value on behaving in ways which enable and maximize pupil learning;
- it places an emphasis on setting targets that are reachable;
- it is relevant to all pupils, irrespective of their stage of learning.

The crucial factor in all these principles is the manner in which a positive climate for learning is established. This is one of the main things in the classroom setting which is directly under your control. You therefore need to select approaches which are more likely to increase the learning behaviour of pupils. Research evidence strongly suggests that these are characterized by the promotion of positive relationships and the development of an appropriate 'emotional climate' in the classroom (EPPI, 2004).

National policies regarding effective classroom management are fully embedded in and sympathetic to a behaviour for learning approach. The role of schools in supporting a movement towards greater social and educational inclusion implies that all teachers – not simply those charged with responsibility for special educational needs (SEN) – are required to have a stake-holding in this aspect of pupil development. And so it is vital that, as a student teacher, you both understand and practise the core principles of a behaviour for learning approach, outlined in this unit, as a routine aspect of your teaching.

OBJECTIVES

By the end of this unit you should be able to:

- recognize the changed policy context for promoting pupil learning in classrooms;
- interrogate a definition of the term 'unacceptable behaviour' and understand the significance of its underlying causes;
- recognize the importance of a behaviour for learning approach and its core principles;
- develop positive approaches to unacceptable behaviour which are based on relationships.

THE CHANGING POLICY CONTEXT

You should be developing an awareness that the last few years has seen an increasing emphasis upon inclusion (DFEE, 1999b; DfES 2001b, 2003). This has had an impact on how teachers now teach and how pupils learn. Educational inclusion is directed towards meeting the needs of all pupils in schools, irrespective of their level of achievement or the nature of their social behaviour. Because of this the range of learner needs you are likely to encounter, both as a student teacher and subsequently as a newly qualified teacher (NQT), is much broader than hitherto. It is therefore crucial that you recognize that the widely used term 'social, emotional and behavioural difficulties' (SEBD) is one which refers to an SEN as described in the *Code of Practice* (DFEE, 2000a). Amongst many other things, the code provides details of provision for pupils who experience SEBD.

It is now recognized that SEBD is a term which refers to a 'continuum' of behaviours, from relatively minor to serious mental illness (Department for Education (DfE), 1994b) – a theme which is developed later in this unit. The present discussion is concerned directly with those pupil behaviours which are viewed as 'low level' unacceptable behaviours. Nevertheless, you should recognize that it is possible that you may encounter pupils who present more challenging behaviours as a routine part of your teaching, including some who may abuse drugs and other substances; pupils with mental health needs and pupils who experience behaviour-related syndromes, such as Attention Deficit/Hyperactive Disorder (ADHD) or Autistic Spectrum Disorder (ASD). All of these behaviours, including those which are sometimes intense and very challenging to teachers, can be more effectively managed if you build proactive, positive strategies into your teaching.

Recent initiatives regarding behaviour and attendance emphasize a 'no blame' approach, built around the development of a positive classroom ethos. Emphasis is also placed on ways in which a repertoire of knowledge, skills and understanding in the field of classroom management can be developed. Moreover, current policy stresses the role played by 'lead behaviour' teachers and other professionals in providing practical support in positively managing behaviour and attendance. You should also be aware of the important work being undertaken in this area by teachers in other educational settings (pupil referral units (PRUs), special schools for pupils experiencing SEBD, teaching assistants and local education authority personnel who have a specific brief for work in SEBD) (Walker, 2004).

The Key Stage 3 (KS3) Strategy for Behaviour and Attendance (DfES, 2003d) is the key guidance document in England in this area, and one which is of paramount importance to you as you begin your career as a teacher. The strategy aims to help schools, and individual teachers, to promote positive behaviour and to support them in tackling issues of 'low-level' unacceptable behaviour. It also emphasizes that attendance is a matter of concern to teachers, in that pupils who choose not to attend a lesson, or school as a whole, are demonstrating important signals of disengagement from formal education (DfEE, 1998d).

The core objective of the behaviour and attendance strategy is to ensure that all schools have the skills and support they need to maintain creative and positive learning environments for all pupils. The strategy promotes the development of *positive* behaviour throughout the school and assists teachers to develop or refine proactive policies in behaviour and attendance. The emphasis, then, is upon establishing an appropriate climate in classrooms, based on the development of positive teacher–pupil relationships, which help to insulate pupils from those factors – discussed later in this unit – which might cause them to behave inappropriately and thereby promote active engagement in learning.

You should also recognize the policy emphasis being placed on tackling bullying in schools. Like other unacceptable behaviours bullying varies in its type and intensity (DfES, 2003c). From September 1999, head teachers of maintained schools in England have been under a duty to draw up measures to prevent all forms of bullying among pupils. A pack entitled *Bullying: Don't Suffer in Silence* (including a video aimed at pupils) (DfES, 2001a) details many aspects of bullying, including the importance of tackling homophobic abuse and bullying and bullying by mobile phone text messages.

Each of these initiatives have recognised that social, emotional and behavioural skills (SEBS) need to be developed by all pupils, and especially by those who, from time to time, present behaviour which is unacceptable or challenging. Pupils move up to KS3 from their primary schools having been exposed to some aspects of SEBS already, through the Primary National Strategy (DfES, 2003f). This states that, where pupils have good SEBS, they are able to:

- be effective and successful learners;
- make and sustain friendships;
- deal with and resolve conflict effectively and fairly;
- solve problems with others or by themselves;
- manage strong feelings such as frustration, anger and anxiety;
- recover from setbacks and persist in the face of difficulties;
- work and play co-operatively;
- compete fairly and win and lose with dignity and respect for competitors (p. 5).

It is clear that each of these represents a goal for teachers in secondary schools, by supporting their efforts to establish an appropriate classroom climate in which learning can take place. Establishing them as guiding principles as a student teacher pays rich dividends as you progress in your teaching career. Discuss with your tutor how you can do this.

Moreover, the concept of SEBS includes an awareness of 'emotional intelligence' (Goleman, 1996). Weare (2004) suggests that 'emotional intelligence' enables pupils to improve their behaviour. She suggests that 'generally a punitive approach tends to worsen or sometimes even create the very problems it is intended to eradicate … punishment alienates children from their teachers and does nothing to build up trust that is the bedrock of relationships' (p. 63).

Moreover, Weare reports several systematic reviews of research which looked at programmes designed to promote mental health in schools in the USA. For example, Wells *et al.* (2003) concluded that many programmes had clear and positive effects on behaviour. Successful programmes taught emotional and social competences and focused on the whole-school environment, not just on an individual behaviour.

Finally, attention has been directed towards the initial education and continuing professional development (CPD) of teachers. Feedback from new teachers indicates that 'behaviour issues' have not featured highly enough in initial teacher education (Teacher Training Agency (TTA), 2002). The TTA has supported the development of a website <http://www.behaviour4learning.ac.uk> which provides a valuable set of resources for student teachers and those in the first years of teaching to enhance understanding of behaviour management. In addition, resources have been allocated for

---

Task 3.3.1
What is behaviour for learning?

You are gathering new information almost daily which assists you, as a student teacher, to develop your professional skills. Respond to each of the questions listed under each of the three behaviour for learning relationships. Reflect on how your responses might compare with those of the pupils you come in contact with. Record your responses in your diary of reflective practice.

Relationship with self
Why do I want to teach?
How do I feel about my general progress so far?
How confident 'in myself' am I about the career I am embarking upon?
What factors motivate me to succeed?
What issues do I view as impacting negatively on my current situation?
Where do I want to be in 1/5/10 years' time?

Relationship with others
How well do I interact with other course members?
Do I empathize with the feelings/views of other student teachers?
How well do I communicate my own views and opinions?
What personal attributes enable me to work as part of a team or group?
Are there any social/interactional skills which I feel I need to enhance?
Do I feel comfortable in both 1:1 and group settings?

Relationship with the curriculum
Am I learning an appropriate range of skills to equip me for my job?
Am I sufficiently aware of the relevant theory underpinning my practice?
Am I coping with the range and amount of work?
Are there any aspects of my ITE course with which I feel less certain?

teachers' CPD. Opportunities are therefore available if you wish to further develop your expertise in the field of behaviour and attendance, or to establish a specific career pathway within it (DfES, 2004j).

WHAT IS UNACCEPTABLE BEHAVIOUR?

The policy approaches described above are concerned with developing new approaches in behaviour management. The term 'behaviour' in these contexts has traditionally been taken to mean 'unacceptable behaviour'. However, it is important to recognize that emerging policy places an equal emphasis upon developing appropriate, *positive* behaviour. Such an approach has significant benefits for all pupils (Harker and Redpath, 1999) and invites teachers to be clear about what behaviour they want pupils to engage in, and modelling this as part of their teaching.

The Elton Report (DES, 1989) refers to misbehaviour as behaviour which causes concern to teachers. The term is one which can variously be replaced by a range of other expressions that teachers use to describe unwanted, unacceptable behaviour by pupils – 'disruptive', 'challenging', 'anti-social', 'emotional and behavioural difficulties (EBD)', and even 'maladjusted'. Each is used by different teachers to describe different behaviour in different settings based on their own personal response to, and understanding of, the actions of pupils.

The term 'unacceptable behaviour', and its companion descriptors (including misbehaviour, challenging behaviour, disruptive behaviour and so on), is a catch-all expression for pupil behaviours that span an elongated continuum (DfE, 1994b). Thus, the so-called 'EBD continuum' can be interpreted as an extended one, ranging from behaviour which is 'low level' at one end (talking out of turn, distracting others, occasionally arriving late in class) to more serious, sometimes 'acting out' behaviour at the other (such as non-attendance, verbal or physical aggression, wilful disobedience, bullying and so on). Indeed, one official definition (DfE, 1994b) recognizes this confusion by describing 'EBD' as all those behaviours which comprise a continuum from 'normal though unacceptable' through to mental illness. A further complication is that the term has recently been expanded to become 'SEBD', with the incorporation of social difficulties into the spectrum (DfES, 2001b).

Elsewhere, the *Code of Practice* (DfE, 1994a) defines 'children and young people who demonstrate features of emotional and behavioural difficulties' as those who are 'withdrawn and isolated, disruptive and disturbing, hyperactive and lacking concentration'. The definition also includes those who display 'immature social skills and those who present challenging behaviours arising from other complex special needs'.

A major difficulty in defining what inappropriate behaviour actually constitutes is that it varies according to the perception, tolerance threshold, experience and management approach of individual teachers. Thus, what might be an unacceptable behaviour in your own classroom may be viewed in another context, or by another (student) teacher, as quite normal. Alternatively, what you accept as normal may be unacceptable in another context or by another (student) teacher. You can infer that such a situation can only lead to confusion in the mind of pupils, and to potential tension between individual teachers in a school or between a student teacher and tutor or other experienced teacher. So it is important to recognize that: (a) pupil behaviour needs to be described explicitly in terms of observable 'actions'; and (b) responses to it have to take full regard of a school's policy concerning behaviour.

In respect of the former, the Qualifications and Curriculum Authority (QCA, 2001b) identified 15 behaviours by which a pupil's emotional and behavioural development might be defined and assessed. These were divided into 'learning behaviours', 'conduct behaviours' and 'emotional behaviours'. Each of these groupings is subdivided into sets of criteria, depicting desirable and undesirable behaviours

Task 3.3.2
School policy on pupil behaviour

Read your school experience school's policy on behaviour. Discuss with another student teacher in a different school similarities and differences in the policies.

(see Figure 3.3.1). DfES (2003d) has sought to support schools to move further towards a common understanding of what comprises appropriate and inappropriate behaviour. The emphasis is placed on a shared ethos and understanding, based on the development of a whole school approach to behaviour.

The task of identifying or defining 'unacceptable behaviour' is an important one if you are going to develop strategies to deal with it in ways which promote learning. There is a need, at the outset, to describe exactly what any unwanted behaviour actually comprises in order that a precise and objective description of what has occurred can be given to others; importantly, the description needs to be of the behaviour itself, not the pupil. A focus on the latter can result in unwarranted negative labelling of the pupil.

Task 3.3.3
What is unacceptable behaviour?

It is important that you arrive at a personal definition of what comprises unacceptable behaviour. Divide a blank sheet of paper into three. Head the left-hand section 'Totally unacceptable' and the right-hand section 'Acceptable'. The middle section is reserved for 'Acceptable in certain circumstances'. Now examine your own classroom teaching, and complete each section. Remember, 'behaviour' is as much about positive, learning behaviour as it concerns those pupil actions which you regard as unacceptable or challenging. Reflect on your responses and discuss with your tutor and record in your diary of reflective practice. You might wish – should the opportunity arise, to undertake this exercise with your pupils, in order to gather their thoughts. Comparing your list to theirs is likely to prove very revealing!

SCOPING THE CAUSAL FACTORS

You should never underplay the importance of causal factors. As Ayers and Prytys (2002: 38) note, 'The way in which behaviour is conceptualised will determine the treatment of emotional and behavioural problems'. There are a number of factors that assist in explaining disaffection and disengagement amongst some pupils. Understanding and recognizing these is important, in that they can give clues as to the teacher action(s) most likely to result in identifying successful strategies. But it is also important that you realize that (a) causal factors are often multivariate and overlapping and (b) the attribution of a 'cause' can frequently result in the acquisition of a negative label by the pupil. To supplement the brief outline of causal factors below, you can find a more exhaustive coverage in a variety of other sources (e.g. Clough *et al.*, 2004; McNamara and Moreton, 1997).

Figure 3.3.1 Desirable and undesirable behaviour (adapted from QCA, 2001b)

DESIRABLE BEHAVIOUR	UNDESIRABLE BEHAVIOUR
L1. Attentive/Interested in Schoolwork	
• attentive to teacher, not easily distracted • interest in most schoolwork • starts promptly on set tasks / motivated • seems to enjoy school	• verbal off-task behaviours • does not finish work / gives up easily • constantly needs reminders • short attention span • negative approach to school
L2.Good Learning Organisation	
• competent in individual learning • tidy work at reasonable pace • can organise learning tasks	• forgetful, copies or rushes work • inaccurate, messy and slow work • fails to meet deadlines, not prepared
L3. Effective communicator	
• good communication skills (peers/adults) • knows when it's appropriate to speak • uses non-verbal signals and voice range • communicates in 1:1 or group settings	• poor communication skills • inappropriate timing of communication • constantly talks • lack of use of non-verbal skills
L4. Works efficiently in a group	
• works collaboratively • turn-takes in communication/listens • takes responsibility within a group	• refuses to share • does not take turns
L5. Seeks help where necessary	
• seeks attention from teacher when required • works independently or in groups when not requiring help	• constantly seeking assistance • makes excessive and inappropriate demands • does not ask 'finding out' questions

C6. Behaves respectfully towards staff	
• co-operative and compliant • responds positively to instruction • does not aim verbal aggression at teacher • interacts politely with teacher • does not deliberately try to annoy or answer the teacher rudely	• responds negatively to instruction • talks back impertinently to teacher • aims verbal aggression, swears at teacher • deliberately interrupts to annoy
C7. Shows respect to other pupils	
• uses appropriate language; does not swear • treats others as equals • does not dominate, bully or intimidate	• verbal violence at other pupils • scornful, use of social aggression (e.g. 'pushing in') • teases and bullies • inappropriate sexual behaviour
C8. Seeks attention appropriately	
• does not attract inappropriate attention • does not play the fool or show off • no attention-seeking behaviour • does not verbally disrupt • does not physically disrupt	• hums, fidgets, disturbs others • throws things, climbs on things • calls out, eats, runs around the class • shouts and otherwise attention seeks • does dangerous things without thought
C9. Physically peaceable	
• does not show physical aggression • does not pick on others • is not cruel or spiteful • avoids getting into fights with others • does not have temper tantrums	• fights, aims physical violence at others • loses temper, throws things • bullies and intimidates physically • cruel / spiteful
C10. Respects property	
• takes care of own and others property • does not engage in vandalism • does not steal	• poor respect for property • destroys own or other's things • steals things

Figure 3.3.1 (continued)

DESIRABLE BEHAVIOUR	UNDESIRABLE BEHAVIOUR
E11. Has empathy	
• is tolerant and considerate • tries to identify with feelings of others • tries to offer comfort • is not emotionally detached • does not laugh when others are upset	• intolerant • emotionally detached • selfish • no awareness of feelings of others
E12. Is socially aware	
• understands social interactions of self and peers • appropriate verbal/non-verbal contacts • not socially isolated • has peer-group friends; not a loner • doesn't frequently daydream • actively involved in classroom activity • not aloof, passive or withdrawn	• inactive, daydreams, stares into space • withdrawn or unresponsive • does not participate in class activity • few friends • not accepted or well-liked • shows bizarre behaviour • stares blankly, listless
E13. Is happy	
• smiles and laughs appropriately • should be able to have fun • generally cheerful; seldom upset • not discontented, sulky, morose	• depressed, unhappy or discontented • prone to emotional upset, tearful • infers suicide • serious, sad, self-harming
E14. Is confident	
• not anxious • unafraid to try new things • not self-conscious, doesn't feel inferior • willing to read aloud, answer questions in class • participates in group discussion	• anxious, tense, tearful • reticent, fears failure, feels inferior • lacks self-esteem, cautious, shy • does not take initiative
E15. Emotionally stable/self-controlled	
• no mood swings • good emotional resilience, recovers quickly from upset • manages own feelings • not easily flustered or frustrated • delays gratification	• inappropriate emotional reactions • does not recover quickly from upsets • does not express feelings • frequent mood changes; irritable • over-reacts; does not accept punishment or praise • does not delay gratification

Key: L = learning behaviour; C = conduct/behaviour; E = emotional behaviour

Individual issues

- A pupil believes that the work is not within their grasp and as a result feels embarrassed and alienated and lacks self-esteem as a learner.
- A pupil may well experience learning difficulties.
- A pupil may have mental health, stress and possible drug misuse issues, all of which are important factors explaining under-achievement and inappropriate behaviour in adolescence.

Cultural issues

- Adolescence can be a period of rebellion or resistance for many young people.
- Possible tension between societal expectation and the beliefs and opinions of the pupil.
- Group/peer pressure can result in various forms of alienation to school.
- Negative experience of schooling by parents, siblings or other family members.

Curriculum relevance – linked to both individual and cultural issues

- The curriculum may be seen by a pupil to be inaccessible and irrelevant.
- The school may give academic excellence more value than vocational qualifications or curriculum options.

School ethos and relationships

- Some schools can be 'deviance provocative' – their organizational structures and procedures are viewed by pupils as oppressive and negative.
- Some schools are less inclusive, both academically and socially to pupils who behave 'differently'.

External barriers to participation and learning

- Family breakdown or illness usually impacts negatively on a pupil's mental health – and often on their sense of priority.
- Poverty and hardship can mean that a pupil's physiological needs are not met – such pupils may be tired, hungry and consequently easily distracted (see also Maslow (1970) in Unit 3.2).
- Sibling responsibilities may mean that some pupils arrive late in your lesson – or not at all.

One aspect of causality which is directly related to behaviour for learning is the recognition of what Bronfenbrenner (1979) called an 'ecosystemic' theory of relationships. In the case of a pupil who is consistently behaving inappropriately, it could be theorized that there has been a breakdown in one (or more) of three areas:

- the pupil's relationship with himself;
- the pupil's relationship with others;
- the pupil's relationship with the learning he is undertaking.

Given that all behaviour occurs within the over-arching context of these relationships, they assume the characteristic of an 'ecosystemic' event, in which all aspects of these relationships need to be taken into account when planning a strategy to ameliorate unacceptable behaviour. The emphasis upon positive relationships is an integral component of a behaviour for learning approach. Establishing good relationships with individual pupils as well as whole classes, from your first encounter with a group of pupils, enables you to establish a climate in which learning can flourish.

Task 3.3.4
Linking causes to possible teaching strategies

Consider a pupil who is in one of the classes you have been allocated during your school experience and who sometimes presents what you regard to be unacceptable behaviour. Write a brief description of each of the behaviours, making sure that the language you use is clear and describes clearly observable pupil actions. Taking each behaviour in turn, and referring to the general set of causal factors identified above, assess which issues you feel impact on the pupil's behaviour. Consider how amenable to change are each of the causal factors you have identified. Finally, reflect on how your interpretation of 'cause' informs the way in which you have chosen to address the behaviour(s) shown.

Discuss your responses with your tutor and record in your diary of reflective practice.

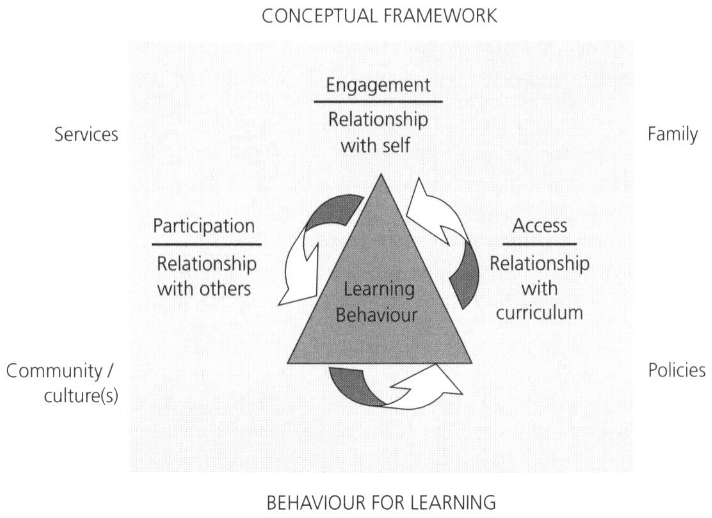

CONCEPTUAL FRAMEWORK

BEHAVIOUR FOR LEARNING

Figure 3.3.2   The behaviour for learning model (After Tod)

KEY ASPECTS OF BEHAVIOUR FOR LEARNING

A behaviour for learning approach accepts that most SEBS are learned. As a theoretical approach (see Figure 3.3.2) it can best be conceptualized as a set of three relationships experienced by pupils. These relate to their relationships:

- with themselves (how they feel about themselves, their self-confidence as a learner and their self-esteem);
- with others (how they interact socially and academically with all others in their class and school);
- with the curriculum (how accessible they feel a lesson is, how best they think they learn).

Each of these relationships is important in developing a positive learning environment in the classroom and you are at the very heart of orchestrating these relationships. In doing this you become increasingly aware that some pupils have relatively advanced skills when they arrive at school; others need support and direct teaching of specific skills they have not yet learned. So your task is to focus on helping to develop appropriate skills which enable each pupil to learn within a variety of learning contexts. This can be in whole class or small group situations in the classroom and elsewhere in the school. Some basic principles inform the way in which this can be done:

- Behaviour for learning is a positive description. It tells pupils what you want them to do and why this helps them to learn – rather than focusing on behaviours that you do not want in your classroom.
- It requires that you place value on (and praise appropriately) pupil behaviour which enables and maximizes learning.
- Effective behaviour for learning strategies range from high level listening or collaborative learning skills to remaining seated for two minutes. The emphasis is upon setting targets that are reachable by pupils.

The crucial factor in a behaviour for learning approach, as implied earlier, is the manner in which you establish a positive climate for learning in your classroom. Evidence strongly suggests that the most successful strategies are those which incorporate the promotion of positive relationships (Burnett, 2002). With these broad principles in mind, four practical features of this approach, each of which is central to a behaviour for learning orientation are explored below.

Leadership in the classroom

Establishing an appropriate climate for learning is your main responsibility. Most pupils come to your classroom wanting to learn, although there are times when some are either unable or unwilling to learn on account of some of the factors described above. So, you need to develop certain classroom leadership skills which contribute to your being able to forge positive relationships with pupils, and thus establish an ethos which allows pupils to demonstrate positive behaviour.

First, and in more general terms, you have to take the 'lead' in promoting three broad elements which help to define the ethos of your classroom. These are:

- motivation – you need to provide time at the start of each lesson to tell pupils what they are learning and why. Pupils need to be involved at every stage in assessing whether these learning intentions have been met (Unit 3.2 looks at motivation in more depth);
- emotional well-being – to help reduce pupil anxiety you should share the lesson structure with pupils at the start, so they know what is going to happen during the lesson;
- expectations – you need to give time at the start of the lesson and before each new activity to make clear what behaviours are needed for this piece of learning to be successful.

These three underpinning principles are embedded in more specific teacher actions, which allow you to demonstrate your role as the 'classroom leader' to your pupils. These include:

- good communication between yourself and your pupils;
- secure subject knowledge;
- providing lively, well paced lessons;
- understanding and meeting the learning needs of all pupils in your class;
- acting on your reflections and evaluations of previous lessons (feedback loop) (see also Unit 2.1);
- demonstrating confidence and direction in managing pupils.

Some of these skills are inevitably developed over several years' experience – therefore it is unlikely, as a student teacher, that everything 'clicks' straight away. Indeed, a deepening understanding of their relevance to pupil learning is part of your CPD on behaviour and attendance issues as your career develops.

Building positive relationships in classrooms

A behaviour for learning approach places emphasis on the relationships you form with your pupils. Moreover, a positive teacher–pupil relationship is a significant factor in encouraging attendance. Ineffective interventions are usually the product of unsatisfactory relationships with individual pupils. These interventions, even though they are ultimately unsuccessful, take up valuable teaching time and impact negatively on the learning of an individual pupil, the rest of the class, and also on your own confidence. Most interventions should take the form of positive actions that fit somewhere on a continuum from positive reinforcement through to positive correction. The actions you select should be those that enable learning to continue. They usually include eye contact, use of pupil name, description of the appropriate behaviour you would like to see, praise and affirmation. For example:

- modelling appropriate behaviour;
- positive reinforcement and the use of praise;
- positive correction;
- consistent and firm application of rules;
- use of verbal and non-verbal communication;
- listening to pupils and respecting their opinions;
- remaining vigilant (pre-empting unacceptable behaviour);
- dealing positively with lateness and non-attendance.

By assimilating these characteristics into your professional repertoire you are more likely to forge meaningful and positive relationships with your pupils. In sum, effective relationships mean that there is 'common ground' between pupil and teacher. This is as vital in securing appropriate conditions for learning as it is for managing those behavioural issues which may be potentially problematic.

Structuring the lesson for positive behaviour and attendance

The design of effective lessons is fundamental to high-quality teaching and learning. This in turn promotes and supports behaviour for learning in the classroom. At its heart is effective lesson design irrespective of the level of achievement of the learner, or the subject or skill being learned. Your teaching should be characterized by:

- focus and structure so that pupils are clear about what is to be learned and how it fits with what they know already;
- actively engaging pupils in their learning so that they make their own meaning from it;
- developing pupils' learning skills systematically so that their learning becomes increasingly independent;
- using assessment for learning to help pupils reflect on what they already know, reinforce the learning being developed and set targets for the future (Units 6.1 and 6.2 look at assessment);
- having high expectations of the effort that pupils should make and what they can achieve (see also Unit 3.2);
- motivating pupils by well-paced lessons, using stimulating activities matched to a range of learning styles which encourage attendance;
- creating an environment that promotes learning in a settled and purposeful atmosphere.

You can further reinforce a behaviour for learning approach by building individual teaching sequences within an overall lesson. The lesson (or a sequence of lessons) needs first of all to be located, in the mind of the pupil, in the context of (a) a scheme of work, (b) pupils' prior knowledge, and (c) their preferred learning styles. It also stresses the importance of identifying clear learning outcome(s) for, and making them explicit to, pupils. It is helpful, then, to structure lessons as a series of 'episodes' by separating pupil learning into distinct stages or steps and then planning how each step should be taught. You can secure overall coherence by providing (a) a stimulating start to the lesson, (b) transition 'signposts' between each lesson episode which reviews pupil learning so far and launches the next episode, and (c) a final plenary session that reviews learning. (Lesson planning is covered in Unit 2.1.)

Rights, responsibilities, routines and rules

A framework for promoting positive classroom behaviours is commonly constructed around rights, routines, rules and responsibilities – the 4Rs (Hook and Vass, 2000). You should recognize that such a focus operates best within an overall context of a fifth, over-arching 'R' of relationships, which are crucial to the successful implementation of any activity in the classroom. Of course, as a student teacher, you need to be very sensitive to the existing protocols of any class you take – these have been established over a longer period of time by the permanent class teacher. But you can begin by being conscious of how each of these 'Rs' can have a positive impact on your teaching.

Rights and responsibilities

These are inextricably linked. They refer to both teacher and pupils and are the basis on which classroom relationships, teaching and learning are built.

- Teacher's responsibilities – you must seek to enable all pupils to learn, to seek out and celebrate improvements in learning, to treat pupils with respect and to create a positive classroom environment in which pupils feel safe and able to learn.
- Teacher's rights – you must be allowed to teach with a minimum of hindrance, to feel safe, to be supported by colleagues and to be listened to.
- Pupils' responsibilities – pupils must be willing to learn, to allow others to learn, to co-operate with teaching and other staff and peers and to do their best at all times.
- Pupils' rights – pupils should be treated with respect, be safe, be able to learn and be listened to.

Rules

These are the mechanisms by which rights and responsibilities are translated into adult and pupil behaviours. They are best constructed collaboratively, so that the views of all pupils are taken into account.

Routines

These are the structures which underpin the rules and reinforce the smooth running of the classroom. The more habitual the routines become the more likely they are to be used. Pupils who behave inappropriately often do so because they are unsure of what is happening in the classroom at a given time.

Choices

Pupils should be encouraged to make choices about their behaviour and thus take responsibility for their own actions. Choice is guided by their responsibilities and leads to positive or negative consequences according to the choice made by the pupil.

Consequences

Pupils know the consequences of sensible or inadvisable choices. Responsible choices lead to positive consequences; conversely, a choice to behave inappropriately leads to a known negative consequence.

For further information about each of these elements see DfES (2003d).

Task 3.3.5
Monitoring your use of praise and encouragement in the classroom

A useful starting point to promote the notion of positive approaches to behaviour is to examine the ways in which you provide encouragement, positive feedback and praise to your pupils. You can assess this by developing a 'log of praise and encouragement' to use as a tool for measuring these positive interactions.

Add to the list of positive pupil behaviours identified below which you can use to give praise. Underneath each one note the words or actions you might use to convey to the pupil that your recognition carries value and meaning.

1. Queuing sensibly and quietly to enter the classroom

    ....

2. Allowing another pupil to go first

    ....

3. Lending an item of equipment to a pupil

    ....

4. Putting waste paper in the bin

    ....

5. ....

6. ....

Identify places where you might have used each of these behaviours, then ask your tutor or another student teacher to observe which of these behaviours you use to promote positive pupil behaviour in one of your classes. Discuss your initial perceptions and the use of each behaviour after the lesson and make changes as needed.

SUMMARY

This unit has focused on the current policy emphasis on positive approaches to managing behaviour. More specifically, it has afforded you the opportunity to examine some individual elements which should give you a more complete understanding of:

*   the changed national policy context for promoting pupil learning in classrooms;
*   the difficulties in arriving at a definition of the term 'unacceptable behaviour';
*   some of the key underlying causes of a pupil's unacceptable behaviour;
*   the characteristics of a behaviour for learning approach and an overview of its core principles;
*   a consideration of a number of practical skills which you can develop or refine, in order to promote pupil learning.

At the heart of this approach is a recognition that old-fashioned notions of authoritarian discipline are no longer – if ever they were – viable or efficacious. This way of working tends to be unsatisfactory for both pupil and teacher. The former is imbued with a greater sense of resistance and alienation, while the latter spends an increasing amount of time controlling particular individuals in the class rather than providing learning opportunities.

In choosing to place emphasis on positive approaches to managing behaviour you need to place a premium on your relationships with pupils. It is axiomatic, such is the centrality of relationship building, that you need to recognize that positive relationships do not happen by chance. Indeed, the opposite is the case: you need to plan for positivity in your interactions with pupils, while at the same time invoking the '4Rs rule' to orchestrate your strategy. Above all, you need to bear two things in mind. First, pupils expect you to assume a leadership role in making 'good behaviour' happen in your classroom. And, secondly, 'behaviour', by its very nature, is complex and ever changing. Establishing a broad set of personal principles is vital groundwork for your CPD.

FURTHER READING

Clough, P., Garner, P., Pardeck, T. and Yuen, F. (eds) (2004) *The Handbook of Emotional and Behavioural Difficulties*, London: Sage. This book provides a systematic, comprehensive and up-to-date overview of a series of themes which underpin a study of 'emotional and behavioural difficulties'. It is divided into four sections, dealing with (i) contexts of problem behaviour, (ii) roots and causes, (iii) strategies and interventions, and (iv) points of tension and development. A range of well-known authors contribute to this resource, providing informative and challenging perspectives and commentaries. Moreover, the international authorship reveals that 'unacceptable behaviour' is not simply an issue that is encountered in a single school or individual country. It has a global dimension, from which all teachers can learn.

Weare, K. (2004) *Developing the Emotionally Literate School*, London: Paul Chapman Publishing. This is a practical and up-to-date account of how schools can use emotional literacy to increase learning and improve relationships between teachers and pupils. The term 'emotional literacy' is discussed in great detail, and its significance to teachers is made clear. It outlines the research base on which the efficacy of 'emotional literacy' is premised, and emphasizes that the concept is as applicable to teachers as it is to pupils.

Useful websites

<http://www.behaviour4learning.ac.uk> This website is supported by both the TTA and the DfES. It functions as a 'collecting point' for information on aspects of promoting a behaviour for learning approach. It contains information to enable you to enhance your understanding of pupil behaviour and to refine approaches which enable them to learn. The site relates much of its resources (which include case-studies, research papers, video extracts and subject-specific materials) to both the standards for qualifying to teach and for induction. From the B4L site you can link to many additional behaviour-related websites, including the DfES's Behaviour and Attendance site. Registration is free, though not compulsory.

4 Pupil Differences

INTRODUCTION

It is a truism to say that each pupil in your class is different but from time to time it is important to remind ourselves of this fact. A class of same-age pupils is likely to contain individuals at different stages of development arising from differences in physical and mental development or cultural experiences, or some combination of all three. Significant differences arise in the achievements of members of a class of pupils, especially in a mixed ability class. Other differences arise from the cultural, religious and economic backgrounds of your pupils which may strongly affect their response to schooling. Some pupils respond to academic challenge while others see no point in such demands. Some pupils are gifted and need special attention, as do many pupils with learning or behavioural difficulties. Some pupils are at ease with adults while others find the experience less comfortable.

This chapter, comprising six units, invites you to consider several aspects of the background and development of your pupils. In practice the features discussed interact, giving rise to the complex and varied behaviours which characterize human beings. For ease of discussion, some factors are discussed separately; we hope this approach helps you subsequently better to integrate your understandings of pupils and their learning and develop better relationships with your pupils.

One response of schools in recent years has been to acknowledge the differences between pupils in their response to school subjects and their associated achievements. Thus Unit 4.1 addresses ways n which pupils are grouped by schools for teaching and learning in the context of differentiation and progression. Central to successful differentiation is the identification of pupil needs; thus case studies invite you to inquire more deeply into the background and response of individual pupils and plan differentiated work. You may want to return to this unit after dipping into other units.

Unit 4.2, on growth, development and diet, focuses on the physical characteristics of pupils as they develop and mature in adolescence and young adulthood and draws attention to the range of 'what is normal'. We address issues of diet and health of young people, the ways in which schools contribute to healthy eating, both academically and socially.

Unit 4.3 addresses the issue of cognition and cognitive development. Logical reasoning is one important aspect of cognitive development, along with others such as problem solving, developing expertise and creative thinking. The notion of intelligence is introduced, including the current theory of 'multiple intelligences'. Some examples of teaching material from secondary school curricula are discussed in terms of their cognitive demand on pupils. You are invited to look specifically at the differences in performance between pupils of different ages on similar tasks. Through set tasks there are opportunities for you to work with pupils and see for yourself how pupils respond to different demands; we address, too, the importance of teaching pupils how to learn and think about their own learning.

In Unit 4.4, on responding to diversity, the cultural background of pupils is considered, including class, gender and ethnicity. The focus here is to highlight some differences in performance of different groups of pupils from different backgrounds, using research evidence, and to speculate on the causes of those differences. Such differences in performance are linked to the implementation of equal opportunities policies in schools and issues of access to the curriculum and career opportunities.

Unit 4.5, moral development and values, links the development of values in young people in the context of the current curriculum structure for schools in England, together with more recent curriculum changes including the subject of citizenship and the growing importance of PSHE programmes. The emphasis lies in the way schools contribute to values education through both the overt and hidden curriculum. While not stressing differences between pupils, the focus of the chapter does acknowledge the range of values and beliefs in our society and how schools not only have to respond to such differences but also to contribute to the spiritual, moral, cultural development of pupils as well as their mental and physical development.

Inclusion and special needs education is the focus of Unit 4.6 and addresses the ways in which those pupils with special physical, behavioural and learning needs may be supported by the 2001 *Code of practice on the Identification and Assessment of Special Educational Needs* for schools in England. The unit draws attention to significant changes in recent years in the way in which pupils with SEN are supported and emphasizes the importance of the classroom teacher in the identification of need and response to need. There is a brief survey of some physical disabilities, mental impairment and behavioural difficulties, pointing to sources of support and guidance, including the support of other professionals.

Unit 4.1

Meeting Individual Differences

Pupil Grouping, Progression and Differentiation

Hilary Lowe

INTRODUCTION

The National Curriculum for England 2000 requires teachers to have due regard to three principles for planning and teaching:

- setting suitable learning challenges;
- responding to pupils' diverse learning needs;
- overcoming potential barriers to learning.

Teachers in training and newly qualified teachers (NQTs) are also set standards with expectations that all beginner teachers must demonstrate their understanding of the principles of inclusion and that they should ensure effective teaching of all pupils through matching the approaches used to the pupils being taught.

There is an increasing acknowledgement of the need for a comprehensive and multi-faceted approach to how we meet pupils' diverse learning needs. This is based on a more complex and inclusive view of ability, of how children learn, of the factors which affect learning and the effectiveness of particular teaching approaches. In the last decade, too, there has been a major shift in expectations about what all pupils can and should achieve.

In this unit we consider how different grouping arrangements have been used and are currently used as a means of coping with differences in pupils' performance. We also consider how progression for all pupils can be achieved through teaching and learning approaches which ensure that account is taken of a range of learning needs. Strategies for developing differentiated units of work are provided, building on the subject specialist focus of the reader. See also Units 2.2 and 3.2.

OBJECTIVES

By the end of this unit you should be able to:

- understand the links between progression, differentiation and pupil grouping;
- evaluate the implications of learning in a range of pupil grouping arrangements;
- discuss definitions of differentiation and their relationship to effective teaching;
- discuss teaching methods which allow for differentiation;
- apply principles of differentiated approaches to learning in lesson planning;
- relate your progress in planning and teaching for differentiation to the competences/standards expected of a newly qualified teacher.

GROUPING PUPILS ACROSS THE SCHOOL

Schools have traditionally sought to cope with differences in pupil performance either through setting, banding and streaming or by setting work at appropriate levels for pupils in *wide*, or *mixed*, *ability* classes. *Streaming* places the best performers in one class for all subjects, the least able performers in the another class, with graded classes in between. *Banding* places pupils in broad performance groups for all subjects and tries to avoid producing classes comprising only pupils showing low attainment or unwillingness to learn. *Setting* describes the allocation of pupils to classes by attainment in each subject, i.e. streaming or banding for each subject. Broad streaming and banding support a notion of a general intelligence whereas setting acknowledges that pupil aptitude and attainment may be different across subjects and contexts. The increased focus currently on the needs of more able or gifted and talented learners has led to renewed interest at a policy and school level in *acceleration* or *fast-tracking*. By this is meant moving a pupil or groups of pupils into a class with an older age group for some or all subjects.

Prior to the Education Act (ERA) of 1988, many state schools grouped their pupils in wide ability classes for teaching purposes. The backgrounds, aptitudes and abilities of pupils, coupled with differences in interest and motivation, can lead to large differences in achievement between pupils which, by age 11, are substantial and widen as pupils grow older. Recognizing these differences without prematurely labelling pupils as successes or failures was regarded as an essential prerequisite for organizing the teaching of secondary pupils. The moves towards de-streaming were most strongly evident in the 1960s, following the Plowden Report (DES, 1967) into primary schooling, some of the recommendations of which spilled over into secondary schooling. The abandonment of selection in schools by the introduction of comprehensive schooling in the 1950s and 1960s caused mixed ability grouping to be seen as the logical way to group pupils in secondary school, thus avoiding selection under one roof and the labelling which selection implied.

There was strong opposition to mixed ability grouping, especially from parents and teachers of able pupils. However, evidence accumulated in the 1970s suggested that differences in the academic performance of pupils in mixed ability groups, compared with those in other groupings, could not be attributed solely to the differences in grouping, especially given the other variables affecting pupil performance (HMI, 1978; Newbold 1977). The research carried out over many years into grouping pupils by ability has been subject to a number of reviews (e.g. Hallam and Toutounji, 1996; Harlen and Malcolm, 1997).

Whilst these reviews bemoan the methodological shortcomings of much of the research into ability grouping and uncertainty concerning the factors affecting the academic performance of pupils, there was evidence that all pupils gained socially from working in wide ability groups. Such groupings allowed pupils from a variety of backgrounds, as well as abilities, to work together, strengthening social cohesion. These arguments were strongly supported in inner-city environments where selection processes often led to separation of pupils along class and ethnic dimensions. Other studies however (Harlen, 1997) showed that teachers with substantial experience of teaching mixed ability groups frequently used whole class methods inappropriate to mixed ability groupings and that teachers retained largely fixed views of ability and intelligence.

A comparative study of pupils in two comprehensive schools has rigorously documented their differences in knowledge and understanding of mathematics and their motivation and attitude towards the subject (Boaler, 1997). The 'progressive' school, which offered more open-ended project work, linked mathematics to the lives of the pupils and encouraged pupils to identify problems in which they were interested, achieved outcomes as good as, and in many cases better than, the school which adopted 'traditional' rule learning and application as the main teaching strategy. The 'progressive' mathematics department did not group pupils in streamed sets, unlike the department working on 'traditional' lines (Boaler, 1997: Ch. 10). There was evidence that in the traditional teaching structure able pupils were anxious, especially those pupils in the top set, and under-performed in the GCSE examination. Many girls were disadvantaged by the traditional teaching approach of this school (Boaler, 1997: Ch. 9). The author points out that the current dismay in government circles at the low standard of mathematics performance by English pupils in international comparative studies has occurred when most mathematics teaching in classrooms is of the 'traditional' type (citing inspection reports as evidence) (OFSTED, 1994).

Harlen (1997) states that the case for ability grouping in mathematics may be stronger given that its hierarchical structure requires different inputs for pupils of different abilities and that the most reliable research studies show all pupils benefiting from within-class ability grouping in mathematics. Other researchers (Hallam and Toutounji, 1996) have found some evidence in favour of grouping by ability for subjects where learning is dependent on a more linear acquisition of skills and knowledge, e.g. in modern languages and science. The same authors suggest that attention should be given to semi-structured forms of pupil grouping, responding to the different strengths and interests of pupils in various areas of the curriculum; and to move away from the notion of one-dimensional and fixed ability. The use of differentiated materials focused on individualized instruction is also suggested as a way forward.

A focus on the needs of more able pupils has led to renewed debates about forms of acceleration and fast-tracking as well as about the benefits of ability grouping for such pupils. Whilst the effects of acceleration is one of the most researched aspects of educational intervention with 'gifted' pupils (for further reading on this see Brody, 2004), research into the effects of ability grouping is based on relatively few studies. Although much evidence is not clear-cut and finds modest effects, a meta-analysis by Rogers (1991) found both gains academically and socially for very able learners and positive attitudes towards subject matters for all learners where they were in ability group settings. Rogers advocates flexibility in grouping with opportunities for very able pupils to work with their peers, but states that ability grouping without differentiation has little or no effect.

Since the introduction of the Education Reform Act (ERA 1988) wide ability grouping has been in retreat. Indeed, government advice from both left and right of the political spectrum has advocated a return to grouping by ability, together with increased whole class teaching. The White Paper 'Excellence in Schools' states that mixed ability grouping has not proved capable of playing to the strengths of every pupil (DfEE, 1997b: 38, para. 3) and that, by setting, advantage can be taken of whole class teaching to maintain pace and challenge of lessons. However, across school attainment data does not support the contention that setting alone contributes to success or that setting improves the standards of those not achieving adequately.

It is said to be less demanding on teachers to prepare lessons for setted groups. However, 'top sets' may contain not only very able pupils, who may be unchallenged by the work expected of the majority, but may also contain a wide spread of ability, given that top sets are often large groups. Organizing learning and teaching to maximize the potential of all pupils requires teachers to acknowledge that their classes, however grouped, are 'mixed ability'.

Streamed and setted classes, however they are formed, are usually based on achievement not on potential, ability or motivation and so contain pupils with a range of attitudes and approaches to learning. Under-performing very able pupils and pupils who are hardworking and perform well on tests can easily be placed in the same achievement group. Such classes must contain many pupils who, for one reason or another, underachieve because of e.g. learning difficulties, behavioural or emotional problems; teachers working with classes formed in this way may have a daunting task. The particular composition of setted classes will to some extent be felicitous, depending on the ability profile of the school population, the resources available, the assessment methods used and is also subject to arbitrary cut off points, given the need to restrict class sizes. At the very least, schools should ask themselves some crucial educational questions about the effectiveness and use of particular groupings of pupils for learning.

The best ways to group pupils has been a vexed question for many years. The Secondary Strategy (DfES, 2001c) has in may ways led to less emphasis on how pupils are grouped and more on strategies which target individual achievement (e.g. the use of data, Assessment for Learning, booster classes, more challenge for some) and at the same time on approaches to learning which can maximize achievement for all pupils (emphasis on thinking processes, learning to learn, intervention via questioning, collaborative learning and literacy across the curriculum). The government's *Five Year Strategy* (DfES, 2004f) places great emphasis on what it terms 'personalised learning' which is intended to allow for greater tailoring of the curriculum to individual needs. The most recent report on the reform of the 14–19 curriculum proposes an approach to pupil progression through a flexible curriculum and qualifications framework and greater emphasis on differentiated approaches to learning and independent enquiry (DfES, 2004f). Whilst these reforms do not spell the end of particular grouping policies they may well make them less significant in learning opportunities and achievement. The NFER report into differentiation (NFER, 1998) and the recent research reports on ability grouping in education (e.g. Ireson and Hallam, 2001) were pre-empting the more flexible approach to grouping promoted by the national strategies and recent policy thrusts. These views also acknowledge the importance and the effectiveness of flexible approaches to grouping within classes, e.g. Harlen, 1997.

At the whole school and class level flexible groupings have a very direct link to how we differentiate to meet individual differences in learning and performance. A common theme in the conclusions to the best evidence studies of research into pupil grouping is that what goes on in the classroom, the pedagogic models and the teaching strategies used, is likely to have more impact on achievement than how pupils are grouped.

Finally, all the research reviews point to the long-lasting effects of particular grouping arrangements not only on self-esteem but also on future engagement in learning.

> **Task 4.1.1**
> **How are pupils grouped in your school?**
>
> Find out the ways in which pupils are grouped in your school experience school, the reasoning behind that grouping and how it works in practice. Grouping arrangements often change after pupils have been in school a term or a year. Different policies may apply often at the transition of KS3–KS4 as well as between subjects.
>
> Are primary records, e.g. NC Achievement Levels used to group pupils? Are any tests, such as the Cognitive Abilities Test (NFER-Nelson) used to assess pupils and assign pupils to groups?

PROGRESSION AND DIFFERENTIATION

By far the greatest challenge to teachers is to ensure progression in the learning of all pupils in their class. Each pupil is different, whether in streamed, banded or wide ability classes. Each pupil brings to school unique knowledge, skills and attitudes formed by interaction with parents, peers, the media and their everyday experience of their world. Pupils are not blank sheets on which new knowledge is to be written. Many pupils may have skills of which the school is not aware: some pupils care for animals successfully; others play and adapt computer games; yet others may work with parents in the family business. Some pupils may know more arithmetic than we dream of as the following parody of stock market practice suggests:

Teacher: 'What is two plus two, Jane?'
Jane: 'Am I buying or selling, Sir?'

Your classroom is a reflection of your pupils' diversity of background and culture. Your pupils' 'cultural inheritance' interacts with their potential for learning, both of which are moulded by experience and affected by the particular learning context. Each pupil responds to the curriculum in a different way.

The values placed by the school on a broad, largely academic education may not be shared by some parents and their children who may value a vocational, relevant education more highly because it is immediately applicable to earning a living.

The teacher must take account of personal interest, ability and motivation to design learning which challenges and interests pupils but, at the same time, ensures for each a large measure of success. Planning and teaching for progression in learning is the core business of teachers. This involves an understanding and consideration of longer-term learning goals for pupils and how these translate into shorter-term goals and outcomes and learning activities. There has been much support in recent years on how we define progression in, e.g. the NC level descriptors, the exemplification of progression in NC guidance and exemplification materials, in examination syllabuses and supporting guidance, in the national strategies and in materials from the Qualification and Curriculum Authority (QCA).

For example, in geography it is suggested that progression involves:

- an increase in the breadth of studies;
- an increasing depth of study associates with pupils' growing capacity to deal with complexities and abstractions;
- an increase in the spatial scale of what is studied;
- a continuing development of skills to include specific techniques and more general strategies of enquiry, matched to pupils' developing cognitive abilities;
- increasing opportunity for pupils to examine social, economic, political and environmental issues (QCA, 2004f).

Developing approaches to differentiating and personalizing learning

Planning learning for pupils, being clear about learning objectives based on knowledge of the pupils and of what constitutes progression in particular curriculum areas, are critical in ensuring pupils' acquisition of the knowledge and skills underpinning progress. Progression and differentiation are therefore two sides of the same coin. The use and success of differentiated approaches depend on teachers knowing their pupils, being secure in their own subject knowledge and having access to a range of teaching strategies. There is no one right way to differentiate for pupils. Effective differentiation is a demanding task which has to take account of pupils' differences in culture, expectation, knowledge and experience.

Differentiation is about raising the standards of all pupils in a school, not just those underachieving or with learning difficulties. The purpose of a differentiated approach is to maximize the potential of the pupil and to improve learning by addressing the pupil's particular needs. But what exactly is meant by differentiation and how is it achieved?

Consider the following definitions:

- Differentiation is the matching of work to the differing capabilities of individuals or groups in order to extend their learning.
- Differentiation is about entitlement of access to a full curriculum in order that every pupil can reach their full potential (McNamara and Moreton, 1997).
- Differentiation means 'shaking up' what goes on in the classroom so that students have multiple options for taking in information, making sense of ideas, and expressing what they learn (Tomlinson, 1999).
- Differentiation is a planned process of intervention by the teacher in the pupil's learning.

What is your definition of differentiation?

However differentiation is defined, the challenge begins with its implementation and practice, which are in turn affected by teachers' beliefs about the ability of their pupils, by expectations of particular groups of pupils, and by understanding of how we learn and of optimal learning environments. Differentiation may also be affected by the nature of the subject itself and the kind of learning it involves.

Differentiation has sometimes had a bad press because at its worst it has implied an unrealistic and daunting demand on teachers to provide consistently different work and different approaches at the level of the individual pupil or has, unwittingly perhaps on the part of teachers, placed a ceiling on achievement for some pupils. Carol Tomlinson (1999) describes what differentiation is not:

> when assignments are the same for all learners and the adjustments consist of varying the level of difficulty of questions for certain students, grading some students harder than others, or letting students who finish early play games for enrichment. It is not appropriate to have more advanced learners … after their 'regular' work be given extension assignments. Asking students to do more of what they already know is hollow.

At its best, given what we know about effective approaches to learning, the influence of high expectations and the potential of all pupils, differentiation may be said to combine a variety of learning options which tap into different levels of readiness, interests, ability and learning profiles with more individualized support and challenge at appropriate times and in appropriate contexts. As we know relatively little about the potential of each pupil, differentiation should be used sensitively and judiciously.

This perspective on differentiation as liberating rather than constraining relies on a number of broader principles informing classroom learning and teaching:

- a focus on key concepts and skills;
- opportunities for problem solving, critical and creative thinking;
- ongoing assessment for learning;
- a balance between flexible groupings and whole class teaching;
- students as active learners with whom learning goals and expectations are shared;
- collaborative and co-operative learning;
- achievable but challenging targets;
- motivating and interesting learning activities;
- supportive and stimulating learning environments.

You may find the discussion of, for example, the work of Vygotsky and Piaget on learning theory of importance and interest here; see Unit 5.1. Both authors identify the importance of relating activities to the experience of the learner and setting targets for pupils that are achievable. Further help on lesson objectives and differentiation may be found in Kerry, 1999.

The National Strategy invites teachers to consider the full range of factors when designing lessons, including lessons where inclusion is a key priority (see Table 4.1.1).

Differentiation starts with a clear view about what you want all pupils to achieve and what individual pupils may need as a particular learning goal, using and acting upon what you know about pupils' previous learning and achievement using assessment from a range of sources of information. Then begins the consideration of appropriate differentiation strategies and how the process can be managed.

Differentiation strategies: stimulus – task – outcome

The outcome of any particular task depends on the way it is presented to the pupil and how they respond. Teaching methods can be restricted by our own imagination; we are inclined to present a task

Table 4.1.1 A sample lesson planning outline

LESSON PLANNING OUTLINE
TOPIC:
TEACHING OBJECTIVES: To enable pupils to:
LEARNING OUTCOMES (What pupils will be able to do – assessable objectives)
HOMEWORK
FORMATIVE ASSESSMENT
DIFFERENTIATION (SEN, IEPs, able pupils, etc.)

STIMULUS	TASK	OUTCOME
Play the role of Mark Antony in a class presentation of excerpts from Julius Caesar	Learn by heart the relevant text	Complete oral recall

X ⟶ X ⟶ X

Stimulus ⟶ Task ⟶ Outcome

Figure 4.1.1 Stimulus task and outcome: rote learning

in just one way with one particular outcome in mind, rather than to look for different ways to achieve our goals or to accept a range of sensible responses.

A traditional teaching goal is to ensure pupils remember things, such as Mark Antony's speech on the death of Caesar. This activity may be described in words (boxed text) or as a flow diagram; see Figure 4.1.1. Much learning depends on recall methods: learning the names of element symbols in science; preparing vocabulary in a language lesson; recalling formulae or tables from mathematics; learning to spell. Recall is necessary, if unexciting.

Task 4.1.2
Lesson planning for differentiation (1): supporting learning

Select two recall tasks for your teaching subject identifying the appropriate age and level. Suggest different ways of helping pupils accomplish the activity successfully.

For example, to stimulate pupils to punctuate a piece of text *which includes recorded* speech you could:

- Engage in a discussion with pupils, tape it and ask pupils to transcribe it.
- Use an interview from a newspaper report; read it out loud and discuss it with the class; give out a report with the punctuation removed and ask for the punctuation to be inserted.
- Ask pupils to gather opinions about a topic of interest and write a report which includes verbatim examples of opinion, e.g. interviewing other pupils about proposed new school uniforms.
- Suggest pupils write their own play.

The strategies in Task 4.1.2 are examples of *active learning*; see Unit 5.2. The flow diagram A in Figure 4.1.2 may represent the way this piece of work was set. This suggests that the outcome is always the same. In the punctuation exercise of Task 4.1.2 is the outcome the same no matter which activity is chosen? Suggest other ways of teaching punctuation.

Consider circumstances from your own teaching subject in which different stimuli could be used to achieve the same ends. In the example you choose, is the task and outcome the same no matter which activity is given to the pupils? Can the same stimulus, or activity, generate different outcomes? (see Figure 4.1.2B). Identify a teaching example from your own subject and explore the possibility of different outcomes arising from the same activity. See Task 4.1.3.

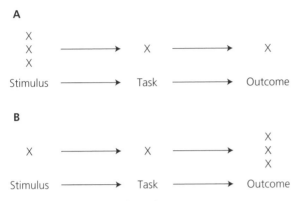

Figure 4.1.2   Stimuli, tasks and outcomes

**Task 4.1.3
Lesson planning for differentiation (2):
using resources**

You have a set of photographs showing the interiors of domestic kitchens covering the period 1850 to the present. Describe two or more ways in which you could use these photographs to teach your subject. Confine your discussion to a class you teach, covering one to two lessons.
For each example, identify:

- how you use the photographs;
- the activities you set your pupils;
- the objectives and learning outcomes;
- how you assess learning outcomes;
- the ways in which the activity can be differentiated.

Analyse your plan in terms of stimulus, task and outcome for the differentiated approaches you develop. If you do not like the choice of photographs, choose your own stimulus, e.g. an astronaut working in a space laboratory; a Salvador Dali painting such as *Persistence of Memory*, 1931.

Beyond task and outcome

The discussion of differentiation in terms of setting tasks or assessing outcomes suggests that work is given to pupils and they get on with it. In practice, of course, you support pupils while they are working. Thus differentiation also takes place at the point of contact with the group or individual. Differentiation is not simply a case of task and outcome. Your response to pupils working in class includes:

- checking that they understand what they are supposed to do;
- listening to a discussion and prompting or questioning when needed;
- helping pupils to brainstorm an idea or problem;
- asking questions about procedure or techniques;
- suggesting further action when difficulties arise or motivation flags;
- giving pupils supporting worksheets or other written guidance appropriate to the problem in hand – the guidance might explain the topic in simpler terms or simpler language;

- checking pupils' notebooks and noting progress;
- marking pupils' work;
- encouraging pupils by identifying success;
- setting targets for improvement;
- increasing the demand of an existing task;
- noting unexpected events or achievements for a plenary session.

Discuss this list of strategies with other student teachers and identify those strategies appropriate to the teaching of your subject; add to the list of responses.

The different ways in which you respond to your pupils' activities affects the quality of their performance; your response to pupils is an important feature of a differentiated approach and knowing how to respond is part of the repertoire of all good teachers. Thus the dichotomy of differentiation, discussed above as 'task versus outcome', hides a host of other ways by which you support your pupils. Knowing how to set such tasks depends on how well you know your pupils.

Identifying different activities or levels within one activity and around the same theme requires some ingenuity. The activity needs to be challenging yet achievable. The ways in which activities can be differentiated include:

- their degree of open-endedness;
- the degree of familiarity with the resources;
- whether the activity is a complete piece of work or a contributory part of a larger exercise;
- the amount of information you give pupils;
- the language level at which it is presented;
- whether the activity is set orally or by means of written guidance;
- degree of familiarity with the concepts needed to tackle the activity;
- the amount of guidance given to pupils; for example, in science lessons, the guidance given on making measurements, recording data or drawing a graph.

Discuss this list and rewrite it in terms of strategies appropriate to your subject and the context of your teaching.

Differences in outcome may be recognized by the amount of help given to pupils and by:

- the extent to which all aspects of the problem have been considered;
- the adoption of a suitable method of approaching the activity;
- the use of more difficult concepts or procedures in planning;
- the recognition of all the factors involved in successful completion of the activity and limiting the choice appropriately;
- thoroughness and accuracy of recording data in a quantitative exercise;
- appropriateness and selection of ways to present information and the thoroughness and depth of analysis;
- use of appropriate ideas (or theory) to discuss the work;
- accuracy and understanding of conclusions drawn from an activity, e.g. are statements made appropriate to the content and purpose of the activity;
- distinction between statements supported by evidence from speculation or opinion;
- the way the report is written up, the selection of appropriate style for the target audience;
- the ability of pupils to express themselves in an increasingly sophisticated language;
- the use of imagination or insight;
- the selection of appropriate diagrams, sketches or pictures;
- sensible use of ICT to support a task;
- recognition of the limitations of the approach to a problem and awareness of ways to improve it.

One model of a differentiated curriculum suggests that the curriculum needs to be differentiated around the following core elements:

- *learning environment or context*, e.g. changes in where learning takes place; open and accepting classroom climate;
- *content*, e.g. greater levels of complexity, abstraction;
- *process*, e.g. promotion of higher level skills, greater autonomy, creative thinking;
- *product*, e.g. encouraging the solving of real problems, the use of real audiences (Maker and Nielson, 1995).

Differentiation can also therefore include different or enriched learning experiences which take place outside the classroom or even the school. The National Curriculum exemplar schemes of work give examples of additional learning opportunities for each subject area (DfES, 2004c). The QCA guidance on teaching gifted and talented pupils also gives guidance on enrichment and extension beyond the classroom, many examples of which are relevant for most pupils (QCA, 2004c).

Grouping within class

Current thinking about effective teaching and learning sees the use of flexible groupings in class as an aid to learning and as a form of differentiation. The reviews on the effects of particular types of pupil grouping on pupils' achievement point to the positive effects of within class groupings which may include grouping by:

- ability;
- mix of ability;
- gender;
- expertise;
- friendship;
- age.

The National Strategy guidance gives examples of learning activities which make use of flexible and different forms of grouping, such as cascading, paired tutoring, jigsawing and rainbowing (DfES, 2004b). Refer to Task 4.1.1 for grouping in your school.

Managing differentiation

Some forms of differentiation may occur spontaneously as part and parcel of the everyday repertoire of effective teaching but differentiation must also be planned and managed if it is to be effective. Lesson planning formats which require consideration of the learning needs of all pupils may assist teachers in ensuring systematic attention to differentiation. It is unrealistic to expect one teacher to plan differentiated work separately for each pupil; it is perhaps better to identify groups of pupils who can work to a given set of objectives using methods suitable to those pupils and the topic in question. It is helpful to some teachers to have a framework in which to plan work. One such plan is shown in Figure 4.1.3, although we recognise that different ITT courses and schools favour different lesson planning frameworks.

Figure 4.1.3 assumes that you know the teaching topic and its place in the school's scheme of work. The framework draws attention to factors to be considered in preparing lesson plans (see also Unit 2.2).

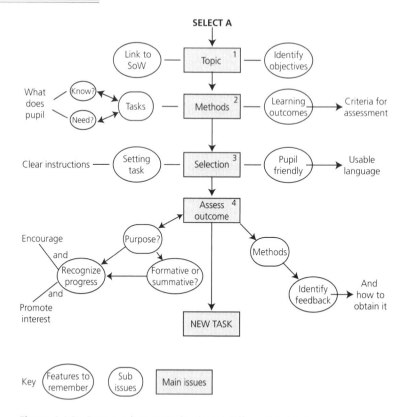

SELECT A

Figure 4.1.3 Framework to assist developing differentiated tasks

The aims and short-term objectives must be broad enough to apply to most pupils in your class. There are often a number of ways of achieving the same goal; Step 2 requires you to consider which activities to give pupils, linking them to what the pupil already knows and then identifying outcomes. Achievable outcomes are one way of ensuring motivation but must set pupils a challenge, i.e. not be too easy. By identifying achievable outcomes for different groups of children, the process of differentiation is set in motion. The final selection of an activity, Step 3, reminds you of some practical issues to consider in selecting or preparing resources, again introducing another feature of differentiation. Step 4 addresses assessment which is achieved in a number of ways, for example by question and answer sessions, taking part in small group discussions, responding to queries in class, asking questions of pupils working on an activity, listening to pupils discussing their work as well as marking books or short tests. The information gained helps you identify the next steps for the pupil. Assessment must reflect your objectives and Step 4 in Figure 4.1.3 draws attention to purpose, timing and methods of assessment. Task 4.1.4 invites you to use this framework.

Models for differentiation often identify different priorities for activities, such as:

- must/should/could;
- core/support/extension.

However, differentiation models should also recognise that pupils' learning needs may not be fixed or permanent and may relate to the learning context or topic at hand. Differentiation may therefore

> **Task 4.1.4**
> **Lesson planning for differentiation (3): using a framework**
>
> Select a topic for a class you teach. Use Figure 4.1.3 to develop an outline for your lesson. Consider whether the main activity is for all pupils or whether the aim of the lesson is best achieved using a small number of different activities. Prepare notes for Steps 1 to 4. If you plan a small number of different activities, identify how many different activities you can manage safely and effectively; check the resource implications.
>   We suggest you approach this task either:
>
> • in a group of specialist student teachers, sharing ideas as they evolve; or
> • on your own, later sharing your ideas with other student teachers and tutors who know the class you are about to teach.
>
> Check your understanding of differentiation against the competences/standards for your course.

involve support or challenge being given to different pupils at different times, for example sometimes to:

• a whole group;
• a targeted group;
• those who work at speed.

Differentiation is good teaching and requires that you know your pupils and how that knowledge helps you devise activities that are achievable but challenging. That same knowledge enables you to judge the extent to which pupils have given an activity their best shot. Left alone, pupils may settle for the easy option. Your role is to persuade the pupil, or group of pupils, to maximize their effort and to judge what is an appropriate outcome. In assessing your pupils, attitudes are as important as cognitive skill.

However well you plan your activities on paper, the response of the pupils is your yardstick of success. Some pupils may present a greater challenge than others and examples are given in case histories below. We suggest you look at the case histories of some pupils below and then attempt Task 4.1.5.

Case studies of pupils

Peter

Peter is a popular member of his group and has an appealing sense of humour. He can use this in a disruptive way to disquiet teachers while amusing his peers.

He appears very bright orally but when the work is of a traditional nature, i.e. teacher led, he often avoids the task in hand; it is at such times that he can become disruptive. His disruption is not always overt; he employs a range of elaborate avoidance tactics when asked to settle to work and often produces very little. His written language and numeracy attainments are significantly lower than those he demonstrates orally.

When given responsibility in groups, Peter can sometimes rise to the challenge. He can display sound leadership ability and, when he is motivated and interested in a group project, can encourage his peers to produce a good team effort. His verbal presentations of such work can be lively, creative, humorous and full of lateral thinking. At such times Peter displays an extensive general knowledge.

Peter's tutor is concerned about Peter's progress. He fears that Peter will soon begin to truant from those subjects in which teaching is traditional in style. He is encouraging Peter's subject teachers to provide him with as much problem-solving work as possible.

Tina

Tina is underachieving across the curriculum in her written work, although orally she appears quite bright. Her concentration span on written work is short. In basic skills she is getting behind her peers. In lessons she can appear quite demanding, as she often appears to need work to be individually set and she finds it difficult to get started and then to sustain and complete pieces of work. She can appear to spend significant amounts of lesson time disrupting the work of other learners. She seems to have a knack of knowing just how to provoke and 'wind up' other learners, so disputes are not unusual. She has been known to be rather confrontational towards teachers, who perceive this to happen when Tina feels threatened.

At the same time, Tina has got what some people describe as 'charm'. Others describe this as being good manipulation. This makes her quite difficult to deal with in school, different teachers develop very different approaches and boundaries in relation to her.

She has a clique of peers who seem to follow her lead. She has a paradoxical relationship with others in the class, who seem to be wary of her, yet also rather courteous towards her.

Filimon

Filimon arrived a year ago from Ethiopia via the Sudan. He had not been at school for at least a year due to his country's war. He speaks Sunharic at home, as well as some Arabic, but knew no English on arrival. Eight months of the year he has spent at school here have been a 'silent period' during which time he was internalizing what he was hearing. Now he is starting to speak with his peers and his teacher. He has a reading partner who reads to him every day and now Filimon is reading these same stories himself.

Joyce

Joyce is a very high achiever. She always seems to respond to as much extension activity as she can get. She puts in a lot of effort and produces very well presented work (e.g. capably using IT), and amply demonstrating her ability to understand, evaluate and synthesize. Joyce's achievements are maximized where she is able to work on her own or in a pair with one of a couple of other girls in the class. In other groups she tends to keep herself to herself. Some teachers are concerned that she is not developing her social and leadership potential.

Joyce's parents put a lot of pressure on her and are keen for Joyce to follow an accelerated programme wherever this is possible. Should she achieve her ambitions for higher education, Joyce will not be the first in her family to make it to Oxbridge.

These case studies were provided by Paul Greenhalgh, adapted by him from Greenhalgh, 1994. You may find it instructive to select one of pupils described above and consider how their presence in your class would modify your lesson planning.

Task 4.1.5
Writing your own case study

Prepare a short case study of two pupils in one of your classes. Identify two pupils for whom further information would be helpful to you in lesson planning and use the examples of case studies to help you identify the information you need to collect. Do not use the pupil's real name in any report you make or discussion outside the school.

Collect information from the class subject teacher and the form teacher. The form teacher can give you background information about the pupils, as much as is relevant to your study.

After collecting the information and writing your report ask the class teacher to read it and comment on it. Finally, use the information to amend Task 4.1.4 or plan a new lesson.

If there are other student teachers in your school share your case studies with them. Use the case studies to identify some learning needs of these pupils and plan teaching strategies to take account of these needs. The study can contribute to your professional portfolio.

Check your understanding of differentiation against the competences/standards for your course.

SUMMARY AND KEY POINTS

Children learn in different ways at different speeds. Some pupils have learning barriers related to behavioural, emotional and cognitive needs. Schools should organize the way in which pupils are taught and teachers should plan their lessons to take account of these differences, as far as is practically possible. Whichever method of grouping pupils is adopted, the choice of task and the range of teaching strategies are key for the successful implementation of a differentiated approach to the curriculum.

At the heart of the debate about standards and differentiation of work for pupils are educational aims. Should all pupils work towards common goals for most of their time in school? Or should the differences between pupils, as measured by their achievement in school, be acknowledged by developing curricula appropriate to their needs? Both courses of action can be justified educationally and socially and can be achieved by the flexible and informed use of grouping, by the use of teaching and learning approaches which stimulate, interest and maximize the potential of all pupils and by the selective use of differentiation strategies to offer greater support or challenge. Differentiation can be achieved through the choice of activities given to pupils and the teachers' expectations about outcomes. Much more, however, depends on the way you respond to your pupils, giving support, encouragement, stimulation and by providing feedback on their progress. Differentiation is embedded in these teaching skills.

Developing those skills depends on getting to know your pupils, both as individuals as well as members of a class. This 'getting to know pupils' is difficult to achieve in a one-year teacher education course involving, as it does usually, school experience in two schools; it is essential to realize the importance of this factor when you start your first post. Pupils need to learn to trust your ability to teach them and develop confidence in your willingness to help; in these circumstances most pupils grow and develop and, most importantly, learn to take responsibility for their own progress.

You should monitor your own progress in developing these skills by reference to the standards/competences which apply to your course of initial training and during your NQT year. The section on Further Reading enables you to widen your knowledge of differentiation, grouping and selection.

FURTHER READING

Hallam, S. and Toutounji, I. (1996) *What do we Know about the Grouping of Pupils by Ability? A Research Review*, London: Institute of Education, University of London. Essential reading for those seeking to understand arguments about grouping pupils in school. Carries an extensive bibliography (c.250 references) which reviews the research carried out in this country and overseas into the effects of pupil grouping on academic performance.

Harlen, W. (1997) *Making Sense of the Research on Ability Grouping*, Newsletter 60 (Spring), Scottish Council for Research in Education (SCRE). This brief summary gives a useful overview of the difficulties in researching ability grouping practices and highlights key issues from some of the major studies.

Hart, S. (ed.) (1996) *Differentiation and the Secondary Curriculum: Debates and Dilemmas*, London: Routledge. For those wishing to dig deeper into the purposes and practice of differentiation.

Kerry, T. (1999) *Learning Objectives, Task Setting and Differentiation*, London: Hodder and Stoughton. This short book contains very useful chapters on differentiation in practice and evidence of research into classroom practice (Chapters 8 and 9). Full of practical ideas.

Unit 4.2

Growth, Development and Diet

Margaret Jepson and Tony Turner

None of the teachers in our school have noticed that I am an intellectual. They will be sorry when I'm famous. There is a new girl in our class. She sits next to me in Geography. She is all right. Her name is Pandora, but she likes being called 'Box'. Don't ask me why. I might fall in love with her. It's time I fell in love, after all I'm 13¾ years old.

(Townsend, 1982: 17)

INTRODUCTION

Adolescence is a period of growth and of physical, mental and emotional change. These changes take place against a background of family life, within a particular society and culture that has expectations of its young people. Young people often bring to school the expectations of their family which may carry both advantages and disadvantages. Disadvantages include parents living on low wages, or who are unemployed or instability within the family, any of which may portend poor career prospects (Child, 1993: 302). Some adolescents bring family pressures to succeed and a burden of high expectation. Yet others have disabilities, some mild and supportable by technology, e.g. wearing glasses, while other young people carry more serious disadvantages, such as dyslexia, less easily overcome.

Sue Townsend's book, quoted above, offers an often amusing but insightful commentary on the pains of growing up. The onset of changes in adolescence comes at a time when society demands that young people attend school and be in continual close contact with their peers where they are reminded constantly of the differences between themselves and others. This extended proximity can place a strain on the adolescent's perception of themselves.

Balancing family and peer pressures is important during adolescence. Parents are anxious that any physical shortcoming should be treated properly whereas adolescents themselves are likely to shy away from drawing attention to themselves. Thus, wearing spectacles or dental braces, for example, become issues for teenagers, because the image they give to others is one of 'difference' and, perhaps, defect. Teachers need to be aware of these difficulties in order to respond sensitively in the classroom and be prepared to initiate remedial action when necessary.

Most young people want to be normal, to conform to what they see in others of their peer group. This gives rise to pressure to conform to peer norms and to question or reject family norms. Conforming, in part, concerns appearance; personal appearance becomes a highly sensitive consideration during adolescence for two reasons. One concerns the notion of normality, shape, size, etc. The second concerns sexuality and emerging relationships.

Many adolescents are trying to 'find their feet', develop an identity and develop new relationships with adults, especially parents. At the same time the academic pressures of school demand that pupils make far reaching choices about careers. Pressures to choose come from home and school, such as through the commonly asked question 'what do you want to do when you leave school?' Many young people, often with good reason, just don't know how to respond, or how to choose.

Schools have a vital part to play in this developmental period. They exist unequivocally to further the development of pupils and must try to provide the environment in which personal autonomy can grow. At the same time and to cope with several hundred young people in a confined space, schools must provide a disciplined context not just for the healthy growth of the individual, but for everyone. Having many young people all together means that these conditions are not necessarily compatible with those for the emergence of the autonomous individual.

This unit enables you to consider the phenomenon of physical growth and development, to consider the range of development that encompasses the 'normal pupil' and to do this in part by observing the pupils in your school. The unit addresses, too, the diet and health of young people and the promotion of healthy eating in school.

OBJECTIVES

By the end of this unit you should be able to:

- discuss the meaning of normal growth and development in relation to adolescence;
- describe and understand some of the physical differences between school age pupils;
- appreciate the effect of external pressures and influences on pupil behaviour and to identify some implications of these differences for teaching and learning;
- discuss healthy eating and the roles of the school in promoting this ideal;
- identify the competences/standards for your course relevant to teachers' responsibilities for growth, development and diet.

About physical growth and development

Variation in the height and weight of humans depends on genetic, health and nutritional factors. In the case of young people, the period from birth to the start of adulthood is critical if the genetic potential of the individual is to be realized. Information about the growth and health of individuals is best obtained by a study of changes in body measurements of individuals and comparing those to reference standards. Patterns of change in height and weight of young people are shown in Figures 4.2.1–4.2.4 and include measurements on young people across the ages 5 to 15+ (Whitehead, 1991).

See also tasks 4.2.1 and 4.2.2. The data are based on observations of a large number of individuals at different age groups, i.e. a cross-sectional study and show the data from the 50th percentile. The 50th percentile corresponds to the mean value and so the graphs 4.2.1–4.2.4 show the average height and weight of pupils in the age groups. Boys and girls are shown separately to contrast their rate of physical development. Figures 4.2.2 and 4.2.4 show in closer detail the mean changes around the period of adolescence.

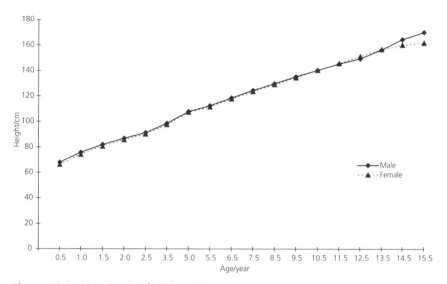

Figure 4.2.1   Mean height of children, 5–16 years

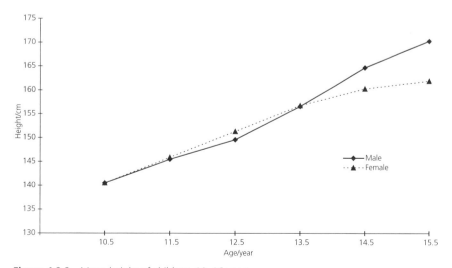

Figure 4.2.2   Mean height of children, 10–16 years

Children who receive enough energy and nutrients in their diet should grow adequately; the growth curve of such a person may be close to the average growth, as shown in Figures 4.2.1–4.2.4. The data in these figures are mean figures; in practice there is considerable spread in the height and weight of children of a given age; see Whitehead (1991: 198–201) for more detailed information. Consistent and large departures from the normal pattern of development may need monitoring. Sudden departures from a regular pattern of growth usually have a simple explanation, related to illness or nutritional factors, to which we return later in this unit.

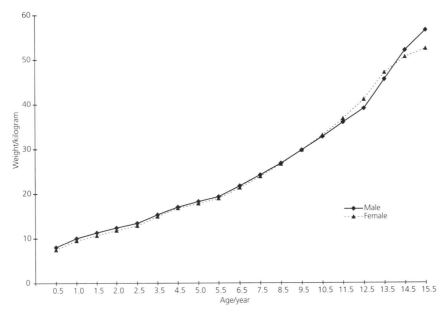

Figure 4.2.3 Mean weight of children, 5–16 years

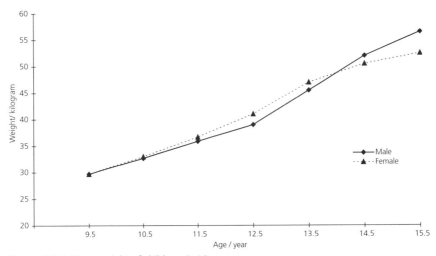

Figure 4.2.4 Mean weight of children, 9–16 years

Task 4.2.1
Pupil growth and development

Using Figures 4.2.1 and 4.2.2, describe the different rate of height increase in boys and girls and identify the probable ages at which these are most obvious. Repeat the exercise to compare weights of boys and girls as they grow older. Do the differences in height and weight occur at the same ages, on average? Further data can be found on the Department of Health (DoH) website <http://www.doh.gov.uk/dhhone.htm> or in Whitehead (1991: 198–201).

Young people tend to have growth spurts, particularly after puberty, the point at which the sex glands become functional; see Figures 4.2.2 and 4.2.4. Most girls mature physically earlier than most boys. There are differences in growth rates between boys and girls at the onset of puberty, some girls showing a growth spurt at an earlier age than most boys. However, there is little difference, for example, in mean height of boys and girls up to age 13 but after 16 years boys on average are over 13 cm taller than girls. Height increases appear earlier than weight increases and this has implications for physical activity. The differential rate of height and weight development is the origin of clumsiness and awkwardness of some adolescent pupils. As well as obvious gender differences between pupils in a coeducational context, the differences between individuals within a group of boys, or a group of girls, can be quite large and obvious. These differences in development can be worrying for the individual and may affect pupil's attitudes and performance to academic work. For example, it can happen that some pupils who have developed physically earlier than their peers may dominate activity in a class, causing a number of pupils to reduce their involvement for fear of being ridiculed by more grown-up members of the class.

Some research suggests that pupils physically maturing faster score better on mental tests than pupils developing more slowly. Girls develop physically and mentally faster than boys on average and it was because of this factor in the 1940s–1950s that the 11+ examination was adjusted to give equal opportunities for boys to gain places in grammar schools in the face of girls' earlier maturation.

There is evidence that environmental factors affect growth (Tanner, 1990). These factors include:

- the size of the family; many larger families have children of below average height;
- where the pupil is raised; urban-reared children are often taller and heavier than those raised in a rural society;
- the socio-economic status of the family (parents); lower social class, defined by the employment status of the parents, correlates with having shorter children;
- prolonged unemployment has a similar effect to socio-economic factors.

There is some evidence, cited above, that physical size and development is linked to social class and economic factors (Tanner, 1990). There may be evidence in your school of a link between 'growth and development' and socio-economic factors such as free school meal provision. The uptake of free school meals is used, for example, by OFSTED in school inspections as a proxy measure of deprivation. The link between health and diet on one hand and academic performance is also recognized in those schools which make available free breakfast for pupils.

These issues of difference in physical development, which taken together with the large differences in performance in school subjects has raised the question of whether pupils should be grouped in classes by age, as they are now or whether some other method should be used to group pupil for teaching purposes, for example, by achievement. Some other educational systems require pupils to reach a certain academic standard before proceeding to the next grade, leading to mixed-age classes. Thus under-performing pupils are kept back a year to provide them with an opportunity to improve their performance. This practice has a big impact on friendship groups and on personal esteem.

The environmental factors, listed above, by themselves do not have a direct causal relationship but reflect complex underlying influences on growth and development. These factors affect also the onset of puberty. It is of interest to consider that any 12-year-old girl might be in a pre-pubertal, mid-pubertal or post-pubertal state; and any 14-year-old boy similarly. Thus it is not sensible to talk of a 14-year-old group of children as though they represented a homogeneous cohort. Task 4.2.2 invites you to explore some characteristics of your pupils.

Task 4.2.2
What will your pupils be like?

The school at which you were a pupil may be quite different from your school experience school. This task is intended to reveal some of those differences and provide you with an opportunity to discuss their implication for your teaching.

In what ways do the pupils in your school experience school resemble or differ from:

- pupils from your own school days;
- your expectations prior to your initial teacher education course?

You might consider:

- family sizes, and extended families in the school;
- socio-economic classes into which most of your pupils' families may fit;
- physical appearance such as height, weight and physical maturity;
- employment rates of parents;
- achievement, as measured by standardized national tests; e.g. Standard Assessment Tasks (SATs) levels or tests of cognitive ability.

Other factors which may help in describing the pupils in your school include:

- how pupils are dressed and adherence to school uniform;
- self-confidence, willingness to talk to teachers and to each other;
- attitude to authority, including respect for other pupils and for teachers.

Collect your own impressions of the pupils in your school, for discussion with other student teachers and your tutor. It may be interesting to repeat this exercise after a period in the school and see how familiarity with the pupils and school has altered first impressions. Keep a record of your work in your professional portfolio.

The variation in physical development of pupils shown, for example, in any year cohort has implications for your management of secondary school classes. These differences are particularly apparent in Years 7–9 and may stand out in activities which prosper on physical maturity or physical control. Boys in early adolescence who develop late often cannot compete with their peers in games; and girls who mature earlier than their friends can be also advantaged in physical education and games but, at the same time, feel embarrassed. Thus competitive activities such as running or throwing or physical confrontation games such as association football, hockey and rugby favour faster developing pupils. Equally important is physical control, the ability to co-ordinate hand and eye and control tools and equipment properly and safely. In the past, some adolescents have been regarded as clumsy which may be related to growth spurts, described earlier. Activity in subjects such as physical education, art and design, technology, science and computing depend, in part, on good co-ordination and psychomotor skills.

You may find it useful to try Task 4.2.3 now and the following notes, sections A to D, suggest the nature and possible sources of information about your pupils.

**Task 4.2.3
The pupils in your class**

Select a class you teach and (1) find out as much as you can about the background of your pupils; (2) shadow the class for a day and try to relate your findings to the ways pupils respond to teachers and different subjects.

Some information towards this task may be obtained in Task 4.2.2.

Respect the confidentiality of information you acquire in any written or oral report. Reports should not quote names. Discuss your plan with your tutor who can direct you to appropriate sources of information such as the form tutor. The school physical education staff may well be able to provide information on physical development. There may be special provisions for some pupils in your school which may provide additional information, e.g. homework club or other provision for pupils unable to work at home.

When you visit classrooms get permission from the teacher, tell him what you are doing, what is to happen to the information and what is expected to emerge. Be prepared to share your findings with him.

The list of suggestions A to D, following this task, indicates the type of information you could gather but you may need to *select* from this list an appropriate *focus* for your task. Section E suggests ways to use the information. Write a short report for your tutor. The report may contribute to your professional portfolio. Record in your diary your personal response to this work and any implications it has for you.

A. Background and attendance

Use the attendance register and personal files to collect information on your pupils. Talk first to the form tutor about your task. Include:

- the names and the numbers of boy and girls;
- the ethnicity of pupils; check the way the school reports ethnicity. If there is no guide to this available, then use the guide in Table 4.2.1;
- the religious or cultural background of pupils; e.g. 7th Day Adventist, travellers' children;
- recent immigrants or children of families seeking asylum;
- patterns of absences and whether absences are supported by notes from parents or guardians;
- the regularity of completing homework and its quality (the class teacher should have such a record).

B. Physical characteristics

Gather data about:

- the height and weight of pupils; are any pupils deemed overweight or obese (see later in this unit);
- the number of pupils who wear spectacles;
- the number that use spectacles for reading or board work (it can be instructive to find out, perhaps from the form teacher, those who should use spectacles, but don't; young people don't usually wear contact lenses but ask about this as well);

Table 4.2.1   A guide to reporting ethnicity

White	Asian – Bangladeshi
Black – African	Asian – other
Black – Caribbean	Chinese
Black – other	Mixed background
Asian – Indian	Other background
Asian – Pakistani	Not known

Source: Graduate Teacher Training Registry, 2004: 11.

- how many use a hearing aid? (Some pupils may be seated near the front of the class for this reason. Find out if any should wear a hearing aid, but don't);
- if any pupils are undergoing prolonged dental treatment, e.g. wearing tooth braces;
- the number of pupils who suffer from anorexia nervosa, asthma, diabetes or epilepsy;
- any other disabilities, but see C below.

C. Special needs

Collect data about the number of pupils in the class who have:

- statements of special need and the reason for this;
- specific learning difficulties, e.g. dyslexia;
- a support teacher, and why;
- no support teacher, but need one. Identify the special need and why it cannot be supported.

D. School meals

Gather data about the number of pupils in the class who are entitled to free school meals. This information is confidential. If the school provides breakfast how many pupils use this service?

E. Using the information

The data may focus on a particular area of interest. Gather together:

- all the data collected;
- read it through;
- identify points of interest;
- identify issues which need clarification.

Meet with your tutor to check and discuss your findings. Questions which could be addressed in this meeting include:

- How representative is the information of the class or group investigated?
- How do the data compare with your impressions of the class? What information or perspective has been added?
- How useful is this information in your future lesson preparation, classroom organization and management?

- Does the sample you have used represent the school? How far does this survey give you a snapshot of all pupils in the school?

The task may help you to be alert to possible hearing or other physical handicaps in your pupils; it may also improve your sensitivity to signs of distress in pupils and to be alert to pupils at risk.

We have discussed the physical development of pupils and drawn attention to the differences in development both within a gender group and between boys and girls. A large influence on physical development is diet, lifestyle and attitude to exercise and games. There is concern about the dietary habits of some young people, in part about risk of disease and in part about the level of fitness of many young people. Yet others draw attention to the increased use of computers in entertainment and the accompanying sedentary habits this entails. Thus we turn to consider diet, development and the curriculum.

DIET AND THE CURRICULUM

Background

In the past one hundred years the average height and weight of children and adults have increased and the age at which puberty arrives has decreased. Such average changes are due in part to increased nutritional standards, better conditions of health and sanitation, as well as better economic circumstances for the majority. It is these changes in society that have given rise to an increased concern about the diet and increasingly sedentary lifestyle of young people

The government issued Eight Guidelines for Healthy Eating over ten years ago. These are:

- Enjoy your food.
- Eat a variety of different foods.
- Eat plenty of foods rich in starch and fibre.
- Eat plenty of fruit and vegetables.
- Don't eat too many foods that contain a lot of fat.
- Don't have sugary foods and drinks too often.
- If you drink alcohol, drink sensibly.
- Eat the right amount to maintain a healthy weight.

To follow these guidelines a level of knowledge and understanding of foods is needed and value judgements made, e.g. How much is a lot of fat? What is a healthy weight?

The current measure of body fatness is the body mass index (BMI). This is defined as a person's weight in kilogrammes divided by the square of their height in metres. Obesity in adults is defined as a BMI of 30 or more and overweight as between 25–29.9. BMI varies with age and there are age and gender specific standards used by the medical profession.

Many adolescents in the UK are not eating healthy diets and many do not meet the recommendations for exercise. The National Diet and Nutrition Survey (2000) carried out by the Food Standards Agency (2000) examined the diets of British schoolchildren aged 4–18 years. It found that adolescents ate more than the recommended level of sugar, salt and saturated fats. The most frequently consumed foods were white bread, savoury snacks, biscuits, potatoes and chocolate confectionery. The results of this type of diet and insufficient exercise are an increase in the weight, leading to overweight and obesity. The Royal College of Physicians (RCP) (2004) described the rapid increase in the prevalence of overweight and obesity in all age groups as 'the obesity time bomb'; see Figure 4.2.5. The estimated

Obesity in 2–4-year-old children almost doubled (5%–9%) in 10 years (1989–99).
Obesity in 6–15-year-olds trebled (5–16%) in 11 years (1990–2001).
Obesity in adult women nearly trebled (8–23%) in 22 years (1980–2002).
Obesity in adult men nearly quadrupled (6–22%) in 22 years (1980–2002).

Figure 4.2.5   Obesity in England 1980–2002: some summary facts (Source: Royal College of Physicians, 2004: 4)

cost to the National Health Service of an increasing number of overweight and obese adults is about £0.5 billion in terms of treatment alone and possibly in excess of £2 billion in the wider economy.

If current trends continue, at least one-third of adults, one-fifth of boys and one-third of girls will be obese by the year 2020.

The most immediate consequences of overweight and obesity in adolescence are social and psychological. Evidence from a longitudinal study in America on self-esteem and obesity shows that at ages 9–10 there were no significantly different scores between obese and non-obese children but by 13–14 years of age significantly lower levels of self-esteem were observed in obese boys, obese Hispanic girls and white girls compared with their non-obese counterparts (Strauss, 2000). This decrease in self-esteem was associated with significantly increased feelings of sadness, loneliness and nervousness and with an increased likelihood to smoke and drink alcohol. There is also an element of social marginali-zation. Asking adolescents to name their friends, Strauss and Pollack (2003) found that whilst obese adolescents nominated similar numbers of friends as normal weight adolescents they received significantly fewer friendship nominations from others than were received by normal weight adolescents. Obese adolescents were also more likely to receive no friendship nominations than were normal weight adolescents. Those who are overweight are often seen as an easy target for bullying, with little peer pressure occurring to prevent it. This social marginalization may aggravate the social and psychological effects of obesity.

The health consequences are also serious. Increasing fatness is closely correlated with the development of type 2 diabetes that used to be diagnosed in middle to later life but is now increasingly seen in young adults and children. Childhood obesity that continues into adult life increases the risk of early death from all disease-related causes, including cancers and cardiovascular disease (RCP, 2004).

Why has there been this increase in overweight and obesity over the last 20 years? A simple answer is to do with energy balance. People are eating too much for the amount of physical activity that they do, see Table 4.2.2.

Energy from food can be measured in calories or joules (4.2 J =1 calorie). It is estimated that the average adult whose daily energy intake is just 60 Calories (60,000 calories) more than their energy output will become obese within 10 years.

In 1997 the Health Education Authority recommended that all young people should participate in one hour of moderate physical activity a day. The National Diet and Nutrition Survey (Food Standards Agency, 2000) estimated that 40 per cent of boys and 60 per cent of girls were failing to meet this target. A survey of Liverpool schoolchildren researching health and fitness found that more than 25 per cent of Year 5 pupils did not participate in any or had low levels of physical activity (equivalent to a slow walk) during the morning and lunchtime break and for Year 7 boys the figure was 40 per cent

Table 4.2.2   Energy balance equations

Energy from food = energy expended in exercise = maintenance of body weight
Energy from food > energy expended in exercise = addition in body weight
Energy from food < energy expended in exercise = loss in body weight.

and for girls 60 per cent (Liverpool Sportslinx Project, 2003). Break times and lunchtimes for about half of all Year 7 pupils are therefore spent either sitting or doing no more than slow walking.

A simple answer to the problem of obesity is therefore that adolescents should eat less and exercise more. But this would be too simplistic. There are many factors that contribute to what has become known recently as an 'obesogenic environment', a term now used to describe environments which encourage and promote high energy intake and inactivity.

By contrast with the growing problem of obesity is a parallel culture that values thinness, with images of men and women in the media, advertising and popular culture that emphasize beauty, youth and thinness. Some adolescent boys but in particular many girls may compare themselves to extremely thin models working in the fashion industry and perceive themselves to be 'fat' in comparison, rather than healthy and attractive. This promotion of the ideal thin body undermines self-confidence. Again, body image and self-esteem are closely connected. An adolescent with high self-esteem will see themselves not necessarily as better than others but not worse, recognizes limitations and expects to grow and improve. An adolescent with low self-esteem will be dissatisfied with themselves and wish that they were different.

Eating habits

The environment outside school, in terms of food habits, has changed in recent years. There has been, e.g.:

* increased consumption of pre-prepared foods and carbonated drinks;
* more 'eating out' in restaurants or 'eating in' through takeaways;
* an increase in snacking, often high in saturated fats, sugar or salt;
* increased pocket money for children; crisps and savoury snacks are the most popular after school snack.

There are advertising and promotional campaigns by the food industry to encourage the sale of their particular brands of food, many targeted at children. The top ten advertised food brands in the UK are dominated by the market leaders in the food industry and represent relatively unhealthy food options and are aimed at children. The food industry gave confidential commercial evidence to the House of Commons Committee of Obesity whose report concluded 'It is clear advertisers use their increasingly sophisticated knowledge of children's cognitive and social development, and careful consumer research into their motivations, values, preferences and interests, to ensure that their messages have maximum appeal' (House of Commons Health Committee, 2004, para. 105). For example, MacDonald's fast food chain spent over £41 million pounds on advertising in 2002 and the other top ten food brands spend between £6m and £16m pounds each in the same period (A.C. Nielson cited in House of Commons Health Committee Report, 2004). By contrast the annual budget for the government's Five a Day campaign to encourage eating of fruit and vegetables is £5 million pounds. Some fast food outlets are now offering more healthy fruit and salad options, which is a welcome move.

There is a link between eating habits and social class and income. Those from the higher socio-economic groups tend to have a more varied diet than those from lower socio-economics groups because the latter group may purchase only food they are sure will be eaten. Those adolescents from low income families eat less fruit and vegetables and more foods high in fat, sugar and salt.

Inside school, nearly half of all 14–18-year-olds bring in a packed lunch from home. A recent lunch box survey found an over-representation of fatty and sugary foods and an under-representation of fruit, vegetables and starchy vegetables (Food Standards Agency, 2004a). The most common items were a cheese or ham sandwich made with white bread, a packet of crisps and a chocolate bar or cake with a high frequency of sweetened fizzy drinks.

School meals in secondary schools are most often provided in the style of cafeteria food outlets and therefore pupils can opt out of healthy choices in favour of unhealthy ones. Schools could use school meals to introduce more healthy foods and to influence the eating habits of adolescents but often they are driven by commercial influences and serve food that they can guarantee adolescents will buy. A school meals survey by a major provider found that 37 per cent of children would select healthy foods if there was a better choice available (DoH, 2004). There are nutritional guidelines for school meals and the catering budgets are the responsibility of the school governors, but there is a disparity of provision across the country. Schools that have installed vending machines are most likely to sell snack foods high in fat, salt or sugar and sweetened fizzy drinks. By contrast, a pilot study by the Food Standards Agency (2004b) has shown that if secondary schoolchildren are given the choice, for example of healthier drinks, such as water, fruit juice and milk, they do make healthy choices.

The school meal may be the first meal of the day since 18 per cent of boys and 29 per cent of 16-year-old girls do not have breakfast before coming to school. School breakfast clubs are said to improve attendance, punctuality, concentration levels, problem-solving abilities and creativity (British Nutrition Foundation (BNF), 2003).

Physical activity

Inactivity starts with getting to school. A minority of secondary school pupils walk to school or cycle to school and few schools offer safe storage for cycles. Children who walk or cycle to school are likely to be fitter than those who journey by car and are therefore more likely to enjoy and benefit from sport. In school, physical education lessons offer the opportunity to expend energy and the DfES has set a target of 75 per cent of school children receiving two hours of high quality PE and sport by 2006. However, as a recent report on obesity points out, 'This two-hour target puts England below the European Union average in terms of physical activity in school, despite the fact that childhood obesity is accelerating more quickly here than elsewhere' (House of Commons Health Committee, 2004: para. 275).

Physical education and school sports form less than 2 per cent of school life but are useful in fostering habits of activity that can last into adult life. Active children tend to be less overweight and achieve more academically, but the HC committee cited above received evidence that organized school sport seems to alienate many children and there is ample evidence to suggest that much bullying begins in the changing room (ibid: par. 256). Other activities such as dance or aerobics could be used to broaden the opportunities for physical activities in school. Again there are fewer opportunities available in terms of access to swimming pools and leisure centres for those in lower socio-economic groups than those in higher socio-economic groups.

Moving forward

The National Curriculum addresses the issues of healthy living. Nutrition is quite firmly based in the science programme of study; in food technology pupils work with food as a material and understand the issues of food marketing and manufacturing; and in Personal, Social and Health Education classes (PSHE) developing a healthy safer lifestyle is a part of the KS3 curriculum. In PE pupils are to be taught knowledge and understanding of fitness and health.

Given all these teaching and learning opportunities why is there still a problem with overweight and obese adolescents? Schools do not exist in a vacuum.

Task 4.2.4
Food and health

Access the National Curriculum documents (DfEE/QCA, 1999) and identify those areas of the programmes of study at KS3 in the your subject area, and others, that address issues of healthy eating and healthy lifestyles. The 'National Curriculum in Action' website is useful (QCA, 2004).

Discuss with your school mentor whether there is a co-ordinated approach in your school experience school between the subjects and PSHE.

Resources for the teaching of nutrition on the British Nutrition Foundation are available online (BNF, 2004). The document 'Establishing a whole school policy' is also useful (BNF, 2003).

There are those would argue that advertising foods high in fat, sugar and salt should be banned during children's television shows. The government Office of Communications (OFCOM) undertook research in 2004 and found that TV advertising had a moderate, direct effect on children's food choices and that indirect effects were likely to be larger. Teenagers were influenced by advertisements that were witty or had subtle messages or featured celebrities as role models. Sponsorship of food products such as crisps and chocolates so that schools can raise money for books or sports equipment give conflicting messages to pupils.

There are a range of initiatives in schools to try to find a means of improving the health of schoolchildren. The National Healthy Schools Strategy is a project where schools can work with pupils, teachers, families and the local community to active promote physical, social and mental well being of all (DoH/DfES, 2004).

Task 4.2.5
The school environment

The definition of an obesogenic environment is one which encourages and promotes high energy intake and inactivity. Use the answers to the following questions and your observations to evaluate your school experience school environment.

- How many of your pupils walk or cycle to school?
- Is there safe storage for cycles?
- Is there a school tuck shop or vending machine and what is sold?
- What proportion of the school curriculum is given to PE and sports activities?

In addition observe the:

- activities of pupils during break and lunchtime for two different weekdays;
- food availability and food choices made at lunchtimes on one or two days.

You may find helpful the document 'Establishing a whole school policy', which has a food in schools audit tool and is available online at British Nutrition Foundation (BNF, 2004). Write a short account of this aspect of the school environment and discuss it with your school tutor.

The government has launched also a campaign to support schools in encouraging a healthy lifestyle called *Healthy Living: The Blueprint* (DfES, 2004a). It is an attempt by the government to bring together a multi-faceted approach to the broad problem of improving the obesogenic environment of modern society. The five objectives of the campaign and how it can be implemented are available online.

Schools need to empower adolescents by the provision of not just knowledge and understanding of diet and a healthy lifestyle but also with confidence in themselves to make the choices that control their lifestyle.

SUMMARY AND KEY POINTS

Adolescence sees dramatic physical changes in young people. These changes cause nervous introspection: 'Am I growing normally, am I too tall, too short, too fat? Will I be physically attractive to others?' Comparison with others becomes the main yardstick of development. Personal appearance assumes a growing importance and causes sensitivity. Girls mature physically earlier than boys, but the range of development of both sexes is wide. Adolescence involves physical, mental and emotional changes leading towards maturity. The range of physical differences between pupils means that, at the same age, pupils react quite differently to tasks and and situations in school.

Young people are taller and heavier than previous generations, in part due to improved diets. But there is growing concern about the rising numbers of overweight and obese pupils and adults and concern about the physical, social and psychological effects on the individual. The obesogenic environment of modern society, the more sedentary lifestyle, increased consumption of unhealthy foods can lead to overweight and obesity. Schools may be giving mixed messages. The teaching of healthy eating in various parts of the curriculum contrasts with the use of tuck shops, vending machines and school meals that sell unhealthy foods. The role of schools in raising awareness of the importance of healthy eating and a healthy lifestyle remains to be fully developed but the Healthy Living Blueprint (DfES, 2004a) for schools may help.

A number of issues affecting the health of adolescents have not been raised including smoking, drinking and drug use, mental health and sexual health. These are discussed further in the report on *Adolescent Health* (BMA, 2003).

Schools have a big role to play in helping young people to move through adolescence with the minimum of disruption, to understand the changes in their bodies, to be comfortable with themselves as they are and how they look. Schools play an important part in ensuring that pupils have access to a healthy diet and that they understand its importance to them now and in the future. This is achieved through a whole-school approach, including teaching and learning in PSHE, citizenship and other areas of the National Curriculum, but more importantly activities in school that encourage active learning, see Unit 5.2. The pupil who feels valued for their contribution is a pupil who is likely to have good self-esteem. All teachers therefore have the opportunity to contribute to the healthy development of their pupils and engender the self-confidence in young people to take control of this aspect of their lives and to resist fashion and peer pressure.

You should now identify the competences/standards for your course relevant to teachers' responsibilities for growth, development and diet.

FURTHER READING

British Nutrition Foundation. Online. Available HTTP: <http://www.nutrition.org.uk (accessed 27 October 2004). This site provides reliable information on diet and health. Particularly useful are the 'Teachers Centre' and 'Pupils Centre' which provide a wide range of resources for teachers, including activities for pupils, which are downloadable free of charge. It also has research papers relating to diet and health. An excellent resource for those teaching about diet and health.

Tanner, J.M. (1990) *Foetus into Man*, rev. and enlarged edn, Cambridge, MA: Harvard University Press. An excellent resource for those interested in the detail of growth and development of humans. The chapters on 'Puberty' and 'Heredity and the environment' are particularly useful.

Coles, A. and Turner, S. (1995) *Diet and Health in School Aged Children*, London: Health Education Authority. A survey of research findings of diet and health of the nation's children. Discusses the work of schools in health education, their provision of meals and what might be done to improve the diet of young people. A short and useful booklet for all teachers concerned with teaching healthy eating.

Unit 4.3

Cognitive Development

Judy Ireson

INTRODUCTION

During the secondary school years, pupils develop their knowledge and understanding of a wide range of subjects and also their ability to perceive, reason and solve problems. All of these are aspects of cognition (literally 'knowing'). A key feature of cognition is that it involves us as learners in making sense of the world around us. As such it is unlike more basic forms of learning such as memorizing a song or rote learning multiplication tables. It includes skills that involve understanding, such as map reading, following instructions to make something and solving problems. Making sense, knowing, understanding, thinking and reasoning develop into adulthood and so cognitive development is an important feature of pupils' mental growth during the secondary school years.

Logical reasoning is one important aspect of cognitive development, along with others such as problem solving, developing expertise and creative thinking. Many school subjects require us to think and reason logically, e.g. when handling evidence, making judgements, understanding when and how to apply rules, untangling moral dilemmas or applying theories. Most western societies in their schooling of children privilege logical, mathematical and linguistic abilities over other ways of knowing about the world. The tests of ability used by some schools to select new entrants or to allocate pupils to teaching groups are often problem-solving exercises involving pattern seeking, pattern recognition and pattern using and the capacity to think logically and quickly.

We consider some of the ways in which pupils' cognitive abilities develop and are identified, particularly logical reasoning, and discuss briefly some ideas about intelligence, including that there are a number of discrete intelligences. We also take a look at the some of the cognitive demands made by activities in different curriculum subjects. This unit is a continuation of Unit 4.2, which considered physical development. Unit 5.1 addresses in more detail theories of how children learn and develop and can be read in conjunction with this unit.

OBJECTIVES

By the end of this unit you should be:

- developing an understanding of cognitive development and the cognitive demands made by curriculum subjects;
- able to explain some ideas about the nature of intelligence;
- able to identify types of thinking and relate them to learning activities;
- developing your use of tasks as a way of finding out about pupils' cognitive level;
- able to evaluate the idea of 'matching' the curriculum to pupils' learning needs.

DIFFERENCES BETWEEN PUPILS

Differences between children are apparent from an early age. Even before they start school, some children pass developmental milestones such as walking and talking more quickly than others. Children may start reading and counting before they begin school, or become very confident in their physical skills. Those who acquire good language and communication tend to be seen as more advanced and may be labelled as brighter than others. At this age it is hard to know whether they have particular linguistic abilities or are more interested in the kinds of activities that encourage this aspect of development.

When children start primary school, teachers soon notice that some are better than others at school tasks. One of the reasons that children may be more advanced is that they are interested in the kinds of learning valued in school. It can be argued that school work is a game that children have not chosen to play, but which others, teachers and society, have chosen for them. If this assumption is correct, it is likely that some pupils will not be highly motivated by the content and focus of lessons and therefore these pupils may be less successful in school. An alternative view is that we all have an intrinsic need for competence and a tendency to protect our sense of self-worth, so children who fall behind in their learning and feel they are not competent act in ways to protect their self-image. Unfortunately this often involves maladaptive activity such as procrastination, denying interest or playing the class joker. This is challenging for teachers who often resort to extrinsic forms of motivation such as threats or praise. These may be effective in the short term but in the long run it is likely to be beneficial to encourage learners to see the point of their work and to emphasize their growing competence. It is well documented that learners work best at activities they themselves identify as worthwhile. A key task for teachers is to generate intrinsic motivation in pupils. See Unit 3.2.

Young people who do well in school subjects are sometimes thought to be 'more intelligent' than others, or more accurately, display more intelligent behaviour. Some people are of the view that intelligence is a fixed capacity or 'entity', which sets a limit on what an individual can achieve. Other people see intelligence as 'incremental', in other words it can grow with learning. An incremental view of intelligence carries with it the potential for change through teaching, whereas an entity view suggests that the effect of teaching is much more limited.

Before reading on, complete Task 4.3.1.

Task 4.3.1
Intelligent people

Think of two people who you would say are intelligent – they could be adults or children. In what ways are they similar and how do they differ? Share your ideas with other student teachers in your group and make a note of characteristics.

Thinking in different curriculum subjects

At this point we turn briefly to some types of thinking and intelligent behaviour called for in different curriculum subjects. A closer look at a few subjects suggests that there are differences but also some overlapping demands. In general, linguistic and logical reasoning seems to be privileged in western school systems.

It is generally thought that the demands of science and arts subjects are rather different. In a recent discussion about the teaching of art and design in secondary school the authors describe cognition in terms of the acquisition, assimilation and application of knowledge (Addison and Burgess, 2000). These processes are based on:

- perception, observation based on experience;
- intuition and reason, both the unconscious and conscious making sense of experience.

These processes require the use of imagination and thinking skills, which are used to transform observations and experiences into material representations. The explicit inclusion of intuition and unconscious making sense of experience is emphasized in art and design in contrast with many other subjects. The authors go on to point out that in the school curriculum knowledge-based, analytical processes are valued in the appreciation and criticism of art and other creative activities (Addison and Burgess, 2000: 26–9).

In contrast, mathematics and science are usually thought to involve logical and mathematical thinking. Indeed for some people mathematics and art lie towards opposite ends of a spectrum or are 'different cultures' as described by Snow (1960).

Intelligent behaviour thus takes different forms in these two subjects. Other curriculum subjects seem to overlap to a greater extent, e.g. the work of artists and designers involves similar skills to those of scientists, requiring the manipulation of materials and use of practical techniques. It may be that artists do more of their thinking in the process of manipulating materials, whereas scientists do more thinking and planning before carrying out their practical work. There is no doubt that new ideas and ways of thinking in science and mathematics involve imagination. For example, Aristotle's insight into floating and Watson and Crick's double helix model for the structure of DNA require imaginative thinking. Creativity is also an important aspect of mathematics (Hardy, 1967:13). Similarly, although the use of imagination and creative thinking is most strongly associated with the arts, creativity may be encouraged in many subjects (see <http://www.ncaction.org.uk/creativity>).

A question of intelligence?

Intelligence is most often linked to a pupil's capacity to exercise linguistic and logical mathematical reasoning. This is what is measured by most tests of intelligence. There is considerable evidence to support classical theories of intelligence, which suggest that there is a general factor underlying our performance in a wide range of activities in school and work. However, Gardner criticizes these theories for being concerned with only a very narrow range of human ability, namely language and mathematics. He argues that they fail to take account of many other aspects that are important in the real world. In his 'theory of multiple intelligences' he proposes that there are a number of relatively autonomous intelligences. He describes intelligence as 'the ability to solve problems or fashion products that are of consequence in a particular culture, setting or community' (Gardner, 1993a: 15). He identified seven intelligences, as follows.

- Linguistic: use and understanding of language, including speech sounds, grammar, meaning and the use of language in various settings.
- Musical: allows people to create, communicate and understand meanings made with sound.
- Logico-mathematical: use and understanding of abstract relationships.
- Spatial: perceive visual or spatial information, to be able to transform and modify this information, to re-create visual images even when the visual stimulus is absent.
- Bodily kinaesthetic: use all or part of one's body to solve problems or fashion products.
- Intrapersonal: knowledge of self and personal feelings. This knowledge enables personal decision making.
- Interpersonal: awareness of feelings, intentions and beliefs of others.

Recently Gardner added an eighth 'naturalistic' intelligence described as 'the kind of skill at recognising flora and fauna that one associates with biologists like Darwin' (Gardner *et al.* 1996: 203). He proposes that these relatively autonomous intelligences can be exerted alone or combined in different contexts at different times. A number of intelligences may be needed in order to carry out some tasks, e.g. in the case of art and design both spatial intelligence and bodily kinaesthetic intelligence might contribute to learning.

At this point you might like to look back at the list of characteristics of intelligent people you identified in Task 4.3.1. How well do they map on to Gardner's seven intelligences?

Gardner's 'intrapersonal' and interpersonal' intelligences capture much of what has recently been called 'emotional intelligence' (Salovey and Mayer, 1990). This is the ability to recognize, express and reflect on our own emotional states and those of other people and also to manage these emotions. There is insufficient space to go into this fairly new idea here, however is worth noting that for most people learning is an emotional experience. It may involve confusion, disappointment, apprehension, fascination, absorption, exhilaration and relief. These emotions can disrupt or facilitate learning and it is easy to see that learners benefit from being able accurately to recognize and manage them effectively.

Some of the ideas behind the theory of multiple intelligences have received critical reviews (White, 1998). It is not yet clear just how autonomous these intelligences are and a common view among experts is that a likely model of intelligence is one that operates through a general underlying intelligence backed up by a small number of special abilities. However, many teachers and advisers find Gardner's ideas very helpful as they alert us to a variety of ways in which we might recognize and develop intelligent behaviour. An influential report on creativity in education refers specifically to the theory of multiple intelligences in its advocacy of a broader approach to education than has existed under the National Curriculum for England and Wales (Robinson, 1999: 34–7).

Over 25 years ago, HM Inspectorate reviewed the state of the secondary curriculum and published a forward-looking document outlining ways of thinking about what pupils might learn in school. They identified eight 'areas of experience' to which pupils should be exposed. These areas were the aesthetic and creative, the ethical, the linguistic, the mathematical, the physical, the scientific, the social and political and the spiritual (HMI, 1977: 6). This publication prompted much debate and several years of discussion about the school curriculum in England and Wales. But the 1988 Education

Act did not reflect any of that thinking. You might like to consider the correlation between the newly emerging theory of multiple intelligences referred to above and the near forgotten 'areas of experience'.

Task 4.3.2
Design and Technology
(D and T)

Locate online the D and T National Curriculum document (DfEE/QCA, 1999a); select the section 'Teaching D and T at KS 3' and read the introduction 'Aims and Purposes of Design and Technology' and 'Content at KS3'. Note, too, the headings of the five attainment targets immediately following.

Discuss the skills and intelligences demanded by D and T by responding to these questions.

1.   In what ways do the demands of D and T link to the importance attached by school to linguistic and logico-mathematical aptitude?
2.   Using Gardner's theory of multiple intelligences, discuss the teaching and learning of D and T as the development and utilization of different intelligences.
3.   Do the skills and intelligences demanded by D and T justify its place as a foundation subject in English schools? For further background to D and T, see Owen-Jackson (2000: chs 1 and 8).

COGNITIVE DEMANDS ON PUPILS

It is worth noting that all subjects are expected to address the following thinking skills (DfEE/QCA, 1999a: 22–3). You should bear this in mind when we turn to some of the cognitive demands made on pupils through the curriculum, below.

Information processing skills. These enable pupils to locate and collect relevant information, to sort, classify, sequence, compare and contrast, and to analyse part/whole relationships.

Reasoning skills. These enable pupils to give reasons for opinions and actions, to draw inferences and make deductions, to use precise language to explain what they think, and to make judgements and decisions informed by reasons or evidence.

Enquiry skills. These enable pupils to ask relevant questions, to pose and define problems, to plan what to do and how to research, to predict outcomes and anticipate consequences, and to test conclusions and improve ideas.

Creative thinking skills. These enable pupils to generate and extend ideas, to suggest hypotheses, to apply imagination, and to look for alternative innovative outcomes.

Evaluation skills. These enable pupils to evaluate information, to judge the value of what they read, hear and do, to develop criteria for judging the value of their own and others' work or ideas, and to have confidence in their judgements.

The first task we have selected (see Task 4.3.3) is taken from a popular quiz book (Brandreth, 1981). The problems in these types of books are often abstract, lack a real context but demand reasoning skills, perhaps not too far from the situation commonly found in school.

Task 4.3.3
A logic problem

Try out the following problem on your own; then compare your answer with other student teachers and share how you set about solving the problem.

When Amy, Bill and Clare eat out, each orders *either* chicken or fish, according to these rules:

1. If Amy orders chicken, Bill orders fish:
2. Either Amy or Clare orders chicken, but not both;
3. Bill and Clare do not both order fish.

Who could have ordered chicken yesterday and fish today? (See Appendix 4.3.1 for solution.)

The problem in Task 4.3.3 is essentially about handling information according to rules of the type 'If A, then B', commonly found in intelligence tests. In this example the rules are arbitrary and it is not a real life problem because people don't behave in this way. The problem cannot be solved by resort to practical activity; it is a logico-mathematical task requiring abstract thinking. The puzzle can be done 'in the head', but many people need to devise a way of recording their thinking as they develop their answer and check solutions.

Another kind of reasoning task is a game used in *Thinking through Geography* (Leat, 1998). Pupils are given sets of words and asked to find the odd one out. See Task 4.3.4.

Task 4.3.4
Odd one out

The following sets of words relate to traffic in urban areas. Which is the odd one out in each set? Try this yourself and then compare your answers with others in your group. What went through your mind as you thought about each set?

1. Park and ride	Shopping trips	Bus passes	Ring road
2. Wheel clamp	Tailbacks	Speed cameras	Sleeping policeman

Leat suggests that this game requires information processing skills, reasoning and creative thinking. Do you agree? How does this task differ from the one above? Make up some sets of words relating to your own curriculum subject and see how well others in your group manage them.

We turn next to an exercise commonly given to pupils in science lessons during Key Stage 3 or early Key Stage 4. Pupils are set a problem-solving task in which they are invited to identify the factors which affect the rate at which a pendulum swings (or 'time period'), see Task 4.3.5. The task is abstract but has real life connections as pendulums are used to control timepieces, such as a longcase clock which contains a pendulum with a heavy weight at one end. The length of the pendulum is adjusted to control the accuracy of the timepiece.

The activity concerns *understanding* and *how understanding is gained* rather than knowing and recall. The pupil's task involves planning an investigation, identifying patterns in data and making deductions, in other words, enquiry skills. The exercise illustrates, too, the ways in which pupils respond to data. The analysis of the data requires abstract thought and the ability to handle a complex situation in which several factors (variables) have to be considered.

Task 4.3.5
Enquiry and understanding

Which factors (variables) affect the swing of a pendulum?

Background information

A pendulum is essentially a rod pivoted vertically at one end and free to swing from side to side. A simple example of a pendulum is a piece of string suspended at one end with a weight at the other; see Figure 4.3.1. Pupils are sometimes expected to use experimental data to deduce factors that influence the rate of swing or 'rules of the pendulum'. They may be given the data, or derive the data for themselves. The task is not to learn the rules, but to understand how the rules derive from observation. The exercise for you and for pupils is to work out what can, or cannot, be deduced from the data.

The pupil's task

Two pupils were given a task to find out which factors affected the time period, or rate at which a pendulum swings. They were not told exactly what to do but the teacher had suggested investigating the effect of length, of weight and the push. They decided to measure the number of swings made by a pendulum in half a minute. They changed variables of the pendulum each time, by varying:

- the length of the pendulum; they had one short pendulum and one long pendulum (Figure 4.3.1a and b);
- the size of the weight on the end of the pendulum, a heavy weight and a light weight (Figure 4.3.1b and c);
- the height it was raised to set it going – the push. One 'push' was high up, the other 'push' low down (Figure 4.3.1c and d).

In their investigation, pupils sometimes changed one variable at a time but occasionally changed more than one. They collected some readings (Table 4.3.1) and then tried to sort out what the readings meant.

Your task

From the evidence *alone* in Table 4.3.1 what do you think the data tell you about the effect of *length*, of *weight* and of *position of release* on the number of swings per half minute of the pendulum? See Appendix 4.3.2 for further information.

Refer to the competences/standards for your course about helping pupils analyse data with several variables.

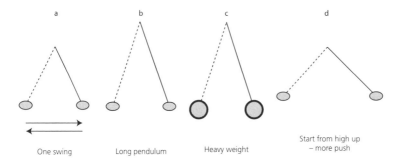

Figure 4.3.1 The pendulum: three variables, length, weight and 'high up'

Table 4.3.1 Data on different pendulums obtained by pupils (for Task 4.3.5)

Experiment	Length of the pendulum	Size of weight on the end	Push at start	No. Swings in ½ minute
1	long	heavy	large	17
2	short	heavy	large	21
3	long	light	small	17
4	short	light	large	21

Note that some further information can be obtained from the data once a decision is made about the effect of weight on the time period of the pendulum; see Appendix 4.3.2. Listening to pupils as they try to solve the problem can be very valuable as it provides clues about their cognitive processes. Some interesting features are as follows.

Intuitively pupils expect the size of the weight and the 'push' to have an effect on the time period, or rate of swing. They tend to expect heavy weights to 'do more' than light weights. The results are contrary to common-sense and pupils often think they are wrong. This conflict with everyday conceptions is not an uncommon experience even for adults. Evidence that the magnitude of the weight at the end of the pendulum has no effect on the time period is often rejected intuitively or put down to error. Common-sense notions are in powerful opposition to logical thinking.

Some pupils also do not accept that if two variables are changed at the same time, then it is not possible on that evidence alone to make a deduction. In this situation, some pupils may then bring in evidence external to the investigation to support their argument, instead of using the data they have.

When pupils are faced with the need to get evidence for themselves they frequently choose trial and error methods rather than logically constructed enquiries. Trial and error methods often lead to data which do not provide clear-cut answers to questions, this can lead pupils to make unwarranted inferences from the data in an attempt to get an answer.

As the data is not always clear cut, judgements may have to be withheld. This may cause mental conflict because there is a powerful expectation (by adults and young people) that experiments yield positive information. Saying 'this enquiry tells us nothing about the question' is not an acceptable answer, especially if the teacher has set up the enquiry. Such feelings mean that attitudes of persistence and honesty are critical for the generation of real understanding.

This investigation, and others like it, suggest that enquiries that involve several variables are difficult for pupils. Teaching is needed to improve achievement in these skills, as has been shown by the Cognitive Acceleration in Science Project (CASE) (Adey and Shayer, 1994: chs 5 and 8). If you would like to try the pendulum task with pupils, furher details can be found in *Science Reasoning Tasks* (Whylam and Shayer, 1978) or the *CASE* materials (Adey *et al.*, 1989).

Common-sense beliefs and misconceptions

Everyday beliefs and misconceptions are common in science, as shown in the pendulum task above, but they also surface in other subjects. Gardner (1991) gives many examples, including a classic case reported by I. A. Richards many years ago. Richards asked undergraduates at Cambridge University to read pairs of poems and then to offer their interpretations and evaluations. He found that the students were heavily influenced by the form of the poem, in other words whether it rhymed, had a regular metre or rhythm, and avoided words that were too common or arcane. Many of them failed to understand the meaning of the poems.

Gardner (1991) suggests that that many of our everyday understandings take the form of 'scripts' and 'stereotypes' that tend to simplify the world around us and make it more manageable. Unfortunately pupils use these to interpret information presented in school subjects. For example, intuitive interpretations of historical events tend to be quite simplistic and stereotypical, there is often a good versus evil narrative, with evil leaders taking on great importance and the good usually winning in the end. Even when students have learned that events such as the Second World War have complex causes and that war is seldom due to the behaviour of a single evil leader they may slip back into simplistic ways of thinking.

It is worth getting to know about common misconceptions in your own subject as this can help you see why pupils have difficulty with some new ideas and ways of thinking. You may be able to plan activities to challenge specific misconceptions.

Understanding percentages

The next task illustrates the demands made by problems involving percentages. Understanding percentage is an important part of everyday economic life, in retail, mortgages, investment and cost of living generally. It is an area of understanding where considerable confusion reigns for both pupils and adults. See Figure 4.3.2.

Another example of a common confusion is financial inflation: many adults expect the cost of living to come down when the inflation rate is reduced from 3 to 2 per cent. Similarly, some adults have difficulty calculating real costs when sales advertising offers percentage discounts; see question c in Table 4.3.2. When pupils are faced with problems involving percentages, it appears that context is as important as the numbers themselves. In addition, the understanding of what constitutes a right answer is confused with 'what answer is good enough, given the context'. We might sympathise with this last point, e.g. when preparing a dish for four people and faced with a recipe which requires 2/3 pint of cream for six people we might estimate rather than calculate exactly. The following example illustrates how context might influence the way questions can be tackled.

Pupils were given three questions on percentages, together with an introduction which explained the meaning of the symbol '%'. The questions (a, b, and c) and the number of pupils getting the right answer (the success rate) for each of three year groups is shown in Table 4.3.2.

We suggest you read through the questions in Table 4.3.2 and check your own answers to the questions. Then consider possible reasons for the variation in the success rate shown by these pupils and the different contexts in which the mathematics is set. If ability is being is judged by responses to questions like these then, clearly, the context in which the mathematics is set matters. The author describes how pupils arrive at their different answers, the different strategies they use and implications for teaching (Hart, 1981: 96–7). See also Task 6.1.2 for further effects of context on assessment.

A supermarket offered olive oil for sale labelled '50% free'. The bottle contained 750 ml and was priced £2.99, the same price as a regular bottle of oil containing 500 ml. A group of adult customers were arguing that this offer was wrong because the price was not cheaper, i.e. £1.50. Despite having the nature of the offer explained to them several times by another customer, most of the group refused to buy the item because it did not cost less than the regular item.

Figure 4.3.2 Percentages in the supermarket

Table 4.3.2 Pupils' performance on questions involving percentage

Q. 8. **%** means per cent or per 100, so 3% is 3 out of every 100.			
a. 6% of pupils in school have free dinners. There are 250 pupils in the school. How many pupils have free dinners?			
Age/years	13	14	15
Success rate/%	36	45	57
b. The newspaper says that 24 out of 800 Avenger cars have a faulty engine. What percentage is this?			
Age/years	13	14	15
Success rate/%	32	40	58
c. The price of a coat is 20. In the sale it is reduced by 5%. How much does it now cost?			
Age/years	13	14	15
Success rate/%	20	27	35

Source: Hart, 1981: 96. For further studies on the performance of pupils see Keys *et al.* (1996).

Evidence from this investigation and others like it show that most of us have several strategies we might use when attempting to solve problems such as these. Even young children may have three different strategies for simple addition problems. Students who are able to use more efficient strategies for the percentage problem above, such as multiplying by a fraction, are generally more successful but they might not always use the most advanced strategy. This might be because they are not very confident with it or it takes time and effort.

Sometimes it is getting the right answer which is the important factor, rather than the understanding of how a right answer can be obtained. Some of these difficulties for pupils may arise from differences in the use of mathematics in and out of school. In everyday life, approximations are often good enough, as in the cooking example above.

Before leaving examples from mathematics, it is worth noting that adults are often quite happy to admit that they 'are not good at maths', whereas they are more reluctant to admit to literacy difficulties. The drive by government agencies to raise standards of literacy and numeracy is a recognition of the importance of these skills. The Teacher Training Agency (TTA), the body responsible in England for teacher supply and qualification has, from 2000, demanded that all trainee teachers be tested in aspects of numeracy as a condition of gaining qualified teacher status and has provided considerable support for teachers (TTA, 2004; Patmore, 2000).

Developing cognitive abilities

In general, pupils' cognitive abilities increase with age, as illustrated by the percentage example in Table 4.3.2. Older pupils are more capable of abstract, symbolic thinking than younger pupils, who tend to use more concrete representations when solving problems (see the discussion of Piaget's theory in Unit 5.1). It is also clear that in any year group there is considerable diversity, with some students able to cope with more demanding work, while others have great difficulty. Several different explanations have been suggested for this diversity and for the general pattern of development during the school years. In the remainder of this section we will briefly outline some of these.

So what might influence the development of cognitive abilities? Most answers to this question emphasize biological or environmental factors, or 'nature' and 'nurture'. 'Nature' refers to our inborn, genetic or inherited characteristics and how these unfold during maturation, while 'nurture' refers to the environment in which we grow and develop. Genetic factors undoubtedly affect development, but the extent of this influence is not entirely clear, as it is difficult to disentangle genetic and environmental determinants. The most influential studies compare twins raised together with twins separated at an early age and raised in different families. These studies show that inherited characteristics do have a strong effect but they do not completely determine measured intelligence, the child's environment also makes an important contribution. Criticisms of the research include the view that the measures of intelligence used in these studies give a particular and quite restricted meaning to the notion of intelligence itself (Gardner *et al.*, 1996).

Turning to the environment, children's attainment on entry to secondary school is influenced by their experiences in the home and in primary school. Evidence has accumulated to suggest that a severe lack of stimulation in early childhood limits the capacity of children to benefit from school and other learning situations. A home life that forms a firm basis for later development is one in which children are well cared for and are encouraged to play, explore and talk and later to enjoy books and learn about the world around them. Children from a good home learning environment have a head start when they enter primary school, as they develop many of the cognitive, communicative and social skills needed in school. Later on, their parents may support them directly and indirectly, e.g. taking them to the local library, explaining homework or enabling them to participate in a wide range of activities. While the majority of parents are able to provide a good home learning environment, some find this difficult, perhaps for economic, social or health reasons. Some parents will be able to find good nursery and primary education for their children, while others find this a problem.

A child's performance in attainment tests, such as Key Stage tests, is thus a reflection of nature and nurture, the child's innate abilities and the influence of the environment. The attainment tests tell you what a child knows, understands and can do at a particular point in time, however they are not necessarily reliable predictors of future attainment. Pupils who have had less support for their learning in the past, or who do not speak English as their first language, may be more capable than suggested by these tests. For this reason it is important to take care not to label pupils in a deterministic way as high, middle or low ability on the basis of attainment tests when they enter the school.

Another important factor that is easily overlooked is the amount of knowledge an individual has acquired. It is sometimes assumed that the more advanced thinking of adults is due to biological maturation, when in fact it may be due to increased knowledge. The power of knowledge is illustrated nicely by comparing children who are very knowledgeable about a subject with adults who are not, e.g. children who are very good at chess and adults who are beginners. When shown a chess board with pieces laid out as they might be during a game the children are better than the adults at remembering the positions. If the board is taken away, they are able to place more pieces in the correct position on another, empty board. However, when the pieces are arranged randomly on the board, there is no difference between the adults and the children. This indicates that the children who are good at chess build up knowledge of patterns and configurations as they play and this knowledge helps them remember (see Bransford *et al.*, 1999).

People who are experts are much better at recognizing patterns in information and using principles to solve problems. This applies in domains as diverse as medicine, music, physics, computer programming and teaching. Experts build up a strong knowledge base and use it effectively to solve problems (for further information see Howe, 1998). For pupils, the development of a strong knowledge base in school subjects is important for remembering and thinking. It also makes learning more enjoyable and satisfying. Good teaching and active learning (see Unit 5.2) should help students to build up a well-structured knowledge base, but this may be undermined by pressure to cover the curriculum, leaving insufficient time for understanding and consolidation (Biggs and Moore, 1993; Howe, 1998).

Several ideas have now been introduced to explain pupils' performance in school. It has been suggested that performance is a product of inheritance and environment. Also that, as they grow, develop and learn, pupils become more able to handle complex problems and situations and abstract thinking. As teachers, we are not in a position to influence inheritance or the home learning environment, but we are able to structure learning experiences so that they are aligned with pupils' current knowledge and understanding. To do this requires a careful analysis of the demands made by a piece of work and the current performance of the pupil or group of pupils with reference to relevant knowledge, skills and understanding needed to do the task. Future learning activities can then be planned so as to guarantee some success while offering a comfortable level of challenge. It has been suggested that curriculum development then becomes a process of matching the curriculum demand so that work is demanding but not too difficult. This depends on being able to analyse the cognitive demands of teaching and learning activities and the relevant capabilities of each pupil in order to achieve a match.

A number of questions arise from proposing such an approach.

- To what extent does the cognitive demand made by the teaching material depend on the way the material is presented? Can most concepts be taught to most pupils if suitably packaged and presented?
- If matching 'curriculum to pupil' is the goal of the exercise, how might you build in development, going beyond the current level of performance? How would pupils progress and is there a danger that reducing the chance of failure may remove challenge?
- Records of pupil performance and development are needed in order to match material to pupil. How should such records be kept?
- If each pupil has different prior knowledge and understanding, how can a teacher cope with a whole class? See Unit 4.1.
- If pupils cannot cope with certain concepts because they are not yet ready for them, does this mean that some areas of the curriculum cannot be taught? Is rote learning an acceptable way to overcome this problem? See Unit 4.1 on differentiated learning, theories of learning and Units 5.1 and 5.2 on active learning.

You may wish to add your own ideas to this list.

An alternative to this approach is to think in terms of 'constructive alignment' (Biggs and Moore, 1993). A basic assumption here is that the learner constructs meaning through relevant learning activities, hence 'constructive'. The 'alignment' part refers to what the teacher does, which is to set up a learning environment that supports the activities appropriate to achieving the desired learning outcomes. The key is that teaching methods and assessment tasks are aligned to the learning activities. Less emphasis is placed on obtaining detailed information about each learner. Such an approach perhaps acknowledges that it is very difficult for a class teacher, given the number of pupils in a class and the variety of differences between pupils, to match work on an individual basis. The key point is that teachers should provide a variety of different types of learning activities carefully designed to enable pupils to achieve the desired outcomes.

The Cognitive Acceleration programme offers a somewhat different approach (Shayer and Adey, 2002) which incorporates several key components. The first is 'concrete preparation' which involves activities to ensure that pupils are familiar with the context of a problem and any technical vocabulary. Pupils are then given problems to discuss in small groups and these problems are designed in such a way that all students are able to contribute to the discussion. An important feature of the programme is that pupils are encouraged to think about their own thinking (metacognition). Teachers and pupils are also encouraged to think about links between their thinking in other aspects of the curriculum.

Results suggest that pupils can be taught to think in generic ways that will help them to learn better across a range of subjects and context (Adey, 2000). Cognitive acceleration started in science but is now being developed in a variety of curriculum subjects (Shayer and Adey, 2002).

CREATIVE PROBLEM SOLVING

In this unit we have taken cognition to encompass acquisition, assimilation and application of knowledge and also problem solving and thinking. Earlier in the unit we used an example from design and technology as fostering capability which is 'the integration of thought and skills into a holistic exercise, rather than a piecemeal exercise of isolated skills'.

A good example of this type of problem solving is shown in a collection by Edward de Bono of children's responses to problems set by adults. The collection shows the spontaneous work by pupils (upper primary, lower secondary) in response to problems related to everyday events (de Bono, 1972). The tasks include:

- 'how would you stop a cat and a dog fighting?'
- 'design a machine to weigh an elephant'
- 'invent a sleep machine'
- 'how would you build a house quickly?'
- 'how would you improve the human body?'
- 'design a bicycle for postmen'

In this work pupils need knowledge of the context from which the problem is drawn and also use knowledge and skills from both inside and outside the classroom. The work of pupils is occasionally unusual and the solutions sometimes impractical. The responses show much imagination and insight into their everyday world. In the author's discussion of the many sketches and solutions made in response to the task, e.g. designing a bicycle for postmen, he noted that children quickly identified what the postmen's problems were. These problems included nasty dogs, getting wet and getting the bike up steep hills. Children recognized that postmen spent a lot of time getting on and off the bike; so solutions were directed to delivery in the saddle. Pupils acknowledged that postmen spent a lot of time outside delivering the post, so some solutions provided the postman with food and drink, even hot drinks. The solutions were usually additive, leading to complexity, without elegance or aesthetic appeal. The important criterion was effectiveness.

You may wish to set a similar task for your pupils; de Bono's text is available in some libraries or can be purchased, e.g. online <http://www.abebooks.co.uk>. You should consider how you deal with your pupils' work; how is it to be marked and the criteria for your response? You could ask pupils to work on the problem in small groups and then explain their thought processes (metacognition). Your pupils could develop criteria for assessing the work. Or you could give them a list of intelligences and thinking skills and ask them to identify the ones they used.

MEASURING COGNITIVE DEVELOPMENT AND INTELLIGENCE TESTS

Much work has been carried out to help us understand children's (and adults') responses to problem situations. For example, Piaget devised many tasks that have been used extensively and adapted by others (see Donaldson, 1978 and 1992; Child, 1997: ch. 7). These tasks provide a window on the type and sequence of thought process adopted by learners and reveal much about how children's thinking develops. Hopefully, if you have tried some of the tasks in this unit you will be starting to see how you might use problems to help you learn more about your pupils' cognitive processes.

In education, the main purpose of many tests and examinations is to assess, rank, select and make predictions about progress (see Unit 6.1). Tests of intelligence were originally designed for this purpose, to assist educational and occupational selection on a fair, meritocratic basis. Most people are familiar with the notion of 'Intelligence Quotient' (IQ) which is reported as a single number. This is derived from test scores and shows the extent to which the pupil is below or above an average score based on a large sample of pupils. The test is norm-referenced and the average score is given an arbitrary value of 100. As indicated above, intelligence tests generally tap a range of cognitive abilities involving language, numerical and non-verbal thinking and reasoning.

Intelligence testing assumed great importance in the UK after the Second World War due to the 1944 Education Act. Pupils were selected for grammar, technical or 'modern' schools by means of the 11+ examination, a type of intelligence test. Despite being developed into a reliable sophisticated tool, the examination failed to take account of late developers or the effects of pupils' social background. The tests also favoured pupils with good linguistic skills, those who had a good vocabulary and were familiar with middle class culture, and girls. Girls on average mature faster than boys and the 11+ entry had to be modified to ensure equal access to grammar school by boys and girls. It was shown, too, that performance on the tests could be improved by training, which suggested that in part at least, learned skills were being tested rather than purely innate intelligence. Confidence in the whole issue of selection was undermined by research showing that it had negative impacts on pupils from less advantaged background. In due course many LEAs abolished grammar schools and moved to a fully comprehensive secondary system on grounds of equity, although some retain selection to this day, e.g. Kent and Buckinghamshire (Crook *et al.*, 1999: 1–3; Ireson and Hallam, 2001). Recently, concerns about the impact of home background on pupils' achievement in national examinations have led to a call for the use of cognitive abilities tests in selecting young people for gifted and talented programmes and entrance to university.

Standardized testing is a skilled process and many commercially available tests must only be used by approved persons. IQ testing is sometimes used by educational psychologists to assess pupils who, in various ways, find school difficult. This may be necessary for the identification of special educational needs such as dyslexia (see Unit 4.6). Other reasons for standardized assessment may be for research purposes as part of monitoring a population. See Unit 6.1 for further information.

SUMMARY AND KEY POINTS

In this unit, cognitive development is introduced as a process through which pupils develop their knowledge, understanding, reasoning, problem solving and creative thinking. It is influenced by maturation and the learning environment provided at home and in school. We have drawn attention to the priority given by schools in western society to linguistic skills and logical reasoning especially that used in the sciences and mathematics. We compared these with the knowledge skills and attitudes needed by arts, design and technology courses and asked you to think about the demands of your own specialist subject.

The nature of intelligence is subject to debate, and here we have done no more than briefly outline some prevailing views. One is that there is a general component and a number of specialized abilities. Another is that there are multiple relatively autonomous intelligences. Also, everyday beliefs about intelligence include both 'entity' and 'incremental' notions. Measures of intelligence or general ability emphasize language and logical-mathematical thinking.

Practical tasks in this unit are offered to encourage you to analyse the cognitive abilities involved in completing them. The tasks also illustrate some ways you might go about finding out more about your pupils' cognitive development. Your classes contain pupils with a wide range of cognitive levels, even if your school has ability grouping. By listening to pupils and finding out about their perspective on learning activities you learn more about their understanding and thinking. This helps you to design activities to assist their development.

We refer you to Unit 5.2 'Active Learning', Unit 3.2 'Motivation' and Unit 5.1 'How Children Learn' for further discussion of those related topics. You should check the competences/standards for your course as they relate to pupil learning and development.

FURTHER READING

Child, D. (2003) *Psychology and the Teacher*, 7th edn, London: Continuum International Publishing Group. A classic text which provides a useful review of cognitive development, theories of learning and intelligence; includes research into classrooms, practice, management and special needs. Source of references.

Donaldson, M. (1978) *Children's Minds*, 1st edn, Glasgow: Collins. Essential reading for anyone interested in developmental psychology and Piaget's work on cognitive growth. Review of work of Piaget. See also Donaldson, 1992.

Gardner, H. (1994) 'The theory of multiple intelligences', in B. Moon and A. Shelton-Mayes (eds) *Teaching and Learning in the Secondary School*, London: Routledge. Readers interested in this model of intelligence might read this introductory paper before tackling his other writing (Gardner, 1993a, 1993b).

Howe, M. (1998) *Principles of Human Abilities and Learning*, Hove: Psychology Press. A very readable introduction to abilities and how they develop. Explores the nature of abilities and challenges some common-sense notions with interesting examples. Also discusses intelligence and motivation.

APPENDIX 4.3.1: ANSWERS TO TASK 4.3.3

From rules a and b, if Amy orders chicken, Bill orders fish and Clare orders fish. This contradicts rule c. So Amy orders only fish. Then from rule b Clare can order fish or chicken. Clare orders chicken, then Bill orders fish or chicken. If Clare orders fish then Bill can order only chicken. So Clare could have chicken yesterday and fish today.

APPENDIX 4.3.2: COMMENTARY ON TASK 4.3.5

The time period of a pendulum depends on the length of the pendulum; neither the magnitude of the weight nor the position from which the pendulum starts swinging (high or low) affects the time period.

From the pupil readings, Table 4.3.1, it follows that investigations 1 and 2 tell you the length has an effect on the time period, since only length was changed, weight and position of release being held the same. Investigations 2 and 4 tell you that weight has no effect on the time period, since length and position of release are held the same. Finally, from 1 and 3, *if weight has no effect*, then since the length is constant in both experiments, the position of release has no effect on the number of swings per half minute.

Unit 4.4

Responding to Diversity

Andrew Noyes and Tony Turner

INTRODUCTION

Teaching is a complex process, made interesting by the vast range of educational, social and political contexts and purposes that shape it. Increasingly, teachers are expected to take account of such diversity in their classroom practices. This chapter helps you to understand better the complex make-up of modern UK society, particularly how social diversity and educational opportunity and attainment are interrelated. As well as considering a big picture perspective you are also encouraged to examine critically the ways in which you respond to diversity in your teaching.

The Standards for Qualified Teacher Status in England begin:

> Those awarded Qualified Teacher Status must understand and uphold the professional code of the General Teaching Council for England (GTC) by demonstrating (that) … they have high expectations of all pupils; respect their social, cultural, linguistic, religious and ethnic backgrounds; and are committed to raising their educational achievement.
>
> (DfES/TTA, 2004: S1)

These standards form the basis of a teacher's development through initial teacher education courses and the newly qualified teacher (NQT) year. The ability to respond appropriately to children's diverse needs and circumstances is of primary importance for teachers. Indeed, the GTC's 'Code of Professional Values and Practice' states that: 'teachers challenge stereotypes and oppose prejudice to safeguard equality of opportunity, respecting individuals regardless of gender, marital status, religion, colour, race, ethnicity, class, sexual orientation, disability and age' (GTC, 2002) This is easy to write but much more difficult to implement. It is important to recognise that teachers are part of that diversity and that your experiences of education and perspectives on a variety of complex social and cultural issues will have a significant influence on the way in which you respond to diversity. In this chapter we focus on issues around ethnicity, gender and class and, although they are examined separately herein, they clearly overlap and intertwine.

OBJECTIVES

At the end of this chapter you should be able to:

- analyse evidence about the relative academic performance of pupils in relation to class, ethnicity and gender;
- discuss issues of discrimination and bias in relation to gender, ethnicity and class;
- consider school policies and critique classroom procedures in order to promote better opportunities for learning for all pupils;
- relate these skills and attitudes to the competences/Standards expected for your course or as an NQT.

A HISTORY OF DIVERSITY

The presence of people originating from other cultures, faiths and backgrounds has been a feature of British society for many centuries. The notion of 'other' suggests that British society is easily described but 'Britishness' is neither a clearly defined nor a fixed concept. Immigration into the British Isles has come in waves. A few examples draw attention to the changing ethnic mix that contributes to present day society. The Roman conquest of England at the dawn of the Christian era lasted some six centuries at the end of which came invasion by Germanic peoples. About two centuries later the Viking invasion brought Danes and Norwegians to the mix of peoples. In 1066, the Normans took over much of England and many French people stayed and were assimilated. In the sixteenth century many people fled mainland European countries to escape, for example, religious persecution.

The ethnic mix was added to by Jewish immigration following their persecution at the end of the nineteenth century. Two world wars saw a further migration of people in mainland Europe away from conflict. As many former colonial countries have gained independence, immigration from Africa and Asia altered the ethnic mix in the UK. The important difference associated with this latter wave of immigration was the visibility of newcomers. Prior to 1948 there was only a trickle of Black immigrants; the 1950s in the UK saw the active recruitment of Black and Asian families to fill the gaps in the work force (Briggs, 1983: 310–12).

Throughout the last century the population of England and Wales grew steadily, from 35.5 million in 1901 to nearly 49 million in 1991. The 2001 census showed that the population of Great Britain was almost 57.1 million. It would appear that steady population growth has been supplemented by immigration. The minority ethnic population is expected to grow to some 10 per cent of the population by 2020.

Up to the early 1950s immigration was largely white. Many immigrants prior to that date were assimilated into the host culture, although a few immigrant groups maintained their distinctive lifestyle, e.g. the Jewish community. At first, the host community adopted the same attitude towards the Black and Asian immigrants and expected them to adopt the values and lifestyle of the host nation. That this policy did not work may be attributed to the influence of racism – Black people were not accepted in the same way as white immigrants of the past. The eugenics movement of the early twentieth century may also have been influential. This movement was supported by some scientists, who claimed to supply 'evidence' of a hierarchy of intelligence among the 'races' as well as between men and women; this hierarchy placed whites above other all ethnic groups and men above women (Gould, 1984; Wersky, 1988: 26–37). The influence of this movement may, at that time, have supported the racist views of some of the host population towards the new immigrants. Such issues still exist in our society and far-right political parties such as the British National Party continue to find support in many parts of England.

EQUAL OPPORTUNITIES AND EDUCATIONAL EQUITY

For many people it is self-evident that the implementation of equal opportunities policies is a reflection of basic human rights, but how does the notion of equality of opportunity relate to a teacher's response to diversity? Should the same curriculum, teaching styles, etc., be used consistently, or does such 'equality' in fact perpetuate inequality? Sociologists have argued for many years that if you assume that all pupils come to school equally prepared, and treat them accordingly, then in reality you advantage those who have been better prepared in their social milieu to succeed at school (Bernstein, 1977; Bourdieu, 1974; Willis, 1977). These authors were writing over a quarter of a century ago but their writing remains pertinent for twenty-first-century Britain. For example, some of their ideas have been used to show how National Curriculum mathematics tests disadvantaged children from lower socio-economic status (SES) groups (Cooper and Dunne, 2000). By a similar process the burgeoning market for home learning resources is widening the gap between the educational 'haves' and 'have nots' (Scanlon and Buckingham, 2004).

Concerns with equity have shifted between different groups over the years. In the 1980s and earlier there was concern about the under-achievement of West Indian pupils (Short, 1986). Now there is growing concern about the low performance of many white working-class boys and pupils from some minority ethnic groups (OFSTED, 2003a). Although much progress has been made in the last three decades as regards equal opportunities for men and women in the workplace and boys and girls at school, there remain substantial differences in the perceived role of men and women in society (EOC, 2001; Myers, 1987, 1990). These issues around gender, ethnicity and class comprise the foci of the remainder of the chapter.

In many cases, explanations of pupil under-achievement have focused on the shortcomings of the pupil or their families, the 'deficit model' explanation. More recently the focus has shifted to addressing the educational system as one of the factors contributing to under-achievement. This focus is not only at the level of government and school policy but also in the classroom where such policies are interpreted and implemented by teachers.

GENDER

The Equal Opportunities Commission (EOC) publications offer a wide-ranging overview of differences in our society. This overview includes performance in Key Stage and GCSE examinations, through take-up and achievement at A level and in further and higher education, to employment patterns and rates of pay and is available online (EOC, 2003). There remains much difference in the ways in which men and women exist and move through our society. Focusing on secondary schooling, both boys and girls have been steadily improving their performance in school examinations over the past 20 years but there is now a clear gender gap. Table 4.4.1 compares the performance of boys and girls at GCSE gaining grades A*–C in many of the popular GCSE subjects in 2003.

Table 4.4.1 GCSE attempts and achievements in selected subjects in schools in 2003

Subject	Girls		Boys	
	Entries (thousands)	% passes at grade C or above	Entries (thousands)	% passes at grade C or above
Maths	290	52	295	50
English	288	68	289	52
English literature	265	72	251	58
Science (any)	283	53	287	52
French	161	56	143	41
German	62	60	58	47
History	97	67	98	61
Geography	88	65	112	58
Art and design	107	76	80	56
Design and Technology (any)	201	62	213	46
Physical education	37	60	74	55
Religious studies	66	68	48	55

Source: Department for Education and Skills, January 2004a, <http://www.dfes.gov.uk/rsgateway/DB/SFR/s000442/SFR02-2004v4.pdf>

Given the different performance at GCSE level, Table 4.4.2 now shows how that cohort of students moved onto General Certificate of Education (GCE) A level courses. There is clear gender delineation in some areas (e.g. physics, English, psychology) between what might be considered masculine and feminine subjects.

The EOC reported that often children have very stereotyped ideas about the roles of men and women, and how these stereotypes are themselves linked to what might be termed class (EOC, 2001). There is much research on the different ways in which boys and girls are positioned by, and respond to, moving schools (Jackson and Warin, 2000), teachers (Younger *et al.*, 1999), learning and the curriculum (Paechter, 2000), the use of physical space and so on. These different modes of being are not simply genetic but are socially constructed identities that gradually influence, and are shaped by, boys' and girls' responses to the opportunities and challenges of school; see also Task 4.4.2. Ruddock explores the challenges of developing and possibilities for gender policies in secondary schools in some detail (Ruddock, 2004).

So far in this section we have been looking at the relationship between sex and performance whereas the notion of gender is more nuanced, including different masculinities and femininities. Traditional stereotypes are being broken down and at the same time are more fragmented. Such differences are increasingly celebrated and this includes children's sexuality. As we said at the outset, teacher's responses to this level of diversity will be influenced by their personal views and experiences. Whatever these are, the issue of homophobic bullying, for example, requires a professional response; see the 'Joint Action Against Homophobic Bullying Project' (JAAHB) website <http://intercomtrust.org.uk/goodschools> (accessed 10 Sept. 2004).

Table 4.4.2 GCE A level examination take-up for men and women in 2003

Subject	Entries (thousands)	
	Women	Men
English	62	26
Mathematics	19	32
Biological Sciences	28	18
Physics	6	21
Chemistry	17	16
French	9	4
Psychology	30	10
Social Studies	28	16
Art and Design	24	11
Business Studies	14	20
History	19	18
Geography	14	17

Source: DfES, January 2004b, <http://www.dfes.gov.uk/rsgateway/DB/SFR/s000441/SFR01-2004v4.pdf>

ETHNICITY

A report in the mid-1990s showed that considerable progress had been made by many, but not all, groups of minority ethnic pupils (Gillborn and Gipps, 1996). That situation remains today. Two recent reports identify the serious under-achievement of Afro-Caribbean pupils and that these pupils have not shared in the rise in standards and achievement shown by many of other pupils, especially white pupils (Fitzgerald *et al.*, 2000; Gillborn and Mirza, 2000). Many pupils of Pakistani background have failed to keep up with the improvements of most pupils in the last ten years. These researchers point out that governments, both central and local, have failed to address adequately the issues of under-achievement of particular groups of pupils. As a consequence the gap between the high and low achievers widens with time. The under-performance of many white working-class boys serves to emphasize the importance of taking into account how class and gender effects are embedded within the data showing attainments of ethnic groups. (Gillborn and Mirza's report is well worth reading and is available online.)

When data from the Youth Cohort Study (DfEE, 1999c) are combined with other data and analysed to look at the effect of gender on performance in each ethnic group, some trends emerge. These need to be treated with caution but suggest that:

- girls are more likely to achieve a higher number of grades than boys in all ethnic groups;
- under-achievement is linked with ethnicity for both girls and boys;
- girls from Indian and white ethnic groups are more likely to achieve five GCSE grade A★–C than any other group of pupils;
- Afro-Caribbean boys show a small decline in an already low relative achievement over the period 1991–5 (Gillborn and Mirza, 2000: 23); and their achievement is marginally lower than in 1988.

The evidence accumulated by the Swann Inquiry suggested that many minority ethnic pupils were underachieving (DES, 1985). The research described above, and by Gillborn and Gipps (1996), shows that although achievement has been raised for most pupils, under-achievement persists and is linked to class and ethnicity.

In eight out of ten LEAs that took part in the Youth Cohort Study mentioned above, and monitored the performance of all their pupils by ethnicity, it was shown that, as a group, Indian pupils attain higher outcomes than their white counterparts. This finding indicates that having English as a second language may not hinder academic achievement. One study has shown that 88 per cent of Indians, 92 per cent of Pakistanis and 97 per cent of Bangladeshis speak a second language (Modood, 1997, in Gillborn and Mirza, 2000: 10). Although some groups of pupils appear to under-perform, the research showed that each ethnic group outperforms all other ethnic groups in at least one LEA responding to the Youth Cohort Study (Gillborn and Mirza, 2000: 9).

For teachers working with pupils from a range of ethnic backgrounds, this issue of supporting those for whom English is an additional language is important and so the standards for QTS mandate that:

> With the help of an experienced teacher, they (trainee and NQ teachers) can identify the levels of attainment of pupils learning English as an additional language. They begin to analyse the language demands and learning activities in order to provide cognitive challenge as well as language support.
>
> (DfES/TTA, 2004: S3.2.5:11)

The issue of language goes far wider than classroom oracy. Many classroom resources are text-based and their use of language requires not only a level of literacy but also cultural awareness. One area impacted by pupils' non-English home languages is homework and coursework tasks. As is pointed out above, the increased use of home-learning resources, and indeed homework, relies to some extent upon the knowledge and support of parents or other family members. If language provides an extra hurdle only for some pupils then homework will have a differential effect. Teachers should consider carefully the language requirements that are made by textbooks, classroom talk and homework tasks.

The above discussion reminds us that the performance of pupils is related to many factors including ethnicity, gender and class. The variables used here, class, ethnicity and gender, are not causes; these variables hide causative factors which contribute to under-achievement. Although Table 4.4.3 does not refer to class, there remains considerable variation in the performance of children from various ethnic groups in 2003 GCSE examinations. It is also evident that gender is a factor across ethnic groups.

Under-achievement in school may be a factor in the higher unemployment rate suffered by many minority ethnic adults. In 2002, 12 per cent of women and 10 per cent of men from minority ethnic groups were unemployed in Great Britain compared to 5 per cent female and 4 per cent male white adults (EOC, 2003). This relatively high level of unemployment has an impact upon the future economic status of those groups and therefore, in some complex way, the chances of their children in school. This is not to say that such inequality of attainment cannot be addressed, or is somehow cyclical, but rather to highlight the limitations of schools' ability to affect social change.

CLASS

Gender is perhaps considered to be the most straightforward category for grouping and analysing pupil performance, although as we have stated a straightforward dichotomy should be challenged. Ethnicity, although considerably more complex, also allows us to analyse the attainments of ethnic categories. The theoretical notion of class is far more complex and contested but the effect that pupils' economic circumstances have upon their education is very real. Moreover, class goes beyond simply

Table 4.4.3 Achievements at GCSE/GNVQ in 2003, by ethnicity and gender

GROUP	% of pupils gaining five or more A*–C grades at GCSE/GNVQ		
	Boys	Girls	Total
White	**46.2**	**56.7**	**51.3**
White British	46.1	56.6	51.3
Irish	58.4	61.8	60.1
Traveller of Irish heritage	43.3	39.1	41.6
Gypsy/Roma	24.4	22.5	23.2
Any other White background	46.3	58.2	52.0
Mixed	**42.7**	**55.4**	**49.3**
White and Black Caribbean	32.3	46.8	39.9
White and Black African	39.5	55.1	47.5
White and Asian	60.6	68.6	64.7
Any other mixed background	44.9	57.7	51.6
Asian	**47.1**	**59.0**	**52.8**
Indian	60.3	70.3	65.2
Pakistani	35.7	48.1	41.5
Bangladeshi	38.5	52.6	45.5
Any other Asian background	53.8	64.6	59.0
Black	**29.1**	**43.1**	**36.3**
Black Caribbean	25.1	40.3	32.9
Black African	34.1	46.8	40.7
Any other Black background	27.2	40.3	33.6
Chinese	**70.9**	**79.2**	**74.8**
Any other ethnic group	**41.3**	**51.2**	**45.8**

Source: DfES, January 2004c, <http://www.dfes.gov.uk/rsgateway/DB/SFR/s000448/NDP_sfr_text_Finished3.pdf>

economic capital but relates to other 'capitals' that children's families possess. This might be social capital or the cultural capital that includes having well-educated parents and ready access to books, computer media or other learning and cultural experiences. There is much evidence to signal the relationship between culturally rich homes and pupil's attainment. This unit has repeatedly referred to the way in which gender, ethnicity and class effects are overlapping and intertwined. In that sense Table 4.4.3, which shows the performance of different ethnic groups, might have as much to do with class as it has to do with gender. Table 4.4.4 below uses the rather crude measure of free school meals to show how socio-economic status relates to GCSE performance. The relative under-performance of these 80,000 pupils is striking.

In the same way that our response to gender issues is needing to become more nuanced, so here we should include the increasing number of children in care and the needs of refugee and asylum seeker

Table 4.4.4 Achievements at GCSE/GNVQ in 2003, by free school meals and gender

	No. of 15-year-olds		% Achieving five or more grades A*–C at GCSE	
	Boys	Girls	Boys	Girls
Non-free school meals	251,134	242,202	49.9	60.8
Free school meals	41,096	40,182	20.4	28.5

Source: DfES, January 2004c, <http://www.dfes.gov.uk/rsgateway/DB/SFR/s000448/NDP_sfr_text_Finished3.pdf>

children. The challenge for teachers is of course that we cannot necessarily see who these children are but they might well require different kinds of support. The use of school uniforms is argued by some to 'level the playing field' by removing the stigma of poverty but perhaps this in fact disadvantages those most in need of targeted help in school because they are now hidden. Class works in many subtle ways to disadvantage those already disadvantaged. Through language, manners, cultural awareness, etc. the middle classes have a better sense of the 'rules of the game' and so can capitalize more on their educational opportunities.

Another aspect of this class discussion is poverty, the effect of which has been described graphically by Davies (2000: 3–22). The second-term Labour government (2001) had a committment to eradicating child poverty by 2020, but many commentators suggest that the gap between rich and poor is increasing (Gold, 2003; Woodward, 2003). This division is happening partly as a result of legislation aimed at the marketization of education by Conservative and Labour governments. Typically more well-educated, middle-class parents have a better understanding of the school system (Power *et al.*, 2003), where to get information from (Hatcher, 1998), how to best support their children's schooling and so generally stand a better chance of maximizing the opportunities afforded by the new educational markets (Ball, 2003). Class remains the main factor in educational disadvantage and yet possibly the most difficult factor to define, identify and respond to in a way that will precipitate meaningful and long-term change.

SCHOOL POLICY AND CLASSROOM PRACTICE

In this section we begin to examine both your school policies and your classroom practice, in the light of the earlier discussion. If schools play a role in the ongoing structuring of inequality in society, albeit not deliberately, then every teacher needs to reflect critically upon his or her own practice. This involves examining how your own position and action in a diverse society both help and hinder you from challenging inequity in the classroom. See Task 4.4.1.

No matter how concerned the school is to promote equity through good policies, implementing them in the classroom is not an easy matter. It is instructive to use lesson observation time to look at specific aspects of teaching and then to report back to your tutor or tutor group. Some ideas are listed in Tasks 4.4.2 and 4.4.3. Ask a class teacher if you can observe some of her lessons.

When you first start teaching, your concern is to promote learning through well-ordered lessons; when you feel more confident ask a colleague to observe one of your lessons, focusing on the questions in Tasks 4.4.2 and 4.4.3. As you develop as a teacher you will be able to consider wider issues of inclusion and diversity. These issues might be regarding language or the textual materials used by pupils. They, like us, are heavily influenced by words and pictures, particularly moving ones. Access to the World Wide Web has opened up all sorts of material to pupils, and not all of this is helpful for their academic or social development.

**Task 4.4.1
Policies towards equal
opportunities (EO)**

1. Obtain a copy of the EO policy in your school. Read it and try to identify:

    *   Who wrote the policy and were parents or pupils involved?
    *   How old is it?
    *   Are there any later documents, e.g. working party reports?
    *   What areas of school life does it cover? Is it the curriculum, playground behaviour, assembly or other aspects of school life? Are any areas of school life omitted from its brief?
    *   What is the focus of the policy? Is it gender, ethnicity, social class or disabilities?

2. Who knows about the policy? Devise a way of sampling knowledge, understanding and opinion of pupils and staff about the policy. For example:

    *   Are copies of the policy displayed in the school?
    *   How many staff know about it; have read it?
    *   How many pupils know about it; have read it?
    *   Who is responsible for EO in the school?

3. Is the policy treated seriously in the school? For example:

    *   Has any in-service programme been devoted to EO issues?
    *   Does the school EO policy influence departmental policy or classroom practice?

See Klein, 1993: 103–10 for further discussion on school policies and equal opportunity issues.

**Task 4.4.2
Responses to gender: classroom
observation**

Ask a class teacher if you can observe her lesson. Explain the purpose of your inquiry, which is to find out which pupils participate in the lesson more than others; and which pupils the teacher invites to answer questions or volunteer information. Be prepared to share your findings with her.

Keep a tally of the frequency of attention to, and the time given to, boys and girls. Devise a recording sheet to collect information about one or two of the following behaviours:

*   Who puts their hand up to answer a question?
*   Who does the teacher select?
*   In class activities, how much time is spent by the teacher with boys, with girls?
*   Does the teacher respond to a pupil with praise, criticism or further questioning?
*   When pupils are reprimanded, is there any difference in the nature of the misdemeanour? (i.e. what is tolerated, or not by the teacher) or in the action taken by the teacher?

You might consider if different messages are conveyed to boys, or girls, by the teacher through his response to classroom interactions.

Task 4.4.3
Responses to ethnicity: classroom observation

Redesign the record sheet you used in Task 4.4.2 to collect data about teachers' response to pupils of different ethnicity. Use the same questions as listed under Task 4.4.2 and observe the same protocols about observing classrooms. You may wish to add to the list of questions:

- Did racist behaviour occur in the class?
- What was the nature of the racism? Was it name calling, inappropriate language or metaphors, stereotyping, inappropriate book or other visual resources?
- How was the racist incident dealt with?

The chapter 'Race and Racism as a classroom topic' in Klein, 1993: 139–45 contains a useful discussion of handling racism in the classroom.

Task 4.4.4
Bias and stereotyping in teaching resources

Interrogate a resource used in teaching in your school for bias and stereotyping. Resources include books, worksheets, wall charts, CD-ROM, video recordings and internet material. Some questions you could use to address this issue include:

- How accurate are the images shown of people and of places?
- Are women and girls shown in non-traditional roles?
- Are men shown in caring roles?
- Who is shown in a position of authority? Who is the employer, the decision-maker, the technologist? Is it always men? What are the roles of women?
- Are people stereotyped, e.g. Black athletes, male scientists, female social workers, male cricketers?
- How and why are people in the developing world depicted? Is it to illustrate malnutrition, or their living conditions or the technology employed? Are the images positive or negative?
- What assumptions, if any, are made concerning minority ethnic citizens in the UK?
- What assumptions, if any, are made concerning under-development in the developing world?

Read 'Printed and published materials in schools' in Klein, 1993: 167–80 for further discussion of teaching resources and equal opportunities.

Task 4.4.5
Who is recruited to post-16 courses?

If your school has a sixth form, compare the number of pupils in the first year academic and vocational courses, by gender and ethnicity and then compare those numbers with the numbers in the previous years' Year 11 cohort. Identify the subject preferences.

How many pupils left school to carry on education in another institution and what are their gender and ethnic characteristics?

RESPONDING TO DIVERSITY IN THE CLASSROOM

Your immediate concerns are focused on the classroom but much of what goes on in the classroom has its origins outside the classroom. These origins include the cultural background of the pupils; the teachers' expectations of pupils; the externally imposed curriculum and the school's ethos realized through its policies and practices.

Expectations of academic performance are often built upon both evidence of what the pupil has done in the past and their social position: male/female; white/Black; Irish/Afro-Caribbean; working/ middle class; stable/unstable family background. A perceived social position is sometimes, if unconsciously, used by teachers to anticipate pupils' progress and their capacity to overcome difficulties (Noyes, 2003). For example, 'Jimmy is always near the bottom of the class, but what do you expect with his family background?' Or 'The trouble with Verma is her attitude, she often seems to have a chip on her shoulder and doesn't respond well to discipline even when she is in the wrong. She never gives herself a chance; I'm always having a go at her.' You might have found yourself thinking these things, or even making assumptions about children from the time you first saw their names on the register. What might you expect of a Chantelle, Saima or Harriet, or of Wayne, Edward or Manbwe?

The interaction of the teacher with pupils in the classroom is often revealing. Some teachers may subconsciously favour asking boys, rather than girls, to answer questions. Once established, the reasons for this behaviour can be explored. Similar questions can arise about the way teachers respond to pupils' answers. Whereas one pupil might make a modest and partly correct response to a question to which the teacher's response is praise and support, to another pupil, offering the same level of response, a more critical attitude may be adopted by the teacher.

Are these different responses justified? Is the pupil who received praise gaining support and encouragement from praise; or is the pupil being sent a message that low-level performance is good enough? It is teacher expectations that direct and control such responses. If, as has been documented in the past about the performance of girls, the praise is implicitly saying 'you have done as well as can be expected because you are a girl' and the critical response is implying 'come on now, you're a boy; you can do better than this', then there is cause for concern.

Such interpretations depend very much on the context. A comparison of teacher behaviours in different lessons might reveal the influences on teaching and learning of the subject and the gender, age and social and cultural background of teachers and pupils. Tasks 4.4.2 and 4.4.3 addressed this suggestion.

SUMMARY

In order to promote equity in educational contexts teachers need to 'understand how pupils' learning can be affected by their physical, intellectual, linguistic, social, cultural and emotional development' (DfES/TTA, 2004: S2.4, 9). But this is only the first step! Beyond 'understanding' needs to come action and this involves noticing, critiquing and changing your own practices if necessary, in order to create learning environments in which all pupils can thrive and succeed, and where prejudice is rooted out. Some of the developments that need to take place might involve changing resources, grouping procedures, developing other teaching styles. Through such actions teachers can begin to challenge some of the inequalities in our society. Alternatively teachers can simply maintain the status quo and although discourses might welcome diversity, practices might just as easily be maintaining inequity.

Sometimes you hear a teacher say 'I didn't notice their colour, I treat them all the same'. Learning opportunities are enhanced by *not* being 'gender blind' or 'colour blind'. We suggest that not recognizing pupil differences, including culture, is just as inadequate a response to teaching demands as the stereotyping of pupils. Pupils learn in different ways and a key part of the differentiated approach to learning is to recognize those differences without placing limits on what can be achieved. This brings us back to expectations, preconceptions and even prejudices (however unintended) of the teacher. If you expect most Asian girls to be quiet and passive and good at written work, then that is not only what they do, but also perhaps all they do. Individuals respond in different ways to teachers; you should try to treat each person as an individual and respond to what they do and say, making positive use of your knowledge of the pupils' culture and background. This chapter has addressed inclusion in relation to class, ethnicity and gender; another dimension of inclusion is addressed in Unit 4.6 on inclusion and special educational needs.

FURTHER READING

Gillborn, D. and Mirza, H.S. (2000) *Educational Inequality: Mapping Race, Class and Gender; A Synthesis of Research Evidence*, London: OFSTED. Online. Available HTTP: <http://www.ofsted.gov.uk/publications/> (accessed 9 Sept. 2004). This report says that black children failed to share in the dramatic rise in attainment at GCSE, which took place in the 1990s, to the same degree as their white peers. Black and ethnic minority youngsters are disadvantaged in the classroom by an education system which perpetuates existing inequalities. Differences in the achievements of boys and girls and children of professional and working-class parents are compared and contrasted.

Equal Opportunities Commission (EOC). Online. Available HTTP: <http://www.eoc.org.uk> (accessed 9 Sept. 2004). The EOC website hosts many easily downloadable statistical summaries of social life in Britain. From these reports you can examine the changing nature of the society in which you live and teach. Many reports are repeated on an annual basis.

Department for Education and Skills (DfES), Research publications. Online. Available HTTP: <http://www.dfes.gov.uk/research> (accessed 9 Sept. 2004). The research section of the DfES website also hosts a wealth of information that will help you to consider pupil diversity. The Youth Cohort Study (DfEE 1999c), which can be accessed through the lists of selected keywords, offers longitudinal data over a number of years.

Unit 4.5

Moral Development and Values

Ruth Heilbronn and Tony Turner

INTRODUCTION

All teachers are expected to uphold the values of their profession, and this is expressed in England, e.g. in the Professional Code of the General Teaching Council for England <http://www.gtce.org.uk>, and in the Standards for the Award of Qualified Teacher Status, S1.1–8 (DfES/TTA, 2002). Schools also uphold certain values and express these in their policies and practices. They may though differ very much from each other in the way they are managed and organized and in the behaviour, attitudes and priorities of the pupils and staff. Research shows that these differences are important to the individual teacher's ability to thrive and develop in school (Totterdell *et al.*, 2002; Heilbronn *et al.*, 2002) and to the pupils' expressions of respect for one another and their socially responsible behaviour in the classroom (Hansen, 1995). Many of the differences can be seen to stem from the values held by the governors and headteacher of the school, which determine what the school promotes as desirable behaviour for all. Ethos can be expressed in the way parents are welcomed into the school; or the relationship of teacher to pupil outside as well as inside the classroom; or staff sensitivity to cultural and faith differences in the school; or how it celebrates the success of its pupils. Philip Jackson (1968) identifies what he calls 'the hidden curriculum': the general social climate of the classroom; the rules, structure, and sanctions which embody the values a school upholds implicitly and nurtures in all its dealings with young people. The ethos of a school contributes as much to values education as does the prescribed curriculum of subjects.

School policies, aims statements, mottos and behaviour are some of the ways in which the values might be expressed. The values are expressed and promoted constantly by the attitudes and behaviour of everyone involved with the school, particularly the way in which teachers behave with, and respond to, pupils through subject teaching, their pastoral role and through extra-curricular activities. The ethos of the school is created largely through the school leadership and the way in which it develops and manages a vision of the kind of school it wishes to maintain. This vision is expressed through the standards it sets and the relationships it nurtures.

In England and Wales, the National Curriculum sets aims which mean that teachers are expected to teach their subject and, while doing so:

- promote the spiritual, moral, cultural, mental and physical development of pupils at the school and of society; and
- prepare pupils at the school for the opportunities, responsibilities and experiences of adult life (DfEE/QCA, 1999a: 12).

These aims were created in the 1988 Education Act (ERA, 1988) and re-affirmed in both the 1996 Education Act (Great Britain, 1996, para. 31) and the current National Curriculum 2000 (DfEE/QCA, 1999a). Citizenship education is also being revised and revitalized in several countries world-wide (Kerr, 1999). This was the case recently in England and Wales with the introduction of statutory citizenship education (DfEE/QCA, 1999b). There is a strong element of values education underlying this initiative to educate pupils to be active citizens.

The focus of much of this unit is on the opportunities in your daily work with pupils to foster and develop values and moral judgement and to help pupils understand the need for a set of common values and what those values might be. We do not address in-depth theories of moral development or their origin but the Further Reading section at the end of this unit offers that opportunity (e.g. Langford, 1995). See also Unit 5.1 on how children learn, which introduces you to theories of how learning happens.

OBJECTIVES

By the end of this unit you should:

- know the legal responsibility of the school towards pupils in the area of moral, spiritual and cultural development;
- be aware of the opportunities in school to promote these aims;
- be able to try out some methods of teaching towards these aims and evaluate them;
- be able to place moral and values education in a subject and school context, including citizenship education;
- be able to relate these aspects of a teacher's role to the standards/competences expected of a newly qualified teacher.

A FRAMEWORK FOR VALUES EDUCATION

Whilst values underlie all aspects of school life, some specific areas of the curriculum lend themselves more readily than others to talking explicitly about values with pupils. These include religious education, personal social and health education and citizenship education. The term 'values' as used in education and in this chapter denotes 'that which is desirable' and is related to the notions of 'worth' and 'goodness'. Talking about 'values' is a development from the philosophical tradition of ethics, which involves enquiry into questions such as the nature of right and wrong, good and bad and how to lead a 'good life'. Providing 'answers' to these questions involves making 'value judgements'. These evidently differ from judgements of fact, for which evidence can provide a foundation. They are formed in a different way. In some schools there is a common understanding about where many of the values come from, as they are based on definable moral codes, e.g. in a faith school there is a clear understanding about what is right and wrong, based on tradition and 'scripture'. In a secular school this understanding is founded on a common moral code relating to a view of individuals in society, of which the school is a part. Even in a faith school, however, there are many areas where value judgements will be made, which are not clearly demarcated from a religious foundation, e.g. judgements about what is 'fair' in a particular situation; or about how to apply limited resources, choosing one claim above another. Value judgements are linked to moral codes, and linked for many with religious belief. In a country whose citizens represent a number of different faiths and beliefs, it is evidently desirable to try to find a set of common values on which all can agree. Later in the chapter we outline one such attempt.

Dealing with pupils you frequently have to decide what you believe is right or wrong in a given situation, and to act on your decision, e.g. if a child steals something from another child you might decide to punish the thief without much discussion or you might decide to talk to the pupil, to get her to understand that what she had done was wrong. Talking with a pupil about the rights and wrongs of an aspect of their behaviour is an essential part of all teachers' (and parents') daily life. Such discussions recognize the child's ability to develop their understanding of themselves through how their actions and behaviour affect others. Most teachers recognize this as one of the aspects of their role which gives them the most satisfaction, feeling that they are not just teachers of a particular subject, but teachers in a general sense, capable of helping pupils' 'moral development'. Pupils can learn that they can change their attitude to themselves and to others, and hence can change their behaviour. In this regard, the policies of the school are the formal interface between the individual child and teacher. For example the behaviour policy will almost always cite the core value of 'respect' and have a 'rule' of some kind that implies that everyone in the school should respect everyone else. So the teacher in the example of the child caught stealing could relate the discussion about why this was wrong to the school's formal statement or rule relating to respect. Schools are concerned with developing young people who value themselves and have a good personal self-image. This self-image includes many things, such as self-confidence and the willingness to tackle new ideas and problems. Equally important is the confidence to listen to the contribution of others and be able to respond knowing that their own contribution is valued.

Engaging pupils in discussion of this kind demonstrates the use of reasoning to respond to undesirable, 'bad' or 'wrong' behaviour. Lickona (1983) has suggested that pupils judge their teachers on the way they respond in such circumstances:

'Students evaluate not only their judgments of teacher responses but also the teachers as respondents. Students rated highest those teachers who responded to moral transgressions with statements focusing on the effects of acts ("Joe, that really hurt Mike")'. Rated lower were teachers who responded with statements of school rules or normative expectations ('That's not the way for a Hawthorne student to act'). Rated lowest were teachers who used simple commands ('Stop it!' or 'Don't hit') (Nucci, 1987).

This finding suggests that the way in which teachers act as value educators and role models has a significant effect on the trust given by the pupils, which itself is a key factor in achieving a good relationship with them. Research has shown how 'everyday classroom life is saturated with moral meaning … even the most routine aspects of teaching convey moral messages to students' (Hansen, 1995).

It is important to note when classroom discussions are in fact not about values but about social conventions. Both have their place in the classroom, and both can be differentiated by pupils. Nucci (1987) reviews a range of research showing that children can distinguish moral judgements, related to justice and fairness, from judgements about social conventions, e.g. how to address people properly or follow dress codes. They are able to do this from an early age (Nucci, 1982; Turiel, 1983). An example is a series of studies involving several hundred children brought up with faith teaching (Catholic, fundamentalist Christian and Jewish) which showed that they made distinctions between matters of morality and religious doctrine and that this was similar to the distinctions which children brought up in secular environments draw between morality and convention (Nucci, 1985). Most of the children in the study agreed that moral transgressions such as stealing, hitting or slander would still be wrong even if there were no religious rules against them, because they are harmful to others. The majority of the children considered the issues of people working on the Sabbath, women preaching in church or synagogue, and the use of contraceptives, to be alright in themselves, except that there were religious rules against them. This research indicates that conceptions of morality (justice and beneficence) are independent of understandings of social conventions and of religious sanctions.

Piaget and Kohlberg are earlier thinkers who investigated the development of moral judgement. (For an introduction to their work see, e.g. Langford, 1995: 69.) Piaget linked the development of moral judgement with cognitive capability, i.e. that mature moral judgement is dependent on a capacity to reason logically. Both writers describe features of the development of moral judgement. They point out that not everyone appears to attain the higher levels of moral judgement and, moreover, if they do, may not practise them. These researchers place emphasis on maturational factors.

The notion of the development of moral reasoning is complex. However, the research quoted above has shown that even very young children differentiate between actions in the moral and conventional domains and reason differently about the two. There are implications for any schools or teachers who wish to establish a formal programme of values education. How to build in progression? How does the programme build up progressively more complex, i.e. 'higher order' understandings?

The National Curriculum

In England and Wales the notion of values education has been firmly linked to the aims of the National Curriculum (NC). The values underpinning these aims are described in the following terms:

> Foremost is a belief in education, at home and at school, as a route to the spiritual, moral, social, cultural, physical and mental development, and thus the well-being, of the individual. Education is also a route to equality of opportunity for all, a healthy and just democracy, a productive economy, and sustainable development. Education should reflect the enduring values that contribute to these ends.
>
> (DfEE/QCA, 1999a: 10)

These values and purposes are to be achieved through two key aims. The first describes its hopes in relation to pupil learning. The second aim is: 'to promote the pupils' spiritual, moral, social and cultural development and prepare all pupils for the opportunities, responsibilities and experiences of life' (DfEE/QCA, 1999a: 11). This second aim is elaborated further by stating that pupils should:

> in particular, develop principles for distinguishing between right and wrong. It (the achievement of the aim) should develop their knowledge, understanding and appreciation of their own and different beliefs and cultures, and how these influence individuals and societies. The school curriculum should pass on enduring values, develop pupils' integrity and autonomy and help them to be responsible and caring citizens capable of contributing to the development of a just society.
>
> (DfEE/QCA, 1999a: 11)

These aims are to be achieved through the opportunities of the statutory subject curriculum, including religious education together with a programme of personal, social and health education (PSHE), including citizenship (DfEE/QCA, 1999b). For further discussion of the NC see Unit 7.3.

When the new National Curriculum for England and Wales was in preparation, the government set up a working party called the National Forum for Values in Education and the Community (see Figure 4.5.1) to give guidance to teachers and managers on values education. An extract from its report is included in the National Curriculum Handbook for Teachers (DfEE/QCA, 1999a: 195–7). The Report set out a 'Statement of Values' which tries to identify common values in society and with which most people would agree, irrespective of culture or belief: see Figure 4.5.1. The values identified in Figure 4.5.1 may be examples of the 'enduring values' referred to above. For further discussion on enduring values, see Warnock (1998: 122–4).

The National Forum moved from the broad general statement of values (Figure 4.5.1) to the translation of those values into practice. For example, under the heading of 'The Self' the National Forum team listed the following goals for pupils:

- develop an understanding of our own characters, strengths and weaknesses;
- develop self-respect and self-discipline;
- clarify the meaning and purpose in our lives and decide, on the basis of this, how our lives should be lived;
- make responsible use of our talents, rights and opportunities;
- strive, throughout life, for knowledge, wisdom and understanding;
- take responsibility, within our capabilities, for our own lives (DfEE/QCA, 1999a: 196).

The values identified can provide a basis for action to be used by the individual or by the teacher as goals for teaching. Similar detailed statements of values for 'relationships', 'society' and the 'environment' were produced by the National Forum.

Successive Education Acts since 1988 have required OFSTED to inspect the contributions which schools make to pupils' spiritual, moral, social and cultural education and how well pupils' attitudes, values and other personal qualities are developed. The latest framework for secondary school inspections requires assessment of:

> the extent to which the school actively enables pupils to:
> - develop self-knowledge and spiritual awareness;
> - understand and respect other people's feelings, values and beliefs;
> - understand and apply the principles that help distinguish right from wrong;
> - understand and fulfil the responsibilities of living in a community;
> - appreciate their own and others' cultural traditions.
>
> (OFSTED, 2003c)

The English National Curriculum for Citizenship is one of the vehicles through which 'moral development' can be channelled, since the subject matter of citizenship education is inherently related to values. As Jeremy Hayward has pointed out (Haydon and Hayward 2004) political and social issues concern the question of how we should collectively live, which is at root an extension of the basic moral question 'How should I live my life?' Although many areas of public life can be taught about in a fairly descriptive manner they remain value-laden in nature and may often call for sensitive handling. So, the new NC in England, with clearly stated aims and values, fortified by the introduction of a strong PSHE programme, including citizenship, fosters moral development and values. These are the main vehicles for engaging in values education in England and Wales although as we say elsewhere the day-to-day actions of teachers and staff display the values we work by.

There have been attempts to teach a specific programme to promote moral development. Lawrence Kohlberg, a noted researcher and theoretician of children's development of moral values commented on the artificiality of separating out such an area within the school curriculum. He evaluated one of his

1 The self
We value ourselves as unique human beings capable of spiritual, moral, intellectual and physical growth and development.

2 Relationships
We value others for themselves, not only for what they have or what they can do for us. We value relationships as fundamental to the development and fulfilment of ourselves and others, and to the good of the community.

3 Society
We value truth, freedom, justice, human rights, the rule of law and collective effort for the common good. In particular, we value families as sources of love and support for all their members, and as the basis of a society in which people care for others.

4 The environment
We value the environment, both natural and shaped by humanity, as the basis of life and a source of wonder and inspiration.

Figure 4.5.1   A set of values (Source: National Forum for Values in Education and the Community. DfEE/QCA, 1999a: 196).

own early projects: 'While the intervention operation was a success, the patient died. When we went back a year later, we found not a single teacher had continued to engage in moral discussion after the commitment to the research had ended' (Kohlberg, 1985: 80). This finding reinforces the comment made in the introduction to this unit that one important way in which a child develops moral understanding and maturity is through experience, mediated by dialogue, e.g. when you talk to a child about something you have both experienced you engage in a process of talking about values in a direct and practical way. You also act at all times as a model of the values which underlie acceptable behaviour, both in terms of social convention and morality. Pupils can also learn from each other by exchanging information, sharing experiences and debating them. The new understandings which are 'constructed' in peer exchange can be powerful in developing children's moral understandings (Berkowitz *et al.*, 1980).

When you facilitate a discussion among pupils some powerful learning can develop. As Nucci puts it:

> The use of discussion acknowledges that social growth is not simply a process of learning society's rules and values, but a gradual process in which students actively transform their understanding of morality and social convention through reflection and construction. That is, students' growth is a function of meaning-making rather than mere compliance with externally imposed values.
>
> (Nucci, 1987)

THE ROLE OF SCHOOLS

Schools have always paid attention to moral education, although often the pupils understanding of the school's values is 'caught', rather than explicitly 'taught'. Research has shown that there are common features of schools that seem to have a positive impact on the development of student values, such as participation in the communal life of the school and the classroom, encouragement to behave responsibly, provision of an orderly school environment, and clear rules that are fairly enforced (Battisch *et al.*, 1998). This same research has reinforced the view that pupils do not automatically 'catch' values or morality but that efforts have to be made to provide opportunities for learning. Other researchers have found that a school's explicitness about its values and the extent to which teachers actually practised shared values had an important influence on the pupils' development in this regard. There is also an agreement that the influence of parents in values formation is of far greater importance than that of the school. This reinforces the importance of a partnership approach between schools and their local communities (Nucci, 1987).

We turn now to consider opportunities through which values education may happen and pupils are helped to consider and develop their moral judgement. Some schools, particularly in the United States, Australia and New Zealand have developed programmes in what has been called 'character education'. These programmes create contexts, topics and examples giving structured opportunities to discuss values. In this unit we identify some areas where values education can take place, focusing on issues of a generic nature rather than those arising from curriculum subject and raised in the companion subject books in this series. Our approach is to make suggestions for tasks from which you select those appropriate to your school and your needs. It is not intended that all tasks be undertaken; see Tasks 4.5.1–4.5.5.

Aims of schools

We address how aims in your school experience school are addressed in Task 4.5.1. Aims are discussed also in Units 7.1 and 7.2; see Task 7.1.1.

Task 4.5.1
Aims of the school and how they are interpreted

This task contains several sub-tasks which focus on the aims of the school. Carry out one or more sub-tasks, either alone or in pairs and discuss your findings with other student teachers or your tutors.

1. Collect together the aims of your placement school and that of another school. Compare and contrast the aims of each school. Does the school in its aims express a responsibility for the moral development of pupils? How are these aims expressed and in what ways do the school statements differ? How do your schools' aims meet the aims of the National Curriculum, described above?
2. Consider these statements of broad aims for a school curriculum. The curriculum should:
    *   allow pupils to make decisions and act on them;
    *   expose pupils to situations in which their contribution is necessary for the success of a project;
    *   foster pupils' self-image, or self-esteem;
    *   help pupils develop independently but without losing contact with their peers;
    *   enable pupils to interact with teachers as young adults with adults.
    Respond to these statements under these two headings:
    In what ways do the statements contribute to the moral and values education of pupils?
    How might the aims of this school curriculum be translated into opportunities for the pupil to achieve them?
3. In what ways does the personal, social and health education (PSHE) programme contribute to the moral and values education of your pupils? Select a topic, e.g.:
    *   acceptable and unacceptable food, and the different practices for its preparation;
    *   the celebration of festivals and holidays across cultures and nations;
    *   preparation for careers, job application and interviews;
    *   identifying bias and stereotyping and developing strategies to deal with it;
    *   care of the environment;
    *   paractices and attitudes towards marriage.

4. How does school assembly contribute to the moral and values education of pupils? You could:
    • Attend assembly; keep a record of its purpose, what was said and the way ideas were presented. After an assembly interview some pupils and compare your perception of the session with theirs. Did they understand the message? Did they believe the message? In what way is the message relevant to their life and their family?
    • Help plan an assembly with a teacher and with the support of other student teachers.

You may find these questions helpful in planning your inquiry.
a. Does the school have a programme for assemblies? How is the content and approach agreed within your school?
b. Does assembly have a Christian bias, a requirement of the 1988 Education Act?
c. How does the content and messages of assemblies relate to the cultural mix of your school?
d. Does assembly develop a sense of community or is it merely authority enhancing?
e. How is success celebrated and whose success is mostly recognized?
f. Is any part of in-service education (INSET) for staff devoted to moral, ethical and values education? How is such work focused and by whom? Your school tutor can direct you to the staff responsible for INSET. See also Cowie and Sharp, 1992; Haydon, 1997.

Subject teaching

Task 4.5.2
The place of subject work in promoting moral development and values education

1. Identify a social, ethical or moral issue that forms part of teaching your subject. Review the issue as a teaching task in preparation for discussing it with other student teachers. Your review could include:

    • a statement of the subject matter and its place in the curriculum;
    • the moral focus for pupils, e.g. the decriminalization of drugs; use of animals for research purposes; road building through the green belt;
    • a sample of teaching material;
    • an outline teaching strategy, e.g. a draft lesson plan;
    • any problems that you anticipate teaching it;
    • any questions that other student teachers might help you resolve.

2. In what ways do the curriculum resources of your department (books, video, film, CD-ROM, worksheets, tests) encourage a moral dimension to the teaching of your subject curriculum? Explore and discuss.

    This task could be tackled alone or with other student teachers on a subject basis, later pooling and comparing information. For example, choose a topic for which you have to prepare lesson plans and consider what might be the moral dimensions of that topic. What visual aids are there to support that topic in this way?
    Make a summary of your response to this task and use it to check the standards/competences for your course.

Class management

We have drawn attention earlier to the importance of teachers setting an example for pupils. If values are preached but not practised, pupils attach little significance to them much less uphold them. Task 4.5.3 illustrates the problem of acting fairly. See also Unit 3.3 on classroom management.

Task 4.5.3
Class control

Pupils dislike being punished for offences which they did not commit or the misdemeanours of others. Under stress, it is easy to respond inappropriately to a misdemeanour.

A class is reading from a set text; from time to time there is a pause in the reading in order to discuss a point. As the lesson progresses, some children get bored and seek distraction by flicking pellets at other pupils seated towards the front. The teacher knows it is happening but is unable to identify the culprit. One or two pupils take offence at being hit by pellets and object noisily. The teacher asks for the action to stop but it continues; noise rises and teacher threatens to keep the person in when they are identified. The lesson is stopped and the culprit asked to own up. No one volunteers; the class is given 5 minutes to sort this out; no one owns up and the whole class is kept in after school for 15 minutes. Some pupils object to detention on the grounds that they did not offend. Some walk out of the detention and refuse to stay.

How might the teacher:

- deal with this situation for those left in detention;
- deal with those who walked out;
- deal with any complaint of unfair practice;
- have responded differently to the whole incident?

How have your responses to this task helped you meet the standards/competences for your course?

Assessing pupils

Cheating in tests, for example, is rare but when spotted involves either collusion (with other pupils) or answers being hidden on the person. This situation may be recognized by direct observation during the test, by comparing pupil scripts or by recognizing a familiar phrase likely to have been copied.

One cause of cheating is fear. The fear may be of the teachers' wrath or punishment in response to poor marks. Some teachers may, for example, give a roll call of marks when the scripts have been marked; or make public comment on individual performances. If mistakes are treated with anger, with punishment or by humiliation, pupils are not encouraged to think freely or attempt solutions. Cheating often means the pupil gets the task correct, instead of wrong. This denies the pupil access to feedback from the teacher about the source of error and it denies them the opportunity to learn from mistakes.

Another cause of pupil anxiety may arise through trying to maintain personal esteem. This situation can arise when the pupil tries to 'keep their end up' at home. Some parents regularly ask their children how they got on and a pupil does not like admitting to low marks. On the other hand, the source of anxiety could be about being moved to a lower set. Where streaming is the method of grouping pupils, failure may lead to demotion, losing friends and having to make new ones; or having to join the class of an unpopular teacher.

Cheating may be a sign that the pupil cares. The misdemeanour may not entirely be their fault; children who don't care are less likely to cheat than those who do. The 'don't care' attitude is a different issue with which to contend. How might teachers respond to a pupil caught cheating? It is not possible to condone the action but at the same time pupils are not mature adults.

Check if there are guidelines in your school about cheating in school work or public examinations? How do these guidelines relate to your views? In what ways do these guidelines contribute to the development of the pupil's understanding of values.

Critical incidents

Many incidents which arise in school have at their heart moral judgements. We mentioned one above, about cheating. How we respond to them taxes our notions of right and wrong; our decisions may guide pupils towards establishing their own moral position. Two examples of incidents are presented in Task 4.5.4; your experience in school may furnish you with others. The incidents attempt to show different aspects of moral judgement that need to be exercised by the teacher and the pupil. The first problem concerns personal morality; the individual has to wrestle with their own conscience and decide what to do. In the second example the teacher is put into a position where their decision is likely to be widely known. The teacher is faced by a situation in which there is a conflict of responsibilities towards the parents on one hand and the pupils on the other.

Task 4.5.4
Critical incidents

Read through the following paragraphs and respond to the questions below. You may wish to prepare your response to these situations prior to talking with other student teachers and your tutor. This procedure may help you get a focus on the legal responsibilities you face as a teacher.

1   Wayne is in school during break in order to keep an appointment with a teacher. On the way, he has to walk past his own form room. As he does so he sees a pupil from his class, whom he recognizes, going through the desk of a classmate. The pupil is not facing Wayne but it seems obvious to him that items are being removed from the desk and pocketed, but he can't identify the items. Wayne walks away unseen by the other pupil. Wayne decides to tell his class teacher.

2   Serena is 15 years old, the daughter of practising Muslim parents and attends the local girls' comprehensive school. Her parents do not approve of her mixing, at her age, with other pupils outside school hours and expect her to return home promptly after school. Nevertheless, in the company of other girls, Serena sometimes walks home part of the way with boys from the adjacent boys' school. Under pressure from peers, she agrees to meet one boy after school. She arranges for an alibi with another girl. On the proposed day of the meeting, the girlfriend panics at the prospect of having to lie to Serena's parents and backs out of the agreement. That afternoon the two girls argue in class to the extent that they are kept back by the teacher after school. The teacher becomes unwittingly privy to the arrangements.

For each case:

- Identify the issues.
- Describe the advice you would give in each situation to the teacher and the pupils.

How have your responses to this task helped you meet the standards/competences for your course?

Valuing diversity

Some schools draw their pupils from families of widely differing backgrounds and ethnicity. This rich mix of pupils can be an opportunity for the school through its curriculum and its policies to help pupils understand the differences between people. In this way, schools can help pupils make judgements about other people based, for example, on knowledge rather than hearsay, on how they behave rather than on racial origin. The importance of recognizing the differences between pupils in preparing lessons has been recognized in the current NC for England; see Unit 4.6 and Unit 7.3.

The same argument can apply to schools in which the ethnic mix of pupils is much more narrow but is the aim of valuing diversity altered because of this difference? A writer on minority ethnic issues made the following remarks:

> If children see only white people around them in their school and locality, they are in danger of acquiring the outdated, inaccurate and racist view that only white people are of account. Schools that do not actively counteract such impressions are misleading and misinforming their pupils, neglecting the cross-curricular themes in the National Curriculum of 'multi-cultural issues' and 'citizenship', and failing to prepare them for their place in multicultural Europe and in a shrinking and independent world in which most people are not white. And the learning materials selected for the school are a major source of information.
>
> (Klein, 1993: 169)

The cross-curricular themes to which the writer refers no longer exist in that form and the knowledge, skills and attitudes embedded in them have been incorporated into the new NC, as described earlier in this unit. See also Task 7.3.2. The message given by the statement and the context it describes remain valid today. How do you respond to this statement by Klein? See Task 4.5.5.

Task 4.5.5
Responding to ethnic diversity

Read the extract of a statement by Klein, above, which is about the importance of educating pupils for life in an ethnically diverse society. Use the following questions to respond to that statement. We suggest that first you consider this statement on your own and then bring your responses to a seminar, either with other student teachers or with your tutor.

What evidence do you have in your daily life that people living in an all-white community develop the views described in the first sentence? What evidence do you have in your school experience school that pupils recognize the views expressed in the first sentence?

1. How and in what ways do the aims of your school address the challenges posed by the statement?
2. What evidence do you have that your school experience school adopts a positive approach to ethnic diversity as advocated in the statement?
3. To what extent do assemblies, PSHE, and extra-curricular activities in your school experience school contribute towards fostering positive cross-cultural attitudes?
4. How does the teaching of your subject allow you to contribute to the development in pupils of positive attitudes towards people of other cultures?
5. How do you select teaching material for pupils which contribute to the development in your pupils of positive attitudes towards people of other cultures.

AIMS AND THE CURRICULUM

Moral judgement, moral behaviour and the values they represent derive from personal, social, cultural, religious and political viewpoints. Social conventions also require that norms are followed, i.e. those norms which are essential for the cohesion and continuity of social life and which guide both interpersonal behaviour and national attitudes towards others. Societies in which the norms of some groups of people differ from the main group have the potential for enrichment or friction. In this respect, the statement of values from the National Forum, cited earlier, are an important step towards local and national harmony.

Very largely, moral standards of the young come from parents, peers and teachers. Eventually some individuals are able to make their own judgement about values, to see the broader picture and consider all the variables in a situation. This mature stage of development may lead to questioning the values they have grown up with. Values are not necessarily useful for all time; they need to be reviewed periodically and modified if no longer valid. For example, in the case of sexual morality, by the end of the twentieth century there was a more open approach to the discussion of sexual behaviours and what is and is not acceptable, than was possible at the start, but the emphasis on love, care and the well-being of one's partner remains an enduring value.

One purpose of education must surely be to enable young people to work towards the mature level of response, described above, in their private lives and their participation in the communal and public world. We see beliefs and conventions (e.g. moral standards and behaviour) changing as we follow and contribute to debates about behaviour (e.g. homosexual rights, abortion) or about intervening in medical decisions which impact on human life (e.g. genetic engineering; or the separation of conjoined twins, where one only could live, resolved legally in the face of conflicting moral viewpoints in the English courts in 2000). Other areas where beliefs and conventions are debated and change relate to the environment (e.g. saving natural organisms, conservation of land and global warming), and balancing the good of society with that of the individual (e.g. road building programmes). Young people need the skills and confidence to engage with these debates.

The first decade of the NC in England and Wales has seen the emphasis in teaching and assessment on the subjects of the curriculum. Only recently has the emphasis begun to shift towards linking the aims with the means. Since the inception of the NC in England and Wales in 1988, it was never made clear how a subject-based curriculum was expected to achieve its broad aims, those related to the spiritual, moral, social and ethical development of young people (O'Hear and White, 1991). In the 1990s it appeared as self-evident that the realization of the aims of the NC was best achieved by the traditional route of English, mathematics, science, etc. Schools found it difficult to address the underlying purposes of the NC while at the same time implementing a subject-based curriculum (and responding to frequent changes in the content and organization of that curriculum).

The new NC for England (DfEE/QCA, 1999a) described in an earlier section of this unit, shows that it has now a respectable set of aims. It remains unclear how the subject-based curriculum is expected to achieve those aims (Bramall and White, 2000b). The link between the aims of the NC and the compulsory teaching of some subjects remains tenuous. The loosening of the domination of compulsory subjects at Key Stage 4 may lead to more choice by pupils and their parents, perhaps a move back to pre-NC days when choice at 13+ was a feature of secondary education (QCA, 2004a).

However, as more choice is introduced, the notion of a balanced curriculum recedes. It is not clear how the promotion of 'the spiritual, moral, cultural, mental and physical development of pupils at the school and of society' can be achieved in the context of a curriculum of academic subjects set in a loose structure which allows choice of subjects. We refer the reader to the discussion of the aims and means of the new NC by Bramall and White, 2000b.

The situations described in this unit have used a variety of contexts. They include interactions which are teacher–teacher; student teacher–student teacher; student teacher–pupil, student teacher–class and student teacher–school. The most common interaction is the student teacher–class relationship. Whereas moral and ethical issues can arise by accident, e.g. dealing with tale telling, there are occasions when moral and ethical issues provide the explicit aim of the lesson. Your subject work may have given rise to such opportunities (Task 4.5.2). To be effective in classroom subject teaching, you need to plan carefully for the introduction of these issues. The use of role-play, games and simulation are good ways of introducing such issues as are organized discussions. We give advice on handling discussion and using role-play, games and simulations in Appendices 4.5.1 and 4.5.2 respectively at the end of this unit.

SUMMARY

Teachers have a responsibility in law for the promotion of 'the spiritual, moral, cultural, mental and physical development of pupils at the school and of society'. In school there are many opportunities for developing these qualities in both subject and pastoral work. The introduction of citizenship as a subject in the curriculum may help schools to meet these demands. The guidance on values, described earlier in this unit, provided by the National Forum on Values in Education is an important step forward in helping teachers.

Elsewhere in the unit we have identified some situations in which your judgement is called into play and may call for the resolution of dilemmas of a moral nature. On occasions, you may find it difficult to know how to respond; in your school experience schools you should refer to experienced and qualified staff for help. These issues are likely to remain on your agenda during your induction period as an NQT. It is important that you know the school policy about the issue that confronts you and the expected response in your school.

In this unit we have tried to help you become aware of the current curriculum situation nationally in relation to values education and invited you to relate teaching situations to helping pupils develop an awareness of morals and values. The section Further Reading gives more detailed advice and background about the development of values education.

APPENDIX 4.5.1: HANDLING DISCUSSION WITH CLASSES

A common technique for raising moral and ethical issues is through discussion. Discussion activities have great potential as a vehicle for moral development through sharing ideas, developing awareness of the opinion of others, promoting appropriate social procedures and profitable debate. It can be a vehicle for learning. On the other hand, discussion can be the mere pooling of ignorance, the confirmation of prejudices and a stage for showing off.

Young people can be taught the protocols of discussion. It is necessary to help them realize that discussion may not end in a clear decision or agreement, but can lead to a deeper understanding of the issues and the position of others. For the teacher, discussion is one of the more difficult strategies to implement. Perhaps that is why it is not often used. See also Unit 3.1 on communicating with pupils.

The following notes may help you develop your strategies for conducting discussion. They adopt the neutral chairperson approach but there are other ways, the 'balanced approach' and the 'stated commitment' (DfEE/QCA, 1998: 10). For further help on running discussions and other ways of introducing moral issues, see Jennings (1995), Wellington (1986) and Tarrant (1981).

Four factors need to be considered. They are: (1) rules and procedures for discussion; (2) provision of evidence – information; (3) neutral chairperson; (4) outcomes expected.

1. *Rules and procedures*; you need to consider:
    - choice of subject and length of discussion (young pupils without experience may not sustain lengthy discussion);
    - physical seating; room size; arrangement of furniture so that most pupils have eye contact;
    - protocols for discourse; taking turns; length of contribution; abusive language;
    - procedures for violation of protocols, e.g. racist or sexist behaviour;
    - how to protect the sensitivity of individuals; pupils may reveal unexpected personal information in the course of a discussion;
    - stance of the chairperson.

2. *Provision of evidence*; in order to stimulate discussion and provide a clear basis for argument, you need to:
    - know the age, ability and mix of abilities of the pupils;
    - know what information is needed;
    - know sources of information;
    - decide at what point the information is introduced (before, during).

3. *Neutral chairperson*; a neutral stance may be essential because:
    - authority of the opinions of the chair should not influence the outcome;
    - the opinions of pupils are to be exposed, not those of the teachers;
    - the chairperson can be free to influence the quality of understanding, the rigour of debate and appropriate exploration of the issues; and
    - pupils will understand the teacher's stance if it is made clear at the start.

4. *Possible outcomes*; the strategy is discussion not instruction. Pupils should:
    - learn by sharing and understand the opinion of others;
    - be exposed to the nature and role of evidence;
    - realize that objective evidence is often an inadequate basis for decision making;
    - come to know that decisions often rely on subjective value judgements;
    - realize that many decisions are compromises.

Action

Try out these rules by setting up a discussion with other student teachers on the topic of 'Equal opportunities for girls enables them to join the power structure rather than challenge it'.

APPENDIX 4.5.2: ROLE PLAY, GAMES AND SIMULATIONS

General and specific subject advice on these strategies can be found in many of the companion subject books in the series. For example, role-play, games and simulations are addressed in the context of promoting collaborative strategies and developing values education in geography (Lambert and Balderstone, 1999: 265–305). See the relevant subject texts in the series *Learning to Teach [subject name] in the Secondary School: A Companion to School Experience*, London: RoutledgeFalmer, listed at the front of this book.

Books giving general help include:

Ellington, H., Fowlie, J. and Gordon, M. (1998) *Using Games and Simulations in the Classroom*, London: Kogan Page.

Jones, K. (1995) *Simulations: A Handbook for Teachers and Trainers*, 3rd edn, London: Kogan Page.

Turner, S. (1995) 'Simulations', in J. Frost (ed.) *Teaching Science*, London: Woburn Press (which includes a full description of simulations as well as their use in science teaching).

FURTHER READING

Bramall, S. and White, J. (2000)*Will the New National Curriculum Live up to its Aims?* IMPACT paper 6, London: Philosophy of Education Society. A case study, in relation to the English National Curriculum, of whether the details of the curriculum requirements are likely to promote the values and aims which (as in many national curricula) are set out in broad terms.

Haydon, G. (1997) *Teaching about Values: A New Approach*, London: Cassell. Sets moral education in the broader context of educational aims and values. Part 5 reviews different conceptions of values education.

Langford, P. (1995) *Approaches to the Development of Moral Reasoning*, Hove: Erlbaum. A survey of approaches to the development of moral reasoning, including the contributions of Freud, Kohlberg and Piaget. The text provides a critical review of stage theory of moral development and alternative approaches are described.

Smith, R. and Standish, P. (eds) (1997) *Teaching Right and Wrong: Moral Education in the Balance*, Stoke on Trent: Trentham. Discusses the work of the National Forum on Values Education. Also argues for alternative approaches to values education.

RESOURCES FOR VALUES EDUCATION

There are now many resources for developing a values education programme in schools, or for finding ideas and materials for work with pupils, where values education appears in a specific curriculum area, such as PSHE, RE, or citizenship. It is worth looking at the following websites:

Belief, Culture and Learning Information Gateway, BeCaL online resources database: <http://www.becal.net>. This is a very useful gateway to international societies and associations working in values education and gives access to research and theory as well as resources.

The Values Education Council: <http://re-xs.ucsm.ac.uk/values/main.html>.

British Humanist Association: 1 Gower Street, London WC1E 6HD: <http://www.humanism.org.uk>.

Citizenship Foundation: <http://www.citizenshipfoundation.org.uk>.

Unit 4.6

An Introduction to Inclusion, Special Educational Needs and Disability

Nick Peacey

INTRODUCTION

The revised National Curriculum sets a commitment to match the needs of all pupils, including those with special educational needs (SEN) and disabled pupils, within the commitment to 'inclusion' of all pupils (DfEE/QCA, 1999a). Inclusion encompasses the right of all to feel they belong and can achieve in school; it underpins the expectation that the mainstream school will be the place in which increasingly all pupils will be educated.

   Understanding approaches to the diverse needs of all their pupils is an essential part of all teachers' professional development. We would expect you, as a student teacher, to be beginning to develop an understanding of the issues relating to inclusion, SEN and disability.

DEFINITIONS

The publication *Index for Inclusion,* which was sent with government support to every school in the country, describes inclusion in these terms:

> Inclusion in education involves the processes of increasing the participation of students in, and reducing their exclusion from, the cultures, curricula and communities of local schools. Inclusion is concerned with the learning participation of all students vulnerable to exclusionary pressures, not only those with impairments or categorised as having special educational needs. Inclusion is concerned with improving schools for staff as well as for students.
>
> (Centre for Studies in Inclusion in Education (CSIE), 2000)

OBJECTIVES

By the end of this unit you should:

- understand how the terms inclusion, SEN and disability are used;
- have an understanding of recent legislation and regulation in this area, in particular teachers' responsibilities at what are known as School Action and School Action Plus of the revised *Code of Practice for the Identification and Assessment of SEN* (DfEE, 2000a) and the Disability Discrimination Act 1995 (revised 2001);
- be aware of the possibility that teacher attitudes may limit pupils' achievement of their potential;
- be developing your knowledge of teaching strategies which may be used with pupils with different SEN within the whole class inclusion approach.

We suggest that you review the competences/standards related to your course to see what is required of you in the area of inclusion/ SEN and disability.

The authors of this document note that schools cannot remove all barriers to inclusion: there are limits, e.g. to how much schools can do about the barriers created by poverty.

Meeting SEN is only a part of inclusion. SEN is essentially a relative term: pupils with SEN are said to require something 'additional to' or 'different from' that offered to other pupils. The definition of disability is rather different: the Disability Discrimination Act 1995 (DDA) describes a disabled person as having 'a physical or mental disability which has an effect on their ability to carry out normal day-to-day activities'. That effect must be substantial (i.e. more than minor or trivial), adverse and long term (has lasted or is likely to last at least a year or for the rest of the life of the person affected). You can see from this statement that the DDA applies to a wider group of pupils than those defined as having SEN For example, it covers those with medical or physical impairments for whom there are no educational barriers to learning.

Some authors feel we are outgrowing the notion of SEN. They feel it places too much emphasis on locating difficulty within the individual, the 'medical model'. This model prevents us seeing diversity as a resource rather than a problem: we have failed, the argument runs, to give proper consideration to the effects and possibilities of the culture, policies and practice of schools in removing barriers to the learning of all. As an example we can consider the deaf pupil with a hearing aid.

For example, the general level of noise in the classroom (the acoustic environment) is highly important when working with any students who have hearing impairments. Hearing aids can distort sound so you may not be heard clearly even if the child is wearing one. If you are working in a very noisy classroom, you should ask colleagues what the school has available to improve this. For example, many schools have what are known as sound field systems; this is a quad-speaker set up to provide good quality sound and ensure that people can hear what is being said, even if there is a main road outside or an airport nearby. Consideration of individual needs can lead to benefits for all.

But much government statute and regulation (including that related to funding) is still set in an SEN model, so the term will be with us for some years. In this unit, we use the terminology adopted in the revised SEN Code of Practice (DfEE, 2000a) which, while not claiming that there are hard and fast categories of special educational need, groups pupils' special educational needs under four main categories:

- communication and interaction;
- cognition and learning;
- behaviour, emotional and social development;
- sensory and/or physical.

The code suggests that

> children will have needs and requirements which may fall into at least one of four areas, although many children will have inter-related needs which encompass more than one of these areas. The impact of these combinations on the child's ability to function, learn and succeed should be taken into account (in planning learning).

We return to these categories later in the unit and consider some of the classroom approaches involved.

REPORTS AND LEGISLATION

The National Curriculum (NC) for England 1999

The revised National Curriculum for England is built on aims, values and principles which support the celebration of diversity (the recognition of everything that diversity of learners brings to a school community) and the rights of all pupils to participate and be partners in their own learning; see Unit 5.3.

More specifically, all NC documents include what has become known as the general Inclusion Statement. This statement has two strands:

* a demand on teachers not to ignore the three principles of inclusion below in their planning and teaching;
* substantial flexibility to allow teachers to match their teaching to the needs of all pupils. For example, secondary teachers can draw on earlier Key Stage Programmes of Study or indeed drop sections of KS3 Programmes of Study if they feel, after proper consideration, this is the best approach for particular pupils.

The inclusion statement is based on the following principles.

1 The need to set suitable learning challenges. A culture of high expectations for all is encouraged within a model of teaching and learning which can suit the approach used to pupils' abilities.
2 Responding to pupils' diverse learning needs. The discussion of this principle emphasizes the need for thought about teaching and learning environments. This includes the physical environment, e.g. the classroom space, its use and its acoustics and making sure that pupils can hear. It also stresses the need for all pupils to feel safe and secure and that views, particularly stereotypical views, about disability and impairment are always challenged.
3 The overcoming of potential barriers to learning and assessment. It includes the statement 'Teachers must address the needs of the minority of pupils who have particular learning and assessment requirements which, if not addressed, could create barriers to learning.'

Some background: the developing legislative framework

There follows a chronological list of recent landmarks in the government's response to the special needs of pupils.

1971 Widening educational opportunity. Legislation in England and Wales to bring those considered 'ineducable' into education.
1981 The 1981 Education Act included specific duties on local education authorities (LEAs) and school governors to make provision for SEN, defining responsibilities and procedures for SEN

and the establishment of parents' participation in special educational assessments, along with a right of appeal.

1988 The 1988 Education Act introduced the National Curriculum and reinforced the duty to consider special educational needs, though many felt that proper attention was not given to the area.

1994 The Code *of Practice on the Identification and Assessment of SEN* (DfE, 1994a) came into effect on 1 September. This is a statutory code of practice (approved by both Houses of Parliament) which cannot be ignored by anyone to whom it applies.

2000 The revised National Curriculum for England (containing the Inclusion Statement) became law.

2001 A revised OFSTED framework for inspection included specific provisions for the inspection of inclusive practices in schools. The current framework can be consulted on the OFSTED website <http://www.ofsted.gov.uk> (accessed 4 Nov. 2004).

2001 The Disability Discrimination Act 1995 was revised by the addition of Part 4. This places duties on schools and other educational institutions not to treat disabled pupils less favourably and to make 'reasonable adjustments' to ensure that disabled pupils are not put at a substantial disadvantage. We should note that disabled staff working in schools have rights under Part 2 of the Act, though these have never been as well publicized and pursued as well as they should have been.

2001 The Revised SEN Code of Practice re-emphasizes the importance of whole-school approaches, including National Curriculum strategies. 'The effective school will identify common strategies and responses across the secondary curriculum for all pupils designed to raise pupils' learning outcomes, expectations and experiences.' The curriculum available for all pupils will directly affect the need to intervene at an individual level (DfES, 2003l).

2004 *Removing Barriers to Achievement: The Government's SEN Strategy.* This document gives a detailed outline of the Government's planning for SEN over the next ten years and provides a useful summary of many areas of development.

Task 4.6.1
The Code of Practice on the identification and assessment of special educational needs and the school's policy

Ask for a copy of the school policy on SEN provision and read this and the extracts from the revised SEN Code of Practice below. If you can, refer also to the revised Code of Practice itself (available in libraries or on the web). Discuss the implementation of the Code of Practice and school policy with your tutor and the SEN co-ordinator (SENCO) in your school. Useful questions include the following. How does the school ensure that the requirements of the SEN Code of Practice are met? How are all the teachers in the school involved in implementing the Code of Practice? Discuss your findings with those of another student teacher who has undertaken the same exercise in another school.

The SEN Code of Practice re-emphasizes the importance of whole-school approaches, including National Curriculum strategies and suggests that 'the effective school will identify common strategies and responses across the secondary curriculum for all pupils designed to raise pupils' learning outcomes, expectations and experiences'. The curriculum available for *all* pupils directly affects the need to intervene at an individual level.

The SEN Code goes further to identify in more detail whole-school approaches to inclusion and SEN, including:

- That all teaching and non-teaching staff should be involved in the development of the schools' SEN policy and be fully aware of the school's procedures for identifying, assessing and making provision for pupils with SEN.
- The importance of practice which encourages high expectations by emphasizing that:

  > All pupils should know what is expected of them. Secondary schools' general marking policies should therefore be consistent in all subjects. Schools should be similarly consistent in other areas, making clear for example how they expect all pupils to behave and to present their work. The emphasis on literacy across the curriculum will help to achieve consistency in handwriting, spelling, punctuation and presentation. Thus for all subject areas and for all pupils including those with SEN, there will be a common set of expectations across the school which are known to everyone, and a further commitment to support those pupils who have difficulty meeting those expectations.

- That schools should not assume that pupils' learning difficulties always result solely, or even mainly, from problems within the young person. Pupils' rates of progress can sometimes depend on what or how they are taught. A school's own practices make a difference, for good or ill'.
- That planning for SEN should consider the views and wishes of pupils 'from the earliest possible age' as well as those of parents and carers; and that 'Partnership between schools, pupils, parents, LEAs, health services, social services, voluntary organisations and other agencies is essential in order to meet effectively the needs of pupils with SEN.'

THE THREE-STAGE APPROACH TO MEETING NEEDS

At the heart of this approach is 'a model of action and intervention designed to help pupils towards independent learning'. The code outlines a three-stage approach to match the needs of pupils with the special education provision available to them.

School Action

The first stage, known as School Action, comes into play when it is clear that 'the pupil requires help over and above that which is normally available within the particular class or subject'. According to the code, the school's SEN co-ordinator should facilitate assessment of the pupil's particular strengths and weaknesses, and plan for support and monitoring of progress.

The pupil's subject teachers remain responsible for working with the pupil on a daily basis and for planning and delivering a programme which takes individual needs into account. Suggestions on how to do this should appear in the Individual Education Plan. Where several pupils have similar needs these are sometimes set out in a Group Education Plan.

Individual Education Plan (IEP)

The IEP will record that which is *additional to* or *different from* curriculum provision for all pupils. Most IEPs will include information about:

- the short-term targets set for the pupil (these are typically reviewed two or three times a year);
- the teaching strategies to be used;
- the provision to be put in place (see next section);
- when the plan is to be reviewed;
- the outcome of the action taken.

Good IEPs are also likely to include some details of the pupil's strengths and interests.

Support and provision on an IEP

This requirement may include (particularly where concerns go beyond School Action) the deployment of extra staff to enable extra help and sometimes one-to-one tuition for the pupil.

The IEP may also prescribe:

- different learning materials or special equipment;
- group support;
- cover for teacher and specialist time for planning support;
- staff development and training on effective strategies;
- support with classroom review and monitoring.

As individual planning for all pupils becomes commonplace, there is less need for plans for pupils with SEN to be special. You may find that you work in a school where there are now few IEPs or where the reviews of IEPs are incorporated into the ordinary review systems for all pupils.

Additional staff in the classroom

Where other adults are supporting pupils in your classroom, you need to liaise closely with them to ensure the pupil gains maximum benefit from this support. The support staff should have the lesson plans well in advance. You can check with them that the materials you are providing are appropriate for a particular child.

Task 4.6.2
Working with support teachers in the classroom

For a pupil with SEN to be fully supported in the classroom, the classroom teacher and the support teacher must develop an effective working relationship. Ask some support teachers for advice about how you can best work together. Observe support teachers working in classrooms and consider what has to be done to ensure the pupils make maximum progress.

School Action Plus

If School Action is not helping a pupil, schools may explore the next stage, School Action Plus. Schools should consult specialists when they set out the strategies for a pupil at School Action Plus. The code states:

At *School Action Plus* external support services, both those provided by the LEA and by outside agencies, should advise subject and pastoral staff on new IEPs and targets, provide more specialist assessments, give advice on the use of new or specialist strategies or materials, and in some cases provide support for particular activities. The kinds of advice and support available to schools will vary according to local policies.

There is of course no reason why specialist advice cannot be taken at any other point.

This IEP will set out revised strategies to promote the pupil's success in the school setting: 'Although developed with the help of outside specialists, the strategies specified in the IEP should usually be implemented, at least in part and as far as possible, in the normal classroom setting.' Once again, the delivery of the IEP's suggestions will largely be the responsibility of subject teachers, supported by their departments or faculties.

Records from transfer between schools

When working with pupils at School Action or School Action Plus you may find useful the school records created at transfer from primary to secondary school. These records can include:

- detailed background information collated by the primary school SEN co-ordinator (SENCO);
- copies of Individual Education Plans prepared in support of intervention through primary School Action or School Action Plus;
- pupil and/or parent views of what is going on;
- your school's assessments of the new entrant.

You can contact the SENCO or the pupil's form tutor if you feel such information would help your planning.

Task 4.6.3
Pupil assessment on entry to school

Ask what, if any, assessments are carried out on pupils on entry to the school and if you can see examples of them. You should also ask what use is made of the information collected by these assessments.

The statement of SEN: the third stage of the Code of Practice for SEN

You may hear staff describe a pupil as 'statemented' or 'having a statement'. If School Action Plus is not succeeding, schools and parents or carers may wish to consider a full multi-disciplinary assessment to examine the possibility of a pupil's having a statement of SEN. Because the process is an expensive one – assessment alone can cost several thousand pounds – LEAs have the duty to consider carefully whether to embark on it. But the statement which can result from such assessment has been popular with parents and schools because it guarantees the resources written into its clauses. Failure to provide can be challenged in the tribunal for SEN and if necessary in the courts. Assessing for a statement and (if it results) a statement's implementation and review are therefore 'high stakes' operations. Unlike

School Action and School Action Plus, these two stages are embedded in a network of statutory rules: schools have very substantial freedom in how they implement the earlier stages.

As a subject teacher you need to aware of pupils with statements of SEN in your class and will almost certainly want to discuss with the head of department or faculty how you can plan for their needs and ensure the resources available are used well.

Task 4.6.4
How does a statement come about in your school?

Arrange a convenient time with the SENCO to discuss the procedure by which a statement of special educational need is drawn up for a child and how it is reviewed. Has the LEA/ school's practice been changed by new funding approaches?

Changes in strategic thinking about statements

The government's SEN strategy in England is increasingly encouraging a move to direct delegation of funding to schools, rather than distribution through the traditional 'statementing' process (DfES, 2004g). It is hoped that this will support more speedy and effective use of the funds. Many voluntary bodies oppose this development which they see as reducing schools' accountability for SEN provision. If you are interested in the arguments, see Pinney (2004).

THE RESPONSE OF SCHOOLS

English as an additional language and SEN

The SEN Code of Practice notes:

> The identification and assessment of the special educational needs of young people whose first language is not English requires particular care. Lack of competence in English must not be equated with learning difficulties as understood in this Code. At the same time, when pupils who have English as an additional language (EAL) make slow progress, it should not be assumed that their language status is the only reason; they may have learning difficulties.

This is an area for you to consult specialist help. The main points to be aware of are:

- pupils learning English go through well-researched stages: they may for instance say little or nothing for some time, but are learning nonetheless;
- pupils learning English benefit from high-quality learning environments: they do not as a rule need individual programmes;
- if the English learning stages are not proceeding as they should, the possibility of a learning difficulty may be considered.

For those wishing to take this area further, see Hall (1996).

Special schools, units and resource bases

A variety of special provision caters for pupils, typically under a designation for a particular group, such as moderate learning difficulties (MLD), behavioural, emotional and social difficulties (BESD) and severe learning difficulties (SLD). Government plans for inclusion are likely to mean that this provision will increasingly be linked more closely to the mainstream. There has been a slow diminution in the number of LEA-maintained special schools, though numbers of pupils educated outside the mainstream have remained almost the same between 1999 and 2004 because of the substantial increase in numbers of pupils educated in pupil referral units, which provide for excluded pupils (OFSTED, 2004c). Mainstream schools may have special units or resource bases attached to them. A resource base provides support within a school to pupils who are normally registered with 'ordinary' classes. A special unit is one step more separate: its pupils will be on the roll of the unit and normally based there.

Special arrangements for examinations and assessments

All awarding bodies for public examinations and the Qualifications and Curriculum Authority responsible for Key Stage 3 assessment make special arrangements for pupils with EAL or learning difficulties. Special arrangements are also available for other pupils with special needs. If you feel that a pupil you are teaching is coming up to an examination or assessment and arrangements are not in place, you should contact the SENCO or the schools examination co-ordinator to find out what can be done.

Concerns about a pupil not recognized by the school as having SEN, i.e. not at one of the stages of the SEN Code of Practice

You may feel a concern about a pupil's progress and wonder if they have unrecognized SEN. It is always worth comparing notes with another teacher to see how the pupil responds in their class. While sensory impairments of hearing or vision are sometimes not picked up until secondary age, the most frequently unrecognized issues relate to delays or difficulties in language development. The Code of Practice notes that: 'Some young people may also raise concerns about their own progress and their views should be treated seriously'. Looking back to your time in secondary school you may reflect that this will frequently require some courage from the pupil. The issues brought to you can be the tip of the iceberg. Once again, discussion with a colleague can help to get the perspective clear. Be alert to signs of eating disorder, particularly anorexia, whether they emerge through observation, written work or conversation; such instances should always be reported for urgent consideration.

HELPING CHILDREN WITH SEN TO LEARN

In this section we provide some guidance on working with pupils with SEN in mainstream classrooms. Overall, you need to remember that the evidence from research supporting the effectiveness of differentiated pedagogies (teaching approaches) for different groups of SEN is slender. Such evidence as there is suggests that 'good normal pedagogy' is the key to success (National Association for Special Educational Needs (NASEN), 2000).

The principles of the inclusion statement of the NC for England and Wales (DfEE/QCA, 1999a) can guide planning for success for all pupils. Part of this planning should involve (at a tactful moment) asking pupils with SEN how they would like to be taught. A good example of how to do this is provided by the British Stammering Association which has produced an excellent video on consulting youngsters worried about a speaking up in class. This resource can guide teachers into making successful approaches to pupils (British Stammering Association, n.d.).

As a student teacher we suggest that you develop your teaching approaches, i.e. concentrate on good normal pedagogy. Seek advice from your tutor. We suggest you approach the issues in this way:

- concentrate on developing your overall teaching style and the best possible learning environments in classrooms you use;
- where a pupil has identified SEN, use the IEP, the knowledge of others in the school and books and websites to build your awareness of the issues in learning for him – do not assume that you need to teach that pupil differently or separately;
- whatever the SEN identified, motivation is a key part of learning – special treatment can 'turn off' adolescents;
- remember what makes a difference is often the timing and intensity of interventions rather than any difference in the pedagogy;
- have high expectations of homework and classwork – clarity in setting homework and care in checking it has been recorded properly helps those likely to find the work difficult.

The SENCO forum on the Virtual Teacher Centre websites provides a space for teachers to discuss general SEN issues; see website addresses at the end of this unit. Using ICT is an important way of helping some pupils with SEN: see Unit 1.4. and Leask and Pachler, 1999 and 2005.

We turn now to discuss briefly the particular of groups of children with specific educational needs. The headings are derived from the draft revised Code of Practice (DfES, 2003p).

Communication and interaction

> The range of difficulties encompass children and young people with speech and language delay, impairments or disorders, specific learning difficulties, such as dyslexia and dyspraxia, hearing impairment and those who demonstrate features within the autistic spectrum. These difficulties may apply also to some children and young people with moderate, severe or profound learning difficulties.

Pupils with language impairment

Pupils in this group may have receptive (i.e. limitations in comprehending what is said to them) or expressive (i.e. they find it hard to put their thoughts into words) language impairments. Obviously, the first impairment is the harder to identify. You need to be aware that:

- emotional and relationship difficulties often go with language and less often with hearing impairments;
- language impairments need specialist attention, normally from a speech and language therapist.

When teaching these pupils you should be sure:

- to check understanding ;
- to use visual aids and cues to the topics being discussed;

- that the pupil is appropriately placed to hear and see;
- that you explain something several different ways if you have not been understood the first time;
- like a good chairperson, you repeat what pupils say in discussion or question and answer sessions (in any case, others in the class may not have heard).

For further information see Adams *et al.* (1997) or the website of the charity 'I Can' (ICAN) <http://www.ican.org.uk>. A resource pack for schools is available, see Blamires *et al.* (2000).

Cognition and learning

Children who demonstrate features of moderate, severe or profound learning difficulties or specific learning difficulties, such as dyslexia (reading difficulty) or dyspraxia (developmental co-ordination disorder), require specific programmes to aid progress in cognition and learning. Such requirements may also apply to some extent to children with physical and sensory impairments and those on the autistic spectrum. Some of these children may have associated sensory, physical and behavioural difficulties that compound their needs.

Learning difficulties

Pupils with learning difficulties are described in the QCA pack *Guidelines for Teaching Pupils with Learning Difficulties* as 'unlikely to reach level 2 of the National Curriculum by the age of 16' (DfEE/QCA, 2001). The package of guidance should be in school and the document is also available online; see reference. The term 'learning difficulties' thus covers a huge range of need and once again you need to check exactly what the pupil's IEP advises and seek specialist advice.

Dyslexia

Some pupils have particular difficulty in developing their literacy skills. You should be aware that:

- the term dyslexia covers a wide range of needs;
- the current emphasis is now on examining the individual's skills, such as phonological awareness, and working on them as a way forward.

Most schools and all LEAs have staff with specialist knowledge in this area. Help can also be sought from the major voluntary organizations working in the field. These include the British Dyslexia Association; the Dyslexia Institute; the Dyslexia Forum and the Professional Association of Teachers of Students with Specific learning difficulties (PATOSS); see website addresses at the end of this unit.

Dyspraxia

Dyspraxia may be defined as difficulty in planning and carrying out skilled, non-habitual motor acts in the correct sequence. Pupils with dyspraxia need the support of whole school systems, particularly in terms of ensuring that they are taking enough exercise. If you are concerned about a pupil with dyspraxia, it may well be worthwhile talking to the PE department as well as to the SENCO.

Difficulties with handwriting are a specific co-ordination issue. The publications and conferences of the Handwriting Interest Group are helpful; further information may be found in Ripley *et al.* (1997). The address of the Dyspraxia Foundation is 8 West Alley, Hitchin, Herts, SG5 1EG.

Autistic Spectrum Disorders (ASD)

Those with autistic spectrum disorders typically lack 'mentalization', i.e. the ability to picture what another person is thinking. This gives them particular difficulty in any social context. You may also hear of Asperger's Syndrome. While authorities differ on whether autism and Asperger's Syndrome are on a continuum or different but overlapping conditions, it is generally agreed that they have strong similarities and that Asperger's is less of an impairment.

Pupils' absorbing interests (such as train timetables) and lack of social focus mean that co-ordinated planning is essential. You need to be aware that:

- many researchers feel the pupils' behaviour is a form of stress management for themselves; they are in a way hyper-sensitive;
- pupils with conditions on the autistic spectrum can learn 'intellectually' how to act socially, e.g. in the matter of eye contact;
- suggestions on approaches to autism vary widely; you need to be absolutely clear what agreed strategies are being used at school and home and work within them.

Further help may be obtained from The National Autistic Society; see useful websites listed at the end of this unit.

Behaviour, emotional and social development

The draft revised Code of Practice indicates that:

> Children and young people who demonstrate features of emotional and behavioural difficulties, who are withdrawn or isolated, disruptive and disturbing, hyperactive and lack concentration; those with immature social skills; and those presenting challenging behaviours arising from other complex special needs.

Emotional and behavioural difficulties (EBD)

Behavioural problems are discussed in Units 3.1, 3.2, 3.3 and 4.1 and tasks are set there to develop your skills in this area. The differentiation case studies in Unit 4.1 are relevant here.

The draft revised Code of Practice states: 'Where a pupil with identified SEN is at serious risk of disaffection or exclusion the IEP should reflect appropriate strategies to meet their need.' This brief sentence scratches a critical issue in secondary school organization. A pupil presenting consistent problems of behaviour may, for instance:

- have special needs: a language impairment or an autistic spectrum disorder;
- have mental health needs: may be depressed, for instance;
- be responding to an unsatisfactory school environment: bullying in the playground, or an irrelevant curriculum.

The definition 'emotional behavioural difficulties' is often applied to pupils whose behaviour is consistently poor and not obviously related to the circumstances and environment in which pupils find themselves. Pupils who are withdrawn also fit into this category. Traditionally, secondary schools have three management approaches to concerns about pupil behaviour. These approaches are: (1) the pastoral teams (form tutor, year/house head, etc.); (2) SEN teams; (3) subject department or faculty.

The inter-relationship of these management teams is critical to a school staff's success with emotional behavioural difficulties. Important points to bear in mind in your response to pupils with EBD include

- understanding that learning, not counselling, is the teacher's contribution to resolving EBD: many heads of EBD schools talk of the 'therapy of achievement';
- being aware that 'scaffolding' success for such pupils can be demanding and you should expect support with your planning (and lessons learnt) from experienced colleagues. Scaffolding is discussed in Unit 5.1.

Your lesson planning should address:

- knowing the strengths and interests of any pupils with EBD;
- knowing the levels of language and literacy of pupils with EBD;
- considering alternatives within lesson plans if one learning project is not succeeding.

Among pupils identified as having EBD you may come across some pupils known as having:

- attention deficit disorder (ADD);
- attention deficit hyperactivity disorder (ADHD).

These terms are medical diagnoses. Medication by means of stimulants is a widely used treatment. The diagnoses in themselves tell you nothing about teaching such pupils. Further help and guidance may be found in Cooper and Ideus (1996) and the useful websites at the end of this unit.

Sensory and/or physical needs

The draft revised Code of Practice advises that:

> There is a wide spectrum of sensory, multi-sensory and physical difficulties. The sensory range extends from profound and permanent deafness or visual impairment through to lesser levels of loss, which may only be temporary. Physical impairments may arise from physical, neurological or metabolic causes that require no more than appropriate access to educational facilities and equipment; other impairments produce more complex learning and social needs; a few children have multi-sensory difficulties. For some children the inability to take part fully in school life causes significant emotional stress or physical fatigue.

Medical conditions

The draft revised Code of Practice notes that:

> a medical diagnosis does not necessarily imply special educational needs. It may not be necessary for a child or young person with any particular diagnosis or medical condition to have a statement, or to need any form of additional provision at any phase of education. It is the child's educational needs rather than a medical diagnosis that must be considered.

A medical condition can affect a child's learning and behaviour. The effect may also be indirect: time in education can be disrupted, there may be unwanted effects of treatment; and through the psychological effects which serious or chronic illness or disability can have on a child and their family. Schools and the pupil's carers and the medical services should collaborate so that the child is not unnecessarily excluded from any part of the curriculum or school activity because of anxiety about his care and treatment.

Deafness and hearing impairment

If you have a deaf pupil in your class, you should be aware that:

- specialist advice is usually not difficult to come by, you should ask the SENCO for direction in the first instance;
- many of the teaching checkpoints set out under language impairment apply;
- pupils have individual communication needs: you need to know what they are.

Further advice can be obtained from the Royal National Institute for the Deaf (RNID) and the National Deaf Children's' Society online; see list of useful websites at the end of this unit. The RNID has produced a valuable series of booklets on teaching deaf and hearing impaired pupils, including material on subject teaching.

Visual impairment

If you have a pupil with visual impairment in your class, again specialist advice is usually not difficult to come by. The SENCO in your school and the individual education plan for the pupil concerned can help in the first instance. Less obvious visual problems may affect pupils' reading. Specialist optometrists sometimes prescribe overlays or tinted spectacles to help with this problem.

There is substantial support to teachers from the Royal National Institute for the Blind online; see list of useful websites at the end of this unit. Further information may be found in Miller (1996).

Task 4.6.5
Analysing the needs of individual pupils

Identify, with the help of your tutor, pupils with whom you have contact who have SEN of different types. Draw up a table similar to the one here in your diary and complete it, drawing on the expertise of different staff as necessary. Use fictional names to preserve confidentiality and compare practice in your school with student teachers from different schools.

Description of pupil's needs	Paul has severe hearing loss. He can lip read reasonably well and his speech is fairly clear.
Pupil's strengths and interests	
Adaptation to classroom work in my subject	
General adaptation to classroom work	
The role of the school/SEN co-ordinator	
The role of outside agencies (LEA, educational psychologists, educational welfare officers)	

SUMMARY AND KEY POINTS

This unit has introduced you to a range of emotional, behavioural and learning difficulties of pupils with special needs and set those needs in the context of the *Code of Practice* for SEN (DfEE, 2000). Understanding the requirements of that Code is important for your practice as teacher. We have not addressed the special needs of the gifted pupil but see Unit 4.1.

Every child is special. Every child has individual educational needs. A major problem experienced by pupils with SEN is the attitudes of others to them. For example, children who have obvious physical disabilities such as cerebral palsy often find they are treated as though their mental abilities match their physical abilities when this is not the case. How will children with SEN find you as their teacher?

Teachers need to ensure that all their pupils learn to the best of their abilities and that pupils with SEN are not further disabled by the lack of appropriate resources to support their learning, including software (Leask and Pachler, 1999).

In your work as a student teacher, we expect you to develop your understanding of the teacher's responsibilities for pupils' SEN so that, when you are in your first post, you are sufficiently aware of your responsibilities and that you ensure that your pupils' SEN are met. The basic rule for you to remember is that you cannot expect to solve all pupils' learning problems on your own. You must seek advice from experienced staff.

You should check your course requirements for SEN in relation to the competences/standards for achieving QTS.

FURTHER READING

Council for Disabled Children/Disability Equality in Education (2002) *Making It Work: Removing Disability Discrimination*, London: National Children's Bureau.

OFSTED (2004) *Special Educational Needs and Disability: Towards Inclusive Schools*, London: OFSTED. Online. Available HTTP: <http://www.ofsted.gov.uk/publications> (accessed 4 November 2004).

Partnership with Parents (1998) *Dealing with Dyslexia in the Secondary School*, Shepway Centre, Oxford Road, Maidstone, Kent, ME15 8AW, tel. 01622 755515.

QCA (Qualifications and Curriculum Authority) (2001) *Planning, Teaching and Assessing Pupils with Learning Difficulties*, Sudbury: QCA Publications. Online. Available HTTP: <http://www.nc.uk.net/ld/GG_content.html> (accessed 4 November 2004).

Useful websites

Attention Deficit Disorder (ADD) Information Service. Online. Available HTTP: <http://www.addiss.co.uk> (accessed 4 November 2004).

Disability Discrimination Act. Online. Available HTTP: <http://www.disability.gov.uk/dda/> (accessed 7 March 2005).

I-Can (a charity for people with speeech and learning difficulties). Online. Available HTTP: <http://www.ican.org.uk> (accessed 4 November 2004).

National Autistic Society. Online. Available HTTP: <http://www.nas.org.uk> (accessed 4 November 2004); tel. 020 7833 2299.

Removing Barriers to Achievement: The Government's SEN Strategy. Online. Available HTTP: <http://www.teachernet.gov.uk/_doc/5970/removing20%barriers.pdf> (accessed 7 March 2005).

Royal National Institute of the Blind. Online. Available HTTP: <http://www.rnib.org.uk> (accessed 4 November 2004).

The British Dyslexia Association. Online. Available HTTP: <http://www.bda-dyslexia.org.uk> (accessed 4 November 2004).

The Dyslexia E-mail Forum, run by BECTA. Online. Available HTTP: <http://www.becta.org.uk/>. Search under discussion forum; (accessed 4 November2004). There are forums on many other areas.

The Dyslexia Institute, Online. Available HTTP: <http://www.dyslexia-inst.org.uk> (accessed 4 November 2004).

The National Deaf Children's Society. Online. Available HTTP: <http://www.ndcs.org.uk> (accessed 4 November 2004).

The Professional Association of Teachers of Students with Specific learning difficulties (PATOSS). Online. Available HTTP: <http://www patoss_dyslexia.org> (accessed 4 November 2004).

The SENCO forum; Virtual Teacher Centre. Online. Available HTTP: <http://www.vtc.ngfl.gov.uk> (accessed 4 November 2004).

See also Unit 1.4, Further Reading, for more web addresses.

5 Helping Pupils Learn

INTRODUCTION

This chapter is about teaching and learning. As you work through these units we hope that your knowledge about teaching and learning increases and that you feel confident to try out and evaluate different approaches.

Unit 5.1 introduces you to a number of theories of learning. Theories about teaching and learning provide frameworks for the analysis of learning situations and a language to describe the learning taking place. As you become more experienced, you develop your own theories of how the pupils you teach learn and you can place your theories in the wider context.

In Unit 5.2 teaching methods which promote learning are examined. How you use these methods reveals something of your personal theory of how pupils learn. At this point in your development we suggest that you gain experience with a range of teaching methods so that you are more easily able to select the method most appropriate to the material being taught.

Unit 5.3 provides you with details about teaching styles. Again we suggest that as you gain confidence with basic classroom management skills you try out different styles so that you develop a repertoire of teaching styles from which you can select as appropriate.

We have talked at various points in this book about the characteristics of effective teaching. Unit 5.4 is designed to provide you with information about methods for finding out about the quality of your own teaching and that of others – through reflection using action research techniques and drawing on the evidence base underpinning educational practice (see http://www.ttrb.ac.uk). These techniques include, for example, the use of observation, pupils' written work, discussion and testing your practice against case studies of effective practice (available on sites such as those listed at the end of Units 7.3 and 7.4). During your initial teacher education course you are using action research skills in a simple way when you observe classes. In Unit 5.4 we explain some aspects of action research and reflective practice.

Unit 5.1

Ways Pupils Learn

Diana Burton

INTRODUCTION

The primary aim of a teacher's work is, fairly obviously, that pupils should learn *how, what, whether* and so on in relation to the subject of study; teaching is therefore a means to an end, not an end in itself. However, the interaction between the activities of teaching and the outcomes of learning is critical. In order to develop presentation and communication techniques that facilitate effective learning a teacher must have some notions of how pupils learn. Course lectures and school experience add to and refine the ideas you already have about learning and reveal the very great differences in how individuals learn. Psychological research is concerned with this individuality of *cognition* – knowing, understanding, remembering and problem solving. Research reveals information about human behaviour, motivation, achievement, personality and self-esteem, all of which impact on the activity of learning.

Several theoretical perspectives contribute to our understanding of how learning happens, e.g. the following seminal theories of:

- behaviourism, which emphasizes external stimuli for learning;
- gestalt theory, which expounds principles of perception predicated on the brain's search for 'wholeness';
- personality theories which are located in psycho-analytic, psycho-metric and humanist research traditions.

Discussion of such work can be accessed quite easily in libraries and journals (see Child, 2004, for a very good overview) so this unit is organized around theories that are currently influential amongst educators in terms of pedagogic strategy. These theories include:

- Piaget's cognitive-developmental theory of maturation;
- the information processing approach to concept development and retrieval;

- social constructivist ideas with their emphasis on social interaction and scaffolded support for learning;
- constructivist ideas about the strength of pupils' existing conceptions;
- metacognition, the way in which learners understand and control their learning strategies;
- learning style theories which serve to question qualitative distinctions between ways of learning, stressing instead the matching of learning tasks to a preferred processing style.

In Unit 4.3 you met Gardner's (1983, 1993a, 1993b) multiple intelligence theory which suggests a multi-dimensional rather than a singular intelligence. This clearly has application when considering how individuals learn. Similarly, emotional intelligence theory – also addressed in that unit and emphasizing the potency of the learner's emotional state – is also of interest to teachers (Mayer and Salovey, 1997; Goleman, 1995; Salovey and Mayer, 1990).

OBJECTIVES

By the end of this unit you should have some understanding of:

- the interaction between ideas about learning and pedagogic strategies;
- a number of psychological perspectives on learning;
- your own approach to learning.

A number of the DfES standards required of NQTs are pertinent to your management of the learning process. Identify these and review how your understanding of how pupils learn helps you to meet them.

HOW IDEAS ABOUT TEACHING AND LEARNING INTERACT

Decisions you make about how to approach a particular lesson with a particular pupil or group of pupils depend on the interplay between your subject and pedagogic knowledge, your knowledge of the pupils and your various ideas about how learning happens. Let us imagine that you have spent 10 minutes carefully introducing a new concept to your class but a few pupils unexpectedly fail to grasp it. You test the reasons for their lack of understanding against what you know about the pupils' and their:

- prior knowledge of the topic;
- levels of attention;
- interest and motivation;
- physical and emotional state of readiness to learn, etc.

You consider also factors relating to the topic and the way you explained it, subject and pedagogic knowledge:

- the relevance of the new material to the pupils;
- how well the new concept fits into the structure of the topic;
- the level of difficulty of the concept;
- your clarity of speech and explanation;
- the accessibility of any new terminology;
- the questioning and summaries you gave at intervals during your explanation, etc.

Finally you draw on explanations from educational psychology which have informed your understanding of how pupils learn and provided you with questions such as the following:

- Does the mode of presentation suit these pupils' learning styles?
- Has sufficient time been allowed for pupils to process the new information?
- Does the structure of the explanation reflect the inherent conceptual structure of the topic?
- Do these pupils need to talk to each other to help them understand the new concept?

A teacher's ideas about learning usually derive from a number of psychological theories rather than from one specific theory. This is fine because it allows for a continual revision of your ideas as more experience is gained. This process is known as 'reflecting on theory in practice'. Some of the psychological theories from which your ideas may be drawn are reviewed in this unit. In order to contextualize that review it may be helpful to think about the types of learning activities that you engage your pupils in.

Gagné (1977) identified five main types of learning (see Task 5.1.1). Each of these is used in the teaching of all subjects of the curriculum, interacting in complex ways. It is helpful to consider them separately so that a particular pupil's learning progress and needs can be monitored and so that teachers can plan lessons that foster all types of learning. Stones (1992) discussed the need to employ different pedagogical strategies depending on the type of learning planned.

Task 5.1.1
Analysing learning activities (1)

Complete the learning activity involved in each of the five areas. An example from science has been provided to guide you.

Activity	Intellectual skills	Verbal skills	Cognitive strategy	Attitudes	Motor skills
Science: a group activity using particle theory of	Discussing how to set up the activity to test an hypothesis	Defining solids, liquids and gases	Recalling previous knowledge about particles	Listening to and sharing ideas	Manipulating equipment

---

Gardner's (1983) multiple intelligences theory may provide a more attractive framework than Gagné's typology for categorizing types of learning. Noble argues that it helps teachers make sense of their observations that students have different strengths and learn in different ways (Noble, 2004: 194). Since each intelligence has a different developmental trajectory, pupils may engage in higher order thinking in areas of intellectual strength and lower order, less abstract thinking in areas of weaker 'intelligence'. He relates this to Bloom's revised taxonomy (Anderson and Krathwohl, 2001) of cognitive educational objectives which orders cognitive processes from simple remembering to higher order creative and critical thinking. From this viewpoint, Noble developed a matrix with Multiple Intelligence (MI) dimensions on the horizontal axis and Bloom's revised taxonomy (RBT) on the vertical axis. Teachers used this to design learning outcomes and activities so that pupils could demonstrate what they had learned at different levels of complexity across intellectual domains. For instance, in a science project about the processes involved in the formation of volcanoes, pupils were given the opportunity to explain the process in a number of ways, such as drawing a flow chart (spatial intelligence) or setting the words to the tune of a well-known song (musical intelligence). In this way the types of learning pupils engaged in were broadened so that each child had greater access to the curriculum and could tackle a task at the relevant level of complexity depending on the strength of a particular intelligence. This approach has clear application in terms of differentiation in the classroom.

PSYCHOLOGICAL PERSPECTIVES ON LEARNING

A determining factor in lesson preparation is the knowledge that learners already possess. Unfortunately, identifying this knowledge is not as simple as recalling what you taught the pupils last time for knowledge is, by definition, individualized. Each pupil's experiences of, attitudes towards, and methods of processing, prior knowledge are distinct. Psychologists are interested in how learners actively construct this individualized knowledge or 'meaning' and different psychological theories offer different notions about what constitutes knowledge. *Cognitive developmental theory* depicts knowledge as being generated through the learner's active exploration of her world (Piaget, 1932, 1954). More complex ways of thinking about things are developed as the individual matures. *Information processing theories* view knowledge as pieces of information which the learner's brain processes systematically and which are stored as abstractions of experiences (Anderson *et al.*, 1996). *Social constructivism* explains knowledge acquisition by suggesting that learners actively construct their individual meanings (or knowledge) as their experiences and interactions with others help develop the theories they hold (Brown, 1994; Rogoff, 1990). The relatively new theory of *situated cognition* does not recognize knowledge as existing outside of situations, but rather as 'collective knowledge', i.e. the shared, ongoing, evolving interaction between people (Lave and Wenger, 1991; Davis and Sumara, 1997).

The first three of these theories have been influential in shaping pedagogy. They are outlined briefly below.

Cognitive developmental theory

Piaget

Jean Piagt was a Swiss psychologist who applied Gessell's (1925) concept of maturation (genetically programmed sequential pattern of changing physical characteristics) to cognitive growth. He saw intellectual and moral development as sequential with the child moving through stages of thinking driven by an internal need to understand the world. His theory implied an investigative, experiential approach to learning and was embraced in many European countries in the 1960s and 1970s.

According to Piaget the stages through which the child's thinking moves and develops is linked to age. From birth to about 2 years the child understands the world through feeling, seeing, tasting and so on. This stage of development Piaget called the sensory-motor stage. As the child grows older and matures he begins to understand that others have a viewpoint. He is increasingly able to classify objects into groups and to use symbols. This second stage, from about 2 to 6 years, Piaget termed the pre-operational stage.

A third stage identified by Piaget is called the concrete operational stage. The child is still tied to specific experience but can do mental manipulations as well as physical ones. Powerful new internal mental operations become available to the child, such as addition, subtraction and class inclusion. Logical thinking develops.

The final stage of development sees the child manipulating ideas in her head and able to consider events that haven't yet happened or think about things never seen. The child can organize ideas and events systematically and can examine all possibilities. Deductive thinking becomes possible. Piaget suggested that this final stage, called the formal operational stage, began at about 12 years of age. For further information about Piaget's ideas on intellectual development see the Further Reading section at the end of this unit, e.g. Bee and Boyd, 2004.

The learner's stage of thinking interacts with his experience of the world in a process called *adaptation*. The term *operations* is used to describe the strategies, skills and mental activities which the child uses in interacting with new experience. Thus adding 2 and 2 together, whether mentally or on paper, is an operation. It is thought that discoveries are made sequentially so, for example, adding and subtracting cannot be learned until objects are seen to be constant. Progress through the sequence of discoveries occurs slowly and at any one age the child has a particular general view of the world, a logic or structure that dominates the way she explores the world. The logic changes as events are encountered which do not fit with her *schemata* (sets of ideas about objects or events). When major shifts in the structure of the child's thinking occur, a new stage is reached. Central to Piaget's theory are the concepts of *assimilation*, taking in and adapting experience or objects to one's existing strategies or concepts, and *accommodation*, modifying and adjusting one's strategies or concepts as a result of new experiences or information (see Bee and Boyd, 2004, for a full description of Piaget's theory).

The influence of stage theory

Piaget's work influenced the way in which some other psychologists developed their views. Kohlberg (1976) saw links between children's cognitive development and their moral reasoning, proposing a stage model of moral development; see also Unit 4.5. Selman (1980) was interested in the way children make relationships, describing a set of stages or levels they go through in forming friendships. Stage models of development were also posited in relation to personality growth, quite independently of Piaget's work. Influenced by Freud's (1901) psychoanalytic approach, Erikson's (1980) stages of psycho-social development explain the way in which an individual's self-concept develops, providing us with important insights into adolescent identity issues, such as role confusion. Harter's research (1985) has since indicated the significance of teacher–pupil relationships for pupils' feelings of self-worth in relation to learning competence. You may be aware of the fragility of an adolescent's self-concept, of the fundamental but often volatile nature of adolescent friendships and of the increased interest adolescents show in ethical issues. It is essential to consider these factors when planning for learning since they impact so heavily on pupils' motivation for, and capacity to engage with, lesson content.

Jerome Bruner, an American psychologist, also developed a stage model of the way people think about the world. He described three stages in learning, the enactive, iconic and symbolic. Unlike Piaget's stages, learners do not pass through and beyond Bruner's different stages of thinking. Instead, the stage or type of representation used depends on the type of thinking required of the situation. It is expected, however, that as pupils grow up they make progressively greater use of symbolic representation (Bruner, 1966).

The stress on the idea of 'stages' in Piaget's theory was far-reaching, especially the implication that pupils need to be at a particular developmental level in order to cope with certain learning tasks. However, research studies have substantially refuted such limitations on a pupil's thinking (Donaldson, 1978). Thus the construct of a staged model of cognitive maturation probably has less currency than the features of development described within the various stages. Flavell (1982), a former student of Piaget, has argued that, while stage notions of development are unhelpful, Piaget's ideas about the sequences learners go through are still valid. They can help teachers to examine the level of difficulty of topics and curriculum material as a way of deciding how appropriate they are for particular age groups and ability levels; see e.g. Unit 4.3. The key task for teachers is to examine the progress of individuals in order to determine when to increase the intellectual demand on them. Bruner (1966) argued that difficult ideas should be seen as a challenge that, if properly presented, can be learned by most pupils.

More recent work by Adey and his colleagues has revealed that learning potential is increased if pupils are metacognitively aware, i.e. if they understand and can control their own learning strategies.

These strategies include techniques for remembering, ways of presenting information when thinking, approaches to problems and so on. Shayer and Adey have developed a system of cognitive acceleration in science education (CASE), which challenges pupils to examine the processes they use to solve problems (Shayer and Adey, 2002; Adey, 1992). In doing so it is argued that pupils are enhancing their thinking processes. In Jordan, researchers have identified statistically significant differences in seventh grade students' achievement in science when using a metacognitive teaching strategy (Namrouti and Alshannag, 2004). Kramarski and Mevarech (1997) showed that metacognitive training helped 12–14-year-old pupils draw better graphs in mathematics. Other researchers reported that transfer of learning between tasks is enhanced where the teacher cues learners into the specific skill being learned and encourages them to reflect on its potential for transfer (Anderson *et al.*, 1996). It seems, then, that the higher order cognitive skills of Piaget's formal operations (stage) can be promoted and encouraged through a focus on metacognition. Claxton (2002) has argued for some time that learners need above all to learn to learn, claiming that teachers' endeavours would be more profitable if they concentrated on teaching pupils how to learn. Certainly, an ever-increasing body of knowledge and more technological ways of accessing it require pupils to have considerable curiosity, confidence and adaptability. You might like to consider how you can give pupils at least one opportunity during each lesson to think about the strategies they are using in their learning. Ask them, for instance, how they reached a particular conclusion, how they tackled the drawing of a 3D shape or how they would undertake a journey from point A to point B.

Social constructivist theory

The ideas of the Russian psychologist, Lev Vygotsky, and of Jerome Bruner in the USA have increasingly influenced educators in recent years. Vygotsky's work dates from between the 1920s and 1930s but was suppressed in Soviet Russia until the 1970s.

Vygotsky

Juxtaposing Piaget's and Vygotsky's theories, Kozulin describes their 'common denominators as a child centred approach, an emphasis on action in the formation of thought, and a systematic understanding of psychological functioning' and their biggest difference as their understanding of psychological activity (Kozulin, 1998: 34). For Vygotsky (1978), psychological activity has socio-cultural characteristics from the very beginning of development. Concepts can be generated from a range of different stimuli, implying a problem-solving approach for pupils and a facilitator role for the teacher. Whereas Piaget considered language a tool of thought in the child's developing mind, Vygotsky held that language was generated from the need to communicate and was central to the development of thinking. He emphasized the functional value of egocentric speech to verbal reasoning and self-regulation, and the importance of socio-cultural factors in its development. In communicative talk, too, the development is not just in the language contrived to formulate the sentence but also through the process of combining the words to shape the sentence because this shapes the thought itself.

Thus Vygotsky's work highlights the importance of talk as a learning tool and reports of some eminence have reinforced the status of talk in the classroom, highlighting its centrality to learning (Bullock Report, 1975; Norman, 1992). Vygotsky believed that such communicative instruction could reduce a pupil's 'zone of proximal development', i.e. the gap between her current level of learning and the level she could be functioning at with adult or peer support: 'What a child can do today in co-operation, tomorrow he will be able to do on his own' (Vygotsky, 1962: 67).

Consider how often you make opportunities for your pupils to talk in lessons, to each other, to you, to a cassette, video recorder or via a CD-ROM? Listen to how the talk develops the thinking of each member of a small group of pupils. Notice how well-timed and focused intervention from you moves the thinking on.

More recent research in this area has indicated that reciprocal peer and cross-age tutoring can also promote learning (Smith *et al.*, 2003; Telecsan *et al.*, 1999; Topping, 1992). Crucially, however, children need to be given specific preparation and guidance by the teacher in order to work effectively. Rogoff (1990) found that homogeneous student grouping and pairing, such as setting provides, have advantages in promoting argument and sharing complex ideas. However, Doise (1990) found that in pair work a slight difference in the intellectual functioning of partners was best because it promoted cognitive conflict. In the USA, Brown (1994) developed the idea of learning communities where group work and seminars provide the main vehicle for learning. The concept of learning communities has become popular as a professional development tool for teachers as well as a means of promoting pupil learning. In both Australia and England networked learning communities have been set up in which teachers can work together to share and develop their practices (Burton and Bartlett, 2004). Unit 5.2 provides information about active learning strategies which support a Vygotskyan approach to learning.

Bruner

Bruner also placed an emphasis on structured intervention within communicative learning models. He formulated a theory of instruction, central to which is the notion of systematic, structured pupil experience via a spiral curriculum where the learner returns to address increasingly complex components of a topic. Current and past knowledge is deployed as the pupil constructs new ideas or concepts. Thus the problem of fractions in Year 5 will be tackled via many more concrete examples than when it is returned to in Year 7. Learning involves the active restructuring of knowledge through experience; the pupil selects and transforms information, constructs hypotheses and makes decisions, relying on a developing cognitive structure to do so.

Teachers should try to encourage pupils to discover principles by themselves through active dialogue with the teacher. Thus, for Bruner, the teacher's job is to guide this discovery through structured support, e.g. by asking focused questions or providing appropriate materials. Bruner termed this process 'scaffolding' (Bruner, 1983). Maybin *et al.* (1992) have used 'scaffolding' in relation to classroom talk. The ideas of pupils emerging through their talk are scaffolded or framed by the teacher putting in 'steps' or questions at appropriate junctures. For example, a group of pupils might be discussing how to solve the problem of building a paper bridge between two desks. The teacher can intervene when he hears an idea emerge which will help pupils find the solution, by asking a question that requires the pupils to address that idea explicitly. Bruner argued that the scaffolding provided by the teacher should decrease in direct correspondence to the progress of the learner. Wood (1988) has developed Bruner's ideas, describing five levels of support which become increasingly specific and supportive in relation to the help needed by the pupil:

- general verbal encouragement;
- specific verbal instruction;
- assistance with pupil's choice of material or strategies;
- preparation of material for pupil assembly;
- demonstration of task.

Thus, having established the task the pupils are to complete, a teacher might give general verbal encouragement to the whole class, follow this up with specific verbal instruction to groups who need it, perhaps targeting individuals with guidance on strategies for approaching the task. Some pupils need physical help in performing the task and yet others need to be shown exactly what to do, probably in small stages.

Task 5.1.2
Analysing learning activities (2)

Wood's ideas can help you think systematically about the nature of the support you should prepare for particular pupils, and to keep a check on whether the level is becoming more or less supportive. This has obvious relevance for differentiation in your classroom, workshop or gym.

For a topic you are planning to teach, use Wood's five levels to prepare the type of support you think might be needed during the first lesson. Once you start teaching the topic choose two particular pupils who need different levels of support. Plan the support for each one, lesson by lesson, noting whether they are requiring less or more support as the topic progresses. What does this tell you about the way you are teaching and the way the pupils are learning?

Constructivism

Another theory called 'constructivism' is that described by Driver and Bell (1986). Whilst sharing a Brunerian and Vygotskyan emphasis on the social construction of meaning, constructivism places much more importance on learners' individual conceptions and gives them responsibility for directing their own learning experiences. It is in the science subject area that constructivist ideas have been most influential. Naylor and Keogh (1999), for instance, have devised concept cartoons, which enable learners to examine the very core of their conceptions.

Information processing theory

This approach to learning originated within explanations of perception and memory processes and was influenced by the growth of computer technology. The basic idea is that the brain attends to sensory information as it is experienced, analyses it within the short-term memory and stores it with other related concepts in the long-term memory.

Psychologists saw the functioning of computers as replicating the behaviour of the brain in relation to the processing of information. Information is analysed in the short-term memory (STM) and stored with existing related information in the long-term memory (LTM). This process is more efficient if material can be stored as abstractions of experience rather than as verbatim events. If I ask you to tell me the six times table, you recite 'one six is six, two sixes are twelve' and so on. You do not explain to me the mathematical principle of multiplication by a factor of six. On the other hand, if I ask you the meaning of the term 'economic enterprise', it is unlikely that you will recite a verbatim answer. Instead, your STM searches your LTM for your 'schema' or idea of enterprise. You then articulate your abstracted understanding of the term, which may well be different from that of the person next to you. In terms of intellectual challenge, articulating the second answer requires greater mental effort, although knowing one's multiplication tables is a very useful tool. Thus teachers need to be absolutely clear that there is a good reason for requiring pupils to learn something by rote because rote learning is not inherently meaningful so cannot be stored in LTM with other related information. Rather it must be stored in its full form, taking up a lot of 'disk' space in the memory. Information stored in this way is analysed only superficially in STM, the pupil does not have to think hard to make connections with other pieces of information.

It can often be difficult in secondary schools for teachers to determine precisely the prior knowledge of their pupils. You observe that good teachers cue learners in to their prior knowledge by asking questions about what was learned the lesson before or giving a brief resume of the point reached in a topic. Such strategies are very important because, if previous learning has been effective, information is stored by pupils in their long-term memories and needs to be retrieved. Psychologists suggest that learning is more effective, i.e. more likely to be understood and retained, if material is introduced to pupils according to the inherent conceptual structure of the topic (Ausubel, 1968; Gagné, 1977; Stones, 1992). Information which is stored using a logical structure is easier to recall because the brain can process it more easily in the first instance, linking the new ideas to ones which already exist in the memory. As a teacher, this requires you to have thought through the structure in advance, and to know how the concepts fit together; hence the importance of spending time on schemes of work even where these are already produced for you. See Task 5.1.3 and concept maps in Unit 5.2.

Task 5.1.3
Structuring topics for effective learning

Choose a topic from your subject area. Brainstorm some of the ideas contained within it for a couple of minutes, jotting them down haphazardly on paper. Now think about how those ideas fit together and whether, in teaching the topic, you would start with the general overarching ideas and then move to the specific ones or vice versa. You can organize your topic by drawing up a conceptual hierarchy of it like the one started below for a PSE topic. This hierarchy moves from the general to the specific.

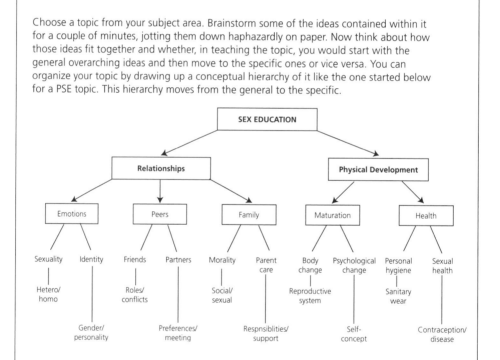

This emphasis on structure and sequence can be found most readily perhaps in the teaching of modern foreign languages (MFL) and mathematics. Mitchell (1994) found that MFL teachers use a 'bottom–up' language learning theory, encouraging recognition and acquisition of vocabulary first, followed by the construction of spoken and written sentences. This approach might be described as moving from the general to the specific but in most subjects the process is the other way around. Chyriwsky (1996) has stressed the importance of working hierarchically through mathematical knowledge. It might be argued that in mathematics we start with the general concepts of addition, subtraction and multiplication, moving to more specific computations like calculating area, solving equations or estimating probabilities.

Concept development

It is helpful to consider briefly how information processing relates to concept development. The material held in the long-term memory is stored as sets of ideas known as 'schemata' ('schema' is the singular). A schema is a mental structure abstracted from experience. It consists of a set of expectations with which to categorize and understand new stimuli. For example, our schema of 'school' consists of expectations of pupils, teachers, classrooms, etc. As teachers, our school schema has been refined and developed as more and more information has been added and categorized. Thus it includes expectations about hierarchies, pupil culture, staffroom behaviour and so on. It is probable that our school schema is different from, and more complex than, the school schema held by a parent, simply because of our involvement in schools.

When children are young their schemata do not allow them to differentiate between pieces of information in the way that those of older pupils do. A one-year-old's schema of dog might include expectations about cats too because she has had insufficient experience of the two animals to know them apart. As she experiences cats as furry, dogs as hairy, cats meowing, dogs barking, etc., greater differentiation is possible. Since the object of school learning is to promote pupils' concept differentiation in a range of different subjects, teachers should encourage comparison between objects or ideas and introduce new ideas by reference to concrete examples. Even as adults, whilst we can think abstractly, we find new ideas easier to grasp if we can be given concrete examples of them.

Critical thinking

Teaching in the context of IP theories stresses the application of knowledge and skills to new situations. The teacher's role is to help pupils find new ways of recalling previous knowledge, solving problems, formulating hypotheses and so on. Montgomery (1996) advocates the use of games and simulations because they facilitate critical thinking and encourage connections to be made between areas of subject knowledge or experience.

We have discussed cognitive development theories, social constructivist theories and information processing theories. In each of these theories about how learning occurs, there has been an emphasis on the individual and the differences between them. Looking at what is known about how learners' styles and strategies differ equips us further to understand individual differences.

LEARNING STYLES, STRATEGIES AND APPROACHES

There is currently a great deal of interest amongst teachers in identifying whether learners are predominantly visual, auditory or kinaesthetic learners (*VAK*, Dryden and Vos, 2001). However, there are a huge number of such classifications based on different psychological constructs and using a range of measurement tools. Some of these ideas, such as the VAK construct and preferred environmental conditions or stimuli for learning, have been incorporated, along with a range of other ideas, such as neuro-linguistic programming, into accelerated learning programmes such as that of Alastair Smith (Smith and Call, 2002); see Burton (2004) for a discussion of these ideas.

It can be attractively simple to feel that we can categorize pupils into fixed learning approaches or styles and then teach to a formula that such a categorization suggests but we know that learning is complex and context-dependent with pupils employing different approaches in different settings. It is important that teachers take an eclectic approach to the growing industry of learning style classification and measurement lest they too readily pigeonhole pupils and fail to provide a range of media and activities to maximize access for all to the curriculum. In this section you are introduced to categorizations that have been researched over a considerable number of years but for a full overview of the range of research in this area consult Riding and Rayner (1998).

There is often confusion about what constitutes learning style as distinct from learning strategy. Psychologists argue that a cognitive or *learning style* is considered to be a fairly fixed characteristic of an individual, which may be distinguished from *learning strategies*, which are the ways learners cope with situations and tasks. Strategies may vary from time to time and may be learned and developed. Styles, by contrast, are static and are relatively in-built features of the individual (Riding and Cheema, 1991).

Learning style

Understanding how in-built features of learners affect the way they process information is important for teachers. Many researchers have worked in this area but Riding and Rayner (1998) have proposed that the various conceptualizations may be grouped into two principal cognitive styles: *Wholist-Analytic Style* – whether an individual tends to process information in wholes (wholist) or in parts (analytics); *Verbal-Imagery Style* – whether an individual is inclined to represent information during thinking verbally (verbalist) or in mental pictures (imagers).

The two styles operate as dimensions so a person may be at either end of the dimension or somewhere along it. Think about what your own learning style might be. Do you:

- approach essay writing incrementally, step by step, piecing together the various parts or do you like to have a broad idea of the whole essay before you start writing?
- experience lots of imagery when you are thinking about something or do you find yourself thinking in words?

Discuss your style with other student teachers. In doing so you are developing your metacognitive knowledge, about your own way of learning.

Riding and Rayner explain that these styles are involuntary so it is important to be aware that your classes contain pupils whose habitual learning styles vary. Teachers need to ensure that they provide a variety of media in which pupils can work and be assessed. It would not be sensible to present information only in written form; if illustrations are added, this allows both 'Verbalizers' and 'Imagers' easier access to it. Similarly, 'Wholist' pupils are assisted by having an overview of the topic before starting whilst 'Analytics' benefit from summaries after they have been working on information.

This is not to suggest that you must determine the style of each pupil, but that there must be opportunities for all pupils to work in the way that is most profitable for them. Unlike the way in which intelligence quotient (IQ) is used, the higher the IQ score the better the performance is expected, the determination of learning style does not imply that one way of processing is better than the other. The key to success is in allowing learners to use their natural processing style. It is important for you to be aware of your own style because teachers have been found to promote the use of approaches that fit most easily with their own styles; see Task 5.1.4.

Task 5.1.4
Determining types of learners

Try to work out which stage of Kolb's cycle describes the way you learn yourself most of the time.
Think about how you process information, e.g.:

•   are you more comfortable reflecting on ideas where you have had lots of concrete experience?
•   do you prefer to draw from abstract theory and experiment with it to solve problems?

Do you think Kolb's ideas could help you to process information differently? Would it be helpful to 'practise' different ways? What are the implications for your work with pupils?

Learning strategy

Learning strategy describes the ways in which learners cope with tasks or situations. These strategies develop and change as the pupil becomes more experienced. Kolb's work describing two dimensions of learning strategy, perceiving and processing, is the most widely known in the area of strategy theory (Kolb, 1976, 1985). Kolb argued that these two dimensions interact and that, although learners use preferred strategies, they could be trained to develop aspects of other strategies through experiential learning. Kolb envisaged a cyclical sequence through four stages of learning arising from the interaction of the two dimensions (see Figure 5.1.1).

Thus Kolb suggests that learners need, at the concrete experience stage, to immerse themselves in new experiences. These experiences are reflected upon from as many perspectives as possible at what Kolb calls the Reflective Observation stage. This reflection enables the learner to create concepts which integrate their observations into logically sound theories at the abstract conceptualization stage, which are then used to make decisions and solve problems at the active experimentation stage (Fielding, 1996). Learners have a predilection for one of the stages. It can be argued that learners should be provided with experiences that ensure their use of *stages in the cycle* additional to their preferred one in order to extend their learning strategies (McCarthy, 1987).

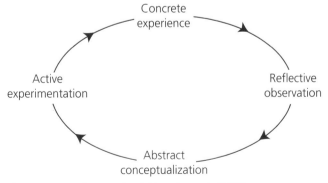

Figure 5.1.1 Kolb's experiential learning cycle (1985)

Learning approaches

Other researchers are interested in the motivations and attitudes pupils and students bring to their learning, described as 'approaches to learning'. Researchers have investigated how learning approaches interact with learning strategies. Biggs (1978, 1987, 1993) and Entwistle (1981 and 1993) have both researched learners' approaches to study.

Entwistle described different orientations to learning, such as being oriented towards discovering the meaning of a topic or being oriented simply to scratch the surface. Combinations of these orientations with extrinsic factors, such as the need to pass examinations or the love of a subject, were thought to lead to learning strategies which characterized certain approaches to study, from 'deep' to 'surface' levels of thinking; see Unit 4.3.

Biggs explained that a student's approach is a function of both motive and strategy and that motives influence learning strategies (Biggs, 1993). Thus, a student with an instrumental (surface) motive is likely to adopt reproducing or rote-learning (surface) strategies. Deep motive results from an intrinsic desire to learn and can inspire the use of deep strategies wherein understanding and meaning are emphasized. An achieving motive might be an egotistical need to pass examinations; from this perspective the learner can derive achieving strategies which stress time management, well-ordered resources and efficiency.

Task 5.1.5
Your own approaches to learning

Refer to the paragraphs on learning approaches. Do you recognize any of these motives and strategies in relation to your own learning? Do your motives and associated learning strategies stay the same over time or do they depend on the task and the reason you are learning it? Prepare some notes on your own ways of learning for discussion with your tutor.

Pupils whose motives and strategies are compatible with the demands made by learning tasks are likely to perform well. Pupils are likely to be less successful where motives and strategy are incompatible with task demand. For example, a pupil with a deep approach to learning is constrained by superficial task design such as a requirement for short answers, whereas a pupil with an achieving motive may be deterred if he is set very long-term, vague objectives.

Successful learning, if defined in terms of understanding and permanence, is linked with deep and deep-achieving approaches, which can be taught. The achievement-driven context within which secondary school pupils in England currently learn, however, could militate against the possibility of teaching deep approaches because of time constraints. An important development in this regard is the UK government's recent emphasis on personalized learning and the use of interactive technology to this end (Leadbetter, 2004). Many research groups have been trying to construct sophisticated hypermedia systems that can identify learners' interests, preferences and needs, and advise them accordingly. Triantafillou *et al.* (2004) describe one such model, called Adaptive Hypermedia Systems (AHS), which adapts web-based educational material to particular users. AHS build a model of the goals, preferences and knowledge of the individual user, and use this to adapt the content of pages and the links between them to the needs of that user. Increasingly such resources will be available to teachers but in the meantime you should endeavour to maintain variety in the learning experiences you design for pupils, in the ways you present information, in the resources pupils use and the tasks they undertake and in the ways you assess their progress.

SUMMARY

The importance of teachers developing their own models of learning and refining these as they gain more experience of pupils and learning contexts has been established. The interaction between your knowledge of the pupils, of the subject and of how learning happens is continually drawn on in the teaching process. The symbiosis between theoretical positions and pedagogic practices has been emphasized. We have seen, for instance, that concept development is enhanced where pupils are introduced to new ideas via concrete examples and that retention is aided if topics are taught according to their inherent conceptual structure.

Key features of three major psychological theories (cognitive developmental, social constructivism and information processing) as they apply to pupil learning have been outlined and your attention has been drawn to the implications of learning style and strategy research for teaching techniques. The benefits of teachers adopting a facilitative, interventionist approach and of aiming for a variety of approaches in presentation, resource, task and assessment can be extrapolated from all the theories that have been discussed. Learning is likely to be most effective where pupils are actively involved with the material through critical thinking, discussion with others and metacognitive awareness of their own learning strategies.

You should review your learning from this unit while referring to the standards for your course.

FURTHER READING

Bee, H. and Boyd, D. (2004) *The Developing Child*, 10th edn, London: Allyn & Bacon.

Child, D. (2004) *Psychology and the Teacher*, 7th edn, New York and London: Continuum. This book and that by Bee and Boyd above are excellent and take you further into theories of learning and child development.

Riding, R. (2002) *School Learning and Cognitive Styles*, London: David Fulton. Riding incorporates recent psychological developments on individual learning differences with practical classroom applications. He presents new approaches in three key areas: processing capacity, cognitive style and understanding the structure of knowledge. These are central to the understanding of pupil differences and they affect our perception of how pupils can be helped to learn; why pupils find some aspects of their school work difficult; and why pupils behave as they do. See also Riding and Rayner (1998).

Shayer, M. and Adey, P. (eds) (2002) *Learning Intelligence: Cognitive Acceleration across the Curriculum from 5 to 15 Years*, Buckingham and Philadelphia: Open University Press. This edited collection describes how children's general ability to process information – their 'intelligence' – can be improved by appropriate cognitive acceleration methods. Through examples of cognitive acceleration in a variety of contexts, from Year 1 to Year 9 and in science, mathematics, and arts subjects, each chapter draws on research or development experience to describe effects of cognitive acceleration programmes. The book also looks at the psychological theory that underlies cognitive acceleration.

Unit 5.2

Active Learning

Françoise Allen, Alexis Taylor and Tony Turner

INTRODUCTION

> As we know from investigations of the process of concept formation, a concept is more than the sum of the certain associative bonds formed by memory, more than a mere mental habit; it is a complex and genuine act of thought that cannot be taught by drilling but can be accomplished only when the child's mental development itself has reached the requisite level.
>
> Practical experience also shows that direct teaching of concepts is impossible and fruitless. A teacher who tries to do this usually accomplishes nothing but empty verbalisation, a parrot like repetition of words by the child, simulating a knowledge of the corresponding concepts but actually covering up a vacuum.
>
> (Vygotsky, 1986: 149–50)

Vygotsky uses the term concepts here to mean 'word meanings'. This extract suggests that the teacher cannot do the learning for the pupil and that in order for understanding to occur the pupil has to be active in the learning process. Active learning is then meaningful learning, in which something of interest and value to the learner has been accomplished and understood. Some writers use the term 'deep learning' instead of meaningful learning, by contrast to 'shallow learning', or surface learning, which is learning with little understanding.

This unit addresses ways in which teachers help pupils to engage in meaningful learning. Active learning supports meaningful learning and enables the learner to take more responsibility for his own learning.

OBJECTIVES

At the end of this unit you should be able to:

- explain the term 'active learning' and discuss the advantage of active learning to the teacher and learner;
- be aware of ways of promoting active learning;
- use resources to their best advantage;
- be able to link these teaching strategies to the standards/competences expected of an NQT.

CASE STUDIES: TWO PUPILS LEARNING MATHEMATICS

> It's not that I haven't learnt much. It's just that I don't really understand what I am doing.
> (Watkins *et al.*, 2000)

Manjeet and Robert are two pupils in Year 8. They are taught the same syllabus at the same school and complete the same activities and assignments. They had similar scores on entry from primary school. Both Manjeet and Robert have worked hard. Here's what they have to say about one of the subjects they take.

Manjeet

I enjoy mathematics because I can think, which is not something I always do in other subjects. I try to see the mathematics that is being taught in other areas as well. For example, I use it at home to help my younger brother and also in the supermarket when we go shopping, and also when I go to town with my friends. I also watch programmes on television – you know, those consumer programmes – and link what we've been doing in class. I never used to like mathematics in my primary school, but I do now. I enjoy doing the homework, and ask the teacher for some additional work. I also try to make up sums and mathematics tasks of my own. This works because I passed the latest mathematics tests. The way I work is to try to understand the information first, then try the activity. If I don't understand I will ask the teacher, or a friend, or my dad – he's good with mathematics! I think that someone who is not so good at mathematics would struggle a bit. You know, to get interested in it. To find different ways to understand it. In our mathematics class we do a lot of group discussions and pair work and the teacher really makes us think by asking some very difficult questions. She also lets us work on our own by getting us to do investigations and surveys and looking on the internet.

Robert

The way I do mathematics is to keep trying the same activity until I get it right …you know trying different techniques to solve the same problem. I know I have to get the mathematics right because my parents say it will be useful for me in the future – to get a good job. I usually try to write down formulas and learn them by heart. I always do the classwork and homework the teacher has given me (I'd get a detention if I didn't!), and also so I can get a good enough mark … but I only spend a short time on it as I like to go out with my friend Sam and play football. The lessons are usually the same.

The teacher explains something to us, then shows us some examples on the board. Then we usually have to do some exercises from a text book or worksheet. We usually work on our own. Sometimes we do past tests papers as practices, but I didn't do well on the last one!

Task 5.2.1
Two pupils' experiences of mathematics

Discuss the observations made by these pupils from the standpoint of (1) their response to the tasks set and possible reasons for those responses; (2) the way the tasks may have been set by the teacher.
Carry out this task before reading on.

The responses of Manjeet and Robert suggest two important things. The first of these is that they experience mathematics differently. Manjeet and Robert appear to approach their learning in two qualitatively different ways. Manjeet appears to take a *deep approach* to his work, while Robert appears to adopt a *shallow (surface) approach.* Nevertheless, Robert's willingness to try different ways of solving problems is a positive feature of his attitude to work. Those who take a *deep approach* tend to have an intrinsic interest in the topic and the tasks and aim to understand and seek meaning. They adopt strategies that help them to satisfy their curiosity and to look for patterns and connections in other areas. They think about the task. Those who adopt a *surface approach* see tasks as work given to them by others. They are pragmatically motivated and seek to meet the demands of the task with the minimum of effort (Entwistle, 1990). Deep and surface learning are discussed further in Units 3.2 and 5.3.

We suggest that Manjeet is engaged mainly in active learning and Robert is engaged more in passive learning. This may mean that Manjeet is able to think abstractly and is actively involved in the process of learning. This may involve, for example, learning through doing, trial and error, trying things out, getting it wrong and knowing why. It is not just the learner's attitude but the way the task is set. Active learning has to be encouraged. Perhaps the way Robert engages with the subject is as much to do with the way the lessons are structured as it is with Robert's own approach to learning. Finally it is important to remember that we are not discussing the ability of the pupils but their response to the subject and the way tasks are set.

WHAT IS ACTIVE LEARNING?

Active learning occurs when the pupil has some responsibility for the development of the activity. Supporters of this approach recognize that a sense of ownership and personal involvement is the key to successful learning. Unless the work that pupils do is seen to be important to them and to have purpose, that their ideas, contributions and findings are valued, little of benefit is learned. Active learning can also be defined as purposeful interaction with ideas, concepts and phenomena and can involve reading, writing, listening, talking or working with tools, equipment and materials, such as paint, wood, chemicals, etc. In a simple sense it is learning by doing, by contrast with being told.

Active learning may be linked to experiential learning. Experiential learning is also learning by doing but with the additional feature of reflection upon both action and the results of action; only where pupils are 'engaged actively and purposively in their own learning is the term experiential appropriate' (Addison and Burgess, 2000: 31). Both active and experiential learning contribute to meaningful learning.

Active learning strategies benefit both teachers and pupils. As a teacher they enable you to spend more time with groups or individuals, which allows better quality formative assessment and feedback to take place (see formative assessment in Unit 6.1). Active learning can also enhance your support of pupils with special needs. Activity methods encourage autonomous learning and problem-solving skills, important to both academic and vocationally based work. There is, of course, an extra demand on you in the planning and preparation of lessons.

The advantages of active learning to pupils include greater personal satisfaction, more interaction with peers, promotion of shared activity and team work, greater opportunities to work with a range of pupils and opportunities for all members of the class to contribute and respond. It can encourage mutual respect and appreciation of the viewpoint of others. Active learning is supportive of co-operative learning, not competitive learning.

It is important to realize that learning by doing, by itself, is not enough to ensure learning. The proverb 'I hear and I forget; I see and I remember; I do and I understand' was reformulated by a prominent educationalist as 'I do and I am even more confused' (Driver, 1983: 9). The essential step to learning and understanding is reflection through discussion with others, especially the teacher; such discussions involve 'thinking' as well as recalling, i.e. experiential learning.

ACTIVE LEARNING AND MOTIVATION

You support pupil learning by identifying clearly defined tasks which have purpose and relevance. Relevance may arise because of personal interest, i.e. it is intrinsic; or the motivation may be extrinsic, e.g. to please the teacher. Outside interests become increasingly important as the pupils get older. If the school task links with some future occupation, employment training or higher education motivation is increased and engagement promoted. Motivation is considered in greater detail in Unit 3.2.

Upper school secondary curricula (Years 10 to 13) often aim to promote higher order thinking. Teaching to promote higher level intellectual skills, however laudable and desirable, cuts no ice with pupils unless the task engages with their need to know. If the task does not meet these needs then learning is on sufferance, leading to problems. Such problems may include poor recall of anything learned or rejection of learning tasks. The latter response may lead to behaviour problems, ranging from disruption to even non-attendance.

LEARNING HABITS

Learning how to learn is a feature of active learning. By promoting activities which engage pupils and require them to participate in the task from the outset, you foster an approach to learning which is both skill based and attitude based. Active learning methods promote habits of learning which it is hoped are valuable in the workplace, the home and generally enhance pupils' capacity to cope with everyday life. The CASE Project sets out to promote thinking skills and to teach pupils how to learn (Adey, 2000: 158–72). CASE provides challenging tasks for pupils and emphasizes the importance for the development of thinking skills that pupils reflect on their own learning.

School can be a place where pupils learn to do things well and in certain ways. Some skills are developed which are used throughout life. For example, pupils learn to consult a dictionary or a thesaurus in book form or through a word processing package, in order to find meanings or to counteract poor spelling. These skills become habits, capable of reinforcement and development. Reinforcement leads to improved performance. Many of our actions are of this sort, like dressing and eating. Important attitudes are developed, such as the confidence to question statements or to believe that problems can be solved and not to be put off by difficulties.

Many professional people depend, in part, on habits and routines for their livelihood; these include the concert pianist who may well practise time and time again a piece of music already well established in her repertoire. Practice commits the sequence of notes and pauses to memory, leaving time to concentrate on expression. Actors, too, depend on learned routines for skilful performance.

ACTIVE LEARNING, DISCOVERY LEARNING AND ROTE LEARNING

Active learning is sometimes contrasted to rote learning to suggest that rote methods do not require the learner to understand what is learned. Rote learning is an active process and often hard work. Discovery learning is also active learning and attempts to motivate pupils by helping them to learn things for themselves.

Discovery learning

Discovery learning at its simplest occurs when pupils are left to discover things for themselves but it is difficult to imagine when such learning happens in the organized classrooms of secondary schools; see also Mosston and Ashworth (2002) in Unit 5.3. Much more common is the use of a structured framework in which learning can occur, sometimes called 'guided discovery'. But is the intention of guided discovery that pupils come to some predetermined conclusion or is it that learning should take place but the outcomes vary from pupil to pupil? See also Unit 5.3. Guided discovery as a method of teaching is a useful strategy for differentiation because the task permits pupils to attain different end points.

You need to be clear, however, about your reason for adopting guided discovery methods. If the intention in discovery learning is to move pupils to a particular end point, then as *discovery* it could be challenged. This approach might preclude, for example, considering other knowledge that surfaced in the enquiry. If discovery learning focuses on how the knowledge was gained, then the activity is concerned with processes, i.e. how to discover and how to learn. The question is one of means and ends. Are discovery methods then concerned with:

- Discovery as 'process' – learning how to learn?
- Discovery as motivation – a better way to learn predetermined knowledge and skills?

Rote learning

It is a fallacy, we suggest, to assume that pupils can learn everything for themselves by discovery methods. Teachers are specialists in their fields of study; they usually know more than pupils and one, but not all, of their functions is to tell pupils things they otherwise might not know but need to know. You need to consider what you want to achieve and match the method with the purpose.

Pupils need to be told when they are right; their work needs supporting. On occasions you need to tell pupils when they are wrong and how to correct their error. How this is done is important but teachers should not shirk telling pupils when they underperform or make mistakes. See Unit 3.2 on motivating pupils, which includes a section on giving feedback.

Rote learning may occur when pupils are required to listen to the teacher. There are occasions when you need to talk directly to pupils, e.g. to give facts about language, of spelling or grammar; about formulae in science; or health matters such as facts about drug abuse or safe practice in the gymnasium. Other facts necessary for successful learning in school include recalling multiplication tables; or remembering vocabulary; or learning the reactivity series of metals; or recalling a piece of prose or poetry. Some facts need to be learned by heart, by rote methods. There is nothing wrong with you requiring pupils to do this from time to time, providing that all their learning is not like that. Such facts are necessary for advanced work; they contribute to the subroutines which allows us to function at a higher level. Habits of spelling, of adding up, of recalling the alphabet are vital to our ability to function in all areas of the curriculum and in daily life.

Sometimes pupils need to use a routine as part of a more important task but which they may not fully understand. You may decide that the end justifies the means and that through the experience of using the routine in different contexts understanding of that routine develops. Many of us learn that way.

Learning facts by heart usually involves a coding process. For example, recalling telephone numbers is easier if it is broken into blocks such as 0271 612 6780 and not as 02716126780. Another strategy is the use of a mnemonic to aid recall, such as recalling the musical scale E G B D F by the phrase 'Every Good Boy Deserves Fun'. Do you know any other mnemonics? What other ways are there of helping pupils to learn by rote?

AIDS TO RECALL

Sometimes information cannot easily be committed to memory unless a structure is developed around it to help recall. That structure may involve other information which allows you to build a picture. In other words, recall is constructed. Structures may include other words, but often tables, diagrams, flow charts or other visual models are used. Other ways of helping learners to remember ideas or facts are to construct summaries in various forms. Both the *act of compiling* the summary and the *product* contribute to remembering and learning.

In Figure 5.2.1 there is a model of learning, based on the idea that personal development proceeds best by reflection on your own actions. Reflection in the model is incorporated in the terms 'review'

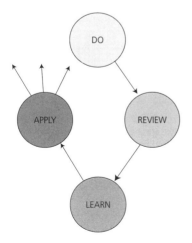

Figure 5.2.1   An active learning model

and 'learn'. This model is presented as a cyclic flow diagram which enables you to keep in mind the essential steps.

To develop your teaching, the key ideas in the model could be interpreted as follows:

Do   Plan and teach a lesson to defined objectives.
Review   Identify where learning took place and what contributed to successful learning. Which ideas or processes gave difficulties? Try to identify factors contributing to success and difficulties.
Learn   Clarify what has been learned about your teaching and what questions remain. Seek help about difficulties, from mentors, tutors, books and colleagues. Identify problems you can solve and those that are more deep rooted.
Apply   How can I use the new knowledge to improve next lessons? Planning and further action.

Spider diagrams and concept maps

It is often helpful to pupils and teachers to 'brainstorm' as a way of exploring their understanding of an idea. One way to record that event is by a spider diagram (or burr diagram) in which the 'legs' identify the ideas related to the topic. Figure 5.2.2 shows a spider diagram constructed by a pupil of some meanings of 'fruit'.

Concept maps are developments from spider diagrams and are used to display important ideas or concepts which are involved in a topic or unit of work and, by annotation, show the links between them. An example is shown in Figure 5.2.3. Concept maps are sometimes referred to as 'mind maps' (Burton, 2004). Concept maps can be made by pupils as a way of summarizing their knowledge of a unit of work. The individual map reveals some of the pupil's understanding and misunderstandings of the topic. An example of a Year 10 pupil's concept map can be found in Lambert and Balderstone (2000: 203). Making a concept map at the start of a unit helps to probe pupils' prior knowledge of the

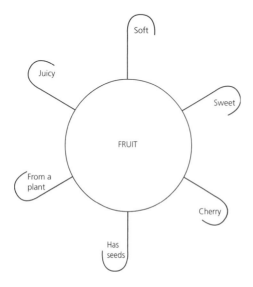

Figure 5.2.2   A pupil's meaning of fruit

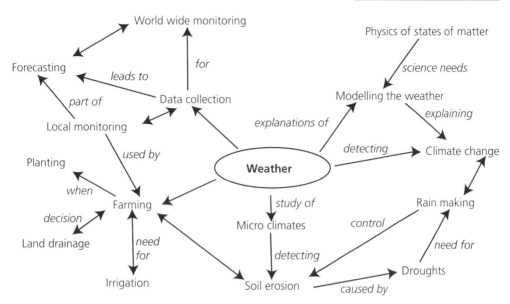

Figure 5.2.3   Concept map: weather

subject. In either case, you may need to provide a list of ideas with which pupils can work and to which they can add their own ideas.

Concept mapping is useful as part of your lesson preparation, particularly when beginning a new unit of work. See also Task 5.1.3 in Unit 5.1 'How Children Learn'. Concept mapping enables you to gain an overview of the unit, to consolidate links between several ideas and may reveal weaknesses or gaps in your own understanding. Your tutor may ask you to prepare a concept map for a Unit of Work as part of your preparation for teaching, using your school's scheme of work. If not, you might like to try this for yourself. Concept mapping is a useful way of linking topics in the curriculum so as to promote continuity and breadth of understanding in your teaching. Concept maps are difficult to construct but the process of drafting one is a valuable exercise. For further discussion see White and Gunstone (1992) or Novak and Gowin (1984). We turn now to a particular group of activities designed to aid recall and learning, familiar to teachers as DARTS activities.

DARTS AND ACTIVE LEARNING

DARTS are ways of involving pupils in active reading, writing and listening. The term is an acronym for 'Directed Activities Related to (the use of) TextS'. A DART involves more than the use of textbooks, but takes in ways of using a variety of written and other visual materials including resources downloaded from the web.

A reading exercise may require pupils to learn from a textbook; then a DART could be used to ensure that pupils interact with the text. Interaction includes, for example, underlining certain types of word; listing important words; drawing diagrams or reformulating a labelled diagram into continuous prose. The level of demand, i.e. differentiation, is adjusted by you to meet the needs of the pupil. A listening DART may be designed to help pupils understand instructions given by the teacher.

The techniques involved in all these interactive processes are known as DARTS activities and some examples are discussed below. For further details see Gilham, 1986: 164; Davies and Greene, 1984.

Giving instructions

This includes activities as diverse as making bread, carrying out a traffic survey or gathering information on the effects of the Black Death. A common complaint by teachers is that pupils do not read instructions or, if they do, are unable to comprehend them. Sometimes the language level is too high; or pupils may understand each step but not the whole or just lack confidence to act. Sometimes it is because pupils do not have any investment in the project; it is not theirs. Ways of alleviating such problems depend on the ability and attentiveness of your pupils but can include:

- Making a list of the instructions on a sheet and given to each pupil; then read out to check understanding. As the instructional steps are completed pupils could be asked to tick off that step.
- Writing instructions on numbered cards. A set of cards can be given to a group who are instructed to put the cards into a working order. The final sequence can be checked, discrepancies discussed and the order checked against the purpose. The acceptable sequence can then be written or pasted in their books.
- Matching instructions to sketches of events; ask pupils to read instructions and select the matching sketch and so build a sequence.
- Discussing the task first and then asking pupils to draft their own set of instructions. After checking by the teacher the pupils can begin.

The same approach can be applied to how to do something or explain a process. For example, helping pupils explain how:

- ice erodes rock;
- a newspaper is put together;
- to interrogate a database;
- to use a thesaurus.

Listening to the teacher

Sometimes you want pupils to listen and enjoy what is being said to them. There are other occasions when you want pupils to listen and interact with the material and keep some sort of record. It may be to

- explain a phenomenon, e.g. a riot;
- describe an event, e.g. a bore in a river;
- describe a process, e.g. making pastry;
- demonstrate a process, e.g. distillation;
- design an artefact, e.g. a desk lamp;
- give an account, e.g. of work experience or a visit to a gallery.

There are a number of ways you can help pupils. For example:

- identify key words and ideas as you proceed, signalling to pupils when you expect them to record them;

- identify key words and ideas in advance on a worksheet and ask pupils to note them, tick, underline or highlight as they are discussed. These words can be written on the board or transparency for reference;
- adopt the above strategy, but develop as a game. Who can identify these ideas? Call out when you hear them;
- by using a diagram which pupils annotate as the lesson proceeds. This diagram might be used to: label parts; describe functions; identify where things happen. Pupils could keep their own notes and then be asked to make a summary and presentation to the class. Some pupils may need a word list to help them.

Another way to effect learning is to give pupils a depleted summary and ask them to complete it. The degree of help is a matter of judgement. For example:

- Give the summary with some key words missing and ask pupils to add the missing words.
- Give the depleted summary with an additional list of words. Pupils select words and put them in the appropriate place. The selection could include surplus words.
- Vary the focus of the omitted words. It could be on key words, or concepts, or focused on meanings of non-technical words, e.g. on connecting words or verbs, etc. (Sutton, 1981: 119; Frost and Turner, 2004: 181–4).

Characterizing events

You may wish to help pupils associate certain ideas, events or properties with a phenomenon. For example, what were the features of the colonization of the West Indies; or what are the characteristics of a Mediterranean-type climate?

As well as reading and making notes:

- List ideas on separate cards, some of which are relevant to the topic and others not relevant. Ask pupils to sort the cards into two piles, those events relevant to the phenomenon and those not directly related. Pupils compare sorting and justify their choice to each other.
- Mix up cards describing criteria related to two phenomena. Ask pupils to select those criteria appropriate to each event. A more complex task would be to compare, for example, the characteristics of the Industrial Revolutions of the eighteenth and twentieth centuries.

Interrogating books or websites or reading for meaning

Learners often feel that if they read a book they are learning and don't always appreciate that they have to work to gain understanding. Learners need to do something with the material in order to understand it. There are a number of ways of interrogating the material in order to assist with learning and understanding. There are some general points to be considered. It is important that pupils:

- are asked to read selectively – the length of the reading should be appropriate;
- understand why they are reading and what they are expected to get out of it;
- know what they are supposed to be doing while they read, what to focus on, what to write down or record;
- know what they are going to do with the results of their reading; e.g. write, draw, summarize, reformulate, précis, tell others, tell the teacher, carry out an investigation.

Homework which says simply 'read through this chapter tonight and I will give you a quick test on it tomorrow' is not helpful to learning because the focus is unclear. The following notes suggest ways of helping pupils read texts, worksheets, posters, etc. with purpose.

Getting an overview

Using photocopies of written material is helpful; pupils annotate or mark the text to aid understanding. Pupils read the entire text quickly, to get an overview and to identify any words they cannot understand and to get help from an adult or a dictionary.

Ask pupils to read it again, this time with a purpose, such as to:

- list key words or ideas;
- underline key ideas;
- highlight key words.

Reformulating ideas

To develop understanding further, pupils need to do something with what they have read. They could:

- make a list of key words or ideas;
- collect similar ideas together, creating patterns of bigger ideas;
- summarize the text to a given length;
- turn prose into a diagram, sketch or chart;
- make a spider diagram;
- design a flow chart, identifying sequence of events, ideas, etc.;
- construct a diagram, e.g. of a process or of equipment with labels;
- turn a diagram into prose, by telling a story or interpreting meanings;
- summarize using tables, e.g. relating structure to function (organs of the body), historical figures' contribution to society (emancipation of women), form to origin (landscapes and erosion).

Where appropriate, pupils could be given a skeleton flow chart, spider diagram, etc., with the starting idea attached and asked to attach further ideas.

Reporting back

A productive way of gaining interest and involvement is to ask pupils to report their findings, summaries or interpretation of the text to the class.

The summary could take one of the forms mentioned above. In addition, of course, the pupil could use the board, overhead projector, poster or computer assisted presentation such a PowerPoint. Pupils need to be prepared for this task and need to be given sufficient time.

Public reporting is demanding on pupils and it is helpful if a group of pupils draft the presentation and support the reporter. The presentation could be narrative, a poem, a simulation, diagram, play, etc. A suggested sequence of events is shown in Figure 5.2.4.

The feedback loop, from 'class discussion' to 'task, …' in Figure 5.2.4, can be introduced depending on the time available and the interest and ability of the class.

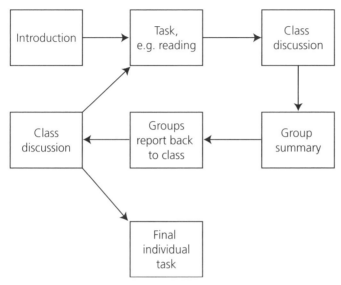

Figure 5.2.4   Reporting back

DARTS and related types of learning activity emphasize the importance of language in learning and in assessing learning. For further discussion on the role of language in learning, see Bennett and Dunne (1994) and Burgess (2004).

LESSON PLANNING FOR ACTIVE LEARNING

It is important to distinguish between 'activities' and 'active learning'. It is relatively easy to fill a lesson with a series of activities which keep pupils busy and apparently enjoying it, yet may provide insufficient learning challenge. Such work may be well within the pupils' grasp and so they do not have to think much about what they are doing or why. Many pupils take seriously copying from the board, book or worksheet but such activities are often superficial and should be used very sparingly, even though they can keep a noisy class quiet.

Some lesson planning in the *early stages of learning to teach* may be to ensure that all your learning outcomes are addressed, or that your discipline is effective; this requirement may lead to a lesson that is teacher dominated. For example, you may have explained orally the lesson and its purpose and have asked some bridging questions; you may have then used a video and asked the pupils to complete a worksheet in response to watching the video; finally, you may have given out homework based on the class work. You, as the teacher, have been very active in the lesson and may well feel exhausted at the end of it! From the pupils' point of view, however, the lesson may have been quite passive because they were told what to do at every step, with little or no input into what they were to do and learn. In these circumstances many pupils may not fully engage in learning except in a superficial sense.

Consider the lesson described in Task 5.2.2 taken from a modern languages lesson.

Task 5.2.2
Active classroom or active learning?

A structured sequence for the learning of new vocabulary in a modern foreign language lesson is presented in Table 5.2.1. You may find this task best discussed in a tutor group.

The pupils seem to be busy but to what extent do you think the pupils are actively engaged in learning?

Identify any changes you would make the lesson and explain why.

After you have carried out this task compare your response to that of an experienced teacher.

Table 5.2.1   An example of a structured sequence for the learning of new vocabulary in a modern foreign languages lesson

Activity	Pupils' physical involvement	Pupils' mental involvement
Teacher presents new vocabulary items with flash-cards	Pupils repeat each word at a time, in chorus and individually at random	As the pupils have just heard the word, the demand on their short-term memory is limited
Teacher asks questions to elicit production of new words	Pupils put their hands up, selected individuals speak	Pupils have to search in their short-term memory to remember what the words are and how they are pronounced
Teacher puts flash-cards up on the board and numbers them; she then calls out the words	Pupils write the number which corresponds to the word they have heard	Demand on short-term memory for recognition only; pupils do not have to pronounce the words
Teacher asks pupils to work in pairs and ask each other the new words	All pupils involved in speaking	Pupils have to search short-term memory to remember what the words are and how they are pronounced

The response of an experienced teacher to this lesson was as follows:

> The lesson sequence provides ample opportunities for pupils to take part, but the cognitive demands remain firmly at word level. For pupils to progress further, they would need to be led gradually, at some stage, towards meeting the challenge of generating whole sentences of their own using this new vocabulary and integrating it into other structures and contexts learnt previously. Furthermore, the memorization techniques illustrated here may well be helpful in the short term but are unlikely to be sufficient to secure deep learning by way of retaining the newly acquired words in the longer term.

Planning for learning requires you to focus on what the pupil is doing as well as what you are doing. To encourage pupils to participate fully in the lesson and hence promote meaningful learning there are some important features to bear in mind when planning your lesson. As well as planning strategies to include input from pupils into the development of the lesson you should:

- share the learning outcomes with your pupils and give an example of what your pupil's finished work will look like, i.e. what counts as a successful piece of work;

- focus some learning outcomes on process rather than content, i.e. on pupil action and contribution to their own learning;
- illustrate your criteria for assessment;
- link the lesson to the pupil's prior knowledge and include your strategies for eliciting it;
- prepare contingency plans for both faster and slower pupils;
- think about ways to help pupils in difficulties, i.e. give support (see scaffolding, Unit 5.1).

Task 5.2.3
Activating pupils' prior knowledge

Select a strategy for probing pupils' prior knowledge of a topic and use it in a lesson in which you are being observed. Evaluate the effectiveness of the activity yourself and also ask your tutor or class teacher to give you feedback on its effectiveness. Strategies you could use include a question and answer session; brainstorming in small groups followed a by a plenary session; asking pupils to prepare a spider diagram summarizing what they know and using them to plan the next lesson. File feedback in your CDP folder.

Active learning goes hand in hand with an approach to teaching which encourages pupils to develop and progress as individuals and not merely to receive information from the teacher. Active learning, therefore, is a process that is:

- structured and organized, a purposeful activity through which pupils can achieve the intended learning outcome as you have planned it;
- transformational, enables pupils to consider alternatives, to think differently and develops attitudes and values;
- communicative, involves engagement with others within and beyond the classroom and develops higher order skills such as analysis, communication, investigation, listening;
- generative, pupils are engaged in the process of their own learning and generates deeper understanding by challenging pupils' understanding;
- supportive of meaningful learning.

If this description is correct then a lesson must invite pupils to participate in the work, contribute to its development and consequently begin to shape their own learning. The demands on the pupil in such a situation move learning to higher order skills to which we now turn. See above under 'What is active learning?' and 'Active learning and motivation'; and Unit 3.1.

Developing pupils' higher order thinking skills

It is now generally acknowledged that the explicit development of thinking skills needs to take place alongside teaching of factual content and that the emphasis in learning is not just on the outcomes, but also on the processes. Teaching, therefore, needs to be designed to enable pupils to:

- develop logical reasoning in order to apply it to new contexts (*formal thinking* approach);
- deconstruct problems in order to find solutions to them (*heuristic* approach);
- reflect on, and evaluate their own learning (*metacognitive* approach) (Muijs and Reynolds, 2001).

These three approaches are at the heart of active learning because they promote the learners' engagement with the task and encourage pupils to make sense of their learning.

Bloom identified six levels of thinking of gradually increasing complexity, which make increasing demands on the cognitive processes of learners (Bloom, 1956; see also Unit 3.1). These six levels are listed in column one of Table 5.2.2. While there is the potential for active learning at every level, the last three levels can be linked to the higher-order thinking skills mentioned above. The Key Stage 3 Strategy guidance for the NC in England makes use of Bloom's taxonomy and you will find this taxonomy useful in your general teaching (DfES, 2003e).

Providing suitable challenges is fundamental to active learning. One strategy used extensively by teachers is questioning; see also Unit 3.1. The importance of questioning as a teaching and learning strategy is long established and well-documented in educational research, e.g. Wragg and Brown (2001), Kerry (2004). Many studies show how questions can take various forms and how they can be adapted to serve a variety of purposes to promote active learning, such as:

- capturing pupils' attention and interest;
- recalling and checking on prior knowledge;
- focusing pupils' attention on a specific issue or concept;
- checking and probing pupils' understanding;
- developing pupils' thinking and reasoning;
- differentiating learning;
- extending pupils' power of analysis and evaluation;
- helping pupils to reflect on how they learn.

To the novice teacher, questions asked by experienced teachers may appear intuitive and instinctive whereas in reality good questioning develops by reflection on experience. Questions should not just be 'off the cuff' but prepared in advance and related to the learning objectives, so that the pupil's learning is structured. A useful observation schedule identifying good principles for effective questioning is available (Good and Brophy, 2000: 412). Experienced teachers have the skill of asking questions beyond those planned in response to pupil's replies. Experience here depends largely on knowing your subject and how to to use it, i.e. pedagogical content knowledge; and knowing your pupils and how they respond to your subject and your teaching.

Effective questioning is central to the teaching and learning process. In Table 5.2.2 we examine how Bloom's taxonomy relates to the use of questions by the teacher. This table identifies the purposes of questioning at the various levels and gives examples of the sort of question that may be asked (DfES, 2003e). For further discussion of questioning techniques, see DfES (2004f).

Task 5.2.4
Developing higher order thinking skills through the use of questioning

Observe a lesson and script the questions used by the teacher to promote learning. Try to classify against Bloom's (1956) taxonomy of educational objectives. How does the type of question used impact upon active learning? Discuss your observations with the teacher or your tutor.

Table 5.2.2 Bloom's taxonomy of educational objectives applied to questioning

Cognitive objective according to Bloom's taxonomy	Use of questioning to develop higher order thinking skills	Examples of possible questions
Knowledge	To help pupils link aspects of existing knowledge or relevant information to the task ahead.	What is the name for? Where in the book would you find ...? What are we looking for?
Comprehension	To help pupils to process their existing knowledge.	What are the key features ...? What is shown about ...? What happens when ...?
Application	To help pupils use their knowledge to solve a new problem or apply it to a new situation.	What do you think will happen? Why? Where else might this be useful? Can you apply what you know now to solve ...?
Analysis	To help pupils use the process of enquiry to break down what they know and reassemble it.	What is the function of ...? What is the evidence ...? What does this symbolize?
Synthesis	To help pupils combine and select from available knowledge in order to respond to unfamiliar situations.	What conclusion can you draw? Can you propose an alternative?
Evaluation	To help pupils to draw upon their knowledge to form opinions or judgements.	Which is more important/moral/logical ...? Why is ... important? What inconsistencies are there in ...?

Source: Adapted from DfES, 2003e, Unit 4, Questioning: 13.

COMMUNICATING WITH PUPILS: VISUAL AIDS

A multisensory classroom experience can also contribute towards active learning. Visual aids can generate interest, bring 'reality' into the classroom and enable an interactive approach to be adopted. Visual aids may take the form of a simple prompt, e.g. a picture, a poster, an object, an overhead projector transparency, a PowerPoint presentation or an interactive whiteboard.

Visual aids are a powerful tool for focusing attention, stimulating memorization and conveying meaning, all of which contribute to active learning. They enable the teacher not only to present information but also to *clarify* concepts and meanings and *build* ideas, models, diagrams, sequences with the class. For example, you can hide definitions that the pupils then complete. Pupils can hypothesize from partly revealed screens, share their ideas and complete some creative writing from these ideas as a class activity. Equally importantly, the pupils can use these aids to display their own understanding.

The interactive whiteboard is a touch-sensitive projection screen which is connected to a computer and a projector. By simply pointing at active elements on the board with a finger or with an appropriate electronic 'pen', you or your pupils can highlight or move what is displayed on the board (BECTA,

ICT Advice for Teachers, 2005). Text can be written on the whiteboard, for instance a whole class correction of an exercise and then saved for further use at a later date. You and your class can also interface with downloaded interactive materials from the internet, or simply use downloaded images, graphs, etc. These added advantages make the interactive whiteboard a powerful tool for engaging pupils in learning. Although it requires a fair amount of preparation time, it helps to make smooth transitions between activities and there is an increasing range of time-saving resources being developed for use in the classroom.

Other equipment, e.g. the overhead projector (OHP) can be equally effective for some activities, and may be more readily available. The use of the word processor helps in producing overhead transparencies that look professional. Such equipment is easy to use, but it is important that its use is effective and not cosmetic.

Whatever visual aids you choose to use, it is worth bearing in mind that they require management. There are practical implications for maximizing the impact of visual aids, including their clarity, lack of ambiguity and appropriateness of the language level to your class. Another practical implication is to make sure all pupils can see and read your visual aid. It is useful, for example, when using an overhead projector to practise where to stand so as not to obstruct pupils' vision. Projectors are cumbersome to carry, are limited in range of use and you may have to book the appropriate space or some equipment in advance.

Task 5.2.5
Using visual aids

In one of your units of work, plan how you can involve pupils in using visual aids themselves. For example, ask a group of pupils to put together a PowerPoint presentation or, if using an overhead projector, complete their own transparencies to report back on group discussion. Teach the lessons incorporating this use of visual aids and then evaluate the effectiveness of this approach and how you might improve their use in future lessons.

SUMMARY

Teaching is an enabling process; teachers can guide pupils' learning but cannot do the learning for them. Pupils need to engage mentally with a task if learning is to take place; thus you need to enthuse and motivate pupils, give purpose to their learning tasks and to provide active learning experiences. Some of these activities, e.g. DARTS, introduced study skills, important for pupils preparing for public examinations.

This unit has used examples of reading, writing, listening and talking activities designed to improve learning and learning skills. There is hands-on activity in practically based subjects, such as art and design, home economics, science and technology. Working with your hands does not guarantee that learning takes place, both hand and brain need to be involved. Pupils need to have a say in the design, execution and evaluation of practical work in the same way as we have stressed the need for their active involvement in reading and listening.

The advantages claimed for the active learning includes, too, an emphasis on co-operative learning which can provide opportunities for the pupil to take some responsibility for her own learning by, for example, active participation in the development of the task. This approach requires pupil self-discipline and may contribute to that wider goal of education. For the teacher, it opens up a wider range of teaching methods to suit different pupil needs, allows the growth of resource-based learning and provides space for monitoring pupil progress. Aims can be widened; as well as encouraging acquisition of knowledge and understanding, active learning can be used to promote process skills and higher order skills.

The key to good teaching is preparation and very important if you select active learning strategies. These strategies are a key part of your teaching repertoire and contribute significantly to your career entry development portfolio. Check the range of teaching strategies expected of you as an NQT, using the list of standards/competences for your course. Further advice and guidance on active learning is in the section on Further Reading.

FURTHER READING

Carnell, E. and Lodge, C. (2002) *Supporting Effective Learning*, London: Sage (Paul Chapman). This book provides a clear outline of various concepts of learning, with a view to helping teachers to provide a rich learning environment.

Joyce, B., Calhoun, E. and Hopkins, D. (2002) *Models of Learning: Tools for Teaching*, 2nd edn, Buckingham: Open University Press. This book presents a range of models of active learning and considers how these inform and develop the teacher's teaching repertoire.

Newton, D.P. (2000) *Teaching for Understanding*, London: RoutledgeFalmer. This book provides a framework of strategies to support the understanding processes. Chapter 5 focuses on the impact of mental engagement on understanding, which is at the heart of active learning.

Useful websites

The British Education Research Association (BERA): <http://www. bera.ac.uk>, a starting point to find out about recent research projects in active learning.

DfES (Department for Education and Skills): <http://www.teachernet. gov.uk>, resources that you may find helpful in developing active learning teaching strategies.

DfES (Department for Education and Skills) (2004) *Pedagogy and Practice: Teaching and Learning in the Secondary School. Unit 7 Questioning*, London: DfES. Online. Available: HTTP: <http://www.standards. dfes.gov.uk/keystage3/respub/sec_pptl0.> (accessed 2 December 2004).

Unit 5.3

Teaching Styles

John McCormick and Marilyn Leask

INTRODUCTION

As mentioned in Unit 2.2, the Hay McBer (2000) research into effective teaching found teachers could control three main factors which significantly influence pupil progress:

- professional characteristics;
- teaching skills;
- classroom climate.

This unit is concerned mainly with professional characteristics, which have two components. The first component, *underlying behaviours*, depends on deep-seated characteristics and drives the things teachers typically do. The second, *microbehaviours*, can be learned and contributes to teaching skills. When combined, these characteristics produce *individual teaching styles*. Although individual teaching styles are very personal, analysis of teaching has identified common approaches in teaching episodes and these provide a framework in which personal styles can develop. The chapter introduces some of these approaches and provides opportunities for you to use theories encountered in other sections of this book in widening your range of teaching styles within them.

OBJECTIVES

By the end of this unit you should:

- understand how behaviour and strategies combine to produce a teaching style;
- be aware of the need for teaching styles to match the different learning strategies of pupils;
- be able to analyse and outline different teaching styles in sequences of your lesson plans;
- appreciate the difference between personal teaching styles and theoretical models of teaching styles;
- appreciate the importance of *mobility ability* (Mosston and Ashworth, 2002), which refers to the capability good teachers have for switching their style to meet different needs of learners.

Appendix 5.3.1 provides an example of peer tutoring as a personalized learning teaching strategy.

TEACHING STYLES AND LEARNING

We refer initially back to pupils' learning styles through Task 5.3.1.

Task 5.3.1
Teaching and learning styles

Consider the following situation.

A student teacher has moved to a second school after a highly satisfactory first school experience.

Knowing the pupils in both schools are of a similar background the student teacher decides to play safe for his first solo lesson. His starter activity has worked well in the first school and he is comfortable with it. A stimulating picture is projected onto a whiteboard and pupils are asked questions, which they are to answer by finding and using information in the picture.

However, the activity does not work. The pupils repeatedly ask for explanations and clarifications, and they interrupt the student teacher so much that he is unable to complete the starter. He has to abandon it and move to the body of the lesson, where he tries to tell the pupils how to carry out an activity. Again, he has trouble in making his instructions clear and he continues to be interrupted by requests for clarification.

For the next lesson, after advice, the student teacher projects a picture onto a whiteboard but, as they enter, pupils are handed a worksheet with six questions and instructions to work in pairs to decide answers. After a few minutes adjacent pairs are asked to spend two minutes deciding the best answers and to choose one member from each of these larger groups to feed back one of their answers to the class. Following this the pupils continue in pairs, using a Directed Activity Related to Text (DART) to decipher the instructions for the next part of their lesson.

The lesson starts well.

What has caused the difference?

Unit 5.1 introduced the notions of pupils' learning styles (preferences), which tend to be fixed and individual, and learning strategies, by which learners 'cope with situations and tasks'. With respect to preferred learning styles, DfES (2003e) asserts only 25 per cent of people are auditory learners, with 35 per cent being visual and 45 per cent kinaesthetic. Sousa (1997, cited by Tilstone, 2000) gives an even lower figure for auditory learners. One possibility in the example in Task 5.3.1 is that, irrespective of their preferences, the learning strategies of the pupils in the student teacher's first school had developed to cope with auditory delivery and individual work. However, in the second school teachers had taken account of preferred learning styles, with the result that learning strategies of the pupils centred on visual and kinaesthetic presentation of work, rather than oral questions and instructions. The student teacher had developed a *teaching style* to match the learning strategies of the first pupils, and the mismatch in the second school was enough to render learning, and teaching, ineffective.

Teaching style is an amalgam of teacher behaviour and teaching strategy. Although, as noted by Hay McBer (2000), teacher behaviour depends to some extent on inherent personal qualities it also depends on more variable factors such as opinions, experience, knowledge and relationship with pupils, which change as you undergo school experience. Strategies correspond to the teaching methods used and these depend on factors such as the ethos of the school and the resources within it, and with teachers' familiarity with them and with the pupils, see also Appendix 5.3.1.

In the case study the student teacher's behaviour may not have changed but his strategies have, resulting in a new and successful style of teaching. As you progress through school experience you should refine your practice to develop teaching styles which suit different circumstances and achieve diverse learning outcomes. Sometimes this requires you to change your behaviour; at other times you try a different strategy. Sometimes you adopt a range of styles within a single lesson in order to ensure all of the pupils achieve the learning outcomes.

However, teachers do not always develop or use the most suitable teaching style for their pupils. Research suggests that mismatch between pupils' preferences and teachers' styles arises from a number of reasons, including a belief on the part of individual teachers that what helps them to learn also helps pupils (DfES, 2003e). The effect is that teachers use a style which is actually best suited to themselves and not necessarily to their pupils. The position may be even worse for student teachers; Calderhead and Shorrock (1997) suggest teachers, especially student teachers, are initially more comfortable with structures and styles they experienced as pupils than with new ideas. Therefore, it is important that you have the support of others when you critically reflect on your own teaching and that you take active steps to incorporate effective practice, including ideas gained from discussion, observation of other teachers and reading, to make your own repertoire of styles as wide as possible.

For example, Her Majesty's Inspectors (HMI) reported on good teaching in good and excellent departments (OFSTED, 2002, online). The report concluded with a short section entitled *improving quality*. This provides a useful checklist of questions for teachers, and reflection on some of them will help your development of your teaching style. Task 5.3.2 illustrates how reflective reading can produce questions which help you improve your practice.

The HMI report also noted that, even in good schools, achieving consistency across the curriculum remains a challenge and lessons are not always good. It is important that you bear this in mind. You should set yourself ever higher targets and aim to improve your repertoire with every lesson you teach but you should also appreciate that some days you do not reach targets and your teaching is not as effective as it could be. One reason for such inconsistency is that a new style you have used has not worked well, or possibly you have used a style without appreciating its shortcomings. If this happens to more experienced teachers it will happen to you and you should not be dissuaded from exploring teaching styles by the occasional apparent failure to engage pupils.

Task 5.3.2
Reflection on effective styles

Think about these questions, derived from HMI observations of successful schools, in the context of your own teaching.

Does my behaviour instil confidence in high attainers? Is it open and encouraging to the less able?

Is my style of presentation formal or informal and what effect does this have on my ability to communicate enthusiasm?

Is my style of teaching personal to every pupil?

Do I build a variety of activities into my lesson plans with a style that incorporates a range of teaching strategies?

Does my style of delivery make my objectives clear at the start and allow me to refer to objectives at key points in the lessons?

When I mark and assess work, is my style of giving feedback personal and informative?

Can you derive similar questions from your own reading?

Teaching style and meaningful learning

Meaningful, or deep, learning (Entwistle, 1990) requires pupils to engage in an active reconstruction of information, to make new links and test old ones, to resolve contradictions and to identify underlying principles. The knowledge and understanding they gain by this activity tends to be retained and it can be applied to new situations. On the other hand, shallow, or surface, learning occurs when pupils do not really understand principles, or when they hold misconceptions. For example, they can often use formulae but do not really understand their derivation and cannot apply them to new contexts; or they hold two conflicting views at the same time. Research and evidence from practice (Mercer, 2000; Wegerif and Dawes, 2004) show that actively teaching pupils how to learn, how to explain themselves, how to ask probing questions, sharing the lesson objectives with them and teaching them how objectives link with activities and assessment tasks leads to raised achievement and motivation (see Appendix 5.3.1 and Unit 5.2 for examples).

The distinction between deep and shallow learning is important. Gipps (1995) suggests the particular learning strategies pupils adopt depends on how they are assessed. Pupils can adopt shallow learning strategies to meet assessment requirements. However, as fundamental principles are not understood, knowledge is not always retained and cannot be applied to new situations. Furthermore, pupils then find it difficult to move to deep learning. Conversely, pupils who are involved with deep learning find it easy to adopt shallow learning strategies when they see the need. While teachers may need to resort to shallow learning at times this should be seen as an expediency and their teaching styles should not encourage it. Rather they should be aimed at promoting meaningful learning. When you reflect on your own and others' teaching, reflect on the degree to which teaching is 'to the test', and use your reflections to develop a style in which your use of assessment promotes meaningful learning.

Meaningful learning happens best where social interaction, particularly between a learner and more knowledgeable others, is encouraged, and where there is a co-operative and supportive ethos. Teaching styles therefore need to take account of the need for discussion, both between pupils and, following constructivist ideas (see Unit 5.1), between pupils and teacher. As pupils' knowledge at the start of a learning activity may not be apparent immediately to you the path they take might not be what you

Table 5.3.1 Teaching styles

| | The participation dimension | | |
	Closed	Framed	Negotiated
Content	Tightly controlled by the teacher. Not negotiable.	Teacher controls the topic, frames of reference and tasks; criteria made explicit.	Discussed at each point; joint decisions.
Focus	Authoritative knowledge and skills; simplified, monolithic.	Stress on empirical testing processes chosen by teacher; some legitimation of pupils' ideas.	Search for justifications and principles; strong legitimation of pupils' ideas.
Pupils' role	Acceptance; routine performance; little access to principles.	Join in teacher's thinking; make hypothesis, set up tests, operate teacher's frame.	Discuss goals and methods critically; share responsibility for frame and criteria.
Key concepts	'Authority': the proper procedures and the right answers.	'Access'; to skills, processes, criteria.	'Relevance': critical discussion of pupils' priorities.
Methods	Exposition; worksheets (closed); note giving; individual exercises; routine practical work. Teacher evaluates.	Exposition; with discussions eliciting suggestions; individual/group problem solving; lists of tasks given; discussion of outcomes, but teacher adjudicates.	Group and class discussion and decision making about goals and criteria. Pupils plan and carry out work, make presentations, evaluate success.

Source: adapted from Barnes *et al.* (1988: 25).

expect. Learners often proceed in a non-linear fashion and go back and forward as they make and test links. Do not be surprised if the immediate outcomes of an activity are not those you predicted. Your teaching style should make allowances for the learning process and should not only promote discussion but encourage pupils to challenge their own and others' ideas and to go back and forth in a non-linear way. To do this you may need to move from a *closed* style (Barnes *et al.*, 1988) where the teacher tightly controls the content of the lesson, the learning environment and the outcomes of the lesson, through a *framed* style, where the teacher controls the topics and has clear expectations of outcomes but allows the pupils to propose and test alternatives, to a *negotiated* style, where the pupils have much more freedom in determining the area of investigation and the way in which work is reported, with, possibly, variable outcomes. Table 5.3.1 describes the main differences between these styles.

Using SACK to develop a style

You may be familiar with the acronym SACK (or CASK), which is intended to remind you to check whether the balance of your lesson objectives between **s**kills, **a**ttitudes, **c**oncepts and **k**nowledge is appropriate. In choosing which of these broad styles to use you need to consider the learning objectives of the lesson. Not all objectives require deep learning. Developing process skills by, for example, training pupils to perform a simple action might best be achieved through use of a closed style, whereas developing an attitude or coming to understand a concept, which does require meaningful learning to take place, might best be achieved through the use of a negotiated style. When one of the objectives for the lesson concerns the development of knowledge it can be more difficult to decide on the best style to use and you might need to refer to other theories, such as information processing models, to help you.

INFORMATION PROCESSING MODELS AND TEACHING STYLE

As well as constructivist models of learning there are models which represent learners as information processing systems. These can run parallel to constructivist views and do not necessarily contradict them; pupils with poor information processing capabilities, who needed a lot of help and progress slowly, would be those who had small 'zones of proximal development' defined as: 'The discrepancy between a child's actual mental age and the level he reaches in solving problems with assistance indicates the zone of his proximal development' (Vygotsky, 1986).

Figure 5.3.1 shows the typical pattern of information flow and processing suggested by a multi-store model of memory proposed by Atkinson and Shiffrin in about 1968. Information-processing models can illustrate why teaching style may need to change depending on whether learning objectives relate to skills, knowledge or attitudes or concepts.

As Figure 5.3.1 suggests, learners can only take in a certain amount of information in a set time. There is limitation of capacity and bottlenecks can occur when a lot of information is transmitted. When bottlenecks occur, not all of the transmitted information is received in the memory. Therefore your teaching style must not deliver too much information too quickly or introduce digressions. Reflect on whether a closed or framed style enables you to get your key points across with most effect. At the start of the lesson, when objectives and activity are outlined or, for example, when demonstrating a technique or ensuring safety, a very focused, closed, instructional style might be required.

After information is received, short- and long-term memory work together dynamically. Information is processed in short-term memory, where fresh information and retrieved existing knowledge are used together to make meaning of new situations. This meaningful learning can then be stored in long-term memory. A teaching style which presents information in different ways and provides a variety of perspectives matches a range of preferred learning styles. More pupils are able both to take in the information and to link it to existing knowledge, increasing the probability that it is processed

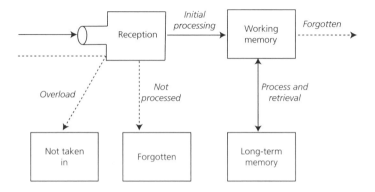

Figure 5.3.1 A flowchart for an information processing model (Source: Adapted from Gross, 2001: 244–8).

rather than disregarded. In this part of the lesson a closed style is not as effective in promoting meaningful learning, even if that learning concerns knowledge rather than understanding of concepts, because it is the links which are important and closed styles tend not to develop these as well as other styles.

Once your style for each objective has been decided consider its behaviour and strategy components. For example, talking too fast or delivering too much information is a common mistake made by inexperienced teachers. Develop open *behaviour* in which information is provided in small amounts and key features are signalled, so pupils can concentrate on what is important, and feel secure when seeking clarification. According to sources cited earlier (DfES, 2003e), the majority of pupils are not likely to be auditory learners. Therefore you should consider an alternative *strategy* to talk, or use talk in conjunction with, for exanple, a PowerPoint reinforcement of key themes.

Task 5.3.3
Using information processing theory

How will you use information processing theory to help you develop a teaching style? Reflect on the pros and cons of closed, framed and negotiated styles in:

- Ensuring you gain pupils' attention, so that they receive information which they are then able to process. Is a closed style the best way of achieving this end?
- Identifying and stressing key information so it is processed. Will a framed style allow pupils to develop a personal perspective and thus make links which will give them a better chance of processing it?
- Making links to known features clear. Alternatively, does a closed style identify the links, with the result that pupils learn more effectively than with a framed style? Or could a negotiated style allow pupils to identify links which you are not aware of?
- Using patterns and mnemonics as memory aids to help pupils remember them. Is it better to provide mnemonics (closed) or allow pupils to make their own (framed)?

Use your reflections when you develop your teaching. Begin with your scheme of work. Can you identify opportunities for different styles? Then develop your ideas in individual lessons. Finally, when you analyse your lessons consider the effectiveness of the styles you used.

EXPERIMENT AND CONSISTENCY

Early school experience should have helped you to realize that routines in the classroom are important. So although you need to experiment in developing a personal style you also need to think about consistency. How will you develop a repertoire of styles yet achieve consistency? One way is to keep your behaviour aspect constant during early school experience and to vary strategy. This helps you to behave consistently towards the pupils while always making your expectations clear. Pupils will know when you are using a closed style which requires, for example, listening and when you are using a different style which allows, for example, enquiry or challenge. You can experiment with your behaviour, the other key element of your teaching style, later. Sharing your styles with the pupils can involve learners more actively, which improves their learning (see e.g. Black *et al.*, 2003: 78). Therefore, explaining to the pupils what styles you are using and why you are using them might be worth consideration.

You also need to think about whether or not you achieve your intended style. Harkin and Turner (1997) contend that a didactic, teacher-centred approach (they use the phrase 'drills and skills') and a more learner-centred approach based on constructivist principles can masquerade as each other. Furthermore, many teachers desire high levels of control and this can affect their style. Task 5.3.4 presents a case study which should help you to reflect on intended and achieved styles.

Task 5.3.4
Case study – electricity bills

The following case study is taken from Key Stage 4 science, on the theme of calculating electricity bills. Electricity consumption is calculated in kilowatt-hours (1 kWh = 1 Unit) and the cost of running an electrical appliance depends how quickly an appliance uses a unit. A 3 kW kettle might use one unit of electricity in 20 minutes. On the other hand, a modern DVD player in standby mode might only use one unit of electricity in six months.

What teaching styles (e.g. closed, framed, negotiated) do you think are attempted and achieved in each stage of the lesson outlined below?

Preparation
Pupils are given a sheet to take home and complete. This requires them to fill in details from the electrical rating plates of some domestic equipment, including a kettle, an iron and their personal audio and video equipment.

Starter activity
As the pupils arrive the first three to enter are given a small script to rehearse. The script centres on parental response to a high electricity bill which is blamed on the use of personal CD and DVD equipment by their children. The script is read after the last member of the class arrives.

Introduction
The teacher introduces the lesson by saying she is going to give the pupils the power to refute parental arguments that high bills are their fault. Lesson objectives are given as:

• to understand the concept of kilowatt-hours and units of electricity;
• to be able to calculate electricity bills.

Exposition
The teacher discusses and, using an OHP, outlines what kWh are and how they are used in calculating bills. A textbook with relevant formula is used to support this – pupils read the page silently and answer questions.

Activity
Pupils work in groups to pool and use their information to work out the cost of running each appliance for one hour. The teacher circulates and helps as appropriate, telling pupils what to do.

Plenary
One member from each group outlines which is the cheapest and most expensive appliance to run and how they could explain this to their parents.

Analyse the activity and decide how much control the teacher has maintained over the teaching agenda. How might the need to maintain control have affected her style?

In the activity in Task 5.3.4 the teacher controls the teaching agenda quite carefully. The styles in use in the lesson tend to be closed. However, analysis is not always simple and determining which styles are intended can further complicate the picture. Therefore, discussion of observations with teachers during school experience should include teaching styles. As well as clarifying actual and intended styles this discussion might help you to appreciate that boundaries between styles are not hard and fast. Styles form a continuum and you need to be able to assess the effectiveness of your chosen style and to move along the continuum to vary it to suit the needs of your pupils. Continue with the case study of electricity bills in Task 5.3.5 to explore the possibilities this episode provides.

Task 5.3.5
Case study – electricity bills
(continued)

Review the electricity case study and think of alternative styles for teaching each activity in the lesson. For example, the starter results from a fairly closed style – pupils are chosen and read the script. A framed style would introduce the idea of the play but might allow the pupils to write and perform the script themselves. A more negotiated style might allow the pupils to vary the delivery, so they might produce a news broadcast instead of a play. Which is the most suitable style, if there is one, and how might it be influenced by teacher behaviour or teaching strategy? Apply the same procedure to some of your own lessons.

Think about the styles you intend to use and the styles you actually do use in your teaching.

Does your need to control the teaching agenda compromise your style? For example, do you plan a lesson with, say, a negotiated style for part of the work but find in your post-lesson analysis that you have not allowed the pupils enough latitude?

You might find you move between closed and framed styles during a lesson but use a negotiated style less often. Negotiated styles are often associated with project or extended work. However, you should not neglect them. There are times in individual lessons when they can be used particularly to challenge the more able pupils.

MOSSTON'S SPECTRUM OF TEACHING STYLES

In analysing your lessons it is helpful to refer to more sophisticated models than those presented by Barnes *et al.* (1988). One such model is characterized by a focus on the decision-making process which is central to planning and teaching. In your teaching you make decisions about what you and your pupils will and will not do. Some of these decisions are made before teaching, some during teaching and some after teaching. Underpinning theory holds that these decisions 'are the pivotal element in the chain of events that form the teaching-learning relationship' (Mosston and Ashworth, 2002: xx) and gives rise to what is known as the *spectrum of teaching styles* (Mosston, 1972). This spectrum is independent of individual or personal style but it can enable teachers to understand fully the effects of their style(s) on pupils' learning. Mosston, and later Mosston and Ashworth, argue that the spectrum is applicable to all subjects and can serve as a guide to selecting the best style for a particular purpose. Therefore, knowledge about the styles contained in the spectrum, and about the decision-making processes within them, allows teachers to develop a repertoire which better promotes learning and helps pupils to become independent learners.

Mosston's spectrum is similar to closed, framed and negotiated styles in that it proposes a continuum of teaching styles in which pupils are able to exercise a greater and greater amount of intellectual freedom, creativity and enquiry, but it has more features. Over the years there have been a number of models of the spectrum. Typically, at one end of the spectrum is *command*, where the teacher makes every decision, before, during and after the teaching episode. Further along the continuum are, for example, *practice* or *task*, where pupils have a limited amount of freedom to decide how they will complete a set activity, and *reciprocal*, where pupils work together and are involved in the evaluation of each other's performance. The *inclusion* style takes account of differences in learners and allows them to decide on the level at which they will perform. As the continuum proceeds there are increasing amounts of freedom and a transfer of responsibility. In *discovery* styles the teacher begins to hand responsibility for all decisions to the learner, who decides what will be studied, for how long, with what resources, how findings will be reported and so on. This results in a *learner initiated* style and, finally, but not in classrooms, a *self-teaching* style. Table 5.3.2 illustrates the differences between these styles.

Within the spectrum no single style is more or less important than another; what is important is that the teacher appreciates the potential of the different styles and can move between them as circumstances demand. This is described by Goldberger as *mobility ability* – 'the ability to shift comfortably from one teaching style to another in order to meet learner objectives' (Mosston and Ashworth, 2002: xi). As a novice, you might approach this from a different perspective. Where are your style(s) on the spectrum and can you widen your range so you can change styles to meet different demands? Task 5.3.6 asks you to look at your own styles of teaching. It may be helpful to carry out this activity with the help of a mentor who observes lessons you have chosen to provide a variety of teaching activities.

Task 5.3.6
Analysing your teaching style

Analyse a number of your own lessons in terms of the decisions you make. What decisions do you take and which decisions are made by pupils? Do the lessons have common features which give you a guide to your prime location(s) on the spectrum?

If you make all of the decisions about the lesson e.g. what will be done, what specific actions will be completed, how big groups will be, what answers will and will not be accepted, how feedback will be provided, this would correspond to the command style.

Giving some latitude, by e.g. allowing pupils to make their own decisions about how they carry out a task you have defined, would correspond to the practice style.

Giving more latitude, by e.g. allowing pupils to work in groups of their own choice to solve a problem which you have defined but where there is a predetermined solution, would correspond to the guided discovery style. Note here that there is a set problem with a predetermined answer, these decisions have been made by the teacher.

Giving pupils a problem with a number of possible outcomes and allowing them to make their own decisions about groups, method and reporting back, followed by neutral feedback which values all of the responses, would correspond to the divergent discovery style.

Now use the table below when evaluating some of your lessons to help you analyse your teaching style and to widen it.

Stage of lesson	Usual behaviour	Usual strategy	Overall style (see Tables 5.3.1 and 5.3.2)	What I can do to widen my range of styles?
Introduction				
Activity 1				
Activity 2				
Activity 3				
Plenary				

Table 5.3.2 Mosston's continuum of teaching styles (2002 version)

The command style:
This style is often described as autocratic or teacher centred. It is appropriate in certain contexts, e.g. teaching safe use of equipment, learning particular routines in dance.

The practice style:
Whilst similar to the command style, there is a shift in decision making to pupils and there is more scope with this style for the teacher to work with individuals whilst the group are occupied with practice tasks such as writing for a purpose in English or practising skills in mathematics.

The reciprocal style:
The pupils work in pairs evaluating each other's performance. Each partner is actively involved, one as the 'doer' and one observing, as the 'teacher partner'. The teacher works with the 'teacher partner' to improve their evaluative and feedback skills. This style provides increased possibilities for the 'teacher partner' to improve their evaluative and feedback skills. This style provides increased possibilities for 'interaction and communication among students' and can be applied when pupils are learning a foreign language or learning routines in gymnastics. Pupils learn to judge performance against criteria.

The self-check style:
This style is designed to develop the learner's ability to evaluate their own performance. The teacher sets the tasks and the pupils evaluate their performance against criteria and set new goals in collaboration with the teacher, for example, some mathematics programmes are organized to allow this type of collaboration with the teacher and this type of personal development. All pupils start at the same level and move up when the teacher deems them ready.

The inclusion style:
In this style, differentiated tasks are included to ensure that all pupils gain some feeling of success and so develop positive self-concepts, for example, if an angled bar is provided for high jump practice, all pupils can succeed as they choose the height over which to jump. They decide at what level to start.

Guided discovery:
Mosston sees this as one of the most difficult styles. The teacher plans the pupil's learning programme on the basis of the level of cognition development of the learner. The teacher then guides the pupil to find the answer, reframing the question and task if necessary but always controlling the teaching agenda. Pupils with special educational needs are often taught in small groups and this approach might be used by the teacher to develop an individualized learning programme for each pupil.

Convergent discovery style:
There is a single desired outcome to the learning episode but the learners have autonomy over processes and presentation.The teacher provides feedback and clues (if necessary) to help them reach the correct outcome.

Divergent discovery style:
Learners are encouraged to find alternative solutions to a question, e.g. in approaching a design problem in art. Multiple solutions are possible and the learners assess their validity, with support from the teacher if necessary.

The learner designed individual programme:
A pupil designs and carries out a programme of work within a framework agreed and monitored by the teacher. Pupils carrying out open-ended investigations to answer a particular question in science provide an example of this style. The knowledge and skills needed to participate in this method of learning depend on the building up of skills and self-knowledge in earlier learning experiences.

Learner-initiated style:
At this point on the continuum, the stimulus for learning comes primarily from the pupil, who provides the question to investigate as well as the method of investigation. Thus the pupil actively initiates the learning experience and the teacher provides support. Giving homework which allows pupils freedom to work on their

Table 5.3.2 (continued)

own areas of interest in their own way might fall into this category. However, Mosston and Ashworth make the point that this kind of learning arises 'only when an individual approaches the teacher (authority figure) and initiates a request to design his/her own learning experiences'; and 'when teachers ask learners to "*do a project*" it cannot be construed to be an example of this style' (Mosston and Ashworth, 2002: 284–5).

Self-teaching style
This style describes independent learning without external support. For example, it is the type of learning that adults undergo as they learn from their own experiences.

Source: Adapted from Mosston and Ashworth (2002).

In some circumstances, such as using resistant materials workshops, working in science laboratories or working with javelins, your choice of actions is quite constrained. Nevertheless, it is unlikely that you adopt a complete command style during school experience and allow pupils no discretion over their work. It is even less likely that you have the confidence or desire to adopt a discovery style, and hand over the majority of the decisions to the pupils. However, Mosston and Ashworth (2002) argue that there is no independent learning before a 'discovery threshold' which only operates when the teaching style incorporates discovery. Therefore, you should take steps to widen your repertoire and incorporate discovery styles if you are to produce independent learners capable of fully exploring issues and developing their own ideas.

Task 5.3.7
Developing independent learners

You should be prepared to use your own reading to support your reflection. For example, applying the idea of locating your position along a spectrum using the advice from QCA (at <http://www.qca.org.uk/14–19/6th-form-schools/index_s3–3–learning-teaching.htm>) might lead to the following reflections.

When you set and clarify learning objectives, expectations and boundaries how do you share these with pupils? Do you instruct or allow pupils to construct their own understanding?

How do you help pupils to acquire knowledge, skills and understanding? Do you tell them or do you ask them open-ended questions? Do you accept different answers as being of equal value?

How structured are the opportunities you provide for pupils to demonstrate, practise and apply what they have learned? Who decides the format for demonstrating learning?

How do you support learners in becoming independent? Is it by helping them to reflect and build on their existing learning through open-ended questions or allowing trial and error? Alternatively, do you have a 'this is how-to-do it' approach?

The questions above are open ended in comparison to some of the tasks outlined earlier. They do not all have hard and fast answers. If your answers are in the vein of 'usually I would … but sometimes …' or 'when I started I would … but now I …' you are beginning to adjust your style in response to your experience and to develop as a teacher. You are beginning to widen your repertoire and developing mobility ability in order to develop independent learners.

SUMMARY AND KEY POINTS

You should appreciate that, although any teaching style is individual, it tends to be identifiable within a continuum of theoretical styles. In this unit we have tried to identify individual factors, behavioural and strategic, which affect teaching and have asked you to analyse them so you can begin to place your own styles on the continuum and then, with support, widen your range. Developing a repertoire of styles to match different needs through different behaviour and the use of a wider range of strategies is important to your development as an effective teacher.

FURTHER READINGS AND ACTIVITY

Geoff Barton has been involved in teacher education and consultancy for the DFES, QCA and TTA. His website at <http://www.geoffbarton.co.uk/> is well worth a visit. In particular, review the PowerPoint presentation 'what do we know about learning'. What are its implications for your teaching style? You can also review Geoff Barton's comments on teaching styles at <http://geoffbarton.co.uk/files/longman/Longman%2012%20–%20Teaching% 20Styles.doc>.

You can read one personal account of teaching styles in Volume 2 Number 3 (November 2001) of *UniTeaching UOW*, the University of Wollongong's teaching and learning newsletter available at <http://cedir.uow.edu.au/CEDIR/uniteach/uniteachv2n3/v2n3a3.html>.

Paul Street, of the University of Greenwich, presented a paper on the impact of personal attributes on teaching at a vocational education conference in 2004. It is now being rewritten for publication but you can read the original, 'Those who can teach – deconstructing the teacher's personal presence and impact in the classroom' at the Triangle Journals website: <http://www.triangle.co.uk/jvet/Resources/Street.pdf>.

Painsley Catholic High School has a webpage of ideas and activities under the heading: *teaching styles*. You can review it at <http://www.painsley.org.uk/re/teaching_ideas.htm>.

There are other ways of characterizing teaching styles: Indiana State University's Centre for Teaching and Learning at <http://web.indstate.edu/ctl/styles/tstyle.html#Teaching> discusses a four-cluster model with similar trends as the models outlined in this section. You can also take an inventory of your own teaching style at <http://web.indstate.edu/ctl/tstyle/tstyles3_instructions.html>. Joyce *et al.* (1999) identify models of teaching and group them into four 'families' which represent different philosophies about how humans learn. This is a comprehensive text designed for those who wish to deepen their knowledge of teaching and learning issues. Gipps and Stobart (1997: ch. 2) provide a useful discussion of deep and shallow learning. Eric Jensen (1998) has written an easy-to-read book, *Super teaching*, with a focus on accelerated learning. It contains many ideas which will help the development of teaching strategies and styles. Freeman (2002) is a short activity booklet which will help both student and qualified teachers to look at their teaching styles and strategies. Beresford (2003) is a thought-provoking article which suggests that teachers in primary and secondary schools tend to have styles which rely on different strategies. Steps taken to widen the repertoire of teaching styles used by Year 7 teachers might ease transition between phases.

For the 'Thinking Together' project website see <http://www.thinkingtogether.org.uk/>, Mercer (2000) and Wegerif and Dawes (2004).

APPENDIX 5.3.1: PERSONALISED LEARNING – THE EXAMPLE OF PEER TUTORING

The help of Lyn Dawes, Middleton Combined School, Milton Keynes and Professor Neil Mercer from the Open University in providing advice for this appendix is gratefully acknowledged.

Introduction

School improvement has been an important focus for research and development in education around the world for decades. Recently the focus for school improvement has shifted to developing strategies for improving the achievement of individual pupils and there have been increased demands on the English school system to adopt teaching and learning approaches which support personalized learning (Miliband, 2004).

New ways of using ICT to support personalized learning are being developed. For example, ICT supports the easy collection of pupil achievement data and its analysis at the individual pupil, class and teacher level. At the same time, there is an increased expectation that pedagogy will be underpinned by evidence and again, ways of accessing evidence are supported through the development of resources on the internet.

As an example of developing pedagogy in personalized learning, in this appendix we introduce peer tutoring as a teaching strategy. The value of peer tutoring in supporting pupil learning is backed up by research and evidence which indicate pupil achievement is raised where pupils are taught the principles of learning underpinning the work they are expected to do, the principles of explaining and questioning, the principles underpinning the structuring of lessons, e.g. the defining of aims, objectives and linking forms of assessment to these. This is an example of theories of learning in action, i.e. social constructivism, metacognition and scaffolding (see Unit 5.1).

Peer tutoring

> Peer tutoring is using one another's minds to do better together than you would do separately.
> (Lyn Dawes, Middleton Combined School, Milton Keynes)

Peer tutoring is a well-established teaching strategy based on sound and established principles of good pedagogy, the principles of social constructivism. Teachers have long employed this strategy when setting paired and group work. You may have used peer-tutoring yourself when preparing for examinations. Students of all ages have long used peer tutoring as an examination revision strategy, working together and testing each other.

The advantages of peer tutoring include the active engagement of children with their own learning and that of others, and increased opportunities for true collaboration. Children learn well if supported by, and supporting, other children who are working at a different level of challenge. The challenges for teachers implementing peer tutoring in classroom contexts include teaching the children how to work most effectively in this way, organizing children into the most suitable pairs or groups, setting tasks which offer the right level of challenge, ensuring that discussions remain focused on the learning task (scaffolding), and helping children to recognize the value of having access to a range of different points of view.

Research and evidence from peer tutoring practice in schools indicates that where systematic and carefully constructed approaches to peer tutoring are applied across the pupils' school experience, there are marked gains in pupils' achievement across a number of measures (see, e.g. the 'Thinking Together' project in Further Reading and below) (OFSTED 2003). The proforma at the end of this appendix illustrates the rules governing talk which pupils are taught by teachers using the 'Thinking Together' teaching strategy. The 'Thinking Together' website contains further examples.

As a teaching strategy, peer tutoring avoids the situation which can easily occur, where teaching is focused on the middle range of ability leaving both weak and bright students unengaged.

The 'Thinking Together' teaching strategy, for example, is being adopted by increasing numbers of LEAs and schools. Pupils are given carefully designed lessons in how to talk and work together, so as to help each other to think and learn. Pupils are given guidance about how to explain their ideas clearly, how to listen, to question and to work together constructively. Teaching and learning activities across the curriculum then utilize the new skills the pupils have gained. Lyn Dawes, a teacher-researcher who has worked on the project developing ideas and materials for ten years, comments: 'The children are learning a lot more collaboratively, and listening to each other rather than just hearing each other and they make sure that everyone in the group is involved. They feel more empowered'.

There is evidence from ten years of pupil data that the 'Thinking Together' teaching strategy raises pupils' achievement. Pupils in schools which have adopted the approach have achieved significantly higher SATs scores in mathematics and science than pupils in matched control schools who have not had the 'Thinking Together' training. They also achieved significantly higher scores in a test of non-verbal reasoning, indicating that the experience has helped the development of their 'thinking skills'.

Eggbuckland Community College also provides examples of the success of peer tutoring. Again, pupils are taught skills (in questioning, listening, etc.) which make peer tutoring more than a conversation between two pupils. OFSTED (inspection report, 2003) described the strategy at Eggbuckland as one where pupils:

- research topics individually and in groups;
- teach one another topics which they have struggled to master and freely question one another about these;
- divide up tasks in order to achieve more in a given time;
- readily share the fruits of their researches or other ideas.

This initiative started some years ago and involves Year 8, 9, 10 and 11 pupils. All pupils have their own wireless laptops and are taught in rooms with wireless connections. Teachers across all subject areas have agreed to adopt very interactive teaching styles which use peer tutoring. At Eggbuckland the model is further developed with NQTs mentoring trainee teachers.

Table 5.3.3 gives an example of the work which pupils might be set to develop their skills in talking and listening. See the 'Thinking Together' website for further examples.

Table 5.3.3 Peer tutoring: working with a partner when one of you is teaching the other

Our names are _____	
The activity we are working on is _____	
Learning objectives _____	
Success criteria _____	

How to teach	How to learn
• Ask what you can help with	• Ask lots of questions
• Try not to take over – give time and space	• Explain what you do understand and say what you do not
• Give a clue or a suggestion rather than the answer	• Accept advice and suggestions in the friendly way they are offered
• Be encouraging and helpful	• Be prepared to try something new
• Be patient – wait and listen	• Say what you have learned
Think how you can show or explain things in a different way. Can you draw a diagram, make it into a story, or use an example, find a picture?	• Think of ways you can show or use what you have learned
• Remember that by explaining, you are learning too!	• Say thank you!
• Listen attentively to each other	
• Try not to get distracted	
• Use your time together well	

Unit 5.4

Improving your Teaching

An Introduction to Practitioner Research and Reflective Practice

Steve Bartlett and Marilyn Leask

INTRODUCTION

In order to improve pupils' learning experiences teachers continually reflect upon their lessons. They consider the content, how it was taught, the involvement of individual pupils and the class as a whole and, ultimately the most important consideration, what the pupils learned. Whilst continuing to cast a critical eye over what they do, it is important that teachers also share and discuss their 'findings' with fellow professionals. It is by doing this that they can refine their teaching methods, discover new approaches and compare how others have tackled similar situations. Thus, evaluation and reflection is central to the development of good teaching.

Other aspects of school life, such as the pastoral care system, work experience, community service and a host of extra-curricular activities, also play a significant part in pupil learning. It is important that these aspects are also reflected upon to ensure that they meet the needs of pupils in creating an orderly and vibrant learning community. Therefore, reviewing and evaluation takes place for all areas of school life in order to make the whole experience more fulfilling for pupils and also teachers.

'How do you know your lesson went well?' is a question you can expect to be asked from time to time and you need to be able to provide answers. The fact that pupils are quiet and look as if they are working industriously is no guarantee that the learning you have intended is taking place. In this unit we introduce you to simple techniques that may help you find answers to questions about your teaching and other school activities. In carrying out the tasks throughout this book you are engaging in 'reflective practice'. Rather than relying on your own opinions or superficial anecdotal observations, you should gather evidence that can be examined critically. In this way your evaluation becomes more rigorous and can be regarded as being practical research into teaching. The work in this unit provides a brief

introduction to this area and we suggest that once you gain qualified teacher status you extend your knowledge and understanding of the tools of teacher research as part of your further professional development.

OBJECTIVES

By the end of this unit you should be able to:

- demonstrate an understanding of practitioner research;
- identify different forms of evidence on which you can draw to enable you to make an informed decision concerning an aspect of practice;
- apply research strategies to evaluate and improve aspects of your teaching;
- begin to use reflective practice based on evidence from practitioner research to acquire higher levels of professional knowledge and judgement.

You should check the competences/standards for your course to see which relate to this unit.

THE PROCESS OF PRACTITIONER RESEARCH

Schon (1983) used the phrase 'reflective practitioners' to explain how enlightened professionals work in modern society. It signifies how those professionals, such as teachers, are able to analyse the effectiveness of their actions and to develop different ways of working as a result. Thus such professionals are constantly learning about what they do and so improving their practice. This in turn benefits their clients who in the case of teachers are the pupils. Investigation into their practice by professionals themselves came to be known as 'action research'. It is the link between action and research that Hopkins (2002) suggests has a powerful appeal for teachers. Thus McNiff says that:

> Action research involves learning in and through action and reflection ... Because action research is always to do with learning and learning is to do with education and growth, many people regard it as a form of educational research.

(McNiff and Whitehead, 2002: 15)

Action research is often presented as a cycle that involves the identification of a problem or issue, information or data is collected on the problem/issue, action is then planned and implemented on the basis of this improved knowledge, resulting changes are monitored and evaluated. This final monitoring and evaluation stage is likely to lead to plans for even further action and so the cycle becomes presented as a continuous process or spiral of development (see the action research models of Kemmis and McTaggart, 1988: 14; Elliott, 1991: 71). One of the criticisms of action research is its implication that teachers can only conduct research if they have a particular problem that needs to be solved and that this is rather a negative approach. It may be, however, that a teacher uses research purely as a way to develop a wider understanding of their practice.

Research conducted by teachers is nowadays more frequently referred to as practitioner research. This is a process that teachers use to find out about the quality of teaching and learning taking place. It may be research by individuals into their own teaching and classrooms, groups of teachers researching into an issue they have noticed such as pupil achievement in a particular subject, or the school monitoring process may have identified areas such as pupil behaviour at lunchtime, truancy or pupil preparation for

Table 5.4.1 Planning a practitioner research project

Research focus
You need to be clear as to the focus of the research. It is a useful exercise to write a paragraph at the outset explaining what is going to be investigated and why this is seen as worth doing. When the focus is decided a number of research questions need to be devised in order to identify precisely what it is you wish to find out. These are the central questions of the research and are important as they provide you with a clear trail to follow.

Data sources
For each research question you can now identify the appropriate sources from which to gather the data. The most likely sources of data for teacher researchers include pupils, teachers from the same or different schools, parents, other adults working with children, documents such as pupil reports, school records and written policies, inspection reports, government or similar publications.

Research methods
After identifying the sources you can now decide upon appropriate methods of data collection. Designing the 'tools' to gather information may at first seem daunting but this should not be the case. In your teaching you are continually using data collection skills through questioning pupils, scanning your classroom, marking pupils' work, and analysing curriculum documents. Carrying out practitioner research will enable you to use and further develop these skills.

Timeline
Now that you have a clear research focus and research questions, the sources of data have been identified and the methods have been decided upon, it is possible to develop a timeline for the collection and analysis of data. A clear plan helps ensure that nothing important has been missed out and gives you more control over the process by fitting the research into your existing work commitments. It is particularly important to have a clear time line when evaluating initiatives where data has to be collected at specific points. For instance, the evaluation of a curriculum initiative on the teaching of a history module, using drama techniques, to a Year 7 class, had to be carefully planned beforehand as data could only be collected during the teaching and immediately after.

assessment at KS3 as being in need of investigation. Very often when a new initiative is introduced in the school, such as a literacy strategy, it is evaluated through the techniques of practitioner research.

Before embarking on practitioner research the teacher, along with other colleagues involved, needs to have thought through and discussed the purpose of the research. This enables them to construct a plan that identifies what is going to be investigated, how the research will be carried out and what will be the expected outcomes in terms of data and analysis. These factors can then be put in a time frame that offers targets to work towards. Whilst it is important to have a clear plan, the teacher researcher must be prepared to adapt and change according to altering circumstances. In this way planning and conducting classroom research mirrors the teaching process itself. The research encompasses some of the methods you have already been using, such as observation, keeping a diary, obtaining the perspective of different interested parties (pupils, staff, parents) by the use of interview and questionnaire, and examining documents. Table 5.4.1 provides you with guidance for planning a practitioner research project.

PRACTITIONER RESEARCH TECHNIQUES

Perhaps the most familiar methods of collecting data are questionnaires, interviews and observations. When used these need to be carefully designed to ensure the information you want is obtained while also considering the feelings of those from whom it is being collected.

Interviewing

Interviews can take many forms depending upon whom you are interviewing, where the interview is being held and what the focus is. Interviews can be very formal, as is the case when a candidate is interviewed for a teaching post, or they can be very informal and part of an everyday conversation, as when a teacher asks a pupil from their tutor group how they are getting on with their GCSE coursework. Different types of interview are a normal part of a school day and teachers can become very skilled at gathering information from pupils by such methods. Consider, for instance, how you might 'interview' a pupil about an incident on the corridor between lessons, or a pupil who is finding work in a particular subject difficult. These are both instances where the teacher employs their professional judgement and skills to find out what has been going on and what the issues are. They will then be in a position to act appropriately. Teachers are used to 'interviewing' or talking with parents when working together to aid the progress of their children. It is also helpful to ask small groups of pupils about particular issues in what can be termed 'focus group interviews'.

When conducting interviews as part of practitioner research, it is important to consider beforehand what questions need to be asked, how they will be asked and how the data will be recorded. The researcher may wish to tape record them though it is often easier to make brief notes under key questions during or immediately after the interviews.

Questionnaires

A questionnaire is useful for surveying pupil or parental views. They can enable the collection of information from a large number of people comparatively quickly. In a questionnaire the wording and layout of the questions is very significant. They need to be framed so that those being asked, Year 7 pupils for instance, can understand and answer appropriately. How the completed questionnaires are collected in also needs to be considered. If they are given to whole groups of pupils it is possible to explain the purpose of the questionnaire at the beginning, read out the questions and then collect them all in at the end.

Observation schedules

Observations should be carefully planned so as to cause the least disruption to the lesson. Unit 2.1 'Observing Classrooms' provides information about observation schedules as does Unit 5.3 'Teaching Styles'. You should by now have used forms of these to observe classroom routines. It is not possible to record everything that happens in a classroom so you need to focus on e.g. a particular group or pupil or aspect of the teacher's work and record behaviour over time. It is important that you devise your own observation schedules to suit your particular purpose. The observation schedule provides a structured framework for recording classroom behaviours. Video recordings provide an additional way of recording of data about classroom activities.

Paired observation

This is a streamlined procedure which enables you to obtain feedback on aspects of your work which are difficult for you to monitor. The example in Unit 5.3, of two students working together with one providing feedback on the topic chosen by the other, is an example of paired observation in practice. Paired observation works in the following way: Two colleagues pair up with the purpose of observing one lesson each and then giving feedback about particular aspects of the lesson or the teaching of the person observed. The person giving the lesson decides the focus of the observation. The three stages of a paired observation are:

Step 1:   You both agree the focus of the observation and what notes, if any, are to be made.
Step 2:   You each observe one lesson given by the other. Your observations and notes are restricted to the area requested.
Step 3:   You give each other feedback on the issue under consideration.

The cycle can be repeated as often as is wished.

You need to be aware that there are in fact many ways of collecting information and it is important to be creative as well as adaptable in considering data collection. For instance, pupil and teacher diaries, analysis of pupil work, asking pupils to write about or draw images of a topic/issue being researched, biographical accounts written by participants, all provide useful insights into life in school and the learning that is taking place. Some of the texts in the recommended reading give more detailed advice on how to design and use the methods noted above.

Task 5.4.1
Designing a practitioner research project

Identify an issue for further investigation associated with your teaching such as, the use of ICT in the classroom, challenging the more able pupils or the development of active learning techniques.

- Outline the focus of the research and explain why this is an important area for you to investigate.
- Write a number of key research questions (about four) that identify what you need to find out.
- List the likely sources of data.
- Identify methods that you would use to collect the data.

If you wish to take this further you could also design the methods, construct a time line and even carry out the research project.

EVIDENCE ABOUT TEACHING AND LEARNING

The evidence available for drawing conclusions about teaching and learning can take different forms. This evidence includes:

- Quantitative data in numerical form collected from, e.g. statistical returns, questionnaires, school management information systems. League tables of school performance are a good example of how quantitative data can be presented and used. This type of data is useful for measurement and comparison on a large scale but often lacks explanation for individual differences and can feel very impersonal.

- Qualitative data which are more descriptive and often include detailed personal explanations. These data are 'richer' and give a feel for particular cases but are sometimes harder to analyse and do not lend themselves easily to measurement. Such data are collected through observation, interview, analysis of documents, diaries, video, photographs, discussions, focus groups brainstorming.

Researchers need to develop a strategy for data collection that is most appropriate for the research focus. This strategy often involves the use of both quantitative and qualitative data. For instance, if you were investigating a problem of pupil truancy at your school, you would be likely to require quantitative data showing the extent of truancy and any relationship this has to factors such as age, gender, pupil performance, the time of day or particular lessons. You may also want qualitative data that gives a more in-depth and personal explanation of truancy from the perspectives of truants, their teachers and parents. Using both types of data helps to give a fuller understanding of the issues.

In your previous classroom observations, you may have started with a clear focus or a question to answer, e.g. what routines does the teacher use in managing the work of the class? You may have collected evidence from various sources to answer that question. In addition, you may have observed and made notes about what the pupils and the teacher actually did during the lesson; you may have looked at the pupils' work and the teacher's lesson plans; you may have cross-checked your perceptions with those of the teacher as a way of eliminating bias, improving accuracy and identifying alternative explanations. So, in such classroom research, data are gathered from different sources, checked for alternative perceptions/explanations and conclusions are drawn from this information so as to develop teaching in the future. This process, whereby the researcher approaches the object of the research from as many different angles and perspectives as possible in order to gain a greater understanding, is called triangulation. Miles and Huberman (1994) have suggested that the constant checking and double-checking involved means that triangulation becomes a way of life in such research.

Task 5.4.2
School-based practitioner research

Schools are developing increasingly detailed information systems to provide data showing how they are performing. Subject departments collect such data as part of the annual reviewing process and to inform future development plans. Find out about the different types of evidence and the processes used in the school to evaluate the effectiveness of teaching, pupils' learning and the monitoring of individual pupil progress. Consider how this data informs the setting of future targets for pupils, teachers, subject departments and the school.

ETHICAL ISSUES

Teachers and other professionals working in classrooms have a duty of care for their pupils. Within this professional way of working there is a need to respect others, share information as appropriate, yet also maintain trust and individual confidentiality. There are ethical considerations to be taken into account when you are collecting data from pupils and teachers. You must have agreement from those who are in a position to give this; your tutor may advise you to get the permission of the headteacher. You need to take your responsibility in this area seriously. It is worth consulting the British Educational Research Association ethical guidelines (2003) for a more detailed consideration of ethical issues. Table 5.4.2 outlines the key areas to consider.

Table 5.4.2 An ethical approach to practitioner research

You must take responsibility for the ethical use of any data collected and for maintaining confidentiality. We suggest that you should as a matter of course:

1. Ask a senior member of staff as well as the teachers directly involved with your classes for permission to carry out your project.
2. Before you start provide staff involved with a copy of the outline of your project which should include:
   - the area you are investigating;
   - how you are going to collect any evidence;
   - from whom you intend to collect evidence;
   - what you intend to do with the data collected, e.g. whether it is confidential, whether it will be written up anonymously or not;
   - who the audience for your report will be;
   - any other factors relevant to the particular situation.
3. Finally, check whether staff expect to be given a copy of your work.
4. If you store data electronically, then you should check that you conform to the requirements of the Data Protection Act. For example, you should not store personal data on computer discs without the explicit authorisation of the individual.

SUMMARY AND KEY POINTS

Developing your teaching skills is one important aspect of your professional development. But other important attributes of the effective teacher that we stress in this book are the quality and extent of your professional knowledge and judgement. Skills can be acquired and checked relatively easily. Building your professional knowledge and judgement are longer-term goals which are developed through reflection and further professional development.

In this unit, we have opened a door on a treasure trove of strategies which you can use to reflect on the quality of your teaching. We suggest that you come back to this work during the year and again later in your career. The application of practitioner research to your work at that later stage opens your eyes to factors influencing your teaching and learning which you may not have known existed. Critical reflection aided by practitioner research, by individuals or by teams, provides the means by which the quality of teaching and learning in the classroom can be evaluated as a prelude to improvement.

You should now have ideas of how to evaluate the quality of your teaching through using a continuous cycle of critical reflection so that you can plan improvement based on evidence. If you intend to develop your research skills, then we suggest that you read several of the set texts and consult with experienced colleagues as, in this unit, we have provided simply a brief introduction into an important area of professional practice and accountability. The following texts all provide a grounding in aspects of practitioner research.

FURTHER READING

Bell, J. (1999) *Doing your Research Project: A Guide for First-Time Researchers in Education and Social Science*, 3rd edn, Milton Keynes: Open University Press. Though written primarily for students carrying out research projects while on academic courses, this book provides a useful introduction for anyone wishing to conduct research in education.

Burton, D. and Bartlett, S. (2004) *Practitioner Research for Teachers*, London: Paul Chapman Publishing. This text discusses the nature of practitioner research and its importance for the professional development of teachers. It also provides useful practical guidance on the designing of research projects and data collection.

Hopkins, D. (2002) *A Teacher's Guide to Classroom Research*, 3rd edn, Milton Keynes: Open University Press. This book is concerned with the development of teachers as researchers as a means to improving classroom practice. It gives clear advice on all aspects of the research process.

Wragg, E.C. (1999) *An Introduction to Classroom Observation*, 2nd edn, London: Routledge. This is one of many useful texts written by Wragg on aspects of teaching and learning. In it he discusses the importance and uses of classroom observation. Wragg gives practical advice on how to design and conduct observation in the classroom.

Useful websites

Networked Learning Communities: <http://www.ncsl.org.uk/index.cfm? pageID=nlc> (accessed 30 Sept. 2004).

National Education Research Forum (NERF): <http://www.nerf-uk.org/> (accessed 30 September 2004).

British Educational Research Association: <http://www.bera.ac.uk/> (accessed 30 September 2004).

6 Assessment

In England and Wales in the 1990s, assessment and its reporting became a central issue in teaching and learning. The 1988 Education Reform Act introduced statutory subjects and statutory assessment procedures into the curriculum for the first time, together with national tests to monitor standards. These factors continue to drive teaching and learning.

This chapter addresses the purposes of assessment and their relationships to teaching and learning and changes in assessment practice and reporting in recent years. The increasing importance of formative assessment as a major factor in supporting learning and raising achievement are extensively discussed. Formative assessment is contrasted with summative assessment as 'high stakes' versus 'low stakes'. The concepts of validity and reliability are addressed, their ongoing tensions and the assessment limits that may apply to objectives which are difficult to assess but are educationally important. Assessment is needed to provide information about individual pupils' progress, help the teacher devise appropriate teaching and learning strategies, give parents helpful information about their child's progress and compare pupils and schools across the country. This chapter discusses the extent to which tests can provide this information.

Unit 6.1 'Assessment and Accountability' gives an overview of the principles of assessment, of formative and summative assessment, diagnostic testing and ideas of validity and reliability. The difference between norm-referenced testing and criterion-referenced testing is introduced and the nationally set tests discussed in the light of these principles. This unit links assessment with the classroom teacher and how the results of assessment can be used to identify progress and diagnose problems. The management of assessment is addressed. The unit touches on the broader issue of what could be assessed, as opposed to what is assessed together with the role of assessment in the public accountability of teachers, school governing bodies and LEAs.

Unit 6.2 'External Assessment and Examinations', preparing pupils for public examinations is an important feature of a teacher's work as well as preparing them for national tests and so considers assessment as exemplified by SATs, GCSE and GCE Advanced level. It links national monitoring of standards with your classroom work, raising issues of accountability. Public examinations grade pupils on a nationally recognized scale and exercise control over both entry to jobs and higher education. Unit 6.2 addresses how national standards are maintained and national grades are awarded. Recent national developments in vocational education and the current drive to improve the status of vocational education in relation to academic education are highlighted. Contrasts are drawn between the assessment methods used for vocational courses and academic courses.

Unit 6.1

Assessment for Learning

Terry Haydn

INTRODUCTION

Assessment covers all those activities which are undertaken by teachers and others to measure the effectiveness of teaching and learning. Assessment includes not only setting and marking pupils' work, tests and examinations but also the recording and reporting of the results. It is important to develop a clear understanding of current mechanisms for assessing, reporting and recording pupils' work and progress in your subject, and also an understanding of the various purposes which assessment serves in the educational process and some of the tensions which arise from these differing purposes.

There has been a revolution in assessment practice over the past 20 years. If you are to teach effectively it is important that you understand the part that assessment can play in making teaching and learning effective; Figure 6.1.1 lists a set of basic ideas you should address in your course of study.

OBJECTIVES

By the end of this unit you should be able to:

- describe and explain the differing purposes of assessment;
- identify the tensions that arise when an assessment instrument is used for multiple purposes;
- explain what is meant by 'assessment for learning';
- use correctly some important assessment terminology;
- identify strategies for making assessment and evaluation purposeful and manageable.

ACQUIRING A 'GROUNDING' IN ASSESSMENT

By the end of your course of professional training, you should have explored the main features of assessment which are outlined in Figure 6.1.1.

DEVELOPING AN UNDERSTANDING OF THE DISCOURSE OF ASSESSMENT

By the end of your course of training, you should have become familiar with some of the more important terminology which is commonly used in talking about assessment issues. We address some of this terminology below.

Formative and summative assessment

Formative assessment provides information which can aid further progress, diagnose reasons for both good and poor performance, and target particular learning needs. Summative assessment measures and reports on pupils' progress, as a 'verdict' on what has been achieved; it summarizes achievement. Summative assessment occurs near the end of a piece of work, such as at the end of a Key Stage or

---

Many assessment issues will arise during your course of initial teacher education; by the end of it you should:

– know
- and understand the vocabulary, e.g. normative, summative, 'baseline' and 'value-added' commonly used in relation to current assessment arrangements;
- the different purposes of assessing pupils' work;
- how to mark a set of books effectively.

– have begun to develop an understanding of the
- different ways teachers can give feedback to pupils;
- factors which are currently thought to contribute to the quality of feedback given to pupils;
- assessment systems used in your school experience schools;
- breadth of ways, including marking to National Curriculum levels, in which assessment can be used to improve teaching and learning outcomes;
- GCSE and AS/A2 assessment objectives for your subject;
- mechanisms used to report to pupils and parents;
- nature of progression in your subject, i.e. what it means 'to get better' at history, mathematics or physics;
- main ideas about 'assessment for learning' and begun to put them into practice in your teaching;
- ways in which technology can contribute to effective practice in assessment.

– be aware of the
- use of 'target setting' for pupils and how to set targets effectively;
- arrangements for assessment of your National Curriculum subject, the attainment level descriptors *and the ways in which they should be used*. In addition, for teachers of English, mathematics and science, the structure and application of the Standard Assessment Tasks;
- assessment instruments currently used in schools, e.g. CATs, PANDAs, MidYIS, Alis, etc.;
- current debates about assessment policy in UK schools.

Figure 6.1.1 A 'grounding' in assessment

GCSE module, or at the end of a course such as the GCE A level or university first degree. Summative assessments are often used to determine access to further levels of education and training, or to employment opportunities where competition is fierce. As one writer said:

> Most examinations exist to distinguish better from worse. With a smaller supply of something than applicants for it, such as university places, training seats in racing cars, oboists' desks in a crack symphony orchestra – we need to pick out those who are to get it.
>
> (Ryan, 2000: 2)

This is education as 'positional goods', i.e. a consumer product; there may not be enough places at University X or in Profession Y for all those who would like to enter them, even if they would be capable of completing the course, so summative assessment is used to decide who should get these places. Lambert makes the point that formative assessment is designed.

> primarily to serve the needs of teachers supporting individual learners, and is thus identified with professional purpose. Summative assessment can be associated more closely with bureaucratic purpose, serving the needs of the system as a whole, the administration and politicians.
>
> (Lambert, 1999: 289)

Norm and criterion referenced assessment

Norm-referenced assessment makes comparisons between a learner's performance and the performance of other learners, either within a teaching group or more widely. So to say that Alan came 18th out of his class of thirty pupils is to make a norm-referenced judgement. If we give Alan a mark out of ten, it does not in itself tell us what Alan can and cannot do, but we can use it to find out how Alan performed compared to the rest of the group. Commercially produced standardized tests can be used to determine where Alan stands in relation to a much broader sample of learners, placing him, perhaps at the 40th percentile of those taking the test, which means that 40 per cent of learners of the same age scored lower than Alan on the test. Normative assessment is helpful when, for example, there are not enough places on a course of further education or employment opportunity, so we have to make decisions as to who to give the places to. If there are 30 places, it may be that the places are allocated to the 30 candidates who scored most highly in the assessment.

Criterion-referenced assessment attempts to determine whether the learner has met pre-specified learning objectives. For example, the driving test tries to determine which candidates fulfil the criteria necessary to drive safely, without endangering others. You are not trying to establish a rank order. Thus:

> It wouldn't matter if nobody failed the driving test, as long as the standard of competence is high enough, and the test is conducted properly. A failure rate of 80 per cent would be fine too, if we thought the standard was right.
>
> (Ryan, 2000: 2)

Criterion-referencing is an important part of formative assessment; teachers try to establish the criteria for 'becoming good' at a subject, and then use assessment to measure learners' progression towards expert levels in the various aspects of that subject. The information gained from assessment can be used to adjust teaching inputs, and act on emerging strengths and weaknesses.

In England, some subjects in the National Curriculum (NC) are divided into 'profile components'; the curriculum for English language, for example, is broken down into reading, writing, speaking and listening. The NC attainment levels attempt to establish criteria for progression in these profile components, which assists teachers in recognizing and recording progression.

Ipsative or 'value-added' assessment

Instead of measuring the performance of a learner against other learners (norm-referencing), or against specified objectives (criterion-referencing), the learner's performance can be measured against the learner's own previous levels of attainment. This is what is meant by 'ipsative assessment'. An example of ipsative assessment would be the concept of 'personal best' in athletics, where the athlete is striving to improve on previous performances.

The current emphasis on accountability in education has raised the profile of ipsative assessment because of the contribution it makes to value-added assessment. Unlike 'raw' achievement and attainment tables, formerly performance tables, and referred to in press as 'league tables', which do not take into account pupils' prior attainment, ipsative assessment measures gains in personal learning and provides data on the extent to which the pupil, the teacher and the school have been able to improve learning. Some educationalists see 'value-added' assessment in terms of school effectiveness and as a way of making more informed comparisons between institutions; others note that if we are seriously to compare schools there are major issues of both validity and reliability in current test instruments; see, for instance, Haylock, 2001.

Validity and reliability

Validity describes the extent to which the exercise assesses exactly what it is intended to assess. If for instance the driving test was based solely on a written exercise, to what extent would we consider it a valid test of people's ability to drive safely? A history examination question, purporting to assess pupils' ability to use sources by providing a picture of Hitler stroking an Alsatian dog, asked 'Why did this man invade Poland?' (Shemilt, 1984). This might be a valid test of historical knowledge or recall, but is it a valid test of the ability to derive information from sources? Pupils who do well at GCSE English examination are said to be 'good' at English, but what does this really mean? Validity is a complex subject because there might not be even general agreement about what it means 'to be good at' a subject. When we devise assessment exercises, we need to keep in mind the idea of validity and, in marking the exercise, to keep in mind whether or not the way in which we constructed the test made it possible for pupils to provide a full and appropriate answer. Sometimes 'deficits' in responses can be the fault of poor question setting, rather than lack of knowledge and understanding on the part of pupils.

Reliability in assessment refers to the extent to which the assessment exercise is trustworthy in providing information about pupils' learning. If the assessment is repeated does the test instrument give a similar result? Considering the reliability of an assessment helps answer questions such as:

- Is the test arbitrary and 'hit and miss' in terms of addressing the content with which the learners have worked?
- Would a different set of pupils with a similar range of abilities and backgrounds gain similar scores?
- Would you get the same result if you repeated the testing at a later date?

Haylock (2001) gives the example of bathroom scales as an instrument for measuring a person's weight to help distinguish between validity and reliability. Bathroom scales are a valid, i.e. appropriate,

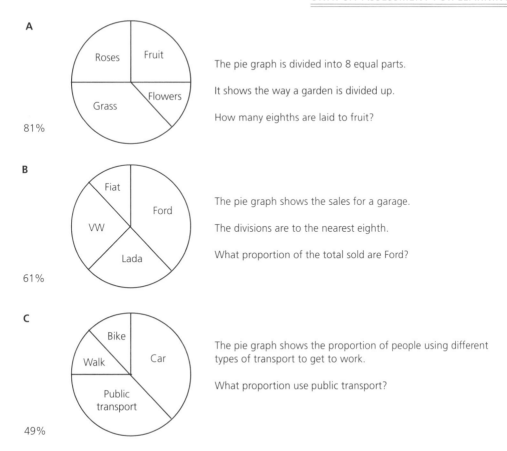

A

The pie graph is divided into 8 equal parts.

It shows the way a garden is divided up.

How many eighths are laid to fruit?

81%

B

The pie graph shows the sales for a garage.

The divisions are to the nearest eighth.

What proportion of the total sold are Ford?

61%

C

The pie graph shows the proportion of people using different types of transport to get to work.

What proportion use public transport?

49%

Figure 6.1.2   Effect of context on assessment

way of finding out someone's weight; the scales can be reliable, i.e. always respond in the same way to a given weight. However, bathroom scales may not be accurate, i.e. record the true weight. In educational assessment accuracy is subsumed into the concept of validity.

Lambert discusses the context of assessment; that is, the way in which the question is posed can influence the outcomes of the assessment (Lambert, 1999: 302). Figure 6.1.2 shows three ways in which pupils were tested on their ability to read information correctly from a pie chart. The number at the bottom left of the graphs gives the proportion (%) of successful pupils in each case.

**Task 6.1.1
The effect of context on
performance**

What explanations can you offer for the different success rates of pupils in reading pie charts (see Figure 6.1.2)? Is it possible to determine which is the most appropriate way of making this assessment?

It is important to remember that assessment is not an exact science. You need to be aware of the limitations and complexities involved in assessment.

'High' and 'low' stakes assessment

'High stakes' assessment occurs when the result is considered important either for the learner, such as deciding the set into which the learner is placed; or for the school, such as influencing its position in league tables of school performance. Driving tests, Standard Assessment Tasks (SATs) and GCSE and A level examinations are examples of 'high stakes' assessment.

'Low stakes' assessment is the informal, routine and low-key day-to-day assessment where the results may not even be formally recorded. Pupils may not even consider that they are being assessed in such activities, it is just part of their work.

WHY DO WE ASSESS PUPILS' WORK? THE PURPOSES OF ASSESSMENT

A great deal of time and effort is spent on assessing pupils' work. There are many reasons for assessing pupils' work; assessment serves a variety of purposes and it is helpful to be aware of them and the tensions which arise from them. It is difficult to devise 'all-purpose' assessment instruments which serve multiple purposes. One common tension is whether the test is more useful for supporting learning (the formative mode), or for making judgements about pupil (the 'summative' mode). Task 6.1.2 asks you to use this classification of assessment as summative or formative to review the various reasons teachers and others give for assessing their pupils.

Task 6.1.2
Purposes of assessment

The subsection headed 'What is assessment for?' describes 12 purposes of assessment. As you read through this list, consider whether the functions of the various items are primarily formative or summative in intent. Do any of the purposes potentially combine both elements of assessment?

WHAT IS ASSESSMENT FOR?

1. To acknowledge pupils' efforts

At a very basic level, but highly important, the purpose is to show pupils that you take an interest in their work. Even pupils who are not avid scholars are often disgruntled if they feel that you have not looked at their work, or if you are slow in returning it. Teachers are not the only ones to differentiate; pupils also differentiate, and 'rate' teachers who mark their work promptly and carefully. One recent survey showed that pupils regarded this as the most important 'professional' characteristic of a teacher's work; see University of East Anglia online: <http://www.uea.ac.uk/~m242/nasc/cross/cman/profchar.htm>.

2. To motivate pupils

Most learners want to know how they are doing, and whether they have done well. It is an opportunity to give encouragement, show your appreciation of their achievement or effort *and to give advice as to how to do better next time*. Marking pupils' work can be a form of extrinsic motivation and can include 'rewards' such as merit marks and commendations, positive written or oral comment, and grades and marks.

3. To monitor progress

The heart of formative assessment is gaining information about pupils' progress. We assess pupils' learning in order to monitor their understanding and to diagnose factors which may be blocking or inhibiting learning. Some assessments are referred to as diagnostic assessment because they are designed specifically to probe misunderstandings or barriers to learning and so provide suggestions for ways forward. Formative assessment can give pupils a self-awareness of their comparative strengths and weaknesses and priorities for future learning. It is also a starting point for establishing a dialogue with your pupil about what they need to do to improve performance in your subject.

You can use the information gleaned from assessing pupils' written work, or oral responses, not just to give the work a mark or a grade, but to provide advice which helps them to respond better next time, or move on to another learning priority. In the longer term, you may be guiding pupils towards being able to monitor and evaluate their own learning and progress, that is learning how to learn.

4. To identify students with special educational needs (SEN)

The class teacher is in the front line of special needs diagnosis. The SEN Code of Practice places responsibility on the classroom teacher to identify pupils who may have specific learning difficulties which are inhibiting them from performing to their full potential. Where such problems are encountered, the information is given to the school's SEN Co-ordinator (SENCO) in order to draw up or adjust the pupil's Individual Education Plan (IEP). This aspect of your work includes identifying particularly able pupils, who may need some differentiated curriculum materials in order to make maximum progress and sustain motivation and engagement in learning. There is fuller discussion of SEN and pupil's IEP in Unit 4.6.

5. To establish baseline evidence of achievement

At the start of a new phase of schooling, an audit of what each pupil can and cannot do is carried out in order to create a baseline against which future progress can be measured. This audit may be in particular subject areas, or by an intelligence test, or both. The information gained can help teachers to plan their teaching to match pupils' individual needs. These data make possible a measurement of the 'value-added' by the teacher or the school, by measuring increments in learning against the baseline score and by estimating progress over and above that expected by pupils of that ability.

Some teachers welcome baseline assessment as it takes into account pupils' prior accomplishments, in a way that 'raw' performance table data do not. Others stress that the imprecision of such testing, and its susceptibility to manipulation make it inappropriate for such 'high-stakes' functions.

6. To detect pupil under-achievement

Assessment can be used to help teachers to be alert to possible under-achievement by pupils who are 'coasting' or who have some temporary difficulties which affect their learning.

In order to monitor progress adequately your assessment of pupils' work should recognize pupils' ability, or potential and previous educational performance. This process identifies pupil under-achievement, or accelerated achievement.

As well as previous school reports and SATs results there is an increasing range of commercial assessment instruments designed to provide a 'baseline' against which future performance can be calibrated. These include:

* Middle-Years Information System (MidYIS);
* A level Information System plus GNVQ (ALis+);
* Year 11 Information System (Yellis),

which are available online from the Centre for Education and Management, University of Durham at <http://www.cemcentre.org>.

A fourth instrument often used by schools is the Cognitive Abilities Test (CAT). The CAT measures a range of abilities using three tests, a verbal reasoning test, a non-verbal reasoning test and a third on number. Scores on CAT can be correlated with subsequent grades in, for example, the GCSE and used to predict GCSE performance. This information contributes to value-added factors in reporting the effectiveness of schooling. The CAT is available from the National Foundation for Educational Research-Nelson online at <http://www.nfer-nelson.co.uk>.

You should enquire whether any of these assessment systems, or others, are used in your school experience school to gain some insight into at least one of them. If a pupil has performed very well on one of these tests, but does not seem to be making appropriate academic progress, it can alert staff towards making an early intervention.

Figure 6.1.3 shows an information chart on the prior attainment of three pupils in a teaching group, in terms of their performance in the Cognitive Ability Tests taken at the start of Year 7, their performance in mathematics and reading tests, their spelling and reading 'ages' and their performance in Key Stage 2 SATs tests for English, mathematics and science. By looking at the chart, the subject teacher can quickly see whether there is a disparity between the pupil's current work and the profile of their previous academic attainment, and explore this further if this is the case.

7. To report to parents

Both formative and summative assessment provide information for teachers to report to parents about their children's progress. Most parents are interested in how their children are doing in school, and good communications between parents, pupils and teachers can help pupils to learn more effectively. The 1988 Education Reform Act made it a minimum statutory requirement for schools to provide an annual report on pupils' progress. Many secondary schools also have a 'diary' system to aid communication between parents and the school. Parents are often required to sign this weekly to establish that they have seen details of homeworks set and comments on pupils' work and overall progress. Government guidance on reporting to parents makes the point that parents are not just interested in academic performance, and want to know about other aspects of their child's progress. The same guidance suggests that parents want to know about the child's performance in relation to the rest of the class, to national standards and how their child is progressing in relation to previous

CONFIDENTIAL – YEAR 8

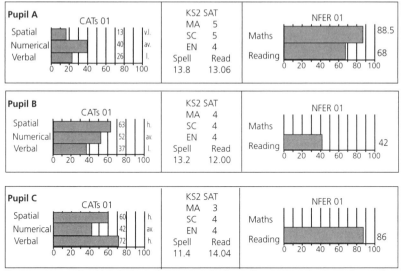

Key: av. – average; h. – high; l. – low; v.l. – very low; Spell – spelling age/year; Read – reading age/year;
EN – English; MA – mathematics; SC – science; followed by the NC levels

Figure 6.1.3   Chart providing teacher with pupil profiles

attainment and perceived potential. Parents should be told about their child's particular strengths and achievements, areas for development and improvement and whether the child is behaving well, and is 'socially' adjusting to school life (DfEE/QCA, 1999a).

8. To 'group' or 'set' pupils

Schools have to make decisions about setting or grouping their pupils. The extent to which pupils are separated into teaching groups of similar abilities varies from school to school (see Unit 4.1 'Pupil Grouping'). Where grouping strategies are used to stream or band pupils, assessment is needed to allocate pupils to groups. This is an important decision, of concern to parents, and it can have a significant impact on a pupil's own self-esteem and friendships. It is essential that there is reliable and transparent evidence to support this decision such as results from end-of-year examinations or end-of-term tests. In the core subjects of English, mathematics and science, the results of end of Key Stage 2 or Key Stage 3 SATs are used. The teacher's overall assessment of the pupil's class work and homework over the course of the year provides further evidence.

9. To measure end-of-course achievement

This summative assessment usually takes the form of an examination grade, a coursework mark, or a (NC) attainment level. Currently, all pupils are ascribed a level of attainment in each profile component of an NC subject at the end of each Key Stage. It is a formal judgement on the level of achievement in a subject, and can determine entry to subsequent stages of education, so it is important that the assessment is 'robust' in the sense of being carefully monitored for validity and reliability.

Not all countries place the same emphasis on external examinations at the age of 16 and 18 as does Britain. For example, Australia has not had public examinations for many years (Gipps, 1997).

10. To compare pupils

As well as simply comparing pupils, assessment is sometimes used to place learners in a rank order. It was once common practice in some schools to rank pupils in each teaching group monthly in each subject, as well as in all subjects by combining their marks for each subject. These rank orders were displayed on a school noticeboard, showing the positions of each pupil. This process did not provide information about what pupils could and could not do, but indicated only their performance relative to other pupils. As well as knowing what their children can and cannot do, parents are (understandably) concerned to know how their child is performing relative to other pupils in the class or school, and comparisons like those described above help parents; the information that they are 'doing well' does not necessarily assuage parental anxiety and concern. There is always the danger, however, that such comparisons may have a negative effect on the motivation of pupils who fare consistently badly in such assessments.

11. To monitor teaching and inform planning

The results of assessment help teachers find out the extent to which their teaching has been effective. This means checking for understanding, both in terms of getting to know *which* pupils have grasped what you were trying to teach and also those *aspects* of the topic learned by pupils. The results also tell you which topics need reinforcement or a change of teaching approach. The information can help to identify weaknesses in your teaching, as well as deficits in pupils' learning. Student teachers usually have to write evaluations of their lessons as part of their experience and many student teachers gain helpful insights into their lessons from their evaluations and reflections. Advice on lesson evaluations can be found in Units 2.2 and 5.4, in your course materials or online, e.g. the University of East Anglia at <http://www.uea.ac.uk/~m242/historypgce/assess/>.

12. To provide information which will make teachers, schools and LEAs accountable for their performance

Recent governments have used the results of assessment to compare schools and LEAs. These assessments include, for example, in England the publication of the achievement and attainment tables (league tables) of examination performance of pupils at GCSE and GCE A level as well as the results of SATs in English, mathematics and science. The publication of these tables has been abandoned in Northern Ireland. Non-academic data about schools are used in the accountability exercise, such as attendance rates. Academic data can be used in a school to compare both departments and teachers.

Teachers, schools and LEAs are publicly accountable for the standards of education of their pupils. Accountability has been a controversial area, not least because of government attempts to make gains in pupils' learning part of the performance management of teachers, affecting their professional pay and advancement. Assessments are used by schools to set targets for improvement, known as 'target setting'. All schools in England receive from the DfES a portfolio of 'Performance and Assessment Data' (PANDA), which enables them to compare their school's performance with 'similar' schools;

similarity based on the number of pupils receiving free school meals. Target setting is designed to raise standards of educational achievement nationally (DfEE, 1998a). Welsh schools have access to national data online at <http://www.schools.wales.gov. uk>. Benchmarking data are provided in Wales similarly online at <http://www.learning.wales.gov.uk/scripts/fe/news_details.asp?NewsID=874>.

ASSESSMENT FOR ACCOUNTABILITY AND ASSESSMENT FOR LEARNING: RECENT DEVELOPMENTS IN ASSESSMENT PRACTICE IN THE UK

Assessment has been one of the battlegrounds of education policy over the past two decades, and the comparative importance attached to assessment for accountability and assessment for learning has fluctuated over this period. Task 6.1.2 was designed to help you appreciate some of the tensions between assessment to provide accountability in the whole education system, and assessment designed to help individual pupils improve their learning.

Accountability in the pre-National Curriculum era was in part through school reports. These were brief and often vague, as Figures 6.1.4 and 6.1.5 show. Further examples of pre-NC assessment models with brief accompanying commentary can be found online at <http://www.uea.ac.uk/~m242/historypgce/assess/welcome.htm>.

This 'vagueness' was one of the factors which led to the introduction of a National Curriculum for England and Wales, more rigorous and precise in specifying and measuring learning outcomes, of

Subject	Position	Remarks	Master's Initials
English	12	Satisfactory progress.	L.G.
History	4	As usual, a very good term's work.	hcb
Geography	9	Progressing satisfactorily	TR.
French	5=	Very good this term.	HcR.
Latin	26=	Just satisfactory, but lacks confidence.	ƒcB
Mathematics			
Chemistry	20	I was delighted with his Grade B in GCE. Possibly a little less happy with organic chemistry	G
Physics	27	Some progress made	aP

Figure 6.1.4 A pupil's school report, 1960s

Name...........

PHYSICAL TRAINING REPORT

Height feet ins.		Weight stns. lbs.		Chest Norm. Exp.		Physical Training	Games	Date
4	7	4	8½	23	25½	Fair work.		7.12.62
						Fair progress		27.3.63
4	7¾	4	9	22¾	25½	Very fair.		7.7.63
4	8½	4	12½	24	26½	Fair		6.12.63
						Fair. Tries		6.3.64
4	9½	5	4			Fair progress. Keen.		13.7.64
4	9½	5	3½	24½	27½	Very fair progress.		1.12.44
						Fair.		1.4.65
						Very fair.		1.12.65
						Satisfactory term.		1.4.66
5	0½	5	10½			Has worked quite well.		7.7.66
						Satisfactory		7.12.66
						Quite good		7.7.67
						Very keen. Table-tennis & cross-country teams		6.12.67
						Keen and willing		26.6.68
						It is good to find a boy so willing to participate.		2.12.68

Figure 6.1.5 A pupil's physical training report 1962–8

greater transparency and making teachers, schools and LEAs more accountable to the public purse. This policy was also seen as a way of 'driving up' educational standards and has led to standardized methods of measuring educational outcomes throughout the period of compulsory education instead of limiting assessment to external examinations at 16 and 18.

The original assessment model of the National Curriculum in England and Wales included in its recommendations a ten-point scale of reporting progress linked to a series of graded level descriptions (levels 1–10) (DES/WO, 1988, the TGAT Report). In 1995 this model was amended to eight levels plus one for 'exceptional performance' (DfE, 1995). For each subject, nine written statements of expected performance were produced, called attainment targets (ATs), to describe progression in achievement between the ages of 5 and 14.

The system of 'levels of attainment', as measured by SATs and teacher assessment in the core subjects of English, mathematics and science, together with public examination results, could then be used to make comparisons of pupil performance across the curriculum. These same data were used also to compare the performance of departments and teachers in a school, of schools within an LEA and, finally, LEAs nationally. This process is an example of one assessment instrument being used to measure many different educational factors. As was said at the time:

> Part of the reason for the acceptance of the TGAT Report by the DES, civil service, and politicians was the fact that it 'delivers' the required bureaucratic data, that is, pupil scores can be aggregated to show results for a class, a school and whole LEA for comparative purposes.
> (Lawton, 1989: 59)

A post-National Curriculum example of a report on a pupil's progress, Figure 6.1.6, gives an indication of the radical nature of changes to assessment and reporting arrangements and shows more specific and detailed feedback on the pupil's progress than the earlier models. The requirement to report a level of attainment in every subject at the end of each Key Stage of education also demonstrates the way in which teacher, school and LEA accountability was now built into the educational system.

This is not to suggest that all recent developments in assessment have been positive and unproblematic in their effects (think how much time it would take the teacher to compile the latter report). A further negative aspect of current practice is the time devoted to preparing for a test or examination which may be at the expense of other learning. Some commentators recognized that teachers might 'teach to the test' and concentrate on what is to be tested and what was easy to test rather than teaching the full breadth of the curriculum (Stobart and Gipps, 1997; Torrance, 2002; Wiliam, 2001). Most teachers and many schools are still wrestling with the problem of how to make best use of assessment, how to ensure that the time and effort involved in assessing teaching and learning is not wasted, or even counterproductive.

There has been increasing concern about some aspects of the current arrangements for assessment and testing; there is now an emerging consensus that the development of assessment for learning is now a very important factor in education policy and practice.

Why is assessment for learning important?

Teachers have to spend many hours assessing, recording and reporting pupils' work. It is not a question of how much assessment you do, or how *much* feedback you provide, but how *intelligently* you use assessment to inform your future teaching and your feedback to pupils. Several commentators have argued that much current assessment practice in schools serves no useful purpose whatever, is a waste of time and may even be counterproductive (Gipps, 1997; Desforges, 2003).

Anytown High School

Subject:	**Science**	Date	**July 1999**
Name	**A pupil**	Form	**9Z**
Effort Grade	**A**	Attainment Grade	**A**
Set (if applicable)	**6 (out of 8)**		

Key: A = Very good, B = Good, C = Satisfactory, D = Poor, E = Very poor (within the set)

Key Stage 3 Teacher Assessment: **Level 7** Key Stage 3 NC SAT Assessment: **Level 5**

Teacher Comment:

Anthony has achieved an average of 87% in the class science tests this year; the class average is 72%. He is a bright boy who has steadily improved and worked hard. His written work is consistently good, but homeworks could be more thorough, methodical and neat. He could also ask and answer more questions in class. At the moment, physics is his weakest area; he must made sure that he puts extra effort in here so that it does not develop into a long-term weakness. His performance in the Standard Assessment Tests (SATs) did not reflect his term performance. This is perhaps because he did not revise thoroughly, or with method and organization. If he continues to work hard, he is capable of a good performance at GCSE.

Signed: A. Teacher

Figure 6.1.6 A School report, 1999

By contrast other research has shown that the use of assessment to develop pupils' future learning makes a substantial difference to pupils' attitude to learning, to their engagement with school subjects, to their motivation as well as their attainment (Black *et al.*, 2003; Black and Wiliam, 1998; Murphy, 1999). Black *et al.* (2003) argue that assessment for learning could do more to improve educational outcomes than almost any other investment in education. Thus good assessment practice may have a profound influence on learning. You may like to refer to Task 6.2.1 to consider aspects of assessment in your own education.

Developing an intelligent understanding of assessment for learning as early as possible in your professional career will make a big difference to how much you are able to find your assessment of pupils' work and progress purposeful and worthwhile. There are some tensions between assessment for learning and other functions of assessment; we turn first to what 'assessment for learning' means.

WHAT DOES 'ASSESSMENT FOR LEARNING' MEAN?

We referred earlier to formative assessment as assessment which provides information which can aid further progress, diagnose reasons for both good and poor performance, and target particular learning needs. Black *et al.* (2003) go further and define 'assessment for learning' as 'any assessment for which the first priority is to serve the purpose of promoting students' learning'. An assessment activity can help learning 'if it provides information to be used as feedback by teachers, and by their students in assessing themselves and each other, to modify the teaching and learning activities in which they are engaged'.

An important feature of good formative assessment practice is the integration of assessment activities into day-to-day teaching activities rather than them being 'tacked-on' as a separate activity. Such assessments can be a worthwhile learning experience for pupils and not just an administrative task to measure learning; they should 'occur in the context of students working on problems, projects or products which genuinely engage them, which hold their interest and which motivate them to do well' (Gardner, H., 1999: 103).

A useful supporting idea is the 'planning loop', which encompasses your learning objectives, how to achieve them, teaching, assessing and evaluating, and from which a revised set of learning objectives emerges; see Figure 6.1.7.

This does not mean that every lesson has to have an in-built test but:

> rather, a more subtle form of ongoing probing and reviewing should be employed which will be sufficient to enable you to feel confident that the intended learning is occurring. Nevertheless, there is a role here for formal tests from time to time and also the use of homework to explicitly probe the learning covered.
>
> (Kyriacou, 1998: 25)

Assessment activities should be varied to gain insights into pupils' understanding of what they are being asked to learn, calling on the wide range of teaching strategies employed by teachers. These include, for example, written tasks, skilful and sustained questioning, and discussion with the whole class of what is to be learned. In addition, teachers look for opportunities to talk to individual pupils about their work. Other assessment strategies include asking pupils to draw mind maps, spider diagrams, giving a short oral presentation or submitting a poster summarizing their work. It is important not to rely on one form of testing, such as pupils' written work, when making judgements on performance.

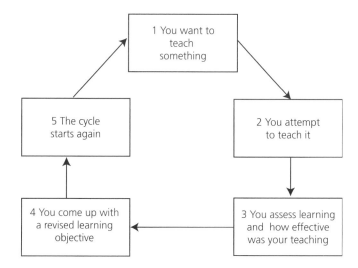

At stage 1 of the cycle, part of your thinking should be about how to assess pupil learning and the effectiveness of your teaching.

Figure 6.1.7   The planning/teaching/assessment/planning loop

Teaching and learning are different activities; you should not assume that 'because you have taught it, pupils have therefore learned it'. In many lessons, some, many or even all the pupils fail to understand some of the things that the teacher is trying to teach. Assessment for learning helps you, for example, to decide:

- Have my pupils really understood what I am trying to teach, or might they forget it in a few days?
- Which bits have they grasped and which bits are still unlearned or only partially understood?
- Do I need to go over the topic again and, if so, with some or all of the pupils?
- What do I teach next?

Task 6.1.3
Evaluation and lesson planning

Student teachers often evaluate their lesson before they have marked pupils' work or before the 'recap' questioning at the start of the next lesson. Mark your pupils' books and question your pupils about the previous lesson *before* writing up your evaluation for the lesson and consider what effect this has on your evaluation.

There is some research evidence to show that both school pupils and university graduates alike can be unsure of their subject; see the QED documentary, 'Simple Minds', about learners' misconceptions in science (Dickinson, 1998: 17).

Assessing for learning must go beyond testing recall to develop understanding and assessment should be seen by pupils as part of learning, rather than as an administered test. The task should test what Harlen terms 'real learning' rather than simply regurgitation of information (Harlen 1995: 14). Learning implies understanding which can be demonstrated by using new knowledge; as one writer has put it, 'The chasm between knowing X and using X to think about Y' (Wineburg, 1997: 256).

Another commentator has said, about understanding:

I feel I understand something if I can do some, at least, of the following:

- state it in my own words;
- give examples of it;
- recognize it in various guises and circumstances;
- see connections between it and other facts or ideas;
- make use of it in various ways;
- foresee some of its consequences;
- state its opposite or converse;

and it may help us in the future to find out what our students really know as opposed to what they can give the appearance of knowing, their real learning as opposed to their apparent learning.

(Holt, 1964: 176)

Thus assessment activities help answer questions such as:

- Can your pupils only answer questions correctly if you asked them exactly the same question as in the lesson, rather than asking them in a slightly different way?
- Can they make connections with contingent aspects of the topic?

As Driver has remarked 'If you want to give someone directions, one of the first questions you would ask is "Where are you now?"' (Driver, 1994: 42). If you want to teach pupils something new, find out first what they know.

An important way to promote learning is develop explicit *learning objectives* and *learning outcomes* (measurable objectives) and share them with your pupils in a way they can understand. This means talking with them about their learning. It helps improve learning for understanding if you share with them, e.g.:

- criteria you use to judge their performance, e.g. quality of preparation and research, marshalling of information, structure, delivery, eye contact, answering of questions, etc.;
- specific performance indicators for judging a task, e.g. a presentation or an essay;
- effective ways of working in a group;
- examples of a good response.

Figure 6.1.8 shows an assessment instrument which attempts to get pupils to think about what is involved in working successfully in groups. There is evidence that, when they had been given clear guidelines about what constitutes good practice in 'working in groups', under-achieving pupils improved (Underwood, 1998).

As well as providing information to pupils about your learning outcomes, you need a clear picture of 'progression' in your subject, i.e. to know what it means 'to get better at geography' in order to help pupils and plan lessons. An example of progression might be the degree of sophistication with which pupils 'appreciate the interdependence of places' (Lambert and Balderstone, 2000: 79); or the 'different levels of explanations for levers' (Frost and Turner, 2004:117). The subject books in the series 'Learning

Name	
People in my group	
TASK	
DID I …	
Make sure I knew what we were supposed to do?	
Make a contribution to discussion?	
Listen to other people's ideas?	
Make suggestions to improve other people's ideas?	
Encourage other people to share their ideas?	
Give people good reasons when I did not agree with them?	
Avoid putting other people down?	
Talk to someone I don't usually talk to?	
Develop my understanding of the task by working with others	
AS A GROUP DID WE …	
Make sure that everyone had something to do and joined in?	
Keep on task?	
Come to agreements on what to do?	
Make compromises about what to do?	
Finish the task on time?	
Feedback our ideas clearly to the rest of the class?	

Figure 6.1.8   A pupil self-assessment exercise

to Teach [subject name] in the Secondary School' (RoutledgeFalmer) provide subject discussion of progression, as do the attainment targets for the NC for England.

A further positive way of improving learning is to involve pupils in their learning and try to develop pupils' understanding of the processes, issues and problems involved in learning. For example, pupils may be asked to:

- make their own judgement on the extent to which they have learned something;
- mark each other's work;
- give 'critical friend' advice to their peers;
- draw up a mark scheme and performance criteria themselves.

Such strategies shift assessment responsibilities towards the pupil and thus emphasize the importance to the pupil of taking more responsibility for their own learning. Teachers need to convey to pupils the nature of the 'gap' which exists between their current level of performance and what is desirable, and what needed to bridge that gap (Clarke, 2001).

Finally, it is important that assessment information is used to move pupils forward in their learning. The full benefits which might be derived from diagnostic assessment only accrue if teachers, having found out about pupil misconceptions and gaps in understanding, go on to use this information in some purposeful way (Black *et al.*, 2003).

Some common weaknesses in current assessment practice

Teaching is something that can be 'delivered', with pupils adopting a fairly passive role; or it can be 'interactive'. Interaction between teacher and pupils, or between pupils, is often the source of useful information about how much learning is going on. Research evidence suggests, however, that many teachers never talk to their pupils about their work, or praise them when they have produced good work (National Commission for Education, 1993: 205); and that much marking is unfocused, often lacking guidance on how to improve (OFSTED, 1996: 40).

There is often an overemphasis on marks, grades and levels at the expense of giving useful advice on how to improve. In particular, the marking of individual pieces of pupils' work to ascribe an NC level to their performance has been criticized (Wiliam, 2001; OFSTED, 2003b; Burnham and Brown, 2004). The NC for England requirement is to give a level for every pupil at the end of each Key Stage, not every few weeks.

Teachers do a lot of marking but the time and effort involved is worthwhile only when it provides clear guidance for pupils on how to improve:

> There's an awful lot of giving smiley faces at the bottom of children's work and very elaborate praise and stars and so on. They are fine for maintaining pupils' motivation and making children feel good about it, but unless it's accompanied by more direct specific advice about what to do to make the piece of work better it's actually of very little help to pupils as a learning activity. It actually helps the pupil to be told directly but kindly, what it is they are not doing very well so that they know how to do it better.
>
> (Gipps, 1997: 9)

Figure 6.1.9 provides examples of teachers' written comments. They should give you some pause for thought about exactly what you might write in pupils' books, given that this is a very time-consuming process. Task 6.1.4 invites you to review your own marking.

Comments over a term on the work of an able Year 9 pupil (Pupil A), and a less able pupil in Year 7 (Pupil B).

Pupil A:
(16/9)   Excellent, well explained and well balanced. 17 out of 20.
(19/9)   Good. 16 out of 20.
(26/9)   Excellent. 26 out of 30.
(10/10)   Neat and well explained. 17 out of 20.
(17/10)   Excellent presentation. 10 out of 10.
(31/10)   Excellent work. 17 out of 20.
(14/11)   Thorough and well balanced, excellent work. 18 out of 20.
(19/11)   Excellent, thorough and well explained. 18 out of 20.
(21/11)   This is the highest mark I have ever given for this test. Relevant, comprehensive and fluently explained. Outstanding work. Well done. 45 out of 50.
(5/12)   Your essay technique is excellent for a Year 9 pupil and you marshal the arguments for and against very fluently. An intelligent and well-balanced assessment. Spelling slightly fallible. 19 out of 20.
(12/12)   Your essay technique continues to impress; concise and relevant. You have a genuine talent for expressing yourself fluently and grasping quite complex historical concepts. 19 out of 20.
(16/12)   Good but too much on Napoleon himself and not enough on the factors which allowed the army to become so powerful. 17 out of 20.
(19/12)   Use paragraphs more. Thorough and well written but too close to the text book in places. 18 out of 20.

Although there is much praise and encouragement, how much feedback is provided which might help the pupil to 'get better' at the subject (history)?

Pupil B:
(5/9)   Get this finished Mark, it's important. No mark.
(10/9)   Good. 8 out of 10.
(12/9)   Try to work more quickly. 2 out of 16.
(17/9)   A good effort. 14 out of 20.
(17/10)   Unfinished.
(24/10)   Rule off! 12 out of 20.
(7/11)   Good on question 1. 9 out of 20.
(14/11)   Neat but try to work faster. No mark.
(4/12)   Use a ruler! 11 out of 20.
(11/12)   A good effort but it doesn't explain WHY William collected all this information. 11 out of 20.
(18/12)   A good homework Mark but use a ruler to draw straight lines. 11 out of 20.

Figure 6.1.9 Comments on an able Year 9 pupil's work, and a less able Year 7 pupil in history over a term

Task 6.1.4
Marking: feedback to pupils

It is easy to be critical of other people's marking of pupils' work: once you have taught a group for several weeks, take a critical look at your own marking. What percentage of comments are genuinely helpful in terms of giving pupils clear guidance on how to make progress in their learning.

SOME TENSIONS AND PROBLEMS IN ASSESSMENT

Fitness for purpose

As you have seen from the earlier sections of this chapter, assessment is made to serve a variety of purposes. For example, the results from one test are used to measure simultaneously the knowledge and understanding of pupils, the quality of teaching and the efficiency of a school. If an assessment instrument is particularly effective for one purpose, it might be very weak for another purpose. It is difficult to devise 'all-purpose' assessment instruments which are both valid and reliable. It is therefore very important that you think about what function you want your assessment activity to achieve.

Are we assessing everything that is worthwhile in pupils' learning or that which is easy to assess?

Some skills are relatively straightforward to identify and others harder to describe and identify. Thus recall is often referred to as lower order skill and may refer to recall of facts, of knowledge 'of' and knowledge 'how'. Lower order skills form the foundation on which many higher order skills function. Being able to *apply knowledge* moves skills up a level but even here one can distinguish applying knowledge to familiar situations, or taught situations, from the context of a new situation which is harder for a learner (higher skill level). See also Table 5.2.2.

Skills used in the analysis of data or of situations, and the synthesis of information into explanations of events both require even higher order skills. The use of imagination, being inventive, thinking laterally are other ways of looking at these higher order skills. These skills are often difficult to assess.

The assessment tension is between validity and reliability. Testing a pupil's ability to do simple addition (either right or wrong) is straightforward compared with assessing the ability to develop reasoned judgements (a subjective decision). The more you gain validity for a test of reasoned judgement the less reliable the test, because such a test becomes complicated, longer and more subjective in its assessment.

You need to be aware that assessing things that are easy to measure may be at the expense of investing time in other worthwhile areas of learning but difficult to assess. A distinction is sometimes made between 'learning outcomes' which are in some way quantifiable, and other educationally worthwhile learning objectives which are difficult to measure.

The key skills of the current NC in England (DfEE/QCA, 1999a) are a good example of this tension. There are tests which reliably measure the application of number, communication and use of information and communications technology (ICT); but it is much harder to devise simple tests of problem solving, or working as part of a team or 'learning how to learn' (metacognition) all equally important skills. The danger for any curriculum is that we might assess only that which is easy to assess rather than that which is important.

Some 20 years ago a set of aims were published in an attempt to counter the overemphasis placed on some achievements through public examinations at the expense of playing down other equally important pupil achievements. They remind us that there is more to assessment than measuring the cognitive development of pupils (Hargreaves, 1984: 2).

The effect on pupils

There is some evidence which suggests that testing pupils from the age of 5 onwards is having a negative effect on some pupils' self-esteem and motivation to learn (Barnard, 2000; Black and Wiliam, 1998). Assessment can be valid and reliable and yet have a profoundly dispiriting influence on pupils' attitude to a subject, and to school in general. Others argue that some assessment practices have contributed to disaffection and disengagement in schools (Elliott, 1998; Macdonald, 2000) and may encourage pupils to truant (Black and Wiliam, 1998: 4). Pupils 'at the bottom of the pile' often do not respond by exhibiting determination to get to the top. It is important, therefore, that you send out a clear message to your pupils that they are capable of learning, improving their performance and benefit from being in your classroom. Positive feedback is part of the support for your pupils' efforts to learn. See Task 6.1.5.

Task 6.1.5
Encouraging weaker and less well motivated pupils

It is not possible to teach pupils without realizing that their *attitude* to learning has a big influence on how successful they are at learning. Talk to teachers in school about:

- how they handle the challenge of providing feedback to pupils who are trying to do well in the subject, but whose progress is limited by lack of ability rather than lack of effort;
- how they try to engage pupils who are reluctant to commit themselves to learning.

High stakes testing and the integrity of assessment

High stakes assessment was discussed earlier in this unit. When much hangs on the outcome of assessment then it is important that the integrity of assessment practice is maintained. Attempts might be made to find ways round the test or to 'lean on' the assessment task to try to make it produce the desired result. One of the dangers of high stakes assessment is that the more important the assessment, the more subject it is to 'corruption processes' (Macdonald, 2000: 31).

When it comes to high stakes testing, there is sometimes pressure on teachers, schools and government agencies to try and present educational outcomes in the most favourable way possible. One facet of reliability in assessment is the extent to which it is 'honest'.

MANAGING ASSESSMENT

We discuss first how to manage your marking and keep your marking under control and, second, to identify your professional development needs now and in the longer term.

Keeping assessment manageable

Teachers have to manage their time effectively and you need to think about how to manage your time, so that assessment does not detract from the rest of your teaching; see also Unit 3.1. It is not practical to mark every piece of pupils' work in the same way without compromising the time available for lesson planning, etc. There are no magic answers to make assessment burdens disappear but there are ways to improve your time management, as listed below. See also Unit 3.1.

Learn to mark flexibly

Some pieces of work require detailed attention and diagnosis; sometimes a light touch monitoring is more appropriate.

Plan marking time

Student teachers tend to set more written tasks than experienced teachers and this produces a heavy marking load. Since lesson planning takes a long time, extra pressure builds. In your planning, try to prepare some lessons which have as one of the objectives not requiring marking to be done in their aftermath or set fewer written tasks which require you to mark them in a time-intensive way. Sometimes pupils can mark their own work, or that of fellow pupils; see below.

Marking codes

Develop a shorthand code for signalling marking corrections, such as symbols for omissions, development, non sequitur, irrelevant, spelling errors, clumsy phrasing.

Common errors

Make brief notes on common errors as you are marking pupils' work so that you can report on them orally to the group as a whole, rather than writing the same comment in several books.

Oral feedback

It takes more than five times as long to write something down compared to saying it so sometimes provide oral feedback to pupils.

Pupil response to tasks

Structure tasks so that sometimes pupils present their work as a poster, a group ICT task or display work. This response may not require you to mark their books although you need to keep records of their performance.

Using ICT

Consider ways in which ICT might help to reduce the administration involved in assessment, recording and reporting. The facility to 'copy', 'cut and paste' and build up an archive of models and exemplars of good and bad responses can save considerable amounts of time (see Leask and Pachler, 1999: ch. 14). In addition, the section of the *Times Educational Supplement* on assessment online at <http://www.tes.co.uk/online/assessit>, and the National Curriculum site online at <http://www.ncaction.org.uk>, are both useful resources.

All marking should let your pupils feel that you care about their progress in your subject. Make room, on occasions, to conduct a rigorous diagnosis of your pupils' written work and provide your pupils with constructive advice and suggestions to improve their learning.

Long-term and short-term goals

You should consider your immediate needs (short-term goals) and your developing needs (long-term goals). The short-term agenda is for you to become effective in your responses to pupils' work, adapting to the demands of the assessment policies of the department in which you are working. The longer-term agenda is for you to develop a sound understanding of the nature and purposes of assessment, how to use the different techniques appropriately and to interpret assessment data and, above all, how to use assessment to improve your teaching, and pupils' learning. These skills are one of the hallmarks of accomplished teachers.

SUMMARY AND KEY POINTS

Although teachers and schools do have to be accountable for their work, the most valuable and important function of assessment is to move pupils forward in their learning. Assessment needs to be built into your planning for teaching and learning, not tacked on as an afterthought. You should be familiar with the idea of assessment as part of the cycle of planning, teaching and assessing, leading into revised planning and teaching.

As well as thinking about how to provide constructive and helpful comments to pupils when responding to their work, you need to use a wide range of strategies which use assessment to develop pupils' learning.

By the end of your course of teacher education, you should be familiar with the range of assessment methods and terminology which are used in schools. You should be aware of the tensions between the different purposes and forms of assessment and of the standards or competences required of you as an NQT in the area of assessment (DfES/TTA, 2004: 10).

Ascribing levels, marks or grades to pupils' work is not unproblematic but it is not the most difficult part of assessment. The most challenging and important part of assessment is saying and doing things which help pupils to make progress in their learning.

FURTHER READING

Black, P., Harrison, C., Lee, C., Marshall, B. and Wiliam, D. (2003) *Assessment for Learning: Putting it into Practice*, Maidenhead: Open University Press. Addresses the practical implications of putting assessment for learning into practice. See also Black and Wiliam (1998) for a concise introduction to formative assessment.

Harlen, W. (1995) 'To the rescue of formative assessment', *Primary Science Review*, 37 (April), 14–15. This article provides suggestions for key principles in effective assessment.

Headington, R. (2000) *Monitoring, Assessment, Recording, Reporting and Accountability: Meeting the Standards*, London: David Fulton. This book is written specifically for student teachers.

Murphy, P. (ed.) (1999) *Learners, Learning and Assessment*, London: Paul Chapman for the Open University. This book is particularly helpful in terms of providing insight into subject specific assessment issues.

Times Educational Supplement (TES) (2000) Online. See websites below. This website focuses on assessment issues and is a good way of keeping up to date with recent developments.

Useful websites

Department for Education and Skills. *National Curriculum for England*: <http://www.nc.uk.net>.

Centre for Education and Management, University of Durham: <http://www.cemcentre.org> (accessed 25 August 2004).

National Foundation for Educational Research. *Cognitive Abilities Test*: <http://www.nfer-nelson.co.uk> (accessed 25 August 2004).

Times Educational Supplement (TES): <http://www.tes.co.uk/online/assessit/> (accessed 25 August 2004).

University of East Anglia Norwich Area Schools Consortium Project (NASC): <http://www.uea.ac.uk/~m242/nasc/cross/cman/profchar.htm> (accessed 7 September 2004).

University of East Anglia. History PGCE Site: <http://www.uea.ac.uk/~m242/historypgce/assess> (accessed 7 September 2004).

Unit 6.2

External Assessment and Examinations

Bernadette Youens

INTRODUCTION

Principles of assessment were introduced in Unit 6.1, which highlighted the importance that this aspect of education has assumed since the Education Reform Act of 1988 (ERA 1988). This Act included the publication of a report by the Task Group on Assessment and Testing (TGAT) recommending strategies for assessing and reporting pupils' progress in the National Curriculum (NC) in England (DES/WO, 1988). This unit looks at the particular role, function and nature of external assessment and examinations. Before reading this unit we suggest you work through Unit 6.1. The relationship between the NC and the subject of this unit is a key one to understand and you should refer also to Unit 7.3 which focuses on the NC of England.

This unit aims to provide you with an overview of the framework for external assessment and examinations in secondary schools. Although you are familiar with the public examinations that you took in school, in recent years there have been significant developments in assessment methods and in the range of external examinations taken by pupils in secondary schools. In England this has been particularly true in the 14–19 sector of education, which has seen the growth of vocationally related courses which are taught in secondary schools alongside the General Certificate of Secondary Education (GCSE) and the General Certificate of Education at Advanced level (GCSE A level).

As well as looking at how pupils are assessed throughout their secondary education, it is important to be aware of the many purposes of external assessment and examinations. These purposes can be usefully divided into those associated with candidates and those that have more to do with educational establishments and public accountability; see Unit 6.1.

Two important, recurrent themes which arise when discussing external assessment and examinations are validity and reliability. These two concepts, together with the agencies, regulations and processes involved in ensuring consistency in these two areas, are discussed in Unit 6.1.

Teaching externally examined classes is a challenge for any teacher and demands particular teaching skills and strategies in addition to the routine elements of good lesson planning and teaching. This aspect of teaching is discussed in the final part of this section.

OBJECTIVES

By the end of this unit you should:

- be familiar with the range of external assessment in secondary schools and with the national framework for qualifications;
- have an understanding of the relationship between the National Curriculum in England and external examinations;
- be aware of the main purposes of assessment;
- know the processes involved in external examining and know of the institutions involved;
- have started to consider the issues relating to teaching examination classes;
- be able to identify the competence/standards for your course related to assessment.

YOUR OWN EXPERIENCE

A good starting point for this chapter is your own experience of external assessment and examinations. Task 6.2.1 invites you to recall this period of your education.

Task 6.2.1
Your personal experience of external examinations and assessment

Think back to your time at school. As a pupil what did you think that the purpose of sitting exams was? How did preparing for examinations impact on your motivation as a learner? Did the teaching strategies of examination classes differ from non-examination classes? Thinking through these points may provide you with a good personal starting point before you go on to develop your understanding of the wider issues pertaining to external assessment and examinations.

TYPES OF ASSESSMENT

In Unit 6.1, we discussed formative and summative assessment and we remind you of those terms. Formative assessment can be defined as assessment *for* learning, and summative assessment as assessment *of* learning (Stobart and Gipps, 1997). External assessment and examinations are generally considered to be forms of summative assessment. There are two important methods used extensively in summative assessment that you will need to be familiar with, namely, norm-referenced assessment and criterion-referenced assessment.

Norm-referenced assessment is the traditional means of assessing candidates and has been used extensively throughout the British education system. In norm-referenced assessment, the value of, or grade related to, any mark awarded depends on how it compares with the marks of other candidates sitting the same examination. The basis for this form of assessment is the assumption that the marks are normally distributed, i.e. if you plot the marks awarded against the number of candidates, a bell-shaped curve is produced, providing the sample is big enough. This curve is then used to assign grade boundaries based on predetermined conditions, e.g. that 80 per cent of all those sitting the examination will pass and 20 per cent will fail. In this way an element of failure is built into the examination. The system of reporting by grades is essentially norm-referenced. For example, if you are awarded the highest grade (A★) in a subject at GCSE this grade does not give any specific information about what you can do in that subject, simply that you were placed within a top group of candidates.

Criterion-referenced assessment, on the other hand, is concerned with what a candidate can do *without* reference to the performance of others, and so provides an alternative method to address the limitations of norm-referencing. A simple example of criterion-referenced assessment is that of a swimming test. If a person is entered for a 100-metre swimming award, and swims 100 metres, then she is awarded that certificate irrespective of how many other people also reach this standard. Vocational courses use criterion-referenced assessment, to which we return later. Academic courses, such as GCSE science, use criterion-referencing when assessing practical skills as part of the coursework element of the course. In this example the results are reported by comparing pupils with other pupils, i.e. norm-referenced. The overall assessment in this case is a mixture of norm- and criterion-referencing.

THE FRAMEWORK OF EXTERNAL ASSESSMENT IN SECONDARY SCHOOLS

We consider in turn Key Stage 3, GCSE and post-16 education in England. Different arrangements are in place in Wales, Scotland and Northern Ireland.

Key Stage 3 assessment

On transfer to secondary school pupils bring with them information obtained from the end of Key Stage 2 assessment, arising from both internal teacher assessment and external assessment. This information is usually reported as NC levels; see Unit 7.3. Pupils are assessed again at the end of Key Stage 3 to determine their attainment and to measure progression, again reported as NC levels.

External assessment at the end of Key Stage 3 takes the form of written tests, called Standard Assessments Tasks (SATs), for the core NC subjects of English, mathematics and science. The form of the SATs now taken by pupils are far removed from the original activity-based assessment tasks advocated by the report of the Task Group on Assessment and Testing (TGAT) (DES/WO, 1988). The TGAT report recommended that assessment should be embedded within classroom practice rather than being 'bolt-on' activities because the latter approach would eventually drive the curriculum; i.e. teaching becomes test-oriented. The integration of assessment with teaching and learning is discussed also in Unit 6.1.

The framework initially proposed by TGAT was of a national assessment system for all pupils up to the age of 16 based on specified criteria, rather than the age-related norm-referenced system which had dominated assessment previously. Teachers were also to be involved in summative assessment and not just formative assessment. Another major change suggested by the TGAT report was that assessment should measure pupils' progress rather continuously measure their relative failure. How these proposals worked out in practice is discussed below. For a more detailed discussion of the TGAT report please refer to Daugherty (1995).

The initial NC tests were criterion-referenced, with each question being ascribed a certain level, and the tests marked by teachers. However, this system proved both unmanageable and unacceptable to the teaching profession. The system was unmanageable because of the heavy additional load on teachers and unacceptable because there was no additional financial reward. Traditionally public examinations are marked externally by paid examiners; the SATs are now set by external agencies and marked by paid, external markers. The SAT tests are written with reference to the subject Programmes of Study of the NC (see Unit 7.3); the questions in the tests are designed so that the demand on the pupil links closely to the level descriptions. Papers are set for each of the core subjects and tiered assessment is used to allow pupils to be entered for the paper most suited to their ability.

In English one common paper is set to assess all pupils working within NC levels 4–7; pupils working at level 3 or below do not sit an external SAT paper. In mathematics and science differentiated papers are set to assess pupils across a narrower range of NC levels. In science two papers are set, one to assess pupils working within levels 3–6 and another to assess pupils working within levels 4–7. In mathematics the papers are even further differentiated, with four papers set to assess pupils working within levels 3–5, 4–6, 5–7 or 6–8. On each paper an allocation of marks is awarded to each question and grade boundaries are decided by a process known as levelling. This procedure involves deciding how many marks on the test are required for the award of each level.

There is an initial process of setting draft thresholds which are confirmed later by marking a sample of papers. Thus the setting of SATs questions is criterion-referenced while the marking is based on normative methods. Schools are statutorily required also to provide teacher-assessed levels for all attainment targets and an overall assessment level for each of the core and foundation subjects. In this way, the progress of each pupil can be identified and reported, which was one intention of the TGAT recommendations as well as being a central tenet of the National Curriculum. In 2004, the proportion of all pupils achieving NC Level 5 or above in written SATs at KS3 in English, with 1999 figures in brackets, was 71 per cent (64), in mathematics 73 per cent (62) and in science 66 per cent (55) (DfES/TTA, 2004: autumn package of guidance, provided annually).

The GCSE

The GCSE was first introduced in 1986 as the examination to be taken at the end of Key Stage 4. The GCSE examination was designed both to replace the General Certificate in Education (GCE) O level and Certificate of Secondary Education (CSE) and to provide certification for a much greater percentage of candidates. Historically, the GCE O level aimed to certificate 20–30 per cent of pupils in any year and the CSE a further 40 per cent. Prior to the introduction of the GCSE, up to 40 per cent of pupils therefore left school without any formal recognition of their achievements. Alternative qualifications, such as the Royal Society of Arts examination, were less prestigious.

One of the aims of the new GCSE examination was to certificate 90 per cent of the cohort in any year. Seven pass grades could be awarded, from A to G and in 1994 an additional grade, A★, was added to recognize exceptional performance. The GCSE examinations also differed from the GCE O level examination in that it was designed to test not only recall, but also understanding and skills. Because nearly all pupils take the GCSE examination, assessment techniques had to be developed to cope with such a broad range of achievement. A range of strategies was introduced to achieve differentiation and so provide all pupils with the opportunity to show what they had learnt through studying the course being examined. To achieve this aim, a tiered assessment pattern was introduced, a strategy later adopted for the NC SATs, to enable pupils to be entered for the paper most appropriate for their ability. This situation requires teachers to assess pupils' progress and potential and to advise pupils on which tier of the examination to enter.

Tiered papers carry grade limits, thus narrowing the opportunities of pupils. For example, a higher paper may enable pupils to be awarded grades A★–D, while a foundation paper may allow only the award of grades C–G. Furthermore, if pupils fail to achieve the marks required for the lowest grade in their tier then they receive an unclassified grade. In the early years of the GCSE examination significant numbers of pupils 'fell off the bottom' of their grade range and were awarded an unclassified grade.

Coursework was also introduced with the GCSE and has proved to be a great motivator for pupils. In the early days of GCSE some of the courses offered were entirely coursework-based. However, the amount of coursework is now restricted by legislation by the Qualifications and Curriculum Authority (QCA) through the subject specifications and depends on the subject. In the more practically based subjects (e.g. music, physical education) a larger proportion of teacher-based assessment contributes to the final mark than in other subjects. In music the upper limit in practice is about 60 per cent, whereas in physical education a maximum of 25 per cent of the total mark is commonly awarded for coursework. No subject is allowed to be assessed only by teacher-assessed coursework.

Thus the GCSE examination, like the external assessment of the NC at the end of Key Stage 3, also combines norm-referenced methods with criterion-referenced methods. Coursework is an integral feature of the GCSE examination and it is important that you have a clear understanding of this part of the examination; Task 6.2.2 asks you to address this issue.

Task 6.2.2
GCSE coursework

Working with another student teacher in your own subject specialism, obtain a copy of a recent GCSE specification. Read the general introduction and then familiarize yourself with the aims, assessment objectives and assessment patterns of the specification. Now turn to the coursework section and find out the following information:

*   how much of the overall mark is allocated to coursework?
*   what form does the coursework take?
*   how is the coursework assessed?
*   what information about course work criteria is given to candidates?

Once you have found out this information, discuss your findings with an experienced teacher in your school experience school. Ask if you can have access to some samples of coursework from pupils at the school, and use them to find out:

*   how the coursework is introduced to pupils;
*   the range of tasks set;
*   how these tasks are made accessible and relevant to pupils.

Now try assessing the coursework samples yourself using the criteria supplied by the examining body and any internal marking schemes used by the school. Discuss your marking with a member of staff and find out how the department internally moderates coursework. Find out, too, from the coursework specifications what processes the examining authority uses to externally moderate coursework.

Check the standards/competences expected of you in your course which relate to coursework in public examinations. A record of your work could be placed in your professional portfolio.

POST-16 ASSESSMENT

Of all of the changes that have followed the ERA 1988 the area that has continued to undergo reorganization is the provision of post-16 courses and their assessment.

GCE A level courses

GCE A level courses were first introduced in 1951 and since then have been regarded as the academic 'gold standard' by successive governments. In 1995, Lord Dearing was commissioned to look at strategies to strengthen, consolidate and improve the framework of 16–19 qualifications. As a result of this review, changes to the post-16 curriculum were introduced in September 2000 (Dearing, 1996).

GCE A level courses remained, but each subject is now composed of six discrete units of approximately the same size. The first three units make up an Advanced Subsidiary course, called AS, representing the first half of an advanced level course of study. The other three units, which make up the second part of the GCE A level, are known as A2. One of the aims of the AS proposal was to provide a more appropriate and manageable 'bridge' between GCSE and GCE A level. The AS course may be taken as a qualification in itself or it may be used as a foundation to study the A2 section of the course.

GCE A levels, like GCSE examinations, may be assessed in stages, as in a modular course, or terminally. The introduction of modular assessment has proved to be very popular with candidates. Dearing listed the main advantages of modularity as:

- motivating pupils to maintain a high, constant commitment throughout their course;
- providing valuable diagnostic information from early results;
- providing the opportunity to have achievement recognized (Dearing, 1996).

Dearing noted also that, on analysis of the examination results, candidates taking the modular route gained higher average point scores in most subjects. Concern about the fact that candidates could resit particular modules any number of times has been addressed and it is now possible to resit any particular module only once.

All GCE A2 courses must include an element of synoptic assessment designed to test a candidate's ability to make connections between different aspects of the course. There is no synoptic assessment at AS level. The synoptic element must normally contribute 20 per cent to the full A level and take the form of external assessment at the end of the course. GCE A level pass grades range from A to E with A the highest grade. As with GCSE examinations there is also teacher assessment of coursework in GCE but there is no upper limit set by the QCA. In practice, the amount of teacher-assessed coursework is set by the QCA subject specification. For example, in GCE A level English there is up to 30 per cent teacher-assessed coursework.

Advanced Extension Awards (AEAs), introduced in 2002 to replace the Special papers at GCE A level, were designed to challenge the most able advanced level students at a standard comparable with the most demanding tests found in other countries. A further stated aim of the AEAs is to assist universities to differentiate between the most able candidates, particularly in subjects with a high proportion of A grades at advanced level.

Vocational courses

The main vocational qualifications traditionally encountered in secondary schools in England have been the General National Vocational Qualifications (GNVQs) which were introduced into schools in 1992 and developed from National Vocational Qualifications (NVQs).

The NVQs are work-related, competence-based qualifications and the courses were designed for people in work or undertaking work-based training. NVQ courses provide job-specific training, the assessment of which takes place in the work environment and is criterion-referenced. Central to the NVQ model is the idea of competence to perform a particular job, where competence is defined as the mastery of identified performance skills.

GNVQs were introduced to provide pupils with an introduction to occupational sectors through school- or college-based courses. Indeed one of the principal aims of the GNVQ was to provide a middle road between the general academic route and occupational courses, such as the NVQs described above.

One of the main stumbling blocks to the uptake of vocational qualifications by schools was the difference in assessment practice and terminology between academic and vocational courses. This situation was acknowledged in the Dearing Report on 16–19 qualifications which identified the need for a coherent qualifications framework encompassing all national qualifications and which provides equivalent status for vocational qualifications (Dearing, 1996). Following that report, vocational GCSE and vocational GCE A levels were introduced, accompanied by a timetable for the phased withdrawal of GNVQ courses. Vocational qualifications at both GCE A level and GCSE are now offered alongside academic qualifications, with pupils at both levels maintaining their study of core curriculum subjects. The purpose of these developments together with the other reforms outlined is to encourage Key Stage 4 pupils and post-16 students to broaden their programme of study to include vocational courses. The National Qualifications framework in Table 6.2.1 shows how the three qualification strands discussed are intended to overlap.

The framework for national qualifications was revised in September 2004 and now has a total of nine separate levels of qualification (entry level to level 8). The Framework is available online at <http://www.qca.org.uk/qualifications/493.html> (accessed 23 Oct. 2004). See also Brooks and Lucas (2004).

GCSE qualifications in vocational subjects were first introduced in September 2002 and are offered in eight subjects, e.g. applied art and design, leisure and tourism. Each course consists of three common, compulsory and normally equally weighted units in each subject. The qualification is equivalent to two GCSEs and is graded, like GCSEs, from A*–U, covering both level 1 and level 2 of the national qualifications framework (Table 6.2.1).

Table 6.2.1   Framework of national qualifications (entry level to level 3 only)

Level of qualification	General qualifications
3	A level grades A–E
2	GCSE grades A*–C
1	GCSE grades D–G
Entry	Certificate of (educational) achievement

Vocational A levels are available at three different levels:

- Advanced Subsidiary Vocational Certificate of Education (3 units);
- Advanced Vocational Certificate of Education (6 units);
- Advanced Vocational Certificate of Education (Double Award) (12 units).

The units assigned to each qualification are intended to be comparable to the GCE A level units described earlier in this section. Vocational GCE A levels are reported using the grade range A–E so that direct comparisons with GCE A level can be made (see Table 6.2.1).

Vocational courses are assessed through an internally assessed portfolio of evidence and externally set tests, projects or case-study work. As with other examinations, the internal assessment is externally moderated. In general, the portfolio contributes two-thirds of the final mark and the external assessment the remaining third. Each unit is graded and these grades are aggregated to produce a mean grade for the whole qualification. Further discussion of vocational courses can be found in Brooks and Lucas (2004).

THE PURPOSES OF EXTERNAL ASSESSMENT

External assessment and examinations feature prominently throughout secondary school education. If the time and resources spent on this form of assessment are to be justified then it is important that the purposes of external assessment are fully understood. There is a long-standing history in the United Kingdom of externally examining pupils at particular stages in their education, which is quite different from the practice in some other countries. For example, Australia has not had public examinations for many years (Gipps, 1997). In recent years in England this practice has extended to the external assessment of pupils at the end of Key Stages 2 and 3. The purposes of external, summative assessment can be thought of in terms of certificating candidates and the public accountability of teachers and schools.

One of the main functions of summative assessment is to categorize candidates. There are a number of reasons why we would want to categorize pupils, which include selecting candidates for higher education, employing people for particular jobs, or to recognize achievement. In the case of national examinations this means providing pupils with a grade that they and other people can use to compare them with other candidates. The grades can then be used to select pupils either for further education or for employment purposes.

A second recognized function of external assessment is that of certification. If you hold a certificate then it is evidence that competence in particular skills has been achieved. For example, if you hold a driving licence this is evidence that in a driving test you successfully performed a hill start, completed a three-point turn, reversed around a corner and so on. The significance to pupils, of both the categorizing and certification purposes, is evidenced by the fact that an impending examination provides an incentive for pupils to concentrate on their studies and to acquire the relevant knowledge and skills required by the examination for which they are entered. Thus a further function of external examinations is to provide motivation for both pupils and teachers. Motivation is discussed in greater detail in Unit 3.2.

Public accountability

One reason why assessment is so high on the political agenda at present is because it is inextricably linked with the notion of raising standards and school improvement. Since 1982 schools have been statutorily required to publish examination results, with the aim of providing parents with more information and of making schools more accountable. The statutory requirements were extended in 1992 to include a detailed breakdown not only of performance but additional statistics such as number of pupils on the roll with SEN, but without statements. This information is published each autumn as achievement and attainment tables, often referred to simply as the 'league tables'; see Unit 6.1. Although a variety of statistical information is published each autumn, currently schools in England are placed in rank order based on just one variable, the percentage of pupils gaining five or more GCSE passes at grades A★–C. The high profile given to the achievement and attainment tables by the different stakeholders in the education process has led schools to implement strategies to increase the percentage of their pupils achieving five or more A★–C grades. For example, schools often target pupils predicted to achieve grade Ds at GCSE for additional mentoring and academic support as part of the school's strategy to increase the number of pupils achieving grade Cs in their GCSE exams. The introduction of external assessment of pupils at the end of Key Stages 2 and 3 has also had a significant impact on the teaching of pupils in this age range, providing further evidence of the effect that so-called 'high stakes' external assessment has on classroom practice. The term 'high stakes' is used to describe assessment that has significant consequences for either the candidate or the school; see Unit 6.1.

In addition to the school achievement and attainment, since September 1998 all schools in England and Wales have had to set and publish targets for all pupils aged 11–16 in order to demonstrate year-on-year improvements. To assist schools with this process, all schools in England are sent annually, in the autumn, a Package of Pupil Performance Information (PPPI). This package includes a summary of national results of assessments and value-added information to enable schools to compare the progress made by individual pupils in their school with progress made by pupils with similar prior attainment in other schools. This package contains benchmark data so that schools can compare whole-school performance with that of schools with similar intakes and profiles.

Additional information in the PPPI is performance and assessment data, usually referred to as PANDAs, which are compiled on the basis of school inspection data. PANDAs are used by OFSTED in their preparation prior to school inspection and are contained in a document called Pre-Inspection and Contextual School Indicators (PICSI) (OFSTED, 1998: 1 and annex 1).

The central government in England also sets national targets to 'build on the progress to date, raise attainment nationally and also narrow the achievement gap'. To help schools to achieve the national targets set, the government has introduced a raft of initiatives aimed at raising pupil attainment at Key Stage 3. For example, over a number of years concern was expressed about the perceived overall lack of progress made by pupils at Key Stage 3 (OFSTED, 2000; QCA, 2000). In response to these observations, the Key Stage 3 Strategy was introduced (DfES, 2001, 2003e). A further, separate set of tests in English and mathematics, the Year 7 progress tests, are available for pupils who did not achieve level 4 at the end of Key Stage 2, and who are assessed to be working at level 3 or 4 during Year 7. These tests set by QCA and are marked by external examiners.

A further example of an initiative in the drive to raise national standards in England is that, from September 2005, schools can purchase additional tests from the Qualifications and Curriculum Authority (QCA), in order to assess pupil's progress. These tests are marked by teachers. By collecting information on pupils' progress in mathematics and English in this way in the school years not covered by statutory tests, i.e. years 7 and 8, schools are supported in monitoring pupils' progress in the years between the statutory tests. The tests are designed to contribute to teaching and learning strategies and enable schools to meet targets for achievement by the end of Key Stage 3 (QCA, 2004e).

VALIDITY AND RELIABILITY

We referred earlier in this unit to the concepts of validity and reliability as central to understanding the examining process. These ideas are also discussed in Unit 6.1. For all external assessment and examinations, frameworks of regulations have been developed to ensure that the examination process and the results produced are both valid and reliable. To understand this framework you need to be aware of the institutions and processes involved in this regulation.

The QCA is the government agency that approves all course specifications as well as monitoring examinations through a programme of scrutinies, comparability exercises and probes. The QCA is accountable to the Department for Education and Skills (DfES). At the end of 2003 the government announced the introduction of a new body, the National Assessment Agency (NNA). This agency is a subsidiary agency of the QCA and its remit is to modernize the examination system and to work alongside the unitary awarding bodies. There are three unitary awarding bodies in England that are authorized by the government to offer GCSE, GCE A and AS and GNVQ courses. These three awarding bodies, formed by the merging of a number of examination boards, are given below, together with the addresses of their websites:

- Assessment and Qualifications Alliance (AQA) <http://www.aqa.org.uk/> (accessed 20 Oct. 2004).
- EdExcel <http://www.edexcel.org.uk/> (accessed 20 Oct. 2004).
- Oxford Cambridge and RSA Examinations (OCR) <http://www.ocr.org.uk/OCR/WebSite/docroot/index.jsp> (accessed 20 Oct. 2004).

Following the Guaranteeing Standards' consultation (DfEE, 1997), the formation of a single awarding body was considered but a group of three was thought useful to retain a measure of competition. The key recommendations of the standards' consultation report were:

- for each externally examined course there is a subject core that specifies the core of content that each specification must cover;
- the publication of a detailed code of practice designed to ensure that grading standards are consistent across subjects and across the three awarding bodies, in the same subject, and from year to year;
- that this code of practice should also set out the roles and responsibilities of those involved in the examining process and the key procedures for setting papers, standardizing marking and grading.

The processes employed by the awarding bodies to address the recommendations above and to ensure that the examinations are valid and reliable are outlined in Figure 6.2.1.

TEACHING EXTERNALLY ASSESSED COURSES

All teachers have to think beyond the particular lesson they are teaching to the end of the unit of work, to ensure that pupils can respond successfully to any assessment scheduled to take place. When pupils are assessed externally the same considerations apply, i.e. how to maximize pupils' achievement. However, you do need to be fully aware of the nature of the external assessment for which you are preparing your pupils. It is important not just to teach to the examination but to hold on to the principles of good classroom practice.

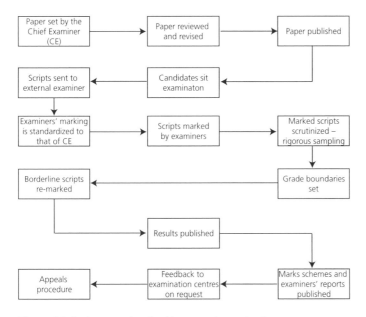

Figure 6.2.1   Processes involved in external examinations

In preparing your pupils for external examinations you need to be familiar with the subject content, the types of questions set in the examination, and the language used in setting questions. Questions are set which often employ words with a specific meaning, e.g. they ask candidates to describe, or explain, or use short notes or summarize. Candidates need to know what these words mean in

---

Task 6.2.3
Using examination papers in your teaching

Collect together a number of GCSE examination papers for your subject together with the mark schemes and specification. Where possible also obtain the relevant examiners' reports which are sent to all schools offering candidates to that awarding body. Read through the specification for the examination arrangements. Then address the questions in the paper in the following way:

- Answer the questions yourself.
- Mark your answers using the mark scheme.
- Evaluate your answers and marking and identify the key knowledge and concepts needed to gain maximum marks. Look back at the examination questions; identify the key words and phrases most often used in the questions.
- Use the examiners' report to refine and review your findings.
- Identify any ideas that might be useful to consider in your day-to-day teaching.
- Repeat the exercise for other years of the same paper; or repeat the exercise using papers set at a different level, e.g. GCE A level.

A completed task should be placed in your professional portfolio.
    Check the standards/competences required in your course which relate to preparing pupils for public examinations.

examination conditions. Task 6.2.3 is designed to help you become familiar with types of questions currently set in examination papers in your own subject and the corresponding reports of examiners.

Once you are familiar with the structure and the language used in past papers you can then integrate this information into your teaching throughout the course. Another important aspect to consider is the development of study skills both in your lessons and throughout the school, see Task 6.2.4. For further advice on developing study skills see Balderstone and King (2004).

Task 6.2.4
Study skills

> Discuss with your tutor or other experienced teacher in your school experience school the whole-school and departmental approaches available to support the development of pupils' study skills. These skills include, e.g. managing coursework, planning and supporting revision, and time management. Use the information you gain to identify strategies to integrate into your teaching. Check the standards/competences required in your course which relate to developing study skills.

SUMMARY AND KEY POINTS

In this unit we have linked the framework for external assessment and examinations with the nature and purposes of summative assessment. Both National Curriculum assessment and external examinations utilize aspects of both norm-referenced and criterion-referenced methods, and this is an important feature of assessment of which you need to be aware and understand. Norm-referencing and criterion-referencing are factors used in discussions seeking to explain the steady increase in the proportion of candidates achieving A★–C grades. The changes recently introduced to the post-16 sector of education aim to encourage students to broaden their studies to include vocational courses alongside traditional academic courses. As this book went to press the long-awaited Tomlinson Report was released proposing a unified framework for 14–19 learning (DfES, 2004i). It will be interesting and important for you to monitor the impact of these reforms on the 14–19 curriculum over the next few years. Check your course requirements for the standards/competences expected of you related to assessment and public examinations.

There are likely to be further innovations in approaches to assessment and, as long as there remains a political focus on raising standards in our schools, external assessment and examinations will maintain their present high profile and powerful influence in educational practice.

FURTHER READING

Stobart, G. and Gipps, C. (1997) *Assessment: A Teacher's Guide to the Issues*, London: Hodder and Stoughton. A very accessible, readable guide to contemporary assessment issues.

James, M. (1998) *Using Assessment for School Improvement*, London: Heinemann. A comprehensive yet very readable book that discusses all aspects of assessment.

Department for Education and Skills <http://www.dfes.gov.uk/> (accessed 20 Oct. 2004). An informative website that is particularly useful for looking at school achievement and attainment tables, autumn package information and for up-to-date information about government initiatives.

Qualifications and Curriculum Authority <http://www.qca.org.uk/> (accessed 20 Oct. 2004). A very useful website for detailed information on the range of qualifications available in secondary school as well as current information on NC tests.

Brooks, V. (2002) *Assessment in Secondary Schools: The New Teacher's Guide to Monitoring, Assessment, Recording, Reporting and Accountability*, Buckingham: Open University Press. A comprehensive introduction, written specifically for new teachers, to all aspects of assessment in the secondary school.

7 The School, Curriculum and Society

This chapter takes you away from the immediacy of teaching to consider the aims of education, how those aims might be identified and, more importantly perhaps, how the curriculum reflects those aims. In the day-to-day urgency of teaching the given curriculum it is easy to push the 'why' into the background and simply get on with the 'how'.

By contrast, some parents do question the judgement of others who insist that their children go to school from '9 to 4', five days a week, for 42 weeks for 11 years and have homework. In your dealing with parents, you may wish to justify this investment in time. Pupils can bring you to a halt when in the middle of a lesson, say on the Great Depression of the 1920s and 1930s, they remark, 'Why have I got to learn this? My mum says that if I'm going to work in "Waitrose" down the road, knowing the economic reasons for the depression won't help me in my job, will it?' As a prospective teacher you need an answer to this observation and similar comments in your subject.

The 1944 Education Act was a landmark in education in the UK. The Act gave a new framework for teaching and learning and it was introduced in the middle of a national crisis – the Second World War. Although the Act gave free secondary education to a wider group of pupils, the several aims of the curriculum were premised on a distinction between three groups of pupils, the academic (grammar schools), the technical (technical schools) and the rest (secondary modern schools). With hindsight we now reject such a simplistic approach.

The 1988 Education Reform Act, which replaced the 1944 Act, identified a common curriculum. The 1988 Act was premised on very narrow aims but with little justification made for the connection between these aims and the subject curriculum that emerged. In the decade following the 1988 Act, several reforms of the curriculum took place and both the aims of the 1988 Act and the latest reforms are addressed in this chapter

In Unit 7.1 'Aims of Education', a comparative and analytical approach is taken to examine assumptions about education. Unit 7.2 'The School Curriculum', examines the school curriculum in terms of aims. Finally in Unit 7.3 on the National Curriculum (NC) we examine the structure of the 1999 NC for England which for the first time has a worked-out set of aims.

Within the general standards laid down in England for student teachers to gain qualified teacher status (QTS) (DfES/TTA, 2004) you are expected to know about the aims of the NC and how your subject supports the general aims of the NC. Different criteria for QTS are laid down for Northern Ireland, Scotland and Wales. An awareness that the aims of education and of subjects within a curriculum are a matter of debate and political decision does not feature in the criteria for the award of QTS. We believe that teachers should be aware of the foundations on which national policy on the school curriculum is based because young people, between the ages of 5 and 16, spend a substantial part of the formative period of their lives in school and a significant slice of the national budget is channelled into education. In addition, it is important to consider why mathematics (or science or history) is justified as a compulsory element of an education from age 11. If education is 'what is left after most of what you have learned in school is forgotten', then what is education for and who decides?

Unit 7.1

Aims of Education

Graham Haydon

INTRODUCTION

Education is very much a value-laden activity; this unit is designed to help you reflect on the values you encounter in your work and the values you yourself bring to it. People's ideas about the aims of education may, in part, be simply 'read off' from the educational traditions of their own society, which already incorporate certain shared values; and they may be formed through an individual's own reflection on their personal values. Not surprisingly, then, in a complex society there is room for differences in views about educational aims. Individuals with, for example, different educational and life experiences, different religious beliefs and cultural traditions, and different political tendencies may all differ in their conceptions of the aims of education. In Britain views about the aims of education in the past have remained often more implicit than explicit, but in recent years there has been some conscious attention to aims at government level. Thus what may at first sight seem rather an abstract question – what should the aims of education be? – is in fact an unavoidable part of the context in which you are working as a teacher.

OBJECTIVES

At the end of this unit you should be able to:

- list a variety of actual and possible aims for education;
- reflect on and formulate your own aims on being a teacher;
- discuss aims of education with other teachers and with parents;
- identify the standards for your course which relate to the broad aims of education.

THE SOCIAL AND POLITICAL CONTEXT OF AIMS

One difference between education systems is that the aims which teachers are expected to pursue may be decided at different political or administrative levels. Many countries today have a national education system, at least partly state-funded and state-controlled. In some cases, as once in the Soviet Union, a clearly defined ideology sets aims which the whole education system is meant to promote. Even in a more decentralized system in which many decisions are left to local level, there may be across the whole society a more or less widely shared sense of what the aims of education should be. Thus in the USA there seems to have been in the early decades of the twentieth century a widely shared sense that one aim of the national education system was to make a single nation out of diverse communities.

In Britain, both historically and today, the picture is mixed. Through much of the twentieth century schools had a good deal of autonomy, from a legal point of view, in setting and pursuing their aims, though in many cases the aims of a particular school were not made explicit. There was also room for some variation at local authority level. For instance, in the 1970s and 1980s there were cases in which particular LEAs pursued more radical equal opportunities policies than were supported centrally. A case in point (though it is not relevant to go into the details here) is the political controversy over 'Clause 28', which began in the 1980s and lasted into the present century. Some LEAs were perceived, rightly or wrongly, as aiming to promote homosexuality through programmes and curriculum materials used in schools, and legislation was brought in to rule this out (section 28 of the Local Government Act 1988). There was a good deal of confusion in the debate over this (particularly since the influence of LEAs over individual schools had been very much reduced), until eventually the relevant legislation was repealed as part of the Local Government Act 2003. Whatever your own view of the rights and wrongs of the issue, it illustrates that the question of whether schools should or should not be pursuing certain aims is potentially controversial.

The more general question of how far there is to be scope for diversity between different localities and different schools is still being played out in Britain in the twenty-first century. A system which in some respects sets up competition between different schools, each aiming to attract and hold onto pupils, encourages each school to make its own aims clear to parents and prospective pupils, and perhaps to present itself as being in some way distinctive from other schools at the level of aims. As obvious examples, we might expect that schools labelled (and funded) as technology colleges, or schools labelled as sports colleges, would give explicit attention in their public statements of aims to the focus of their activities. At the time of writing, the tendency in England, in line with government policy, is towards the majority of secondary schools having a curricular specialization (while still teaching the National Curriculum). There are also likely to be increasing numbers of faith schools, and one would expect that if a school has been set up by a particular religious community and is dedicated to offering education within a particular faith, this would be reflected in its aims. If you have school experience within a faith school, or if you yourself attended one, keep this in mind in the tasks that follow.

While in some respects the last two decades have seen increasing room for variation in aims between schools, there has also been increasing attention to aims at the level of national politics. Though there has not been widespread public debate about the aims of education, politicians often express their views on the matter. These views will not always be put explicitly in the terminology of aims, but when politicians say that schools should enable Britain to compete economically with other nations, or that schools should inculcate moral standards or should promote active citizenship, they are in effect recommending certain aims for schools. At this broad level it will generally be assumed that the same aims are shared by all schools.

Thus there is always a potential tension between (a) the possibility of a diversity of aims in different schools, perhaps because they are serving rather different communities, and (b) the promotion of common aims across the school system as a whole. At the end of the twentieth century the focus on common aims became more prominent in England, for reasons connected with the revision of the NC, as we shall see in a later section. But the political situation is fluid, and it may be that by the time you read this you are hearing more about different aims in different schools.

As a student teacher, then, you are working in a context in which many expectations about aims are already in place. Even if aims were not mentioned in legislation, or in the prospectus of our school, you would still have to recognize that other teachers, your pupils, their parents, and the wider society all have their views about what you should be doing, and a legitimate interest in what you are doing. What aims you pursue as a teacher are clearly not just up to you.

Is there, in that case, much point in your doing your own thinking about the aims of education? It is a premise of this unit that there is a lot of point in this, in fact that any good teacher has some view about the aims of education. (This doesn't mean that your view is different from anyone else's, but it does mean that it is a view that you have thought through and endorsed for yourself.)

Here are two reasons why your own thinking about aims is relevant (you may well think of further reasons). First, within the constraints, your own thinking about aims influences the way you approach your task as a teacher of a particular subject (we discuss this aspect of aims of education further in the next unit). Second, as a citizen, you have the same right as any other citizen to form and express your own view about the aims of education in general; but at the same time other people might reasonably expect that as a member of the teaching profession you will be in a better position than the average citizen to make your views clear and be prepared to argue for them.

THINKING ABOUT AIMS

Tasks 7.1.1 and 7.1.2 are intended to give you some insight into the nature and variety of aims in education, as well as some experience in thinking about aims and their implications and discussing this with others.

WHY BOTHER WITH AIMS?

> Education as such has no aims. Only persons, parents and teachers, etc., have aims, not an abstract idea like education
>
> (Dewey, 1916: ch. 8, 'Aims of education').

Your experience in doing the tasks may have backed up Dewey's point. You may have seen that different people can have different aims for education. You may also have considered how much difference aims can make. A statement of aims on paper does not, of course, make any difference by itself (there is an example of this below in the context of the NC). But what people do and how they do it is certainly influenced by what they are themselves aiming at. Aims, at their different levels, can affect:

- How a whole school system is organized. (For example, the movement towards comprehensive education which began in the 1960s was driven at least partly by explicit aims of breaking down class barriers and distributing opportunities for education more widely.)
- How an individual school is run. (For example, various aspects of a school's ethos and organization may be motivated by the aim that pupils should respect and tolerate each other's differences.)
- How curriculum content is selected and taught (there is more on this aspect of aims in the next unit).

Task 7.1.1
School aims: a comparison

When you have carried out this task by yourself, try to compare your findings with those of other student teachers. The two schools for comparison are:

* the school in which you received your own secondary education (or the majority of it, if you changed schools);
* your current school experience school.

For the first school, your data will be wholly or largely from your own memory. Answer the following questions as far as you can:

* Did your school have an explicit statement of its aims?
* Were you as a pupil aware of the school's aims?
* In what ways did the particular aims of your school impinge on your experience as a pupil?

For your school experience school, ask:

* Does your school have an explicit statement of aims – if so, what does it say?
* Are the pupils you are teaching aware of the school's aims?
* Does the existence of these aims appear to make any difference to the pupils' experience in the school?

If you are a parent, you could also identify the aims of your child's school, using the school's documentation and, perhaps, discussion with staff.

Answering these questions in the case of your present school experience school gives scope for some small-scale empirical research. Depending on your subject, you may be able to incorporate some research into your teaching, e.g. in a discussion about school aims or through pupils themselves conducting a survey into how far their fellow pupils are aware of the school aims. You should discuss first with your school tutor any inquiry you plan.

Compare your findings for the two schools. Do you find that aims have a higher profile in one school or the other? Is there any evidence that the existence of an explicit policy on aims enhances the education the school is providing? Check the standards for your course which identify with the aims of schools.

MAKING SENSE OF THE VARIETY OF AIMS

Because aims can be so diverse, it is useful in thinking about aims to be able to categorize them in some way. There is no single right way of dividing different aims into categories; in fact it is more helpful to be able to work with different categorizing schemes.

Some approaches assume that education is aiming to develop personal qualities and capacities of one sort or another, and therefore divide aims up into the categories of knowledge, attitudes and skills. A distinction between academic, personal and vocational aims is related to this, but does not coincide exactly with it. Part of the importance in practice of the academic/personal/vocational division is that it can be recognized to some extent in ways in which different types of school historically have conceived their task.

But even if you are confident that education should be developing certain qualities or capacities in individuals, there is the wider question – still one about aims – of why this should be done. Is it just for the benefit of each individual, or for the general good of society? In other words, what should the aim be of the educational system as a whole? Should it be to do the best that can be done for each individual?

Task 7.1.2
The governing body: aims for a
new school

This is a group task involving role play. It is suitable for a group of several student teachers in the same school, or for a tutorial session with student teachers from several schools.

With other student teachers, role-play a governors' meeting which is intended to put together a statement of aims for a new school (imagining that it is a new school allows you to start with a relatively clean sheet). Within the allotted time (say, one hour) you must try to produce a statement of aims to be included in the prospectus, to help show prospective pupils and their parents what is distinctive about the new school and its educational priorities.

Before you start the role-play, you should agree on any special characteristics of the area in which the school is located. It may be best to make it a school which has to serve a wide range of interests, i.e. a comprehensive school with a socially and ethnically varied intake.

Depending on the number in your group, you can assign individuals to some of the following roles as governors. (You may think there is some stereotyping in the brief descriptions of these roles. If you have experience of role-play, you should be able to distance yourself from the stereotypes.)

- a Conservative-voting company director;
- a Labour-voting trade union leader;
- a Church of England vicar;
- a spokesperson for the main local ethnic community;
- a parent of a bright child, with high academic ambitions for their child;
- a teacher-governor;
- the headteacher.

One of you should be elected to chair the meeting and another to take notes on the points made and record anything which is agreed.

After the role-play, if you have not arrived at an agreed statement, talk about what it was that prevented agreement. In what ways does the disagreement within your group reflect the actual diversity of interests and cultures within our society?

The standards of your course require you to know about the roles of the governing body of a school.

Or should it be to promote and maintain a certain kind of society – perhaps a democratic society, or a just society, or an economically successful society?

This question introduces another distinction which has its uses but which, like any categorization, can be misleading if not used carefully. If you had to make a sharp choice, say between developing in people the capacities which enable each individual to lead a fulfilling life, and giving them the skills and attitudes which fit them to be cogs in an impersonal system, then there would be a real divide between aiming at the good of the individual and aiming at the good of society. But it is not necessarily like that. If, for instance, your view of a good society is that it is the kind of society in which all individuals have the capacity to lead fulfilling lives and there are no obstacles in the way of people exercising those capacities, then there need be no contradiction between aiming at the good of the individual and aiming at the good of society.

In fact, even without being idealistic, many aims do cut across the individual/society division. Giving people skills which enable them to get productive jobs, for example, is in many instances of benefit to the individuals concerned and to others in society. Other cases may be more difficult. Certain types of academic knowledge might benefit individuals who have that knowledge, if only because they happen to find it interesting, without having any spin-off for others. Certain types of moral socialization might benefit others while on balance having a negative effect for the self-fulfilment of the individuals concerned. Historical examples of this might include working-class boys being brought up to assume they would follow in their father's kind of employment, or girls being brought up to be always deferential to the male members of their families. Few people now would explicitly endorse such aims as these (see the section below 'Equal aims for everyone?') but prejudices can still survive and make a difference. This is one reason both for making aims explicit and for paying attention to the 'hidden curriculum' (see Unit 7.2).

JUSTIFYING AIMS

In your role plays and discussions people have been trying to defend their own conceptions of what the aims of education should be. What sorts of argument have they been using?

One approach which used to be favoured by philosophers was to say that certain aims are incorporated into the *concept* of education. So, if someone aimed at inculcating in pupils particular religious or moral beliefs, this could be rejected on the ground that inculcating unquestioned beliefs is simply not part of our concept of education. In fact (it might be said) it is part of our concept of *indoctrination*, whereas the concept of *education* implies the promotion of rationality and critical thinking.

You may agree with this. Its limitation as an argument, though, is that it does not allow you to meet on their own ground people who might argue that what they want teachers and schools to do *is* to inculcate certain unquestioned beliefs. They may not mind if you don't *call* this education; it is what they want you to aim at.

In the end, argument about educational aims is not about concepts, or how people use words. It is also not a matter that can be settled empirically by surveying what people actually think the aims of education should be. The history of education shows how much ideas about the aims of education can change from one generation to another (as the next section illustrates); if certain ideas about educational aims are widely accepted now, that does not show they are beyond criticism (see also Bottery, 1990: chs 1 and 2). Discussion about educational aims is fundamentally discussion about values, an ethical discussion about the responsibilities of adult members of society towards the young members of society and towards the next generation. In some way probably almost everyone would agree that education should be seeking to improve the quality of life of individuals or of the society in general – otherwise why bother about it? – but there is room for dispute over what is important in a good quality of life. Do we do more for someone's quality of life by enabling them to earn a good income, or by developing, say, their scientific curiosity or their appreciation of art (even if these do not help them to work productively)?

Argument about the aims of education, then, may come down in the end to questions of what matters most in life. But it also has to be about the distinctive contribution that teachers and schools can make to promoting what is important in life. If we agree, for instance, that health is important in everyone's life, this does not mean that the aim of teachers in relation to health is the same as the aim of nurses and doctors, but it may be that there are particular kinds of contribution that teachers can make to improving people's chances of having a healthy life.

The individual/social dimension affects the issue of justification. If some aspect of education is seen as being of value only for (some) individuals, there may be questions about why society – people in general – should support it. If some aspect is seen as being of value only for the majority of people, but not everyone, there may be questions about whether it should be imposed on individuals if they do not freely choose it. Such questions, though, may often stem from a simplistic contrast between society and individual; for a more sophisticated view, see Dewey (1916).

Some writers today would argue that aims for education should be derived explicitly from a conception of the kind of society in which young people will be living. If this is to be a liberal, democratic and multicultural society, then education should be preparing people to live in that kind of society, and other more particular aims will follow from this.

The last two sections of this unit discussed the variety of aims for education and ways in which aims can be justified. To explore further these two aspects of aims of education we suggest you address Task 7.1.3.

Task 7.1.3
Why teach information and communication technology (ICT)

ICT is a relatively new subject in the curriculum but is much more influential than just a subject. ICT is conceived of as contributing to other subjects, to introducing new ways of learning and influencing the way teachers teach.

Discuss the place of ICT in the school curriculum in terms of possible aims, such as the personal, academic and vocational. How might those aims be justified to the pupil, the parents or the wider society? You may wish first to reread the previous two sections of this unit.

EQUAL AIMS FOR EVERYONE?

Through much of the history of education, it would have been an unquestioned assumption that the aims of education should be different for different people. Plato built his conception of an ideal state (*The Republic*) on the argument that the people in power would need a much more thorough education than anyone else. A similar position was apparent in Victorian Britain, where the expansion of education was driven in part by the aim that the mass of the population should be sufficiently well educated to form a productive workforce but not so well educated that they might rebel against the (differently educated) ruling classes. In the mid-twentieth century, within a system selecting by ability, there were different aims behind the education offered in different types of schools: secondary modern, technical and grammar. Also, through much of the twentieth century, differences in aims were apparent between boys' and girls' schools, and between religious foundations and schools which were effectively secular.

Today the unquestioned assumption is often the reverse: that the basic aims of education are the same for everyone, even if different methods have to be used with different people in pursuing the same aims, and even if some people go further in the process than others. This assumption underlies many important developments in the promotion of equal opportunities. One of the basic reasons for being concerned with equal opportunities is that, if what you are aiming at is worthwhile, no one should be excluded from it because of factors, like race or gender, which ought to be irrelevant to achieving these worthwhile aims. But this basic assumption is still not without its problems.

In the area of special educational needs in England and Wales, for instance, the Warnock Committee, which was set up in the late 1970s to look into the education of pupils with physical and mental disabilities, argued that the fundamental aims of education are the same for everyone (DES, 1978). This was part of the thinking which led in the 1980s to the integration of an increasing proportion of pupils with special educational needs (SEN) into mainstream schools, rather than their segregation in special schools. (See Unit 4.6 for the current position.) Schools require, for example, to be specially equipped to respond to some needs and to appoint additional specialist staff. This requirement has led to funding problems and to inadequate provision due to a shortage of suitably trained teaching staff.

As regards gender, few people would now suggest that the aim of education for girls should be to produce wives and mothers while the aim of education for boys should be to produce breadwinners. When people today argue for single-sex schooling or for dividing teaching groups according to gender, it is usually not because they think there are separate aims for the education of boys and of girls, but because they recognize that giving boys and girls an equal opportunity to achieve those aims requires attention to practical conditions, and this may make a difference to the means though not to the ends. So, for instance, the teaching of boys and girls may be more effective if they are taught without the distractions or pressures present in mixed-sex groups (whether this actually is so is a matter for research). Even so, some might argue that a degree of differentiation in aims is needed; perhaps, for instance, there should be an attempt to develop assertiveness in girls and sensitivity in boys. See Unit 4.4 for further discussion of gender issues.

Turning to different cultural, religious or ethnic groups, it is not surprising if governments expect the same aims to be pursued for all groups; anything else would seem grossly discriminatory. But at the same time the members of particular groups may have special aims they would like to see pursued for their own children. To some religious believers it may be more important that their children are brought up within the faith of their community than that they are brought up as citizens of a secular society; such differences lie behind the demands that some religious groups make for separate schools.

These examples illustrate again the point made earlier, that while at one level statements of the aims of education can appear rather platitudinous and bland, there is the potential for controversy when aims are considered in more detail and the attempt is made to see how the pursuit of certain aims can be implemented in practice.

AIMS IN THE NATIONAL CURRICULUM

You may be working within the constraints of an NC, such as that for England (DfEE/QCA, 1999a). How much scope does this leave you and your colleagues in deciding on your aims?

A first stage in answering this is that you should be aware of what the documentation of your NC actually says about aims. When the NC for England and Wales was first brought in, in 1988, its explicit aims were limited to the following: 'to promote the spiritual, moral, cultural, mental and physical development of pupils at the school and of society; to prepare pupils for the opportunities, responsibilities and experiences of adult life'.

As a statement of aims, this was not very controversial (with the possible exception of the idea of spiritual development). Its problem was that it was so broad and general that it gave very little guidance. And in fact there was no indication within the rest of the original documentation of the NC for England and Wales that its content had been influenced at all by the statement of aims. That statement seemed to be an example of an error which it is easy for government agencies, and also schools, to slip into: setting out a statement of aims which looks good, but which makes no apparent difference to what actually happens.

During the late 1990s, when the NC was being reviewed, the Qualification and Curriculum Authority (QCA) decided to pay explicit attention to aims. This resulted in a much expanded statement of aims (see Unit 7.3). What does this statement say about aims?

First, the statement acknowledges that aims rest in values, and refers to a number of values which are taken to be shared across our society. It also acknowledges that in influencing and reflecting these values schools need to work with other parts of society.

Second, so far as the school curriculum of England is concerned, two aims are set out and more particular statements (objectives) are made about how the curriculum can promote these aims. A summary of these aims is given below; the full statement can be found in DfEE/QCA, 1999a: 11–12.

Aim 1: The school curriculum should aim to provide opportunities for all pupils to learn and achieve

The curriculum should:

- promote pupils' commitment to learning and confidence in their capacities to do so – equip them with basic skills;
- cultivate capacity to solve problems, think rationally, critically and creatively – help pupils to become creative, innovative, enterprising and capable of leadership – develop physical skills and see the importance of a healthy lifestyle;
- develop pupils' sense of identity through understanding of cultural heritage and of local, national, European and international dimensions – appreciate human aspirations and achievement in aesthetic, scientific and other fields.

Aim 2: The school curriculum should aim to promote pupils' spiritual, moral, social and cultural development and prepare all pupils for the opportunities, responsibilities and experiences of life

The curriculum should:

- pass on enduring social values, promote pupils' integrity and autonomy – help them become caring citizens in a just society – help them challenge discrimination – promote spiritual, moral, social and cultural development – develop knowledge of different beliefs and cultures – promote respect for environment and commitment to sustainable development at local through to global levels;
- promote pupils' self-esteem and emotional well-being – help them form satisfying relationships – develop their ability to work for the common good – help them respond positively to challenges and to change and adversity;
- prepare pupils for the next steps in learning and employment – equip them to make informed choices (Bramall and White, 2000b: 10–12).

As a statement of aims, it could be said that this has 'something for everyone'. There is probably not much there that anyone could dissent from. At the same time there are ideas which are open to interpretation, and there is scope for balancing one aim against another in all sorts of ways.

As a teacher in schools in England (or also elsewhere, even if the same legislation does not apply to you), you could consider this statement of aims as a resource you can draw on. The next unit suggests ways in which you might do this in relation to your own curriculum subject.

So is this a statement of aims that actually makes a difference in schools? At least we can say that there is enough detail there to make it possible to ask whether a school is actually working in a way that helps to promote these aims. Is enough attention being paid, for instance, to different beliefs and cultures, or to the environment, or to the requirements of citizenship, or to developing pupils' self-esteem?

In the end it is for you and other teachers to determine how much difference this statement of aims makes. But the next two units in this chapter, on the curriculum in general, and on the NC in particular, gives you a basis to begin thinking about how far the curriculum you are working with is likely to promote such aims as these.

Task 7.1.4
Aims and education – the NC for England and Wales

Working either from the summary given, or preferably from the full statement of values and aims for the NC of England (DfEE/QCA, 1999a; or the NC website <www.nc.uk.net>) consider the following points.

- Do all these aims seem to you to fit together into a coherent idea of what education is about?
- Is there is anything in this statement of aims which you would not have expected to see there? Is there anything which is likely to prove controversial? Is there anything you think should be mentioned which is not mentioned?

Discuss your responses with other student teachers, or with your tutor. Use the findings from your discussion to check the standards for your course.

SUMMARY

In working as a teacher you necessarily have some aims, and these are more likely to be coherent and defensible if you have thought them through. At the same time, you are operating within the context of aims set by others. Aims can exist at different levels, local or national. In Britain, in recent years, the dominant tendency has been towards a common conception of aims for everyone, and most recently in England a broad set of aims has been incorporated into the documentation for the NC. But this still leaves room for you to form your own view as to the most important priorities for education, and to discuss with others how these aims can best be realized.

It is always possible to raise questions about the justification of educational aims. Ultimately our aims for education rest on our values – our conceptions of what makes for a good life both for individuals and for our society as a whole. Because we do not share all of our values with each other, there will always be room for debate about the aims of education.

You should cross-check this unit with the standards of your course, particularly sections dealing with wider professional requirements.

FURTHER READING

Aldrich, R. and White, J. (1998) *The National Curriculum beyond 2000: The QCA and the Aims of Education*, London: Institute of Education. An argument for basing the curriculum on an explicit consideration of aims, and for deriving these aims from democratic values.

Bottery, M. (1990) *The Morality of the School*, London: Cassell. A wide-ranging discussion relevant to any teacher thinking about aims. Chapter 1 gives you an exercise to help you classify your own beliefs about education into one of four categories: the cultural transmission model, the child-centred model, the social reconstruction model, and the 'GNP (gross national product) code'.

Dewey, J. (1916) *Democracy and Education*, New York: Free Press. A classic book (often reprinted) which is still well worth reading. Though Dewey is often thought of simply as an advocate of child-centred education, his educational theory is part of a well worked out theory of the relation between individual and society and of the nature of knowledge and thought. See especially Chapters 1 to 4, 8 and 9.

Wringe, C. (1988) *Understanding Educational Aims*, London: Unwin Hyman. An introductory text by a philosopher of education, reviewing a variety of positions about aims in education concerned with: (i) the development of qualities and capacities in the individual for the individual's own good; (ii) what is good from the point of view of society; (iii) the pursuit of aims seen as intrinsic to education and valuable in their own right.

Unit 7.2

The School Curriculum

Graham Haydon

INTRODUCTION

The curriculum is an important part of the context within which you work as a teacher. The planned or formal curriculum is the intended content of an educational programme set out in advance. We refer later to the informal and hidden curriculum. Like other aspects of the context of your work (the school buildings, say, or the administrative organization of the school), the curriculum forms a 'frame' to what you are doing even when you are not explicitly thinking about it. But often you find that you do refer to the curriculum, in your everyday conversations with colleagues, and less frequently perhaps in meetings with parents or in talking to pupils in a pastoral role.

It might seem that the curriculum is so clearly part of the context of your work that it must be obvious what the curriculum is. In which case, why does a book of this nature need a unit on the curriculum (in fact two units, since the next unit is specifically about the National Curriculum (NC) in England, but see the next paragraph).

The purpose of this unit is to show you that, once you think about it, it is not so obvious what the curriculum is, and that it is not something you should, as a teacher, take for granted. Rather than relying on implicit assumptions about the curriculum, you should be able and willing, as part of your professional role, to think about the curriculum, about its role in education and about ways in which it is controversial and might be open to challenge. In doing this, you will, of course, need to keep in mind the relevant legislation and government documentation for the country within which you are working. The 1988 National Curriculum was for England and Wales, but the 1999 legislation made changes specifically for England: see Unit 7.3 for details. The Welsh National Curriculum is adapted from that in England (ACCAC, 2000); Scotland and Northern Ireland have their own curricula.

Similar remarks applied to the topic of aims, discussed in the previous unit. The strategy of this unit is to discuss the curriculum as one of the most important 'tools' through which educational aims can be realized. But we shall need first to be clearer about what the term 'the curriculum' refers to.

OBJECTIVES

At the end of this unit you should be able to:

- distinguish a number of different conceptions of the curriculum;
- discuss ways in which the curriculum may or may not help to realize educational aims;
- see why the content of the curriculum, even if often taken for granted, is potentially controversial;
- discuss the place of your particular teaching subject within the broader curriculum.

THE CURRICULUM IN GENERAL AND WITHIN PARTICULAR SUBJECTS

It helps to avoid confusion in the rest of this unit (and hopefully in your thinking more generally) if we distinguish between the curriculum of a school (or even of schools in general) and the curriculum within a particular subject. We can often mark this distinction by speaking of the 'syllabus', rather than curriculum, of a particular subject. In the way the words are actually used in professional discourse and wider debate the distinction is not clear-cut. The term 'syllabus' usually refers to a specific programme in a specific subject set out in detail in advance, possibly designed by a particular teacher, but often laid down by an examination board or other body external to the school. But people do also speak of, say, 'the science curriculum' or 'the arts curriculum', when they want to focus on a part of the curriculum in general, though not necessarily at the level of the details of a specific syllabus.

The documentation of the NC for England (DFEE/QCA, 1999a) which is the focus for the next unit, does not make it easy to keep any sharp distinction in terminology, since in that documentation some level of detail of Programmes of Study and targets for particular subjects has always been seen as part of the English NC.

For most of this unit, though, the focus is on the broad curriculum. Questions are raised about the role of particular subjects within the curriculum in general, more than about what goes on *within* the teaching of particular subjects. But we shall have to say something about the latter point as well, because the role of a subject within the curriculum partly depends on what is done within that subject. (So far, the term 'the whole curriculum' has been avoided because that too may carry some ambiguity.)

Task 7.2 1
School curricula: a comparison

(This task is deliberately parallel to Task 7.1.1 on aims in Unit 7.1.) When you have carried out this task by yourself, try to compare your findings with those of other student teachers.

The two schools for comparison are:

- The school in which you received your own secondary education (or the majority of it, if you changed schools);
- Your current school experience school.

From memory, write down on one side of paper what was in the curriculum of the school you attended as a pupil. Then (without referring to documentation at this stage) write down what is in the curriculum of your school experience school. Compare the two accounts.

THE FORMAL CURRICULUM

There *could* be considerable variety in what you and other student teachers have written, because the term 'curriculum' can be used in various ways. But it is likely that what you have written down, for both schools in the comparison, is a list of subjects. What this illustrates is that when people refer to 'the curriculum' without qualification, most often they think of what we can usefully label 'the formal curriculum'. This is the intended content of an educational programme, set out in advance.

At a minimal level of detail, the formal curriculum can be stated as a list of names of subjects. Thus the statement that we expect pupils to learn 'reading, writing and arithmetic' would itself be a curriculum statement (about the thinnest possible). So would be the extended and modified version adopted in the school attended by Lewis Carroll's *Mock Turtle*:

> 'Reeling and Writhing, of course, to begin with … and then the different branches of Arithmetic – Ambition, Distraction, Uglification and Derision … Mystery, ancient and modern, with Seaography: then … Drawling, Stretching, and Fainting in Coils (but the Mock Turtle didn't do 'Laughing and Grief' though they were on the curriculum; they must have been options).
> (Gardner, M., 1965: 129–30, with explanations)

While the formal curriculum can be listed simply as a set of subjects (and the requirement that you write it down on one side of paper may have encouraged this approach), it is always possible to set out in more detail under both headings the content which is supposed to be taught and learned. Even when the curriculum is stated simply as a list of subjects, those who write it and those who read it have some implicit understanding of what goes into each subject. It is important to keep this in mind when comparing the curriculum offered in schools at different times. It is likely that your lists contain a number of items, probably the majority, that are common to both lists. In fact we can go further. The NC in England at the beginning of the twenty-first century can be compared with the secondary school regulations for England of 1904 (Aldrich, 1998: 48), and even with the mid-nineteenth-century curriculum which Lewis Carroll was parodying, we find many items in common (the most noticeable absence from Carroll's list, which appears in all the subsequent ones, is science).

This finding does illustrate something about the extent to which the formal curriculum in schools in England has *not* gone through revolutionary changes. At the same time, it would be a mistake to conclude from the similarity of the lists that the curriculum has hardly changed at all. Even if we could set aside all changes in teaching method and concentrate solely on the content of the subjects, what is taught under the heading of history or science in 2005 is obviously going to be very different in many ways from what was taught under the same headings in 1904.

Another point to note under 'formal curriculum' is that the curriculum may contain parts which are optional. Even before the introduction of an NC in England and Wales in 1988 made certain subjects compulsory, it was normal for most of the curriculum in a secondary school to consist of subjects which all pupils were expected to take. But there may also be options within the curriculum, particularly in the later years of secondary school.

Related to the idea of a compulsory curriculum are the notions of a 'common curriculum', that is, one taken by everyone in practice, whether or not it is actually compulsory; and a 'core curriculum', the part of a whole curriculum which everyone takes, around which there is scope for variations.

THE INFORMAL CURRICULUM AND THE HIDDEN CURRICULUM

The notion of the formal curriculum refers to the content which is, quite deliberately, taught by teachers in a school, usually in periods structured by a timetable and labelled according to subject. So the fact that something is on the curriculum means that it is taught (or at least that the intention of the curriculum planners or of the school management is that it shall be taught). But since some pupils may fail to learn what teachers are intending to teach, the fact that something is a non-optional part of the formal curriculum does not guarantee that pupils learn it.

On the other hand, pupils may learn things in school which are not taught as part of the formal curriculum. There are two ways in which this can happen. One is that the school intends that pupils should learn things which cannot be directly taught in lessons. Many of the possible aims of a school, which you were thinking about in the previous unit, involve matters of this kind. If a school wants, for instance, to promote co-operation and consideration for others, then (if these are to be more than pious aspirations) it needs to do something to try to bring about co-operation and to encourage pupils to behave in considerate ways. (See also Unit 4.5 'Moral Development and Values' for further discussion of promoting common values.) Teachers might agree to build co-operative work into their lessons, whatever the subject; teachers and pupils might draw up a code of behaviour; there may be some system of rewards and sanctions; the school management may pay attention to the way that pupils move around the school during break times; and so on. All such arrangements can be counted as part of the 'informal curriculum' of the school.

Taking into account both the formal and the informal curriculum, the curriculum can be defined in some way such as this: 'The school curriculum comprises all learning and other experiences that each school plans for its pupils' (DfEE/QCA, 1999a: 10).

But pupils may also learn things at school that the school does not intend them to learn. For several decades sociologists have pointed out that many pupils at school were learning, for instance, to accept passively what they were told or to see themselves as failures; while some were learning to identify with and follow the mores of a rebellious subculture; and some were learning racist and sexist attitudes, and so on. Such learning was not normally part of what the school was intending its pupils to learn, and the school may not have been aware of many of the things that its pupils were learning; from the school's point of view, these outcomes were side-effects of the pupils' time in school. So the term 'hidden curriculum' was invented to cover such learning.

The side-effects just mentioned are undesirable ones, and it has often been undesirable effects that people have in mind when they used the term 'hidden curriculum'. But side-effects could also be desirable ones; for instance, a side-effect of students of different ethnic backgrounds learning and playing together might be the development of understanding and respect. The point about the idea of the hidden curriculum is not that its content is necessarily bad, but that the school is not aware of it. Today, teachers are far more likely to be aware of the likely side-effects of all aspects of the school's activity. In that way, what might once have been part of a hidden curriculum comes to be hidden no longer. This does not mean that schools today have no hidden curriculum; it means that a school has to be careful to try to uncover and become aware of side-effects of what it does deliberately in its teaching and its organization.

If these side-effects are unwelcome – if, say, they work against the school achieving its intended aims – then the school may make deliberate attempts to counteract them. Often a school does this by paying attention to aspects of its teaching and organization outside of the formal curriculum. So, where the learning of racist or sexist attitudes might once have been part of the *hidden* curriculum in some schools, it is more likely today that the *informal* curriculum includes anti-racist and anti-sexist policies. And it may also be that such policies alter what is done within the *formal* curriculum, e.g. within a PSHE course or citizenship education (an area often referred to as the pastoral curriculum).

Mention of the informal curriculum shows that the curriculum as a whole is not, for any teacher, a rigid framework within which there is no room for flexibility or planning. Even when the formal curriculum is determined largely in advance, as in the NC for England, there is still scope open to the school in designing the details of the curriculum and the way that links between curriculum subjects are (or are not) made; and there is space outside the NC since that is not supposed to occupy the whole timetable.

You should, then, see it as part of your professional role as a teacher that you can take an overview of the curriculum, have a sense of 'where it comes from' and be able to engage in discussion on whether it could be improved and, if so, in what ways.

CURRICULUM AS A SELECTION FROM CULTURE

A number of writers have referred to the curriculum as a selection from the culture of a society. 'Culture' here refers to 'everything that is created by human beings themselves: tools and technology, language and literature, music and art, science and mathematics – in effect, the whole way of life of a society' (Lawton, 1989: 17). Any society passes on its culture to the next generation, and in modern societies schooling is one of the ways in which this is done. But obviously no school curriculum can accommodate the whole of human culture; so a selection has to be made.

A natural question to ask next is how do we make that selection? Different curriculum theories give different answers.

A first move is to recognize that, since some aspects of culture are passed on or picked up independently of schools, it may make sense for schools in general to concentrate on matters which will not be learned if they are not included in the school curriculum; and secondary schools in particular have to try to build on, but not to duplicate, what pupils have learned by the end of primary school. Even these points give rise to many questions. For example, many young people of secondary age pick up much of what they know about computers, sport or popular music independently of school; does this mean there is no point in including study of these areas in the curriculum?

After putting on one side things which pupils learn independently of school (if we can identify such things), there are principles by which we might try to make a selection from culture. In this unit there is space to mention just three: to select what is *best*, or what is *distinctive* of a particular culture, or what is in some way *fundamental*.

The idea of selecting, and enabling people to appreciate, what is *best* goes back at least to Matthew Arnold. Arnold was not only a Victorian poet and a commentator on the culture of his day, but also a school inspector. Historically, this principle has been linked with the idea of whole areas of culture – 'high culture', centred on arts and literature – being of greater value than the rest of culture, and also perhaps being accessible only to a minority of society. The principle does not have to be interpreted in that way (see Gingell and Brandon, 2000, for an updated interpretation). Whatever area of culture we are dealing with, including for instance football and rock music, we may well want people to be able to appreciate what is good rather than what is mediocre. It does not follow, though, that the school curriculum should always be focused on what is best in any area. If we suppose, for instance, that the greatest science is that of Einstein or Stephen Hawking, it does not mean we place this science at the centre of the school curriculum. In many areas, if people are ever to be able to appreciate the best, they need to start by understanding something more basic.

Another principle of selection which is sometimes favoured is to pick from the whole of human culture what is *distinctive* of a particular culture – the way of life of a particular nation, or ethnic group, or religion. This may apply more to the detailed content within areas of the curriculum than to the selection of the broad areas. We do not just learn language, we learn a particular language; and while it is possible to study historical method, any content of history is that of particular people in a particular part of the world. One question for curriculum planning, then, is how far to select from what we see as 'our' culture, and how to interpret what is 'our' culture. That question, in England, has to be resolved in a context of a multicultural society, within a world in which there is increasing interaction between different cultures.

Rather than looking to what is best, or what is distinctive, we may try to look to what is *fundamental*. This idea may apply both across the curriculum and within areas of the curriculum. Within the sciences and mathematics, for instance, the idea of what is culturally distinctive may have little application (which is not to say that these subjects as actually taught are culture-free), and the idea of teaching the best may be inappropriate. We need to think about what is fundamental. In the educational context, this does not mean what is fundamental in the whole structure of human knowledge; it means what people need to learn if they are to have a foundation on which further knowledge or skills can be built.

Thinking about the curriculum in general, we can also try to ask what is fundamental in the whole human culture in which people are living. But this question depends in turn on some particular understanding of what is important in human life. Is it the development of the capacities for rational thought and judgement? Then we might argue, as the philosopher of education Paul Hirst (1974) once did, that there are certain basic forms of human understanding – science, mathematics, interpersonal understanding and so on – which are not interchangeable and each of which is necessary in its own way to the development of rational understanding.

Or is human life more fundamentally about providing the material necessities of life? Then we might stress what can be economically useful, and our curriculum might be primarily a vocational one. Or is the essential aspect of human life, so far as education is concerned, the fact that people live together in groups and have to organize their affairs together? Then preparing people to be citizens might turn out to be most fundamental.

So far, none of these approaches looks as if it takes us very far, by itself, in selecting which aspects of culture should make up a school curriculum. Of course, there is much more to the arguments than can be considered in detail here. But even this much discussion suggests that the attempt to select from human culture does not take us far without an explicit consideration of the aims of education. We do not, after all, have to transmit culture just as it stands (and in any case it is constantly changing). We may have views about what kind of society we wish to see, or about what kind of persons we hope will emerge from education.

RELATING CURRICULUM TO AIMS

The previous unit raised the question about the aims of education in general terms, suggested some approaches to answering it, and looked briefly at the current stated aims of the NC in England. The important point to emphasize is that the curriculum of schools is a major part of the way in which we attempt to realize educational aims. So, rationally, the planning of a curriculum should depend on how the overall aims of education are conceived. Historically, as was pointed out in the last unit, this has not always happened. Even when, as now, there is an NC in England incorporating an extended statement of aims, there is room to question how far the required curriculum is actually likely to realize the stated aims.

The aims set out in Unit 7.1 contain many that we would not expect to be realized primarily through anything in the content of the curriculum subjects. Think for instance of the promotion of self-esteem and emotional well-being; challenging discrimination; developing a sense of identity. It is

**Task 7.2.2
Linking curriculum content to
aims**

Look again at the statement of aims of the NC for England, as used for task 7.1.3. You may
wish to use a different NC for this task.

If you were responsible for planning a curriculum which could realize these aims, what
would you think should go into that curriculum?

Look at the next unit for the details of the current English NC. How far do you think the NC
for England as we have it now is likely to promote its stated aims? Discuss with other student
teachers or your tutor.

Notice that this question about the NC is asking you to consider the formal curriculum with
which schools in England now operate (apart from the small amount of time available to
schools for pursuing activities outside the NC). But we can also think about ways in which a
school's informal curriculum may further the same aims.

clear that the informal curriculum has a large role to play here; any school which gave its attention
only to the formal curriculum would be realizing these other aims only incidentally if at all.

How far, then, *can* the formal curriculum promote the kinds of aims set out? It is clear that the
traditional curriculum subjects have a role in promoting pupils' learning and achievement (achievement
within those subjects, that is, although there are other kinds of achievement as well), and in promoting
their intellectual development. What is not so clear is the role of the traditional subjects in promoting
the broader aims of a moral and social kind which were always recognized in NC documents since
1988 and have now gained greater prominence than before.

The first version of the NC in England and Wales, brought in by the Education Reform Act 1988,
attempted to address such aims by incorporating a number of cross-curricular themes: health education,
citizenship education, careers education and guidance, environmental education, and education for
economic and industrial understanding. These themes did not have the statutory force of the core and
foundation subjects, and it was left largely to individual schools (with limited published guidance) to
decide how to teach them. In fact, in many schools the cross-curricular themes were not systematically
taken up at all.

In the current NC for England (DfEE/QCA, 1999a) a number of the stated aims relate to topics
which the cross-curricular themes had been intended to address: economic understanding, careers
choice and education about the environment, for instance, are clearly incorporated in the aims. But of
the original cross-curricular themes, only citizenship has gained the status of a statutory subject, and
the other areas are no longer there as distinct themes. It is clear from this that, in relation to the
declared aims, citizenship education carries a heavy burden, as does PSHE, even though that is not
statutory. The role of citizenship is raised also in Unit 4.5 'Moral Development and Values'.

What of the subjects which still form the bulk of the curriculum? It is no surprise that subjects such
as English, mathematics, and science have a central place in most curricula; as we saw above, they have
been in the curriculum of schools in Britain (and many other countries) for a long time. But it remains
true that the current NC documents for England do not attempt any detailed arguments to show in
which ways particular subjects help to promote particular aims (DfEE/QCA, 1999a). Indeed, some
writers have questioned whether subjects such as mathematics and foreign languages do deserve the
prominence they have in the curriculum if the overall purpose of that curriculum is to promote the
kinds of aims set out in the documents; see Bramall and White, 2000b. More detailed arguments both

for and against the prominence of mathematics in the curriculum can be found in Bramall and White, 2000a; and Tikly and Wolf, 2000. On the other hand, it may be argued that an understanding of the history of one's own society has such an important role in underpinning informed citizenship that it should not cease to be compulsory at Key Stage 4 (Bramall and White, 2000b).

How a subject relates to overall aims may affect not only its place in the overall curriculum but also how it is taught. In science and mathematics, what is the balance between equipping pupils with skills which they can put to practical use (thus furthering training and employment opportunities) and trying to show pupils something of the sheer fascination which mathematics and science can hold quite apart from their applications? In history, what is the balance between trying to promote a sense of a common British inheritance and exploring the history which has led to Britain being the multicultural society it now is?

Mathematics and history have been used as two examples here, but similar questions can be raised about other subjects. *Rethinking the School Curriculum: Values, Aims and Purposes* (White 2004) devotes a chapter to each subject of the National Curriculum, with the exception of PSHE, citizenship and ICT, and also to religious education. The discussions in that publication will help you in thinking about the role of your own subject within the whole curriculum.

Task 7.2.3
Justifying your subject in the school curriculum

This can be a two-part task, with an individual stage followed by a group stage. The task is to contribute to a school prospectus (it might be for the same imaginary school which you used in Task 7.1.2). Suppose that the school has adopted the statement of aims from a national curriculum.

Your individual task is to write a paragraph of not more than one hundred words setting out for prospective parents the ways in which your teaching subject fits into the whole curriculum, and thus contributes to realizing the overall aims of the curriculum. (Remember that some parents – and pupils – may wonder what the point of studying certain subjects is at all.)

The group task for you and your fellow student teachers, representing different subjects, is to make sure that the individual subject statements fit together into a coherent description of a whole curriculum, complementing and not competing with each other.

Reflect on this task and check your development against the standards for your course.

SUMMARY AND KEY POINTS

The curriculum is an important part of the context in which you work as a teacher. It includes both the formal curriculum, which sets out in detail the subjects to be taught; the informal curriculum, which covers the variety of ways in which a school can attempt to achieve the kinds of aims which cannot be captured in the content of timetabled subjects and the hidden curriculum which is way the school relates to pupils and parents, sometimes referred to as the ethos of a school.

The curriculum is perhaps the most important means through which educational aims can be pursued. Although much of the curriculum exists already as a framework within which you work, you may well have the opportunity to contribute to discussion about the curriculum, and you should be able to take and argue a view both on the whole curriculum and on the place of your own subject within it.

Any curriculum is a selection from the culture of a society, but any way of selecting elements from culture – the attempt to select what is best, or what is distinctive or what is fundamental – may not by itself be adequate without a view of the overall aims of education.

While the current National Curriculum for England includes a statement of aims, there is still room for discussion over the contribution which individual subjects make to the achievement of those overall aims.

In this unit no more has been done than to introduce a few of the questions that can be raised and approaches that can be taken. Within educational research and theory, 'curriculum studies' has come to be a subject area in its own right on which there is a large literature; some of this literature is in the further reading below. You should refer to the statement of standards for your course and check how this unit contributes to your professional development.

FURTHER READING

Bramall, S. and White, J. (2000b) *Will the New National Curriculum Live up to its Aims?* London: Philosophy of Education Society of Great Britain. A short pamphlet (No. 6 in a series called IMPACT) which offers an evaluation of the content of the National Curriculum in the light of its own aims, reaching some sceptical conclusions about some of the traditional subjects.

Lawton, D. (1996) *Beyond the National Curriculum: Teacher Professionalism and Empowerment*, Sevenoaks: Hodder and Stoughton. From one of the major British contributors to curriculum studies, this as the title implies considers not just the National Curriculum, but how the curriculum impinges on teachers and how teachers can be involved in curriculum planning.

White, J. (ed.) (2004) *Rethinking the School Curriculum: Values, Aims and Purposes*, London: Routledge Falmer. The first two chapters and the conclusion are about the relationship between aims and curriculum, going in more depth into many of the issues raised in Units 7.1 and 7.2. The intervening chapters are about individual subjects, covering the NC for England (except PSHE, citizenship and ICT) and RE.

Unit 7.3

The National Curriculum for England and Wales

Graham Butt

INTRODUCTION

The National Curriculum (NC), as implemented in state maintained primary and secondary schools in England and Wales from September 1989, represented a bold step towards standardizing the school curriculum. Introduced as part of the Education Reform Act 1988 (ERA 1988) the National Curriculum has dominated state education in England and Wales in a way that contrasts sharply with earlier practice, for governments had previously made few interventions into the curriculum taught in schools. Indeed, up until the late 1980s, schools themselves largely determined what and how they taught – the only statutory requirement being that religious education was provided for children, as a consequence of the Education Act 1944. The ERA 1988 was therefore a very significant piece of legislation, the effects of which are seen in schools to this day. It paved the way for the publication of schools' examination results, the creation of national 'league tables' based on schools' performance, the greater availability of information on all pupils' attainment, and the restructuring of the subject-based curriculum taught in all state schools.

The National Curriculum defines the educational entitlement for pupils of compulsory school age – as a trainee teacher in England you will have to teach lessons that meet the requirements of the National Curriculum and support pupils in line with the national standards it defines. It describes each subject's content, the expected levels of pupil performance at different stages of their schooling, and the means of assessing and reporting on such performance. However, although the National Curriculum applies to all pupils in state-maintained schools it is not statutory for the independent sector, although many independent schools currently choose to structure their curricula around it.

Despite the existence of this 'common curriculum' many would now argue that the grip of the National Curriculum on the structure and content of what is taught in schools is weakening. Legislation introduced this century enables all secondary schools to become 'specialist' schools and may herald the death not only of the National Curriculum but also of comprehensive education as a whole. Therefore, although the purpose of the National Curriculum remains – to give teachers, pupils, parents and the wider community a shared understanding of the knowledge, understanding and skills pupils will gain at school – many would now argue that it only partly achieves this goal.

This chapter provides you with an overview of the implementation, modification and impact of the National Curriculum on state education in England and Wales. It also poses questions about the scope, content and structure of the curriculum (see Beck, 2000).

OBJECTIVES

At the end of this unit you should be able to:

- understand the key terms associated with the National Curriculum;
- understand the nature, scope and content of the National Curriculum;
- understand why changes have been made to the National Curriculum since its inception;
- appreciate the effects of the National Curriculum on the curriculum experienced by pupils in state schools;
- appreciate the place of your own subject within the National Curriculum framework.

BACKGROUND

The original rationale for the National Curriculum was that it should:

> provide teachers with clear objectives for their teaching; children with identifiable targets for learning; parents with accurate, accessible information about what their children can be expected to know, understand and be able to do and what they actually achieve.
>
> (NCC, 1989)

Working groups were established by the government in the late 1980s and early 1990s to create the National Curriculum. Significantly the first group to be set up was the Task Group on Assessment and Testing (TGAT), whose recommendations created the framework for an assessment-driven curriculum, built upon a foundation of national testing and teacher assessment (DES, 1988). Subject working groups were also formed, composed of teachers, educationists, subject experts, 'lay' people and advisers. Each of these working groups was directed to comply with the assessment structure determined by TGAT. They often worked to tight time schedules to produce their statutory subject orders.

The curriculum structure was to be in four Key Stages, with formal assessments to be reported at the end of each stage. Expectations of levels of performance for pupils in each Key Stage were also outlined (see Table 7.3.1).

The National Curriculum, as originally established by ERA, consisted of ten compulsory subjects for secondary schools: three core and seven non-core, or foundation, subjects.

Core subjects, introduced from September 1989:

- English (or Welsh, where Welsh was the first language);
- mathematics;
- science.

Table 7.3.1 Key stages, pupil ages, year groups and range of levels of performance determined by the National Curriculum

Key Stage	Ages	Year groups	Original range of levels within which the majority of pupils were expected to work	Current range of levels within which the majority of pupils are expected to work	Expected attainment for the majority of pupils at the end of the Key Stage
1	5–7	1–2	1–3	1–3	At age 7 = 2
2	7–11	3–6	2–5	2–5	At age 11 = 4
3	11–14	7–9	3–7	3–7*	At age 14 = 5/6
4	14–16	10–11	4–10	National qualifications are the main means of assessing attainment	National qualifications are the main means of assessing attainment

* A level 8 description and description for 'exceptional performance' also exists.

Non-core or Foundation subjects, introduced in phases from 1990 to 1992:

- history;
- geography;
- technology;
- music;
- art;
- physical education;
- modern foreign language (secondary).

Religious education, based on a locally agreed syllabus, also had to be included in the school curriculum, but was not formally part of the National Curriculum. Cross-curricular themes were added later, although these were not uniformly adopted by schools.

Associated with each of these subjects was a framework of associated attainment targets (ATs), programmes of study (PoS) and statements of attainment (SoAs) (see Table 7.3.2) appropriate for each of the Key Stages. The first subject working groups were set up for the core subjects, with the non-core groups being created later with the aim of introducing their curricula into schools on a rolling programme. Unfortunately, this staggered timing meant that groups could not discuss their work with each other, leading to an inevitable lack of coherence and comparability between subjects.

Assessment at Key Stage 4 was to be through the existing General Certificate of Secondary Education (GCSE). However, because of the expansion of the curriculum as a result of the introduction of a subject-based National Curriculum, pupils who would previously have taken up to (say) nine subjects at GCSE would now be expected to take a minimum of eleven under the new proposals.

Table 7.3.2   Some terms associated with the National Curriculum

Attainment Target (AT)
The knowledge, skills and understanding that pupils of different abilities and maturities are expected to have by the end of each Key Stage.

Programmes of Study (PoS)
The matters, skills and processes that should be taught to pupils of different abilities and maturities during the Key Stage.

Statement of Attainment (SoA)
Statements used to define subject content more precisely than the Attainment Target within which they were contained. SoAs were removed after the Dearing Report in 1994.

Level Description (LD)
Level descriptions describe the types and range of performance that pupils working at that level should characteristically demonstrate. They indicate progression in the knowledge, skills and understanding as set out in the programmes of study.

SCOPE OF THE NATIONAL CURRICULUM

The ERA 1988, and the subsequent Education Act 1997, requires all state schools to provide a curriculum for pupils which:

- is broad and balanced;
- promotes spiritual, moral, cultural, mental and physical development;
- prepares pupils for the opportunities, responsibilities and experiences of adult life; and
- includes religious education and, for secondary pupils, sex education.

In essence, the National Curriculum is therefore a framework of subjects and other requirements representing a minimum curriculum entitlement for pupils. Schools can develop their own, fuller curriculum which reflects their particular ethos, needs and local requirements but this must also enable the delivery of the statutory curriculum.

It was soon apparent in the early 1990s that the National Curriculum was overloaded with content and was creating considerable problems for teachers, particularly with respect to assessment. The subject-based curriculum was so large that it dominated any other curricular activities, giving schools little latitude to make the curriculum their own. These issues, alongside limited industrial action by teachers in response to the introduction of Key Stage 3 tests in 1993, led to the first review of the National Curriculum.

DEARING REPORT ON THE NATIONAL CURRICULUM

The fact that the National Curriculum required such a substantial review of its content, assessment and administrative arrangements so soon after it had been introduced revealed the extent of its problems. Sir Ron (later Lord) Dearing was appointed by the government to lead this process, which resulted in the curriculum content of many subjects being slimmed substantially, statements of attainment being removed from subject orders and level descriptions being introduced (Dearing, 1994). The greatest impact of the review was in the area of assessment, where teacher assessment and national testing had already encountered difficulties. By the time of the review, national tests had been implemented for the core subjects at Key Stages 1 and 2, but boycotted by most schools at Key Stage 3. Some piloting of national tests for non-core subjects had also taken place, although these tests were soon abandoned.

Dearing also suggested that the National Curriculum should be reviewed again for the year 2000 – a process which was to be intentionally 'light touch', with the aim of mainly 'rebalancing' the curriculum. For the five years up to 2000 the government agreed that there would be no more major alterations to the National Curriculum, although the change of government in 1997 and the subsequent implementation of other curricular initiatives made this a rather hollow promise.

The pragmatic and sensible recommendations made by Dearing (Table 7.3.3) were largely welcomed by schools. They consisted of a revised set of subject orders for all subjects, to be introduced in September 1995 for Key Stages 1 to 3 and September 1996 for Key Stage 4. In essence Dearing had achieved his aim of freeing around 20 per cent of the time schools had previously committed to teaching the National Curriculum.

Following consultations with teachers, unions and subject associations, which proved largely uncontroversial, Dearing's changes were implemented by schools.

It can be argued that some of the consequences of the Dearing Report were unforeseen and unintended (see Watson, 2002), particularly the creation of a three-tiered ranking of subjects (Table 7.3. 4).

Despite this implicit rank ordering, non-core subjects still proved popular amongst pupils at GCSE, A and AS level, but only where option systems in schools allowed pupils to make the subject choices they wished.

Importantly, both in his 'Report on the National Curriculum' (Dearing, 1994) and his later 'Review of 16–19 Education' (Dearing, 1996), Dearing flagged the increasing importance of providing vocational

Table 7.3.3 A brief summary of the Dearing changes

Key Stages 1 to 3
- Reduced content of all subject orders to 'free up' 20% of curriculum time. This was most significant in non-core subjects, leaving something of an imbalance between core and non-core orders.
- Information technology (IT) was separated from design and technology, creating an additional National Curriculum subject. IT was to be a core entitlement for pupils.

Key Stage 4
- Due to the expansion of the number and content of subjects to be studied under the National Curriculum at Key Stage 4 it was decided to make a number of subjects optional.
- From 1996 pupils would study for GCSE in the core subjects (English, mathematics and science), as well as one modern foreign language and design technology. They were expected to take a full GCSE in the former and at least a GCSE short course in the latter.
- All pupils would be taught, but not necessarily examined in: physical education; religious education; personal, social and health education (PSHE); sex education; and IT.
- Other non-core subjects become optional.

Assessment
- Simplification of the TGAT system. In many subjects the number of attainment targets were substantially reduced, whilst within each AT the statements of attainment were replaced by level descriptions.
- The original 10 level scale across the Key Stages was reduced to eight, with an additional category for 'exceptional performance', to be applied only at Key Stages 1 to 3.
- National assessment of the core subjects at Key Stages 1, 2 and 3 to be externally assessed as 'pencil and paper' tests. No national testing of non-core subjects.
- The results of National Curriculum assessments at Key Stages 2 and 3 to be published. Also teacher assessments against attainment targets, using level descriptions, for all other subjects at the end of Key Stage 3 to be published.
- Attainment at Key Stage 4 to be assessed and reported through public examinations (GCSE, GNVQ and/ or NVQ).

Table 7.3.4 Effects of the Dearing Report on subject status

Rank	Subject	Key Stages taught	Assessment
1	English, Maths, Science	Compulsory at Key Stages 1 to 4	National tests at Key Stages 1 to 3. Results used as basis for primary school league tables.
2	PE, Design and Technology, ICT, Modern foreign language, RE	Compulsory at Key Stages 1 to 4	No national tests at Key Stages 1 to 3. Teacher assessment.
3	Music, Art, Geography, History	Compulsory at Key Stages 1 to 3. Optional at Key Stage 4.	No national tests at Key Stages 1 to 3. Teacher assessment.

options for pupils. He recommended a strengthening of the vocational pathways for pupils post-14, primarily leading to General National Vocational Qualifications (GNVQ) and National Vocational Qualifications (NVQ). These intentions have subsequently been supported by the work of the Tomlinson Committee on 14–19 education (Working Group on 14–19 Reform, 2004), which was set up to achieve greater coherence in 14–19 learning programmes, to strengthen the structure and content of vocational programmes, and to provide a unified framework of qualifications. A new diploma framework was proposed based on four levels – entry, foundation, intermediate and advanced – with implications both for the National Curriculum and for existing external examinations.

CURRICULUM 2000

A change of government often leads to significant changes in policy-making. In 1997 the election of a New Labour government, partly on a pledge to move education to the centre of policy initiatives, led to a reassessment of state education. The new government confirmed previous intentions to conduct a review of the National Curriculum for 'Curriculum 2000', but also introduced ambitious measures to raise the standards of literacy and numeracy amongst primary pupils. The Curriculum 2000 review focused on the whole school curriculum, some would say for the first time, rather than concentrating too closely on revising the separate subjects which made up the curriculum.

In the late 1990s the national literacy strategy (NLS) and national numeracy strategy (NNS) took government-led curriculum initiatives further than ever before, changing the whole emphasis of the National Curriculum at primary level (see Unit 7.4). These strategies not only prescribed the teaching approaches to be adopted by teachers – something which the National Curriculum had never explicitly attempted – but also specified the amount of time to be spent on the teaching of literacy and numeracy. Although not statutory, most maintained schools simply adopted these strategies in an attempt to meet the ambitious achievement targets laid down for them at Key Stage 2. As a result the non-core subjects suffered a further reduction in status between 1998 and 2000, for in an attempt to give schools more space to achieve their literacy and numeracy targets the government suspended all programmes of study in non-core subjects. This sharp focus on literacy and numeracy meant that the time most primary schools had spent on the non-core subjects was now substantially reduced, with an obvious 'knock on' effect when pupils came to study them again at Key Stage 3. As a result, many pupils may undertake very little work in the non-core subjects before transferring to Key Stage 3, creating obvious pressures on teachers to achieve expected attainment levels for their pupils at the end of that key stage.

By 1998 Key Stage 4 pupils still had to take examinations in mathematics and English, but schools could 'disapply' certain pupils from up to two of the compulsory National Curriculum subjects (science, design technology, modern foreign language) in order that they might take vocational studies. A new subject was also added to the National Curriculum when citizenship became a compulsory part of the Key Stages 3 and 4 curriculum in September 2002, and a non-statutory part of PSHE at primary level.

The Curriculum 2000 review of the National Curriculum had given an opportunity to reassess how appropriate the curriculum was for the twenty-first century and to reappraise the effectiveness of individual subject orders. Teachers still felt the pressures of initiative overload and were not keen on further changes, seeking continuity rather than change. Nonetheless, the overall purpose of the review – to maintain stability, to keep change to a minimum, to make the National Curriculum more flexible and less prescriptive and to raise standards – was largely achieved.

Task 7.3.1
Reviewing the National Curriculum for England

Obtain a copy of the *National Curriculum Handbook for Secondary Teachers* <http// www.nc.uk.net>. This outlines the values, aims and purposes of the National Curriculum.

- To what extent do you consider the National Curriculum to be successful in educating young people in the values, beliefs and cultural aspects of the society in which it is based?
- What aims do you think underpin the National Curriculum? Is it a curriculum which specifically prepares pupils for adopting useful roles in society based upon achieving gainful employment or are the aims focused on education more broadly?
- Does the National Curriculum achieve a sensible balance between centralized control and local interpretation? Is the curriculum primarily driven by what is 'good for the state' or by what is 'good for the individual'?
- Ideally, what should a National Curriculum aim to do?

CURRENT STRUCTURE OF THE SUBJECT ORDERS

Each of the current subject orders in the National Curriculum follows a common format. Initial guidance is given about the structure of the National Curriculum, about learning across the curriculum, and about the place of the subject within this framework. The section on learning across the curriculum highlights each subject's contribution to promoting spiritual, moral, social and cultural development, as well as citizenship, key skills and other aspects of the curriculum. At the start of the programmes of study are some limited examples of pupils' work alongside quotes from media personalities, academics and other notaries, giving a context for the subject. The orders distinguish, by using either black or grey typeface, between those sections of the curriculum that are statutory and those which are non-statutory. The latter occur either as notes in the margins, or as examples in the main text – with marginal notes being used to define certain terms used in the programmes of study or to create links with other subjects in the curriculum. Whether this approach actually reduces prescription, or whether teachers simply assume that everything that is written in the order must be taught, is debatable.

The concluding section of each order, which focuses on general teaching requirements, gives detailed information on inclusion, use of language across the curriculum, use of ICT across the curriculum and (if applicable) on health and safety (see Table 7.3.5). The final section details the attainment target for each subject in terms of its level descriptions.

Table 7.3.5   National Curriculum guidance on inclusion, use of language, use of ICT and health and safety

---

Inclusion

The statements on inclusion, within the 'general teaching requirements' section, is by far the largest and most comprehensive of the four subsections. The provision of effective learning opportunities for all pupils – including those with special educational needs, disabilities, English as an additional language, and from different ethnic and cultural backgrounds – is a foundation of the National Curriculum and guidance is given in each subject order about the ways in which teachers can modify the PoS to make learning relevant and appropriately challenging at each Key Stage. Three principles are established for a more inclusive curriculum:

1   setting suitable learning challenges;
2   responding to pupils' diverse learning needs;
3   overcoming potential barriers to learning and assessment for individuals and groups of pupils.

The statement reminds teachers that these principles should avoid the need for pupils to disapply from the National Curriculum and that other curricular opportunities can be provided beyond the National Curriculum to meet the needs of individuals and groups (such as speech and language therapy and mobility training). Advice states that only 'a minority of pupils will have particular learning and assessment requirements which go beyond the provisions described' but that these requirements will usually arise as a consequence of a pupil having a special educational need or disability, or may be linked to a pupil's progress in learning English as an additional language (EAL).

Use of language

This section explains that pupils in all subjects should be taught to express themselves correctly and appropriately and be able to read accurately and with understanding. Since standard English is the predominant language in which knowledge and skills are taught and learned, pupils should be taught to recognize and use this. Brief sections on writing, speaking, listening and reading follow.

Use of ICT

This section explains that pupils should be given opportunities to apply and develop their ICT capabilities through the use of ICT tools to support their learning in all subjects.

Health and safety

The health and safety section applies mainly to science, design and technology, ICT, art and design and PE. It highlights hazards, risks and risk control by and for pupils.

Task 7.3.2
Review your subject order

Look closely at your subject order <http//www.nc.uk.net>.

Does it adequately reflect what you want pupils to learn about your subject at Key Stage 3? Discuss this with two other colleagues and try to achieve a consensus about what the aims of education within your subject should be at Key Stage 3.

Talk to your tutor about what you perceive to be the strengths and weaknesses of your existing subject order at Key Stage 3.

Table 7.3.6   Themes for Key Stage 3 strategy

Planning and assessment	Teacher repertoire
• Assessment for learning in everyday lessons • The formative use of summative assessment • Planning lessons	• Questioning • Explaining • Modelling
Structuring lessons	**Knowing and learning**
• Starters • Plenaries • Challenge • Engagement	• Principles for teaching thinking • Thinking together • Reflection • Big concepts and skills

SCHEMES OF WORK

The DfES and QCA have also published schemes of work related to the National Curriculum requirements in all subjects at Key Stages 1, 2 and 3. These are optional and exemplify how the programmes of study for each subject might be taught in the medium term and how they could be modified for pupils with particular needs. Although it was the intention that schools would draw upon these schemes to meet their own needs, rather than adopting them wholesale, there is evidence that some teachers apply them as though they are a statutory part of the National Curriculum.

KEY STAGE 3 STRATEGY

The Key Stage 3 Strategy (see Unit 7.4) focuses on how children learn and how teachers intervene in the learning process, rather than on *what* they learn. It consists of five strands:

- teaching of English and promoting literacy across the curriculum;
- teaching of mathematics and promoting numeracy across the curriculum;
- science;
- ICT;
- foundation subjects.

It therefore does not alter the nature of the subject orders which make up the National Curriculum, but performs similar functions to the NNS and NLS as applied at primary level. Training materials and additional LEA support has been provided to schools to help them implement the strategy, which is organized under four themes (see Table 7.3.6).

CHANGES TO THE KEY STAGE 4 CURRICULUM

Following the report of the Tomlinson Committee and consultation over the White Paper '14–19: Opportunity and Excellence', the Key Stage 4 curriculum changed again from September 2004. The statutory changes for Key Stage 4 are highlighted below:

- revised science programme of study (from 2006);
- study of design and technology and a modern foreign language no longer compulsory;
- entitlement curriculum areas established – arts, design and technology, humanities, modern foreign languages – which schools must make available to pupils who wish to study them;
- establishment of work-related learning (with a non-statutory framework setting out minimum work-related experiences schools should provide);
- disapplication of pupils from National Curriculum subjects discontinued (from 2004 for design and technology and a modern foreign language, from 2006 for science).

As such the statutory National Curriculum at Key Stage 4 (at the time of writing) comprises of: English, mathematics, science, ICT, physical education, citizenship, religious education, sex education, careers education, work-related learning.

Additionally, the continuing encouragement by the government for secondary schools to become 'specialist' in some way – mirroring the weakening of LEA control of schools when grant-maintained (GM) schools were created by the ERA 1988 – has been a feature of New Labour policy this century.

SUMMARY AND KEY POINTS

The National Curriculum established for itself an ambitious remit. It currently provides an entitlement for pupil learning; the development of literacy and numeracy skills; creativity; and the flexibility for teachers to plan ways to teach that will inspire pupils to make a long-term commitment to learning. Since 2000 it has made explicit the rights of all children to be included in the learning process and to be given chances to succeed – whatever their individual needs or barriers to learning. Principles of equality of opportunity, shared values, recognition of diversity and the need for sustainable development are also mentioned, while education for citizenship is a notable recent addition to the National Curriculum.

In 2004, under a Five Year Strategy for Children and Learners, the government urged every secondary school to become an 'independent specialist' school (or city academy in inner cities), specializing in at least one subject by 2008. Such schools have 'foundation' status – employing their own staff, applying admissions policies, and controlling their own land, building and assets. In an attempt to win back middle-class parents, all schools are being encouraged to adopt school uniforms and a house system, with popular schools being given freedom to expand their pupil intake. The implications of such changes are potentially huge – creating a system of 'grant-maintained'-style schools (which Labour itself abolished in 1997) outside the control of the LEA, which teach a weakened version of the National Curriculum.

There is also an increasing emphasis on a 14–19 orientation of the curriculum. The government is keen to develop 'world class' academic routes and better vocational options, with stronger partnerships between schools, colleges and employers.

As a result of the focus on 'wider initiatives' there is no intention to complete a further wholesale review of the National Curriculum in the near future. A rolling programme of subject reviews has updated subject content and seeks to reflect current trends in teaching and learning. The government seems satisfied with changing the National Curriculum 'around the edges', while allowing new policies to alter the overall curriculum framework in schools as they become specialist institutions. Increasing the flexibility of the conditions under which schools work, while concentrating on curriculum initiatives rather than on reviewing the subjects themselves, inevitably means a loosening of the National Curriculum.

Teachers are broadly positive about the current National Curriculum. The reasons for this have been outlined in the chapter – the relaxation of the grip that the National Curriculum once held on the whole school curriculum and the flexibility for greater teacher-led curriculum development is widely supported. However, a question now arises as to how far the National Curriculum can be allowed to become reformulated and customized by schools before it ceases actually to *be* a National Curriculum in any real sense. The provision of a common learning experience for all children in state schools was always ambitious and now appears to be further away than at any time since 1988.

NOTE

This chapter is based partly on an earlier version published in the 3rd edition of *Learning to Teach in the Secondary School: A Companion to School Experience* written by Gill Watson.

FURTHER READING

Beck, J. (2000) 'The School Curriculum and the National Curriculum', in J. Beck and M. Earl (eds) *Key Issues in Secondary Education*, London: Cassell. A useful overview of what we mean by the term 'curriculum', as well as the nature of its scope, content and structure. Beck raises issues about the control of the curriculum in schools and focuses on the various 'ideologies' that influenced how the National Curriculum originally developed, and continues to develop.

DfEE/QCA (1999) *The National Curriculum: Handbook for Secondary Teachers in England*, London: DfEE/ QCA. A compendium of all the National Curriculum subject orders and guidance on the National Curriculum.

Useful websites

Department for Education and Skills. QCA/DfES schemes of work: <http://www.standards.dfes.gov.uk>. All the schemes of work for subjects are available on the DfES standards website.

The National Curriculum Online: <http://www.nc.uk.net>. This provides direct links to the QCA/ DfES schemes of work and other online resources relevant to each part of the programmes of study for each subject.

National Curriculum in Action: <http://www.ncaction.org.uk>. Uses pupils' work to exemplify the National Curriculum at Key Stages 1 and 3. New materials are added to the site as they become available. Work exemplifying creativity and the use of ICT are also included.

Qualifications and Curriculum Authority: <http://www.qca.org.uk>. Provides guidance on the curriculum, assessment and the range of qualifications offered in schools and colleges.

Unit 7.4

Pedagogy and Practice

The Key Stage 3 and Secondary National Strategy in England

Rob Batho

INTRODUCTION

The Key Stage 3 National Strategy in England is a vital component of the government's drive to transform secondary education. The Strategy aims to raise standards by strengthening teaching and learning across the curriculum for all 11–14-year-olds. In 2006 this will become the Secondary National Strategy.

   The challenges at Key Stage 3 are particularly demanding. These are vitally important years for laying the foundations for life-long learning and influencing the crucial decisions pupils will make at age 14. The English and mathematics strands of the Key Stage 3 National Strategy were introduced to all schools in England in 2001 with science, foundation subjects and information and communication technology (ICT) following in 2002 and behaviour and attendance in 2003. In addition, the Strategy also addresses a number of elements such as literacy, numeracy and ICT across the curriculum and assessment for learning. The content and coverage of the secondary school curriculum is the responsibility of the National Curriculum(NC), not the Strategy. The Strategy's responsibility is to advise and guide senior leaders and teachers about effective strategies, techniques and skills to improve teaching and learning in classrooms. It is designed to support schools and teachers in addressing the learning needs of 11–14-year-old pupils. The support for schools and teachers is twofold; first, through local education authority (LEA) consultants who work directly with schools and teachers to improve teaching and learning in the classroom, and second, through issuing training and guidance materials, most of which you should be able to find in your school if you are in England or alternatively on the Key Stage 3 website (details below).

OBJECTIVES

At the end of this unit you should be able to:

- understand the Strategy's main principles of teaching and learning;
- know the main features of a good lesson at Key Stage 3;
- know where and to whom to go to find guidance and materials on teaching and learning at Key Stage 3.

MAIN PRINCIPLES

The Strategy's main principles of teaching and learning are as follows:

- To focus on teaching to objectives: teachers and pupils need to have a clear focus and purpose for their teaching and learning.
- To make concepts and conventions explicit through teacher modelling and demonstration: pupils often find difficulty in understanding the concepts within a subject or the writing conventions of a particular type of text used in a subject, and teachers can help by explicitly demonstrating or modelling (which includes thinking out loud to give pupils access to their thought processes) the convention or the explanation of the concept.
- To structure the learning explicitly: teachers can, through planning and careful explanation, help pupils see and understand the links between the different parts of a lesson and how they contribute to their learning.
- To make the learning active and interactive: pupils are more likely to be motivated and gain genuine understanding if the teacher plans for them to be interactive with their peers and with her in their discussions and tasks, and if the activities demand that pupils actively seek meaning and knowledge rather than simply receive it.
- To make learning enjoyable and stimulating with an appropriate degree of challenge: pupils at this age can become easily bored and reluctant to learn, and the teacher needs to consider such matters as the suitability of the content, stimulating and enjoyable activities, instigating and maintaining an appropriate pace for learning and setting an appropriate degree of challenge for all pupils.
- To scaffold and support learning: when pupils are confronted by a new task and new learning, they may often be unsure of how to proceed if the leap is too big from their existing understanding, and so the teacher can help by providing suitable scaffolds and support (e.g. writing frames★, guided group work) to enable those pupils to take small, secure steps towards their learning goal.
- To teach pupils how to reflect on their learning and to take responsibility for future learning: effective learners of all ages are usually able to reflect on their own learning, what they have learned and how they have learned, and are able to use that facility to identify what they need

---

★ Note: A writing frame is commonly an outline of a text type that the teacher expects the pupils to write. Writing frames help pupils to structure a text and often contain the opening words for key paragraphs and indications as to how to connect each paragraph. Writing frames, as Roger Beard explains, 'are intended to be used as a kind of prompt, eventually to be dispensed with, as children begin to adopt the features of the genre for themselves' (Beard, 2000: 113).

to do next to improve their learning. Many pupils do not have that facility but teachers can teach them how to be able to reflect on their learning and to plan their future learning, in order that they become more independent learners.

The Strategy asks teachers to adopt these principles to inform their planning and teaching of lessons in order that their pupils are motivated, suitably challenged and make progress in their learning.

WHAT MIGHT A GOOD KEY STAGE 3 LESSON LOOK LIKE?

We want you to consider what a good Key Stage 3 lesson might look like where these principles have been applied.

Task 7.4.1
Planning a Key Stage 3 lesson

Look back at the main principles of the Key Stage 3 Strategy and consider what a lesson might look like the where they have been applied.

- What would you expect the teacher to be doing at the various stages of the lesson?
- What would you expect the pupils to be doing?
- How might the pupils be organized at the different stages?
- Observe a Key Stage 3 lesson and note down the key features and where they match the main principles.
- Now compare your thoughts and findings with Table 7.4.1 and consider if there are any elements that you could usefully introduce into your own teaching.

PLANNING AND SETTING LEARNING OBJECTIVES

The Strategy is keen to emphasize the importance of teachers setting clear teaching and learning objectives for their pupils so that they, the pupils, will know and understand what it is they are expected to learn and how that might be achieved, monitored and assessed. To assist teachers in their planning and in their setting of teaching and learning objectives the Strategy has published frameworks for teaching in each of the core subjects, in ICT, modern foreign languages and design and technology. I suggest you locate and consider some of those teaching and learning objectives for your own classroom teaching.

The Strategy advises teachers to use the teaching objectives from the frameworks to assist them in planning for progression in pupils' learning and also to help them in setting clear learning objectives and learning outcomes (what pupils will produce during a lesson or series of lessons) for their pupils. To give one example; in the English framework for Year 7 there is a teaching objective for reading that states:

> Know how to locate resources for a given task, and find relevant information in them, e.g. skimming, use of index, glossary, key words, hot links.

(DFEE, 2001: 24)

Table 7.4.1 Features of a good Key Stage 3 lesson

Phase	Features
Start	**Starter activity** The first 5 minutes or so are spent on a brisk mini-activity to catch the imagination. This could be linked directly with the work to come or to previous homework as a 'tester'. This is the place to establish early teaching points or to position 'little and often' objectives which require revisiting and practising skills or consolidating knowledge. It also allows the teacher to quickly establish any gaps in pupils' knowledge or understanding.
Introduction	**Learning objectives and outcomes** The teacher introduces the lesson by sharing with the pupils what they are going to learn and what outcomes are expected. The focus is on the learning: 'Today we're going to look into the factors that affect how quickly enzymes work', or '... learn how to substitute an integer into a simple formulae', or '... consider how the writer builds suspense' or '... look at the benefits and drawbacks of using ICT to automate processes'.
	Active teaching New learning is introduced by teacher input. For example, the teacher may model or demonstrate on the board how to compose a particular type of writing, and the pupils will be drawn in to contribute. The teacher is not afraid to be an expert.
	Pupil participation Pupils are expected to participate; to respond to questions, to think, make suggestions and explain. For example, they might have a moment to talk to a partner and come up with an idea. They might have to work on a problem and hold up answers on individual whiteboards.
Development	**Pupils applying what they've learned** Pupils may apply what they've learned in group work or paired work, or an individual exercise. This part of the lesson may last around 15 to 20 minutes. In the past teachers may have waited for pupils who 'get stuck' to put their hands up. Now, they are more likely to sit with one group for several minutes and guide them through the work, helping them to apply new skills.
	Teaching assistant usefully deployed Any teaching assistant is well prepared, has helped the teacher to plan the lesson and is familiar with their special role. The assistant may be sitting with a group of pupils to help them keep up with the work, or making notes for the teacher on how pupils are setting about a task.
End	**Plenary session** The lesson closes with a plenary session in which the teacher draws out the key points. It is here that learning is reviewed and there is an opportunity to reflect on the learning process itself. Pupils do most of the work. They are encouraged to explain what they've learned and how it can be used in the future, perhaps in other lessons. There may be a series of shorter plenaries to review learning at the end of specific episodes throughout the lesson.
	Homework Regular homework helps individuals to reinforce and consolidate what they have learned in the lesson or to prepare for the next one. Homework tasks can be differentiated as appropriate to the needs of individuals. They should be planned for and used to enhance or extend work in the lesson, not as a fill-in or finishing-off exercise.

This might be translated by the teacher into a learning objective for the pupils in a specific lesson:

Know how to use the table of contents and index of a range of non-fiction texts to find the information you need.

In turn, that learning objective could be transformed into the following learning outcome:

By the end of the lesson you will have used the table of contents and index of a range of non-fiction texts and made a record of the information you need and its source in your exercise book.

Learning outcomes are commonly written but they don't need to be. They could for instance be oral; a talk to the whole class or to a small group, or even a spoken answer in the plenary session to the teacher. Or the outcome could be visual such as a drawing, plan or diagram.

Task 7.4.2
Linking objectives to your planning

Find a copy of the framework for your subject (your training provider should be able to supply you with one for your subject, your department should have some and it is also available for download from the Key Stage 3 website <www.standards.dfes.gov.uk/keystage3/> or, if you teach a subject where there is no framework (e.g. geography, history), locate a copy of the English framework (DFEE, 2001) to focus on possible literacy objectives.

Find a copy of the scheme of work (SOW) and any lesson plans for a Key Stage 3 class that you are teaching or are likely to teach during your school experience. Your subject department will have its own SOWs, many of which will be based on those from the Qualifications and Curriculum Authority (QCA) and which are accessible on their website <www.qca.org.uk>. In the framework, locate the section that contains the teaching objectives and those for the year group you are or will be teaching.

Try now to identify those teaching objectives for the year group that would match the learning intentions you have for those pupils that are implied or indicated in the SOW and lesson plans.

Task 7.4.3
Teaching and learning objectives

Locate a scheme of work and any associated lesson plans for a Key Stage 3 class that you are teaching or are likely to teach during your school experience (they could be the same ones that you used for Task 7.4.2).

Identify one particular teaching objective that will apply to a particular lesson.

Ask yourself, 'Considering the teaching objective, what is it that I want the pupils to learn by the end of this lesson?' Now change the wording of the teaching objective into a learning objective that reflects what you want the pupils to learn and is expressed in words that the pupils will quickly understand.

Next, ask yourself, 'In considering what I want the pupils to learn this lesson, what am I expecting them to produce by the end of it to show me and them what they have learned?' Now write down what it is you want the pupils to produce by the end of the lesson.

If in your planning, your scheme of work and lessons clearly state the teaching objective, the learning objective and the learning outcomes, then you and your pupils will be sharply focused on not only what needs to be learnt and taught but also on what needs to be assessed. Task 7.4.3 gives you the opportunity to try transforming teaching objectives into learning objectives and outcomes.

SUPPORT FOR YOUR TEACHING AT KEY STAGE 3

As has been mentioned, the Key Stage 3 Strategy provides a wealth of practical support and guidance for teachers to improve teaching and learning in the classroom, and you may be wondering how you can access that support and guidance. There are a number of ways. Most of the materials are available for downloading on the Key Stage 3 website <http://www.standards.dfes.gov.uk/keystage3/>. In addition, you should find that all of your school experience schools have copies of all of the Strategy training and guidance materials.

The person in the school who will know where the training and guidance materials are and who has a responsibility for organizing Strategy training in the school is the Key Stage 3 Strategy manager. The Strategy manager should be an excellent source of information and advice for you about Key Stage 3. He can tell you about the training that has taken place and is about to take place in your subject area as well as providing you with data and information concerning the achievement and attainment of pupils you might be teaching. The data and information can help you to plan more effectively. It is important therefore that you make the acquaintance of the Key Stage 3 Strategy manager in your practice school.

Task 7.4.4
Contacting the Key Stage 3
Strategy manager

Find the name of and arrange to meet the Key Stage 3 Strategy manager at your school experience school.

At the meeting ask the Strategy manager the following:

- What Key Stage 3 training has your subject department taken part in over the past two years, what are they likely to be involved in during your time at the school and is it possible and appropriate for you to be included?
- What Key Stage 3 whole-school initiatives and training has the school been involved in, what are they likely to be involved in during your time at the school and is it possible and appropriate for you to be included?
- Where are Strategy whole-school and your subject area materials held?
- What pupil achievement data are held concerning the Key Stage 3 pupils you are scheduled to teach, and which of it might be useful in helping you to know the pupils and in supporting your planning?

In addition to the Strategy manager, your subject head of department should also be able to tell you where the Strategy resources for the subject are kept, the initiatives and training that the department's teachers have been involved in and will be involved in during your time at the school. She should also be able to tell you what the department's key development priorities are, so that you can address some of those priorities in your own planning and teaching and thus be an important part of the department's drive to improve teaching and learning.

THE IMPACT OF THE STRATEGY

There is research evidence that indicates that the Key Stage 3 Strategy has had an impact on teaching and learning in secondary schools. For example, the Office for Standards in Education (OFSTED) in its evaluation of the third year of the Strategy points to the following successes (HMI, 2004):

- the Strategy is helping to improve teaching, in particular through the use of specific objectives for learning and better planning, which add greater challenge and purpose to lessons;
- teachers welcome the training and many are enthused by the developments the Strategy is bringing about in their schools;
- the improvements in teaching are leading to better attitudes to work, especially, but not only among boys;
- there is an increasingly positive effect, albeit uneven, on pupils' attainment.

In 2003 the National Foundation for Education Research (NFER) undertook a study of the perceptions of LEA officers and teachers of the implementation and effectiveness of the Key Stage 3 National Strategy and in its main findings published in May 2004 reported the following:

- the Key Stage 3 National Strategy was well received by LEAs and schools;
- it was an important component of the School Development Plan, a tool to improve teaching and learning in the classroom and, thereby, ultimately raise attainment;
- LEAs and schools felt well supported during the implementation of the Strategy and described the Strategy materials as good quality, useful resources;
- LEAs and schools perceived that the Strategy was making a significant contribution to the improvement of teaching and learning and had contributed to the improvement of lesson structures including pace of lessons, the variety of teaching methods used and the focus on the learner.

SUMMARY AND KEY POINTS

The Key Stage 3 Strategy was introduced in England to improve teaching and learning for 11–14-year-olds, but most of its suggested teaching strategies, techniques and approaches are also applicable and suitable when you teach any secondary age class of pupils. The Strategy aims for teachers to move pupils from dependence on the teacher to being independent and autonomous learners.

In this unit, we have introduced you to the Strategy's main principles for teaching and learning and to the key features of a good Key Stage 3 lesson which engages and motivates pupils and develops their learning. We have also emphasized the importance of careful planning to set pupils clear learning objectives and learning outcomes so that they are able to understand what they are expected to learn and produce. To support your own professional development, we have also indicated the key personnel (such as the Key Stage 3 Strategy manager) in any school who will be able to advise and guide you on matters to do with teaching and learning at Key Stage 3. And remember, there are also plenty of Strategy training and guidance materials which should be readily accessible to you in your training institution and school experience school and most of which are also freely available on the Strategy website.

FURTHER READING

Key Stage 3 Strategy frameworks

The following Strategy frameworks (in England, your ITT provider should be able to give you your own subject copy) not only provide yearly progressive teaching objectives for each of the subjects, but they also include suggestions and advice on approaches to teaching and learning, planning and assessment and they can all be found on the Key Stage 3 website <http://www. standards.dfes.gov.uk/ keystage3/>:

DfEE, *Framework for Teaching English: Years 7, 8 and 9* (2001).

DfEE, *Framework for Teaching Mathematics: Years 7, 8 and 9* (2001).

DfES, *Framework for Teaching Science: Years 7, 8 and 9* (2002).

DfES, *Framework for Teaching ICT Capability: Years 7, 8 and 9* (2002).

DfES, *Framework for Teaching Modern Foreign Languages: Years 7, 8 and 9* (2003).

DfES, *Framework for Teaching Design and Technology: Years 7, 8 and 9* (2004).

Key Stage 3 Strategy foundation subjects training materials

DfES, *Training Materials for the Foundation Stage*, DfES Publications (2002). These training materials contain some excellent ideas and advice for teachers of all subjects on areas such as assessment for learning, planning, questioning, explaining, modelling, starters and plenaries.

Unit 7.5

Secondary Schools and Curriculum in Scotland[1]

Allen Thurston and Keith Topping

INTRODUCTION

Scotland's social and cultural identity is defined largely by its geography and history. Its political, educational, legal and religious systems make Scotland unique within the UK (Humes and Bryce, 2003). This chapter aims to identify the distinguishing structures and characteristics of the Scottish education system. It explores the nature and functioning of the various stakeholders in Scottish education. It illustrates the systems of governance of education in Scotland. The structure and nature of the curriculum and assessment in Scotland are examined. It also explores the standards for initial teacher education and discusses the preparation necessary for a newly qualified teacher to enter the profession in Scotland.[2]

SCOTTISH EDUCATION

Elementary schooling in Scotland was first placed on a statutory basis by an Act of 1872 – education became compulsory for children between the ages of 5 and 13 (Anderson, 2003). Owing to the actions of various philanthropists, some education had been available prior to this. After this, various Acts and Orders passed in Westminster shaped the nature of Scottish education, until the Scottish Parliament passed its first Education Act in 2000. The 2000 Act stated the entitlement to free compulsory schooling for children aged 5 to 16, and has driven new educational developments for pre-school children, students and adult learners. This separate legislative framework seems one of the most potent expressions of the distinctiveness of Scottish education (Humes and Bryce, 2003).

OBJECTIVES

By the end of this unit you should:

- be familiar with the distinctive features of the structures of governance in Scottish schools;
- know what principles have shaped curriculum design in Scotland in the recent past;
- understand the structure, balance and distinctive features of the Scottish secondary school curriculum;
- have a clear understanding of the standards for initial teacher education and a basic understanding of the standards for full registration of teachers in Scotland.

This separate legislative framework has allowed and indeed encouraged a number of differences to develop between the Scottish education system and that of England. Of particular note was the introduction and subsequent adaptation of Curriculum Guidelines for pupils in Scotland within the age ranges of 5–14 in the 1990s (Paterson, 2003), quite different from the so-called 'National' Curriculum in England. No core subjects are identified, which gives more breadth and flexibility in curriculum and pedagogical methods. The guidelines are advisory recommendations and not prescriptive.

Provision for assessment is also different between England and Scotland. The Conservative government in Westminster tried to introduce similar regimes of national testing in Scotland as had been implemented in England and Wales. However, this met with considerable resistance from parents, local authorities and teaching unions. Different legislation was subsequently enacted for Scotland, leaving teachers free to conduct assessments at a time of their choosing. As a result of this, constructing performance league tables is impossible in Scotland until pupils sit national examinations at the ages of 16–18, and even then they are not published by government. One reason why the teaching unions were able to resist is that 80 per cent of teachers in Scotland are members of a single teaching union (the Educational Institute for Scotland).

Another difference is that school boards exist in Scotland, as compared to governing bodies in England. In Scotland school boards have a role in the appointment of senior management staff and in supporting the head teacher to raise standards within a school (Jeyes, 2003). Much of the finance for Scottish schools remains in the hands of local authorities, as compared to more local, school-based, financial management in England.

A cornerstone of the Scottish Parliament's vision for education is 'equality and inclusion linked to active citizenship'. 'Education for All' is a fundamental principle. This is at the core of the recently published 'National Priorities' for Scotland (dealt with in greater detail later in this unit). The Scottish Executive Education Department (SEED) sees three keys to the maintenance of quality in education (Scottish Executive Education Department, 2004a) namely:

- all school teachers must be qualified and registered with the General Teaching Council for Scotland (GTCS);
- examinations and qualifications are nationally accredited through the Scottish Qualifications Authority (SQA);
- all schools and colleges are open to Her Majesty's Inspectorate in Education (HMIE) who are employed by, and report to, SEED.

In Scotland pupils will normally be able to attend state nursery as an ante-preschool year and as a preschool year. Children usually start primary school in August when they are aged between 4½ and 5½. If parents choose to educate their children by sending them to school, they must start in the August after their fifth birthday. Children born between September and February can, however, start school in the August preceding their fifth birthday, or they can defer to the following August. Pupils complete seven years at primary school before going to secondary school for four years. The seven years in primary are named Primary 1 through Primary 7 (P1–P7) and the four years in secondary school S1–S4. At the end of S4, pupils finish compulsory education, but may stay on for fifth and sixth year to gain further qualifications. These years are termed S5 and S6. Importantly, SEED sees secondary schools as the route to work and continuing education whether pupils leave at 16 or stay until the end of the sixth year.

Pupils study for awards at two broad levels in Scotland, Standard Grade and Higher Grade, conferred by the SQA. The Scottish Certificate of Education (known as Standard Grade) is normally gained after S4. Standard Grade is available at three levels – Foundation, General and Credit. Higher Grades (known as Highers and Advanced Highers) follow on from Standard Grade, generally taken in S5 and S6. Both Higher and Advanced Higher awards use a combination of external examination and internal assessment. Additional national qualifications are available to pupils in S5 and S6, including courses at Access 1, 2 and 3, and Intermediate 1 and 2 levels. More details of these will be found later in this unit.

Secondary schools in Scotland have a senior management structure that includes a headteacher, depute headteachers and principal teachers. The latter may be responsible for managing departments and curriculum initiatives.

Overview of the curriculum in Scotland

In S1/S2 the curriculum generally follows SEED's 5–14 Programme (Learning and Teaching Scotland, 2004a). Pupil choice is a fundamental principle at this stage. The transition from S1 to S2 is often characterized by increasing specialism, e.g. a move from general science to courses more aligned with chemistry, physics and biology (Gavin, 2003). The S3/S4 curriculum is strongly influenced by study for Standard Grade awards. A typical pupil will study for seven or eight subjects at Standard Grade. In S5/S6 (the 16–18 age range), schools offer a varied range of Higher Grade awards, sixth year study awards and Scottish Vocational Education Council (SCOTVEC) awards.

SEED's 5–14 Programme, monitored by HMIE, lays down guidelines for the progress and performance of children at different stages through primary and early secondary school. Each stage allows for different levels of development. Each school is free to create its own curriculum with advice from the guidelines, local authority education departments and specialist agencies. The detail of this is dealt with later in this unit. The stated aims of the 5–14 curriculum (Scottish Executive Education Department, 2000) are that it should help each pupil to acquire and develop:

- knowledge, skills and understanding in literacy and communication, numeracy and mathematical thinking;
- knowledge, understanding and appreciation of themselves and other people and of the world around them;
- the capacity to make creative and practical use of a variety of media to express feelings and ideas;
- knowledge and understanding of religion and its role in shaping society and the development of personal and social values;

- the capacity to take responsibility for their health and safe living;
- capability in ICT and an awareness of the uses of ICT in the world at large;
- the capacity to treat others and the world around them with care and respect;
- the capacity for independent thought through enquiry, problem solving, information handling and reasoning;
- positive attitudes to learning and personal fulfilment through the achievement of personal objectives.

The structure and nature of the 5–14 curriculum in Scotland appears to offer teachers much greater freedom and professional responsibility than the National Curriculum in England. Even within curriculum areas the guidance is not prescriptive, and there is latitude for teachers to exercise professional judgement in deciding what to teach and when. Programmes of study for individual pupils vary greatly, but pupils up to the age of 16 study English, mathematics, science, one modern foreign language and a social subject. In the fifth and sixth years, study expands to include a wide range of modular courses in vocational subjects. Scotland's school-based qualifications are awarded by SQA, a quango answerable to SEED. The SQA develop assessments at Standard Grade and Higher Grade.

THE STRUCTURE AND GOVERNANCE OF EDUCATION IN SCOTLAND

Local authorities

There are 32 local authorities in Scotland. The most recent reorganization of local government resulted in a larger number of smaller authorities. Each has a degree of autonomy over educational issues. To a large extent the provision of education in Scotland is still governed by the Education Scotland Act 1980 which emphasised:

- the right of pupils to be educated as far as is reasonable in accordance with the wishes of their parents;
- the duty of parents to provide efficient education by ensuring their children regularly attend school or receive efficient education by other means;
- the duty of education authorities to secure adequate and efficient provision of school education.

Scottish Executive Education Department (SEED)

SEED is the central government agency administering education in Scotland. It promotes quality in education through three principal channels. First, it develops guidance on curriculum in Scotland in the form of the 5–14 curriculum guidelines. Second, it has an agency that has a cross-sector responsibility for standards and quality assurance throughout the Scottish education system (HMIE). Third, it supports a nationally accredited qualifications and assessment framework managed by the SQA.

The roles and responsibilities of SEED in relation to the other stakeholders in Scottish education are represented in Figure 7.5.1. Further information on the structure of governance of Scottish Education is available from: <http://www.scotland.gov.uk/Resource/Doc/923/0004718.pdf>.

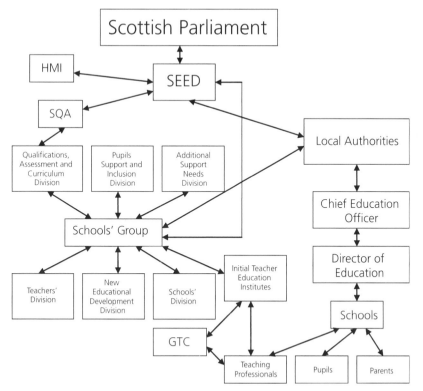

Figure 7.5.1   Interrelationships between stakeholders in Scottish education

Her Majesty's Inspectorate of Education (HMIE)

HMIE is responsible for undertaking inspections of the standards and quality of services in pre-school centres, schools and post-compulsory education. It also inspects providers of initial teacher education. Inspections are carried out as a statutory requirement. A representative sample of establishments from across the country is selected for inspection each year.

One of the differences between the roles of OFSTED in England and HMIE in Scotland is that OFSTED inspectors are contracted in order to undertake specific inspections whereas HMIE inspectors come from a public appointment process. There are also a number of differences in the inspection process itself. It is really in ethos and style that the major differences lie. HMIE places great emphasis on self-evaluation by schools and the focused professional development of teaching professionals, seeking to offer support in addition to critique.

Learning and Teaching Scotland (LTS)

LTS is a quango with an advisory role. Its Advisory Council offers advice to Scottish Ministers on issues affecting the learning experiences of children and young people aged 0–18. It is supported by five Advisory Council Reference Groups who develop advice on specific areas of education. It is funded by SEED. LTS also aims to provide support, resources and staff development opportunities for teachers to enhance achievement and attainment and promote life-long learning. Its Chair and Board are appointed by SEED, as are its Advisory Council Reference Groups. It is LTS who produce the National Curriculum Guideline documentation for SEED and the additional supporting material for teachers.

NATIONAL PRIORITIES FOR EDUCATION IN SCOTLAND

Throughout 2000 SEED undertook a national consultation exercise. This was termed the 'Great Debate' in Scottish education. The aim was to consult widely on the future and nature of education in Scotland. As a result of the debate the National Priorities for School Education in Scotland were defined and incorporated into the Education (National Priorities) Order 2000. The Order was approved by resolution of the Scottish Parliament. The National Priorities were defined under the following headings:

- Achievement and Attainment;
- Framework for Learning;
- Inclusion and Equality;
- Values and Citizenship;
- Learning for Life.

The National Priorities (Scottish Executive Education Department, 2003) are:

1   to raise the standards of educational attainment for all in schools, especially in the core skills of literacy and numeracy, and to achieve better levels in national measures of achievement including examination results;
2   to support and develop the skills of teachers, the self-discipline of pupils and to enhance school environments so that they are conducive to teaching and learning;
3   to promote equality and help every pupil benefit from education, with particular regard paid to pupils with disabilities and special educational needs, and to Gaelic and other lesser used languages;
4   to work with parents to teach pupils respect for self and one another and their interdependence with other members of their neighbourhood and society and to teach them the duties and responsibilities of citizenship in a democratic society; and
5   to equip pupils with the foundation skills, attitudes and expectations necessary to prosper in a changing society and to encourage creativity and ambition.

Task 7.5.1
Integrating the national priorities into professional practice

Examine the National Priorities above. Choose one to think about in more detail. How could you integrate the aims of this National Priority into your professional practice?

THE SCHOOL CURRICULUM

In Scotland the school curriculum aims to develop certain dispositions in pupils towards learning. These dispositions (Scottish Executive Education Department, 2000) are stated as:

- a commitment to learning as a life-long process;
- a respect and care for self and others, having a positive self-image as well as respect for diversity of people, cultures and beliefs;
- a sense of social responsibility and a willingness to take a positive role in society;
- a sense of belonging and a feeling that one is a stakeholder in society.

The 5–14 curriculum identifies core skills and capabilities that should be developed by the formal curriculum in school. These are listed as including:

- personal and interpersonal skills including working with others;
- language and communication skills;
- numeracy skills;
- ICT skills;
- problem-solving skills;
- learning and thinking skills.

In addition to the learning dispositions and the development of the core skills the 5–14 curriculum aims to foster the acquisition of knowledge and the development of understanding in the main curriculum areas.

Structure and balance of the 5–14 curriculum

The 5–14 national guidelines are non-statutory guidelines for Scottish local authorities and schools. They cover the structure, content and assessment of the curriculum in primary schools and in the first two years of secondary education. The stated aim of the 5–14 programme is to promote the teaching of a broad, coherent and balanced curriculum that offers all pupils continuity and progression as they move through school (Learning and Teaching Scotland, 2004a).

The 5–14 curriculum aims to offer a breadth of experience and a balance of opportunity for learning for every pupil. In order to fulfil this aim the 5–14 curriculum provides clear pathways though the areas of learning. These pathways provide the framework for personal growth and progression in learning for pupils. The curriculum aims to build on pupils' experience and learning and tries to be responsive to their needs. The 5–14 guidelines (Scottish Executive Education Department, 2000) state that the curriculum is intended to:

- relate to events and facets of pupils' everyday lives;
- help pupils develop intellectually, aesthetically, socially, emotionally, spiritually, imaginatively and physically;
- prepare pupils to face the challenges of life in a rapidly changing society. It should help guide them through the transition from childhood to adulthood.

To these ends the 5–14 curriculum in Scotland has been developed so that:

- *Breadth* ensures coverage of a sufficiently comprehensive range of areas of learning.
- *Balance* ensures that appropriate time is allocated to each area of curricular activity and that provision is made for a variety of learning experiences.

- *Coherence* emphasizes links across the curriculum so that pupils make connections between one area of knowledge and skills and another.
- *Continuity* ensures that learning builds on pupils' previous experience and attainment and prepares them for further learning.
- *Progression* provides pupils with a series of challenging but attainable goals.

Breadth of the 5–14 curriculum

The 5–14 curriculum is divided into a number of areas:

- English language;
- mathematics;
- environmental studies;
- expressive arts;
- religious and moral education;
- health education;
- personal and social development;
- modern languages;
- ICT.

For each area there are attainment outcomes, each with a number of strands or aspects of learning that pupils experience. Most strands have attainment targets at five or six broad levels: A–E or A–F.

Task 7.5.2
Auditing curriculum content knowledge in preparation to teach

Are you ready to teach? Look at the 5–14 curriculum guidelines for the area that you teach. Examine the attainment targets at levels E and F. Do you have the subject knowledge necessary to teach all the subject matter? Conduct a brief audit and identify any areas that are a development need for you.

Balance of the 5–14 curriculum

Time allocation for each subject in schools has an element of flexibility built into it. Within secondary schools in S1 and S2 the suggested time allocations are represented in Table 7.5.1.

Schools can use the remaining 20 per cent of time flexibly to meet development needs of pupils and the development priorities of the school.

Table 7.5.1 Time allocations for curriculum subjects

Curriculum Areas	Minimum time over two areas (%)
English language	20
Mathematics	10
Environmental studies	30
Expressive arts	15
Religious and moral education	5
Total core	80

Coherence in the 5–14 curriculum

The 5–14 guidelines suggest that links between the curricular areas should be developed in order to give the curriculum coherence. Cross-cutting themes suggested by the 5–14 guidelines as appropriate areas where this could be attempted include:

- personal and social development;
- education for work;
- education for citizenship;
- the culture of Scotland;
- information and communications technology.

Each cross-curricular aspect requires careful planning and teaching. This allows its distinctive contribution to be made both within and across the curriculum areas. It is important that these are taught in ways that allow pupils to make connections to other parts of the curriculum. This strengthens coherence in pupils' learning and avoids unhelpful fragmentation of the curriculum. It also provides an important basis for the personal and social development of all pupils.

Continuity within the 5–14 curriculum

The principle of continuity within 5–14 is that the curriculum should build on pupils' experience and attainment and prepare them for further learning. Continuity also deals with important issues relating to transition from primary to secondary school, issues within the secondary school curriculum, and transition from secondary school to life after school. Scotland is similar to the rest of the UK in that transition from primary to secondary has often been associated with a dip in attainment (Galton *et al.*, 1999). Transition programmes have been established between secondary and feeder primary schools, and have been reported to have a beneficial effect in counteracting attainment dips (Waldon, 2000). However, evidence is growing that since the introduction of 5–14 curriculum more children are coping better with the primary–secondary transition, and report positively on preparation programmes (Graham and Hill, 2003).

SEED suggest that bridging topics, jointly taught by both primary and secondary staff, can strengthen continuity during transition. In addition, the guidelines suggest that continuity will be enhanced if curriculum planning and programmes in feeder primary schools and receiving secondary schools are based on the 5–14 guidelines. It is common to have regular cluster group meetings between staff of feeder primary and associated secondary schools. It is desirable that there is continuity in expectations and approaches to learning and teaching within and between schools. This is expected in respect of both classroom organization and the management of the learning experience, and in respect of the contexts for learning which are established. Schools normally develop policies to help staff develop a shared ethos and approach to managing the learning experience. In recent years the effective communication of information and arrangements to support pupils and parents have developed. Both formal parents' evenings (where assessment and pupil progress will be reported to parents) and curriculum evenings (where aspects of the curriculum will be explained and exemplified to parents) are common. Liaison meetings between schools and pre-transition visits by primary pupils to high school help in preparing them for the transition. The introduction of the 5–14 curriculum, the consistent approaches to assessment and shared understanding of levels of pupils' level of attainment means that information is more easily passed on as children move class either within or between schools.

Within the secondary school, continuity in pupils' learning is based (Scottish Executive Education Department, 2000) on:

- an active and ongoing partnership between home and school, where the distinctive contributions of home and school to pupils' learning are recognized and valued;
- a positive school/classroom ethos being established where praise, encouragement, challenge and the celebration of achievement increase motivation and create a learning environment in which pupils become confident and enthusiastic learners ready to make the most of school;
- teachers' planning recognizing prior learning and whole-school programmes being matched tightly to national guidelines and syllabuses of standard grades and national units/courses;
- consolidation of learning and an understanding that teachers make time for pupils to review and consolidate their prior learning at the beginning and end of lessons and topics;
- sustaining appropriate intervention strategies to support learners by giving, as appropriate, more direction, opportunities to talk about problems and solutions, and time for reflection, further experience, or more practice;
- evaluation of lessons, topics and teaching strategies with assessment information, feedback from pupils (through self-assessment activities or learning diaries) and discussions with colleagues involved in collaborative teaching, providing important sources of evidence for evaluating the effectiveness of teaching and learning.

Progression within 5–14

There is a link between high attainment in schools and a pupil's ability to see progression in the curriculum (Harland *et al.*, 2002). The curriculum is a route plan for pupils' learning. The 5–14 guidelines feature strands, pathways and attainment targets. Within the strands progressively more demanding attainment targets have been developed (A–F). These provide specific statements of what pupils should know and be able to do at each level for each of the attainment outcomes. In each subject area each of the six levels of progression of the attainment targets are based on the following descriptions of levels:

Level A: should be attainable in the course of P1–P3 by almost all pupils.
Level B: should be attainable by some pupils in P3 or even earlier, but certainly by most in P4.
Level C: should be attainable in the course of P4–P6 by most pupils.
Level D: should be attainable by some pupils in P5–P6 or even earlier, but certainly by most in P7.
Level E: should be attainable by some pupils in P7–S1, but certainly by most in S2.
Level F: should be attainable in part by some pupils, and be completed by a few pupils, in the course of P7–S2.

ASSESSMENT

National tests

SQA have developed an online bank of national assessment materials which are based on Assessment of Achievement Programme (AAP) tests and tasks. These national assessments are used by teachers to confirm their judgements about pupils' levels of attainment in the key areas of reading, writing and mathematics, for each of 5–14 levels, A–F. The professional judgement of the teacher is very important. The national assessments should support valid and reliable judgements of attainment against published attainment targets, when results are considered alongside other available evidence. The basic premise is that pupils should be tested when a teacher deems them ready to pass the test.

Formative assessment

One of the major assessment initiatives in Scotland has been the Assessment for Learning (AFL) programme, emphasizing formative assessment to shape teaching in process (rather than summative assessment to assess the effect of teaching after it has happened). The programme has tried to develop a unified process of assessment and feedback so that pupils, parents, teachers and other professionals can plan effectively for pupils' developmental needs. The specific aims of the programme (Learning and Teaching Scotland, 2004b) have been to:

- develop one unified system of recording and reporting, the Personal Learning Plan (PLP), which will bring together the current PLP, progress file, transition records and Individualized Educational Programmes (IEPs);
- bring together current arrangements for assessment, including the Assessment of Achievement Programme, national tests and the annual 5–14 Survey of Attainment;
- provide extensive staff development and support through its project-based approach.

It is hoped that the programme will promote better and more timely feedback for pupils, leading to improved achievement. It is also intended that simplified systems of assessment should be adopted, making it possible to provide more effective support for teachers (and therefore a reduction in workload). Teachers should also be able to provide clearer information for parents.

The programme was developed as a result of a number of reviews and debates in Scotland surrounding the introduction of the 5–14 programme. A review by HMIE led to recommendations that assessment should be used to support learning and provide information for monitoring, review and evaluation of a school's performance against national levels of attainment (HMIE, 1999). A report on the consultation process and surrounding research emphasized the importance of formative assessment in promoting pupil attainment (Hayward et al., 2000). As a result, an Assessment Action Group was formed and from this developed the AFL programme.

The AFL programme has three main components. These components emphasize:

- assessment *for* learning;
- assessment *as* learning;
- assessment *of* learning.

The programme has provided guidance in each of these key areas. AFL explores the collection of evidence by assessment to inform onward planning. It also explores how to form effective partnerships with parents and pupils. In addition it explores the roles of pupils as learners, teachers as learners and the management and role of assessment (5–14 national tests, the Assessment of Achievement Programme (AAP) and alternatives). The AAP has monitored the attainment of a representative sample of pupils in P3, P5, P7 and S2 in specified areas of the Scottish 5–14 curriculum through the use of tests since 2002. The curricular areas monitored have included social subjects (2002), science (2003), mathematics (2004) and English language (2005). Pupils' performance in the core skills of communication, numeracy, ICT, problem solving and working with others has been assessed in the surveys since 2002. Further information about the AFL programme is available from <http://www.ltscotland.org.uk/assess/about/aims/index.asp>.

Scottish Qualifications Authority (SQA)

SQA is the national body in Scotland responsible for the development, accreditation, assessment, and certification of qualifications other than degrees. It is answerable to SEED.

The stated functions of the SQA (Scottish Qualifications Authority, 2004) are to:

- devise, develop and validate qualifications, and keep them under review;
- accredit qualifications;
- approve education and training establishments as being suitable for entering people for these qualifications;
- arrange for, assist in, and carry out, the assessment of people taking SQA qualifications;
- quality assure education and training establishments which offer SQA qualifications;
- issue certificates to candidates.

The SQA offers a number of national qualifications. Within the secondary school sector these are generally Standard Grades, National Units and National Courses. Standard Grade is generally taken over the third and fourth year of secondary school. An exam usually takes place at the end of fourth year. There are three levels of study from credit (the highest), to general and foundation (the lowest). Students usually take examinations at two of the three levels, e.g. credit and general or general and foundation. This enables pupils to try and get the highest level of qualification that they can achieve.

National Courses take place at seven levels: Access 1, Access 2, Access 3, Intermediate 1, Intermediate 2, Higher and Advanced Higher.

Access 1 courses are designed for students who require considerable support with their learning, while Access 2 courses are designed for those with moderate support needs. Access 3 courses are comparable to Standard Grade Foundation level, but there is not a requirement to sit an exam. Intermediate 1 and 2 courses are for students who have completed Standard Grades or Access 3 courses. Intermediate 2 is used sometimes as a stepping stone to Higher Grade by students (or even by students who are starting a new subject in school). Highers are generally taken by students who have passed subjects at Standard Grade Credit level or have successfully completed a course at Intermediate level 2. Highers are normally needed to allow entry to a university or college course that leads to a degree or Higher National Diploma. Advanced Highers are generally for those students who have passed Highers. Normally taken in sixth year, they are additional qualifications for entry into higher education or the workplace. National Units are qualifications in their own right. They are usually of about 40 hours' duration and are assessed by the student's own teacher. Assessment for National Courses from Intermediate 1 to Advanced Higher includes an external examination. Performance in the external assessment determines the grade awarded for the course. Pass grades are awarded at grades A (top grade), B and C (lowest 'pass grade'). Grade D is awarded to students who just fail to obtain a grade C.

Task 7.5.3
Preparing pupils for national
assessments

Obtain a copy of the Standard Grade and Higher Grade (and 5–14 National Test if you teach mathematics or English language) examinations for last year. Look at the nature and structure of the examination papers. How could you ensure pupils are prepared for undertaking examinations of this nature?

A teaching profession for the twenty-first century

In January 2001 the findings of the McCrone Report into teaching in Scotland *A Teaching Profession for the 21st Century*, were published (SEED, 2001a). The report detailed the recommendations of an enquiry into the pay and conditions of teachers in Scotland. The report recommended the following career structure for teachers in Scotland:

Progression to Chartered Teacher is via qualification at masters level. Progression to principal teacher, depute headteacher and headteacher is by application for specific jobs. Promotion to depute headteacher and headteacher is normally preceded by study towards the 'Standard for Headship'.

The only accredited route to achieving the Standard for Headship is through the Scottish Qualification for Headship (SQH). As from August 2005 achievement of the Standard for Headship is a prerequisite for all first-time appointments as a headteacher (SEED, 2004b). A summary of the career structure is given in Figure 7.5.2.

The report recommended a working week of 35 hours for teachers, of which not more than 22.5 hours should be class contact time. Importantly, probationer teachers were guaranteed one year's on-the-job training leading to full registration with the GTCS. During this probationary period their maximum class contact time should be no greater than 0.7 of the working week (one and a half days of non-contact time). Further details of the McCrone Report can be found at:
<http://www.scotland.gov.uk/education/teaching/pages/mccrone_report.htm>.

General Teaching Council for Scotland

In order to teach in a Scottish state sector school teachers are expected to maintain a current valid registration with the GTCS. The GTCS has three levels for registration:

1. Standard for Initial Teacher Education – which providers of initial teaching qualifications must build into their programme design. Students must then demonstrate competence against the benchmarks of education practice in order to register as a probationer teacher in Scotland.
2. Standard for Full Registration – which individual probationer teachers must attain to achieve full registration with the GTCS.
3. Standard for Chartered Teacher – to be attained by individual teachers. Aspects of this are covered earlier in this unit.

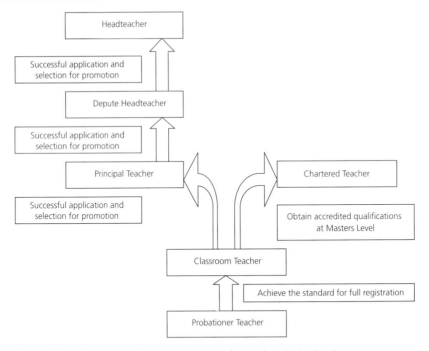

Figure 7.5.2 Summary of the career structure for teachers in Scotland

Task 7.5.4
Achieving the Standard for Initial Teacher Education

Look at the Standard for Initial Teacher Education. As you progress through your programme of initial teacher education, your tutors are likely to ask you to keep brief notes regarding your development in each of these Standards. Try to evidence your notes by developing a personal portfolio drawing in personal thoughts, examples of plans and pupils' products from school experience and examples of summative and formative feedback from tutors, teachers and mentors.

CHALLENGES FACING SCOTTISH EDUCATION

The education system in Scotland faces a number of challenges for the future. Declining populations in rural areas of Scotland mean that it is becoming fincially difficult to sustain schools that can have a roll in single figures. Balanced against this are the huge costs of transporting rural pupils to centralized facilities. Delivering effective CPD to teachers in rural locations presents similar problems.

Another major challenge for Scottish education is the development of effective strategies to counteract the effects of poverty and low income. Scotland has one of the highest rates of childhood poverty in the western world, in both urban and rural communities. One-third of Scotland's households live in poverty. One in five Scottish children is entitled to a free school meal. In Scotland many children under 16 become homeless every day and 360,000 children live in property affected by dampness (Mackenzie, 2003).

Mainstreaming of pupils with special education needs as the default expectation was made explicit in the Education Act 2000. The legislative framework that deals with SEN in Scotland focuses on rights and responsibilities (pupils' rights to be educated and educators' responsibilities to educate them) (Scottish Office Education and Industry Department, 1999). Pupils with SEN have Records of Needs (rather than Statements as in England). These are being replaced by Co-ordinated Support Plans (CSPs), emphasizing multi-agency co-operation. Whether these administrative changes deliver better services on the ground remains to be seen.

Like the rest of the UK, Scotland been tackling behavioural problems in schools. A task group on discipline in Scottish schools reported to SEED (SEED, 2001b), and as a result £10 million per year over four years was allocated to establish restorative justice schemes (SEED, 2004b). Effective educational provision for children of asylum seekers and refugees is a related issue. A survey of 2000 Scots revealed that a high proportion self-reported themselves as having racist views and over one-quarter openly admitted to being racist (Humes and Bryce, 2003). In 2002 the Scottish Executive launched a major initiative to combat racism in Scotland – the 'One Scotland, Many Cultures' campaign. Problems of bullying associated with racism and minority language use have been recognized by SEED (2002). Support materials have gone to all schools and an anti-bullying network has been established (see <http://www.antibullying.net>).

Given its historical tradition of excellence in education, Scotland pays attention to international comparisons of educational performance. In the results published by the Programme for International Student Assessment (PISA) Scottish secondary pupils performed reasonably well in mathematics and science (PISA, 2000). In mathematics Scottish pupils ranked equal fifth amongst the Organization for Economic Co-operation and Development (OECD) countries and in science they ranked ninth amongst the OECD countries (SEED, 2004c). However, Scotland did not perform as well as England in either mathematics or science. The Progress in International Reading Literacy Study (PIRLS) with pupils at the end of primary education showed that while Scotland was well above the international average in literacy, it had lower scores than England (DfES, 2003a). This suggests the Scottish education system has little room for complacency and considerable further room for improvement.

SUMMARY AND KEY POINTS

This chapter has sought to identify key features that make the Scottish education system distinctive from that in the rest of the UK. It has also tried to raise awareness of the structure and balance of the curriculum in Scotland and highlight the preparation that may be required to teach within that framework. The intention has been to stimulate thinking about some of the issues that are likely to impact upon the professional practice of teachers in Scotland.

The challenge for the newly qualified teacher in Scotland is to teach their subject well, but not to lose sight of the overview of how they fit into the larger picture of education in Scotland. In addition to this, in order to enhance standards in Scottish education it is imperative that research is used to inform practice. In order to facilitate articulation with research to allow it to inform and shape professional practice in this way, making early connections with interested research groups such as Scottish Education Research Association (SERA) or Scottish Council for Research in Education (SCRE) is desirable. This will allow research evidenced based practice to develop rather than more intuitive methods of working in the classroom. This should lead to more effective learning and teaching.

NOTES

1 An extended version of this unit is available on the website linked with this text: <http://www.routledge.com/textbooks/0415363926>.
2 The Standards for Initial Teacher Education in Scotland are available on the Quality Assurance Agency website <http://www.qaa.ac.uk/crntwork/benchmark/itescot/individual%2Dtext%2Ddocs/introduction.htm>.

FURTHER READING

Bryce, T.G.K. and Humes, W.M. (2003) *Scottish Education*, 2nd edn, Post-Devolution, Edinburgh: Edinburgh University Press.

Paterson, L. (2003) *Scottish Education in the Twentieth Century*, Edinburgh: Edinburgh University Press.

Useful website

Scottish Executive Education Department (2000) *The Structure and Balance of the Curriculum 5–14 National Guidelines*. Online. Available HTTP:<http://www.ltscotland.org.uk/5to14/htmlguidelines/saboc/page3.htm>.

8 Your Professional Development

In this chapter we consider life beyond your student teaching experience. The chapter is designed to prepare you for applying for your first post and to be aware of the opportunities available to continue your professional development as a teacher after you have completed your initial teacher education course. It contains three units.

Getting a job at the end of your initial teacher education is important, time-consuming and worrying for student teachers. Unit 8.1 is designed to help you at every stage of the process of getting your first post. It takes you through the stages of deciding where you want to teach, looking for suitable vacancies, sending for further details of posts that interest you, making an application, attending an interview and accepting a post.

The success of any school depends on its staff. However, although you have successfully met the requirements to qualify as a teacher at the end of your initial teacher education course, you still have a lot to learn about teaching to increase your effectiveness. Unit 8.2 considers the transition from student teacher to newly qualified teacher, immediate induction into the school and the job, ongoing induction throughout the first year and continuing professional development which helps you continue to learn and develop professionally throughout your career.

Unit 8.3 is designed to give you an insight into the system in which many of you will be working as teachers. We look briefly at the structure of the state education system in England and then at teachers' accountability: professional, moral and contractual. This leads into a slightly fuller consideration of the legal and contractual requirements and statutory duties that govern the work of teachers.

Unit 8.1

Getting your First Post

Alexis Taylor, Julia Lawrence and Susan Capel

INTRODUCTION

Obtaining your first teaching post involves a number of stages, each of which is equally important. You need to be clear about why you want to enter the teaching profession, and then decide where you want to teach, look for suitable vacancies, select a post which interests you and send for further details, prepare your curriculum vitae (CV), write a generic and then specific letter of application, contact potential referees to make sure that they are prepared to act for you and to confirm their address, make an application, prepare for an interview (and undertake a mock interview, if possible), attend the interview and accept the post. This unit is designed to help you with that process.

OBJECTIVES

At the end of this unit you should be able to:

- consider critically why you want to enter the teaching profession;
- understand the procedure for and process of applying for your first teaching post;
- make a written application which is received favourably;
- be prepared for an interview for a teaching post.

CONSIDER WHY YOU WANT TO ENTER THE TEACHING PROFESSION

Obtaining your first teaching post may be one of the most important decisions of your life, so it needs to be taken carefully. Think for a moment why you want to enter the teaching profession. Teaching is an attractive choice of career for many reasons. You may have heard about the long holidays and short working days and that it fits around commitments, such as family. However, now you have undertaken some school experience, you are also aware that in reality teaching is a demanding career. Even though student teachers are already committed to a programme of initial teacher education (ITE) it is not automatic that all wish to enter the teaching profession. Smithers and Robinson (2000) found that almost a quarter of secondary student teachers do not continue into the profession.

Over the last decade the issue of entry into ITE in England has been high on the government's agenda. The top priority of the Teacher Training Agency (TTA), the government's regulatory body for ITE is teacher recruitment. The TTA's Corporate Plan (TTA, 2003: 3) states that its first strategic aim is to 'increase the number of able and committed people to teaching'. A number of mechanisms have been introduced by the TTA to manage recruitment at a central level, e.g. extensive advertising campaigns. There are also a range of financial support schemes to counteract the economic difficulties facing some new entrants and to compare favourably with training schemes for other professions.

As committed teacher educators, we think that there is no point in you learning to become effective teachers if you do not obtain a teaching post at the end of your ITE course, but we realise that there are many factors that you have to consider when thinking about applying for your first post. The remainder of the chapter explores these. The procedures for applying for teaching jobs in Scotland and Northern Ireland are different. If you are interested in teaching in these areas, you should obtain further information from your institution, and/or the relevant government office.

DECIDING WHERE YOU WANT TO TEACH

For most student teachers, deciding where to apply is your first major decision. If you are committed to living in one place because, for example, you have family commitments, you need to consider the distance it is possible to travel to a job in order to determine the radius in which you can look for a post. You need to think about the travel time to and from school, as you probably will not want a long journey in your first year of teaching when you are likely to be tired at the end of each day or when you have had school commitments in the evening.

For other student teachers, deciding where to apply is your first major decision. If you opt for a popular area it could be difficult to obtain a post. The reasons for popularity may be that there are few schools, turnover from schools is low or there are a number of applications from student teachers at a local higher education institution. It is therefore worth considering if your preferred areas are popular areas and, if so, whether there are other areas to which you could go or whether you could be totally flexible as to where you teach. It is worth doing some research about other areas of the country rather than basing your decision on assumptions about certain areas – unless, of course, you are committed to a restricted geographical area due to personal reasons. Alternatively, you may want to teach abroad, either in a paid or voluntary capacity, such as Voluntary Service Overseas (VSO). Some teaching jobs abroad require you to have teaching experience before you can apply.

**Task 8.1.1
Where do you want to teach?**

Think about where you would like to teach and how flexible you are able to be in where you can look for a post. List all areas in which you would consider working and find out something about them. If you know anyone from the area, talk to them about it. Visit the area if at all possible to get a general 'feel of the place' and further information.

Think about the type of school in which you want to teach. You probably have a list of criteria for the type of school you would be happy to teach in. For example:

- primary/middle/secondary;
- maintained or voluntary;
- specialist school;
- sixth form college.

However, it is advisable not to close your mind to other options. During your school experiences you see or hear about a range of types of school and you may surprise yourself by enjoying teaching in a type of school that you had not previously considered.

**Task 8.1.2
What type of school do you want
to teach in?**

Think back to the types of schools you experienced/are experiencing during your ITE. List the aspects you find positive about working in them and list the opportunities you were/are not able to experience in these different types of schools.

List criteria for schools you would be happy to teach in. Find out about different types of school and discuss these with other student teachers or teachers in your school experience school who have gone to or taught in these different types of school. Find out what types of school there are in those areas in which you would like to teach. You can start by looking at the *Education Authorities Directory and Annual* and the *Education Year Book* (see Further Reading at the end of this unit). If you visit the area(s) in which you would like to teach, try to arrange to visit some schools.

LOOKING FOR SUITABLE VACANCIES

The majority of advertisements for teaching posts are for specific posts in specific schools. Advertisements generally start around January or February. However, the majority of advertisements are around April or May because teachers who are leaving at the end of the academic year are required to hand in their notice by the end of May. Independent schools often advertise earlier, from December onwards.

Teaching posts are advertised in a number of different places: in the national press, sometimes the local press (especially for part-time posts). The major source of information about teaching posts is the *Times Educational Supplement* (published every Friday). However, jobs are also advertised in other national newspapers, such as the *Guardian* (the Tuesday edition). There are also advertisements in religious and ethnic minority newspapers such as the *Asian Times*, *Catholic Herald* and the *Jewish Chronicle*.

Letters from headteachers are often sent to teacher education institutions. These give advance notice of posts about to be advertised and information about making applications.

Local Education Authorities (LEAs) sometimes advertise posts themselves. Sometimes information is sent by subject inspectors or advisers to institutions which have courses offering that specific subject. Some LEAs produce lists of vacancies which they send on request, some send information and guidance about applications for posts to teacher education institutions. Some (although a decreasing number) advertise for general applications to the LEA rather than to an individual school. Many LEAs produce recruitment literature, e.g. brochures and/or videos, which are designed to show what it is like to work for the authority. Practices vary; therefore check current practice in LEAs in which you might be interested.

Recruitment strategy managers (RSM) have, in a recent initiative, been appointed in some LEAs. One of the roles of the RSM is to establish strategic recruitment (and retention) projects in response to teacher supply needs identified in their LEA. A list of contact names is available from the Teacher Training Agency (TTA). You may wish to contact an RSM of an LEA in which you are interested in teaching as they may be aware of local needs.

Online there are agencies with whom you can register. Such agencies match up, for student teachers registered on an ITE course, preferences for posts (e.g. location, type of school, and type of contract) with vacancies at schools, and forward information about suitable posts to student teachers. One such initiative is the Student Teacher Employment Programme (STEP: <http://www.stepjobs.com>).

If you are interested in applying for teaching jobs in Scotland and Northern Ireland, the procedures are different. You should obtain further information from your institution.

SELECTING A POST WHICH INTERESTS YOU AND SENDING FOR FURTHER DETAILS

If an advertisement interests you then write for further details. Write briefly and to the point, for example:

> Dear Sir/Madam (or name if given in advertisement)
>
> I am interested in the vacancy for a (subject) teacher (quote reference number if one is given) at ABC School, advertised in (publication, e.g. the *Times Educational Supplement*) of (date) and would be grateful to receive further details of this post.
>
> Yours faithfully (*if you use Sir/Madam* or Yours sincerely *if you use a name*)

MAKING AN APPLICATION

As you read details of all posts to which you are interested in applying, highlight key words and phrases, and the requirements specified, which indicate whether the post is suitable for you as a first post, e.g. whether you have the knowledge, skills, qualities and experience the school is looking for and whether the school meets some or all of your requirements. If you decide to apply, remember that first impressions are very important and applications are the first stage in the selection process. You need to present yourself effectively on paper. Plan the content of your application before you complete an application form or CV or write a covering letter for a specific post. You use the same basic information for all applications, however, you cannot have a standard application form, CV or letter of application which you use for every application. Each application needs to be slightly different as you want to match your experience and qualifications to the requirements of the post, highlighting different points and varying the amount of detail you provide according to specific requirements of the post and the school. You should find it useful to look back at the key words, phrases and requirements you underlined in the details for the post. These help you to customize and personalize the application. A customized application shows that you have taken the time to find out about a specific post in a specific school, and should help your application to stand out from the others. An application which fails to explain why you are interested in the specific post in the specific school is unlikely to be considered further.

Thus, completing an application form for each post takes time. Two hours is probably the minimum time to complete an application properly without rushing it if you have prepared beforehand and have all the information available. It takes longer if you have not prepared in advance. It is a good idea to keep all your information on a computer. This helps you to customize your applications more easily and also enhances your information and communications technology (ICT) skills.

Referees

When applying for teaching posts you are normally asked to supply the names and addresses of at least two referees. Before you complete an application, contact potential referees to make sure that they are prepared to act for you, to confirm their address contact details and if there are any dates when they are away and unable to respond should a request arrive. Your first referee is normally someone associated with your teacher education course. Check if there is one particular person within your institution who you should name as the first referee and, if not, decide who you would like this to be and then ask that person. This reference covers all areas of your professional and academic work on the course. It is often helpful for the person compiling your reference to have additional information about you which might be included in a reference, e.g. other activities in which you are involved. Therefore, check whether it would be helpful for your referee to have a copy of your CV. Your second referee should be someone who knows you well and is able to comment on your character, qualities, achievements and commitment to teaching as a career. Your mentor (or other member of staff) at the school where you were placed for your final block school experience may well be an appropriate person, otherwise an employer from any work you have undertaken. It is not normal practice to include open testimonials with your application as schools or LEAs value confidential references more highly. Some LEAs have a policy of open references, i.e. the reference is shown to the applicant in certain circumstances. The referee knows this at the time of writing the reference.

Methods of application

Schools normally require job applicants to submit a letter of application and completed application form or a CV.

Letter of application

A letter of application should state clearly your reasons for applying for the post, matching your qualifications, experience, particular skills and personal qualities to the post as described in the information sent to you from the school. The letter is normally between one and two sides of A4 in length, on plain white notepaper. A suggested format for a letter of application is given in Figure 8.1.1.

Address
(at top right hand side)
Date

Name of headteacher
Address

Dear Sir/Madam or Name of headteacher

Paragraph 1
In reply to your advertisement in (name of publication) of (date) I would like to apply for the post of (subject(s)) teacher (quote reference number if one is given) at (name of school).
   Or
I have been informed by my University/College that, in September, you will have a vacancy on your staff for a teacher of (subject(s)) and I would like to apply for this post.

Paragraphs 2/3
This section should begin by explaining why you are applying for this particular post. It should then carefully match your qualifications, experience, particular skills and personal qualities to those required by the school, indicating what you could contribute as a teacher of the subject(s) specified.

Paragraphs 3/4
These might begin:
The enclosed curriculum vitae provides details of the content of my teacher education course. I would also like to draw your attention to … (*here outline any special features of your course and your particular interest in these, anything significant about your teaching and any other work experience, anything else you have to offer above that required specifically by the post, including being able to speak a language other than English, extra-curricular activities, a second subject; skills in ICT; pastoral work; etc. that you wish the school to be aware of and any other information about interests and activities related to the post or to you as a teacher, including additional qualifications, awards and positions of responsibility you have held*).
   If you are unavailable for interview on any days, this is the point to mention it. You might indicate this by including a statement such as 'It may be helpful to know that my examinations (or other event) occur on the following date(s) (quote actual dates). Unfortunately this means that I am not able to attend for an interview on those dates. I hope this does not cause inconvenience as, should you wish to interview me, I could come at any other time.'

   Yours faithfully (or Yours sincerely if you use the head teacher's name)

            (signature)

Figure 8.1.1 Format for a letter of application

An application form

The information required on an application form closely matches that identified for a CV (below). Read through any application form before you write anything on it. To help you focus on what you are going to write and check that the information fits into the space provided, we recommend that you make a photocopy of the blank form and complete this in pencil as a practice before completing the original form. It may be possible for you to obtain an electronic copy of the application form. Follow exactly any instructions given. Check that there is no missing information, dates or other detail or questions which have not been answered. Do not leave any sections of the form blank. If there are sections which you cannot complete write N/A (not applicable).

One page of the form is often blank and in the space provided you are required to explain why you are applying for the post and to elaborate on the skills and experience that equip you for it. This section should be written in continuous prose as if it is a section of a letter, following the suggested format and containing the type of information given for a letter of application (above). It is usually acceptable to use additional sheets of paper and attach them to the form. This section requires information that would otherwise be included in a letter of application; therefore a letter of application with such an application form is normally very brief, indicating that you have included your application for the post of (subject) teacher as advertised in (publication). A longer letter of application would be needed if the application form does not include such a section.

CV

A CV should always be accompanied by a longer letter of application. A CV summarizes your educational background, qualifications, teaching and other work experience, interests and activities and any other relevant qualifications and information. A sample format for a CV is provided in Figure 8.1.2.

Notes about applications

Applications should be laid out well and presented clearly, completed neatly, with legible writing and without using jargon. Check your application to ensure that there are no basic errors such as typing errors, mistakes in spelling, grammar or punctuation; and that the information is accurate and consistent. If there is time, it is worthwhile asking a colleague, friend or tutor to read through your final application. We recommend that, if you do not word process an application form, you use black ink as applications are often photocopied for members of an interview panel.

Indicate clearly any dates that you are unable to attend for interview, e.g. because you have an examination. Examinations must normally take precedence over interviews. However, holidays do not take precedence and most schools do not wait until you return from holiday to interview you; therefore do not book holidays at times when you are likely to be called for interview.

Remember that if you put down additional skills or experiences, for example, that you can sing, you may be invited to use those skills in school, e.g. in the school choir. Therefore, do not make exaggerated claims about your skills or additional experiences.

Always send the original application, but keep a copy of every letter of application, application form or CV so that you can refresh your memory before an interview.

Task 8.1.3
Your curriculum vitae

Draft a specimen letter of application and CV and obtain and complete an application form. Ask your tutor to check these for you. Use these as the basis for all your job applications.

CURRICULUM VITAE

Name: Date of birth:
Term time address: Home address:
Telephone number: Telephone number:
e-mail address: e-mail address:

(*indicate dates when you are at your term time address and when your home address should be used*)

Academic qualification(s): (your first degree and above, with subject, institution and class)

Professional qualification (for teaching): *If you are yet to qualify write* I am currently on a PGCE/ BEd (or other) course and expect to qualify in July 200?.

Previous relevant experience:

(*provide only very brief details here to highlight the most important points to help the reader; expand on these later in the CV*)

EDUCATION
(*list institutions from Secondary School on, in reverse chronological order*)
Institution   Dates attended
(*you might want to include some detail about your degree and/or teacher education course, particularly emphasising those aspects of your course which match the requirements of the post*)

QUALIFICATIONS
(list qualifications from 'O' levels/GCSEs on, in reverse chronological order)

Qualification gained   Date awarded
(with subject(s), grades or classification)   (or date to be awarded)

TEACHING EXPERIENCE
(*list any prior teaching experience and the school experiences on your course, in reverse chronological order*)
School and subject(s) taught   Year(s) and length and focus of experience
e.g. ABC school. Final block school experience of 7 weeks' duration, comprising: hockey (Year 7); gymnastics (Year 8); swimming (Year 9); GCSE PE (Year 10).

OTHER WORK EXPERIENCE
(*list permanent full- or part-time jobs and holiday jobs separately, each in reverse chronological order*)

Job   Dates (start and finish)
(*include anything special about each job, particularly where it relates to children and/or teaching*)

INTERESTS AND ACTIVITIES
(*e.g. membership of clubs or societies, details of offices held, achievements, e.g. sport, music, hobbies; group these together if appropriate, with the most relevant first and if giving dates, in reverse chronological order*)

ADDITIONAL QUALIFICATIONS
(e.g. ability to use ICT, additional languages, music grades, coaching or first aid awards)

OTHER INFORMATION
(*include anything else that you think is important here in relation to the post for which you are applying*)

REFERENCES
First referee   Second referee
Position   Position
Address   Address
Telephone number   Telephone number
e-mail address   e-mail address

Figure 8.1.2   Sample curriculum vitae

ATTENDING AN INTERVIEW

If you are offered an interview, acknowledge the letter at once, in writing if there is time, indicating that you are pleased to attend for interview on that date. If you are offered two interviews on the same day, you probably have to choose which one you attend, unless they are at different times and close enough together to enable you to attend both. Write and decline the interview you decide not to attend. If there is a problem with an interview date, for example, it coincides with an examination, let the school know immediately.

Preparing for the interview

Prepare for an interview in advance. Read through the advertisement, job description and any other information about the school and post again. Also try to find out if there is anyone at your institution or school experience school who knows the school. If possible, visit the school beforehand to find out more about it and about the local area. Most schools welcome this – as long as you ask in advance. Do not just turn up at the school and expect to look around. Decide what to look for when shown round the school. If possible, talk to a newly qualified teacher in the school. You might find it helpful to reflect on why you applied for this particular post, so that you can put across the relevant information convincingly at the interview. Read through your application again so that you can communicate effectively the information and evidence you consider to be relevant to the post. It also helps you avoid any contradictions between what you say and what you wrote in your application, as each member of the interview panel has a copy of your application and so can compare answers. If you are not reading the *Times Educational Supplement* on a regular basis, we recommend that you do so before your interview so that you can talk about and answer questions on the latest educational issues and debates. It is useful to have a portfolio of, for example, good lesson plans, examples of pupils' work, worksheets, evaluations, review of resource(s), ICT skills. This is derived from the professional development portfolio you have been keeping throughout your ITE course (see Unit 8.2 for further information).

Plan what you are going to wear to the interview as your appearance is important. Knowing something about the school is useful, for example, if the staff dress formally you should dress formally. If you are unsure, it is advisable to be conservative in your dress.

Attending the interview

It is difficult to generalize about interviews because these vary considerably. In many schools, all people invited to interview arrive at the school at the same time, are shown round the school, sit and wait, while everyone is interviewed in turn, for a decision to be made and for the successful candidate to be told. In other interviews, candidates are invited at different times so that they do not meet. The format for interview days also varies. It may, for example, comprise a tour of the school, an informal talk or interview with the head of department or a senior teacher, lunch and a panel interview. An example of an interview day is shown in Figure 8.1.3.

9.15 a.m.	Arrive at school	At this stage you are normally welcomed, along with other candidates, by the headteacher and are given the schedule for the day, if this has not already been sent to you.
9.35 a.m.	Meeting with head of faculty and/or head of department	At this stage information about the school and department is explained to you. For example, structure and organization; curriculum; roles and responsibilities; assessment policies; examination results; procedures about school routines and expectations. You may well receive further documentation. If there is more information you would like to have, please take the opportunity to ask questions.
10.00 a.m.	Coffee	This might be with other members of the department or staff. Again, use this as an opportunity to learn more about the school and the post.
10.15– 10.45 a.m.	Tour of the school	You may well be escorted by a member of staff or by pupils. This provides an opportunity to take note of what may be your working environment. For example, the layout of the school and department; display work; facilities; the learning and working atmosphere in the lessons.
10.45– 12.30 p.m.	Teaching a lesson	There is normally a rota for this with other candidates. You should be prepared for this part of the interview in advance. It is not normal practice for this to be sprung on you without warning! For further information see the section on teaching a lesson at interview.
12.30 p.m.	Lunch	This may well be in the school canteen with other members of the department. Again, use this period of the day as an opportunity to ask questions.
1.30 p.m.	Formal interviews	Candidates are interviewed individually, normally in alphabetical order. If you have a legitimate commitment (e.g. a train to catch) and need to leave before your allocated time, it is best to say so, and the school usually accommodates this request.

Figure 8.1.3   Possible interview schedule

Teaching a lesson as part of the interview

It is now regular practice for candidates to be asked to teach a lesson as part of the interviewing process. If required make sure that you know the age and size of the class, what you are expected to teach and the pupils' prior knowledge, the length of the lesson, what resources and equipment are available, i.e. all the information you require before teaching any class. You should be told this in the letter of invitation to the interview. If not, telephone and ask. Plan this lesson carefully, giving attention to learning outcomes, purpose of content and activities, and resources. It is useful to have copies of the lesson plan available to give to those observing you. This is an opportunity to show the quality of your preparation and planning. Lessons taught as part of the interviewing process also provide you with the opportunity to demonstrate the level of your subject knowledge, so, again, prepare well, particularly if you have been asked to teach a topic with which you are not totally familiar. It is probably best to try to base your interview lesson on something that has been successful on a previous occasion with similar classes. The lesson is also an opportunity to show your enthusiasm for teaching and pupils' learning. Try to appear confident and relaxed, although those observing you understand that you probably feel a little nervous!

It is a good idea to talk with relevant staff about the lesson; for example, how you feel it went; what the pupils learnt; how you know that they learnt this; and what you might change. Do not be anxious about mentioning if some things have not gone to plan. For example, your timing might have gone astray, or your instructions were not as clear as you had anticipated. Use the opportunity to show that you have realized this and analyse why it happened and how you might change this in the future. This demonstrates that you are reflective and thoughtful and serious about your own practice.

As the format for interview days varies so does the panel interview. In some interviews you are faced by a panel comprising anything between two to three and six to seven people, in others you have a series of interviews with different people. In either case these people normally include some of the following: the head teacher, a governor, another senior member of the school staff, head of department and possibly LEA subject adviser. The length of time for a panel interview can vary from about half an hour to one-and-a-half hours.

An interview is a two-way affair. At the same time as being interviewed you are, in effect, interviewing the school and deciding if this is a school in which you could work and therefore if this is a post for you. Take the opportunity to learn as much as you can about the school, the post and the working environment. This requires you to be alert to what is being said and to be prepared to ask as well as to answer questions. If not included as part of the interview day, be firm in requesting an opportunity to look round the school prior to interview, including sitting in on a lesson if possible.

The initial impact you make is very important as interviewers tend to form an overall impression early. The interview starts as soon as you walk into the school and you are assessed throughout the day. Your performance, including your verbal and non-verbal communication, in each activity is therefore important and could make the difference between the job being offered or not. Particular attention is paid to the impression you create in the formal interview. For example, do not sit down until you are invited to do so and then sit comfortably on your chair looking alert; do not sit on the edge of your chair looking anxious or slouch in your chair looking too relaxed. Look and sound relaxed and confident (even if you are not). Try to be yourself. Try to smile and to look at the panel during discussion. Do not talk too much. If you are unsure about how much information to give when answering questions it is probably better to keep an answer brief and then ask the panel if they would like further information. Avoid repetition but do not worry if you repeat information included in your application, as long as you do not contradict what you wrote. Interviewers have various degrees of specialist knowledge and understanding. Avoid jargon in explanations but assume interviewers have some knowledge and understanding of your subject area. Aim to provide a balanced picture of yourself, being on the whole positive and emphasizing your strengths, but being aware of areas for development.

Interviewers are trying to form an impression of you as a future teacher and as a person and have a number of things they are looking for. These include:

- Your knowledge and understanding of your subject and your ability to teach it. Interviewers assess your ability to discuss, analyse, appraise and make critical comment about ideas, issues and developments in your subject and subject curriculum, your personal philosophy about and commitment to the teaching of your subject(s).
- Your professional development as a teacher. This is based partly on your school experiences. Interviewers assess your ability to analyse observations of pupils' behaviour and development, your own development and your involvement in the whole life of the school on school experiences, and your ability to discuss, analyse, appraise and make critical comment about educational issues.

- Your ability to cope with the post. Interviewers assess how you would approach your teaching, for example, your understanding of the different roles you are required to undertake as a teacher, how you have coped or would cope, in a number of different situations, for example, disciplining a difficult pupil or class, dealing with a difficult parent or with teaching another subject.

- Your ability to fit into the school and the staffroom and to make contact with and relate to colleagues and pupils. Interviewers assess your verbal and non-verbal communication skills (your written communication skills have been assessed from your application).

- Your commitment to living in that particular area and to the specific post. Interviewers assess the interest and enthusiasm you show for the post to try to find out if this is a post you really want or whether you see this post as a short-term stop-gap before you can find a post in an area where you really want to teach.

After introductions and preliminaries, most interviews ask why you have applied for this particular post. They then focus on the information in your application, including your personal experiences, your education, qualifications, teaching skills gained from school experiences and other teaching and/ or work experience, your interests and activities and other qualifications. You are normally also asked what you feel you can contribute to the school and general questions about professional or personal interests, ideas, issues or attitudes. Therefore, think about areas you want to emphasize or any additional evidence of your suitability for the post that you did not have room to include in your application. Draw on both your teacher education course and school experience and on other experiences, e.g. other work with children such as work in a youth club or voluntary work. This demonstrates your commitment to working with children.

You also need to show that you realize you still have things to learn and that you are committed to continuing your development as a teacher. You should be able to talk about areas for development. For example, you need to consolidate your learning in your first year, perhaps gain further experience of other areas, such as teaching Years 12 and 13 or taking on a tutor group. There may also be specific areas of subject knowledge you will need to enhance. Depending on when your interview takes place, it might be possible for you to refer to your career entry and development profile which indicates your strengths towards the end of your ITE and also areas for development in your induction year. It is helpful to have a career plan, but not to appear so ambitious that you give the school the impression that you will leave at the first opportunity.

Questions asked at interview vary considerably; therefore it is not possible for you to prepare precisely for an interview. However, it is helpful if you identify possible questions in your preparation and prepare some possible outline responses to such questions. It is useful to give a general response to the question to show you are aware of some of the principles and issues and also to refer to examples of your own practice. For example,

> Interviewer: How did you set about planning differentiated learning for a class you have taught recently?

> Candidate: This is an important way of enabling all pupils to have equal access to the curriculum so that they learn as much as possible. There are a number of strategies that can be used; for example, differentiation by outcome, by task or by rate of work. During my last school experience I was teaching a Year 7 class about religious festivals. I did not want to give out several different worksheets as this might have embarrassed some pupils, so I made one worksheet which had some core tasks for all pupils and also some option tasks, which involved different levels of work and different types of activities. I also developed differentiation through my use of questioning …

Some further questions which might be asked:

Your commitment to teaching

Why did you choose teaching as a career?

Why did you choose to teach the secondary (middle/upper) age range?

Why did you choose this particular course?

Tell me what you have learnt about teaching from your school experiences.

What have been the most difficult aspects of your school experiences and why?

Tell me about any other experiences of working with pupils which you think are relevant. What have you learned from these?

Your knowledge and understanding of your subject and subject application

What experience do you have of teaching your subject(s)?

Which aspects of your subject have you taught on school experience and to what years?

How would you introduce topic X to a Year 9 class?

Recall a lesson that went well and/or one that went badly. Describe why this lesson went well or badly. How would you improve the lesson that went badly?

How would you deal with, say, three pupils misbehaving during a lesson in which there are safety implications?

Do you think that your degree subject prepares you to teach A level?

How has your development in your subject during your course contributed to your work in the classroom?

How do the theory and practice on your course relate?

How can you tell if pupils are learning in your subject?

Can you describe one incident where a pupil was not learning and what you did about it?

What experience have you had of setting targets for pupils?

Have you used ICT in your teaching? If so, how and if not, how do you think you might incorporate them into your teaching?

What other subjects could you teach and to what level? What background/teaching experience do you have in these subjects?

Your views about education, philosophy of education and educational ideas

What do you think education is about (individual development or to acquire skills to get a job)?

Do you view yourself as a teacher of children or of X subject?

Why should all pupils study X subject?

What do you think the aims of secondary (middle/upper) education should be?

How did you set about planning differentiated learning for a class you have taught recently?

How do you think your subject can contribute to the education of all pupils?

What are your views about the way that the National Curriculum should develop?

What are your views on assessment?

On what should pupils' achievements be based?

Your ability to cope as a teacher

What do you think are the qualities of a good teacher?

What do you consider to be your strengths and weaknesses as a teacher at this stage in your career?

How are you working to overcome your weaknesses?
How would you maintain good discipline in the classroom?
How would you motivate a group of Year 9 pupils who do not have much interest in your subject?

Other roles you may be asked to undertake

What experience do you have of being a form tutor?
How do you feel about taking on the responsibilities of a form tutor?
How do you feel about taking extra-curricular activities?
What experience do you have of dealing with parents?

Your future development as a teacher

What are your targets for development during your first year of teaching?
How do you see your career developing?
How do you think you will go about achieving your career goals?
How long do you expect to stay in this school?
How do you aim to widen your experience as a teacher?

Other interests, activities etc.

What interests/ hobbies do you have and how involved are you in these? Do you see yourself being involved with any of these at school?

Other questions

At the end of the interview you may be asked: If you were to be offered this post would you be in a position to accept it? (At some interviews you may be asked this question earlier. You can say that you decline the offer to respond at that point but will respond after the interview.)

At the end of the interview you are normally asked if you have any questions. Asking one or two questions shows a genuine interest in the school and the post; therefore do ask questions (not too many), if you have any. You are likely to forget the questions you wanted to ask if you are nervous; therefore, do not be afraid to take a checklist of questions with you to an interview. It is quite acceptable to refer to this during the interview itself. You may also wish, at this stage, to clarify issues that have arisen during the interview day. You should enquire what arrangements there are for induction of newly qualified teachers in the school and what you might expect. However, do not ask questions just to impress. If all your questions have been answered during the course of the day and you do not have any questions, just say politely that all the questions you wanted to ask have been answered during the day (or in the interview).

At some point you may want to ask about your starting salary. In a private school and in some situations in the state sector you may have to negotiate your salary. In the state sector you are on a national rate of pay, but your starting point on the scale depends on your degree classification. Any previous relevant experience may also be taken into account, and you may be able to negotiate your starting salary. If you feel you are in a strong position, you may want to negotiate your starting point on the scale during your interview and ask for confirmation of this before you accept a post. In other situations, for example, if you feel you are not in a very strong position to be offered the post, but really want the post, it may be appropriate to discuss the starting salary at a later date. How you describe experience in an application and at interview, therefore, is very important as it may be used to support any claim for increments above the starting salary.

Task 8.1.4
Mock interviews

Arrange for a mock interview with your tutor or another student teacher. If possible, either have an observer or video the interview so that you and the interviewer can use this to analyse your verbal and non-verbal communication after the interview. If, on analysis, you or the interviewer feel that there is a great deal on which you can improve, arrange for another interview after you have worked at improving your weaknesses.

ACCEPTING A POST

Where all candidates are invited for interview at the same time, you may be offered a post on the same day as the interview. You are normally expected verbally to accept or reject the offer at that time. Schools rarely give you time to think about an offer. Therefore, it is important that you consider all the implications of accepting the post before you attend the interview. On rare occasions it may be that you feel you really need some time to think about the offer. You may want to ask if you can think about the offer overnight and telephone first thing in the morning. If your request is refused, you have to make a decision there and then or be prepared for the post to be offered to another candidate. Your decision depends on how much you want a particular job and how strong a position you think you are in.

If candidates are invited for interview at different times, you may have to wait for a few days before being offered a post. However, normally you do not know which format an interview is going to take until you arrive at the school, so you cannot rely on being able to do this.

It is normal practice to be asked to confirm your verbal acceptance of a post in writing. It is unprofessional to continue to apply for other teaching posts after you have verbally accepted a post, even if you see one advertised that you prefer. Offers of a post are made on certain conditions. You may be asked to have a medical before you start a job, in which case, the school or the LEA send you details. As you have access to children and young people, you are required to disclose all previous criminal convictions as part of the check by the Criminal Records Bureau (CRB). The government has established the CRB, which checks applicants working with children through a service called 'Disclosure'. This service provides recruiting organizations with additional information on which to base employment decisions, and also covers student teachers on courses of ITE placed in schools in England and Wales. A final assessment of a (student) teacher's suitability for teaching is made on the basis of a Disclosure obtained.

Expenses (including basic overnight accommodation where necessary) are usually paid for attending an interview. However, you might want to check in advance as rules vary between schools and LEAs. You should receive a travel and expenses claim form with the letter notifying you of the interview or at the interview itself.

The transition from student teacher to teacher is not easy. Being a teacher involves you coming to terms with your new role within a new institutional context and an awareness of the complexities of its organization, structures and routines, as well as ethos and expectations. This transition may be easier if you make arrangements – with your future mentor, for example – to visit the school again to make preparations to start your post. This is not dissimilar to the preparations you make when you go on school experience. You are able to meet members of the department and find out about facilities in the school. You also need to collect information about classes you will be teaching and what you will be teaching, as well as your teaching timetable. You may find it useful to make a few visits to get to know the school culture. For example, you may become involved in some school activities such as sports day or perhaps observe some classes or teach some lessons before you start your post proper.

IF YOU ARE NOT OFFERED THE POST

It is disappointing when a post is offered to another candidate. However, try not to think of this in terms of failure on your part. There may be many legitimate reasons why the post was offered to the other candidate in preference to you. For example, the other candidate might have relevant teaching experience (which you did not have) in an aspect of the curriculum required for the post. If you are not successful, build this into your learning experience. Most interview panels routinely offer feedback to candidates. If not, you can ask if this is possible as it helps you identify strengths and areas to develop in preparation for your next interview.

SUMMARY

This unit is designed to help you realize that, just as with your teaching, you must prepare for obtaining your first post; you cannot leave it to chance or rely on your innate ability to perform well at interview. In this unit we have tried to lead you through the steps, skills and techniques you need to prepare actively for obtaining your first post.

FURTHER READING

National Union of Teachers (NUT) (annually) *Your First Teaching Post*, London: NUT. This guide is designed to answer some of your questions about where to look and what to look for in your first teaching post. It contains information supplied by education authorities and can be obtained from the NUT.

The Education Authorities Directory and Annual (annual) Redhill, Surrey: The School Government Publishing Co. Ltd. *The Education Year Book* (annual), London: Longman. These books list all the LEAs in England and Wales, along with names, addresses and telephone numbers of secondary schools and sixth form colleges in their areas.

Times Educational Supplement (annually, around the middle of January) *First Appointments Supplement*, TES. This supplement is published yearly. It contains articles and features on processes and procedures to help you get your first post and what to expect when you start your first post. It also contains many advertisements from LEAs about general applications.

Unit 8.2

Developing Further as a Teacher

Julia Lawrence, Alexis Taylor and Susan Capel

INTRODUCTION

The success of any school depends on its staff. Although you have successfully met the requirements to qualify as a teacher at the end of your initial teacher education (ITE) course, you still have a lot to learn about teaching to increase your effectiveness. Professional accountability includes a commitment to keeping abreast of changes in education, in order to develop your knowledge and teaching skills. Continuing professional development (CPD) helps you continue to learn and develop professionally throughout your career. The first part of your CPD is your induction. Induction includes immediate induction into the post and ongoing induction throughout the first year. After induction, early professional development (EPD, in the second and third years of teaching), then CPD continues throughout your career. This sequence of development can be shown as follows:

$$\text{ITE} \text{———} \text{CPD} \text{———} \text{EPD/CPD}$$
$$\text{induction}$$

You must take responsibility for your own professional development, supported by school managers. If you are teaching in England your Career Entry and Development Profile (CEDP) is the beginning of active planning for your future career, identifying appropriate areas for development and activities and/or experiences appropriate to achieve these.

This unit considers life beyond your student teaching experience. It considers the transition from student teacher to newly qualified teacher (NQT), induction into the school and the job and during the first year of teaching and EPD/CPD beyond the first year.

OBJECTIVES

By the end of this unit you should:

- understand the need to undertake continuous learning and development;
- begin to recognize the induction and EPD/CPD opportunities available to you;
- begin to be able to set goals for your CPD early in your career.

PROFESSIONAL DEVELOPMENT PORTFOLIO

Throughout your ITE course you should develop a professional development portfolio or portfolio of achievement. In order to keep this professional development portfolio, you might find it useful to compile a diary of reflective practice in which you record evidence of reflection and evaluations of yourself and those you teach (for further information refer to the introduction to this book).

Your professional development portfolio contains evidence of your developing professional knowledge and judgement to complement your subject knowledge. Specifically, it documents your performance in relation to the requirements to qualify as a teacher, your strengths and successes and areas for development, and gives examples of your work as part of your ITE course. Guidance on evidence you may wish to include in your professional development portfolio comes from a number of sources, including your tutors and the Teacher Training Agency (TTA). The TTA list suggests content, along with a suggested layout. See Figure 8.2.1 and <http://www.tta.gov.uk>.

Many ex-student teachers of ours have commented that they did not see the relevance of certain information, theories or activities while they were student teachers, but began to see their relevance as they developed as teachers. They then referred back to the notes they took or work they did as student teachers. Therefore the information contained in your portfolio is useful in its own right. However, it is also important that information is gathered together so that you have evidence to take to interview

---

Reflections on lessons you have observed

Records of observations of your teaching

Your medium-term and short-term curriculum planning

Targets you have set for pupils and their progress towards meeting them

Individual Education Plans that you have helped prepare and review

Pupils' work you have assessed

Reports to, and feedback from, parents and carers (be aware of confidentiality issues)

Learning logs you have maintained

Reflections on the range of professional development opportunities you have accessed

Evaluations of your professional development, including its impact on pupils' learning

Reflections on the ways in which you have promoted creativity in your teaching

Evaluation of your contribution to collaborative working within your school, and to the work of the school beyond the classes you teach.

Figure 8.2.1   What you may wish to include in your professional development portfolio (Source: TTA, 2003b: 5)

(if needed) and, for those of you learning to teach in England, to complete your CEDP. It may also be used to provide evidence for prior learning if you apply to study for a higher degree or further professional qualification (accreditation of prior experiential learning (APEL)). In order to claim exemption you must provide evidence. This is usually requested in a portfolio, therefore if you are in the habit of keeping your professional development portfolio up to date, you will have the evidence ready to hand for consideration. Task 8.2.1 is designed to encourage you to keep your professional development portfolio and diary of reflective practice throughout your ITE course.

Task 8.2.1
Your professional development portfolio

If you are reading this unit near the beginning of your ITE course, start to develop your professional development portfolio for tasks you undertake as you read through this book and as part of your ITE course, using evidence suggested by your tutors and by the TTA. (If you are near the end of your course and have not been developing a portfolio, collect together evidence from the tasks and assignments you have undertaken on your course.) Within the professional development portfolio also keep a diary of reflective practice. Reflect on the evidence you have collected and write down what you perceive to be your strengths and your areas for development as a student teacher. Develop and implement a strategy for enhancing these.

CAREER ENTRY AND DEVELOPMENT PROFILE (CEDP)

A CEDP is a working document required of all NQTs in England that reflects what you have achieved during your ITE course and identifies subsequent EPD/CPD requirements. The TTA (2003a: 7) identify the purpose of your CEDP as:

- to help you to make constructive connections between your ITE, induction and later stages of your development as a teacher;
- to focus your reflection on your achievements and goals in the earliest stages of your teaching career;
- to guide the processes of reflection and collaborative discussion about your professional development needs that take place as part of your ITE and induction programmes.

There are three transition points at which you complete your CEDP. Table 8.2.1 summarizes the key focus of the CEDP at each of these three transition points.

TRANSITION FROM STUDENT TEACHER TO NEWLY QUALIFIED TEACHER

When you complete your ITE course successfully and get your first teaching post, you are likely to feel immense relief at having 'made it'. You may feel very confident and believe that you are going to be able to solve any problem you are faced with, e.g. motivating an unmotivated pupil or class or changing the teaching approaches in the department to encourage more active learning. You may also fear failing in your new job. Different people have different fears, e.g. fear of not being able to control pupils, of being thought to be lacking skill or ability, of not being accepted by other members of staff,

Table 8.2.1   The key focus of the CEDP at each transition point

	Transition point	Focus of the CEDP
1	End of your ITE course	Reflecting on your experiences during ITE, identifying your strengths, as well as identifying and setting targets in areas for further development
2	Beginning of your induction year	Discussing your priorities and how these are linked to and further develop the targets outlined at transition point 1
3	End of induction year	Reflecting upon your induction year and identify further EPD/CPD requirements

of not liking the school or the people you work with. See Chapter 1 in Capel, *et. al.* (2004) for further information about the transition from student teacher to newly qualified teacher.

As the new person in a school and department, you may not be sure of how to behave or of the rules or procedures to follow. You will have some successes and some failures and will soon realize that you cannot solve every problem or change the world. As a result, your confidence may decrease and you may not be fully effective until you are settled in the school and the job. A well-structured induction programme should help you make this transition. See Chapter 1 in Capel *et al.* (2004) for further information on your immediate professional needs.

INDUCTION

In England you must complete successfully the requirements of the statutory induction in order to continue teaching in a maintained school or a non-maintained special school beyond your induction year. If you complete induction arrangements for Wales, Scotland or Northern Ireland, you are able to teach in a school in England. Websites containing information about induction in all four countries are included in the Further Reading section at the end of this unit.

The induction period in England comprises three school terms or equivalent. For example, if you are teaching two-and-a-half days a week, your induction period lasts six terms. However, only appointments that last a term or more count towards your induction period. It must be completed satisfactorily within five years of starting. You would be wise to clarify at your interview the induction arrangements, especially if you are appointed to a position on a part-time basis.

You may have commitments that prevent you beginning your teaching career immediately after your course (e.g. family obligations or further study). In such cases, you commence your induction as soon as you begin teaching in a maintained school. However, although there is no time limit to when you start the statutory induction it is advisable to begin your teaching career and statutory induction period as soon as possible after qualifying to teach. The world of education is dynamic, with changes occurring constantly and swiftly (e.g. in subject knowledge, in curriculum development, in teaching approaches and in assessment) and a school making an appointment needs to consider the 'freshness' of your school experience.

Induction can be divided into two main parts: immediate induction into the school and the job, which gives you vital information to help you through the early days; and ongoing induction throughout the first year, providing the link between ITE and EPD/CPD. We consider immediate induction first.

Immediate induction

Immediate induction applies only to the first few days and weeks of any job and focuses on general familiarization and welfare aspects that all teachers (not only NQTs) in that school need. Immediate induction should, therefore, help you to understand, as quickly as possible, how you fit into the school and the department, building on information gained previously from the school literature, your interview and any further visits to the school after you were appointed. This covers a range of issues, e.g.:

- management and administrative arrangements, e.g. staff responsibilities, terms and conditions of employment, sickness policy, issuing of keys;
- structure and departments, e.g. staff responsibilities, line managers, meeting other members of staff;
- rules, regulations and procedures within the school and your department, e.g. behaviour policy, equal opportunities, lesson planning;
- health and safety requirements, e.g. fire drill, medical policy.

Ongoing induction throughout the first year

In our experience many NQTs report that school experience gave them an indication of the demands of teaching, but had not prepared them fully for the demands of a full-time post. They had felt that, as they would not be constantly observed, evaluated and assessed, tiredness and stress would reduce. However, they discovered that the first year of teaching was just as tiring and stressful as their school experience, if not more so.

In one way, being an NQT in your first teaching post is not much different from being a student teacher: you are still a beginner, albeit a beginner with more experience. In other ways, however, your first teaching post is a very different experience from school experience. You may feel differently about yourself as a 'real' teacher, which may influence the way you behave. Further, staff and pupils may treat you differently as a full member of staff.

Although your ITE course prepares you to reach the standards for entry into the teaching profession you still have a lot to learn and inevitably feel unprepared for some aspects of the teacher's role. It is likely that as a student teacher you do not undertake all the activities that teachers undertake, for example, you are unlikely to be involved with developing schemes of work for a year or a Key Stage or with administering examinations. In your first year of teaching you undertake a greater range of responsibilities than as a student teacher, for example, you have your own groups and classes and can establish your own procedures and rules for classroom management right from the beginning of the school year. You therefore undertake the full role of the teacher in your classroom.

During the first few weeks or first term in your new post, you will probably find that you concentrate mainly on becoming confident and competent in your teaching so as to establish yourself in the school. You are busy getting to know your classes, planning units of teaching from the school's schemes of work, preparing lesson plans, teaching, setting and marking homework, undertaking pastoral activities with your form and getting to know the rules, routines and procedures of the school.

Over the course of the first year you will face situations that you did not experience as a student teacher. This includes undertaking activities for the first time, for example, discussing progress with pupils as part of their Record of Achievement, setting questions for examinations, undertaking supervisory duties, or sustaining activities that you have not had to sustain over such a long period of time previously, e.g.:

- Planning and preparing material for a year to incorporate different material, teaching strategies and approaches to sustain pupil interest and motivation.
- As you should be aware from your school experiences, you cannot plan one set of material and deliver it in exactly the same way to different groups of pupils. Adapting your planned unit of work and lessons to meet the needs of different groups of pupils requires careful planning and being able to think on your feet in order to meet the needs of particular pupils and classes.
- Setting targets to maintain progress in learning over the period of a year.
- Maintaining discipline over a whole year. This is very different to maintaining discipline over a short period of time on school experience. You cannot 'put up with' things that you may have been able to put up with for a relatively short period of time on school experience.

Although taking extra-curricular activities may be expected of you, we advise you not to take on too many (certainly not every lunch time and evening as many physical education teachers do). In your first year you need to concentrate initially on developing into an effective teacher.

However, as an NQT, you may not be expected to undertake the full range of roles and responsibilities of teachers, for example, you may not be expected to deal with some of the more serious pastoral problems or to undertake the full range of administrative demands, this:

> confirms and contradicts the assertion that probationers are invariably thrown in at the deep end of teaching. They might be thrown in, but it is a rather small pool in which they have to swim, since most of the administrative and managerial responsibilities do not come their way. Nonetheless, to continue the metaphor, it is possible to drown in a very small pool and … the classroom is notoriously hazardous. The major consolation is that much of the classroom-based work will have been encountered during the teaching practice term.
>
> (Marland, 1993: 191)

Thus, you may feel that teaching is more difficult than you first thought and realize that you still have a lot to learn. As a result, you may become frustrated and have doubts about whether you can teach and what you are achieving with the pupils. You may need help and understanding from other members of staff to overcome these doubts and continue to develop as a teacher. Whilst in England an induction period is statutory, you should find that wherever you first teach some form of induction occurs. This may be informal or you may be assigned a tutor who provides support. You can draw on your tutor's experience to help you to answer the numerous questions you have as new situations arise, and to overcome problems with aspects of your teaching. Your tutor can help you to learn as part of your normal job, by identifying and using opportunities available in your everyday work to develop further your skills, knowledge or understanding. You may discuss a problem and then go away and try to put some of the suggestions into practice. In an ideal world a tutor is proactive, making a conscious effort to look for opportunities for development. However, your tutor is busy and you spend much of your time in a classroom on your own with pupils, therefore there may be limited opportunities to work with your tutor. You may therefore use your tutor reactively by identifying areas where you feel you would benefit more from further development or where something has gone wrong. You can set up a situation where your tutor can help to address or correct that particular issue, for example, ask your tutor to observe a lesson and comment on a particular aspect of your teaching; or observe a lesson taken by your tutor or another member of staff, or team-teach particular topics on which you lack confidence.

Most other staff are helpful and understanding, especially if you establish good relationships with them. Relationships take time to develop and you need to be sensitive to the environment you are in. You will not get off to a good start if, for example, you sit in someone's usual chair in the staffroom, try to impress everyone with your up-to-date knowledge, ideas and theories, try to change something immediately because you think things you have seen in other schools could work better, ask for help before you have tried to solve a problem yourself or do not know when to ask for help, or do not operate procedures and policies and enforce school rules. If you do not operate procedures and policies or enforce school rules, you undermine the system and create tensions between pupils and teachers and between yourself and other members of staff.

However, as you settle into the job and work with your classes and learn the procedures, rules and routines, other staff may forget that you are new. As they become ever more busy with their own work as the term and year progress, they treat you as any other member of staff and do not offer help and advice. If you need support, approach staff and talk to them about your concerns and ask for help. You may form a support group with other NQTs. You can share your concerns and problems, support and learn from each other and remind each other that, despite the amount you still have to learn, you also have much to offer and are enthusiastic. In England support is the role of the Induction Tutor, who is provided with clear guidance as to their roles and responsibilities for the NQT as part of the induction support programme.

Induction support programme in England

In England an induction support programme is in place throughout the first year. The Department for Education and Skills (DfES, 2003) defines this as an 'individualised programme of support, monitoring and guidance when you begin to teach in schools, following the award of QTS. It aims to help you build on the knowledge and skills you have already acquired, and provide (following your ITE) the foundation for your continuing professional and career development' (DfES, 2003k: 7).

The induction support programme includes:

- A reduction in your timetable commitments. Normally, you are expected to undertake 90 per cent of a full-time teaching load. Your non-contact time is, therefore, over and above what the school normally allocates. This time should be used wisely to focus on activities that are part of your induction programme.
- A dedicated tutor throughout your induction programme in that school. This tutor has responsibility for implementing your induction support programme.
- A programme that is planned to suit your needs. You work collaboratively with your induction tutor to ensure that your programme is appropriate. You are expected to play an active role in your own induction, and therefore need to develop skills of self-reflection, target setting and action planning. The important principle is that your induction programme is individualized and that it should meet *your* needs in trying to demonstrate the National Induction Standards, which link to the QTS standards you are already familiar with (DfES, 2003n). The starting point for your induction is the information in your CEDP. It identifies targets for your induction period and specifies actions to achieve these, along with resources needed and colleagues to help you. Success criteria and review dates are also identified. When discussing your CEDP with your induction tutor, try to think of what support you need to achieve your targets. For example, this could include collaborative work with other teachers in the department; visiting other schools for focused tasks; participation in formal training courses; or subject-specific tasks such as planning particular schemes of work or assessment activities.
- Observation of your teaching. The first observation normally takes place in the first four weeks in post, then normally occurs at least once each half term. Your induction tutor and others

undertake observation. Following each observation there is a collaborative review of your progress towards the Induction Standards, and your targets, programme and action plan are revised as necessary.

- Formal assessment meetings with your induction tutor. These take place at least once each term. After each of the first two formal assessment meetings, your headteacher makes a report to the Local Education Authority (LEA) (or the Independent Schools Council Teacher Induction Panel (ISCTIP), for independent schools). This report records your achievements in line with the National Induction Standards. If you are identified as needing further help to reach these, the school will arrange for this.

For more information regarding induction see DfES (2003k: 16–17).

Task 8.2.2
Preparing for induction

Before you begin your first teaching post, find out what is expected of you by the end of your induction period by reading the National Induction Standards. Using your professional development portfolio and diary of reflective practice, identify in your CEPD areas that you wish to focus on during your induction year. This should help you to gain an idea of what you need to prepare for your discussions with your induction tutor.

CPD (BEYOND THE FIRST YEAR)

Your CEDP identified areas for development during your induction year. However, successfully addressing these areas of development and completing the statutory induction period does not mean the end of your learning; indeed, it marks the start of a new period of your career, your EPD. This is a new scheme currently being piloted in 12 LEAs in England, which focuses on your development in the second and third years of teaching. CPD (including EPD) is part of your professional accountability as a teacher. Although not comprehensive, several aspects of your EPD/CPD to be considered are identified below.

Monitoring and evaluation

In order to continue to learn in the teaching situation, as well as get the most out of your EPD/CPD, continue the active, reflective approach to learning that you started during your ITE course. Monitor and evaluate your development as a teacher against specific objectives identified for development and continue to question what you are doing and identify alternative approaches. Record your progress in your professional development portfolio. Discuss this informally and/or through the appraisal process.

Your own individual development needs

As an NQT you spend the first couple of years in teaching establishing yourself. However, as you develop you will probably want to develop areas of expertise and take on posts of responsibility, either within the subject area or department or within the school. For example, you may wish to think about becoming an Advanced Skills Teacher (AST). This means that you remain in the classroom but spend a day a week assisting fellow teachers to develop their teaching further. In order to qualify for AST status you must complete external assessment requirements that demonstrate your excellence in the classroom. Further information can be accessed from <http://www.teachernet.gov.uk/ast>. Alternatively, you may wish to become involved in pastoral work or work placements, or even aspects of ITE. In the final assessment meeting of your induction period, you target areas for development for your second (and early) years of teaching.

It is important to recognize that, just as when you started your first post, when you take up a new responsibility or post, you go through a period of transition as you adjust to the new situation. You are likely to adjust more quickly if you have identified areas for development in a new post. This enables you to undertake appropriate CPD to develop an understanding of the role and the skills you will need to undertake the role successfully. There are many CPD opportunities, for example, short or long courses, a higher degree or a further professional qualification and being involved in development and change activities in the school.

As part of the drive for school improvement in England the government has developed national standards (these start with the standards to qualify as a teacher and for successful completion of your induction). There are also standards for those wishing to become special educational needs co-ordinators (SENCOs), subject leaders and headteachers. The main aims of the National Standards are to:

- set out clear expectations for teachers at key points in the profession;
- help teachers at different points in the profession to plan and monitor their development, training and performance effectively, and to set clear, relevant targets for improving their effectiveness;
- ensure that the focus at every point is on improving the achievement of pupils and the quality of their education;
- provide a basis for the professional recognition of teachers' expertise and achievements; and
- help providers of professional development to plan and provide high quality, relevant training which meets the needs of individual teachers and headteachers, makes good use of time and has the maximum benefit for pupils (TTA, 1998: 1).

More detail about the National Standards can be accessed on <http://www.tta.gov.uk>.

All new heads of department and headteachers in England are required to undertake training for their responsibilities (see TTA, 1998). For further information about this training see the National College for School Leadership website at <http://www.ncsl.org.uk>.

Task 8.2.3
Your continuing professional development

During your first year of teaching, maintain your diary of reflective practice. Within it identify your strengths, areas for development and how you might work to overcome them. Join your subject association in order to keep up to date with changes in your subject.

Appraisal

Teacher appraisal is part of making explicit teacher accountability. It is a crucial part of the school's performance management arrangements. Your CEDP should be used to provide a focus for discussion in your first appraisal (at the end of your induction period). Appraisal normally consists of observation of your teaching and an appraisal interview. An appraisal interview should provide you with valuable dialogue. It may start with discussion of your observed teaching performance, then progress to your performance over the past year (particularly in relation to pupils' progress). In addition to your teaching, other topics may be discussed, for example, pastoral work, curriculum development work, management and administrative activities and membership of committees and working parties. In all of these areas you discuss your strengths and areas for development, CPD undertaken to address these or ways in which any identified needs might be met, e.g. by attending conferences, studying for a higher degree or other opportunities for CPD within the school.

As well as informing CPD, in England appraisal also informs decisions about teachers' pay, with good teaching being rewarded with access to higher pay scales.

Linking CPD to the priorities of the school

Although not discussed in detail here, a valuable opportunity for CPD is provided through involvement in school development planning. Discuss with your tutor the school development plan and how you might be involved in this in relation to your development targets and your career aspirations.

SUMMARY AND KEY POINTS

This unit has considered the sequence of development as a teacher through:

$$ITE \text{ ------ } CPD \text{ ------ } EPD/CPD$$
$$\text{induction}$$

You are already on the professional development road and it is your professional responsibility throughout your career to seek opportunities for development. Your CEDP helps you to build on your strengths in your first year of teaching and to target and address areas for development. It also helps you to take responsibility for your own professional development from the beginning of your career, by establishing the practice of target setting and review. Your targets may include targets for wider aspects of your role as a teacher. For example, do you know what to do if a pupil has an epileptic fit or an asthma attack? Would you feel more in control if you knew how to deal with such situations in your teaching? If so, would you benefit from undertaking a first aid course? Similarly, although competence in information and communications technology (ICT) is a requirement if you are learning to teach in England (Department for Education and Employment (DfEE), 1998b), do you, for example, need to develop further the use of ICT in teaching and learning or are there aspects that you need to update?

The practice of target setting and review establishes a good foundation for appraisal, EPD and your ongoing CPD. However, it is important not to take on too much at once. Your first year of teaching is very demanding and you will want to ensure that you are fully established as a teacher first. Therefore it is important that you pace yourself when planning for your EPD/CPD. However, in order to develop your career further you need to identify CPD opportunities to enable you to develop your knowledge and skills so you can successfully reach and achieve your career goals.

FURTHER READING

Bleach, K. (2000) *The Newly Qualified Secondary Teacher's Handbook: Meeting the Standards in Secondary and Middle Schools*, London: David Fulton. This book provides an overview of professional development during the first years of teaching, with practical examples aimed at encouraging you to reflect on your current practice and highlight your individual developmental needs.

Capel, S., Heilbronn, R., Leask, M. and Turner, T. (2004) *Starting to Teach in the Secondary School: A Companion for the Newly Qualified Teacher*, 2nd edn, London: RoutledgeFalmer. This book is designed to support NQTs in their first year of teaching to provide a firm foundation for ongoing development throughout their career.

Trolley, H., Biddulph, M. and Fisher, T. (1996) *Beyond the First Year of Teaching: Beginning Teaching Workbook 6*, Cambridge: Chris Kington Publishing. This book provides practical examples of reflection on teaching after qualifying to teach, and how personal development plans can be developed.

Information about induction and CPD in each of the countries of the United Kingdom (useful websites)

England: Documentation regarding the induction of NQTs and EPD/CPD for teachers as they progress within the profession is on the TTA website: <http://www.tta.gov.uk>.

Wales: *Induction for NQTs in Wales: Circular No: 18/03* (2003, National Assembly for Wales <http://www.learning.wales.gov.uk>) provides an overview of induction procedure in Wales, identifying the roles and responsibilities of those involved.

Scotland: *Guidelines for Initial Teacher Education Courses in Scotland* (1998, Scottish Office <http://www.scotland.gov.uk>) identifies the competences that must be met in Scotland to qualify as a teacher.

Northern Ireland: *The Code of Values and Professional Practice* (2004, General Teaching Council of Northern Ireland). This publication can be accessed at <http://www.gtcni.org.uk>.

Unit 8.3

Accountability, Contractual and Statutory Duties

Marilyn Leask

INTRODUCTION

Teachers' work is guided and regulated in different ways by national and local government, the school, school governors, parents and pupils – so you are accountable to a whole range of interested parties for the quality of your work.

To help you understand the context in which teachers work, this unit outlines how the education system operates in the state system in England. See Unit 7.5 for Scotland.

OBJECTIVES

By the end of this unit you should:

- understand the structure of the state education system;
- be aware of the legal and contractual requirements that govern the work of the teacher.

WHERE DO TEACHERS FIT WITHIN THE EDUCATION SYSTEM?

The structure of the education system in England is set out in Figure 8.3.1, showing the relationships between the education system and teachers. The Secretary of State, ministers and staff at the Department for Education and Skills (DfES) do not usually have teaching experience. They are provided with professional advice by advisory bodies such as the Qualifications and Curriculum Authority (QCA), the British Education Communications Technology Agency (BECTA), and the Training and Development Agency for Schools (TDA – previously the Teacher Training Agency, TTA) which have some members with a wide range of expertise in the profession. However, local education authority officers and professors and lecturers in higher education institutions normally start their careers as trainee teachers like yourself and so are likely to have been classroom teachers for some time before taking on these other roles.

Whilst the responsibilities within the school, listed in Figure 8.3.1, are shared out differently in different schools, the structure is not too dissimilar, although the terminology used is in some cases different. There are also numerous support staff whose contribution to school life is essential to the smooth running of the school, e.g. teaching assistants; school's premises' officer; nurse; administrative staff; technical staff; cleaners; lunch time supervisors; the bursar. Staff from other professions are also linked with the

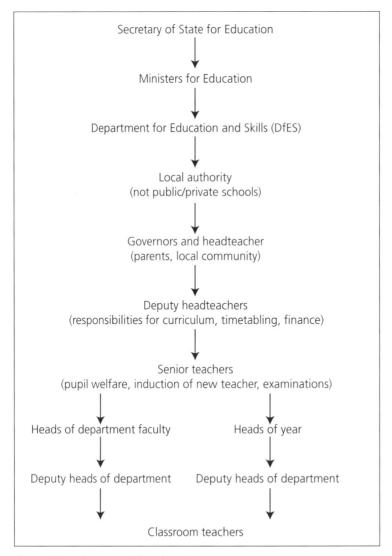

Figure 8.3.1   Structure of the education system

school, e.g. the education welfare officer, school psychologists and some pupils have social workers who are responsible for overseeing their progress. Parents and members of local communities will often have roles in schools – as governors or in providing support in a wide range ways.

Accountability

Within the structure of the education system and individual schools, teachers are accountable for what they do and the Office for Standards in Education (OFSTED) plays a major part in monitoring the work in schools. As an individual teacher, however, you are also accountable – to parents, to colleagues, to pupils, to your employer.

Bush (in Goddard and Leask, 1992: 156–8) identifies three ways in which a teacher experiences accountability. Bush calls these: moral accountability, professional accountability and contractual accountability. *Moral accountability* is about your conscience about how you should carry out your work. You are 'morally accountable' to students, parents and to society. Your *professional accountability* is your responsibility to your colleagues and to the teaching profession, to do your work to the highest standard of which you are capable. *Contractual accountability* is defined by legal requirements set down by your employer as well as in legislation passed by Parliament.

Whilst this may seem an oversimplification of a teacher's accountabilities, these three aspects provide a useful framework for developing your own understanding of your accountability. However, the way moral and professional accountability is personally perceived depends on the values of the individual teacher and on the standards they set themselves (see Task 8.3.1). The following section sets out in some detail your legal duties, both contractual and statutory.

Task 8.3.1
Moral accountability and
professional accountability

Consider what being morally and professionally accountable means for you and for the way you approach your work. Discuss this with other student teachers or your tutor.

Legal duties

Teachers have various legally binding contractual responsibilities and statutory duties. In addition you also have, as do all citizens, 'common law duties' which mean, among other things, that you have a duty of care towards other people. Teachers, again as citizens, are subject to criminal law. One aspect of criminal law you should note is that if you hit a pupil, or if a pupil hits you, this constitutes assault. It also is common sense to protect yourself against allegations by ensuring that you do not spend time alone in closed environments with individual pupils (see also the appendix to Unit 1.2).

Contractual and statutory duties

Contractual duties are negotiated between a teacher and their employer. Statutory duties are those which the government has established through legislation.

In the case of teachers employed in state schools in England, the document that sets out teachers' contractual duties is *School Teachers' Pay and Conditions* which is produced by the DfES and updated annually. In *School Teachers' Pay and Conditions* <http://www.teachernet.gov.uk/paysite/> guidelines are laid down for the exercise of your professional duties under the headings of teaching, other activities (which covers pastoral work), educational methods, assessment and reports, public examinations, appraisal, review, continuing professional development, discipline, health and safety, staff meetings, cover (for absent colleagues), management, administration and working time. Conditions of service, legal liabilities and responsibilities, child protection and other important aspects of a teachers' role are discussed in Cole (1999).

Additional conditions may apply in individual schools. There may also be 'implied terms' to your contract, i.e. terms which are not written down, for example, that you behave in a manner befitting your role – some schools operate a dress code. The *Headteacher's Guide to the Law* (annually updated, Croner) is recommended further reading for those with a particular interest in this area.

Specific advice on teaching contracts is available from the teaching unions and more guidance is provided in the extension to this unit on the website <http://www.routledge.com/textbooks/0415363926>.

**Task 8.3.2
Your contractual and statutory duties**

Obtain a copy of the conditions likely to govern your employment as a teacher. In England, the *School Teachers' Pay and Conditions* contains this information. Discuss this with other student teachers or your tutor and ensure that you understand what is required of you when you become a qualified teacher.

SUMMARY AND KEY POINTS

As a student teacher, you need to be aware of the full range of a teacher's duties. Whenever you are working in a school, you are acting with the agreement and support of qualified teachers. When you take over their classes, you are accountable for the work in the classroom in the same ways they are.

FURTHER READING

Cole, M. (ed.) (1999) *Professional Issues for Teachers and Student Teachers*, London: David Fulton. This text contains chapters on conditions of service, legal liabilities and responsibilities, child protection and other important aspects of a teacher's role.

Croner (updated annually) *The Headteacher's Guide to the Law*, New Malden: Croner Publications. Croner produce a range of publications which provide up-to-date advice for headteachers and other staff.

Department for Education and Skills (updated annually) *School Teachers' Pay and Conditions*, London: HMS). Online. Available HTTP: <http://www.teachernet.gov.uk/paysite/>. The provisions in this document are based on the statutory conditions affecting the employment of teachers (in all sectors primary, secondary, special) who are employed by local education authorities or governing bodies of voluntary or most grant-maintained schools. It provides useful information about salary scales and conditions of work.

OFSTED (2000) *Improving Schools: The Framework*, London: OFSTED. Some OFSTED publications set out the statutory basis for the work of teachers. The main requirements affecting the work of newly qualified teachers have been summarized in this unit. We suggest that you become familiar with the latest OFSTED publications for your subject.

9 And Finally

Marilyn Leask

This text has drawn on the evidence base for educational practice in providing information and background linked with tasks and enquiries. The tasks are intended to provide opportunities to examine the practice of other teachers, of yourself and the organization of schools. The enquiry-based tasks generate the data or ideas upon which an understanding of and an explanation for the complex world of teaching and learning in schools is built.

The relationship between explanation and practice is a dynamic one; explanations are needed to make sense of experience and inform practice. Some explanations will be your own, to be tried and tested against the theories of others, often more experienced teachers and educators. At other times you may use directly the explanations of others. Explanations in turn generate working theories, responsive to practice and experience. Theory is important, it provides a framework in which to understand the complex world of the classroom and to direct further research into improving the quality of learning. It provides, too, a reference point against which to judge change and development, both of yourself and schools. It is the encompassing of these ideas, the interplay of theory and practice, which underpins the notion of the reflective practitioner.

We ask you, as one last task, to consider the message in the following poem which we have occasionally found displayed on staffroom walls.

CHILDREN LEARN WHAT THEY LIVE

> If a child lives with criticism,
>   he learns to condemn,
> If a child lives with hostility,
>   he learns to fight,
> If a child lives with ridicule,
>   he learns to be shy,
> If a child lives with shame,
>   he learns to feel guilty,

If a child lives with tolerance,
    he learns to be patient,
If a child lives with encouragement,
    he learns confidence,
If a child lives with praise,
    he learns to appreciate,
If a child lives with fairness,
    he learns justice,
If a child lives with security,
    he learns to have faith,
If a child lives with approval,
    he learns to like himself,
If a child lives with acceptance and friendship,
    he learns to find love in the world.
                (Dorothy Law Nolta)

As a teacher you will have an impact – beyond what you will ever know – on people's lives and thus on the community and society. We hope that what your pupils learn from you will help them make positive contributions to their world. We hope too that you will help pupils to build personal self-confidence and skills to cope with adult life and to become autonomous learners and caring members of society.

To achieve these goals, you should expect to carry on learning throughout your professional life. Joining your subject association (<http://www.tta.gov.uk/eprd> provides a list) will ensure you receive publications outlining good practice and attending the annual subject conference will introduce you to the network of educators taking thinking in your subject forward.

You will also need the ability to balance society's continual demands on teachers with your personal needs and to lead a fulfilling life beyond school.

Appendix

Guidance for Writing

Susan Capel and John Moss

INTRODUCTION

In order to gain qualified teacher status at the end of your initial teacher education (ITE) course you are required to meet both teaching and other course requirements, e.g. written assignments through which you demonstrate your ability to produce academic work worthy of a graduate or postgraduate qualification. These assignments are designed to encourage you to make connections between educational theory and practice. This is to ensure that when you complete your ITE course you have begun to develop an understanding of how to:

- make use of educational research and theory to inform and improve your practice;
- develop your own theories about teaching and learning, reflecting on and evaluating established practice;
- develop and assess innovative practice in your own classroom;
- respond creatively and critically to local and national educational initiatives.

It is very likely that your education to date has provided you with many opportunities to find out what processes you need to work through in order to produce good written assignments. One literacy expert, Margaret Meek, has often argued that if we want to know what literacy practices will benefit our pupils, we should start by considering what works for us. Consequently, working on the assignments for your ITE course also provides you with an opportunity to reflect on how you can support your pupils in undertaking the writing tasks you set them. If something helps you, it may well help them. Research on writing suggests that paying attention to the following issues is particularly significant.

UNDERSTANDING THE GENRE

Genre is the term used to define a type of text which has a set of agreed conventions. These conventions apply at different levels, including the kind of vocabulary and voice it is appropriate to use, the structure and organization of sentences and paragraphs, and larger required structural elements. In academic writing these elements may include:

- an *introduction*, which should normally identify the focus of the assignment and outline the structure of what is to follow, i.e. the sequence in which material will be presented in the assignment;
- a *literature review*, which usually analyses the academic writing which is relevant to the topic, identifying common or contrasting views and current issues;
- a *statement of a question or hypothesis* to be investigated, which explains the scope of the investigation and the reasons for it;
- a *description and analysis of the methodology used*, which explains how an issue was investigated, the reasons for this and the advantages and disadvantages of the methods chosen;
- *data presentation and analysis*, which should enable a reader to see what is established fact in the work, where interpretation begins and how and why it has been made;
- *conclusions* should arise from the investigation and its results, and compare findings with established theory or positions; matters which are unresolved should be identified; recommendations for future practice may be included if appropriate.
- a *bibliography* which lists all references used in the assignment.

You bring preconceptions about academic writing from your earlier studies to assignments on your ITE course. However, the genre 'essay' contains many 'subgenres', just as the genre 'novel' includes science fiction, romance and detective stories among many other kinds of novel. You should establish which of the elements of academic writing listed above, and others, must be contained in the genre(s) you are expected to write in on your ITE course.

Just as it helps your school pupils if you do this, it is good practice for your tutors to teach you explicitly what is appropriate. Some methods which may be used for this include modelling and providing examples of successful work. Good modelling involves a practical demonstration of how an assignment can be constructed, e.g. by developing a plan or a paragraph on an overhead transparency or interactive whiteboard. Formative feedback on plans or first drafts also helps writers to understand what is required of them, and consequently to improve. The assessment criteria for the assignment should be made explicit from the outset: these should always make reference to the kind of writing that is expected as well as the required content. It will also help you as a writer if you are given more than one opportunity to write a particular kind of assignment, so that you develop experience in using the genre.

UNDERSTANDING THE PURPOSE AND MODE OF WRITING

Writing may, of course, have many different purposes. In the pupil National Curriculum for English, for example, these range from description and narration to argument and persuasion. The primary purpose of many written assignments in ITE is to develop a capacity for *reflection*. This means that you are encouraged to use your writing to think about your experiences in school; your own teaching; your observations of, or discussions with, others; your analysis of school documents or activities or events that occur in school; and the content of lectures, seminars and academic literature, in order to reach a higher standard of awareness about your teaching and the ways in which pupils learn.

Reflection requires you to stand back from a specific lesson, observation, activity or event and question it. You draw on your knowledge about, and understanding of, the work of others, research and theory, and consider it in relation to the practice on which you are reflecting. Reflection is as integral to your teaching as your ability to manage a class and pupil behaviour. It is a process which should continue into your first year of teaching and throughout your teaching career.

Evaluation of your teaching at the end of each lesson is an example of reflection. Evaluation can be carried out alone or with your tutor. When you evaluate a lesson, you question what went well in addition to what did not go well, what might have worked better and what you might do next time that will enable you to improve what you are doing. As evaluation and reflection involve recall of what took place, you need to focus your evaluation and reflection in advance. So much is going on in a lesson that unless you select one or two things on which to focus you are unlikely to collect the detailed data necessary for an in-depth evaluation. You also need to write a few notes and identify points of relevance as soon as you can after the lesson or observation so that you record your perceptions when they are fresh in your mind. There are checklists, guidelines and series of appropriate questions included in many of the texts concerned with helping teachers to develop into reflective practitioners (see the further reading list at the end of Unit 5.4).

Your reflections can then be used as the basis for explicitly linking the work of others to your practice in your assignments. You should aim to show how the work of others, research and theory, informs your practice and vice versa, rather than leaving the two separate, isolated from and not informing each other. Reflection allows you to give your own opinions, but you should underpin these with reference to research and theory. An assignment title which requires you to reflect does not imply that you should not include theory; nor does it mean that you should not include references. Rather, the expectation is that you should include examples from practice to support or challenge the research and theory. When drawing on examples from your practice in assignments, you should not use the name of the school or any individual. All such references should be made anonymous.

Common pitfalls in reflective writing include discussing the issues entirely at a theoretical level so that the work fails to engage with your practical experience in school or discussing only practical experience without making any reference to the theoretical context in which your own work is inevitably set. To avoid these and other pitfalls, detailed planning and preparation, and thorough drafting and academic referencing are necessary. These processes take time in themselves, and writing is also often improved if there are time gaps between the different stages of its production. These gaps help you, as the writer of an assignment, to approach it as a reader will do, and to judge your work to date more objectively. It follows that an important first step is to plan how you will pace your coverage of the planning, preparation and drafting stages indicated below, to allow you to meet the assignment deadline comfortably.

PREPARATION AND PLANNING

Identifying the title, focus and audience

Before you begin an assignment, you need to be very clear about what you are writing about, i.e. the title and focus of the assignment. You may be given a title or you may have to choose your own topic or focus. In either case, you should be very clear about the topic and focus before you start. It is often helpful to have a short title which clearly focuses on the issue you are going to address. The title can be written as a problem or a question and may be intentionally provocative. Phrasing the title in this way clarifies and reminds you of the focus when you are writing the assignment. Ask yourself: 'What am I seeking to find out by writing this assignment?'

You should also establish who the intended audience for the work is. Although many assignments in ITE are primarily reflective, you may be asked to produce work which can benefit the schools in which you undertake school experience or your peers on your ITE course. If there is an intended audience other than your tutor, as a monitor of your development as a reflective practitioner, this will influence how the assignment is written.

Collecting information

You should make a list of the sources of information that will help you to address the topic. You will be used to identifying and collecting together relevant notes from higher education institution (HEI) based sessions, books and articles from journals. However, you should also collect together information from school, such as lesson plans and evaluations of lessons you have taught or observed, and records of observations or interviews conducted in school, so that your written work can refer to, and link, published sources and your developing practice in school. It is helpful to keep this in your professional development portfolio.

Make sure that you are familiar with the library system at your HEI. You will probably have an induction briefing about this. If not, find out what books and journals are available to support your course. Ask what databases for education are available (e.g. BEIndex (British Educational Index)) and find out how to use them.

DRAFTING

Drafting is given high status in the National Curriculum for English. You should give it high status also. However, it is sometimes poorly interpreted as 'writing it out' and 'writing it out again with the spelling (and perhaps some grammar) corrected'. In fact, effective drafting is a complex process involving several stages.

Gathering ideas

Brainstorm ideas and collect key points from your reading notes, seminar or lecture notes, teaching file and material from school. At this point, include everything you think of that appears to be even slightly relevant. A spider diagram (see Unit 5.2) or arrows may be used, perhaps at a second stage, to begin to group points and ideas. It is a good idea also to identify examples and illustrations and note them next to key points and ideas: this will help you to work out which points you have most to say about and whether others should be eliminated or need more research before you start writing.

Selecting and sequencing ideas in a plan

Produce a plan which supports visually the organization of ideas in a way which is appropriate to the content and structure of the assignment. For example, flow charts are useful if the core of the assignment is concerned with a process; columns can be used to list pairs of contrasting points or ideas and illustrations; a matrix provides a means of charting complex matters in which combinations of factors need to be taken into account. It can help to add numbers as you work out the order in which you will deal with the material. At this stage, it is possible to check whether you have appropriate amounts of information for each stage of a process to be discussed, each side of an argument, or each combination of factors. If not, you may decide you need to research or develop your thinking about part of the subject matter.

Drafting

Write parts of the assignment as fluidly as possible. Allow ideas to develop rather than stopping too often to check detail or refine wording. It is not necessary to write in sequence: in fact, it may help to work on the different main sections of the assignment concurrently. This can help you to work out what each section needs to include and, for example, to sort out what belongs appropriately in the introduction and conclusion. If you have a section reviewing literature or discussing examples of practice, writing about one text you have read or lesson you have taught can help you to see how much space you have for each example, and so help you to balance the whole assignment. Clearly, sequencing and resequencing the writing as it develops is easy using a word-processor as you can move chunks of text so easily. You need to use this facility effectively. The aim of this stage is a continuous draft.

Redrafting

This stage should involve careful checking of the structure and balance of the assignment. A good exercise is to make notes from your own writing, paragraph by paragraph. This will draw attention to repetition, arguments which are left unsupported or incomplete, and the overall balance or imbalance in the work. Some questions to consider include: Does the introduction cover what the reader needs to know about the context of the work? Are the arguments, illustrations and examples given appropriate space? Do the points in the conclusion really arise from the earlier discussion? Are there some unresolved issues which could only be addressed in another piece of work? Where you have used information selectively, is it clear that it has been selected from a larger set of information and for a particular reason? It may be appropriate to move or re-sequence whole paragraphs or larger sections of the text during this stage.

Editing and proofreading

Editing should always involve some consideration of what can be deleted from the work to improve it. Many assignments exceed word limits and you may be penalized for this. A GCSE English chief examiner once said how impressed he was by a candidate who had the courage to cross out a long paragraph from an answer in examination conditions: because the piece was better balanced and the arguments flowed better as a result, this action had made the answer worthy of an A★ grade rather than an A.

Proofreading, or checking for technical accuracy, is often enhanced by reading aloud, which forces you to slow down, and draws attention to matters such as overlong sentences and word omissions. Reading each paragraph in turn from the end of the assignment to the beginning can also help you to focus on technical accuracy rather than the development of the content. Spelling and grammar checkers in word processors are useful tools, but remember, if this is appropriate, to use UK rather than US spelling which may be the preset option. Grammar checkers have a preference for active rather than passive constructions which may not always be appropriate in academic writing. It is also easy to click on 'change' rather than 'ignore' by mistake and vice versa when working quickly, so a final read through is still needed. We know this does not always happen from the number of times we find, for example, 'offside' in assignments rather than 'Ofsted'.

Some other technical points to consider are as follows. Academic writing is normally written mainly in the third person. However, if you are reflecting on your own practice you may want to use the first person – I – when referring to your own practice. This helps to distinguish your practice and thoughts from those of other writer(s) to whom you refer.

The first sentence of a paragraph usually identifies the main point of the whole paragraph; this is a useful signal for readers. Make sure that each sentence contains a main verb. You should use a new paragraph to mark the introduction of a new point or idea. It is important to use a variety of sentence structures. Words and expressions like: 'however', 'nevertheless', 'on the other hand', and 'in addition' provide useful openings which help a reader to understand how sentences are related to each other.

The word 'the' tends to be overused. A statement that includes 'the', for example, 'the fact that' or 'the answer is', is a categorical statement that portrays certainty or definitiveness which may not be appropriate. Words such as 'a', 'one of', 'there is a suggestion that' or 'one possible answer is' may be better instead because they are less definite. Another overused word is 'very', for example, 'very large' when 'large' would do.

Choose your words carefully. Do not use slang, jargon, colloquialisms, abbreviations or words that need to be put into quotation marks, unless quoting somebody else. For example, the use of 'kids' is slang.

Be careful about punctuation, i.e. full stops, commas, colons, semi-colons, dashes (e.g. for an aside) and brackets (e.g. for an explanation). By using punctuation appropriately, you help the reader to make sense of what you are saying. Underuse of commas is probably the most common error. Leaving out a comma can alter the meaning of a sentence. Dashes or brackets (normally curved brackets), used at the beginning and end of a phrase or clause, may help a reader to better understand the relative importance of different parts of a sentence.

Many writers make errors when using or omitting apostrophes. Remember that apostrophes are used to indicate possession or letter omission, but not plural nouns.

ACADEMIC REFERENCING

In academic writing, ideas, descriptions and explanations should not be taken for granted, even if everything you have read about the issue seems to provide a consensus. Ideas, assertions, descriptions, explanations or arguments should be supported by evidence from the work of others – from research and theory, appropriately referenced (e.g. you might say that: 'the research undertaken by Bloggs (2000) suggests that … This supports/contradicts the findings of Smith (1997)'). However, alongside references to the work of others, research and theory from texts or articles, you should draw on your own teaching or observations in school, giving examples of activities or events you have observed or participated in to provide evidence from practice, where appropriate.

By 'the work of others' and 'theory' we mean explanations of teaching and learning, and descriptions of research, as well as any theories which have been developed from such work. You should use the evidence of others and your own evidence to advance your own understanding and formulate your own theories. Your own theories evolve by bringing your critical faculties to bear on the work of others and what has been happening in your teaching.

When referring to other research or to texts, a reference should always be given, together with a page number if quotations are used. It is important to show, by appropriate citation, what is your work and what is the work of others. Direct quotations should be used sparingly; otherwise they disrupt the flow of the assignment. Do not put in a quotation for the sake of it: only use quotations with a clear purpose. You need to explain whether a quotation is being used as evidence which supports or disagrees with your point of view. If you are not clear why you are using a quotation, you may be better to paraphrase the point.

References cited in the text must be included in a *bibliography* at the end of the assignment. Your HEI will give you information about how to present your bibliography. This may be different from the way you were required to present bibliographies on your degree course. If you are not given information, ask the library which system is used in the HEI to present bibliographies. Otherwise use a recognized system such as the Harvard system. Details of this should be available in the library.

STRATEGIES FOR MAKING NEUTRAL REFERENCE TO GENDER

Your writing is governed by social customs and conventions. One such custom and convention in the UK is to make sure that there is no gender bias in your writing, that men and women are regarded as equal. This translates into not making assumptions that certain jobs (e.g. lawyer, doctor, lorry driver, primary teacher, nurse) are either male or female and, therefore, not using words such as *he, him, his* to refer to someone in one of these jobs.

Thus, in your writing you need to avoid such gender bias. Three methods of overcoming the difficulty have been identified: (i) *avoidance*, (ii) *disclaimer* or (iii) *inclusion*. Unless your HEI prescribes one method for you to use, you may use any of the three methods. Avoidance is probably the most popular and effective of these methods; inclusion, the least popular method.

Avoidance

'Avoidance' avoids using male or female words altogether when reference is made to a person who could equally be male or female. Some strategies for avoidance include:

Strategy	Example	
	Avoid this	*by writing this*
Change to plural	… when a teacher meets his class for the first time	…when teachers meet their classes for the first time
Change to an article	… so that every member of the group can give his opinion	… so that every member of the group can give an opinion
Recast the clause so that a different noun becomes the subject	if the student cannot understand his feedback …	If the feedback is difficult to understand …
Use neutral words like *the other, an individual, the author*	Each student must read what his partner has written	In pairs, each student must read what the other has written
Omit the male/female word	… working with each individual to ascertain her needs	… working with each individual to ascertain needs

Disclaimer

A disclaimer is a statement at the beginning of the assignment that you are using words like *he*, *him* and *his* throughout without wanting to convey gender bias. In other words you claim that the male words are to be read as neutral in their reference. Alternatively you might state that you are using *she*, *her* and *hers* throughout the assignment for some particular purpose, without wanting to convey gender bias. This might be appropriate, for example, when referring to primary teachers, as most primary teachers are female. Thus, the statement disclaims that any gender bias is intended. Without such a statement, you are likely to offend others. Even with a disclaimer, some readers may find this strategy offensive.

Inclusion

Some people prefer to get round the difficulty by using the phrase *he or she*, or *he/she* or *s/he*. If used occasionally, such phrases may be appropriate, but they affect the style and interrupt the flow of the assignment when used frequently. It may be best to avoid using this approach to avoid such difficulties.

CONCLUSION

To sum up, assignments set as part of your ITE course require good academic writing, but are also designed to enable you to show that you are reflecting on research and theory of teaching and are applying this to your own developing practice as a teacher, i.e. that you are developing as a reflective practitioner. You therefore need to combine academic writing and evidence of reflection in your written assignments.

Teachers need good writing skills. You write on the board, write notices, write reports, send letters to parents and undertake numerous other written communications. Whatever your subject, you have a responsibility to promote in your lessons the development of key literacy skills. Therefore, you need good spelling, grammar, punctuation, sentence construction and paragraph formation. If your writing skills are not as good as necessary to write effectively for a variety of audiences in school, you should ask for help during your time in ITE. HEIs will be able to direct you to study support units and to self-study materials available on the internet.

Good luck with writing your course assignments and the written communications you make as part of your teaching.

NOTES

The section on strategies for making neutral reference to gender is adapted from a paper produced by the Department of Language Studies, Canterbury Christ Church University College.

FURTHER READING

Burchfield, R. (ed.) (1996) *The New Fowler's Modern English Usage*, Oxford: Clarendon Press.

Creme, P. and Lea, M. (2003) *Writing at University*, Buckingham: Open University Press.

Greenbaum, S. and Whituit, J. (1988) *Longman Guide to English Usage*, Harlow: Longman.

Meek, M. (1988) *How Texts Teach What Readers Learn*, Stroud: Thimble Press.

Palmer, R. (1996) *Brain Train: Studying for Success*, London: Spon.

Palmer, R. (1993) *Write in Good Style: A Guide to Good English*, London: Spon.

Redman, P. (2001) *Good Essay Writing: A Social Sciences Guide*, Milton Keynes: Open University Press/ Sage.

Smith, P. (2002) *Writing an Assignment*, Oxford: How to Books.

Glossary of Terms

All items with ★ are used with specific reference to England and are taken from: OFSTED, *Handbook for the Inspection for Schools, Part 6: The Statutory Basis for Education* (London: Office of Her Majesty's Chief Inspector of Schools, 1994). All items with ★★ are taken from: Department for Education, *Code of Practice on the Identification and Assessment of Special Educational Needs* (London: DFE, 1994). All items with ★★★ are taken from *The Education Year Book*, London: Longman, 2003). All items with ★★★★ are taken from R. Dearing *The National Curriculum and its Assessment: Final Report* (London: SCAA, 1994). Terms shown in bold within a definition have their own entry in the glossary.

ACCAC   Awdurdod Cymwysterau, Cwricwlwm ac Asesu Cymru (Qualifications, Curriculum and Assessment Authority for Wales). The English equivalent is **QCA**.

AEB   Associated Examining Board. Now part of **AQA**.

Annual Review★★   The review of a statement of special educational needs which an **LEA** must make within 12 months of making the statement or, as the case may be, of the previous review.

AQA   Assessment and Qualifications Alliance. An awarding body comprising **C and G**, **NEAB** and **AEB**, for **GCSE**, **GCE** A and AS levels and **GNVQs**. <http://www.aqa.org.uk>

Attainment Targets (ATs)   The knowledge, skills and understanding that pupils of different abilities and maturities are expected to have by the end of each Key Stage. Except in the case of **citizenship** attainment targets consist of eight **level descriptions** of increasing difficulty, plus a description for exceptional performance above level 8. See also **Programmes of Study**.

Awarding Body   There are now three awarding bodies, formed by merging a number of examination boards. These are: Assessment and Qualifications Alliance (**AQA**) <http://www.aqa.org.uk>; **EdExcel** <http://www.edexcel.org.uk>; Oxford and Cambridge Regional (**OCR**) <http://www.ocr.org.uk>

BA/BSc (QTS)   Bachelor of Arts/Bachelor of Science with **QTS**. A route to QTS.

Banding★   The structuring of a year group into divisions, each usually containing two or three classes, on grounds of general ability. Pupils are taught within the band for virtually all the curriculum. See also mixed ability group, setting and streaming.

Baseline Testing   The assessment of pupils in Year 1 and reception classes for speaking, listening, reading, writing, mathematics and **PSE**. (See the DfEE website).

Basic curriculum   Religious education plus the three core subjects, plus the foundation subjects of the English National Curriculum. From August 2000 seven subjects at Key Stages 1 and 2 are compulsory. From August 2002 nine subjects at Key Stage 3 and five at Key Stage 4 are compulsory.

Beacon schools   Beacon schools are schools identified as representative of the best practice which can be disseminated to other schools. Such best practice might focus on a wide range of areas, including individual curriculum subjects; assessment of pupils; school management; parent/ community partnerships; special educational needs; gifted and talented pupils.

BEd   Bachelor of Education (a route to **QTS**).

BTEC   Business and Technician Education Council. Joined with **London Examinations** to form **EdExcel Foundation**. The BTEC label is still used for certain purposes.

C and G   City and Guilds.

Career Entry and Development Profile   A document to help newly qualified teachers and their first teaching post schools to identify and address targets, to target monitoring and provide support during induction. All **ITT** providers in England are required to provide newly qualified teachers with a career entry and development profile produced by the **TTA**.

Careers Education   Careers education is designed to help pupils to choose and prepare for opportunities, responsibilities and experiences in education, training and employment that will contribute to their own fulfilment and to the well-being of others, including the wider society and the economy. See also cross-curricular elements.

CCW   Curriculum Council for Wales; now **ACCAC**.

CEDP   See Career entry and development profile.

Certificate of Achievement (COA)   An examination designed to give a qualification to pupils who may not gain a GCSE grade. Courses are available in many subjects. The COA is awarded at pass, merit and distinction, corresponding to levels 1, 2 and 3 respectively of NC. Details available from the websites of **AQA**, **Edexcel** or **OCR**.

Citizenship   A compulsory element of the English National Curriculum at Key Stages 3 and 4 from August 2002. See also cross-curricular elements.

Collaborative group★   A way of working in which groups of children are assigned to groups or engage spontaneously in working together to solve problems; sometimes called co-operative group work.

Combined course★   A course to which several subjects contribute while retaining their distinct identity (e.g. history, geography and RE within combined humanities).

Comprehensive school★   A secondary school which admits pupils of age 11 to 16 or 19 from a given catchment area, regardless of their ability.

Continuity and progression★   Appropriate sequencing of learning which builds on previous learning to extend and develop pupils' capabilities.

Core skills   Skills required by all students following a vocational course, e.g. **GNVQ**.

Core subjects★   English, mathematics and science within the National Curriculum. Strictly speaking these are both core and foundation subjects.

Coursework   Work carried out by pupils during a course of study marked by teachers and contributing to the final examination mark. Usually externally moderated.

CPD   Continuing professional development.

CRE   Commission for Racial Equality.

Criterion-referenced Assessment   A process in which performance is measured by relating candidates' responses to pre-determined criteria.

Cross-curricular elements   These run across the whole curriculum and are not confined to one subject. Introduced in the National Curriculum in 1988 as dimensions, themes and skills. In National Curriculum 2000 these were replaced by careers; citizenship; personal, social and health education; key skills; thinking skills.

CSE   Certificate of Secondary Education (replaced by **GCSE** in 1988).

CTC   City Technology College.

Curriculum★★★   A course of study followed by a pupil.

Curriculum guidelines★   Written school guidance for organizing and teaching a particular subject or area of the curriculum. See also **Programmes of Study**.

D and T   Design and technology (in National Curriculum, technology).

Dearing Report   A review of the 'National Curriculum and its assessment' (1994). Recommended review of subject orders and five-year moratorium on further change.

Department★   Section of the curriculum/administrative structure of a (secondary) school, usually based on a subject.

DES   Department of Education and Science in England (became Department for Education (**DfE**) in 1992).

DfE   Department for Education (previously **DES**); became Department for Education and Employment (**DfEE**) in 1995.

DfEE   Department for Education and Employment (previously **DfE**); now Department for Education and Skills (**DfES**).

DfES   Department for Education and Skills (since 2001) (previously **DfEE**) until 2001).

DfES Circular   Advice issued by the Department for Education and Skills to **LEAs**. Circulars do not have the status of law.

Differentiation★   The matching of work to the differing capabilities of individuals or groups of pupils in order to extend their learning.

Disapplication★   Arrangement for lifting part or all of the National Curriculum requirements for individuals or for any other grouping specified by the Secretary of State.

EAL   English as an Additional Language.

EBD★   Emotional and behavioural difficulties and disorders. Used with reference to pupils with such difficulties or schools/units which cater for such pupils.

EdExcel Foundation   An awarding body formed from **BTEC** and **London Examinations** (previously **ULEAC**) <http://www.edexcel.org.uk>.

Education welfare officer (EWO)★   An official of the LEA concerned with pupils' attendance and with liaison between the school, the parents and the authority.

EOC   Equal Opportunities Commission.

ERA   Education Reform Act (1988).

ESL   English as a second language.

Examination Group   Public examination bodies which agreed to work together to provide a range of syllabuses for examination. These have been replaced by **awarding bodies**.

Exclusion★   Under section 22 of the Education (No. 2) Act 1986 the headteachers of county, voluntary and maintained special schools are empowered to exclude pupils temporarily or permanently when faced with a serious breach of their disciplinary code. The Act sets out procedures relating to the three categories of exclusions: fixed term, indefinite and permanent.

Faculty★   Grouping of subjects for administrative and curricular purposes.

Formative assessment   Assessment linked with teaching; describes pupils' progress and used to identify the next stage of teaching and learning; it uses diagnostic approaches, employing a wide range of methods, including formal and informal methods.

Forms of entry (FE)★   The number of forms (of 30 pupils) which a school takes into its intake year. From this can be estimated the size of the intake year and the size of the school.

Foundation subjects★★★★   Ten subjects in England (eleven in Wales) which state-maintained schools are required by law to teach. The foundation subjects of English, mathematics, science and, in Wales, Welsh, are designated as **core subjects**. The other foundation subjects are art, geography, history, modern foreign language, music, physical education, technology and, in Wales, Welsh as a second language. Different subjects are compulsory at different Key Stages.

GCE   General Certificate of Education

GCSE★   General Certificate of Secondary Education. National external qualification usually taken at age 16 after a two-year course. Introduced in 1988 to replace **GCE** 'O' level and Certificate of Secondary Education (CSE) examinations.

GNVQ   General National Vocational Qualifications.

Grade-related criteria   The identification of criteria, the achievement of which are related to different levels of performance by the candidate.

Group work★   A way of organizing pupils where the teacher assigns tasks to groups of children, to be undertaken collectively although the work is completed on an individual basis.

GTC   General Teaching Council.

HEI   Higher Education Institution.

HMCI   Her Majesty's Chief Inspector of School in England.

HMI   Her Majesty's Inspectors of Schools in England.

HOD   Head of Department.

House system★   A structure for pastoral care/pupil welfare within a school in which pupils are grouped in vertical units, i.e. sections of the school which include pupils from all year groups.

HOY   Head of Year.

IB   International Baccalaureate. A post-16 qualification designed for university entrance.

ICT   See Information and Communications Technology.

In-class support★   Support within a lesson provided in the classroom by an additional teacher, often with expertise in teaching pupils with special educational or language needs.

Inclusion   Inclusion involves the processes of increasing the participation of pupils in, and reducing their exclusion from schools. Inclusion is concerned with the learning participation of all pupils vulnerable to exclusionary pressures, not only those with impairments or categorized as having special educational needs.

Independent school   A private school that receives no state assistance but is financed by fees. Often registered as a charity. See also **public school**.

Information and Communications Technology (ICT)   Computer hardware and software which extend beyond the usual word-processing, databases, graphics and spread-sheet applications to include hardware and software which allow computers to be networked across the world through the World Wide Web, to access information on the internet and which supports other communication activities such as e-mail and video-conferencing.

Information Technology (IT)★★   Methods of gaining, storing and retrieving information through microprocessors. Often encompassed within **Information and Communications Technology**. IT is a compulsory subject in the National Curriculum for England.

INSET★   In-service Education and Training. Now generally called 'continuing professional development'.

Integrated course★   A course, usually in a secondary school, to which several subjects contribute without retaining their distinct identity (e.g. integrated humanities, which explores themes which include aspects of geography, history and RE).

Integration★★   Educating children with special educational needs together with children without special educational needs in mainstream schools wherever possible and ensuring that children with special educational needs engage in the activities of the school together with children who do not have special educational needs.

Ipsative assessment   A process in which performance is measured against previous performance by the same person. See also criterion-referenced assessment, normative assessment.

IT   See **information technology**.

ITT   Initial Teacher Training.

Key Skills   Six skill areas of the National Curriculum for England which help learners to improve their learning and performance in education, work and life are identified as key skills: communication; application of number; IT; improving own learning and performance; problem solving and working with others. See also cross-curricular elements.

Key Stages (KS)★   The periods in each pupil's education to which the elements of the National Curriculum apply. There are four Key Stages, normally related to the age of the majority of the pupils in a teaching group. They are: Key Stage 1, beginning of compulsory education to age 7 (Years R (Reception), 1 and 2); Key Stage 2, ages 7–11 (Years 3–6); Key Stage 3, ages 11–14 (years 7–9); Key Stage 4, 14 to end of compulsory education (Years 10 and 11). Post-16 is a further Key Stage.

Language support teacher   ★A teacher provided by the LEA or school to enhance language work with particular groups of pupils.

LEA   See **Local Education Authority**.

Learning support★   A means of providing extra help for pupils, usually those with learning difficulties, e.g. through a specialist teacher or specially designed materials. See also **learning support assistants**.

Learning support assistants   Teachers who give additional support for a variety of purposes, e.g. general learning support for **SEN** pupils, **ESL**; most support is given in-class although sometimes pupils are withdrawn from class. See also **learning support**, **withdrawal**.

Lesson plan   The detailed planning of work to be undertaken in a lesson. This follows a particular structure, appropriate to the demands of a particular lesson. An individual lesson plan is usually part of a series of lessons in a **unit of work**.

Level Description   In the National Curriculum for England a statement describing the types and range of performance that pupils working at a particular level should characteristically demonstrate. Level descriptions provide the basis for making judgements about pupils' performance at the end of Key Stages 1, 2, 3. At Key Stage 4, national qualifications are the main means of assessing attainment in National Curriculum subjects.

Levels of attainment   Eight levels of attainment, plus exceptional performance, are defined within the National Curriculum attainment targets in England. These stop at **Key Stage** 3 (before 1995 there were ten levels, which continued until Key Stage 4). In deciding a pupil's level of attainment teachers should judge which description best fits the pupil's performance (considering each description alongside descriptions of adjacent levels).

Local Education Authority   Each local education authority (**LEA**) has a statutory duty to provide education in their area.

London Examinations   An examining body previously known as **ULEAC**, which joined with **BTEC** to form **EdExcel Foundation**.

MEG   Midland Examining Group. Now part of **OCR**.

Middle school   A school which caters for pupils aged from 8–12 or 9–13 years of age. They are classified legally as either primary or secondary schools depending on whether the preponderance of pupils in the school is under or over 11 years of age.

Minority ethnic groups★   Pupils, many of whom have been born in the United Kingdom, from other ethnic heritages, e.g. those of Asian heritage from Bangladesh, Pakistan, India or East Africa, those of African or Caribbean heritage, or of Chinese heritage. The groups are often closely associated with countries in the British (New) Commonwealth, although non-Commonwealth refugee pupils are also to be found in schools.

Mixed ability group★   Teaching group containing pupils representative of the range of ability within the school. See also **banding**, **setting**, **streaming**.

Moderation   An exercise involving teachers representing an awarding body external to the school whose purpose is to check that standards are comparable across schools and teachers. Usually carried out by sampling coursework or examination papers.

Moderator★★ An examiner who monitors marking and examining to ensure that standards are consistent in a number of schools and colleges.

Module★   A definable section of work of fixed length with specific objectives and usually with some form of terminal assessment. Several such units may constitute a modular course.

National Curriculum (NC)★   The core and other foundation subjects and their associated attainment targets, programmes of study and assessment arrangements of the curriculum in England.

National induction standards   Standards that all newly qualified teachers in England are required to demonstrate at the end of their induction period. See also **statutory induction**.

NCC   National Curriculum Council. Merged with **SEAC** to form **SCAA**. Now **QCA**.

NCVQ   National Council for Vocational Qualifications. Joined with **SCAA** in 1997 to form **QCA**.

NEAB   Northern Examinations and Assessment Board (now part of **AQA**).

NFER   National Foundation for Educational Research. Carries out research and produces educational diagnostic tests.

Non-contact time★   Time provided by a school for a teacher to prepare work or carry out assigned responsibilities other than direct teaching.

Norm-referenced assessment   A process in which performance is measured by comparing candidates' responses. Individual success is relative to the performance of all other candidates.

Normative assessment   Assessment which is reported relative to a given population.

NQT   Newly qualified teacher.

NSG   Non-statutory guidance (for National Curriculum). Additional subject guidance for the National Curriculum but which is not mandatory; to be found attached to National Curriculum Subject Orders.

NVQ   National Vocational Qualifications.

OCEAC   Oxford and Cambridge Examination and Assessment Council (see **OCR**).

OCR   Oxford and Cambridge Regional (a merger of **MEG**, **OCEAC** and **RSA** examinations groups) <http://www.ocr.org.uk>.

OFSTED   Office for Standards in Education. Non-ministerial government department established under the Education (Schools) Act (1992) to take responsibility for the inspection of schools in England. OFSTED inspects pre-school provision, further education, teacher education institutions and **local education authorities**. **Her Majesty's Inspectors (HMI)** form the professional arm of OFSTED. See also OHMCI.

OHMCI   Office of Her Majesty's Chief Inspector (Wales). Non-ministerial government department established under the Education (Schools) Act (1992) to take responsibility for the inspection of schools in Wales. **Her Majesty's Inspectors (HMI)** form the professional arm of OHMCI. See also **OFSTED**.

PANDA   Performance and Assessment Reports (used by **OFSTED**).

Parent★   This is defined in section 114 (1D) of the Education Act 1944, as amended by the Children Act 1989. Unless the context otherwise requires, parent in relation to a child or young person includes any person:

- who is not a natural parent of the child but who has parental responsibility for him or her, or
- who has care of the child.

Section 114 (1F) of the 1944 Act states that for the purposes of subsection (1D):

- parental responsibility has the same meaning as in the Children Act 1989, and
- in determining whether an individual has care of a child or young person any absence of the child or young person at a hospital or boarding school and any other temporary absence shall be disregarded.

Parental responsibility★   Under section 2 of the Children Act 1989, parental responsibility falls upon:

- all mothers and fathers who were married to each other at the time of the child's birth (including those who have since separated or divorced),
- mothers who were not married to the father at the time of the child's birth, and
- fathers who were not married to the mother at the time of the child's birth, but who have obtained parental responsibility either by agreement with the child's mother or through a court order.

See *Code of Practice on the Identification and Assessment of Special Educational Needs* (DFE, 1994a) for further details.

Partnership teaching★   An increasingly common means of meeting the language needs of bilingual pupils in which support and class teachers plan and implement together a specially devised programme of in-class teaching and learning. It is used as a criterion for the allocation of **Section 11** grants. See also **support teacher**.

Pastoral care★   Those aspects of a school's work and structures concerned to promote the general welfare of all pupils, particularly their academic, personal and social development, their attendance and behaviour.

PGCE   Post Graduate Certificate in Education. The main qualification for secondary school teachers in England and Wales recognized by the **DfES** for **QTS**.

PICSI   Pre-Inspection Context and School Indicator (used by **OFSTED**).

Policy★   An agreed school statement relating to a particular area of its life and work.

PoS   See **Programmes of Study**.

Pre-vocational courses★   Courses specifically designed and taught to help pupils to prepare for the world of work.

Profile   Samples of work of pupils, used to illustrate progress, with or without added comments by teachers' and/or pupils.

Programmes of study (PoS)★   The subject matter, skills and processes which must be taught to pupils during each **Key Stage** of the **National Curriculum** in order that they may meet the objectives set out in **attainment targets**. They set out what pupils should be taught in each subject at each Key Stage and provide the basis for planning **schemes of work**.

Project★   An investigation with a particular focus undertaken by individuals or small groups of pupils leading to a written, oral or graphic presentation of the outcome.

PSE   Personal and social education - mainly concerned to promote pupils' personal and social development, and to help educate pupils for life outside and following school. See also **PSHE**.

PSHCE   Personal, social, health and citizenship education. **PSHE** with a specific additional citizenship component.

PSHE   Personal, social and health education. **PSE** with a specific additional health component. See also **PSHCE**.

PTA★   Parent-teacher association. Voluntary grouping of parents and school staff to support the school in a variety of ways (financial, social, etc.).

PTR★   Pupil: Teacher Ratio. The ratio of pupils to teachers within a school or group of schools (e.g. 17.4:1).

Public school   Independent secondary school not state funded. See also independent school. So-called because they were funded by public charity at their inception.

QCA   The Qualifications and Curriculum Authority. Formed as a result of the Education Act 1997, its remit is to promote quality and coherence in education and training. It brings together the work of **NCVQ** and **SCAA**, with additional powers and duties that give it an overview of the curriculum, assessment and qualifications across the whole of education and training, from pre-school to higher vocational levels. QCA advises the Secretary of State for Education and Skills on such matters. The Welsh equivalent is **ACCAC**.

QTS★   Qualified teacher status. This is usually attained by completion of a Post Graduate Certificate in Education (**PGCE**) or a Bachelor of Education (**BEd**) degree or a Bachelor of Arts/Science degree with Qualified Teacher Status (**BA/BSc (QTS)**). There are other routes into teaching.

Record of achievement (ROA)★   Cumulative record of a pupil's academic, personal and social progress over a stage of education.

Reliability   A measure of the consistency of the assessment or test item; i.e. the extent to which the test gives repeatable results.

RSA   Royal Society of Arts.

SACRE★   The Standing Advisory Council on Religious Education in each LEA to advise the LEA on matters connected with religious education and collective worship, particularly methods of teaching, the choice of teaching materials and the provision of teacher training.

SATs   See **standard assessment tasks**.

SCAA   School Curriculum and Assessment Authority. Formed in 1993 from a merger of **NCC** and **SEAC**. Joined with **NCVQ** in 1997 to form **QCA**.

Scheme of work   This represents long-term planning as it describes what is planned for pupils over a period of time (e.g. a Key Stage or a Year). It contains knowledge, skills and processes derived from the **Programmes of Study** and **Attainment Targets**.

School Development Plan (SDP)★   A coherent plan, required to be made by a school, identifying improvements needed in curriculum, organization, staffing and resources and setting out action needed to make those improvements.

SEAC   School Examination and Assessment Council. Merged with **NCC** to form **SCAA**.

SEG   Southern Examining Group. Now part of **AQA**.

Section 11 staff   Teachers and non-teaching assistants additional to the school's staffing establishment whose specific function is to provide language and learning support for pupils of New Commonwealth heritage.

SEN★   Special educational needs. Referring to pupils who for a variety of intellectual, physical, social, sensory, psychological or emotional reasons experience learning difficulties which are significantly greater than those experienced by the majority of pupils of the same age. The Warnock Report (DES, 1978) envisaged support for very able pupils but they are excluded from the definition of SEN and support is rarely provided.

Setting★   The grouping of pupils according to their ability in a subject for lessons in that subject. See also **banding**, **mixed ability group**, **streaming**.

Short course★   A course in a National Curriculum foundation subject in Key Stage 4 which will not by itself lead to a GCSE or equivalent qualification. Two short courses in different subjects may be combined to form a GCSE or equivalent course.

Sixth Form College   A post-16 institution for 16–19-year-olds. It offers GCSE, GCE A level and vocational courses.

SLD   Specific learning difficulties.

SOA   Statements of attainment (of National Curriculum subjects).

Special school★   A school which is specially organized to make educational provision for pupils with special educational needs and is approved by the Secretary of State under section 188 of the Education Act 1993.

Specialist schools   Maintained schools in England can apply for specialist school status in one of ten subjects: arts; business and enterprise; engineering; humanities; language; mathematics and computing; music; science; sports; technology. These schools are supported by government funding and, while teaching the National Curriculum, establish distinctiveness in their chosen area.

Standard assessment tasks (SATs)★   Externally prescribed **National Curriculum** assessments which incorporate a variety of assessment methods depending on the subject and **Key Stage**. This term is not now widely used, having been replaced by 'standard national tests'.

Statements of special educational needs★   Provided under the 1981 Education Act to ensure appropriate provision for pupils formally assessed as having **SEN**.

Statutory induction   Introduced in 1999 in England, this provides an individualized programme for newly qualified teachers to monitor, support and assess their progress during their first year of teaching. See also **National induction standards**.

Statutory order★   A statutory instrument which is regarded as an extension of an Act, enabling provisions of the Act to be augmented or updated.

Streaming★   The organization of pupils according to general ability into classes in which they are taught for all subjects and courses. See also **banding**, **mixed ability group**, **setting**.

Summative assessment   Assessment linked to the end of a course of study; it sums up achievement in aggregate terms and is used to rank, grade or compare pupils, groups or schools. It uses a narrow range of methods which are efficient and reliable, normally formal, i.e. under examination conditions.

Supply teacher   Teachers appointed by **LEAs** to fill vacancies in maintained schools which arise as a result of staff absences. Supply teachers may be attached to a particular school for a period ranging from half a day to several weeks or more.

TDA   Training and Development Agency in 2005 superseded the **TTA** with an extended remit for overseeing standards and qualifications across the school workforce.

Teacher's record book★   A book in which a teacher plans and records teaching and learning for his or her class(es) on a regular basis.

Team teaching★   The teaching of a number of classes simultaneously by teachers acting as a team. They usually divide the work between them, allowing those with particular expertise to lead different parts of the work, the others supporting the follow-up work with groups or individuals.

TES   *Times Educational Supplement*. Published weekly and contains articles on educational issues, information about developments in education, job vacancies, etc.

TGAT   Task Group on Assessment and Testing (of National Curriculum). Produced the *TGAT Report* (1988), which led to some of the assessment procedures for the **National Curriculum**.

Thinking skills   Additional skills to be promoted across the **National Curriculum** for England. See also **cross-curricular elements**.

Travellers★   A term used to cover those communities, some of which have minority ethnic status, who either are or have been traditionally associated with a nomadic lifestyle, and include gypsy travellers, fairground or show people, circus families, New Age travellers, and bargees.

Traveller education★   The development of policy and provision which provides traveller children with unhindered access to and full integration in mainstream education.

TTA   Teacher Training Agency. Established in 1994 to take over the work of the Council for the Accreditation of Teacher Education (CATE). The TTA was responsible for the quality of teacher education in England and the supply of teachers. In 2005, the TTA became the **TDA**.

Tutor group★   Grouping of secondary pupils for registration and pastoral care purposes.

ULEAC   University of London Examinations and Assessment Council (formerly **LEAG** – of examination groups), became **London Examinations** and now part of **Edexcel**.

Unit of work   Medium-term planning as it describes what is planned for pupils over half a term or a number of weeks. The number of lessons in a unit of work may vary according to each school's organization. A unit of work usually introduces a new aspect of learning. Units of work derive from **schemes of work** and are the basis for **lesson plans**. The number and length of units of work varies from school to school (QCA recommend units of work are 12 weeks long).

Validity   A measure of whether the assessment measures what it is meant to measure – often determined by consensus. Certain kinds of skills and abilities are extremely difficult to assess with validity via simple pencil and paper tests.

Voluntary school   School which receives financial assistance from the **LEA**, but which is owned by a voluntary body, usually religious.

Withdrawal★   Removal of pupils with particular needs from class teaching in primary schools and from specified subjects in secondary schools for extra help individually or in small groups. In-class support is increasingly provided in preference to withdrawal.

WJEC   Welsh Joint Education Committee (of awarding bodies).

Work experience★   The opportunity for secondary pupils to have experience, usually within school time, of the world of work for one or two weeks, during which a pupil carries out a particular job or range of jobs more or less as would regular employees, although with emphasis on the educational aspects of the experience. It may only take place after Easter in Year 10 (i.e. in the final year of statutory schooling).

World class tests   Devised by the government for gifted and talented pupils aged 9–13 years (see **QCA** website <http://www.qgc.org.uk>.)

Year system★   A structure for pastoral care/pupil welfare within a school in which pupils are grouped according to years, i.e. in groups spanning an age range of only one year.

Years 1–11   Year of schooling. Five-year-olds start at Year 1 (Y1) and progress through to Year 11 (Y11) at 16 years old. This comprises four **Key Stages** (KS): KS1 = Y1 to Y3; KS2 = Y4 to Y6; KS3 = Y7 to Y9; KS4 = Y10 to Y11.

References

ACCAC (Awdurdod Cymwysterau, Cwricwlwm ac Asesu Cymru) (2000) *Welsh National Curriculum KS3*. Online. Available HTTP: <http://www.accac.org.uk/eng/content.php?mID=170> (accessed 8 Oct. 2004)

Adams, C., Brown, B. B. and Edwards, M. (1997) *Developmental Disorders of Language*, London: Whurr.

Addison, N. and Burgess, L. (2000) *Learning to Teach Art and Design in the Secondary School: A Companion to School Experience*, London: Routledge.

Adey, P. (1992) 'The CASE results: implications for science teaching', *International Journal of Science Education*, 14: 137–46.

Adey, P. (2000) 'Science teaching and the development of intelligence', in M. Monk and J. Osborne (eds) *Good Practice in Science Education*, Buckingham: Open University Press.

Adey, P. and Shayer, M. (1994) *Really Raising Standards*, London: Routledge.

Adey, P., Shayer, M. and Yates, C. (1989) *Thinking Science*, London: Macmillan.

Aldrich, R. and White, J. (1998) *The National Curriculum beyond 2000: The QCA and the Aims of Education*, London: Institute of Education.

Ames, C. (1992a) 'Achievement goals and the classroom motivational climate', in D.H. Schunk and J.L. Meece (eds) *Student Perception in the Classroom*, Hillsdale, NJ: Erlbaum, pp. 327–48.

Ames, C. (1992b) 'Classrooms: goals, structures and student motivation', *Journal of Educational Psychology*, 84: 261–71.

Amos, J.-A. (1998) *Managing your Time: What to Do and How to Do it in order to Do More*, Oxford: How to Books.

Anderman, E.M. and Maehr, M.L. (1994) 'Motivation and schooling in the middle grades', *Review of Educational Research*, 64: 287–309.

Anderman, L.H. and Anderman, E.M. (1999) 'Social predictors of changes in students' achievement goal orientations', *Contemporary Education Psychology*, 25: 21–37.

Anderson, J.R., Reder, L.M. and Simon, H.A. (1996) 'Situated learning and education', *Educational Researcher*, 25: 5–11.

Anderson, L.W. and Krathwohl, D. (eds) (2001) *A Taxonomy for Learning, Teaching and Assessing: A Revision of Bloom's Taxonomy of Educational Objectives*, New York: Longman.

Anderson, R. (2003) 'The history of Scottish education, pre-1980', in T.G.K. Bryce and W.M. Humes (eds) *Scottish Education Post-Devolution*, 2nd edn, Edinburgh: Edinburgh University Press.

Arikewuyo, M.O. (2004) 'Stress management strategies of secondary school teachers in Nigeria', *Educational Research*, 46 (2): 196–207.

Arnold, R. (1993) *Time Management*, Leamington Spa: Scholastic Publications.

Atkinson, J.W. (1964) *An Introduction to Motivation*, Princeton, NJ: Van Nostrand.

Ausubel, D. P. (1968) *Educational Psychology: A Cognitive View*, New York: Holt, Rinehart & Winston.

Ayers, H. and Prytys, C. (2002) *An A to Z Practical Guide to Emotional and Behavioural Difficulties*, London: David Fulton Publishers.

Balderstone, D. and King, S. (2004) 'Preparing pupils for public examinations: developing study skills', in S. Capel, R. Heilbronn, M. Leask and T. Turner (eds) *Starting to Teach in the Secondary School: A Companion for the Newly Qualified Teacher*, 2nd edn, London: RoutledgeFalmer.

Ball, S. (2003) *Class Strategies and the Education Market: The Middle Classes and Social Advantage*, London: RoutledgeFalmer.

Bandura, A. (1977) 'Self-efficacy: toward a unifying theory of behavioral change', *Psychological Review*, 84: 191–215.

Bandura, A. (1997) *Self-Efficacy: The Exercise of Control*, New York: Freeman.

Barnard, N. (2000) 'Tests are so, so, so boring Mr Blunkett', *Times Educational Supplement* (18 August).

Barnes, D., Johnson, G. and Jordan, S.S. (1988) *Learning Styles. TVEI: Evaluation Report Number 3*, Leeds: Manpower Services Commission.

Batchford, R. (1992) *Values: Assemblies for the 1990s*, Cheltenham: Stanley Thorne.

Battisch, V., Solomon, D. and Watson, M. (1998) 'Sense of community as a mediating factor in promoting children's social and ethical development', paper presented at the meeting of the American Educational Research Association, San Diego, CA, April 1998. Online. Available HTTP: <http://tigger.uic.edu/~lnucci/MoralEd/articles/battistich.html> (accessed 14 July 2004).

Beard, R. (2000) *Developing Writing 3–13*, London: Hodder and Stoughton.

Beck, J. (2000) 'The school curriculum and the National Curriculum', in J. Beck and M. Earl (eds) *Key Issues in Secondary Education*, London: Cassell.

BECTA (British Educational Communications and Technology Agency) (2001) *Information Sheet: Parents, ICT and Education*, Coventry: British Educational Communications and Technology Agency. Online. Available HTTP: <http://www.becta.org.uk/leaders/leaders.cfm?section=9_1andid=2189> (accessed 28 June 2004).

BECTA (British Educational Commnications and Technology Agency) (2005) *ICT Advice for Teachers: The Interactive Whiteboards Project*. Online. Available HTTP: <http://www.ictadvice.org.uk> (accessed 4 March 2005).

Bee, H. and Boyd, D. (2004) *The Developing Child*, 10th edn, London: Allyn & Bacon.

Benmansour, N. (1998) 'Job satisfaction, stress and coping strategies among Moroccan high school teachers', *Mediterranean Journal of Educational Studies*, 3: 13–33.

Bennett, N. and Dunne, E. (1994) 'How children learn: implications for practice', in B. Moon and A. Shelton-Mayes (eds) *Teaching and Learning in the Secondary School*, London: Routledge.

BERA (British Educational Research Association) (2003) 'Ethical guidelines for educational research: consultation of members', *Research Intelligence, No. 82*, Southwell, Notts: BERA.

Beresford, J. (2003) 'Minding the gap', *Managing Schools Today*, 12 (6): 38–44.

Berkowitz, M., Gibbs, J. and Broughton, J. (1980) 'The relation of moral judgment stage disparity to developmental effects of peer dialogues', *Merrill-Palmer Quarterly*, 26: 341–57.

Berndt, T.J. and Keefe, K. (1995) 'Friends' influence on adolescents' academic achievement motivation: an experimental study', *Journal of Educational Psychology*, 82: 664–70.

Bernstein, B. (1977) *Class, Codes and Control*, Volume 3, *Towards a Theory of Educational Transmissions*, 2nd edn, London: Routledge & Kegan Paul.

Biggs, J. and Moore, P. (1993) *The Process of Learning*, London: Prentice Hall International.

Biggs, J.B. (1978) 'Individual and group differences in study processes', *British Journal of Educational Psychology*, 48: 266–79.

Biggs, J.B. (1987) *Student Approaches to Learning and Studying*, Hawthorne, Victoria: Australian Council for Educational Research.

Biggs, J.B. (1993) 'What do inventories of students' learning processes really measure? A theoretical review and clarification', *British Journal of Educational Psychology*, 63: 3–19.

Black, P. and Wiliam, D. (1998) *Inside the Black Box*, London: King's College.

Black, P. and Wiliam, D. (2002) *Working Inside the Black Box: Assessment for Learning in the Classroom*, London: King's College.

Black, P., Harrison, C., Lee, C., Marshall, B. and Wiliam, D. (2003) *Assessment for Learning: Putting it into Practice*, Maidenhead: Open University Press.

Blamires, M., Brookes, H., Lacey, R. and Roux, J. (2000) *Communication Difficulties, the Classroom and Curriculum*, London: Special Educational Needs Joint Initiative and Training (SENJIT), Institute of Education, University of London.

Bleach, K. (2000) *The Newly Qualified Secondary Teachers Handbook: Meeting the Standards in Secondary and Middle Schools*, London: David Fulton.

Bloom, B.S. (1956) *Taxonomy of Educational Objectives, Handbook 1: Cognitive Domain*, London: Longman.

Boaler, J. (1997) *Experiencing School Mathematics: Teaching Style, Sex and Setting*, Buckingham: Open University Press.

Bottery, M. (1990) *The Morality of the School*, London: Cassell

Bourdieu, P. (1974) 'The school as a conservative force: scholastic and cultural inequalities', in J. Egglestone (ed.) *Contemporary Research in the Sociology of Education*, London: Methuen & Co., pp. 32–56.

Bourdieu, P. (1989) 'How schools help reproduce the social order', *Current Contents: Social and Behavioural Science*, 21 (8): 16.

Bramall, S. and White, J. (eds) (2000a) *Why Learn Maths?* London: Institute of Education, University of London.

Bramall, S. and White, J. (2000b) *Will the New National Curriculum Live up to its Aims?*, IMPACT paper 6, London: Philosophy of Education Society of Great Britain.

Brandreth, G. (1981) *The Puzzle Mountain*, Harmondsworth: Penguin Books.

Bransford, J. D., Brown, A. and Cocking, R.C. (eds) (1999) *How People Learn: Brain, Mind, Experience and School*, Washington, DC: National Academy Press.

Briggs, A. (1983) *A Social History of England*, London: Book Club Associates.

British Medical Association (2003) *Adolescent Health*, London: BMA. Online. Available HTTP: <http://www.bma.org.uk> search on home page (accessed 27 Oct. 2004).

British Nutrition Foundation (2003) *Establishing a Whole School Policy*. Online. Available HTTP: <http://www.nutrition.org.uk> go to Education (accessed 27 Oct. 2004).

British Nutrition Foundation (2004) *School Breakfast Clubs*. Online. Available HTTP: <http://www.nutrition.org.uk> go to Education, then access the 'Shifting the Balance' section in the Teachers Centre (accessed 27 Oct. 2004).

British Stammering Association (n.d.) *A Chance to Speak: Teachers Information Pack* (Video and leaflets). Information available online. HTTP: <http://www.stammering.org> (accessed 4 Nov. 2004).

Brody, L. (ed.) (2004) *Grouping and Acceleration Practices in Gifted Education*, Thousand Oaks, CA: Corwin Press and National Association for Gifted Children.

Bronfenbrenner, U. (1979) *The Ecology of Human Development*, Cambridge, MA: Harvard University Press.

Brooks, J. and Lucas, N. (2004) 'The school sixth form and the growth of vocational qualifications', in S. Capel, R. Heilbronn, M. Leask and T. Turner (eds) *Starting to Teach in the Secondary School: A Companion for the Newly Qualified Teacher*, 2nd edn, London: RoutledgeFalmer.

Brooks, V. (2002) *Assessment in Secondary Schools: The New Teacher's Guide to Monitoring, Assessment, Recording, Reporting and Accountability*, Buckingham: Open University Press.

Brown, A.L. (1994) 'The advancement of learning', *Educational Researcher*, 23: 4–12.

Brown, M. and Ralph, S. (2002) 'Teacher stress and school improvement', *Improving Schools*, 5 (2): 55–65.

Brown, S. and McIntyre, D. (1993) *Making Sense of Teaching*, Buckingham: Open University Press.

Bruner, J. (1966) *Towards a Theory of Instruction*, New York: W.W. Norton.

Bruner, J. (1983) *Child's Talk: Learning to Use Language*, Oxford: Oxford University Press.

Bryce, T.G.K. and Humes, W. M. (2003) *Scottish Education Post-Devolution*, 2nd edn, Edinburgh: Edinburgh University Press.

Bubb, S. and Earley, P. (2004) *Managing Teacher Workload: Work–Life Balance and Wellbeing*, London: Sage.

Bull, S. and Solity, J. (1987) *Classroom Management: Principles to Practice*, London: Croom Helm.

Bullock Report (1975) *A Language for Life*, London: HMSO.

Burgess, T. (2004) 'Language in the classroom and curriculum', in S. Capel, R. Heilbronn, M. Leask and T. Turner (eds) *Starting to Teach in theSecondary School: A Companion for the Newly Qualified Teacher*, 2nd edn, London: RoutledgeFalmer.

Burnett, P. (2002) 'Teacher praise and feedback and students' perceptions of the classroom environment', *Educational Psychology*, 22 (1): 5–16.

Burnham, S. and Brown, G. (2004) Assessment without level descriptions', *Teaching History,* 115: 5–15.

Burton, D. (2001) 'Ways pupils learn', in S. Capel, M. Leask and T. Turner (eds) *Learning to Teach in the Secondary School: A Companion to School Experience*, 3rd edn, London: RoutledgeFalmer, pp. 235–49.

Burton, D. (2004) 'Developing teaching and learning strategies', in S. Capel, R. Heilbronn, M. Leask and T. Turner (eds) *Starting to Teach in the Secondary School: A Companion for the Newly Qualified Teacher*, 2nd edn, London: RoutledgeFalmer.

Burton, D. and Bartlett, S. (2004) *Practitioner Research for Teachers*, London: Paul Chapman Educational Publishing.

Cains, R.A. and Brown, C.R. (1998) 'Newly qualified teachers: a comparative analysis of the perceptions held by BEd and PGCE-trained primary teachers of the level and frequency of stress experienced during the first year of teaching', *Educational Psychology*, 18 (1): 97–110.

Calderhead, J. and Shorrock, S.B. (1997) *Understanding Teacher Education*, London: Falmer.

Capel, S. (1994) 'Help – it's teaching practice again!', paper presented at the 10th Commonwealth and International Scientific Congress, Victoria, BC, Canada.

Capel, S. (1996) 'Changing focus of concerns for physical education students on school experience', *Pedagogy in Practice*, 2 (2): 5–20.

Capel, S. (1997) 'Changes in students' anxieties after their first and second teaching practices', *Educational Research*, 39 (2): 211–28.

Capel, S. (1998) 'A longitudinal study of the stages of development or concern of secondary PE students', *European Journal of Physical Education*, 3 (2): 185–99.

Capel, S., Leask, M. and Turner, T. (2001) *Learning to Teach in the Secondary School: A Companion to School Experience*, 3rd edn, London: RoutledgeFalmer.

Capel, S., Heilbronn, R., Leask, M. and Turner, T. (2004) *Starting to Teach in the Secondary School: A Companion for the Newly Qualified Teacher*, 2nd edn, London: RoutledgeFalmer.

Carnell, E. and Lodge, C. (2002) *Supporting Effective Learning*, London: Sage (Paul Chapman).

Carpenter, P.J. and Morgan, K. (1999) 'Motivational climate, personal goal perspectives and cognitive and affective responses in physical education classes', *European Journal of Physical Education*, 35: 31–44.

Centre for Studies on Inclusion in Education (CSIE) (2000) *Index for Inclusion: Developing Learning and Participation in Schools*, ed. T. Booth, Bristol: CSIE with CEN (University of Manchester) and CER (Canterbury Christ Church University College, Canterbury).

Chalmers, G. (ed.) (2001) *Reflections on Motivation*, London: Centre for Information on Language Teaching and Research (CILT).

Child, D. (1993) *Psychology and the Teacher*, 5th edn, London: Cassell.

Child, D. (1997) *Psychology and the Teacher*, 6th edn, London: Cassell.

Child, D. (2004) *Psychology and the Teacher*, 7th edn, London and New York: Continuum.

Chirkov, V.I. and Ryan, R.M. (2001) 'Parent and teacher autonomy-support in Russian and U.S. adolescents: common effects on well-being and academic motivation', *Journal of Cross-Cultural Psychology*, 32 (5): 618–35.

Chyriwsky, M. (1996) 'Able children: the need for a subject-specific approach', *Flying High* (Worcester, The National Association for Able Children in Education) 3: 32–6.

Clarke, S. (2001) *Unlocking Formative Assessment: Unlocking Practical Strategies for Enhancing Pupils' Learning in the Classroom*, London: King's College.

Claxton, G. (2002) *Building Learning Power: Helping Young People Become Better Learners*, Bristol: TLO.

Clough, P., Garner, P., Pardeck, T. and Yuen, F. (eds) (2004) *The Handbook of Emotional and Behavioural Difficulties*, London: Sage.

Cockburn, A. and Haydn, T. (2004) *Recruiting and Retaining Teachers: Understanding Why Teachers Teach*, London: RoutledgeFalmer.

Cockburn, A.D. (1996) 'Primary teachers' knowledge and acquisition of stress relieving strategies', *British Journal of Educational Psychology*, 66: 399–410.

Cole, M. (ed.) (1999) *Professional Issues for Teachers and Student Teachers*, London: David Fulton.

Coles, A. and Turner, S. (1995) *Diet and Health in School-aged Children*, London: Health Education Authority.

Conway, P.F. and Clark, C.M. (2003) 'The journey inward and outward: a re-examination of Fuller's concerns-based model of teacher development', *Teaching and Teacher Education*, 466–82.

Cook, M.J. (1998) *Time Management: Proven Techniques for Making the Most of your Time*, Holbrook, MA: Adams Media Corporation.

Cooper, B. and Dunne, M. (2000) *Assessing Children's Mathematical Knowledge: Social Class, Sex and Problem Solving*, Buckingham: Open University Press.

Cooper, P. and Ideus, K. (1996) *Attention-Deficit/Hyperactivity Disorder: A Practical Guide for Teachers*, London: David Fulton Publications.

Council for Disabled Children/Disability Equality in Education (2002) *Making it Work: Removing Disability Discrimination*, London: National Children's Bureau.

Covington, M.V. (2000) 'Goal theory, motivation and school achievement: an integrative review', *Annual Review of Psychology*, 51: 171–200.

Cowie, H. and Sharp, S. (1992) 'Students themselves tackle the problem of bullying', *Pastoral Care in Education*, 10 (4): 31–7.

Cox, M. (1999) 'ICT and pupil motivation', in M. Leask and N. Pachler (eds) *Learning to Teach Using ICT in the Secondary School*, London: Routledge.

Croft, C. (1996) *Time Management*, London: International Thomson Business Press.

Crook, D., Power, S. and Whitty, G. (1999) *The Grammar School Question: A Review of Research on Comprehensive and Selective Education*, London: Institute of Education, University of London in the series 'Perspectives on Education'.

Cunningham, M., Kerr, K., McEune, R., Smith, P. and Harris, S. (2003) *Laptops for Teachers: An Evaluation of the First Year of the Initiative*, London: Department for Education and Skills/British Educational Communications and Technology Agency.

Curtis, S.J. (1967) *History of Education in Great Britain*, Foxton, Cambs: University Tutorial Press.

Daugherty, R. (1995) *National Curriculum Assessment: A Review of Policy 1987–1994*, London: Falmer Press.

Davies, F. and Greene, T. (1984) *Reading for Learning in Science*, Edinburgh: Oliver and Boyd.

Davies, N. (2000) *The School Report: Why Britain's Schools are Failing*, London: Vintage Books.

Davis, B. and Sumara, D.J. (1997) 'Cognition, complexity and teacher education', *Harvard Educational Review*, 67: 105–21.

de Bono, E. (1972) *Children Solve Problems*, London: Penguin Education.

Dearing, R. (1994) *The National Curriculum and its Assessment. Final Report*, London: HMSO.

Dearing, R. (1996) *Review of Qualifications for 16–19-Year-Olds (Full Report)*, London: School Curriculum and Assessment Authority.

Deci, E.L. and Ryan, R.M. (1985) *Intrinsic Motivation and Self-Determination in Human Behavior*, New York: Plenum.

Deci, E.L., Koestner, R. and Ryan, R.M. (1999) 'A meta-analytic review of experiments examining the effects of extrinsic rewards on intrinsic motivation', *Psychological Bulletin*, 25: 627–68.

DES (Department for Education and Science) (1967) *Children and their Primary Schools* (The Plowden Report). London: HMSO.

DES (Department of Education and Science) (1978) *Special Educational Needs*, London: HMSO.

DES (Department of Education and Science) (1985) *Education for All: The Final Report of the Committee of Inquiry into the Education of Children from Ethnic Minority Groups*, Cmnd. 9469, (The Swann Report), London: HMSO.

DES (Department of Education and Science) (1989) *Discipline in Schools* (The Elton Report), London: HMSO.

DES/WO (Department of Education and Science and the Welsh Office) (1988) *National Curriculum Task Group on Assessment and Testing* (the TGAT Report), London: DES/WO.

Desforges, C. (2003) *On Teaching and Learning*, Cranfield: NCSL.

Dewey, J. (1916) *Democracy and Education*, New York: Free Press.

DfE (Department for Education) (1994a) *Code of Practice on the Identification and Assessment of Special Educational Needs*, London: DfE.

DfE (Department for Education) (1994b) *The Education of Children with Emotional and Behavioural Difficulties* (Circular 9/94), London: DfE.

DfE (Department for Education) (1995) *The National Curriculum* (1995 revision), London: HMSO.

DfEE (Department for Education and Employment) (1997a) *Guaranteeing Standards: A Consultation Paper on the Structure of Awarding Bodies*, London: DfEE.

DfEE (Department for Education and Employment) (1997b) *Excellence in Schools*, London: DfEE.

DfEE (Department for Education and Employment) (1998a) *Target Setting in School* (Circular 11/98), London: DfEE.

DfEE (Department for Education and Employment) (1998b) *Teachers Meeting the Challenge of Change*, London: HMSO.

DfEE (Department for Education and Employment)) (1998c) *The National Literacy Strategy*, London: HMSO.

DfEE (Department for Education and Employment) (1998d) *Truancy and School Exclusion Report*, London: DfEE.

DfEE (Department for Education and Employment) (1999a) *Minority Ethnic Pupils in Maintained Schools by Local Education Authority Area in England*, DfEE: Statistical First Release (SFR 15/1999).

DfEE (Department for Education and Employment) (1999b) *Social Inclusion: Pupil Support* (Circular 10/99), London: DfEE.

DfEE (Department for Education and Employment) (1999c) *Youth Cohort Study: The Activities and Experiences of 16 Year Olds; England and Wales 1998*, London: Stationery Office. Issue 4/99, March – Statistical Bulletin. Online. Available HTTP: <http://www.dfes.gov.uk/rsgateway/DB/SFR/s000230/contents.shtml> (accessed 9 Sept. 2004).

DfEE (Department for Education and Employment) (2000a) *SEN Code of Practice on the Identification and Assessment of Pupils with Special Educational Needs*, London: DfEE. Online. Available HTTP: <http://www.teachernet. gov.uk/teachinginengland/> (accessed 4 Nov. 2004).

DfEE (Department for Education and Employment) (2000b) *Transforming Key Stage 3: National Pilot English at Key Stage 3 Training 2000*, London: DfEE.

DfEE (Department for Education and Employment) (2001) *Framework for Teaching English, Years 7, 8 and 9*, London, DfEE.

DfEE/QCA (Department of Education and Employment/Qualifications and Curriculum Authority)(1998) *Education for Citizenship and the Teaching of Democracy in Schools: Final Report of the Advisory Group on Citizenship*, London: QCA.

DfEE/QCA (Department for Education and Employment and Qualification and Curriculum Authority) (1999a) *The National Curriculum for England. Handbook for Secondary Teachers: Key Stages 3 and 4*, London: The Stationery Office. Online. Available HTTP: <http://www.nc.uk.net/index.html> (accessed 28 Oct. 2004).

DfEE/QCA (Department for Education and Employment and Qualifications and Curriculum Authority) (1999b) *Citizenship: The National Curriculum for England*, London: Stationery Office.

DfEE/QCA (Department for Education and Employment/Qualifications and Curriculum Authority) (2001) *Guidelines for Teaching Pupils with Learning Difficulties*, London: DfEE. Online. Available HTTP: <http://www.nc.uk.net/ld> (accessed 4 Nov. 2004)

DfES (Department for Education and Skills) (2001) *The Key Stage 3 Strategy*. Online. Available HTTP: <http://www.standards.dfes.gov.uk/key stage3> (accessed 23 Oct. 2004).

DfES (Department for Education and Skills) (2001a) *Bullying: Don't Suffer in Silence*, London: DfES.

DfES (Department for Education and Skills) (2001b) *Inclusive Schooling*, London: DfES.

DfES (Department for Education and Skills) (2001c) *Education and Skills: Delivering Results – A Strategy to 2006*, Sudbury, Suffolk: DfES.

DfES (Department for Education and Skills) (2003a) *England's Success*, London: DfES.

DfES (Department for Education and Skills) (2003b) *Every Child Matters*, London: HMSO.

DfES (Department for Education and Skills) (2003c) *Guidance on Bullying*, London: DfES.

DfES (Department for Education and Skills) (2003d) *KS3 National Strategy (Behaviour and Attendance)*, London: DfES.

DfES (Department for Education and Skills) (2003e) *Key Stage 3 Strategy: Key Messages about Assessment and Learning*, London: DfES.

DfES (Department for Education and Skills) (2003f) *Primary National Strategy (Social, Emotional and Behavioural Skills)*, London: DfES

DfES (Department for Education and Skills) (2003g) *Teaching and Learning in Secondary Schools: Pilot – Guidance. Units 4–7*, London: Crown Ref: DfES 0344/2003-0347/2003.

DfES (Department for Education and Skills) (2003h) *Teaching and Learning in Secondary Schools: Pilot. Unit 3: Modelling*, London: Crown, Ref: DfES 0343/2003.

DfES (Department for Education and Skills) (2003i) *Teaching and Learning in Secondary Schools: Pilot. Unit 4: Questioning*, London: Crown, Ref: DfES 0344/2003.

DfES (Department for Education and Skills) (2003j) *Teaching and Learning in Secondary Schools, Pilot. Unit 10: Learning Styles*, London: DfES.

DfES (Department for Education and Skills) (2003k) *The Induction Support Programme for Newly Qualified Teachers*, London: HMSO.

DfES (Department for Education and Skills) (2003l) *The Code of Practice*, London: DfES.

DfES (Department for Education and Skills) (2003m) *Time for Standards*, London: DfES.

DfES (Department for Education and Skills) (2003n) *Qualifying to Teach: Handbook of Guidance*, London: DfES.

DfES (Department for Education and Skills) (2004a) *Healthy Living: the Blueprint*. Online. Available HTTP: <http://www.teachernet.gov.uk> use search facility 'Healthy Living' (accessed 27 Oct. 2004).

DfES (Department for Education and Skills) (2004b) *Key Stage 3 National Strategy Materials*. Online. Available HTTP: <http://www.standards.dfes.gov.uk/keystage3/> (accessed 1 Nov. 2004).

DfES (Department for Education and Skills) (2004c) *National Curriculum Exemplar Schemes of Work*. Online. Available HTTP: <http://www.standards.dfes.gov.uk/schemes3/> (accessed 1 Nov. 2004).

DfES (Department for Education and Skills) (2004d) *National Curriculum for England*. Online. Available HTTP: <http://www.nc.uk.net/index.html> (accessed 1 Nov. 2004).

DfES (Department for Education and Skills) (2004e) *National Curriculum in Action; Pupil's Work, Exemplar Material*. Online. Available HTTP: <http://www.ncaction.org.uk/> (accessed 1 Nov. 2004).

DfES (Department for Education and Skills) (2004f) *Pedagogy and Practice: Teaching and Learning in the Secondary School. Unit 7 Questioning*, London: DfES. Unit 7, Questioning is online. Available HTTP: <http://www. standards.dfes.gov.uk/keystage3/respub/sec_ppt10>. (accessed 2 Dec. 2004)

DfES (Department for Education and Skills) (2004g) *Removing Barriers to Achievement: The Government's SEN Strategy*, Nottingham: DfES Publications.

DfES (Department for Education and Skills) (2004h) *The 14–19 Gateway: Information on the 14–19 Curriculum Reforms*. Online. Available HTTP: < http://www.dfes.gov.uk/14–19/ (accessed 1 Nov. 2004).

DfES (Department for Education and Skills) (2004i) *The Final Report of the Working Group on 14–19 Reform* (The Tomlinson Report). Online. Available HTTP: <http://www.14–19reform.gov.uk/> (accessed 20 Oct. 2004)

DfES (Department for Education and Skills) (2004j) *National Programme for Specialist Leaders in Behaviour and Attendance – Pilot*, London: DfES.

DfES (Department for Education and Skills) Research publications. Online. Available HTTP: <http://www.dfes.gov.uk/research> (accessed 9 Sept. 2004).

DfES/TTA (Department for Education and Skills and the Teacher Training Agency) (2003) *Qualifying to Teach: Professional Standards for Qualified Teacher Status and Requirements for Initial Teacher Training*, London: TTA.

DfES/TTA (Department for Education and Skills and Teacher Training Agency) (2004) *The Autumn Package 2004 Guidance*. Online. Available HTTP: <http://www.standards.dfes.gov.uk/performance> (accessed 11 March 2005).

DfES/TTA (Department for Education and Skills/Teacher Training Agency) (2004) *Qualifying to Teach: Professional Standards for Qualified Teacher Status and Requirements for Initial Teacher Training*, London: TTA. Online. Available HTTP: <http://www.tta.gov.uk/php/read.php?sectionid=110andarticleid=459> (accessed 9 Sept. 2004).

Dickenson, P. (1999) *Whole Class Interactive Teaching*. Online. Available HTTP: <http://s13a.math.aca.mmu.ac.uk/Student_Writings/Masters/PaulDickenson.html> (accessed 12 June 2004).

Dickinson, A. (1991) 'Assessing, recording and reporting children's achievements: from changes to genuine gains', in R. Aldrich (ed.) *History in the National Curriculum*, London: Kogan Page, pp. 66–92.

Dickinson, A. (1998) 'History using information technology: past, present and future', *Teaching History*, 93: 16–20.

Dillon, J. and Maguire, M. (eds) (2001) *Becoming a Teacher: Issues in Secondary Teaching*, 2nd edn, Buckingham: Open University Press.

Dillon, J.T. (1981) 'To question or not question in discussion', *Journal of Teacher Education*, 32: 51–5.

DoH (Department of Health) (2004) *Food in Schools*. Online. Available HTTP: <http://www.doh.gov.uk> go to 'The need for food in schools' (accessed 29 Nov. 2004).

DoH (Department of Health). Online. Available HTTP: <http://www.doh.gov.uk/dhhone.htm> (accessed 27 Oct. 2004).

DoH/DfES (Department of Health/Department for Education and Skills) (2004) *Wired for Health*. Online. Available HTTP: <http://www.wiredforhealth.gov.uk> (accessed 27 Oct. 2004).

Doise, W. (1990) 'The development of individual competencies through social interaction', in H. Foot, M. Morgan and R. Shute (eds) *Children Helping Children*, Chichester: Wiley.

Donaldson, M. (1978) *Children's Minds*, Glasgow and London: Collins/Fontana and Croom Helm.

Donaldson, M. (1992) *Human Minds: An Exploration*, London: Allen Lane.

Driver, R. (1983) *The Pupil as Scientist*, Milton Keynes: Open University Press.

Driver, R. (1994) 'The fallacy of induction in science teaching', in R. Levinson (ed.) *Teaching Science*, London: Routledge.

Driver, R. and Bell, J. (1986) 'Students thinking and learning of science: a constructivist view', *School Science Review*, 67 (240): 443–56.

Dryden, G. and Vos, J. (2001) *The Learning Revolution: to Change the Way the World Learns*, Stafford: Network Educational Press in association with Learning Web.

Duda, J. (1993) 'A goal perspective theory of meaning and motivation in sport', paper presented at the World Congress on Sport Psychology, Lisbon, June.

Dunham, J. (1995) *Developing Effective School Management*, London: Routledge.

Dunham, J. and Varma, V. (eds) (1998) *Stress in Teachers: Past, Present and Future*, London: Whurr.

Dussault, M., Deaudelin, C., Royer, N. and Loiselle, J. (1997) 'Professional isolation and stress in teachers', paper presented at the Annual Meeting of the American Education Research Association, Chicago, March.

Dweck, C. (1986) 'Motivational processes affecting learning', *American Psychologist*, 41: 1040–8.

Dweck, C.S. and Leggett, E. (1988) 'A social-cognitive approach to motivation and personality', *Psychological Review*, 95: 256–73.

Eccles, J.S. (1984) 'Sex differences in achievement patterns', in T. Sonderegger (ed.) *Nebraska Symposium on Motivation, 32*, Lincoln, NE: University of Nebraska Press, pp. 97–132.

Edwards, A.D. and Furlong, V.J. (1978) *The Language of Teaching*, London: Heinemann.

Eisenberg, R. with Kelley, K. (1997) *Organise Yourself*, London: Macmillan.

Ellington, H., Fowlie, J. and Gordon, M. (1998) *Using Games and Simulations in the Classroom*, London: Kogan Page.

Elliott, J. (1991) *Action Research for Educational Change,* Milton Keynes: Open University Press.

Elliott, J. (1998) *The Curriculum Experiment: Meeting the Challenge of Social Change*, Buckingham: Open University Press.

Entwistle, N. (1990) *Handbook of Educational Ideas and Practices*, London: Routledge.

Entwistle, N.J. (1981) *Styles of Learning and Teaching*, Chichester: Wiley.

Entwistle, N.J. (1993) *Styles of Learning and Teaching*, 3rd edn, London: David Fulton.

EOC (Equal Opportunities Commission) (2001) *Women and Men in Britain: Sex Stereotyping – from School to Work*, London: EOC. Online. Available HTTP: <http:// eoc.org.uk/cseng/research/ wm_sex_stereotyping.pdf> (accessed 2 July 2004).

EOC (Equal Opportunities Commission) (2003) *Facts about Men and Women in Great Britain, 2003*, London: EOC. Online. Available HTTP: <http:// eoc.org.uk/cseng/research/factsgreatbritain2003.pdf> (accessed 2 July 2004).

EOC (Equal Opportunities Commission). Online. Available HTTP: <http://www.eoc.org.uk> (accessed 9 Sept. 2004).

EPPI (2004) *A Systematic Review of How Theories Explain Learning Behaviour in School Contexts*, London: Institute of Education, EPPI Centre.

ERA (Education Reform Act) (1988) *Education Reform Act, 29 July 1988; Section 1,2 Aims of the School Curriculum*, London: HMSO.

Erikson, E.H. (1980) *Identity and the Life Cycle*, New York: Norton.

Fielding, M. (1996) 'Why and how learning styles matter: valuing difference in teachers and learners', in S. Hart (ed.) *Differentiation and the Secondary Curriculum: Debates and Dilemmas*, London: Routledge.

Findley, M.J. and Cooper, H.M. (1983) 'Locus of control and academic achievement: A literature review', *Journal of Personality and Social Psychology*, 44: 419–27.

Fine, M. (1986) 'Why urban adolescents drop into and out of public high school', *Teachers College Record*, 87: 393–409.

Fine, M. (1989) *Framing Drop-outs: Notes on the Politics of an Urban High School*, Albany, NY: State University of New York Press.

Finn, J.D. (1989) 'Withdrawing from school', *Review of Educational Research*, 59: 117–42.

Finn, J.D. (1993) *School Engagement and Students at-risk*, Washington, DC: National Center for Educational Statistics.

Fitzgerald, R., Finch, S. and Nove, A. (2000) *Black Caribbean Young Men's Experiences of Education and Employment*, Report No. RR186, London: DfEE.

Flavell, J.H. (1982) 'Structures, stages and sequences in cognitive development', in W.A. Collins (ed.) *The Concept of Development: The Minnesota Symposia on Child Psychology*, 15: 1–28.

Flink, C., Boggiano, A.K. and Barrett, M. (1990) 'Controlling teaching strategies', *Journal of Personality and Social Psychology*, 59: 916–24.

Fontana, D. (1993) *Managing Time*, Leicester: British Psychological Society Books.

Food Standards Agency (2000) *National Diet and Nutrition Survey: Young People aged 4–18 Years*, London: Stationery Office.

Food Standards Agency (2004a) *School Lunch Box Survey 2004*. Online. Available HTTP: <http://www. food.gov.uk> search on home page (accessed 27 Oct. 2004).

Food Standards Agency (2004b) *Vending Healthy Drinks*. Online. Available HTTP: <http://www.food.gov.uk> search on home page (accessed 27 Oct. 2004).

Ford, D.Y. (1992a) 'Self-perceptions of under-achievement and support for the achievement ideology among early adolescent African-Americans', *Journal of Early Adolescence*, 12: 228–52.

Ford, D.Y. (1992b) 'The American achievement ideology as perceived by urban African-American students: explorations by gender and academic program', *Urban Education*, 27: 196–211.

Franks, A. and Jowett, C. (2001) 'The meaning of action in learning and teaching', *British Educational Research Journal*, 27 (2): 201–18.

Freeman, P. (2002) *Teaching and Learning Styles for KS3*, Milton Keynes: Chalkface Project.

Freud, S. (1901) 'The psychopathology of everyday life', (ed.) J. Strachey in *The Standard Edition of the Complete Psychological Works of Sigmund Freud*, Vol 6, London: Hogarth, 1953.

Frost, J. and Turner, T. (2004) *Learning to Teach Science in the Secondary School: A Companion to School Experience*, 2nd edn, London: RoutledgeFalmer.

Fuller, F.F. and Bown, O.H. (1975) 'Becoming a teacher', in K. Ryan (ed) *Teacher Education (Seventy-Fourth Yearbook of the National Society of Education)*, Chicago: University of Chicago Press, pp. 25–52.

Gagné, R.M. (1977) *The Conditions of Learning*, New York: Holt International.

Gall, M.D. (1970) 'The use of questioning in teaching', *Review of Educational Research*, 40: 707–21.

Galton, M., Gray, J. and Ruddock, J. (1999) *The Impact of School Transitions and Transfers on Pupil Progress and Attainment*, London: Department for Education and Employment.

Gardner, H. (1983) *Frames of Mind: The Theory of Multiple Intelligences*, New York and London: Basic Books and Heinemann.

Gardner, H. (1991) *The Unschooled Mind*, London: Harper Collins.

Gardner, H. (1993a) *Frames of Mind: The Theory of Multiple Intelligences*, 2nd edn, London: Fontana.

Gardner, H. (1993b) *Multiple Intelligences: the Theory in Practice*, New York: Basic Books.

Gardner, H. (1994) 'The theory of multiple intelligences', in B. Moon and A. Shelton-Mayes (eds) *Teaching and Learning in the Secondary School*, Milton Keynes: Open University Press.

Gardner, H. (1999) 'Assessment in context', in P. Murphy (ed.) *Learners, Learning and Assessment*, Buckingham: Open University Press, pp. 90–117.

Gardner, H., Kornhaber, M. and Wake, W. (1996) *Intelligence: Multiple Perspectives*, Fort Worth, TX: Harcourt Brace.

Gardner, M. (1965) *The Annotated Alice*, Harmondsworth: Penguin.

Garner, P. (1999) *Pupils with Problems: Rational Fears, Radical Solutions*, Stoke-on-Trent: Trentham Books.

Gavin, T. (2003) 'The structure of the secondary curriculum', in T.G.K. Bryce and W.M. Humes (eds) *Scottish Education Post-Devolution*, 2nd edn, Edinburgh: Edinburgh University Press.

Gessell, A. (1925) *The Mental Growth of the Preschool Child*, New York: Macmillan.

Gilbert, I. (2002) *Essential Motivation in the Classroom*, London: RoutledgeFalmer.

Gilham, B. (ed.) (1986) *The Language of School Subjects*, London: Heinemann.

Gillborn, D. and Gipps, C. (1996) *Recent Research on the Achievements of Ethnic Minority Pupils: OFSTED Reviews of Research*, London: HMSO.

Gillborn, D. and Mirza, H.S. (2000) *Educational Inequality: Mapping Race, Class and Gender: A Synthesis of Research Evidence*, London: OFSTED. Online. Available HTTP: <http://www.ofsted.gov.uk/publications/ > (accessed 9 Sept. 2004).

Gingell, J. and Brandon, E.P. (2000) *In Defence of High Culture*, Oxford: Blackwell.

Gipps, C. (1995) *Beyond Testing*, London: Falmer Press.

Gipps, C. (1997) 'Principles of assessment', unpublished lecture, Institute of Education, University of London, 7 Feb.

Gipps, C. and Stobart, G. (1997) *Assessment: A Teacher's Guide to the Issues*, 3rd edn, London: Hodder and Stoughton.

Goddard, D. and Leask, M. (1992) *The Search for Quality: Planning for Improvement and Managing Change*, London: Paul Chapman Publishing.

Gold, K. (2003) 'Poverty *is* an excuse', *Times Educational Supplement* (7 March): 22.

Gold, Y. and Roth, R.A. (1993) *Teachers Managing Stress and Preventing Burnout*, London: Falmer Press.

Goleman, D. (1995) *Emotional Intelligence*, New York: Bantam.

Goleman, D. (1996) *Emotional Intelligence*, London: Bloomsbury.

Good, T. and Brophy, J. (2000) *Looking in Classrooms*, 8th edn, New York: Addison-Wesley Longman.

Goodenow, C. (1993) 'Classroom belonging among early adolescent students: relationship to motivation and achievement', *Journal of Early Adolescence*, 13: 21–43.

Gould, S. J. (1984) *The Mismeasure of Man*, London: Pelican.

Graduate Teacher Training Registry (GTTR) (2004) *Entry: How to Apply*, Cheltenham: GTTR.

Graham, C. and Hill, M. (2003) *Spotlight 89: Negotiating the Transition to Secondary School*, Glasgow: Scottish Council for Research in Education.

Great Britain (1996) *Education Act 1996: Elizabeth II. Chapter 56*, London: HMSO. Online. Available HTTP: <http://www.hmso.gov.uk/acts1996/1996056.htm>.

Greenhalgh, P. (1994) *Emotional Growth and Learning*, London: Routledge.

Grolnick, W.S., Deci, E.L. and Ryan, R.M. (1997) 'Internalization within the family: the self-determination theory perspective', in J.E. Grusec and L. Kuczynski (eds) *Parenting and Children's Internalisation of Values: A Handbook of Contemporary Theory*, New York: John Wiley, pp. 135–61.

Gross, R. (2001) *Psychology: The Science of Mind and Behaviour*, 4th edn, London: Hodder and Stoughton.

GTC (General Teaching Council) (2002) *Code of Professional Values and Practice for Teachers*, GTC (England). Online. Available HTTP: <http://www. gtce.org.uk/gtcinfo/code.asp> (accessed 2 July 2004).

GTC (General Teaching Council) (2003) *Teacher Survey*, London: General Teaching Council.

Guay, F., Boggiano, A.K. and Vallerand, R.J. (2001) 'Autonomy support, intrinsic motivation and perceived competence: conceptual and empirical linkages', *Personality and Social Psychology Bulletin*, 27 (6): 643–50.

Hall, D. (1996) *Assessing the Needs of Bilingual Pupils*, London: David Fulton Publishers.

Hallam, S. and Toutounji, I. (1996) *What do we Know about the Grouping of Pupils by Ability? A Research Review*, London: Institute of Education, University of London.

Handy, C. (1993) *Understanding Organisations*, 4th edn, London: Penguin.

Hansen, D. (1995) 'Teaching and the moral life of classrooms', *Journal for a Just and Caring Education*, 2: 59–74. Online. Available HTTP: <http://tigger.uic.edu/~lnucci/MoralEd/articles/hansen.html> (accessed 15 July 2004).

Hardy, G.H. (1967) *A Mathematician's Apology*, Cambridge: Cambridge University Press.

Hargreaves, A. (1984) *Improving Secondary Schools: Report of the Committee on the Curriculum and Organisation of Secondary Schools*, London: ILEA.

Harker, M. and Redpath, R. (1999) 'Becoming solution-focused in practice', *Educational Psychology in Practice*, 15 (2): 116–21.

Harkin, J. and Turner, G. (1997) 'Patterns of communication styles of teachers in English 16–19 education', *Research in Post-Compulsory Education*, 2 (3): 261–80. Reprinted in B. Holmes, B. Tagney, A. Fitzgibbon. and S. Mehan (eds) (2001) *Communal Constructivism: Students Constructing Learning For as Well as With Others*, Dublin: Centre for Research in IT in Education, Trinity College, Dublin.

Harland, J., Moor, H., Kinder, K. and Ashworth, M. (2002) *Is the Curriculum Working? The Key Stage 3 Phase of the Northern Ireland Curriculum Cohort Study*, Slough: National Foundation for Educational Research.

Harlen, W. (1995) 'To the rescue of formative assessment', *Primary Science Review*, 37 (April): 14–15.

Harlen, W. (1997) *Making Sense of the Research on Ability Grouping*, newsletter 60 (Spring), Edinburgh: Scottish Council for Research in Education (SCRE).

Harlen, W. and Malcolm, H. (1997) *Setting and Streaming: A Research Review* (Using Research Series, 18), Edinburgh: Scottish Council for Research in Education (SCRE).

Harrison, C., Comber, C., Fisher, T., Haw, K., Lewin, C., Lunzer, E., McFarlane, A., Mavers, D., Scrimshaw, P., Somekh, B. and Watling, R. (2003) *The Impact of Information and Communication Technologies on Pupil Learning and Attainment: Full Report*, London: DfES/BECTA.

Hart, K (1981) *Children's Understanding of Mathematics*, London: Murray.

Hart, S. (ed.) (1996) *Differentiation and the Secondary Curriculum: Debates and Dilemmas*, London: Routledge.

Harter, S. (1985) 'Competence as a dimension of self-evaluation: toward a comprehensive model of self-worth', in R.L. Leay (ed.) *The Development of the Self*, Orlando, FL: Academic Press.

Hatcher, R. (1998) 'Class differentiation in education: rational choices?', *British Journal of Sociology of Education*, 19 (1): 5–24.

Hay McBer (2000) *Report into Teacher Effectiveness*, London: DfEE. Online. Available HTTP: <http://www.teachernet.gov.uk/educationoverview/briefing/strategyarchive/modelofteachereffectiveness/>.

Haydon, G. (1997) *Teaching about Values: A New Approach*, London: Cassell.

Haydon, G. and Hayward, J. (2004) 'Values and citizenship education', in S. Capel, R. Heilbronn, M. Leask and T. Turner (eds) *Starting to Teach in the Secondary School: A Companion for the Newly Qualified Teacher*, 2nd edn, London: RoutledgeFalmer, pp. 161–75.

Haylock, D. (2001) *Teaching Children 3–11: A Students' Guide*, London: Paul Chapman.

Hayward, L., Kane, J. and Cogan, N. (2000) *Report on the Consultation on the Review of Assessment Pre-School and 5–14*, Glasgow: University of Glasgow.

Head, J., Hill, F. and Maguire, M. (1996) 'Stress and the post graduate secondary school trainee teacher: a British case study', *Journal of Education for Teaching*, 22 (1): 71–84.

Headington, R. (2000) *Monitoring, Assessment, Recording, Reporting and Accountability: Meeting the Standards*, London: David Fulton.

Heilbronn, R. (2004) 'From trainee to newly qualified teacher: your immediate professional needs', in S. Capel, R. Heilbronn, M. Leask and T. Turner (eds) *Starting to Teach in the Secondary school: A Companion for the Newly Qualified Teacher*, 2nd edn, London: RoutledgeFalmer.

Heilbronn, R., Jones, C., Bubb, S. and Totterdell, M. (2002) 'School based induction tutors: a challenging role', *School Leadership and Management*, 22 (4): 371–89.

Hirst, P. (1974) *Knowledge and the Curriculum*, London: Routledge.

HMI (Her Majesty's Inspectorate) (1977) *Curriculum 11–16*, London: Department of Education. and Science.

HMI (Her Majesty's Inspectorate) (1978) *Mixed Ability Work in Comprehensive Schools*, London: HMSO

HMI (Her Majesty's Inspectorate) (2004) *The Key Stage 3 Strategy: Evaluation of the Third Year*, London: OFSTED.

HMIE (Her Majesty's Inspectorate in Education) (1999) *Review of Assessment in Pre-school and 5–14*. Online. Available HTTP: <http:// <www.scotland.gov.uk/3–14assessment/rapm-00.htm> (accessed 11 Oct. 2004)

Holmes, B., Tagney, B., Fitzgibbon, A. and Mehan, S. (2001) *Communal Constructivism: Students Constructing Learning For as Well as With Others*, Dublin: Centre for Research in IT in Education, Trinity College, Dublin. Paper presented at the SITE Conference, 2001.

Holt, J. (1964) *How Children Fail*, New York: Pitman.

Holt, J. (1984) *How Children Learn*, New York: Penguin.

Hook, P. and Vass, A. (2000) *Confident Classroom Leadership*, London: David Fulton.

Hopkins, D. (2002) *A Teachers Guide to Classroom Research*, 3rd edn, Buckingham: Open University Press.

House of Commons (1997) 'Teacher recruitment: what can be done?' *First Report of the House of Commons Education and Employment Select Committee HC 262*, London: HMSO.

House of Commons Health Committee (2004) *Obesity: Third Report of Session 2003–04*, London: Stationery Office.

Howe, M. (1998) *Principles of Human Abilities and Learning*, Hove: Psychology Press.

Humes, W. and Bryce, T. (2003) 'The distinctiveness of Scottish education', in T.G.K. Bryce and W.M. Humes (2003) *Scottish Education Post-Devolution*, 2nd edn, Edinburgh: Edinburgh University Press.

Hutchings, M., Menter, I., Ross, A. and Thomson, D. (2002) 'Teacher supply and retention in London: key findings and implications from a study of six boroughs in 1998–9', in I. Menter, M. Hutchings and A. Ross (eds) *The Crisis in Teacher Supply*, Oakhill: Trentham, pp. 175–206.

Ireson, J. and Hallam, S. (2001) *Ability Grouping in Education*, London: Paul Chapman Publishing.

Jackson, C. and Warin, J. (2000) 'The importance of gender as an aspect of identity at key transition points in compulsory education', *British Educational Research Journal*, 26 (3): 375–91.

Jackson, P.W. (1968) *Life in the Classroom*, New York: Holt, Rinehart & Winston.

James, M. (1998) *Using Assessment for School Improvement*, London: Heinemann.

Jeffrey, B. (2003) 'Countering learner "instrumentalism" through creative mediation', *British Educational Research Journal*, 29 (4): 489–503.

Jennings, A. (1995) 'Discussion', in J. Frost (ed.) *Teaching Science*, London: Woburn Press.

Jensen, E. (1998) *Super Teaching*, 3rd edn, San Diego, CA: The Brain Store Inc.

Jerome, L., Hayward, J., Easy, J. and Newmanturner, A. (2003) *The Citizenship Co-ordinator's Handbook*, Cheltenham: Nelson Thornes.

Jeyes, G. (2003) 'The local governance of education, an operational perspective', in T.G.K. Bryce and W.M. Humes (eds) *Scottish Education Post-Devolution*, 2nd edn, Edinburgh: Edinburgh University Press.

Jones, K. (1995) *Simulations: A Handbook for Teachers and Trainers*, 3rd edn, London: Kogan Page.

Joyce, B., Calhoun, E. and Hopkins, D. (2002) *Models of Learning: Tools for Teaching*, 2nd edn, Buckingham: Open University Press.

Joyce, B., Calhoun, E. and Weil, M. (1999) *Models of Teaching*, 6th edn, Boston and London: Allyn & Bacon.

Juvonen, J. and Murdock, T.B. (1993) 'How to promote social approval: the effect of outcome and audience on publicly communicated attributions', *Journal of Educational Psychology*, 85: 365–76.

Juvonen, J. and Murdock, T.B. (1995) 'Perceived social consequences of effort and ability attributions: Implications for developmental changes in self-presentation tactics', *Child Development*, 66: 1694–705.

Kassin, S.M. and Lepper, M.R. (1984) 'Oversufficient and insufficient justification effects: cognitive and behavioural developments', in J. Nicholls (ed.) *Advances in Motivation and Achievement*, vol. 3, Greenwich, CT: JAI.

Kavale, K., Forness, S. and Mostert, M. (2004) 'Defining emotional or behavioral disorders: the quest for affirmation', in P. Clough, P. Garner, T. Pardeck and F. Yuen (eds) *The Handbook of Emotional and Behavioural Difficulties*, London: Sage.

Kemmis, S. and McTaggart, R. (1988) *The Action Research Planner*, 3rd edn, Geelong: Deakin University Press.

Kerr, D. (1999) *Re-examining Citizenship Education: The Case of England*, Slough: National Foundation for Educational Research.

Kerry, T. (1999) *Learning Objectives, Task Setting and Differentiation*, London: Hodder and Stoughton.

Kerry, T. (2004) *Explaining and Questioning*, Cheltenham: Nelson Thornes.

Keys, W., Harris, S. and Fernandes, C. (1996) *Third International Mathematics and Science Study: First National Report – Part 1. Achievement in Mathematics and Science at Age 13 in England*, London: National Foundation for Educational Research.

Klein, G. (1993) *Education towards Race Equality*, London: Cassell.

Kluger, A. and DeNisi, A. (1996) 'The effects of feedback interventions on performance: a historical review, a meta-analysis and a preliminary feedback intervention theory', *Psychological Bulletin*, 119 (2): 254–84.

Kohlberg, L. (1976) 'Moral stages and moralization: the cognitive-developmental approach', in T. Lickona (ed.) *Moral Development and Behavior: Theory, Research, and Social Issues*, New York: Holt, Rinehart & Winston.

Kohlberg, L. (1985) 'Resolving moral conflicts within the just community', in C. Harding (ed.) *Moral Dilemmas: Philosophical and Psychological Issues in the Development of Moral Reasoning*, Chicago: Precedent Press.

Kolb, D.A. (1976) *The Learning Style Inventory: Technical Manual*, Boston:, MA McBer & Co.

Kolb, D.A. (1985) *The Learning Style Inventory: Technical Manual*, rev. edn, Boston, MA: McBer & Co.

Kozulin, A. (1998) *Psychological Tools: A Sociocultural Approach to Education*, Cambridge, MA: Harvard University Press.

Kramarski, B. and Mevarech, Z.R. (1997) 'Cognitive-metacognitive training within a problem-solving based Logo environment', *British Journal of Educational Psychology*, 67: 425–45.

Krapp, A., Hidi, S. and Renninger, K.A. (1992) 'Interest, learning and development', in K.A. Renninger, S. Hidi and A. Krapp (eds) *The Role of Interest in Learning and Development*, Hillsdale, NJ: Erlbaum, pp. 3–25.

Kyriacou, C. (1998) *Essential Teaching Skills*, 2nd edn, Cheltenham: Stanley Thornes.

Kyriacou, C. (2000a) *Effective Teaching in Schools*, Cheltenham: Stanley Thornes.

Kyriacou, C. (2000b) *Stress-Busting for Teachers*, Cheltenham: Stanley Thornes.

Kyriacou, C. (2001) 'Teacher stress: directions for future research', *Educational Review*, 53 (1): 27–35.

Kyriacou, C. and Stephens, P. (1999) 'Student teachers' concerns during teaching practice', *Evaluation and Research in Education*, 13 (1): 18–31.

Kyriacou, C., Kunc, R., Stephens, P. and Hultgren, A. (2003) 'Student teachers' expectations of teaching as a career in England and Norway', *Educational Review*, 55 (3): 255–63.

Lam, S.-F., Yim, P.-S., Law, J.S.F. and Cheung, R.W.Y. (2004) 'The effects of competition on achievement motivation in Chinese classrooms', *British Journal of Educational Psychology*, 74: 281–96.

Lambert, D. (1999) 'Assessing and recording pupils' work', in S. Capel, M. Leask and T. Turner (eds) *Learning to Teach in the Secondary School: A Companion to School Experience*, 2nd edn, London: Routledge, pp. 283–323.

Lambert, D. and Balderstone, D. (2000) *Learning to Teach Geography in the Secondary School: A Companion to School Experience*, London: Routledge.

Langford, P. (1995) *Approaches to the Development of Moral Reasoning*, Hove: Erlbaum.

Lave, J. and Wenger, E. (1991) *Situated Learning: Legitimate Peripheral Participation*, Cambridge: Cambridge University Press.

Lawton, D. (1989) *Education, Culture and the National Curriculum*, Sevenoaks: Hodder and Stoughton.

Lawton, D. (1996) *Beyond the National Curriculum: Teacher Professionalism and Empowerment*, Sevenoaks: Hodder and Stoughton.

Leadbetter, C. (2004) *Personalisation through Participation: A New Script for Public Services*, London: DEMOS/ DfES Innovations Unit.

Learning and Teaching Scotland (2004a) 'About 5–14'. Online. Available HTTP: <http://www.ltscotland.org.uk/5to14/about5to14/index.asp> (accessed 26 Aug. 2004).

Learning and Teaching Scotland (2004b) 'Assessment is for learning', Online. Available HTTP: <http://www.ltscotland.org.uk/assess/about/aims/index.asp> (accessed 26 Aug. 2004).

Leask, M. (ed.) (2001) *Issues in Teaching with ICT*, London: Routledge.

Leask, M. and Pachler, N. (eds) (1999) *Learning to Teach Using ICT in the Secondary School*, London: Routledge.

Leask, M. and Pachler, N. (eds) (2005) *Learning to Teach Using ICT in the Secondary School*, 2nd edn, London: Routledge.

Leask, M. and Williams, L. (2005) 'Whole school approaches: integrating ICT across the curriculum', in M. Leask and N. Pachler (eds) *Learning to Teach using ICT in the Secondary School*, 2nd edn, London: Routledge.

Leask, M., Dawes, L. and Litchfield, D. (2000) *Keybytes for Teachers*, Evesham: Summerfield Publishing.

Leat, D. (1998) *Thinking through Geography*, Cambridge: Chris Kington Publishing.

Lickona, T. (1983) *Raising Good Children*, New York: Bantam Books.

Liverpool Sportslinx Project (2003) *Report on the Health and Fitness of Liverpool Primary and Secondary School Children 01–03*, Liverpool: Liverpool City Council, Education, Libraries and Sports Services.

Lloyd, J. and Fox, K.R. (1992) 'Achievement goals and motivation to exercise in adolescent girls: a preliminary intervention study', *British Journal of Physical Education Research Supplement*, 11: 12–16.

McCaleb, J. and White, J. (1980) 'Critical dimensions in evaluating teacher clarity', *Journal of Classroom Interaction*, 15: 27–30.

McCarthy, B. (1987) *The 4MAT System*, Barrington, IL: Excel.

McClelland, D.C. (1961) *The Achieving Society*, Princeton, NJ: Van Norstrand.

McClelland, D.C. (1972) 'What is the effect of achievement motivation training in the schools?', *Teachers College Record*, 74: 129–145.

Macdonald, B. (2000) 'How education became nobody's business', in H. Altricher and J. Elliott (eds) *Images of Educational Change*, Buckingham: Open University Press, pp. 20–36.

McGregor, D. (1960) *The Human Side of Enterprise*, New York: McGraw-Hill.

McInerney, D.M., Yeung, A.S. and McInerney, V. (2001) 'Cross-cultural validation of the inventory of school motivation (ISM)', *Journal of Applied Psychological Measurement*, 2: 134–52.

Mackenzie, J. (2003) 'Disaffection with schooling', in T.G.K. Bryce and W.M. Humes (2003) *Scottish Education Post-Devolution*, 2nd edn, Edinburgh: Edinburgh University Press.

McNamara, S. (1999) *Differentiation: An Approach to Teaching and Learning*, Cambridge: Pearson Publishing.

McNamara, S. and Moreton, G. (1999) *Understanding Differentiation: A Teacher's Guide*, 2nd edn, London: David Fulton.

McNiff, J. and Whitehead, J. (2002) *Action Research: Principles and Practice*, London: Routledge.

McSherry, J. (2001) *Challenging Behaviours in Mainstream Schools*, London: David Fulton.

Maehr, M.L. and Anderman, E.M. (1993) 'Reinventing schools for early adolescents: emphasizing task goals', *Elementary School Journal*, 93: 593–610.

Mager, R. (1990) *Preparing Instructional Objectives: A Critical Tool in the Development of Effect Instruction*, London: Kogan Page.

Maitland, I. (1995) *Managing your Time*, London: Institute of Personnel and Development.

Maker, C.J. and Nielson, A.B. (1995) *Teaching Models in the Education of the Gifted*, 2nd edn, Austin, TX: Pro-Ed.

Manouchehri, A. (2004) 'Implementing mathematics reform in urban schools: a study of the effect of teachers' motivational style', *Urban Education*, 39 (5): 472–508.

Marland, M. (1993) *The Craft of the Classroom*, London: Croom Helm.

Marton, F. and Saljo, R. (1976) 'On qualitative differences in learning: 1, Outcome and process', *British Journal of Educational Psychology*, 46: 4–11.

Maslow, A.H. (1970) *Motivation and Personality*, 2nd edn, New York: Harper & Row.

Maybin, J., Mercer, N. and Stierer, B. (1992) 'Scaffolding learning in the classroom', in K. Norman (ed.) *Thinking Voices: The Work of the National Oracy Project*, London: Hodder and Stoughton.

Mayer, J.D. and Salovey, P. (1997). 'What is emotional intelligence?', in P. Salovey and D. Sluyter (eds) *Emotional Development and Emotional Intelligence: Implications for Educators*, New York: Basic Books, pp. 3–31.

Mercer, N. (2000) *Words and Minds: How We Use Language to Think Together*, London: Routledge.

Mickelson, R.A. (1990) 'The attitude–achievement paradox among Black adolescents', *Sociology of Education*, 63: 44–61.

Midgley, C.M., Feldlaufer, H. and Eccles, J.S. (1989) 'Student/teacher relations before and after the transition to junior high school', *Child Development*, 60: 981–92.

Miles, M. and Huberman, M. (1994) *Qualitative Data Analysis: A Sourcebook of New Methods*, Thousand Oaks, CA: Sage.

Miliband, D. (2004) 'Personalised learning', speech by the Minister of Education for School Standards to the North of England Education Conference, January 2004, Befast. Online. Available HTTP: <http://www.dfes. gov.uk/standards>.

Miller, O. (1996) *Supporting Children with Visual Impairment in Mainstream Schools*, London: Franklin Watts.

Mills, S. (1995) *Stress Management for the Individual Teacher*, Lancaster: Framework Press.

Mitchell, R. (1994) 'The communicative approach to language teaching: an introduction', in A. Swarbrick (ed.) *Teaching Modern Languages*, London: Routledge/Open University, pp. 33–42.

Montgomery, D. (1996) 'Differentiation of the curriculum in primary education', *Flying High* (Worcester, National Association for Able Children in Education), 3: 14–28.

Morgan, N. and Saxton, J. (1994) *Asking Better Questions: Models, Techniques and Classroom Activities for Engaging Students in Learning*, Markham, Ontario: Pembroke Publishers.

Morton, L.L., Vesco, R., Williams, N.H. and Awender, M.A. (1997) 'Student teacher anxieties related to class management, pedagogy, evaluation, and staff relations', *British Journal of Educational Psychology*, 67: 68–89.

Mosston, M. (1972) *Teaching: From Command to Discovery*, Belmont, CA: Wadsworth Publishing Co.

Mosston, M. and Ashworth, S. (2002) *Teaching Physical Education,* 5th edn, San Francisco: Benjamin Cummings.

Muijs, D. and Reynolds, D. (2001) 'Effective Teaching, Evidence and Practice', in P. Prosser and K. Trigwell (eds) *Understanding Teaching and Learning*, Buckingham: Open University Press.

Munn, P., Johnstone, M. and Holligan, C. (1990) 'Pupils' perceptions of effective disciplinarians', *British Educational Research Journal*, 16 (2): 191–8.

Murdock, T.B. (1999) 'The social context of risk: Social and motivational predictors of alienation in middle school', *Journal of Educational Psychology*, 91: 1–14.

Murdock, T.B., Anderman, L.H. and Hodge, S.A. (2000) 'Middle-grade predictors of students' motivation and behavior in high school', *Journal of Adolescent Research*, 15 (3): 327–51.

Murphy, P. (ed.) (1999) *Learners, Learning and Assessment*, Buckingham: Open University Press.

Myers, K. (1987) *Genderwatch!*, Cambridge: Cambridge University Press.

Myers, K. (1990) *Sex Discrimination in Schools*, London: Advisory Centre for Education.

Namrouti, A. and Alshannag, Q. (2004) 'Effect of using a metacognitive teaching strategy on seventh grade students' achievement in science', *Dirasat*, 31 (1): 1–13.

NASEN (National Association for Special Educational Needs (UK)) (2000) *Specialist Teaching for Special Educational Needs and Inclusion: Policy Paper 4 in the SEN Fourth Policy Options series*, London: NASEN. (See the NASEN website <http://nasen.org.uk>; select book list, then policy options.)

National Commission for Education (1993) *Learning to Succeed: A Radical Look at Education Today*, London: Heinemann.

Naylor, S. and Keogh, B. (1999) 'Constructivism in the classroom: theory into practice', *Journal of Science Teacher Education*, 10 (2): 93–106.

NCC (National Curriculum Council) (1989) *An Introduction to the National Curriculum*, York: National Curriculum Council.

Neill, S. (1991) *Classroom Nonverbal Communication*, London: Routledge.

Newbold, D. (1977) *Ability Grouping: The Banbury Inquiry*, Windsor: NFER-Nelson.

Newton, D.P. (2000) *Teaching for Understanding*, London: RoutledgeFalmer.

NFER (National Foundation for Educational Research) (1998) *Learning from Differentiation: A Review of Practice in Primary and Secondary Schools*, Slough: NFER.

NFER (National Foundation for Educational Research) (2004) *The Key Stage 3 National Strategy, LEA and School Perceptions*, LGA Research Report 11/04, Slough:NFER.

Nicholls, J.G. (1984) 'Achievement motivation: Conceptions of ability, subjective experience, task choice and performance', *Psychological Review*, 91: 328–46.

Nicholls, J.G. (1989) *The Competitive Ethos and Democratic Education*, Cambridge, MA: Harvard University Press.

Nicholls, J.G. (1990) 'What is the ability and why are we mindful of it? A developmental perspective', in R.J. Sternberg and J. Kolligan (eds) *Competence Considered*, New Haven, CT: Yale University Press, pp. 11–40.

Noble, T. (2004) 'Integrating the revised Bloom's Taxonomy with multiple intelligences: a planning tool for curriculum differentiation', *Teachers College Record*, 106 (1): 193–211.

Norman, K. (ed.) (1992) *Thinking Voices: The Work of the National Oracy Project*, London: Hodder and Stoughton.

Novak, J.D. and Gowin, D.B. (1984) *Learning How to Learn*, Cambridge: Cambridge University Press.

Noyes, A. (2003) 'Moving schools and social relocation', *International Studies in Sociology of Education*, 13 (3): 261–80.

Nucci, L. (1982) 'Conceptual development in the moral and conventional domains: implications for values education', *Review of Educational Research*, 49: 93–122.

Nucci, L. (1985) 'Children's conceptions of morality, societal convention and religious prescription', in C. Harding (ed.) *Moral Dilemmas: Philosophical and Psychological Issues in the Development of Moral Reasoning*, Chicago: Precedent Press.

Nucci, L. (1987) 'Synthesis of research on moral development', *Educational Leadership*, 86–92. Online. Available HTTP: <http://tigger.uic.edu/~lnucci/MoralEd/articles/nuccisynthesis.html> (accessed 15 July 2004).

NUT (National Union of Teachers) (annual) *Your First Teaching Post*, London: NUT.

OFSTED (Office for Standards in Education) (1993) *The New Teacher in School: A Survey by Her Majesty's Inspectorate in England and Wales*, 1992, London: HMSO.

OFSTED (Office for Standards in Education (1994) *Mathematics Key Stages 1, 2, 3 and 4*, London: HMSO

OFSTED (Office for Standards in Education) (1996) *Subjects and Standards. Issues for School Development Arising from OFSTED Inspection Findings, 1994–5*, London: HMSO.

OFSTED (Office for Standards in Education) (1998) *Judging Attainment: An Occasional Paper on the Relationship between Inspectors Judgements and School Results*, London: OFSTED

OFSTED (Office for Standards in Education) (2000) *Progress in Key Stage 3 Science*, London: OFSTED.

OFSTED (Office for Standards in Education) (2001) *ICT in Schools: The Impact of Government Initiatives: An Interim Report*, London: OFSTED.

OFSTED (Office for Standards in Education) (2002) *Good Teaching; Effective Departments*, London: OFSTED.

OFSTED (Office for Standards in Education) (2003a) *Boys' Achievement in Secondary Schools*, London: OFSTED.

OFSTED (Office for Standards in Education) (2003b) *Good Assessment Practice in History*, HMI 1475, London: OFSTED.

OFSTED (Office for Standards in Education) (2003c). *Inspecting Schools: Handbook for Inspecting Secondary Schools*. Online. Available HTTP: <http://www.ofsted.gov.uk/publications/>.

OFSTED (Office for Standards in Education) (2004a) *ICT in Schools: The Impact of Government Initiatives Five Years on*, London: Office for Standards in Education.

OFSTED (Office for Standards in Education) (2004b) *OFSTED Subject Reports 2002/03: Information and Communication Technology in Secondary Schools*, London: OFSTED.

OFSTED (Office for Standards in Education) (2004c) *Special Educational Needs and Disability: Towards Inclusive Schools*, London: OFSTED. Online. Available HTTP: <http://www.ofsted.gov.uk/publications> (accessed 4 Nov. 2004).

O'Hear, P. and White, J. (eds) (1991) *A National Curriculum for All: Laying the Foundations for Success*, London: Institute for Policy Research.

Olweus, D. (1993) *Bullying at School*, Oxford: Blackwell.

Owen-Jackson, G. (2000) *Learning to Teach Design and Technology in the Secondary School: A Companion to School Experience*, London: Routledge.

Paechter, C. (2000) *Changing School Subjects: Power, Gender and Curriculum*, Buckingham: Open University Press.

Papaioannou, A. (1995) 'Differential perceptual and motivational patterns when different goals are adopted', *Journal of Sport and Exercise Psychology*, 17: 18–34.

Partnership with Parents (1998) *Dealing with Dyslexia in the Secondary School*. Available from Shepway Centre, Oxford Road, Maidstone, Kent, ME15 8AW (tel: 01622 755515).

Pateman, T. (1994) 'Crisis, what identity crisis?', *First Appointments Supplement, Times Educational Supplement* (14 Jan.): 28–9.

Paterson, L. (2003) *Scottish Education in the Twentieth Century*, Edinburgh: Edinburgh University Press.

Patmore, M. (2000) *Achieving QTS : Passing the Numeracy Skills Test*, Exeter: Learning Matters and University of Exeter for the Training Agency.

Peacey, N. (2005) 'Special educational needs and ICT', in M. Leask and N. Pachler (eds) *Learning to Teach Using ICT in the Secondary School*, 2nd edn, London: Routledge.

Peddiwell, J. (1939) *The Sabre Toothed Curriculum*, New York: McGraw-Hill.

Perrenoud, P. (1991) 'Towards a pragmatic approach to formative evaluation', in P. Weston (ed.), *Assessment of Pupils' Achievement, Motivation and School Success*, Amsterdam: Swets & Zeitlinger, pp. 79–101.

Phelan, P., Davidson, A.L. and Cao, H.T. (1991) 'Students' multiple worlds: negotiating the boundaries of family, peer and school cultures', *Anthropology and Education Quarterly*, 22: 224–50.

Piaget, J. (1932) *The Moral Judgment of the Child*, New York: Macmillan.

Piaget, J. (1954) *The Construction of Reality in the Child*, New York: Basic Books.

Pinney, A. (2004) *Reducing Reliance on Statements: An Investigation into Local Authority Practice and Outcomes*, DfES Research Report 508, Norwich: HMSO. Online. Available HTTP: <http://www.dfes.gov.uk/research> (accessed 4 Nov. 2004).

Pithers, R.T. and Soden, R. (1998) 'Scottish and Australian teachers stress and strain: a comparative study', *British Journal of Educational Psychology*, 68: 269–79.

Plato (1955) *The Republic*, tr. H.D.P. Lee, Harmondsworth: Penguin Books.

Postlethwaite, K. (1993) *Differentiated Science Teaching: Responding to Individual Differences and Special Educational Needs*, Milton Keynes: Open University Press.

Power, S., Edwards, T., Whitty, G. and Wigfall, V. (2003) *Education and Middle Class*, Buckingham: Open University Press.

PriceWaterhouseCoopers (2001) *A Study into Teacher Workload*, London: PriceWaterhouseCoopers.

Priyadharshini, E. and Robinson-Pant, A. (2003) 'The attractions of teaching: an investigation into why people change careers to teach', *Journal of Education for Teaching*, 29 (2): 95–112.

Programme for International Student Assessment (PISA) (2000) 'Programme for International Students 2000: Scotland Analysis'. Online. Available HTTP: <http://www.scotland.gov.uk/stats/bulletins/00343.pdf> (accessed 15 Oct. 2004).

QCA (Qualifications and Curriculum Authority) (2000) *Research into the Dip in Performance in English of Children Entering Key Stage 3 (Secondary School for Most)*. Report commissioned by QCA and carried out by the University of Cambridge Local Examinations Syndicate Evaluation Team. London: QCA.

QCA (Qualifications and Curriculum Authority) (2001a) *Planning, Teaching and Assessing Pupils with Learning Difficulties*, Sudbury: QCA Publications. Online. Available HTTP: <http://www.nc.uk.net/ld/GG_content.html> (accessed 4 Nov. 2004).

QCA (Qualifications and Curriculum Authority) (2001b) *Supporting School Improvement: Emotional and Behavioural Development*, London: QCA.

QCA (Qualifications and Curriculum Authority) (2004a) *14–19 Learning – Courses in Subjects and Disciplines Comprising the Entitlement Areas*. Online. Available HTTP: <http://www.qca.org.uk/14–19/developments/index.htm> (accessed 15 July 2004).

QCA (Qualifications and Curriculum Authority) (2004b) *14–19 Learning: Guidance on Teaching 14–19 Phase.* Online. Available HTTP: <http://www.qca.org.uk/14–19> (accessed 1 Nov. 2004).

QCA (Qualifications and Curriculum Authority) (2004c) *Guidance on Teaching Gifted and Talented Pupils.* Online. Available HTTP: <http://www.nc.uk.net/gt/index.html> (accessed 1 Nov. 2004). Also *Gifted and Talented.* Online. Available HTTP: <http://www.qca.org.uk/ages3–14/inclusion/302.html (accessed 1 Nov. 2004).

QCA (Qualifications and Curriculum Authority) (2004d) *Key Stage 3 Assessment and Reporting Arrangements,* London: QCA.

QCA (Qualifications and Curriculum Authority) (2004e) *National Curriculum in Action.* Online. Available HTTP: <http://www.ncaction.org.uk> (accessed 27 Nov. 2004).

QCA (Qualifications and Curriculum Authority) (2004f) *Progression in Geography.* Online. Available HTTP: <http://www.qca.org.uk/geography/innovatingwithgeography-matters/continuityand progression/> Search 'progression' (accessed 1 Nov. 2004).

Reeve, J. (1996) *Motivating Others,* Needham Heights, MA: Allyn & Bacon.

Reeve, J. and Deci, E.L. (1996) 'Elements of the competitive situation that affect intrinsic motivation', *Personality and Social Psychology Bulletin,* 22: 24–33.

Reid, I. and Caudwell, J. (1997) 'Why did PGCE students choose teaching as a career?', *Research in Education,* 58: 46–58.

Riding, R. (2002) *School Learning and Cognitive Styles,* London: David Fulton.

Riding, R.J. and Cheema, I. (1991) 'Cognitive styles: an overview and integration', *Educational Psychology,* 11: 193–215.

Riding, R.J. and Rayner, S. (1998) *Learning Styles and Strategies,* London: David Fulton.

Ripley, K., Daines, B. and Barrett, J. (1997) *Dyspraxia: A Guide for Teachers and Parents,* London: David Fulton.

Robertson, J. (1996) *Effective Classroom Control: Understanding Teacher–Student Relationships,* 3rd edn, London: Hodder & Stoughton.

Robinson, K. (chair) (1999) *All our Futures: Creativity, Culture and Education. Report of the National Advisory Committee on Creative and Cultural Education,* London: DfEE.

Roger, R. (1994) *How to Write a Development Plan,* Oxford: Heinemann.

Rogers, C. (1982) *A Social Psychology of Schooling: The Expectancy Process,* London: Routledge & Kegan Paul.

Rogers, K.B. (1991) *The Relationship of Grouping Practices to the Education of the Gifted and Talented Learner,* Storrs, CT: The National Center on the Gifted and Talented, University of Connecticut.

Rogoff, B. (1990) *Apprenticeship in Thinking: Cognitive Development in Social Context,* Oxford: Oxford University Press.

Rosenthal, R. and Jacobson, L. (1968) *Pygmalion in the Classroom,* New York: Holt, Rinehart & Winston.

Rowe, M.B. (1986) 'Wait time: slowing down may be a way of speeding up!', *Journal of Teacher Education,* 37: 43–50.

Royal College of Physicians (RCP) (2004) *Storing up Problems, the Medical Case for a Slimmer Nation: Report of a Working Party,* London: Royal College of Physicians.

Ruddock, J. (2004) *Developing a Gender Policy for Secondary Schools,* Buckingham: Open University Press.

Ryan, A. (2000) 'Comment', *Independent* (9 Nov.).

Ryan, R.M. and Deci, E.L. (2000) 'Self-determination theory and the facilitation of intrinsic motivation, social development and well-being', *American Psychologist,* 55: 68–78.

Salovey, P. and Mayer, J.D. (1990) 'Emotional intelligence', *Imagination, Cognition and Personality,* 9: 185–211.

SCAA (School Curriculum and Assessment Authority) (1996) *Teaching English as an Additional Language: A Framework for Policy,* London: SCAA.

Scanlon, M. and Buckingham, D. (2004) 'Home learning and the educational marketplace', *Oxford Review of Education,* 30 (2): 287–303.

Schiefele, U. (1996) *Motivation and Learning with Text,* Jotting, Germany: Hogrefe.

Schon, D. (1983) *The Reflective Practitioner,* Aldershot: Ashgate.

School Teachers' Review Body (2002) *A Review of Approaches to Reducing Teacher Workload,* London: School Teachers' Review Body.

Scottish Executive Education Department (2000) *The Structure and Balance of the Curriculum 5–14 National Guidelines*. Online. Available HTTP: <http://www.ltscotland.org.uk/5to14/htmlguidelines/saboc/page3.htm> (accessed 30 Aug. 2004).

Scottish Executive Education Department (2001a) *A Teaching Profession for the 21st Century*, agreement reached following recommendations made in the McCrone Report. Online. Available HTTP: <http://www.scotland.gov.uk/library3/education/tp21a-01.asp> (accessed 20 Sept. 2004).

Scottish Executive Education Department (2001b) *Better Behaviour, Better Learning*, Edinburgh: Scottish Executive Education Department.

Scottish Executive Education Department (2002) *Welcoming Asylum Seekers to Schools*. Online. Available HTTP: <http://www.scotland.gov.uk/pages/news/2002/01/p_SE5159.aspx> (accessed 15 Oct. 2004).

Scottish Executive Education Department (2003) *National Priorities in School Education*. Online. Available HTTP: <http://www.scotland.gov.uk/education/nationalpriorities/> (accessed 26 Aug. 2004).

Scottish Executive Education Department (2004a) *About the Scottish Executive Education Department*. Online. Available HTTP: <http://www.scotland.gov.uk/About/Departments/ED> (accessed 3 Oct. 2004).

Scottish Executive Education Department (2004b) *Action to Tackle Discipline in Schools*. Online. Available HTTP: <http://www.scotland.gov.uk/News/Releases/2003/09/4212> (accessed 14 Oct. 2004).

Scottish Executive Education Department (2004c) *Programme for International Student 2000: Scotland Analysis*. Online. Available HTTP: <http://www.scotland.gov.uk/stats/bulletins/00343–00.asp> (accessed 15 Oct. 2004).

Scottish Executive Education Department (2004d) *The Standard for Headship*. Online. Available HTTP: <http://www.scotland.gov.uk/education/teaching/pages/cpd_head.htm> (accessed 20 Sept. 2004).

Scottish Office Education and Industry Department (1999) *A Manual for Good Practice in Special Educational Needs*, Edinburgh: Scottish Office Education and Industry Department.

Scottish Qualifications Authority (2004) *Role and Functions*. Online. Available HTTP: <http://www.sqa.org.uk/> (accessed 26 Aug. 2004).

Selinger, M. (1999) 'ICT and classroom management' in M. Leask and N. Pachler (eds) *Learning to Teach Using ICT in the Secondary School*, London: RoutledgeFalmer.

Selman, R.L. (1980) *The Growth of Interpersonal Understanding*, New York: Academic Press.

Shayer, M. and Adey, P. (eds) (2002) *Learning Intelligence: Cognitive Acceleration across the Curriculum from 5 to 15 Years*, Buckingham: Open University Press.

Shemilt, D. (1984) *In-service Training Course for History Teachers*, London: Eltham, July.

Short, G. (1986) 'Teacher expectation and West Indian underachievement', *Educational Research*, 27 (2): 95–101.

Skinner, B.F. (1953) *Science and Human Behavior*, New York: Macmillan.

Skinner, E.A. (1995). *Perceived Control, Motivation and Coping*, Thousand Oaks, CA: Sage.

Smith, A., Douglas, W., Campbell, J. and Topping, K. (2003) 'Cross-age peer tutoring in mathematics with seven- and 11-year-olds: influence on mathematical vocabulary, strategic dialogue and self-concept', *Educational Research*, 45 (3): 287–308.

Smith, A. and Call, N. (2002) *The ALPS (Accelerated Learning in Primary School) Approach*, London: Accelerated Learning in Training and Education (ALITE).

Smith, R. and Standish, P. (eds) (1997) *Teaching Right and Wrong: Moral Education in the Balance*, Stoke-on-Trent: Trentham.

Smithers, A. and Robinson, P. (2000) *Attracting Teachers: Past Patterns, Present Policies, Future Prospects*, Liverpool: Centre for Education and Employment Research University of Liverpool.

Snow, C.P. (1960) *The Two Cultures and the Scientific Revolution*, Cambridge: Cambridge University Press (The Rede Lecture, 1959).

Solmon, M.A. (1996) 'Impact of motivational climate on students' behaviors and perceptions in a physical education setting', *Journal of Educational Psychology*, 88 (4): 731–8.

Spear, M., Gould, K. and Lee, B. (2000) *Who would be a Teacher? A Review of Factors Motivating and Demotivating Prospective and Practising Teachers*, Slough: National Foundation for Educational Research (NFER).

Steinberg, L., Dornsbush, S.N. and Brown, B.B. (1992) 'Ethnic differences in adolescent achievement: an ethological perspective', *American Psychologist*, 47: 723–9.

Stobart, G. and Gipps, C. (1997) *Assessment: A Teacher's Guide to the Issues*, London: Hodder and Stoughton.

Stokking, K., Leenders, F., De Jong, J. and Van Tartwijk, J. (2003) 'From student to teacher: reducing practice shock and early dropout in the teaching profession', *European Journal of Teacher Education*, 26 (3): 329–50.

Stones, E. (1992) *Quality Teaching: A Sample of Cases*, London: Routledge.

Strauss, R.S. (2000) 'Childhood obesity and self-esteem', *Pediatrics*, 105 (1): e15. Online. Available HTTP: <http://www.pediatrics.org/cgi/content/full/105/1/e15> (accessed 3 Nov. 2004).

Strauss, R.S. and Pollack, H.A. (2003) 'Social marginalisation of overweight children', *Archives of Pediatrics and Adolescent Medicine*, PubMed 12912779.

Sukhnandan, L. with Lee, B. (1998) *Streaming, Setting and Grouping by Ability*, Slough: NFER.

Sutton, C. (1981) *Communicating in the Classroom*, London: Hodder and Stoughton.

Tanner, J.M. (1990) *Foetus into Man*, Cambridge, MA: Harvard University Press.

Tarrant, G. (1981) 'Social studies in the primary school: the place of discussion', *Social Studies Teacher*, 13 (3): 63–5.

Taylor, A. (2003) 'Perceptions of prospective entrants to secondary teaching', unpublished paper, School of Education, Brunel University.

Telecsan, B.L., Slaton, D.B. and Stevens, K.B. (1999) 'Peer tutoring: teaching students with learning disabilities to deliver time delay instruction', *Journal of Behavioural Education*, 9 (2): 133–54.

Terry, P. M. (1997) 'Teacher burnout: is it real? Can we prevent it?', paper presented at the annual meeting of the North Central Association of Colleges and Schools, Chicago, IL, April (ERIC Document Reproduction Service No. ED 408 258).

Thacker, J. (1995) 'Personal, social and moral education', in C. Desforges (ed.) *An Introduction to Teaching: Psychological Perspectives*, Oxford: Basil Blackwell.

The Education Authorities Directory and Annual (annual) Redhill, Surrey: School Government Publishing Co.

The Education Year Book (annual) London: Longman.

Tikly, C. and Wolf, A. (2000) *The Maths we Need Now: Demands, Deficits and Remedies*, London: Institute of Education, University of London.

Tilstone, D.W. (2000) *10 Best Teaching Practices*, Thousand Oaks, CA: Corwin Press.

Todorovich, J.R. and Curtner-Smith, M.D. (2002) 'Influence of motivational climate in physical education on sixth grade pupils' goal orientations', *European Physical Education Review*, 8 (2): 119–38.

Tomlinson, C. (1999) *The Differentiated Classroom: Responding to the Needs of All Learners*, Alexandria, VA: Association for Supervision and Curriculum.

Topping, K.J. (1992) 'The effectiveness of paired reading in ethnic minority homes', *Multicultural Teaching to Combat Racism in School and Community*, 10 (2): 19–23.

Torrance, H. (2002) 'Can testing really raise educational standards?', inaugural professorial lecture, University of Sussex, 11 June.

Totterdell, M., Heilbronn, R., Bubb, S. and Jones, C. (2002a) *Effectiveness of the Statutory Arrangements for the Induction of Newly Qualified Teachers*, Nottingham: DfES.

Totterdell, M., Heilbronn, R., Bubb, S. and Jones, C. (2002b) *Evaluation of the QCA 14–19 Learning: Courses in Subjects and Disciplines Comprising the Entitlement Areas*. Online. Available HTTP: <http://www.qca.org.uk/14–19/developments/index.htm> (accessed 15 Sept. 2004).

Townsend, S. (1982) *The Life of Adrian Mole*, London: Methuen.

Travers, C.J. and Cooper, C.L. (1996) *Teachers under Pressure: Stress in the Teaching Profession*, London: Routledge.

Treasure, D. (1997) 'Perceptions of the motivational climate and elementary school children's cognitive and affective responses', *Journal of Sport and Exercise Psychology*, 19: 278–90.

Trend, R., Davis, N. and Loveless, A. (1999) *QTS Information Communication Technology*, London: LETTS Educational.

Triantafillou, E., Pomportsis, A., Demetriadis, S. and Georgiadou, E. (2004) 'The value of adaptivity based on cognitive style: an empirical study', *British Journal of Educational Technology*, 35 (1): 95–106.

Trolley, H., Biddulph, M. and Fisher, T. (1996) *Beyond the First Year of Teaching: Beginning Teaching Workbook 6*, Cambridge: Chris Kington Publishing.

TTA (Teacher Training Agency) (1998) *Subject Leaders Standards*, London: TTA.

TTA (Teacher Training Agency) (2000) *QTS Skills Tests*, London: Teacher Training Agency. Online. Available HTTP: <http://www.teach.gov.uk/> (accessed 28 Oct. 2004).

TTA (Teacher Training Agency) (2002) *Newly Qualified Teachers Survey*, London: TTA.

TTA (Teacher Training Agency) (2003a) *Career Entry and Development Profile: Maintaining a Professional Portfolio*, London: TTA.

TTA (Teacher Training Agency) (2003b) *Corporate Plan*, London: TTA.

TTA (Teacher Training Agency) (2003c) *Supporting Induction for Newly Qualified Teachers: Overview*, London: TTA.

TTA (Teacher Training Agency) (2003d) *The Role of the Induction Tutor*, London: TTA.

TTA (Teacher Training Agency) (2004) *Behaviour4Learning*. Online. Available HTTP: <http://www.behaviour4learning.ac.uk>.

Turiel, E. (1983) *The Development of Social Knowledge: Morality and Convention*, Cambridge: Cambridge University Press.

Turner, S. (1995) 'Simulations', in J. Frost (ed.) *Teaching Science*, London: Woburn Press.

Underwood, J. (1998) 'Making groups work', in M. Montieth (ed.) *IT for Learning Enhancement*, Exeter: Intellect.

Vallerand, R.J. (1997) 'Toward a hierarchical model of intrinsic and extrinsic motivation', in M.P. Zanna (ed.) *Advances in Experimental Social Psychology*, vol. 29, San Diego: Academic Press, pp. 271–360.

Vallerand, R.J., Fortier, M.S. and Guay, F. (1997) 'Self-determination and persistence in a real life setting: toward a motivational model of high school dropout', *Journal of Personality and Social Psychology*, 72: 1161–76.

Vygotsky, L.S. (1962) *Thought and Language*, Cambridge, MA: MIT Press.

Vygotsky, L.S. (1978) *Mind in Society: The Development of Higher Psychological Processes*, London: Harvard University Press.

Vygotsky, L.S. (1986) *Thought and Language*, trans. and ed. A. Kozulin, Cambridge, MA: MIT Press.

Waldon, A. (2000) 'Bridging the gap', *Journal of Design and Technology Education*, 6: 158–60.

Walker, S. (2004) 'Interprofessional work in child and adolescent mental health services', *Emotional and Behavioural Difficulties*, 9 (1): 189–204.

Warnock, M. (1998) *An Intelligent Person's Guide to Ethics*, London: Duckworth.

Waterhouse, P. (1983) *Managing the Learning Process*, Maidenhead: McGraw-Hill Series for Teachers.

Watkins. D., Carnell, E., Lodge, C., Wagner, P. and Whalley, C. (2000) *Learning about Learning*, London: Routledge.

Watkins, D., McInerney, D., Akande, A. and Lee, C. (2003) 'An investigation of ethnic differences in the motivation and strategies for learning of students in desegregated South African schools', *Journal of Cross-Cultural Psychology*, 34 (2): 189–94.

Watson. G. (2002) 'The National Curriculum', in S. Capel, M. Leask and T. Turner (eds) *Learning to Teach in the Secondary School: A Companion to School Experience*, London: Routledge.

Weare, K. (2003) *Developing the Emotionally Literate School*, London: Paul Chapman Publishing.

Wegerif, R. and Dawes, L. (2004) *Thinking and Learning with ICT: Raising Achievement in Primary Classrooms*, London: Routledge.

Weiner, B.J. (1972) *Theories of Motivation*, Chicago: Markham.

Weiner, B.J. (1992) *Human Motivation: Metaphors, Theories and Research*, London: Sage.

Wellington, J. (ed.) (1986) *Controversial Issues in the Curriculum*, Oxford: Blackwell.

Wells, J., Barlow, J. and Stewart-Brown, S. (2003) 'A systematic review of universal approaches to mental health promotion in schools', *Health Education*, 103(4), 197–220

Wentzel, K. (1997) 'Student motivation in middle school: the role of perceived pedagogical caring', *Journal of Educational Psychology*, 89: 411–17.

Wersky, G. (1988) *The Visible College: A Collective Biography of British Scientists and Socialites from the 1930s*, London: Free Association Books.

Weston, P., Taylor, M., Lewis, G. and MacDonald, A. (1998) *Learning from Differentiation: A Review of Practice in Primary and Secondary Schools*, Slough: NFER.

White, J. (1998) *Do Howard Gardner's Multiple Intelligences Add up?*, London: Institute of Education (in the series 'Perspectives on Education Policy').

White, J. (ed.) (2004) *Rethinking the School Curriculum: Values, Aims and Purposes*, London: RoutledgeFalmer.

White, R.T. and Gunstone, R. (1992) *Probing Understanding*, London: Falmer Press

Whitehead R.G. (chairperson) (1991) *Report on Health and Social Subjects No. 41. Dietary Reference Values for Food Energy and Nutrients for the United Kingdom: Report of the Panel on Dietary Reference Values of the Committee on Medical Aspects of Food Policy*, London: HMSO for the Department of Health.

Whylam, H. and Shayer, M. (1978) *CSMS Reasoning Tasks: General Guide*, Windsor: NFER.

Wilhelm, K., Dewhurst-Savellis, J. and Parker, G. (2000) 'Teacher stress? An analysis of why teachers leave and why they stay', *Teachers and Teaching: Theory and Practice*, 6: 291–304.

Wiliam, D. (2001) *Level Best? Levels of Attainment in National Curriculum Assessment*, London: Association of Teachers and Lecturers (ATL).

Willis, P. (1977) *Learning to Labour: How Working Class Kids Get Working Class Jobs*, Aldershot: Gower.

Willis, P. (1983) 'Cultural production and theories of reproduction', in L. Barton and S. Walker (eds) *Race, Class and Education*, London: Croom-Helm, pp. 107–38.

Wineburg, S. (1997) 'Beyond breadth and depth: subject matter knowledge and assessment', *Theory into Practice*, 36 (4): 255–61.

Wood, D. (1988) *How Children Think and Learn*, Oxford: Blackwell Press.

Woodward, W. (2003) 'Poverty hits exam scores', *Guardian* (21 April 2003): 8.

Working Group on 14–19 Reform (2004) *14–19 Curriculum and Qualifications Reform: Interim Report of the Working Group on 14–19 Reform (Tomlinson Report)*, London: HMSO.

Wragg, E. (ed.) (1984) *Classroom Teaching Skills*, London: Croom Helm.

Wragg, E.C. and Brown, G. (2001) *Questioning in the Secondary School*, London: RoutledgeFalmer.

Wringe, C. (1988) *Understanding Educational Aims*, London: Unwin Hyman.

Younger, M., Warrington, M. and Williams, J. (1999) 'The gender gap and classroom interactions: reality and rhetoric?', *British Journal of Sociology of Education*, 20 (3): 325–41.

Younie, S. and Moore, T. (2005) 'Using ICT for professional purposes' in M. Leask and N. Pachler (eds) *Learning to Teach Using ICT in the Secondary School: A Companion to School Experience*, 2nd edn, London: Routledge.

Name Index

Subject Index

BRUNEL UNIVERSITY LIBRARY

Bannerman Centre,
Uxbridge, Middlesex,
UB8 3PH

Renewals: www.brunel.ac.uk/renew
OR
01895 266141

1 WEEK LOAN